KEEPING YOUR SCHOOL SAFE & SECURE:
A PRACTICAL GUIDE

- Drugs and Alcohol
- Weapons
- Student Searches

- Bullying
- Crisis Management
- Intruders

Center for
Education & Employment Law

Center for Education & Employment Law
P.O. Box 3008
Malvern, Pennsylvania 19355

> "This publication is designed to provide accurate and authoritative information in regard to
> the subject matter covered. It is sold with the understanding that the publisher is not engaged
> in rendering legal, accounting or other professional service. If legal advice or other expert
> assistance is required, the services of a competent professional person should be sought."—
> *from a Declaration of Principles jointly adopted by a Committee of the American Bar
> Association and a Committee of Publishers and Associations.*

ISBN 978-1-944331-01-6

Published 2016   by: Center for Education & Employment Law

Library of Congress Control Number: 2008937927

Cover Design by Patricia Jacoby

Cover photo ©GettyImages.com/deystudio (School building)
Cover photo ©GettyImages.com/SolStock (Fight in hallway)
Cover photo ©GettyImages.com/Steve Debenport (Teacher/Security officer)

Other Titles Published By
Center for Education & Employment Law:

Deskbook Encyclopedia of American School Law
Higher Education Law in America
Legal Update for Teachers: The Complete Principal's Guide
Private School Law in America
Students with Disabilities and Special Education
Deskbook Encyclopedia of Public Employment Law
Deskbook Encyclopedia of Employment Law

TABLE OF CONTENTS

TABLE OF CONTENTS

CHAPTER TWO
Emergency Preparedness and Response

CHAPTER THREE
School Safety and Liability

CHAPTER FOUR
Campus Law Enforcement

CHAPTER FIVE
Employment

CHAPTER SIX
Extracurricular Activities

CHAPTER SEVEN
Health Issues

TABLE OF CONTENTS

CHAPTER EIGHT
Statutes and Regulations

CHAPTER NINE
Forms

TABLE OF CONTENTS

TABLE OF CONTENTS

TABLE OF CONTENTS

TABLE OF CONTENTS

REFERENCE SECTION

INTRODUCTION

We are excited to introduce this updated edition of *Keeping Your School Safe & Secure: A Practical Guide*. Designed for the busy education professional, this easy-to-use resource presents a unique combination of materials designed to help administrative professionals formulate and implement a comprehensive plan to keep schools a safe place to learn. Case summaries, source materials, forms, checklists and practical guidance are organized into chapters by subject area for easy reference. A comprehensive index and case tables make it easy to quickly find the information you need.

Now more than ever, school security and related issues predominate the education landscape. Rely on *Keeping Your School Safe & Secure: A Practical Guide* with confidence as a valuable tool to avoid legal liability and protect the health and safety of your students.

ABOUT THE EDITORS

Curt J. Brown is the editorial director of the Center for Education & Employment Law. Prior to assuming his present position, he gained extensive experience in business-to-business publishing, including management of well-known publications such as *What's Working in Human Resources, What's New in Benefits & Compensation, Keep Up to Date with Payroll, Supervisors Legal Update,* and *Facility Manager's Alert.* Mr. Brown graduated from Villanova School of Law and graduated magna cum laude from Bloomsburg University with a B.S. in Business Administration. He is admitted to the Pennsylvania bar.

James A. Roth is the editor of *Legal Notes for Education* and *Special Education Law Update.* He is a co-author of *Students with Disabilities and Special Education Law* and an adjunct program assistant professor at St. Mary's University in Minnesota. Mr. Roth is a graduate of the University of Minnesota and William Mitchell College of Law. He is admitted to the Minnesota bar.

Thomas D'Agostino is a managing editor at the Center for Education & Employment Law and is the editor of *Higher Education Legal Alert.* He graduated from the Duquesne University School of Law and received his undergraduate degree from Ramapo College of New Jersey. He is a past member of the American Bar Association's Section of Individual Rights and Responsibilities as well as the Pennsylvania Bar Association's Legal Services to Persons with Disabilities Committee. Mr. D'Agostino is admitted to the Pennsylvania bar.

Elizabeth A. Wheeler is editor of the monthly newsletter *Private Education Law Report* and the *Private School Law in America* deskbook. She's also a contributing editor for the newsletters *Higher Education Legal Alert* and *School Safety and Security Alert.* A graduate of Macalester College and Capital University Law School, she's a member of the Massachusetts bar. Before joining the Center for Education and Employment Law, she was a legal editor for a South Boston publisher, where she edited employment law and education law newsletters.

Carol Warner is the editor of *EducationTechNews.com* and two monthly newsletters: *School Safety & Security Alert* and *Legal Update for Teachers.* She is also a contributing editor for *HigherEdMorning.com* and *Higher Education Legal Alert.* Before joining the Center for Education & Employment Law, she was an editor for two employment law newsletters: *What's Working in Human Resources* and *What's New in Benefits & Compensation.* Ms. Warner is a graduate of The New York Institute of Technology and holds a Bachelor of Arts in English with an emphasis in professional writing.

HOW TO USE YOUR GUIDE BOOK

We have designed *Keeping Your School Safe & Secure: A Practical Guide* in an accessible format for both attorneys and non-attorneys to use as a research and reference tool toward prevention of legal problems.

Research Tool

As a research tool, our guide book allows you to conduct your research on two different levels – by topics or cases.

Topic Research

♦ If you have a general interest in a particular **topic** area, our **table of contents** provides descriptive chapter headings containing detailed subheadings from each chapter.

➢ For your convenience, we also include the chapter table of contents at the beginning of each chapter.

Example:
For information on MRSA infection, the table of contents indicates that a discussion of this topic begins in Chapter Seven on page 325:

HOW TO USE YOUR GUIDE BOOK

◆ If you have a specific interest in a particular **issue**, our comprehensive **index** collects all of the relevant page references to particular issues.

Example:
 For information on entranceway security, the index provides references to all of the text dealing with building security instead of only the text dealing with entranceways:

Building security, 2-43
 Coordinating with first responders, 19
 Doors, 9-10
➤ Entranceways, 12-15
  Biometrics, 14-15
  Card readers, 14
  Closed-circuit television (CCTV), 12-13
  Metal detectors, 12
  PIN codes, 14
  Security personnel/greeters, 13
 Eye-scanning systems, 15
 Fingerprinting, 15
 Legal decisions, 21-43

Case Research

◆ If you know the **name** of a particular case, our **table of cases** will allow you to quickly reference the location of the case.

Example:
 If someone mentioned a case named *Daniels v. City of New York,* looking in the table of cases, which has been arranged alphabetically, the case would be located under the "D" section.

D

D.S. v. East Porter County School Corp., 85
Dailey v. Los Angeles Unified School Dist., 109
Daniel v. Hancock County School Dist., 269
➤ Daniels v. City of New York, 23, 65
Danso v. Univ. of Connecticut, 129

✓ Each of the cases summarized in the guide book also contains the case citation, which will allow you to access the full text of the case if you would like to learn more about it. *See How to Read a Case Citation, p. 579.*

HOW TO USE YOUR GUIDE BOOK

♦ If your interest lies in cases from a **particular state**, our **table of cases by state** will identify the cases from your state and direct you to their page numbers.

> **Example:**
> If cases from California are of interest, the table of cases by state, arranged alphabetically, lists all of the case summaries contained in the guide book from California.
>
> ➡ **CALIFORNIA**
>
> American Nurses Ass'n v. Torlakson, 312
> Avila v. Citrus Community College Dist., 260
> Broney v. California Comm'n on Teacher Credentialing, 291
> C.A. v. William S. Hart Union High School Dist., 109
> C.B. v. City of Sonora, 188
> Castaneda v. Inglewood Unified School Dist., 216
> Chavez v. Martinez, 186

✓ Remember, the judicial system has two court systems – state and federal court – which generally function independently from each other. *See The Judicial System, p. 575.* We have included the federal court cases in the table of cases by state according to the state in which the court resides. However, federal court decisions often impact other federal courts within that particular circuit. Therefore, it may be helpful to review cases from all of the states contained in a particular circuit.

We hope you benefit from the use of *Keeping Your School Safe & Secure: A Practical Guide*. If you have any questions about how to use the guide book, please contact Thomas D'Agostino at tdagostino@pbp.com.

TABLE OF CASES

TABLE OF CASES

TABLE OF CASES

TABLE OF CASES

TABLE OF CASES

TABLE OF CASES

Z

TABLE OF CASES BY STATE

TABLE OF CASES BY STATE

TABLE OF CASES BY STATE

TABLE OF CASES BY STATE

CHAPTER ONE

Access and Building Security

I. INTRODUCTION

An important key to maintaining school safety and security is controlling access to school facilities. A variety of tools are available to help schools ensure that access to school facilities is gained only by authorized personnel. A one-size-fits-all approach to controlling school access is inappropriate. Although some issues relating to school access are common to most schools, an individualized assessment must be undertaken to determine which specific security steps are best-suited for your particular facility.

Several factors should be taken into consideration when determining how best to ensure safe access to school facilities. These include:
- the grades that the school serves
- the layout of the school campus
- the enrollment level
- the location of the school (e.g., urban vs. suburban or rural), and
- the crime level in the neighborhood where the school is located.

II. ENVIRONMENTAL DESIGN

It is important to note the value of incorporating environmental design elements that ensure school safety and security to the maximum extent possible. While this is a benefit that can be most fully utilized by incorporating environmental design principles into new facilities at the design stage, some of these design elements can also be incorporated into existing school campuses. In addition, expansion and reconstruction plans create a valuable opportunity to increase school safety by incorporating environmental design elements that take school safety into account. In all of these cases, the likelihood of crime can be reduced via an effective use of the school's physical environment.

A. Crime Prevention Through Environmental Design

An approach to increasing safety called Crime Prevention Through Environmental Design (CPTED) recognizes the important role that the design of the built environment can play in reducing the risk of criminal activity. CPTED is not intended to replace traditional crime prevention approaches. Instead, it should be thought of as a complementary tool that can be incorporated into an overall comprehensive plan to make schools safer.

The CPTED approach incorporates several concepts that are applied to increase the security level of the studied facility. The approach has been used to provide an increased measure of security at facilities such as government buildings, commercial complexes and parks. Although not originally developed specifically with schools in mind, the approach is particularly useful in school settings, partly because application of its principles can substantially increase the safety of school premises while preserving a welcoming environment and avoiding a prison-like atmosphere. CPTED is also relatively cost-effective.

CPTED has a strong record of success. The Broward County, Florida school district experienced a dramatic reduction in crime after implementing CPTED, and some state legislatures have mandated its use in schools.

The CPTED approach involves several discrete components, including natural surveillance, natural access control, and territoriality.

1. Natural Surveillance

The natural surveillance component of CPTED seeks to maximize the safety advantage that is gained when the environment's physical features keep obstacles to surveillance to a minimum and enable authorities to observe the facility's entire physical environment without undue interference and without a need to resort to advanced technological measures. Essentially, this component seeks to maximize the ability of authorities to observe the environment, in general, and especially higher-risk areas, such as parking lots and building entrances. Several potential barriers impede the ability to maximize surveillance capabilities, such as solid walls, overgrown shrubbery, and inadequate lighting.

2. Natural Access Control

Natural access control, a second important component of CPTED, refers to the benefit obtained by taking steps to design the facility's physical environment in a way that deters criminal activity by creating a perception of risk to potential offenders. This is accomplished, for example, by constructing the physical environment so that visitors are guided through the physical space of the facility by means of clear routing, signage, and other steering features.

3. Territorial Reinforcement

A third component of CPTED is territorial reinforcement. This component seeks to create an environment that encourages authorized users of the space to develop a sense of territoriality or ownership over the space. When users develop this sense of territoriality, potential offenders are discouraged from engaging in criminal activity. An example of a design feature that encourages territoriality is clear border definition.

Professional resources are available to aid schools in conducting a CPTED analysis. School personnel also can perform a CPTED analysis by undertaking a comprehensive study of criminal behavior and other misconduct that occurs on campus. Such a study can identify and categorize the types of problems that take place and ascertain whether patterns exist with respect to time and/or location. Ideally a comprehensive study will yield information that can be used to change the physical environment in a way that reduces the incidence of criminal behavior or other improper conduct.

4. Case Study: Effective Use of CPTED

The Broward County, Florida school district was one of the first in the country to effectively utilize CPTED concepts in the school environment. After completing an evaluation, the district applied a number of CPTED strategies. Based on the assessment, the district considered changes relating to vehicle access and border definition. It also considered relocating parking lots and replacing restroom entrance doors with open mazes. In addition, it evaluated strategies relating to the maintenance of landscaping and the effective use of lighting and color in and around school facilities. The district's use of CPTED techniques resulted in a significant reduction in school-related crime.

B. Specific Environmental Elements

The following are examples of ways in which schools can help prevent crime in the school environment by controlling specific environmental elements in ways that increase the security of entrance areas.

1. Entrances

A basic key to maintaining a safe school environment is controlling access to the school campus. The school campus should be designed (or redesigned) so that students and visitors must pass through a particular designated entrance or entrances. The school's main entrance should be the school entrance that is closest to the school's main parking lot. It should be clearly marked and in the front of the school near the administrative areas of the building. By locating the main entrance in this manner, visitors will be steered toward it and not to another less prominent entry point. In addition, main entry points should be located in areas of high visibility so people entering and exiting can be observed easily by school personnel. Glazing of windows and doors enhances the ability to conduct effective surveillance. Windows should be kept free of announcements and other postings that impede the ability to conduct effective surveillance of the entrance area. It is preferable for both the entrance area and the parking area to be observable from the school's administrative area. The entrance should be wide enough to minimize pedestrian traffic congestion during peak periods. For many schools, an opening of at least 20 feet will be required to enable smooth ingress and egress.

Minimizing the number of entry points is a critical key to maintaining building security. Providing just one entry point is not a feasible option for most schools and, in fact, can be counterproductive to the overall effort to maintain safety. Decisions relating to the number of entrance points that should be provided in addition to the main entrance must be made with reference to each school's particular characteristics, keeping in mind that it is desirable to maintain a number of entry points that allows for manageable ingress and egress without unnecessarily creating the added risk that each additional entrance point potentially represents. Secondary entrances are an area of particular concern, and they require special attention because they are often a problem area. Secondary entrances should be placed in visible locations and should be monitored. They should be subject to all the security controls that apply at the main entrance point.

☑ CHECKLIST – *Entrances*

☐ The main entrance is located close to the school's main parking lot.
☐ The main entrance is marked by clear and adequate signage.
☐ The main entrance and parking lot can be easily monitored
   by administrative personnel from inside the school building.
☐ Windows and doors near the main entrance include glazing.
☐ Windows are kept free of postings and other impediments
   to visibility.
☐ The entrance is wide enough to accommodate pedestrian traffic
   at peak times.
☐ The number of entrances is kept to a minimum.
☐ Signage steers visitors to a particular entrance.
☐ Secondary entrances are monitored.

2. Traffic Control/Parking

School parking areas require extra attention because they frequently are locations where vandalism and other crimes take place.

Access to the school and its parking areas should be controlled by limiting the number of entrance and exit points to campus. The number of access points to parking areas should be limited. This reduces the likelihood that the parking area will be perceived as a public space. Vandal-proof lighting in parking areas should be provided, and the use of gates to limit or prevent access to parking areas during low-use times should be considered.

Controlling the flow of both vehicular and pedestrian traffic is of critical importance. Vehicular and pedestrian traffic should be routed in a manner that separates the two and minimizes congestion while also enabling easy observation. Where feasible, traffic lanes of ingress and egress should be separated by a landscaped median. In addition, automobile traffic should be separated from bus traffic once entry to the school campus is gained. Bus parking should be configured so that buses can maneuver the lot without needing to back up to park or turn. It is preferable to avoid long and straight stretches of roadway on the campus. Avoiding long straight stretches helps to keep down the speed of vehicles and reduce the risk of injury to pedestrians. Where appropriate, traffic-control devices, such as speed bumps, can help reduce the probability of vehicles traveling at excessive speeds on the school campus.

Visitor parking should be designated as such via proper signage, and signage should further define authorized uses within the parking area. The ability of students to gain access to parking areas at times other than arrival time and dismissal time should be restricted. In addition, parking areas and vehicular routes should be observable from a point or points within the building's interior that include administrative areas and/or classrooms.

It is necessary to maintain proper access routes for emergency service personnel. Service and delivery routes should be separated from other traffic routes.

☑ CHECKLIST – *Traffic Control/Parking*

- ☐ Vehicular routes and parking areas can be observed from administrative areas and/or classrooms inside the school.
- ☐ Access to parking areas is restricted to a limited number of entrances.
- ☐ Automobile traffic is separated from bus traffic by barriers and/or routing.
- ☐ Pedestrian traffic is separated from motor vehicle traffic by barriers and/or routing.
- ☐ Undesignated spaces within parking areas are minimized.
- ☐ Traffic control devices are used to control speeds as needed.
- ☐ Long, straight stretches of roadway are minimized.
- ☐ The parking area includes signage that sets out the authorized use of the assigned space.
- ☐ The parking area has vandal-resistant lighting.

3. Signage and Sightlines

Signage serves the dual role of helping to control access and providing notice of prohibited behavior.

The campus should include clear signage that directs all visitors to the school's main office, where they can be screened to make sure they have a legitimate reason to be on the campus. Preferably, the main entrance should be visible from both the administration area and main point of vehicular access.

Maintaining open sightlines is another important key to campus security. Building placement, landscaping, the placement of signage and lighting should all take into account the need to maintain open sightlines.

This is especially true in higher-risk areas of the school campus, such as parking lots, pickup/drop-off points, bus stops, hallways and stairwells. These higher-risk areas can be identified by analyzing the school's incident history.

Borders within the school's campus should be clearly defined.

☑ CHECKLIST – *Signage*

☐ There is a sign or marquee that identifies the school by name and is visible from a point beyond the school's physical borders.
☐ Signs include large lettering.
☐ Signs are well lit.
☐ Directional signage is used as needed to control traffic flow.
☐ Signage directs visitors to a main point of entry.
☐ Signage does not create a place to hide.
☐ Signage does not block lines of sight.
☐ Signage indicates restricted areas.
☐ Signage indicates bus-loading and drop-off zones.

4. Preventing Roof Access

A number of steps can be taken to reduce the likelihood of unauthorized access to the roof of a campus building. Access to rooftop areas should be available only from inside the building, preferably from a locked point. Placement of landscaping and trees should not enable access to the roof of any building.

Covered walkways should be designed in a manner that does not create opportunities for unauthorized access to a building's roof or other upper-level area. In addition, if the campus includes columns that potentially could be scaled to gain unauthorized access to a roof or upper-level area, the columns should be made from smooth building materials. Alternatively, a slippery finish or coating should be applied to the columns. Campus walls and other architectural features should be designed in a manner that does not allow for footholds or handholds to create an ability to gain unauthorized roof access. Niches in exterior walls should be avoided or eliminated, as these can create hiding places for unauthorized and dangerous materials.

5. Landscaping

As previously noted, landscaping should take into account the need to maintain open sightlines and to deny unauthorized access to rooftop areas. There are additional important points to keep in mind regarding the important role that landscaping can play in maintaining building security.

It generally is advantageous to delineate space throughout the school campus both internally and externally. Delineating space as a defined area with a particular purpose helps to remove any perception that the space is available and open. It also makes it easier to assign security responsibilities for specific areas within a school's campus. One way to delineate space in the outside areas of a school campus is through the effective use of landscaping.

Landscaping can be used to define the outer boundaries of school property without the use of fences. Where fences are used, landscaping can be added to help create a more welcoming look while maintaining the security that the fences provide.

It is important to make sure landscaping is maintained so that it does not create hiding places. Shrubbery should be trimmed to a height of less than two feet. Tree canopies should be kept at a minimum height of eight feet, and hedges should be kept low enough to avoid serving as a hiding space. Controlling the growth of landscaping plants is also important to enabling clear lines of sight. Landscaping also can serve as a way to direct and control traffic, giving direction to vehicles and pedestrians, or limiting access to particular areas.

☑ CHECKLIST – *Landscaping*

- ☐ The school's landscape design does not create hiding places.
- ☐ The school's landscape design maintains open sightlines.
- ☐ The school's landscaping is well maintained and is not overgrown.
- ☐ The school's landscaping does not block lighting.
- ☐ Shrubbery is kept at a maximum height of less than two feet.
- ☐ Tree canopies are trimmed to a minimum height of eight feet.

III. TRAINING AND EDUCATION

School staff, students and parents all play an important role in preventing criminal activity that results from unauthorized access. Staff should be trained to intercept strangers and to report them to administration if they do not feel safe approaching a stranger on campus. Students should be instructed not to open doors or otherwise enable access by strangers. Students also should be instructed that they are not to assist other students in circumventing prescribed access procedures or routes. Parents should be provided with detailed information regarding the access control strategies the school utilizes. Parents need to understand the importance of following the school's rules and procedures governing access to school facilities.

It is helpful to take inventory of particular skills or expertise staff members possess that would be useful in the event of an emergency, such as experience in firefighting, or search and rescue. Such individuals can be added to the school's crisis team. For examples of forms that can be used to conduct a staff skills inventory and to create a crisis team member list, see Form I-1 and Form I-2 in Chapter Nine.

The Pennsylvania Department of Education has set out school safety recommendations that encourage school staff and students to be watchful for and to report suspicious activities, including the following:

- an unusual interest in entry points, security points and/or access controls
- an interest in gaining site plans, bus routes, attendance lists or other sensitive information
- an unusual degree of interest in personnel or vehicles approaching or leaving facilities or parking areas
- observation of security drills and procedures
- prolonged surveillance by people appearing to be vendors or others not usually seen in the area, and
- an unexplained presence of people in areas where they should not be.

While safety drills certainly play an important role in employee training, a lack of adequate communication in this regard can lead to a variety of unforeseen problems. For example, a former elementary school teacher in Oregon sued her school district, claiming that an unannounced active shooter safety drill caused her to develop an anxiety disorder. The former teacher claimed that she was not warned in advance about the drill, during which a school resource officer allegedly burst into her classroom and pointed a gun at her head.

Having staffers assume roles other than the ones they normally play can be an effective training tool. One Nevada school district had principals act as teachers and teachers act as students during security drills. The drills were recorded and reviewed. Participants reported benefiting from seeing the crisis from a different viewpoint.

IV. DOORS AND WINDOWS

A. Doors

Exterior doors should be designed to prevent unauthorized building access. The National Clearinghouse for Educational Facilities offers a checklist that lists a number of desirable attributes for exterior school doors, including the following:

- Doors should have a minimal degree of exposed hardware and should be installed using non-removable pins.
- Although exit-only doors do not need outside locks and handles, access should be possible in some manner in an emergency, such as by using a proximity card.
- Doors should be made from steel, aluminum alloy, or solid-core hardwood. If constructed of glass, doors should be fully framed and equipped with tempered glass that is breakage-resistant.
- To prevent doors from being pried open, door frames should

be installed without excess flexibility.

- Exterior locks should be mounted flush to the door surface and should not rely on protruding lock devices such as a key-in-knob device.
- Exterior swinging doors should be equipped with a deadbolt lock that is at least one inch with a one-inch throw bolt and hardened steel insert, as well as a free-turning glass or steel-tempered guard, and double-cylinder locks if glass is located within 40 inches of the locking mechanism.
- Panic bar latches should be protected by pick plates.
- Panic push bars should be equipped with tamper-proof deadbolt locks and a metal plate covering the gap between the doors.
- Strike plates should be securely fastened to door frames.
- If the door is key-controlled, it can be equipped with contacts so it can be tied into a central monitoring and control system.
- Double doors should be equipped with heavy-duty, multiple-point long flush bolts.
- If a door is particularly vulnerable to unauthorized use, consider installing door alarms or delayed opening devices, or using sensors or cameras to monitor it from a central location.

Exterior doors should permit a view of the outside via narrow windows, sidelights, fish-eye viewers or cameras, while preventing intruders from opening any door from the inside by breaking a window or sidelight.

If schools fail to implement the listed safety measures, injuries can occur. Here's an example: An Oregon middle school student was walking into school on a rainy day when she suddenly slipped. Her foot slammed into and shattered the glass door. The broken glass severed her Achilles tendon and left her permanently injured.

A common and potentially devastating problem is that of students who open locked doors for outsiders seeking entry to the interior of a school building. Oftentimes, students do so thinking they are being helpful and polite. School administrators need to make students understand how important it is to follow the strict rule against opening outside doors for people seeking entry. But how? Mark Baker, a school superintendent in Indiana, developed a plan to get the message across to students without scaring them. Baker ensured that students received frequent reminders about the rule, including during assemblies, in homeroom, by way of morning announcements, and from special advisers such as guidance counselors.

Even the most secure exterior doors won't be very effective if staffers or others on the inside open them for unauthorized visitors. To address this danger, the principal of a New Jersey school aimed a school surveillance camera at a locked door and had two outsiders – a college-age man and a young mother – knock on the door every 10 minutes for an hour. The camera caught images of students and faculty opening the door. The principal then used the video as "teachable moments," thus reducing the frequency with which the doors were opened to outsiders.

In response to the tragic mass shooting at Sandy Hook Elementary School in December of 2012, Connecticut Gov. Dannel Malloy created a 16-member public safety panel called the Sandy Hook Advisory Commission. In March of 2013, the commission issued an interim report that included a number of specific recommendations relating to school doors. The panel recommended that all K-12 classrooms be equipped with doors that can be locked from the inside by the teacher. It also recommended that all exterior doors in K-12 schools be equipped with hardware that can implement a full perimeter lockdown.

Some devices are designed to create an additional layer of security by making it more difficult for an intruder to breach a locked interior door. One such tool is called a "Bearacade." The Bearacade is a door control system that creates another layer of protection between students and would-be attackers. The device can be installed on doors without leaving the classroom. It slides on the bottom of the door and secures the classroom with a 1/4" stainless steel pin. Reflective markings on the outer portion of the device let authorities know that the device is in use, and its makers say it can withstand up to 4,000 pounds of external pressure.

A similar device is called "The Sleeve." The Sleeve is a 12-gauge steel case that fits around an interior door's closer arm, securing it from the inside. The closer arm is installed at the top, in the inside of classroom doors. The device covers the closer arm, preventing it from being opened from the outside. It can withstand more that 550 foot-pounds of pressure.

An Illinois high school with 65 doors on its main floor decided to improve security by reducing the number of those doors used during the school day. It locked many of the exterior doors and restricted access to them with key controls. The school explained to staffers that keys had to be limited to make sure the security team knew exactly when normally locked doors were opened.

Also in Illinois, two school districts began using a system that installs safety magnets in door frames. When the magnet is removed, a locking mechanism is engaged. Use of the magnets allows teachers to secure classrooms without having to go outside into hallways to lock the doors with keys.

B. Windows

School administrators who want to provide staff and students with the advantages afforded by natural lighting should do so with an awareness of the security risks that windows can create, especially with respect to unauthorized entry.

Placement of windows plays a key role in minimizing unauthorized entry. Ideally windows are placed where they enable easy surveillance of school grounds, and especially higher-risk areas. For example, it is important to include windows that enable staff to monitor the school's main entrance. These windows should be kept free of announcements or other postings that create an obstacle to effective surveillance.

Windows that are operable (that is, ones that can be opened and closed) should have locks that can secure them in a closed position. Window film can be used to reinforce window glass and hold it in place should it be subjected to impact. Second-floor windows should be inaccessible from the outside. Ideally, each room should include at least one designated window that can be used to escape in the event of an emergency.

Basement windows are an area of particular concern and should be protected by window well covers or grills.

V. SPECIFIC MEASURES AT ENTRANCEWAYS

Specific security measures implemented at entrance areas will depend on factors such as budget and incidence history. These measures are not undertaken singly but are part of a comprehensive overall security plan.

A. Metal Detectors

The use of metal detectors at school entrance points is an extreme measure that can help prevent unauthorized access but is often subject to criticism. Walk-through metal detectors can be utilized in conjunction with handheld detectors, which can be used to investigate further when an individual triggers the walk-through detector. Use of a walk-through detector requires a significant investment of space. The detector itself will typically fill a space approximately three-feet wide and two-feet deep. Of course, the staging area is much larger. It must allow enough room to provide a comfortable environment for those waiting to pass through. Space also is needed for people who are being scanned to place items in a pass-through container and to turn around and pass through a second time, if needed. Care must be taken to locate the system in an area where it will not be subjected to potential sources of interference, such as nearby electromagnetic equipment or even plumbing in the walls.

Opponents say metal detector use is overly intrusive and creates an atmosphere of fear. Because metal detectors cannot distinguish between items that are prohibited (such as a knife) and items that are not (such as a set of keys), trained personnel are needed to operate and monitor them. This need, in combination with the cost of the detectors, the cost of hiring trained personnel to man them, and the fact that the layout of many schools makes it difficult to efficiently implement a metal-detection system, makes the use of metal detectors impractical for many schools. But metal detectors can also be an effective tool for reducing the likelihood of an unauthorized intrusion.

B. Closed-Circuit Television (CCTV)

Closed-circuit television technology can deter unauthorized access and help prevent crime throughout the school campus. A CCTV system intended to prevent access by intruders must be designed with reference to, and in coordination with, conditions that exist at the school with respect to external lighting and landscaping conditions. When cameras are placed at external locations, steps should be taken to minimize the likelihood of compromises to performance that can arise due to vandalism and exposure to outdoor elements. These systems typically monitor entrance points and parking areas, recording images that can be preserved electronically. Decisions relating to placement are made with reference to the level of risk associated with particular areas. Although full-time monitoring of CCTV cameras is not financially feasible for many schools, CCTV creates a record of any suspicious or illegal activity and can serve as an effective deterrent.

Case in point: In Wisconsin, a school's CCTV system recorded a student spraying a sticky substance on the steps of his high school as a senior prank. But the prank stopped being funny after two people were hurt after slipping and falling on the steps. The student was charged with two counts of recklessly endangering safety and was subjected to up to 20 years in jail and a $50,000 fine.

Many school administrators have seen the benefits of security cameras, and in a November 2010 release the National Center for Education Statistics and Bureau of Justice Statistics reported that the percentage of public schools using security cameras increased from 19% to 55% between the 1999-2000 school year and the 2007-08 school year. But despite the benefits, some students and parents express concerns that surveillance cameras may violate students' privacy rights. Calming concerns is a crucial step. One of the most effective ways to get parents and students on board is to develop a written policy outlining how and where security cameras will be used. Consider including the following information in the policy:

- list specific areas in school that will be monitored by the cameras
- list areas of the school where cameras will not be used, such as bathroom stalls and locker rooms, and
- say whether recordings from cameras will be produced as well as how long they will be kept and who has access to the recordings.

C. Security Personnel/Greeters

The use of security guards and/or greeters is a low-tech but effective tool for preventing unauthorized access to a school's campus. Located at entrance points, security guards can check identifications and respond immediately to suspicious activities. Greeters, who are often parent volunteers, can serve a similar function at entrance points. Grandparents, caregivers, and retired community members also serve as good sources of greeters. The greeter's role is not to directly intervene to stop criminal activity. Instead, greeters can determine whether a visitor has a legitimate reason to be on the school's grounds and can direct the visitor to a specific location where he can complete applicable sign-in procedures. Ideally, greeters should also receive training relating to the school's evacuation plans and emergency procedures. Students should not be used as greeters.

D. Card Readers

Access-control card systems can be used to help keep track of who is entering a school facility. When this technology is used, an identification card is encoded and recognized by a card reader. When the reader recognizes the card, access is gained, such as by lifting a mechanical arm to permit access to a parking area. This system carries the advantage of not requiring live personnel to operate. But there are drawbacks. Cards can be passed from one person to another person, and more than one individual or vehicle may be able to enter at the same time using just one authorized card.

1. Case Study: Use of 'Smart Cards'

Cards can also be used to regulate the movement of students inside the school. At New Jersey's Dumont High School, for example, students are given "smart cards" that allow administrators to control specific areas the students can access. For example, access to a gym can be limited to sports team members. The cards also permit administrators to track the use of bathrooms and computers. In addition, they can be used to pay for meals and to take books from the school's library.

E. Use of PIN Codes

Access can also be limited by requiring individuals to enter a personal identification number (PIN) code into a keypad in order to gain entrance to a designated area of the school. The use of PIN codes is more effective as a security measure when it is combined with the use of identification cards and card readers. Their use includes potential drawbacks, including a vulnerability to vandalism and the ability of authorized users to permit entry by unauthorized personnel.

F. Biometrics

Biometric devices permit access only upon identification of a particular physical trait associated uniquely with the authorized user. Examples include fingerprint readers, systems that verify identity by measuring the size and shape of the entering individual's hand, and technology that reads retinal impressions. This technology works in essence by collecting data relating to a specific individual's physical or behavioral characteristics and comparing it to data that already is on file. These devices carry the advantage of allowing authorized users to enter without having to remember any type of identification card. Because they rely on unique individual characteristics, they also carry the advantage of being more reliable than identifiers such as identification cards. Although biometric devices are more commonly used in applications that require the highest level of security, such as prisons and international border points, they may become more prevalent in school applications as technologies improve.

1. Case Study: Eye-Scanning System

A 2006 evaluative study of an eye-scanning system used in three New Jersey elementary schools highlighted the advantages and shortcomings of relying on this particular type of biometric technology as an access security measure in the school setting. Teachers and staff, and more than 700 school parents had their eye images scanned into a computer system. To gain access to the school, they were required to have a camera on school grounds scan images of their irises. Five cameras were placed in exterior locations, and another six were placed in interior locations. The study found that the system provided an accurate identification and unlocked the door 78% of the time. Another 6% of attempted entries were properly denied because the individuals' eye scans were not in the computer. But 16% of the time, there were problems with scanning due to outdoor lighting conditions or a failure of the individual to line up his eyes properly with the camera. Despite the shortcomings, parents and staff indicated a perceived increase in school security.

2. Case Study: Fingerprinting

One of the nation's largest providers of child care and early educational services has installed biometric security systems at all of its corporate locations. Tutor Time, which has more than 100 locations nationwide and serves more than 28,000 students, began requiring fingerprint information and a PIN number from individuals seeking access to its facilities. The organization does not maintain a database of actual fingerprints. Instead, fingerprints are scanned into a system and converted into a series of numbers to produce something similar to a bar code. The "bar code" is then matched with a specific authorized user.

VI. LIGHTING

Proper illumination of entry areas and parking areas is a key to preventing unauthorized access to facilities. Because light fixtures are vulnerable to vandalism, they should be mounted as high as possible and covered with a material or housing that prevents breakage of lenses. Lighting fixtures can be controlled by clocks or by photocells that turn them off at dawn and on at dusk, although a manual override feature should be included. Lighting controls and switches must be protected, and the accessibility of electrical panels must be restricted.

Lights should be placed so as to minimize glare and the creation of shadows. Ideally, the lighting near entrance points should cast a pattern of light horizontally rather than vertically. Flush-mounted or recessed light fixtures should be used when possible. Because light-colored surfaces reflect light more efficiently than dark-colored surfaces, the presence of light-colored surfaces at entry points will increase the overall level of entry-point security. Maintaining a fixed schedule for maintenance of all outdoor lighting, including lighting at entrance points, is another important safety key. Decisions relating to the provision of lighting must be made with reference to the need of lighting to work effectively with other security measures that may be in place, such as the use of closed-circuit television.

☑ **CHECKLIST –** *Lighting*

☐ There is a regular schedule of maintenance for outside lights.
☐ Special attention is paid to adequacy of lighting at entrance points and other high-risk points of potential intrusion.
☐ Light lenses are protected by an impact-resistant material.
☐ Lighting fixtures do not provide handholds that can be used to climb into the building.
☐ Exterior lighting minimizes glare and shadows.

VII. CONTROLLING ACCESS BY VISITORS

A detailed procedure for controlling access to the school by authorized visitors is essential. Visitors should be steered to a main entrance by clear appropriate signage and by the layout of the school's exterior. Ideally, they will be intercepted by a greeter or security officer outside the school building before they can proceed to sign in at a main office, where school personnel can verify that they are at the school for a legitimate purpose. A similar measure was implemented in the Burke County School District in Waynesboro, Georgia. School visitors there are identified and cleared with the help of a camera outside of the building. Once inside, visitors complete the check-in process and receive an identification badge.

Schools should strongly consider implementing a requirement that visitors produce photo identification to verify identity. Visitor badges, which must be located outside the reach of visitors in a secure area, should be dated and issued once authorization for the visit is confirmed. The date, time, name, purpose, and intended destination of the visitor should be recorded in a log that each visitor should sign. School personnel should accompany visitors to the specific area of the visit. An important but sometimes overlooked feature of a visitor access policy is the incorporation of a "checkout" procedure whereby the visitor surrenders his pass or badge before leaving and the time of the visitor's departure is noted in the school's log. The log should be checked periodically during the day to determine whether any visitor appears to be remaining at the school for an inordinate amount of time.

A relatively extreme measure is to ban unannounced parent visits. The step was taken by Nathan Parker, the superintendent of the Summit Public Schools in New Jersey. Saying the move would improve safety, Parker told parents that unannounced school visits were being banned, regardless of the reason for the visit. For a sample authorization to release a student, see Form I-3 in Chapter Nine.

A check-in policy that relies simply on a visitor typing in a name is vulnerable to exploitation. Brad Kent, an assistant principal at a middle school in Arkansas, was faced with the task of improving this system. With his assistance, the school upgraded to a system called "KeepnTrack." Using this system, visitors had to give their IDs to the school receptionist, who scanned their ID cards. The system works with any state driver's license. It prints a photo scan on a yellow sticker, which creates a photo ID for visitors to wear while on campus. The scan also runs visitors' licenses through the national registry of sex offenders. In addition, the system can be used to run criminal background checks. For more information on the program, go to *www.keepntrack.com.*

It is important for all staffers to be trained on how to approach people who look like they do not belong in the building. School resource officer Michael Rudinski of the Hyattsville (Maryland) Police Department explained a universal greeting staffers use. Staffers say, "Hi, I am [name and title] at [school]. I see that you [circumstances]. How can I help you with that"? Having this plan in place beforehand helps staff approach people with confidence, and faculty and staff are more likely to speak up rather than look the other way.

Following court-ordered custody agreements is sometimes easier said than done. Mike Cowsert, a school resource officer at Timber Ridge Schools in Arlington Heights, Illinois, described the problem of having non-custodial parents trying to sign out their children without the custodial parent's consent. To combat the problem, the school issued identification badges to parents at student orientation and explained that the badges would have to be shown to sign children out of school. Where custody was an issue, badges were provided to custodial parents only. The use of the badges enabled office staffers to determine whether the parent had the authority to pick up the student.

A. Case Study: Visitor Screening

More and more schools are adding another layer of protection to visitor screening policies by checking the identities of visitors against lists of sexual predators. Typically, the prospective visitor's driver's license is swiped through a computer that searches for a match against lists of offenders. Some systems also allow administrators to search for a match against lists of court orders that restrict parental custody of students. The Charter School for Applied Technologies, located in Tonawanda, New York, has utilized the tool. When a license does not show a match against the lists, the school issues a pass that includes the visitor's photograph. In the event of a match, school officials are notified immediately by phone and email.

Schools considering implementation of a background check system should be aware of a new associated threat: lawsuits challenging the legality of the systems under the Constitution.

A couple filed a suit against a Texas school district, claiming its background check system violated their rights to freely associate with their children. They also added a claim of unreasonable search and seizure.

The couple cited concerns about identity theft. They didn't like the idea of a private company collecting their personal information. One of the plaintiffs asked the school to check her status against a database maintained by the Justice Department. She said the school denied her request. The school district's director of police and public safety said before the suit was filed, there had been no complaints about the system.

Schools must be extremely vigilant to ensure students are picked up only by authorized individuals. Sandra White, principal at a Mississippi school, explained how a simple procedure effectively met this goal in a specific case. When a teacher did not recognize a man who tried to pick up a student, the teacher kindly but firmly explained that she needed to check his identification and confirm it on a pickup sheet. At the office, the man's name was not on the list. The teacher called the child's mother to confirm that the man had authority to pick up the child. The mother confirmed the man's authority to do so. The next day, the mother went to the school to add the man's name to the list.

☑ CHECKLIST – *Visitor Policy*

☐ School entrance points include signage that steers visitors to an office location.

☐ Sign-in areas are adequately staffed.

☐ Visitors must produce photo identification.

☐ Visitors are required to wear dated visitor passes or badges once authorization is confirmed.

☐ Visitors are escorted to their specific visit location.

☐ Visitor identification passes and badges are kept in a secure area.

☐ Visitors are required to sign a log indicating date, time, and intended destination.

☐ Visitor identification passes and badges are collected from visitors upon exit.

☐ Time of building exit is recorded in a log.

For steps key personnel should take in response to a school intruder, see Form II-12 in Chapter Nine. Information about specific steps to take in situations involving a weapon, and in potentially violent situations in general, can be found on Form I-4 and Form I-5 in Chapter Nine. For resources for victims and families in child abduction cases, go to the federal Office of Juvenile Justice and Delinquency Prevention's Web page, located at *http://www.ojjdp.gov*.

VIII. COORDINATING WITH FIRST RESPONDERS

Coordinating with first responders, such as police, fire and EMS personnel, is key to maintaining building security. In September 2007, the Attorney General of Pennsylvania introduced a tool schools can use to improve coordination between schools and first responders in the event that security at a school's entrance is breached and an emergency response is required. The Attorney General's Office created a School Safety Project CD-ROM. Based on a program that was developed by a local school district within the state, the CD-ROM helps schools create building safety plans that first responders can access on websites in an emergency. The CD-ROM helps districts create a secure website that includes information relating to many aspects of the facility, such as floor plans, photographs of school grounds, and a contact list of school administrators. The program on which the Attorney General's guide is based was developed by the Susquenita School District at a cost of approximately $1,000. First responders can access a password-protected website and view floor plans, school access roads, and photographs of classrooms and corridors. They can even access a real-time view of classrooms and offices, as the website includes images taken from school security cameras. This feature enables first responders to gain an inside view of the school building before entering.

IX. EFFECTIVE LOW-TECHNOLOGY ALTERNATIVES

Ideally, technological measures designed to protect entry points should be combined with less technical, but effective strategies and techniques to decrease the risk of criminal behavior. The U.S. Department of Justice's Office of Justice Programs has compiled the following list of low-technology but effective tools for deterring unauthorized entry to school facilities. Some of these measures are discussed elsewhere in this chapter. Utilizing the combination of them that best fits a particular school's needs can have the effect of increasing entry-point security.

- Post signs warning that unauthorized trespassers are subject to arrest.
- Post signs indicating that all vehicles on campus are subject to search.
- Provide a guard to check identifications at the main entrance to the school.
- Provide authorized vehicles with parking stickers so that unauthorized vehicles can be more easily identified and removed.
- Require student uniforms so that outsiders can be easily identified.
- Implement a school policy that bars hats, shirts that include messages related to alcohol, drugs, violence or gangs and exposed tattoos.
- Provide greeters at all open entrances.

- Provide a minimal number of entrances.
- Implement a policy under which students walking around the school campus during class time are challenged for a pass and are potentially subjected to search.
- Close off the main student parking lot during the day.
- Provide fencing that defines school property and discourages casual intruders.
- Confiscate the student ID of students who are suspended or expelled and make their photographs available to security staff.

Here's an instance that proves low-tech preventive measures are effective ways to keep students safe: A swift, coordinated response to warning signs enabled school officials and law enforcement authorities to thwart a shooting plot at a Pennsylvania high school. Local police had been informed that guns had been stolen from the home of a 15-year-old student. When school officials realized the student fit the profile of a potential shooter – a white teenage loner with few friends – they took action quickly.

School officials began to check students' backpacks and lockers. They also talked to students who knew the possible suspect. The superintendent notified school board members about what was going on, and the faculty met with its emergency response team.

The student's plan to go on a shooting rampage near the start of the new year unraveled when one of his friends told a teacher that he knew the location of the missing guns. The teacher immediately reported the information to school officials, and police recovered the guns. The student was arrested – before causing any harm.

X. CASE STUDY: INSTALLATION OF FACILITY MANAGEMENT SYSTEMS

The Harrison County School District Two, located near Colorado Springs, Colorado, serves more than 11,000 students and has 23 schools. In 2002, the district decided to upgrade its security systems at all of its schools, which included elementary schools, middle schools, high schools, alternative schools and charter schools. After soliciting several proposals, the district decided to install a security system that included closed-caption television, digital video recording, and card access control.

A vendor installed card readers on perimeter doors of schools, and all staff members were issued combination identification badges and access cards. All exterior building locks were re-keyed, and key distribution was limited. A digital video recording unit was installed at every district school. All front lobbies were outfitted with cameras. Surveillance was added for exteriors and some interior areas. Digital video recorders replaced VCRs, and some secondary buildings were outfitted with pan-tilt-zoom cameras.

A policy was implemented whereby all perimeter school doors, except the ones at front lobby entrances, remained locked at all times. Cameras began recording all activity at lobby entrances at all times, with monitors enabling school staff to observe those areas. Each school's security system was linked to a central location, where monitors at all the school facilities could be viewed at all times. The installed system also enabled administrators and security personnel to view video from a remote location by using a Web browser.

The system was installed in a way that enabled it to interface with the district's pre-existing burglar alarm system. This alarm system alerted the district's private security company whenever an alarm was triggered after hours.

In cases of a security breach, the system enables personnel to export video clips to a CD-ROM for delivery to local law enforcement authorities. The system includes an authentication process which verifies that stored video has not been altered.

A lockdown capability is also included. Staff can activate a button in the front office that locks perimeter doors and deactivates card readers. When a school is placed in lockdown, entry can occur only via the front door after staff has had the opportunity to view the person or persons seeking access, and chooses to permit access by manually unlocking the door.

The system also provides wireless personal panic control devices that are distributed to key personnel. These devices can be activated to signal a need for assistance from any location on the school grounds. When activated, the devices cause a white strobe light to turn on in the school's front office and send emails and pages to members of a designated response team.

The district reported great success with the new system. Soon after installation was completed, an individual who entered three different school buildings during a lunch hour, and stole cash and credit cards from teachers' purses, was caught on tape. The system also reduced fighting and vandalism.

XI. LEGAL DECISIONS

A. Intruders

◆ A 17-year-old non-student intruder sexually assaulted an elementary school student in a school bathroom. About 14 years later, the student sued the school district and claimed a violation of her equal protection rights. **The court rejected her claim because she did not show that the district discriminated against her** and that the district treated her worse than students who were not in her protected group. *McGuire v. Northwest Area School Dist.*, No. 3:11-CV-1022, 2011 WL 5444084 (M.D. Pa. 11/8/11).

◆ An intruder entered an elementary school through its main entrance. A teacher asked him if he needed help, but he ignored her. She then went to the office to see if he had signed in. Two other teachers also saw the intruder in the hallway. When one of them questioned him, he said he needed to use a restroom. The teacher pointed out a restroom and told the intruder he needed to return to the office after using it. The teachers then lost sight of the intruder, who entered another restroom and sexually assaulted a five-year-old student. The student's mother filed a negligence claim against the school district. A trial court ruled against her on the basis that the assault was not foreseeable. An appeals court reversed, finding **reasonable minds could differ as to whether the district's response to the presence of the intruder constituted a breach of its duty of care** and as to whether the assault was a foreseeable consequence of the district's failure to initially note the intruder's entry and monitor the situation more closely. *A.W. v. Lancaster County School Dist. 0001*, 784 N.W.2d 907 (Neb. 2010).

◆   A non-student entered a high school and requested a visitor's pass. When his request was denied, he became angry. School employees escorted him from the school building, but they did not make sure he left the premises. The man then re-entered and stabbed a former schoolmate in a hallway. The schoolmate and her parents sued the school, its principal and others, claiming they were negligent. A trial court granted a defense motion for summary judgment, and an appeals court upheld the trial court's ruling. The appeals court explained that the defendants owed a duty of reasonable supervision to the student who was attacked. However, **they could not be liable for negligence because the attack was not reasonably foreseeable and preventable**. The attacker did not go to the school looking for the student he attacked, and he did not even know she was a student there. There was no evidence that the defendants had any warning indicating the attacker would come into the building and stab a student. The stabbing occurred suddenly and without warning, and the defendants' failure to prevent it was not negligent. *Boudreaux v. St. Tammany Parish School Board*, No. 2007 CA 0889, 2007 WL 4480703 (La. Ct. App. 12/21/07).

◆   While teaching a volleyball class, a teacher noticed two young men come into the gym. She recognized one as a student at the school, but she did not recognize the other. When the teacher walked toward the men and blew her whistle, the unknown man struck her in the left temple. The man left but returned a short time later and punched her in the back of the head, causing her to lose consciousness. She suffered serious injuries. **The teacher sued the city, claiming it was negligent as a landlord of the school when it allowed the attacker to gain unauthorized access.** She also claimed the city breached a special duty to protect her from harm and breached a contract with a teachers' union by failing to properly implement a school safety plan. The court granted the city's motion for summary judgment. Because the city was acting as a public government entity and not as a landlord when it undertook efforts to provide security, it was immune to the teacher's negligence claim. The court also rejected the teacher's claim that the city breached a special duty it owed to her by failing to implement a school safety plan and protect its teachers. Neither the maintenance of a comprehensive security system nor school officials' representations that they "take security seriously" created a special duty. Finally, the court rejected the contract claim because the city could not be held liable to individual teachers for any alleged contract breach between it and the teacher's union. *Daniels v. City of New York*, No. 04-CV-7612 (CM), 2007 WL 2040581 (S.D.N.Y. 6/26/07).

◆   A deranged convicted felon entered a school building holding a picture of a young girl. The school principal confronted the intruder, who then left. The school subsequently instituted a new access control policy. An individual was stationed in the school's lobby to screen people entering the school, and visitors were instructed to sign in at the principal's office. The policy further required staff to monitor visitors through a floor-to-ceiling window in the principal's office. About a year after the incident involving the intruder, a different intruder gained unauthorized access to the school and attacked a 10-year-old student with a hammer. The attack caused serious injury. The student's parents sued the school's principal, the county school superintendent, the board of education and others, alleging they were negligent in failing to develop a school safety plan as required by state law and allowing the attack to occur. A trial court granted the defendants' motion for summary judgment, and an appeals court affirmed. **The school had prepared and put into place a school safety plan** before the attack. Because the plan was in place before the attack occurred, the defendants were entitled to immunity on the negligence claims. The ruling of the trial court was affirmed. *Leake v. Murphy*, 644 S.E.2d 328 (Ga. Ct. App. 2007).

◆   A father drove his 12-year-old son to a high school that the boy and his brother attended. The father waited outside while the boy entered the school to find his brother, who was participating in a school event. The 12-year-old was sexually assaulted in the school by a convicted sex felon who had gained unauthorized access. The incident took place on a Saturday, when school was not in session. The parent sued the school, its president and its principal, **claiming they were negligent in leaving the school doors unlocked and unattended during school-sponsored activities**. The court upheld a ruling against the parent, finding that he failed to show the defendants owed him a duty of care. There is generally no duty to protect others from the criminal acts of third parties. Although a duty may exist when there is a special relationship between the defendant and the plaintiff, a special relationship giving rise to a duty did not exist in this case. School was not in session, and the 12-year-old was not participating in any school-sponsored event at the time of the assault. In addition, the parent did not show the assault was foreseeable. *Roe v. Univ. of Detroit Jesuit High School and Academy*, No. 264269, 2006 WL 475285 (Mich. Ct. App. 2/28/06).

◆   A high school student sued a board of education, a high school and others after she was raped in a school bathroom by a non-student intruder. **The student alleged that the defendants wrongfully failed to provide**

security guards in the area of the alleged attack and near exterior doors.
She said students frequently opened exterior doors to allow other students to
enter. The board of education, high school and private security firm appealed
a trial court's decision to deny their motions for summary judgment. The
appeals court reversed the trial court's ruling. The alleged security
deficiencies arose from the allocation of security resources, which was a
governmental function. Because such decisions are in the nature of a
governmental function, the district and high school could not be held liable
unless they had a special relationship with the student that created a special
duty to protect her. No special duty existed, as there was no direct contact
between the student and the school defendants before the alleged attack.
Also, the school defendants did not have notice of prior sexual assaults at the
school and had no reason to anticipate an intruder would enter and commit a
violent crime against a student. Finally, the claim against the private security
firm failed because the school defendants controlled the security guards at
the school. The lower court's ruling was reversed. *Doe v. Town of Hempstead
Board of Educ.*, 795 N.Y.S.2d 322 (N.Y. App. Div. 2005).

◆   A substitute teacher sued a board of education after she was attacked by
a school intruder, claiming the board negligently failed to provide adequate
security. The court reversed a trial court's decision to deny summary
judgment to the board. **Because the provision of security against attacks
by school intruders is a governmental function, there is no liability
unless there is a special duty to protect.** In this case, there was no special
duty to protect the substitute teacher. The implementation of security
measures did not create a special duty, and the board made no special
promise of protection to the substitute teacher. *Bain v. New York City Board
of Educ.*, 702 N.Y.S.2d 334 (N.Y. App. Div. 2000).

◆   A high school secretary noticed a neatly dressed man carrying what
appeared to be flower boxes near a school entrance. The secretary asked the
man if she could help him. He uttered an incoherent response, thanked her,
and moved along. A short time later, the man was observed by an individual
who worked at the school as a water safety instructor. At the time, the man
was standing between a swimming pool and bleachers. **The layout of the
school building made it easy to become disoriented, and it was not
unusual for male visitors to become disoriented and walk through the
girls' locker room.** The water safety instructor, who also believed the man
was delivering flowers, concluded that he had reached the area by walking
through the girls' locker room. She began to walk toward him to ask why he
was in the building. While doing so, she met a school custodian who had
also seen the man exit from the girls' locker room into a lobby area. When
the custodian saw the man, he commented that it was odd to see someone
coming out of the girls' locker room. The man again uttered an incoherent
remark and moved on. About an hour after the secretary first saw the man,
she observed him again near a school entrance. This time, the man was

talking to a student. She did not confront him, even though she later admitted that he did not belong in that location because it was not the school's main entrance. A short time later, the man sexually assaulted a student in the locker room. The student's parents sued the school district, claiming it failed to provide adequate supervision and security. A lower court granted immunity to the individual school employees but not to the school district, and the school district appealed. The appeals court affirmed, finding that the school district was not entitled to immunity. **The employees engaged in discretionary acts that deserved the protection of official immunity. However, this immunity did not extend to the school district. If it did, the district would be rewarded for failing to develop and implement a basic security policy.** *S.W. v. Spring Lake Park School Dist. No. 16*, 592 N.W.2d 870 (Minn. Ct. App. 1999).

◆   A teacher was killed when a local resident with a history of mental illness entered her daycare center through an unlocked rear entrance and shot her. The center was operated out of a wing of a local high school. The rear entrance was open because it was being used by construction contractors. The teacher's husband sued the school district and owner of the daycare center, claiming they created the danger that resulted in the teacher's death by unlocking the back entrance. A trial court ruled against him, and he appealed. The appeals court affirmed the ruling against the teacher's husband. The state generally has no obligation to protect citizens from the violent acts of private individuals. Although an exception applies when the state creates a danger that causes harm, the exception was not applicable. **The district could not have foreseen that allowing construction workers to use the back entrance would result in the shooting, and it did not willfully or deliberately disregard a foreseeable danger.** *Morse v. Lower Merion School Dist.*, 132 F.3d 902 (3d Cir. 1997).

◆   While providing instruction in her classroom, a teacher was confronted by four intruders. One of the intruders accused the teacher of having physically abused a student. The intruder then assaulted the teacher with a metal chair, causing back injuries. **The teacher sued the board of education, claiming it was negligent because it failed to monitor and control the people who entered the school.** The teacher also claimed that the school negligently failed to provide proper security and created a dangerous condition. In addition, she claimed the board breached a union contract that required school principals to develop safety plans. The court granted the board's motion for summary judgment. The board was immune to the negligence claim because the provision of security was a governmental function rather than a proprietary function. The court rejected the teacher's claim that the school assumed a special duty to protect her and thus was not immune to the negligence claims against it. The teacher alleged that this special duty arose when the school's principal told her not to worry because she was "in a good school." She also alleged that a special duty arose based on the collective bargaining agreement between the teachers' union and the board. The court held that neither the principal's statement nor a collective bargaining agreement provision requiring principals to develop safety plans created a special duty. Therefore, the teacher's negligence claims failed and summary judgment was awarded to the board. *Genao v. Board of Educ. of the City of New York*, 888 F.Supp. 501 (S.D.N.Y. 1995).

◆ While leaving her high school following her last class for the day, a student inadvertently bumped shoulders with another student. The second student told the first that "she was going to kill her." The first student then met her sister, who also attended the school, in another area of the school. She attempted to report the incident at a security office, but she received no response when she knocked at the door. She and her sister were then assaulted as they tried to leave the school. **The second student struck one of the sisters in the head and elbow with a hammer, and the second student's brother, who was not a student at the school, stabbed the other.** The sisters sued the city's board of education and others, claiming negligent supervision. A jury returned a verdict of $50,000 for one of the sisters and $750,000 for the other. A lower court set aside the verdict and dismissed the complaint, finding the evidence did not prove negligent supervision. On appeal, the court reinstated the verdict, finding the jury could permissibly find that the board failed to provide adequate supervision. *Mirand v. City of New York*, 190 A.D.2d 282 (N.Y. App. Div. 1993).

◆ A teacher selected a fourth-grade student to supervise a classroom of second-graders while their teacher went to retrieve supplies from another part of the building. While the teacher was away, the fourth-grader was lured from the classroom by an intruder. The intruder exited the school with the student by proceeding through an unlocked rear door and through an open gate of a security fence. He then forced her into a wooded area and raped her. The student's mother sued the school district, claiming negligence. A jury found in her favor and awarded nearly $251,000. The district appealed, arguing that it could not be held liable because the actions of the intruder were not foreseeable. The appeals court rejected the argument and upheld the jury's verdict. There was enough evidence for the jury to find that school officials were on notice that students were in danger of being assaulted by intruders. The school was located in a statistically high crime area, and there had been sexual assaults and other violent crime in the surrounding area. Also, school security was deficient. **The gate on a security fence at the rear of the school was left open and unlocked, and a set of doors at the back of the school did not close and lock properly due to an alignment problem. Doors at the front of the school did not close properly, and an intercom system was not functioning properly at the time of the assault.** Further, unaccompanied and unknown adult males were permitted to roam school hallways. All of these things raised a factual issue of foreseeability that was properly submitted to the jury. The trial court's judgment was affirmed. *District of Columbia v. Doe*, 524 A.2d 30 (D.C. Ct. App. 1987).

B. Search and Seizure

◆   An Ohio bus driver approached a school security guard with a book bag that had been left on the bus. In a quick initial search, the guard opened the bag and determined it belonged to student Joshua Polk. Because he had heard rumors that Polk had ties to a gang, the guard took the bag to the office and searched it further. Inside, he found bullets. The guard, the principal and a police officer then took Polk to an empty classroom and searched another bag Polk had. In it, they found a pistol. Polk later asked a court to suppress the evidence. A trial court granted the request, and an appeals court affirmed. **Though the initial quick search of the bag was reasonable, the follow-up searches were not.** After the initial search, there was no justification to proceed with a more detailed one. Rumors regarding gang affiliation were not enough, the court said. *State of Ohio v. Polk*, No. 14AP-787, 2016 WL 102005 (Ohio Ct. App. 1/7/16).

◆   An Iowa student suffered a serious injury during a school football game and was taken to a hospital by ambulance. His coach said he was very concerned about his equipment bag and wanted to make sure only one specific person could get it. The coach became suspicious and told the superintendent, who searched the bag and found a loaded gun as well as drug paraphernalia. The student was found guilty of possession of a firearm, carrying weapons on school grounds and possession of a controlled substance. An appeals court rejected his appeal. It noted that **student-athletes using school-issued equipment bags have a reduced expectation of privacy**. In addition, the student had a history of drug and weapons charges, and his preoccupation with it under the circumstances was a red flag that "the bag contained something illicit." *State v. Lindsey*, 868 N.W.2d 881 (Iowa Ct. App. 2015).

◆   A knife was found in a Minnesota high school student's locker during a random search. The student said she forgot to remove the knife from her purse after using it to do farm chores. Initially she was suspended for three days, but the school board then expelled her for the rest of the school year. She sued, saying the suspension violated state law. **The state's highest court invalidated the expulsion.** Though the school board said it expelled the student for "willful conduct that endangers" others, this conclusion was not supported by the evidence. The expulsion was reversed. *In re Expulsion of A.D. From United South Cent. Public Schools*, No. A14-1587, 2016 WL 4126377 (Minn. 8/3/16).

◆   A Nebraska special education coordinator at a middle school helped a student with his backpack and heard a clunking sound when she set it down on a counter. Because she thought the sound "was not what a backpack should sound like," she opened the bag and searched it. Inside she found three bottles of cologne and then a switchblade knife. When the student was charged in juvenile court, he moved to suppress the evidence. The juvenile court overruled the motion, finding that **"the search was reasonably related to the circumstances justifying the opening of the backpack, permissible in its scope, and reasonably related to the objectives of the search."** A state appeals court affirmed. The clunking sound justified the initial search, and the eventual scope of the search was reasonably related to its original objective and not excessively intrusive. *In re Interest of Dana H.*, No. A-15-246, 2015 WL 7733998 (Neb. Ct. App. 12/1/15).

◆   A cell phone and watch were reported stolen from a boys' locker room, and surveillance video showed a student leaving the locker room with something shiny and then exiting the building to go to his car. An assistant principal brought the student to his office, and the student admitted going to his car to smoke. The assistant principal then searched the car and found the stolen items. At his criminal trial, the student said the evidence should be suppressed because there was no probable cause for the search and because he was not read his *Miranda* rights. The court rejected his claim, finding **there was probable cause for the search**. It also found the student was not entitled to *Miranda* warnings because the questioning by the assistant principal was not a custodial interrogation. *State of Kansas v. Moses*, 327 P.3d 1052 (Table) (Kan. Ct. App. 2014).

◆   A student at a California high school informed campus security officers that she had witnessed a classmate shoot someone on a public bus. School administrators instructed a campus security officer to find the student. The officer often saw the student hanging around another student's locker. That locker was searched, but no weapons were found in it. The locker next to it was also searched, and that search revealed a sawed-off shotgun. Other officers located the alleged shooter, who had a gun in his backpack. In criminal proceedings, the student who had the shotgun asked the court to suppress the evidence of the shotgun. He claimed the search violated his Fourth Amendment rights. The court rejected the claim, finding that **the decision to search the locker with the shotgun was reasonable under the circumstances**. *In re J.D.*, 225 Cal.App.4th 709 (Cal. Ct. App. 2014).

◆   Police in Florida received a tip that a student might have a gun at school. After the tip was passed along to the school, an assistant principal and two security guards brought the student to a conference room and opened his book bag. **A loaded handgun was in the book bag.** At his criminal trial, the student argued that the search was unreasonable because it was based on an anonymous tip. The court rejected his argument. It found the search was justified because an extraordinary danger was present and because students at school are entitled to less privacy than free adults in other settings. *K.P. v. State*, 129 So.3d 1121 (Fla. Dist. Ct. App. 2013).

◆ A high school student reported that a classmate was driving in an unsafe manner in the school parking lot. The assistant principal called the classmate to the office, where he detected an odor of cigarette smoke. Pursuant to school policy, the assistant principal and the school resource officer searched the classmate's car. They found brass knuckles and a glass pipe that was coated with marijuana residue. In criminal proceedings, the classmate sought to suppress the evidence, arguing that the search of the car violated his rights under the Fourth Amendment. He said that since he was old enough to use tobacco legally, the odor did not justify the search. The court rejected his claim, because **even though he was old enough to use tobacco the use of it on school grounds was a violation of school policy**. *State v. Voss*, 267 P.3d 735 (Idaho Ct. App. 2011).

◆ Pursuant to a high school's policy, a student who left school and returned during the same day was searched. When he was told to empty his pockets, he pulled out a bag containing 44 tablets of ecstasy. The student later claimed that the search violated his Fourth Amendment rights. He asked the judge in a juvenile proceeding to suppress the evidence uncovered by the search. The judge denied the request, and the student appealed. The appeals court upheld the judge's ruling. It decided that the school did not violate the student's Fourth Amendment rights. The search was conducted pursuant to a written policy, and the policy applied to all students. Also, **the policy was justified by legitimate safety concerns, and the search was not overly intrusive**. *People v. Sean A.*, 120 Cal.Rptr.3d 72 (Cal. Ct. App. 2010).

◆ An alternative learning center, which was attended by students who had been removed from other school campuses due to disciplinary problems, subjected all entering students to a search. The daily search required students to pass through a metal detector, be patted down, remove their shoes for inspection and empty their pockets. All students and parents attended an orientation session that included a description of the search policy. During a search, an examining officer found a marijuana cigarette inside the shoe of a student. At a trial held to determine whether he should be adjudicated delinquent, the student filed a motion to suppress the evidence. The motion was denied, and the student was adjudicated delinquent. He appealed, renewing his argument that the evidence should have been suppressed because it was discovered as a result of an unlawful search. The court rejected the student's argument and affirmed the lower court's decision. **Even though the search was not conducted based on individualized suspicion, it was justified by the school's need to maintain a safe learning environment in a high-risk setting.** Public school students are subject to a greater degree of supervision than adults, and the state had a compelling interest in maintaining safe schools. In addition, the uniform nature of the searches guarded against an abuse of discretion by administrators. The search was an administrative search that intruded on the privacy of students only to the extent necessary to satisfy the state's interest in maintaining safety. The lower court's ruling was affirmed. *In re O.E.*, No. 03-02-00516-CV, 2003 WL 22669014 (Tex. Ct. App. 11/13/03).

◆   A public high school in Philadelphia periodically subjected all students to a point-of-entry search for weapons. When the searches were conducted, students were required to stand in line and empty their pockets while their backpacks, coats and other personal effects were searched. Students were also scanned by a handheld metal detector. During one such search, a student removed a Swiss army-type knife from his pocket. He was arrested for bringing a weapon onto school property and was adjudicated delinquent after a juvenile hearing. After a court affirmed the disposition, the student appealed again. On appeal, he renewed his argument that the evidence should have been suppressed because the search was made without any individualized reasonable suspicion. The court rejected the argument and affirmed the lower court's decision. **The search was justified because it affected a limited privacy interest and was minimally intrusive.** In addition, the student population and parents were notified of the purpose of the search and the manner in which it was conducted via a school policy and procedure manual, mailings, and notices that were posted throughout the school. The purpose of the search – to keep weapons out of public schools – was compelling. Therefore, the search did not violate the student's constitutional rights. *Ex rel. F.B.*, 726 A.2d 361 (Pa. 1999).

◆   A high school subjected students to random searches for weapons using a handheld metal detector. It provided students and their parents with notice of this practice before it was instituted. On one day, the school decided to search all students who entered the attendance office without hall passes or who were late. A knife was found in the pocket of one of the students who was searched, and she was charged with the crime of bringing a knife onto school grounds. The trial court denied her motion to suppress the evidence and sustained the petition against her. She appealed, challenging the denial of her motion to suppress the evidence. The appeals court affirmed the lower court's decision. **Special needs administrative searches can be conducted without individualized suspicion so long as the government need is great, the privacy intrusion is limited in nature, and it would be unworkable to require a more rigorous standard of suspicion.** In this case, the searches were minimally intrusive, and it would be unworkable to institute a system that relied more on suspicion. Therefore, the search did not violate the student's rights under the Fourth Amendment. *People v. Latasha W.*, 70 Cal.Rptr.2d 886 (Cal. Ct. App. 1998).

◆   To keep weapons out, a public high school set up metal detectors that students passed through shortly after they entered. A student turned around to leave when he saw other students lined up to pass through a metal detector. When he was stopped by a police officer and told he would be required to go through the detector, he raised his shirt to reveal a pistol and said "someone put this gun on me." The student was arrested, and he filed a motion to suppress the evidence. The trial court sustained the motion, finding that **the student could have turned around for innocent reasons that were unrelated to the metal detector**. The state appealed, but the reviewing court affirmed. A person is seized when his freedom of movement is restrained, and the student's detention constituted an illegal seizure. Although the state argued that the officer was performing an administrative search, the cases it relied on to support its argument did not prevent people from choosing not to pass through a checkpoint. In addition, the officer did not have a reasonable suspicion to believe the search would turn up incriminating evidence. Instead, the decision to order the student to pass through the detector was based on a hunch. *People v. Parker*, 672 N.E.2d 813 (Ill. App. Ct. 1996).

◆   The parent of a student who was fatally shot at his high school sued the city, the board of education and others. The parent claimed the city and board negligently allowed people who were armed and dangerous to gain unauthorized access to the school and failed to use metal detectors on the day of the shooting. The parent further claimed that by placing metal detectors at the school, the city and board voluntarily assumed a duty to provide special protection against criminal acts by third persons. She separately claimed that the city and board owed a special duty to the student because he was in their control and because they were uniquely aware that he was at risk. A lower court ruled against the parent, and she appealed. The appeals court affirmed. The city's decision to use metal detectors did not negate the immunity it enjoyed under a tort immunity statute. Nor did a special duty exception to immunity apply, because the parent did not show that a special relationship existed between the city and the student. For similar reasons, the decision favoring the board was affirmed. **The decision to use metal detectors did not make the board an insurer against all criminal activity.** In addition, there was no showing that the decision not to use the metal detectors every day increased the incidence of crime at the school. *Lawson v. City of Chicago*, 662 N.E.2d 1377 (Ill. App. Ct. 1996).

◆   As he entered his public high school in Philadelphia, a student was instructed by a school employee to remove his coat and place his book bag on a table to be searched. The employee then scanned the student with a metal detector and patted him down. All entering students were subjected to the same scan and pat-down procedure that day. When the employee felt a bulge resembling a knife in the student's coat, he searched the coat and found a box cutter in one of its pockets. The student was later arrested and charged with possession of a weapon on school property. At the criminal trial, his motion to suppress the physical evidence was denied, and he was convicted and placed on probation. He appealed, claiming the physical evidence should have been suppressed because he had been subjected to an unlawful search and seizure. **The student claimed the search and seizure**

were unlawful because there was no reasonable suspicion or probable cause to believe he had violated any law or school regulation. The court held that the search did not violate the student's constitutional rights. Administrative searches are permitted even in the absence of individualized suspicion when they are conducted as part of a general regulatory scheme to ensure public safety. The search was reasonably related to the school's interest in promoting student safety, and it was justified because of the high rate of violence that was present in the Philadelphia public schools. All students were subjected to the search, and the uniform procedure that was followed assured that officials would not improperly exercise discretion with respect to the searches. The order adjudicating the student delinquent was affirmed. *Ex rel. S.S.,* 680 A.2d 1172 (Pa. Super. Ct. 1996).

◆   A school chancellor adopted guidelines for searching students as they entered public high schools, and several schools were selected for periodic scanning. At the start of the school year, students at the selected schools were told they would be subjected to a search at some point. The students were not told ahead of time when the searches would take place. Although all entering students could be searched, the guidelines allowed personnel to limit the search, such as by searching every second or third student. Any student chosen to be searched was asked to place bags and parcels on a table, and to remove any metal objects from pockets. Students were then scanned with a metal detector. When a bag or parcel activated the detector, students were asked to open it. If a body scan activated the detector, students were again asked to remove metal objects. Students were taken to a private area if a second body scan activated the detector again. They were then asked a third time to remove metal objects before being subjected to a pat-down search. A student who was subjected to a search under the guidelines was arrested after a metal detector activated on her bag and a knife was discovered inside. She filed a motion to suppress, arguing it was discovered in violation of the Fourth Amendment. The court denied the motion. **The search was permissible because the need to maintain school safety outweighed the minimally intrusive nature of the searches.** In addition, the searches were permissible even though the guidelines did not include any provision requiring administrators to gain the consent of students before conducting a search. Children are required to attend school, and a consent element "would be all but impossible to administer." *People v. Dukes*, 580 N.Y.S.2d 850 (N.Y. Crim. Ct. 1992).

C. Release of Students

◆   A student's father had custody, and his mother had visitation rights. His mother was allowed to pick him up from school on certain days. The mother and his stepfather tried to sign the boy out on a non-allowed day. While a school office employee tried to call the father, the mother and stepfather became angry and the stepfather threatened to kill everyone at the school with an AK-47. The stepfather was later arrested and convicted of attempted terrorism. But an appeals court reversed the conviction on the basis that **the stepfather's statement did not create an imminent danger**. *State v. Watts*, No. M2013-02750-CCA-R3-CD, 2015 WL 3863242 (Tenn. Ct. Crim. App. 6/23/15).

◆ A mother said a teacher at her daughter's elementary school released the daughter to a person who was not authorized to pick her up. The person then allegedly sexually assaulted the child, who was later found on a playground. The mother sued the school district and others, asserting a due process violation. The defendants filed a motion to dismiss, but the court denied it. **The allegations of the complaint were sufficient to plead that the alleged sexual assault was a foreseeable result of the teacher's actions** and were also sufficient to plead that the teacher took affirmative steps to place the child in danger. *L.R. v. School Dist. of Philadelphia*, 60 F.Supp.3d 584 (E.D. Pa. 2014).

◆ A father dropped his son off at school. Later that day, a woman identifying herself as the boy's mother called the school. She claimed that the boy had an appointment and that her boyfriend would pick him up. The boyfriend was not on a list of people who could pick up the child, and the school allowed the man to leave with the child. The child was then taken to Mexico, where his mother lived. The father sued, and **a jury awarded $2 million to him and $850,000 to the child**. It also added $3,500 in punitive damages. *Ramirez v. Escondido Unified School Dist.* (S.D. Cal. 2013).

◆ The guardians of a nine-year-old female student filled out a school form that listed the adults who had permission to remove the child from the school. Six times, the school released the child to a man who said he was the student's father. **The school did not ask the man for identification, and on several occasions he sexually abused her and then returned her to school.** The student's parents sued the school district and other defendants, claiming a violation of the student's due process rights under the federal Constitution. A district court granted a defense motion to dismiss, and a federal appeals court affirmed. The district did not create or knowingly increase the danger to the student, so there was no constitutional violation. *Doe v. Covington County School Dist.*, 675 F.3d 849 (5th Cir. 2012).

◆ A man entered a high school and told a front-office employee that he was the uncle of a student at the school. The man told the employee he was at the school to pick up the student and take her to an appointment. School policy called for the staffer to ask the man for picture identification and to verify that the adult was listed in the student's file as a person who was authorized to remove her from school. However, **the staffer did not ask for picture identification or check the student's file, which would have revealed that only the student's parents were authorized to remove her from school**. The student was released to the man, who took her to a house and molested her. When the student's mother sued the staffer for negligence, a trial judge ruled for the staffer. However, an appeals court reversed. It said that although public school employees in the state can't be sued for negligently performing discretionary acts, the student-checkout policy made her acts "ministerial." Therefore, the staffer could be sued. However, a jury was needed to decide whether the molestation of the student was a reasonably forseeable consequence of the staffer's failure to adhere to the policy. *Cotton v. Smith*, 714 S.E.2d 55 (Ga. Ct. App. 2011).

◆   A high school custodian repeatedly sexually molested a student. The custodian would remove the student from class with written permission he obtained from the school's main office. Then, the custodian would proceed to sexually abuse the student. The abuse was discovered when school surveillance video showed the custodian taking the student into a custodial closet. The custodian was criminally charged, and he was incarcerated. The student's parents sued the local board of education, alleging claims under the federal Constitution based on the board's alleged failure to ensure students were free from sexual assaults, its alleged deprivation of educational services and its alleged failure to supervise a safe and open environment for educational services. **The parents claimed their son was sexually molested as a result of the board's policy of granting permission to the custodian to repeatedly remove the student from class.** The complaint also asserted a federal statutory claim and state tort and constitutional claims. The board of education filed a motion to dismiss. The court refused to dismiss the claims the parents raised under the Fourteenth Amendment. The law recognizes liability for sexual molestation, and it also recognizes a property interest in educational benefits that are temporarily denied. Further, the law recognizes that in some circumstances the state has an affirmative duty to care for and protect particular individuals. In this case, it would be premature to dismiss the parents' claim that the board failed in its duty to protect the student. The state law tort claims were barred by immunity, and the claim under the state constitution was dismissed because there was an adequate state remedy. Finally, the court dismissed claims of breach of contract and violation of the Americans with Disabilities Act. *Cooper v. Brunswick County Board of Educ.*, No. 7:08-CV-48-BO, 2009 WL 1491447 (E.D.N.C. 5/26/09).

◆   A mother enrolled her six-year-old daughter at a school and informed the school secretary that her estranged husband had abducted the child in the past and was not to have contact with her. The secretary did not note the warning on the child's registration form, and it was not entered into the school's computer system. School procedures required the receptionist to check a student's registration card before releasing any child to make sure the person picking up the child was authorized to do so. If a particular child's registration card did not list the person attempting to pick up the child from school, the receptionist was to consult a school administrative official. During school one day, the receptionist received a call and a fax from someone who posed as the child's mother. The impostor instructed the receptionist to release the child to the estranged husband. The receptionist looked for the child's registration card but could not locate it. She then released the child to the estranged husband. The school reprimanded the receptionist for failing to consult with an administrator before releasing the child. The child's mother sued the principal and receptionist. The trial court concluded that the principal and receptionist were immune from liability under state law. The mother appealed, but only as to the ruling regarding the receptionist. The appeals court explained that public officials are generally immune from damages caused by their performance of discretionary functions. However, they are not entitled to immunity if harm is caused by their negligent performance of ministerial acts. In this case, the receptionist was performing a ministerial act when she released the student. **The policy regarding the release of students did not allow for the exercise of any discretion on her part.** She had been specifically told that she was to consult an administrator if she received a fax request to release a child from school. Because the receptionist's conduct did not involve discretion, she was not entitled to immunity. The lower court's ruling in favor of the receptionist was reversed. *Smith v. McDowell*, 666 S.E.2d 94 (Ga. 2008).

◆   A high school teacher brought a 14-year-old special education student to the assistant principal's office, stating that she had found the student walking in the hallways. The student provided the telephone number of a man she said was her uncle. **School policy barred the release of students to anyone other than a parent, legal guardian, police authority, or a person designated in writing by a parent. Nonetheless, the assistant principal allowed the student to call the man to arrange for her to be picked up from school.** He then left the student alone in the lobby of the school's main office. The man picked her up from school and allegedly sexually abused her at his home. The student's mother sued the vice principal and the school district, asserting due process and state-law claims. A magistrate judge granted summary judgment in favor of the assistant principal, finding that he was immune from suit. The mother appealed. The appeals court affirmed the decision in favor of the assistant principal. The assistant principal was entitled to qualified immunity on the student's federal claims because the student did not adequately allege a violation of substantive due process. The assistant principal was not obligated to protect the student due to a special relationship. The student could not prove her claim that the assistant principal had a duty to protect her because he created the danger that led to her alleged harm. The assistant principal did not restrain the student in a way that created a constitutional obligation to protect her. In addition, he did not act with deliberate indifference. The student's state-law claims failed as well, because the assistant principal's actions did not result in the student's alleged injury. The decision of the lower court was affirmed. *Doe v. San Antonio Independent School Dist.*, 197 Fed.Appx. 296 (5th Cir. 2006).

◆ The father of two children sought a divorce from his wife. The wife obtained a temporary restraining order splitting custody of the children. A school policy allowed students to leave with their parents if the approval of the principal was first obtained. The date and time of student departure and return was to be recorded with the reason for leaving school. The father became upset when he came to school and learned his mother-in-law had taken the children to their mother. The mother told staff not to release the children to their father, but a staff member said that would require a court order. The next day, the father came to the school for both children. The reasons he gave for signing them out were "keeping promise by mother" for the daughter and "pay back" for the son. Police later arrived at the father's house to find it ablaze. The father brandished a knife, and the police killed him. The children's bodies were found inside the house. The mother sued the school board in a state court for negligence.

The court held for the board, and the mother appealed. The state court of appeals held that schools, teachers, and school administrators have a duty to exercise ordinary care for student safety. The board was not liable for negligently violating its own sign-out policy. There was no evidence that staff knew about a dispute until the mother called the day before the murders. Without a court order, a school has no legal duty to follow the instruction of one parent not to release a child to the other parent. The court affirmed judgment on a claim based on the father's violent nature. However, failure to read his reasons for signing out the children was evidence of breach of the duty to exercise ordinary care. **The court rejected the board's claim that it had no legal duty to examine a parent's reason for signing out a child.** The reasons the father gave for signing out the children might cause a reasonable person to suspect he intended to cause them harm. The state Governmental Tort Liability Act did not protect the board, since the decision to release the children did not involve planning. The decision was reversed, and the case was remanded. *Haney v. Bradley County Board of Educ.*, 160 S.W.3d 886 (Tenn. Ct. App. 2004).

D. Other Cases

◆ An attorney visited a private school to interview witnesses on behalf of clients he was representing. He entered by a road leading to a parking lot, neither of which had "no trespassing" signs. The attorney interviewed two student witnesses inside a campus building. When school staff learned of the his presence, they called police. The next day, a local police officer called the attorney and said he was not to return to the school. He also told him he would be receiving a citation for trespass. **The citation was issued, and the attorney sued the officer for malicious prosecution and violation of his rights under the First Amendment.** The court rejected the malicious prosecution claim because the attorney was not subjected to a seizure and there was probable cause to issue the citation. It also rejected the First Amendment claim because the attorney did not engage in constitutionally protected conduct when he interviewed the witnesses. He did not have a First Amendment right to interview witnesses wherever he chose. *Considine v. Jagodinski*, No. 13-7263, 2015 WL 1573391 (E.D. Pa. 4/9/15).

◆ A mother arrived at a high school to pick up her son from Saturday detention. They walked through interior double doors directly onto the school's baseball facility, and the doors locked behind them. The entrance/exit gates to the baseball facility were locked, and the pair tried to exit by climbing a six-foot-high fence. The student did so successfully, but the mother was injured. She sued the school for negligence, but she lost. Although there were no signs near the double doors indicating that they were for exit only, the school did not breach any duty to the mother. **It was not foreseeable that she would exit the double doors and get trapped in the baseball facility.** She also had other options: She could have used her son's cell phone to get help, and she could have had him re-enter the building and let her out. *Gutchewsky v. Westside Community Schools*, No. A-14-446, 2015 WL 1243207 (Neb. Ct. App. 3/17/15).

◆ A school's entrance doors had glass panes. A seventh-grader pushed on the glass and it shattered, cutting him. He and his mother sued, claiming the school had maintained a dangerous and defective condition. The court denied the school district's motion for judgment without a trial. Though safety glass wasn't required when the school was built and no current law required retrofitting, the district was in the habit of replacing broken glass with Plexiglass. Therefore, **a question existed as to whether the district knew it was dangerous to leave glass in the doors**. A trial was needed. *Karathanasis v. Union Free School Dist.*, No. 56217/2011, 2013 WL 3828389 (N.Y. Sup. Ct. 7/24/13).

◆ A high school student's father objected to a school's plan to have students use "Smart IDs," which include a radio frequency chip to track students. The father rejected the district's offer to let the child use an ID without the chip. **The student and her father sued, claiming a violation of their religious rights.** They alleged that they would be "condemn[ed] to hell" if they allowed tracking of the girl at school. The court rejected the father's request to order the district to let the girl stay at school without the ID while the case proceeded. It said the father was not likely to win, as the offer of a chip-free ID was sufficient. *A.H. v. Northside Independent School Dist.*, No. SA-12-CA-113-OG, 2013 WL 85604 (W.D. Tex. 1/8/13).

◆ A high school student's mother said she told school officials that a schoolmate was getting violent with her son. The student said that while he was standing outside a school office, the schoolmate and the schoolmate's father physically attacked him. He sued the school district officials, alleging a violation of his substantive due process right to be free from harm. The court ruled against him, finding that "the failure to create greater security barriers for entry to a public school" did not support a substantive due process claim. **School officials generally do not have a constitutional duty to protect students from attacks by third parties.** Though an exception to this rule would apply if the district created the danger that caused the injury, the district did not create the danger in this case. *Campbell v. Brentwood Union Free School Dist.*, No. CV 12-1582(LDW), 2012 WL 5564405 (E.D.N.Y. 11/13/12).

◆   A high school student was seriously injured in her school's parking lot when the car she was sitting in was rear-ended by a student who was driving another vehicle. The injured student's parents sued the school district for negligence, claiming it was liable for failing to ensure safe driving conditions in the lot. **The court ruled for the district, finding it was immune to the claim raised against it** because an element of judgment was involved with respect to regulation of school parking lot traffic and because the judgment involved economic concerns and public policy. *J.S. v. Lamarr County School Dist.*, No. 2011-CA-00260-COA, 2012 WL 2895914 (Miss. Ct. App. 7/17/12).

◆   A ninth-grader was expelled for having a knife at school. He was allowed back on the condition that he would not again violate any major rule, but he subsequently threatened one student and punched another. He also wrote a threatening message on his backpack. His readmission was finally rescinded after he became irate at a meeting and the principal concluded he had violated a rule barring intimidation and harassment. After his expulsion, he continued visiting the school to pick up friends and use the weight room. When a teacher told him to leave, he punched a locker and was banned from campus. He was cited for trespassing after he ignored the ban. He sued, claiming the district wrongfully failed to provide him with notice and a hearing before instituting the ban. He lost, because once he was expelled from the school he had the same right as any other member of the general public to access it. At that point, **he had no constitutional right to access the campus**. *Hannemann v. Southern Door County School Dist.*, 673 F.3d 746 (7th Cir. 2012).

◆   Parents of students divorced, and the father was granted physical custody. Following the divorce, the mother needed the father's permission to see the children. The father informed the children's school that he did not want the mother to visit the children at school. When the school denied the mother access, she sued and claimed a violation of her constitutional right to control the education of her children. The court rejected her claim. **Parents do not have a constitutional right to make decisions relating to how a school is run.** The school's actions did not prevent the mother from raising her children as she saw fit. *Schmidt v. Des Moines Public Schools*, 655 F.3d 811 (8th Cir. 2011).

◆   A woman drove to a high school to drop off her son at a field house that was located on the high school's grounds. As she was leaving, she drove her vehicle into a free-swinging metal gate. The gate penetrated the vehicle and injured the woman. She and her husband sued a school resource officer, alleging he violated a duty to secure the gate, report its broken latch to authorities, and have the gate equipped with a working latch. Under state law, the school resource officer could be sued if the acts of inspecting the gate and reporting/repairing any damage to it were discretionary. If the acts were ministerial and did not involve the exercise of discretion, the school resource officer was entitled to immunity unless he acted with malice or intent to injure. **The court ruled that the school resource officer was entitled to immunity.** The parties agreed that he did not act with malice or intent to injure, and there was no formal policy or procedure that created a ministerial duty on the part of the school resource officer to inspect the gate. *Scott v. Waits*, 703 S.E.2d 419 (Ga. Ct. App. 2010).

◆   A school district regulation required all visitors to present state-issued photo identification before entering secure areas of the school where students were present. Information on the visitor's identification document was photographed and checked against lists of registered sex offenders. The parent of elementary school students visited their school but refused to allow school officials to scan her driver's license or input her information manually. As a result, the parent was not permitted to access areas of the school that she wished to visit. Instead, she met with her children's teachers in a conference room. The parent subsequently was similarly blocked from accessing particular areas of the school when she visited to attend a musical, a volleyball game and a Thanksgiving lunch. The parent sued the district, claiming violations of her constitutional rights to speech, assembly, association, freedom from unreasonable search of seizure, privacy, procedural due process and substantive due process. She also asserted claims under state law. A trial court ruled against her, and a federal appeals court affirmed. **The parent did not have a fundamental right to access the secure areas of the school, and she was not denied the ability to make fundamental decisions about her children's education.** Further, the regulation was narrowly tailored to achieve the compelling state interest in determining whether a potential visitor was a registered sex offender. *Meadows v. Lake Travis Independent School Dist.*, 397 Fed. Appx. 1 (5th Cir. 2010).

◆   A high school student was suspended for three days for packing snow into the gas cap of a schoolmate's car. The student's father went to the school and acted in a loud and threatening manner. The father left at the request of the vice principal, but he said he planned to complain to the superintendent and local media. He also reportedly told the vice principal he "better look for another job." The father was later arrested for creating a disturbance at the school, but the charge against him was eventually dismissed. The father and student filed a lawsuit. The student claimed he was suspended without due process, and the father accused the police of malicious prosecution. The court rejected the claims. The student's due process rights were not violated because the vice principal spoke to the student about the incident three times and allowed him to tell his side of the story. And **the father's claim of malicious prosecution failed because witness reports supported the conclusion that the police had ample cause to arrest him for creating a disturbance at school**. *Scrocca v. Alton Police Dep't*, No. 1:08-cv-0042-JL, 2009 WL 2246753 (D.N.H. 7/28/09).

◆   A 17-year-old high school student was killed in his school's parking lot when a vehicle driven by another student struck him. The administrator of the student's estate sued the school district and a security company employed by the district, claiming negligent supervision of the parking lot where the accident happened. **The court held that the district was not liable because it did not have specific notice or knowledge of a particular danger at a particular time.** Therefore, the district could not have reasonably anticipated the accident. The security company could not be held liable because there was no evidence it failed to perform its duties under its contract with the district. Even if it failed to supervise its security guards at the school, such a breach could not be deemed a proximate cause of the accident. *Ravner v. Autun*, 876 N.Y.S.2d 453 (N.Y. App. Div. 2009).

◆   A parent entered a school gymnasium to pick up his stepson. He left the gymnasium by going through double doors that led to a commons area. One of the doors came off a closing mechanism and fell on the parent's head. He sued for negligence, and a trial court ruled for the district. It found a state tort claims act recreational use exception to liability was applicable. Under the exception, a claim could not be brought if injury occurred while the property was being used for recreational purposes. After a state appeals court affirmed the trial court's decision, appeal reached the state's highest court. The parent argued that the recreational use exception was inapplicable because the injury occurred in a commons area and not in the gymnasium. The lower court had found the school commons was a "transitional area" from outside the school into the gymnasium. The lower court found the commons was an appendage to the gymnasium and was therefore a part of a "recognized recreational use area." **The state's high court explained that the legislative purpose of the tort claims act was to immunize government entities so as to encourage them to build recreational facilities without fear of lawsuits.** To be immune, the school district had to show the parent was claiming only ordinary negligence and that the injuries resulted from the use of a "qualifying property," meaning a property that was "public" and was intended to be used for recreational purposes. Although the commons was not used exclusively for recreation, the court found it was "an integral part of the use of the gymnasium." The commons was used to sell tickets and concessions during events, and it was not "incidentally connected" to the gymnasium. The commons was necessarily connected to the gymnasium as a principal means of access and for purchasing tickets and concessions. The parent's use of the commons at the time of the injury was consistent with the plan of the building. **Extending immunity was consistent with legislative intent. A school would be discouraged from opening a gymnasium for recreational use if liability was permitted in an area that was integral to its recreational usage.** The school district was immune from liability under the recreational use exception. *Poston v. Unified School Dist. No. 387, Altoona-Midway, Wilson County*, 189 P.3d 517 (Kan. 2008).

◆ After a fire alarm sounded at a high school, a guidance counselor was severely injured when a student pushed open a door. The guidance counselor sued several defendants, including the city where the school was located. He relied on the theory that the swinging double doors were negligently designed. A jury issued a verdict in his favor, and the defendants appealed. The appeals court negated the jury's verdict and issued a ruling in favor of the defendants. It explained that the issue in the case was whether the building design complied with safety standards that were in place when the school was constructed. The guidance counselor's expert testified that the design of the double doors was unsafe because it placed people going through the left door into the path of the door on the right. The expert also testified that the lack of a restricting mechanism allowed the doors to be opened too quickly. The court explained that the expert's testimony did not establish that the design of the doors violated the building code that was applicable when the school was built in 1970. **Rather, expert testimony offered by the defense showed that the doors complied with the building code that was in effect at the time of construction. In addition, the guidance counselor did not show the design of the doors was unsafe in light of the design standards that applied when the school was built.** The guidance counselor did not prove his claim of negligent design. Therefore, the judgment entered on the jury's verdict was reversed. *Hotaling v. City of New York*, 866 N.Y.S.2d 117 (N.Y. App. Div. 2008).

◆ A parent volunteer was asked by another parent to check on the other parent's child at the school. The volunteer parent said she signed a volunteer sign-in sheet and then went to the classroom of the other parent's daughter. She said a teacher's aide nodded her approval to enter the classroom, and the volunteer parent visited with the girl and a paraprofessional for about two minutes. The volunteer parent then left the building before returning at lunch time to perform volunteer duties. During lunch, the other parent asked the volunteer parent to check on the other parent's daughter again. On her way out of the building that day, the volunteer parent looked in the window of the girl's class but did not go in because the door was closed. **The same day, the school sent the volunteer parent a letter banning her from the school for five weeks.** It claimed the volunteer parent had violated a state law that banned "interfering with peaceful conduct of activities." The volunteer parent objected. After a hearing, the length of the ban was reduced. The volunteer parent sued the school district, claiming a violation of her due process interest in the care, custody and control of her children. She also asserted other claims, including a claim of emotional distress. The court granted the school's dismissal motion. It noted that **public education is committed to the control of school authorities, and parents do not have a right to total control over every aspect of their children's education**. Instead, school authorities have broad discretion when it comes to operating their schools, and the school permissibly limited the volunteer parent's access to its premises. *Mayberry v. Independent School Dist. No. 1 of Tulsa County, Oklahoma,* No. 08-CV-416-GKF-PJC, 2008 WL 5070703 (N.D. Okla. 11/21/08).

◆   A school parent, who was the president of the Parent Teacher Student Organization (PTSO) at her son's elementary school, criticized the school's performance and safety policies. The school's principal said the parent threatened administrators and teachers and violated visitation policies. He banned her from school, prevented her from distributing flyers and cancelled a PTSO meeting. The parent sued the principal and other school officials, **claiming the actions taken against her violated the First Amendment because they were designed to prevent her from criticizing the school**. She claimed the defendants' actions were a retaliatory response to her criticisms. The court denied cross-motions for summary judgment, finding factual issues were present. There was conflicting evidence about whether the principal took adverse action against the parent for a permissible reason. Also, it was not clear whether the school had created a public forum for speech. Therefore, it was too soon to issue a definitive ruling on the First Amendment claim. *Williamson v. Newark Public Schools*, No. 05-CV-4008 (WJM), 2008 WL 1944849 (D.N.J. 5/1/08).

◆   A parent who was visiting a school got into a confrontation with a school employee. A school safety agent witnessed the confrontation and attempted to separate the parent and the school employee. The school safety agent advised the school employee to walk away from the confrontation. The school employee walked to a staircase to return to her classroom. Moments later, the parent followed her into the stairwell and attacked her. The school employee sued the board of education to recover for her injuries. A trial court denied the board's motion for summary judgment, but the appeals court reversed. **The appeals court held that the school employee did not show that the school safety agent had assumed an affirmative duty to act to prevent the attack.** The school employee did not show that the school agent was aware that the parent posed a threat of violence. Therefore, the board was not liable for the school employee's injuries. *France v. New York City Board of Educ.*, 834 N.Y.S.2d 193 (N.Y. App. Div. 2007).

◆   The parent of a high school student complained to the school's principal after the student broke his leg during a school football practice. The parent claimed that the student received no medical attention from any of the coaches present at the practice. Two years later, the parent complained to the principal again after the student was inserted into a football game even though he was feeling ill. A short time after he made the complaint, the principal barred the parent from entering any school district property except to drop off and pick up his son. The principal also circulated a memo stating that he physically feared the parent and that the parent was "the most out-of-control parent [the principal] had witnessed in 31 years of education." The parent later sued the school district, claiming it violated his constitutional rights by barring him from school property. The court granted the district's motion to dismiss the claim. The court was unable to locate any authority for the proposition that the parent had a constitutional right to enter school property. To the contrary, **school officials have a right to assure that parents conduct themselves properly while they are on school property**. The parent did not show that the decision to bar him from school property violated his constitutional rights. *Van Deelen v. Shawnee Mission Unified School Dist. #512*, 316 F.Supp.2d 1052 (D. Kan. 2004).

CHAPTER TWO

Emergency Preparedness and Response

I. INTRODUCTION

From school shootings to weather emergencies to public health concerns like the Zika virus, schools have to plan for a whole variety of worst-case scenarios – because sometimes the worst-case scenario is what

you get. You'll have a serious leg up on handling the worst if your school
has prepared by brainstorming on potential risks, plotting out the best
responses, training with first responders and incorporating lessons learned
from your own and other schools' experience.

You don't want to be caught short when glass is shattering around you,
or the halls are filled with smoke, or you've just been notified a serious
storm is heading your way – and suddenly the power goes out in the
building. If a crisis hits, you want to already know what to do next.

Legally, school emergency operations plans are governed by state law
and local regulations.

Federal law typically factors in as the kind of compliance *always*
expected of your school. For just a few obvious examples, schools can't
assign students to shelter-in-place rooms based on race, ignore the special
needs of those with disabilities, or post confidential student records to the
school's Facebook page just to make sure the records survive the crisis.

Apart from your usual compliance issues, school emergency operations
plans aren't legally mandated on the federal level.

That said, the federal government takes the matter so seriously that it
has issued guidance to schools and districts: the *Guide for Developing High-
Quality School Emergency Operations Plan*, a collaboration by the
departments of Education, Health and Human Services, Homeland Security
and Justice along with the Federal Bureau of Investigation and the Federal
Emergency Management Agency.

The guide is available online at *rems.ed.gov* – as is "EOP ASSIST," a
free software application intended to be installed on a school's or school
district's server and made available to those responsible for creating the
emergency operations plan.

In this chapter we'll touch on the federal guidance as well as other best
practices for school emergency operations plans. We'll also look at two issues
raised by real-life school disasters: school intruders and tornado safe rooms.

We'll conclude with court decisions in which students, parents and
school employees brought lawsuits connected to school crisis planning or a
school's response to an emergency.

II. SCHOOL EMERGENCY OPERATIONS PLANS

A. Federal Guidance

1. Overview

The developers of the *Guide for Developing High-Quality School
Emergency Operations Plan* understand your school is almost certain to
already have an emergency operations plan in place.

The way they envision you using the guidance is to perform needed
tweaks by comparing your existing M.O. to the info and procedures
suggested in the guide.

The main focus of the guidance is on planning, but that's intended to be seen in the context of these five mission areas:

- **Prevention** of threatened or actual school emergencies
- **Protection** of students, teachers, visitors, school networks and property
- **Mitigation** of threatened or actual harm at school
- **Response** that establishes a safe and secure school environment, saves life and property there, and facilitates the transition to:
- **Recovery**, which means a restoration of the learning environment

2. Your Planning Team

Having set the example by having six federal agencies team up to produce the *Guide*, the guidance emphasizes the importance of collaboration in school safety planning.

It suggests your "core planning team" should include not only administrators but also:

- teachers
- school psychologists and nurses
- facilities and transportation managers
- food personnel
- representatives of students, parents, persons with disabilities, racial minorities, and religious minorities, and
- first responders, such as: police officers, SROs, fire officials, EMTs, and also public health and mental health practitioners.

And don't forget to include students. See Chapter Nine for Form II-24, a checklist about involving students in prevention.

3. The Feds' Standard for 'High Quality'

The guidance also contains benchmarks to help you assess the quality of your plan.

As a basic matter, your plan has to comply with the state laws and local requirements that pertain to school emergency operations plans.

Beyond that, the guidance says plans are:

- **adequate** if they effectively address critical courses of action
- **feasible** if tasks can be accomplished with the available resources, and
- **acceptable** if they get tasks done on time and within budget and the plan complies with the law.

The guide calls a plan **complete** if it:

- "Incorporates all courses of action to be accomplished for all selected threats and hazards and identified functions"
- "Integrates the needs of the whole school community"
- "Provides a complete picture of what should happen, when, and at whose direction"

- "Estimates time for achieving objectives, with safety remaining as the utmost priority"
- "Identifies success criteria and a desired end state" – and
- "Conforms with planning principles outlined in this guide."

4. Useful Features

The guidance also has helpful info on complying with federal law in the context of a school crisis.

It contains an overview of the Family Educational Rights and Privacy Act (FERPA) to address concerns schools have found confusing in the past.

The guide also contains info on the Health Insurance Portability and Accountability Act of 1966 to help you with matters of confidential health records.

There is also information about how to make sure your plan complies with the Americans with Disabilities Act.

As we discuss later in this chapter, it also contains a helpful "Active School Shooters" section.

Now let's move on to best practices.

B. Plan Considerations

1. Basic Plan Elements

There is no one-size-fits-all approach to crisis management plans.

Each school has a unique school community with unique needs, and schools in different parts of the country face different risks. For example, if your school is in an earthquake-prone area, you'll want to check out FEMA's Earthquake Preparedness Checklist in Chapter Nine (Form II-19).

Even schools in the same area can face very different challenges if one is in a big city and the other's in a quiet suburb.

Importantly, each state has different laws that its schools must follow.

All of this means that for a crisis management plan to be truly effective, it must be tailored to your school's specific needs.

That said, some things are true of all plans. For example, each one has to comply with its state and local laws.

Also, every crisis management plan should be considered a work in progress. That's because the day-to-day realities at school are constantly changing.

One important preparedness step is to assign crisis duties to personnel – but staff come and go. You may lose (or gain) a CPR expert. It's important to keep that in mind in case a pregnancy leave, a resignation, or a new hire means you need to change up key go-to responsibilities.

Students also come and go, shifting the established needs of your community. That can mean making sure different disabilities are accommodated or new languages are covered to make effective communication with students and their parents possible.

Also, lessons learned from a previous incident can mean that the plan should be tweaked to take advantage of real-life experience.

☑ CHECKLIST – *Basic Plan Elements*

☐ complies with state and local laws
☐ is periodically reviewed and updated as needed
☐ includes provisions relating to students with disabilities
☐ addresses potential language barriers, and
☐ is updated based on real-life experiences
   when appropriate.

For a checklist to help you assess your risks for purposes of your emergency operations plan, see Form II-25 in Chapter Nine. For a checklist on assessing hazards in your facilities, see Form II-26.

2. Students Not on Campus

Have you planned for the possibility that some students and staff might not be on campus when a crisis occurs – but you still have responsibility for them? For example, a class might be on a field trip or a team might be in transit to an away game.

Concerns to address here include:
- establishing communication protocols ahead of time – not just between the school and the away-group, but also between the school and the student's parents
- making sure staff always have emergency supplies before they leave campus – which might include water, energy bars, first aid supplies, a flashlight and a reliable communication device, and
- anything else that seems appropriate given the circumstances of the away trip and the risks the travelers are likely to encounter along the way.

It's also important to remember to take before- and after-school programs and events into account in emergency plans. Do you and your staff know what to do if an event occurs while clubs are meeting or when there's a packed house in the auditorium for the annual talent show?

3. Communicating With Parents

Are you sure you can access contact info as needed in an emergency?

It's a good idea to keep contact info in multiple places – both online and in hard copies that are laminated or kept in reliably waterproof containers.

Also, having compiled this info in the first place, you'll want to make sure to make it someone's responsibility to update it regularly.

Another important consideration is letting parents know where and how to get information about an ongoing incident. For a sample letter to parents on how your emergency planning affects them, see Form-II-23 in Chapter Nine.

One thing you may want to let families know in advance is that they should not come to campus during an emergency as they and their cars could physically block ambulances, fire trucks and emergency personnel.

Does it make sense to use social media to communicate with parents during an emergency? If so, you'll want to consider how to go about that, whose responsibility to make it, and how best to get the word out to families.

Even if you're planning to be all over social media, you'll probably want to provide as many other sources as you realistically can. Many parents have smartphones and access to the Internet, but it's nothing like 100%.

Alternative ways for parents to get information about an incident in progress include calling a pre-arranged phone number to hear a recorded message that will be updated as often as possible under the circumstances. You may also be able to direct them to a local TV or radio station that has agreed to broadcast info about your school in case of an emergency.

See Chapter Nine for a Reunification After a Crisis checklist (Form II-20).

4. Emergency Supplies

Do you store emergency supplies at school in case of an emergency?

There are many approaches for schools that do, but they all tend to fall under two categories: either the school gathers all the emergency supplies, or the school gathers some of the supplies while parents and students, or some other party, supplies the rest.

Under one model plan, for example, parents are instructed to pack up specified drinks and snacks and a few other items (such as a laminated copy of the student's emergency card, a reassuring message and photo from the family, pocket-sized tissues and a small book or game) in a gallon zip-lock bag placed inside a 50-gallon plastic snap-top container and then bring it to school for storage.

The American Red Cross reports that some schools make it a practice to donate their emergency stockpiles of food to a charity at the end of each school year.

In addition to food and water, emergency supplies typically include first aid gear, radios and flashlights.

5. Evacuation and Lockdown

Evacuation and lockdown plans are basic – but that's because they're so important. It's never a bad idea to take another look at yours.

Evacuation requires pre-determined routes and on-site assembly sites (to evacuate from) and off-campus assembly sites (to evacuate to). You need several of each as the first choices might be unreachable or unusable due to the emergency.

Schools generally expect to evacuate staff and students by using school buses, but the roads may be impassable or buses may be unavailable. Therefore, alternate ways to remove students from danger should be discussed.

The evacuation provisions in model plans stress the importance of making sure students remain accounted for by:

- keeping classes together during the evacuation so that teachers can continue to keep track of their own students, and
- having teachers take roll both immediately before the evacuation and as soon as they arrive at the evacuation destination.

Keep in mind that authorities may ask that a school be evacuated during a broader crisis. On September 11th, for example, Stuyvesant High School was near ground zero, but that was not why it was evacuated – the FBI wanted to use the school building as a command center.

Lockdowns are used to keep students safe inside from a danger outside. Your school will have its own procedures based on building features and other unique considerations, but one procedure many schools follow is to train staff in soft and hard lockdowns. The difference depends on the threat level. A mild threat may only require a soft lockdown – perhaps locked doors only. A serious and immediate threat calls for a hard lockdown: locked doors, lights and computers off, everyone silent, blinds closed (or everyone otherwise kept out of an intruder's line of sight). In a hard lockdown, it's possible every one is hiding while poised to run or fight.

An example of a sample notice to parents regarding a school lockdown drill is provided in Chapter Nine (Form II-2).

6. Sheltering-in-Place

Sheltering-in-place is a response to the more specific danger of needing to minimize students' exposure to contaminants in the environment – a chemical accident, for example. Sheltering-in rooms should have as few windows as possible. Basic necessities, such as food, water and bedding, should be stored there in advance, along with emergency supplies, such as flashlights and radios, as well as first aid supplies and medicine.

For sheltering-in-place, the American Red Cross suggests an interior room that's located above the ground floor and has no windows. This is because some dangerous chemicals are heavier than air. Even with precautions, heavy chemicals could seep into basement rooms. As an extra safety measure, provide people a wet cloth to keep over their noses and mouths.

The Red Cross also says all HVAC and fans should be turned off and all vents and cracks around doors should be sealed with duct tape. If only a room with windows is available, it should be covered with plastic and sealed over completely with duct tape. Checklists showing specific steps to take in the event of a gas leak or hazardous spill are provided on Form II-3 and Form II-4 in Chapter Nine.

7. Planning for Your Staff in a Crisis

Virtually every crisis presents twists no one could have imagined – and therefore no one could have planned for. That's one reason training staff on the plan is so important. Having the basics down makes it a lot likelier staff will be able to intelligently adapt the original plan to cover unexpected events.

Sometimes the unexpected element is people's reactions. No one knows what they'll be like under pressure until they actually experience it. Also, people are different – and so are their responses to a crisis. Some people may find themselves cool-headed and decisive, while others might have to fight the tendency to panic or freeze. Training can help tilt the scale toward cool-headed decisiveness.

Another thing that can help is having easy-to-read-and-understand checklists on hand. Many plans call for them – and some call for them to be laminated to make them not only more durable but also more legible, since you can wipe off a laminated surface.

Simple, straightforward checklists that contain basic action plans and also relevant contact info can help get frozen people up and going again and on to the next step.

Even if you trust everyone to stay calm, focused and move quickly, it's a good idea to have simple reminders that can be easily scanned and followed. Examples of a crisis team member list and a list of emergency telephone numbers are provided in Chapter Nine on Form I-2 and Form II-6.

Here's something else to keep in mind and possibly include in the plan: One common mistake experts have cited is schools waiting too long to call in emergency services and alert its own crisis team.

The best bet is to go ahead and call for help and alert the team even if there's a chance the situation might be resolved by the time help arrives. If that turns out to be the case, that's actually a good thing. And if there's any risk of injury or loss of life or property, it's best to err on the side of safety.

8. Planning for After the Crisis

Experience has shown that there are several predictable recovery needs that many schools experience after an emergency is over.

Because they're predictable, they can be planned for and addressed in the crisis plan. They include:

- helping students, families and staff cope with trauma
- repairing any physical damage to the facility
- addressing insurance requirements, and
- dealing with the media.

Perhaps the most predictable recovery need in the wake of a crisis at school is that students, families and school staff are likely to need help coping with the emotional fall-out that accompanies living through a disaster. One way to support staff is by utilizing a thank you letter such as the one provided on Form II-10 in Chapter Nine.

You may want to get before-the-fact advice from experts in whatever field is needed. And don't forget in planning for coping with the after-effects of trauma that you may have your own onsite experts. School counselors have the added advantage of already having a relationship with many of the people who might be needing help.

Schools that go to off-campus professionals for preliminary advice for the plan might use the advice-gathering process as a kind of audition to determine if the expert might also be a good person to bring back to help the school if the worst happens.

Another predictable recovery need concerns the brick and mortar of the school building. Even apart from additional safety considerations – such as leaking roofs that could lead to slip-and-fall accidents or falling rubble that could cause injuries – the physical damage left after a disaster can be a potent reminder of a traumatic experience. Apart from other pressing reasons, making repairs can be an important psychological way to start moving beyond the event.

One thing you can do to prepare for property damage is make sure you have plenty of "before" pictures. Still images work, and so do videos. If you can manage it, aerial photos are also a good idea if FEMA is likely to be involved. You'll probably also want to make sure some kind of camera is on hand to take "after" photos of property damage as well.

It can also be a good idea to find out in advance exactly what other kind of insurance requirements the school is likely to have to comply with in case it has to make claims on any policies.

Another predictable recovery-stage need is for a spokesperson or spokespeople to deal with the media. Many schools already have staff and established procedures in place for this.

For a sample statement to the media concerning school violence, see Form II-22 in Chapter Nine.

Finally, the plan should call for debriefing sessions with school staff and emergency personnel after any actual crisis so the school can incorporate lessons learned from the incident into the plan.

C. Special Considerations

The Governmental Accountability Office (GAO) is the agency that acts as the investigative arm of Congress.

The GAO made a 2007 study of school planning and preparedness and found that the overwhelming norm among schools was an emergency operations plan that addressed multiple specific scenarios.

It found virtually all plans addressed bombs or bomb threats, hostage situations, and the natural disasters likely for the locality. Those bases are pretty thoroughly covered in the majority of school crisis management plans. Even if that's true of yours, you still may want to check out the bomb threat report form in Form II-11 in Chapter Nine and the bomb threats procedure and checklist in Form II-21.

Schools should also be prepared to follow-up on environmental risks, such as chemical spills. For a parental consent form for mercury testing, see Form II-15 in Chapter Nine.

The GAO also found that city-based school districts were more likely than rural school districts to plan crisis responses for terrorism (86% as opposed to 70%) and much more likely to plan for incidents involving radiation (60% compared to 29%) or anthrax (57% of urban districts versus 26% or rural districts).

In addition to those findings, the GAO study also identified four areas in which many plans weren't following recommended practices by:

- including procedures to ensure the safety of special needs students
- including a plan to continue teaching students in case the school closed due to a pandemic or other emergency
- conducting school drills and exercises, and
- training with first responders and community partners.

This section will focus on the topics that many schools and districts may still need information in addressing.

1. Special Needs Students' Safety

Just as a good crisis management plan is tailored to address the crises a school is likely to face, a good plan for students with disabilities is drafted to take into account the special needs of the students the school actually has in its own community.

The GAO found that 28% of school districts with plans had not included specific provisions for students with disabilities. Of those that had, the provisions were not in writing.

The GAO's report focused on the following recommended practices concerning special needs students:

- keeping track of where special needs students are located throughout the school day
- identifying the staff assigned to evacuate or shelter with these students, and
- providing any devices needed to transport them to evacuation areas.

Educators told the GAO that districts devise their own procedures for keeping special needs students safe in a crisis because disability groups don't agree on the best practices.

One reason for this might be that while all students are unique, students with disabilities tend to be the most unique of all. Some need motorized wheelchairs to cross a room, while others need specialized laptops to communicate. Still others – Down syndrome or autistic children, for example – have cognitive limitations that may require a teacher with real experience of what works with a particular student in order to get him or her on the evacuation bus or to keep the child from panicking during lockdown or sheltering-in. And while first responders can tell at a glance if a student has Down syndrome, the same isn't true if a student is autistic.

The CDC puts the average number of children with an autism spectrum disorder at one in every 68 children. The number of children diagnosed with an autism spectrum disorder is increasing – increasing the need for crisis planning to specifically address these students.

Info provided by The Autism Society for paramedics and ER staff warns of typical reactions that could be especially problematic in a crisis.

Children with autism may over-react to loud noise and bright lights – running away or turning aggressive if confronted by a siren accompanied by flashing lights, for example. They also may not understand the significance of first responders' badges or uniforms, not follow directions, refuse to make eye contact, get inappropriately close, fail to respond to requests for information or else respond in confusing ways: saying "Yes!" to every question or using gestures instead of language.

The unique problems posed by autistic children during emergencies have led several groups to create specialized training for first responders in dealing with this population – something you may want to discuss when you liaise with your own first responders for planning or practice drills.

For more on first responder training on dealing with individuals with autism, go to *autismalert.org*.

Autistic students and other special needs students often need extra help under normal circumstances, and this need for extra help can be greatly increased during a crisis. As the National Organization on Disability has said, perhaps the most effective tactic for special needs individuals to survive an emergency is to have strong relationships with nondisabled people.

Disabilities are categorized differently by different groups, but there are some special needs experiences that may be common enough to take account of for crisis management planning. For example:

- People who use wheelchairs, crutches or other mobility devices are going to need special help if an emergency disables elevators or leaves piles of rubble blocking paths – especially if a speedy exit is required.
- Individuals who are blind are likely to be badly disoriented by loud, overwhelming noises – like sirens. Extremely loud noises drown out the ambient sounds that normally give blind people cues about who and what is in their immediate environment and what is happening there.
- People with cognitive or developmental disabilities like ADHD, Down syndrome and Tourette's are likely to have trouble following instructions.

☑ CHECKLIST – *Special Needs Planning*

☐ Establish a pre-set location to which special needs students can be escorted so they can be rescued.

☐ Consult with emergency responders about their own protocols for dealing with special needs individuals – and adopting them, if appropriate.

☐ Alert emergency responders to the presence of any special needs students likely to need additional help, such as the mobility-impaired.

☐ Obtain devices – such as specialized, light-weight chairs – to help evacuate students with severe mobility problems.

☐ Train staff to use any specialized devices deemed necessary to evacuate these students, and play it safe by assigning more people to operate them than are actually needed.

☐ Provide (or train) a sign-language interpreter, if needed.

☐ Provide written instructions in Braille, if needed.

☐ Make sheltering-in arrangements for service animals. Although pets aren't permitted in shelters, federal regulations allow service animals – although they can be excluded if they threaten others' lives or safety or if they become a nuisance. That said, anyone with known allergies to animals should be assigned to a different room.

☐ Store pet foods, medicines, plastic bags and disposable gloves for service animals along with other emergency supplies – and earmark water for them.

☐ Store backup devices of any vital special-needs device.

☐ Store spare or alternative power sources for the devices.

☐ Store needed medicine along with emergency supplies.

☐ Provide cards for special needs students to wear to alert first responders of their condition and the limitations it causes them. For example, a card for a person with a cognitive disability might state that this person has trouble understanding language, so patience and a simple vocabulary are needed.

A form to help build a list of students and staff who require special assistance for evacuation can be found at Form II-13 in Chapter Nine.

2. Planning for a Pandemic

Another area of crisis planning that the GAO identified as neglected was planning for a pandemic flu event and how to continue to educate students in case of the extended school closure likely to accompany it.

Given recent health scares and outbreaks – including Zika, Ebola and measles – you'll want to keep other infectious diseases on your radar, too. See *rems.ed.gov/KeepSchoolsSafeFromDiseases.aspx*. But never underestimate the flu.

Flu pandemics are caused by a highly contagious flu virus so new (or so long since it last circulated) that many people have little or no immunity to it. A virus-specific vaccine may not be available for at least six months, and this heightens the chance people will become seriously ill or die.

The risk is significant even without a pandemic. Pneumonia and the flu are eighth on the Centers for Disease Control and Prevention's (CDC's) most recent list of leading causes of death.

The 1918 flu pandemic killed 500,000 Americans. Pandemic numbers aren't always that dramatic. The 1957-58 pandemic caused 70,000 fatalities. The 1968-69 pandemic caused only 34,000.

Researchers estimate the 2009-10 H1N1 pandemic killed 2,634 more people than would have died if it had been a regular flu season.

Thanks to widespread public outreach associated with H1N1, most schools have taken onboard the recommendations from the U.S. Department of Health and Human Services (HHS) and the CDC.

They suggest pandemic flu planning could include education campaigns to prevent spread of the virus by:

- frequent hand washing
- sneezing and coughing only into either a tissue which is then immediately disposed of, or against the upper arm if a tissue isn't available, and
- encouraging everyone in the school community to stay home at the first sign of illness.

Guidance from *flu.gov* and the CDC forms the basis for the following checklist.

☑ CHECKLIST – *Flu Virus Avoidance*

☐ Focus on protecting high-risk students and staff, such as anyone who's pregnant or has asthma or diabetes

☐ Establish a plan to cover key personnel if they're out sick

☐ Work out ways to make it harder for the virus to spread – such as by holding class outside when feasible, regularly washing much-handled surfaces (like door knobs and computer equipment) with the usual cleaning supplies and moving student desks farther apart

☐ Cut any program that might encourage staff or students to come to school when sick – for example, prizes for good attendance

☐ Set up a special room to care for anyone who's sick until they can be sent home

☐ Have a supply of gloves and masks on hand for those who care for them

Based on experiences schools had with the H1N1 virus, it also might be a good idea to get a supply of disposable thermometers. A fever is associated with the flu, and some schools dealing with H1N1 outbreaks had several students displaying flu symptoms at once.

You should also be aware that some students displaying flu symptoms may be in your care longer than you expect. In fact, some schools had a serious problem with parents sending sick children to school during the spring 2009 outbreak. That's probably not too surprising, given the economic pressures many parents face plus the difficulty of finding child-care. In any event, realities being what they are, this may be something you want to anticipate and plan for.

The CDC also advises schools to contact and work with local health authorities in anticipation of a pandemic.

The GAO identified these procedures for educating students when the school is closed:

- electronic or human telephone trees to convey academic information
- web-based instruction
- mailed lessons and assignments, and
- classes broadcast over local TV or radio stations.

Depending on the availability of electricity during a crisis and the level of Internet access among your school community, you may want to consider some kind of web-based delivery of education.

Alternative-education plans are extremely important because experts can anticipate circumstances in which schools could be closed for longer than a year – although a more conservative estimate is that pandemic-related school closures could last from a few weeks up to three months.

The spring of 2009 saw schools closed to protect public health by limiting the spread of the virus. These closures weren't long, but future closures could be – not just to limit spread of a virus but because there might be so few teachers available due to illness that there aren't enough to supervise the students.

Much more info on school planning is available at *flu.gov.*

3. Training

Based on its survey of school districts, the GAO estimated that 27% of districts had never trained with first responders on implementing the school's crisis management plan and that approximately three-quarters of all districts were not training at least once a year with each of the following three resources: law enforcement, firefighters and emergency medical services.

Hopefully the numbers are better now.

The danger of not conducting this participatory training is that it can lead to confusion over who's doing what during an actual event.

Training, on the other hand, can provide responders basic and necessary information, such as how to get into the school, where to turn on (or off) utilities, and how to find their way around. It can speed up response time and may save lives if, for example, the medics told to report to the gym already know where the gym is.

For a sample list to be used to compile phone numbers of first responders and other emergency response personnel, see Form II-6 in Chapter Nine.

a. Training With First Responders

It is important to keep in mind that law enforcement, firefighters and emergency medical services have their own protocols. By training with them, schools can learn whether any protocols conflict or are otherwise counterproductive. Also, first responders have a level of training and experience that most school staffs lack. This is a valuable resource. Schools should take advantage of it.

Training with first responders can also clarify whether you're likely to have communication problems. FEMA suggests always using plain language to make sure everyone understands what is needed. It may be obvious to someone very familiar with the campus that "Ken-one" is short for No. 1 Kendall Street and means the auditorium, but it won't be obvious to Officer Rodriguez who just moved here from two states away.

Plain language is a good idea even when it comes to communicating effectively with staff inside the school. A first-time substitute teacher will have no idea that the "Code Purple" announcement over the intercom means she's supposed to lock her classroom door and tell students to lie flat on the floor.

Training with first responders can also help schools make sure in advance that their technology will work with emergency responders' equipment so that they can communicate in a crisis. Incompatible equipment can lead to the school and responders failing to connect or even jamming each other's gear and shutting down communication entirely.

Eight of the 27 districts that the GAO interviewed in researching its 2007 study said that their one-way radios and other equipment didn't work with the first responders' equipment. School officials in Iowa told the GAO that their district had a special problem in that it shared a radio frequency with only some of the first responders, not all of them.

It's vital to fix such disconnects *before* an emergency.

b. Training With Community Partners

While the police, the fire department and emergency medical services spring immediately to most school staffs' minds, not as many think of working with public health professionals and benefiting from the training and expertise they can provide. These community partners can be especially helpful in the event of a biological and radiation emergency.

In addition to other help, public health professionals can help schools plan the best response to biological and radiation events. They can provide expert guidance on specific hazards as well as such info as when sheltering-in-place is called for and how to care for children who may have been outside when an event occurred.

Biological weapons ultimately make people very ill, but the initial symptoms can fall within the normal range of everyday complaints. Therefore, one of the greatest risks of a biological attack is that it will not be recognized as such until after there has been a significant loss of life. The more quickly a biological attack is recognized, the more casualties can be prevented by distributing the available vaccines and antidotes.

In the case of anthrax, for example, the initial signs of the gastrointestinal form of the disease look a lot like food poisoning. The preliminary symptoms of the inhalation form of anthrax could easily be mistaken for a cold or the flu. Symptoms could appear within a month after contact with the bacterium, but they can take longer than a month to appear.

There is a vaccine to prevent anthrax. Even after it's contracted, a 60-day course of antibiotics can sometimes provide a cure.

Schools can help reduce the lag time between seeing symptoms and recognizing a biological attack – and thus save lives – by assigning a staff member to monitor diseases at school and look for patterns. It also helps to have staff who:

- can distinguish between normal illnesses and anomalies caused by biological weapons
- keep in close touch with the public health department, and
- know how and where to report unusual symptoms.

In terms of crisis management planning for an actual incident, a supplement to the Report of the National Advisory Committee on Children and Terrorism suggests:

- training staff in Blood Borne Pathogen Standards
- training staff to use personal protective gear and respirators and conduct a decontamination
- having one accessible switch to perform an emergency shutdown of the HVAC system in order to keep anything airborne from spreading, and
- having a procedure in place to let parents know about the illness and the best way to treat it.

As with pandemics, a biological attack might require schools to close – with all that this implies – in order to avoid the spread of disease.

The CDC's website has an A-Z listing of bioterrorism agents posted at *emergency.cdc.gov/bioterrorism*. This listing includes information about how the diseases are contracted, the symptoms, and if vaccines or cures are available.

With respect to radiation, ideally schools would be prepared to administer potassium iodide in case of radiation exposure within two hours of a "dirty bomb" explosion or a catastrophic incident at a nuclear plant.

A radiation event could require either sheltering-in-place or an evacuation. Public health professionals can help schools to determine when each of these options is the most appropriate choice.

D. Issues Raised by Real-Life Crises

1. School Intruders

Twenty first-graders and six school staff members were killed by an armed intruder at the Sandy Hook Elementary School in Newtown, Connecticut, in December 2012.

The school had a security system in place, but the gunman, a disturbed 20-year-old, shot his way into the building.

What happened was horrific – but safety experts say it could have been even worse if teachers hadn't followed lockdown procedures and if police hadn't arrived quickly. The gunman killed himself as they approached.

The Sandy Hook tragedy prompted a national discussion about whether school personnel should be armed and whether schools should be required to have active shooter drills.

States went on to pass laws saying yes to each.

The feds' *Guide for Developing High-Quality School Emergency Operations Plans* comes out in favor of active shooter drills but urges schools to tailor them to the students' ages. The guide includes an "Active Shooter Situations" section that provides a lot of useful information. Again, the guide is available online at *rems.ed.gov*.

For specific steps key personnel should take in the event that an intruder gains unauthorized access, see Form II-12 in Chapter Nine.

2. Tornado Safe Rooms

In May, 2013, a massive tornado in Moore, Oklahoma, destroyed two elementary schools and killed seven second- and third-graders.

This opened up widespread debate on whether tornado safe rooms should be required in schools.

According to info provided by FEMA: "A safe room is a hardened structure specifically designed to meet FEMA criteria and provide 'near absolute protection' in extreme weather events, including tornadoes and hurricanes."

On the pro side of the debate, requiring safe rooms in schools – especially in states where severe storms are common – could save lives. On the con side, the cost would be astronomical. One school safe room can cost as much as $1 million.

Currently, there are few mandates requiring schools to have safe rooms. Alabama law requires new schools to have safe rooms, and a few school districts have also decided to find a way to make safe rooms happen – but those are the exceptions.

For more info, check out FEMA's Safe Room Funding page at *fema.gov/safe-room-funding*.

III. LEGAL DECISIONS

A. Intruder- and Student-Attack Cases

Students and teachers have tried to hold schools responsible for injuries caused by students or school intruders by arguing that the school's crisis planning somehow created a duty to ensure their safety.

When the claim is brought as an alleged constitutional violation, courts virtually never find "the state" (here, a public school or the police) legally responsible for the violent acts of private individuals.

There are two very narrow exceptions, not recognized by every jurisdiction. The first is the state-created danger (or enhanced danger) doctrine. The second is the special relationship doctrine.

Under the **state-created danger doctrine**, the state can be held responsible for a person's injury if the state did something that either created the danger that caused the injury or significantly increased it.

Under the second exception, the **special relationship doctrine**, an injured party can prevail by showing that the government took actions that created a legal duty to protect him or her. (The special relationship doctrine can also create liability under states' personal injury laws.)

The decision in a case filed after the Columbine shootings clearly illustrates the operation of the legal framework described above.

The Colorado federal court dismissed most of the injury lawsuits brought by students and teachers in the wake of the Columbine shootings, finding the state was not legally responsible for private individuals' violent acts. But the court refused to dismiss the following case, finding both the state-created danger and special-relationship exceptions applied.

◆   The police created a legal duty to protect a Columbine teacher who bled to death after medical attention was delayed for four hours. **The police interfered with the teacher's ability to save himself and took actions that increased his danger of bleeding to death.**

A teacher was standing outside a cafeteria packed with early lunch period students when he saw two students approaching with guns. The teacher went into the cafeteria and shouted for the other students to run. He lagged behind until the last of the students escaped up a stairway. As he was urging the last ones up the stairs, one of the gunmen shot him twice in the back. The teacher managed to shepherd approximately 50 students into an upstairs classroom before he collapsed.

The teacher had spotted the gunmen at approximately 11:35 a.m. and was shot about five minutes later. Perhaps half an hour after that, rooftop police sharpshooters with high-powered binoculars saw the gunmen commit suicide in the library.

Although the officers in command knew about the suicides almost immediately, they incorrectly characterized the state of affairs inside the school as a "hostage situation" and followed "hostage situation" procedure by allowing no one in or out of the building – including the firefighters and SWAT team that wanted to rescue the teacher and the emergency medical staff that wanted to provide him onsite care.

Inside the classroom, another teacher and several students applied makeshift compresses to staunch the injured teacher's bleeding. By 12:30 p.m., at least two people had made 911 calls – which were relayed to the responding officers – to report how seriously the teacher had been injured and to tell emergency responders exactly where to find him. They also hung a large sign in the window reading: "1 BLEEDING TO DEATH."

An uninjured teacher spent the afternoon keeping 911 operators informed of the deterioration of the injured teacher's condition. Starting at around noon and continuing for more than three hours, the 911 operators kept relaying the police's message that help was "on the way" and would arrive soon, and that no one should leave the classroom to seek medical help.

At around 2:00 p.m., a 911 operator alerted the police that the people in the classroom were threatening to throw chairs through the windows to attract help for the injured teacher. Although the police knew the gunmen were dead, they told the operator to say this plan was more likely to draw the gunmen than medical help. About half an hour later, an uninjured teacher tried to leave the school to find a medic, but a SWAT team member, acting under police orders, forcibly pushed him back inside.

Once rescue personnel did enter the building, the injured teacher was the last wounded person they reached – even though he was the only person identified as someone who could be saved by emergency medical treatment and they had been told exactly where to find him. A SWAT team finally reached him at 4:00 p.m. By that time, his originally survivable injuries had become fatal. He died.

The deceased teacher's personal representative sued the board of county commissioners, the sheriff's department and several individual officials, alleging deprivation of life in violation of the deceased teacher's right to due process. The United States District Court for the District of Colorado denied the government defendants' request to dismiss the suit.

The district court explained that the U.S. Supreme Court held in 1989 that the Fourteenth Amendment's Due Process Clause does not impose a duty on a state to protect individuals from private acts of violence. Its purpose is "to protect the people from the State, not to ensure that the State protects them from each other." *DeShaney v. Winnebago County Dep't of Social Services*, 489 U.S. 189, 109 S.Ct. 998, 103 L.Ed.2d 249 (1989).

However, the district court continued, the Tenth U.S. Circuit Court of Appeals – which has jurisdiction over Colorado – had adopted two exceptions to this rule, both of which applied here. The special relationship doctrine applied because the government created a duty to protect this teacher by interfering with his ability to save himself, falsely assuring those caring for him that help was coming soon and ordering them not to seek other aid. **The state-created danger exception also applied because the police took actions that increased the teacher's danger of bleeding to death** by keeping him from the medical treatment that could have saved his life. Because these exceptions applied, the court refused to dismiss the case. *Sanders v. Board of County Commissioners of County of Jefferson, Colorado*, 192 F.Supp.2d 1094 (D. Colo. 2001).

As the following cases show, courts have not been persuaded by arguments that schools should be held legally responsible for injuries caused by a student or a school intruder because the schools had – or didn't have – a crisis plan.

It's also worth noting that the federal *Guide for Developing High-Quality School Emergency Operations Plans* makes a point of specifying up front that it is meant as "informal guidance" and doesn't create legal duties or rights.

Instead, to hold the schools liable, courts have insisted the injured parties must establish that either the special relationship doctrine or the state-created danger exception applies.

◆ A student injured in a gang-related attack claimed administrators increased the risk of his attack by covering up past attacks on others instead of entering them in a record and reporting them to the police. A Pennsylvania federal judge granted the school district judgment, finding the facts didn't bear out his claim.

Onesimus Gayemen had been at his new high school only a few days when four students asked for his black, red and white bead necklace. They said it was connected to a gang. He didn't know what they meant. They attacked him, leaving him with a fractured jaw and a concussion.

One assailant was incarcerated for the assault. The other three were prosecuted through the juvenile justice system. A detective later explained the necklace had made them think Onesimus was in a gang.

Onesimus sued the school district under a state-created danger theory, alleging it had violated his Fourteenth Amendment right to bodily integrity.

To state a valid claim, he had to show the district did something that made him more vulnerable to danger than if it hadn't acted at all. He didn't.

Under the school's Positive Behavioral Support System, assaults and violations of the district's gang policy called for suspension or expulsion. **School administrators were supposed to use an online system to document student discipline – and use it to track students who flashed gang signs, wore gang colors or otherwise signaled gang membership.** They were also supposed to report crimes to the police.

Onesimus claimed the district concealed gang-related fights and attacks instead of recording them in the online system and reporting crimes to the police – but produced no valid evidence to back his claim that the district failed to appropriately address gang-related violence and that this made him more vulnerable to suffering a gang-related attack. *Gayemen v. School Dist. of the City of Allentown*, No. 14-CV-1518, 2016 WL 3014896 (E.D. Pa. 5/26/16).

◆ A gym teacher hospitalized after an intruder's attack couldn't sue the city for her injuries. **The city didn't create a special relationship with her by putting safety measures in place or breach a duty of protection to her by not complying with its own school safety plan.**

A strange man appeared in the gym during class. He struck the teacher and then left. The teacher sent a student to alert a security guard about the intruder, but the student came back to say he couldn't find a guard. The intruder returned unnoticed and hit the teacher from behind, knocking her unconscious. Her injuries included a fractured skull, a fractured rib and hemorrhaging around her left temple.

The teacher sued the city for personal injury, but the court granted the city summary judgment.

New York law almost always found the city immune to personal injury suits based on the operation of a school's security system. The only exception was if the injured party could prove a special relationship that created a duty of protection. The teacher couldn't.

She claimed the school assumed a special duty to protect her because it implemented safety measures, such as metal detectors, door locks, panic bars, video surveillance, patrols by school aides and safety agents, and security telephones in the classrooms.

But the rule in New York was that police protection was owed to the community at large, not to specific individuals.

The teacher needed to show someone with the authority to make promises on the city's behalf created a special relationship with her by promising the city would keep her safe. Instead, she admitted the safety training she received from city employees was for all teachers, not just her. *Daniels v. City of New York*, No. 04-CV-7612(CM), 2007 WL 2040581 (S.D.N.Y. 2007).

◆ A student at a high school with escalating violence and chronic security shortages couldn't hold the school district responsible for injuries he suffered in another student's attack.

A tenth-grader was punched in the eye by a student in a school stairwell. The other student was aiming at someone else, who ducked. The injured student had a fractured facial bone and traumatic hyphema of the eye. He spent six days in the hospital.

Violence at the high school had gotten worse over the previous four years. The principal described the school as "out of control" with fights, fires and other serious issues.

The student said there should have been a surveillance camera in the stairwell. Also, the school was short four security officers and had not had full security staffing in 83 of the 85 previous days.

The student sued the school district, alleging it violated his Fourteenth Amendment right to bodily integrity and safety. The court granted the school district summary judgment. The student appealed to the Third U.S. Circuit Court of Appeals, but it affirmed judgment for the school district.

The student couldn't hold the school district responsible for his injury because the district didn't create the danger he faced.

The general atmosphere of violence at the school made it foreseeable any student might be attacked by another student, but the court didn't find the attack was a direct result of the district's actions.

The student also didn't show a surveillance camera in the stairwell would have prevented the attack or that security staff shortages increased the danger he'd be injured. Even if all the guards had been there that day, there was no guarantee one would have been in the stairwell at the time of the attack. *Mohammed v. School Dist. of Philadelphia*, 196 Fed.Appx. 79 (3d Cir. 2006).

◆   A teachers' union contract and an official circular creating a school security plan didn't create a special relationship that let a teacher hold the state responsible for his injuries from an attack in a school hallway.

A teacher was assaulted in the hall outside his classroom. He sued the school board, alleging his union contract and the state's official circular adopting and implementing a school security plan created a duty for the school to protect him.

A jury found in the teacher's favor, but the trial court set the verdict aside, finding the teacher's union contract and **the state's adoption of a school security plan didn't create a special relationship** between school authorities and the teacher. Without a special relationship, he couldn't hold them liable for not protecting him from third-party violence on school property. The teacher appealed, but the appellate court affirmed. *Krakower v. City of New York*, 217 A.D.2d 441 (N.Y. App. Div. 1995).

B. Negligence Claims

In the cases below, students and parents had mixed success in convincing a court to find their schools were negligent for not following a security plan.

◆   A student-supervision schedule didn't say principals had to make sure each patrol post was manned, so the principal had immunity to a suit that alleged a student got hurt because the teacher assigned to the hall where he was attacked was absent that day.

A classmate put high school freshman Cody Whitaker in a chokehold in the hall outside Cody's first class of the day. Cody fainted and hit his head on the floor, sustaining severe head trauma.

Kentucky law required schools to have a code of student behavior and discipline – and Cody's school adopted a student supervision schedule. The teacher responsible for supervising the hall where Cody was injured wasn't at school that day, and no one covered for him.

Cody sued then-principals James Beward and Gary Emberton for negligence and negligent supervision. They asked the court for judgment without a trial, claiming immunity. The judge found they weren't entitled to qualified official immunity under state law because their failure to enforce the student supervision schedule was "ministerial" (a duty to do what the law says in the way it says to do it). The principals appealed, arguing the duty was "discretionary" (a duty an actor can decide how – and sometimes whether – to do). The trial court found this duty was ministerial, meaning the principals didn't have immunity. The appeals court agreed, but the state's supreme court reversed.

The law gave the principals the general duty of ensuring school safety, but the student supervision schedule didn't give them the specific duty of seeing that all teachers assigned to supervise were either at their assigned posts or had arranged for a sub. The principals were entitled to immunity – and excused from the case. *Emberton v. Whitaker*, No. 2013-CA-000773-MR, 2016 WL 2609308 (Ky. Ct. App. 5/6/16).

◆ The mother of a charter school student raped at an off-campus end-of-year party claimed the school board was negligent in not ensuring the school crisis plan was implemented – but a Louisiana appeals court held the claim failed. The board had no duty to supervise students off campus after the end of the school year.

Freshman Unique Hayes went to an end-of-year party hosted by a classmate's mother at a hotel. There, a boy Unique had never met before raped her in a stairwell. Unique's mother sued multiple defendants, including the school board – but the trial court dismissed the school board from the case. The mother appealed, but the appeals court affirmed.

State law gave the board immunity to this suit unless its negligence breached a legal duty it owed Unique. The board had no legal duty to protect Unique here as it was well established under Louisiana law that **a board's duty to exercise reasonable supervision over a student was limited to situations where the student was under its supervision or control**. Unique wasn't under the school board's supervision or control at an off-campus party that occurred after the end of the school year and where no school official was present. The school board was properly dismissed from the suit. *Hayes v. Sheraton Operating Corp.*, 156 So.3d 1193 (La. Ct. App. 2014).

◆ A student sued her school district, saying it was responsible for her on-campus rape by a classmate because it didn't follow safety procedures, but a California appeals court affirmed a legal duty couldn't be premised on a school safety manual.

Special ed student R.G. met classmate James in algebra class. They talked sometimes. When James got a one-day suspension, the school's safety provisions called for the school to notify his parents and add his name to the list of suspended students it emailed to security staff and posted to teachers' computerized record programs.

The school tried to call James' guardian but couldn't reach her. James also didn't tell her. He went to school as usual the day he was suspended. School security guards that saw a suspended student were supposed to take steps to remove the student from campus. Around four guards saw James on campus that day but only told him to go to class or get a pass.

James ran into R.G. He convinced her to come with him to the student parking lot. He raped her between two cars.

R.G. sued the school district for negligent supervision, arguing the school's failure to follow its safety procedures caused her injury, but the court agreed with the district that her claim couldn't go forward. It granted the district a nonsuit, and an appeals court affirmed.

California's constitution gave students the "inalienable right to attend campuses which are safe, secure and peaceful" – but state courts had found that didn't create a legal duty for schools to establish any specific procedures or for "any government agency to guarantee the safety of schools." While a state law gave school districts responsibility for developing "comprehensive school safety plans[,]" that was a statement of public policy – which couldn't create a mandatory legal duty under California law. **Previous decisions had determined that mandatory legal duties couldn't be based on school safety manuals.** "Thus," the court wrote, "any claim defendant owed duties to plaintiff based on its safety manual alone fails." *R.G. v. San Bernardino City Unified School Dist.*, No. G049924, 2014 WL 5320262 (Cal. Ct. App. 10/20/14).

◆   Finding state education department regulations had "the force and effect of law," the Delaware Supreme Court OK'd a negligence per se claim based on an alleged breach of rules concerning suicidal students.

The Delaware Department of Education's (DOE's) Regulation 621 required school districts to have written emergency plans that followed the DOE's Emergency Preparedness Guidelines.

A "Quick Referral Reference" posted on the DOE's website said schools with a suicidal student should contact the student's parents or guardian immediately.

To comply with the guidelines. the school district adopted the policy: "Crisis Intervention Procedures for Suicide Threats." Third on its list of six protocols was: "Contact Parent[.]"

After 16-year-old Roger Ellerbe's friend told a teacher and then a school counselor that Ellerbe was suicidal and had attempted suicide two days earlier, the counselor called Ellerbe into the office.

The counselor was working under a contract with the district. She didn't know the district had a protocol for dealing with suicidal students.

She spent four hours with Ellerbe and sent him back to class when she decided his crisis had ended. She sent an email to teachers, counselors and an assistant principal to tell them about the incident. She didn't call the boy's grandmother, his guardian.

That night, Ellerbe hanged himself at home.

Ellerbe's family sued the district for wrongful death. This claim required them to show the district was negligent. Finding they couldn't, the trial court granted the district judgment without a trial.

The family appealed to the state's highest court. It reversed, finding the case could go forward because the family stated a valid claim of negligence per se.

In Delaware, violating a statute or ordinance enacted for the safety of others constituted negligence per se. **The family claimed the district violated a school policy, but the court found it had "the force and effect of law."** As the family could make a valid negligence claim, their wrongful death claim could go forward. *Rogers v. Christina School Dist.*, 73 A.3d 1 (Del. 2013).

◆   A trial was needed for a student's personal injury suit because factors – including the school's failure to follow its security plan – indicated a New

York district may have breached its duty to supervise students.

The district was aware of escalating aggression between two students.

First, a teacher had to restrain seventh-grader Ashley Bivens from physically attacking ninth-grader Tajoura Walley. A week later, the students got into a physical fight on a school bus, and a volleyball coach had to break it up. The next day, Bivens and Walley started a fight as soon as they got to school. Teachers had to separate them, and both girls were suspended.

The day their suspensions ended, Bivens went straight from the school bus to Walley's locker and stabbed Walley in the leg with a knife.

Walley sued the district, alleging it breached its duty to supervise them. She argued their escalating dispute put the district on notice that another incident could occur when they returned to school from their suspensions for fighting. She also **argued the school had failed to follow its security plan** by not:

- providing counseling, and
- having teachers stand outside their classrooms at the start of the school day to prevent problems.

The district agreed it breached its duty to supervise, but asked for judgment without a trial as its negligence wasn't the proximate cause of Walley's injury. It argued Bivens' attack was so sudden and spontaneous no amount of supervision could have prevented it.

The judge agreed and granted the district judgment. But Walley appealed, and the appellate court reversed.

As a prior New York decision held, the test for proximate cause was "whether under all the circumstances the chain of events that followed the negligent act or omission was a normal or foreseeable consequence of the situation created by the school's negligence." If it wasn't foreseeable, the school couldn't be held liable for it. But if that wasn't clear, a jury was needed – and that was the case here. *Walley v. Bivens*, 81 A.D.3d 1286 (N.Y. App. Div. 2011).

◆ The Nebraska Supreme Court rejected a mother's argument that the state education department's regulations for school safety plans created a legal duty that could be violated if a school district didn't follow the regs.

An intruder entered an elementary school's unlocked door and ignored a sign telling all visitors to check in at the office.

Two teachers spotted him and reported him to the office.

Meanwhile, five-year-old C.B. came back from the bathroom to tell his teacher "a bad man" was in there. C.B. later said the man pulled down his pants and performed oral sex on him.

The district's "Safety and Security Plan" and the school's "Emergency Procedures and Security" guidelines called for dealing with an intruder by talking to the person and then deciding whether to lock down the school and call 911.

The administrator went inside the restroom and found the man sitting in a stall. After C.B.'s teacher told the administrator what C.B. said, the administrator locked down the school and called 911. Police arrived and arrested the intruder.

C.B.'s mother sued, alleging the district was negligent because its security system was ineffective. The trial court granted the district summary judgment. It found the assault on C.B. wasn't foreseeable and the district had made a *prima facie* showing that its security plan was adequate.

On appeal, the Nebraska Supreme Court sent the case back for a trial to decide if the attack was foreseeable – but **rejected the mother's argument the school should be held liable because its safety plan allegedly didn't follow the state education department's regulations**.

The regulations set the standard for school security plans but didn't create an extra legal duty that went beyond the district's existing duty to act with reasonable care to protect students from a sexual assault. *A.W. v. Lancaster County School Dist. 0001*, 280 Neb. 205 (Neb. 2010).

◆   The district's state-law-required transportation safety plan (TSP) may have triggered a legal duty to stop a six-year-old from getting off a school bus before it left to drive the children home.

Eric M. was a first-grader. His parents signed him up for the school bus, but sometimes drove to school and picked him up instead. Whether he took the bus or drove home with a parent changed from day to day.

About a month into the school year, Eric got on the bus but then told the bus driver he was getting off because he'd just seen his father's car. The bus driver grabbed Eric's arm to stop him and asked if he was sure. Eric said he was – but he was mistaken.

After Eric couldn't find his father, he started to walk with other students. He was struck by a car while crossing a busy street.

Eric sued the district for personal injury, alleging it breached its duty of care when it "negligently permitted, allowed, and let [him] wander away from school." The court dismissed his claim. He appealed, and the appellate court reversed.

California law required districts that provided transportation to prepare a TSP that set out procedures for school personnel to follow "to ensure the safe transport of pupils." The procedures for grades preK-8 were supposed to include "boarding and exiting a schoolbus[.]" Based on this and provisions giving drivers and school personnel responsibility for supervising students, the court found the district had undertaken a duty of care toward students.

The court decided a trial was needed to determine if the duty of immediate and direct supervision of pupils was breached here. *Eric M. v. Cajon Valley Union School Dist.*, 174 Cal.App.4th 285 (Cal. Ct. App. 2009).

C. Claims Based on State Requirements

◆   California laws require public schools to have school safety plans. The plans must include anti-harassment and anti-discrimination policies.

An appeals court found the father of a boy who was allegedly bullied for being disabled and Hispanic could seek to enforce those laws against a school district his son no longer attended.

Hector F.'s seventh-grade son Brian was eligible for special education based on emotional disabilities, including bipolar disorder. English wasn't Brian's first language, and he was in the school's only bilingual classroom.

Hector went to administrators after seeing Brian had large bruises and scratches. Brian went on to file reports with the school to say other students were physically and verbally abusing him, including with ethnic slurs.

The principal's proposed solution was to move Brian out of the bilingual classroom. His parents rejected this proposal.

Hector and Brian sued the school district. **The father claimed the district hadn't adopted state-required safety plans.** He also alleged the district wasted taxpayer money by responding to harassment complaints in a way that discriminated against Hispanics and the disabled. He wanted a "writ of mandate" to enforce the laws. After Brian moved on to a high school in another school district, a trial court decided Hector couldn't seek this remedy – but an appeals court found he could.

Generally, the state allows writs of mandate only to "beneficially interested" persons, but Hector fell within a public interest exception. The appeals court wrote that the laws "articulate a well identified public interest in maintaining a system of taxpayer funded public education which is free of the destructive influence of discrimination, harassment and bullying." Here, the writ was intended to enforce a public duty. The court found Hector had a right to seek enforcement of the law both as a taxpayer and a member of the public. *Hector F. v. El Centro Elementary School Dist.*, 227 Cal.App.4th 331 (Cal. Ct. App. 2014).

In 2007, Georgia courts heard three appeals involving the interplay between the state's requirement that schools have crisis management plans and lawsuits brought by students who were seriously injured at school. In two cases, the school was sued because it didn't have a plan in place. In the third, the school was sued, although it did have a plan in place. In each case, the court found the school was immune to the student's lawsuit.

◆   A student who was nearly raped at school couldn't sue the members of the school board for negligence based on the board's failure to implement a school safety plan at her school because the board had state immunity to this claim.

A female student was sexually molested at school by a male student who also tried to rape her. Despite a state law requiring schools to have safety plans, there was no such plan in place at her school.

The student brought a Title IX claim against the school board. She also sued the individual board members, alleging they were negligent for failing to implement a school safety plan. The board members objected to her lawsuit, arguing they couldn't be held negligent because they had no individual legal duty to create the safety plan.

In Georgia, state employees were immune to lawsuits alleging negligence only if the duty they allegedly failed to perform was discretionary rather than ministerial. Discretionary duties called for greater personal authority and judgment, whereas ministerial duties were more like those performed pursuant to orders.

Because the *Murphy v. Bajjani* case (reported below) had determined Georgia school boards and superintendents had a discretionary duty when it came to preparing school safety plans, this court agreed with the board members that the student could not sue them for negligence based on their failure to develop a school safety plan. As a result, the court invited the board members to ask the court to grant it summary judgment. *Snethen v. Board of Public Educ. for the City of Savannah*, No. 406CV259, 2007 WL 2345247 (S.D. Ga. 2007).

◆   The Georgia Supreme Court held that a student severely injured by another student at school couldn't sue school administrators or members of the school board for negligence based on their failure to create a school safety plan as required by state law. Georgia law granted them immunity to negligence claims unless they acted with actual malice or intent to cause injury – which they did not.

In June 2007, the Supreme Court of Georgia reversed a lower court's judgment in favor of a high school student who was seriously injured at school by another student. The lower court determined the individuals sued by the student – including his principal, vice principal and members of the school board – were responsible for the student's injuries because the school hadn't created a school safety plan as required by Georgia state law. The law called for schools to devise a plan to respond to the following potential emergencies: natural disasters, hazardous material or radiological accidents, terrorism and violence.

The state supreme court reversed the judgment for the student and dismissed the case against the school defendants because it determined **these public employees had qualified immunity under the state's constitution with respect to safety plans**. This meant that they could not be sued for negligence unless they had acted maliciously or with intent to injure.

This decision hinged on which kind of duty the safety-plan law created: ministerial or discretionary. The court determined that drafting safety plans was a discretionary act (an exercise of educated, personal judgment) as opposed to a ministerial act (something more akin to following established procedures). Ministerial acts weren't covered by qualified immunity for negligence, but discretionary acts were.

The court dismissed the case against the school defendants because it found that creating a school safety plan was a discretionary act and the school defendants hadn't acted with actual malice or intent to cause injury. This meant they were immune to the student's claims. *Murphy v. Bajjani*, 647 S.E.2d 54 (Ga. 2007). A Georgia appellate court adopted the supreme court's judgment in another proceeding based on the same incident. *Bajjani v. Gwinnett County School Dist.*, 651 S.E.2d 366 (Ga. Ct. App. 2007).

◆ A county board of education, its individual members, the superintendent and **a school's principal and staff were entitled to official immunity because there was a valid safety plan in place at the school when a psychologically disturbed stranger gained unauthorized entry to it and attacked a 10-year-old with a hammer**.

Georgia law requires schools to create safety plans. This school provided evidence that it did have a safety plan in place before the intruder attacked the 10-year-old, but the child's parents argued that the plan wasn't valid because it had been developed by the Georgia Emergency Management Agency (GEMA) and other third parties instead of the school itself. But the Georgia Court of Appeals found that the law specifically sanctioned input from approved third parties and that it required GEMA to provide public schools training and technical assistance, which included safe school planning and model school safety plans.

This case pre-dated the state's supreme court decision that settled the law by finding creation of a school safety plan was a discretionary duty instead of a ministerial duty. But it also held the duty was discretionary and therefore shielded school officials from negligence charges. *Leake v. Murphy*, 644 S.E.2d 328 (Ga. Ct. App. 2007).

D. Evacuating Students With Disabilities

◆ A student with a disability couldn't sue the school board for disability discrimination based on school personnel's failure to properly execute the emergency evacuation plan for children with disabilities.

A middle school student had a form of dwarfism that limited her strength and mobility. She operated a computer with voice recognition software so that she didn't have to type. She also had a motorized wheelchair and a full-time aide.

In 1996, her school was evacuated because of a bomb threat. For just over an hour, this student and another student with disabilities were left alone in the building under adult supervision. No bomb was discovered.

Her parents filed a complaint with the state department of education, alleging the school board discriminated against her based on her disability by not evacuating her from the building during the bomb threat. After mediation, the parents agreed to drop their complaint in exchange for the school board's agreement to adopt a new emergency preparedness plan for students with disabilities.

This plan called for sending students with disabilities to one of several "safe rooms" during school emergencies. Each safe room was assigned a responsible adult (plus an alternate) and was equipped with a special flag to alert emergency responders of their presence and also a cell phone. In case evacuation was necessary, the plan called for emergency personnel to rescue the students from the safe rooms.

The school instituted the plan based on advice from local fire and police officials and then explained it to staff and students. It also held a successful practice drill. But two months later, the school had an unscheduled fire drill and the student was left alone for two minutes until the student's math teacher – not assigned as a responsible adult for that room – stopped by to make sure the student was OK. The math teacher stayed with the student for the rest of the fire drill.

The student's parents sued the school board, alleging disability discrimination in violation of Section 504 of the Rehabilitation Act and Title II of the Americans with Disabilities Act based on the bomb-threat and fire-drill incidents.

The court granted the school board summary judgment. The parents appealed, but the Fourth U.S. Circuit Court of Appeals affirmed judgment for the school. The parents couldn't sue concerning the bomb-threat incident because the parents definitively resolved that dispute with the school board when they agreed to drop the complaint in return for institution of the new safety plan.

Based on only the fire-drill incident, the parents couldn't show the school board excluded the student from safe evacuation procedures during an emergency. The school had developed a plan, based on expert advice, specifically aimed at safely evacuating children with disabilities. It had equipped its safe rooms and run a successful drill. **Although the student was left alone for two minutes in a safe room, the imperfect execution of an otherwise reasonable evacuation plan did not constitute disability discrimination.** *Shirey v. City of Alexandria School Board*, 229 F.3d 1143 (4th Cir. 2000).

E. Cases Involving Staff

◆   An Oregon federal judge refused to dismiss emotional distress and assault claims against a school district and members of its safety committee that sprang an unannounced live shooter drill on unsuspecting teachers.

The 2012 Sandy Hook school shooting prompted a rural school district in Oregon to plan for a similar event. It was of special concern that emergency response time to these schools could take more than an hour.

The school board formed a safety committee to plan a response to a school intruder or active shooter.

Committee members, the superintendent and teachers attended "Run, Hide, Fight" presentations on the recommended response to active shooter incidents. After it, the elementary school principal told teachers to develop "Run, Hide, Fight" plans for their classrooms.

Unbeknownst to teachers, members of the safety committee decided to hold an unannounced active shooter drill during the teachers' in-service day. Their classroom "Run, Hide, Fight" plans were due that day and no students were expected to be at school.

For the drill, two of the committee members covered their faces with paintball mask goggles. One wore military pants and boots. The other wore a hoodie. They carried firecrackers and starter guns loaded with blanks.

The principal told the teachers to work on their safety plans in their classrooms. Teacher Linda McLean was in her classroom when she heard a loud bang (a firecracker). Then a masked man burst into her room, pointed a gun at her and pulled the trigger. It sounded like a real gun and McLean thought she was going to die. The man said, "You're dead" and ran out.

The drill took about 90 seconds total. Two teachers collided while running for the exit. One fell, hitting her knee. Another wet herself.

McLean sued the district and members of the safety committee on multiple claims. Her constitutional claims failed, but the court refused to dismiss her intentional infliction of emotional distress and civil assault claims. A reasonable jury could find the defendants intended to cause the teachers severe emotional distress and that their actions were outrageous – and that the civil assault requirements were met in that the defendants intended McLean to believe the "shooter" was going to harm her. *McLean v. Pine Eagle School Dist., No. 61*, No. 3:15-cv-654-SI, 2016 WL 3574017 (D. Or. 7/1/16).

◆ A New York appellate court affirmed a ruling that a board of education acted in bad faith by replacing a union position with a virtually identical – but nonunion – position.

After a school district abolished its Director of Emergency Planning position, the union of the person who lost the job sued the district's board of education.

The union accused the board of acting in bad faith, claiming it replaced the emergency planning position with a nearly identical one called Homeland Security Coordinator – which union members couldn't hold because it was civil-service exempt.

Both positions required a comprehensive understanding of emergency management and involved responsibilities relating to emergency preparedness, including implementing safety plans and organizing training programs.

The board argued it was entitled to abolish a position at any time – but prior New York decisions had held "a position may not be abolished as a subterfuge to avoid the statutory protection afforded to civil servants." The court found that was the case here and held the board acted in bad faith. The board appealed, but the appellate court affirmed. *Gallagher v. Board of Educ. for Buffalo City School Dist.*, 81 A.D.3d 1408 (N.Y. App. Div. 2011).

◆ The Ninth U.S. Circuit Court of Appeals found a school district's former security specialist stated a valid First Amendment claim.

Robert Posey's job as a high school security specialist included liaising with police, enforcing truancy policies, searching students and investigating student misconduct – until the new principal relieved him of those duties. After that, he mainly monitored the parking lot, grounds and hallways. The principal asked him to update the school's emergency plan – but later reassigned the job, finding "Mr. Posey was not in full charge of those issues." **Posey met with the principal to say he was worried about the way discipline and safety issues were being handled.** The principal didn't respond directly, and Posey became increasingly worried.

Posey had a friendly relationship with the district's chief administrative officer (CAO). About a year after his meeting with the principal, Posey gave the CAO a long letter about school safety issues, hoping it would prompt the district to "correct the problems before somebody gets seriously hurt." In it, he detailed concerns about the administration's lack of responsiveness to safety problems, inadequate staff training, failure to properly document safety violations, ineffective truancy and sexual-harassment policy enforcement, and inadequate fire safety and school evacuation planning.

Posey substantiated each concern with specific examples. The letter was copied to the superintendent and two school administrators.

At the end of the year, Posey was told the district was combining his and two other employees' job duties to create a new "preventative specialist" position. Posey applied for it but wasn't hired.

He filed a grievance, and the school district found he'd been retaliated against because of his letter – but the district's governing board overrode that determination and refused to rehire Posey.

Posey sued the district, alleging it violated his First Amendment rights by firing and then not rehiring him in retaliation for raising safety concerns. But the court granted the district summary judgment. The Supreme Court decision *Garcetti v. Ceballos*, 547 U.S. 410 (2006), had held public employees don't have free speech rights in statements made concerning their official duties. The court determined Posey's letter wasn't protected speech because it concerned his official duties.

On appeal, the Ninth Circuit reversed. It found the safety concerns Posey raised were matters of public concern, protected speech under *Garcetti*, and disagreed that Posey's remarks concerned his official duties. It returned the case to the lower court for further proceedings. *Posey v. Lake Pend Oreille School Dist. No. 84*, 546 F.3d 1121 (9th Cir. 2008).

CHAPTER THREE

School Safety and Liability

I. BULLYING AND HAZING

Liability in bullying cases is typically determined under traditional negligence and constitutional law principles. In negligence cases, a school district or board of education may be held liable for student-on-student violence only if it had "specific, prior knowledge of the danger that caused the injury." An exception was made by the Court of Appeal of California in *Hector F. v. El Centro Elementary School Dist.*, 227 Cal.App.4th 331,173 Cal.Rptr.3d 413 (Cal. Ct. App. 2014). The court held a parent had standing as both a citizen and taxpayer to enforce a comprehensive law requiring safety plans in all schools. It found a "manifest public interest in enforcing the antibullying statutes" and no countervailing reasons not to enforce them.

In contrast to the court's decision in *Hector F. v. El Centro Elementary School Dist.*, a Connecticut court held there is **no private cause of action** to enforce the state's anti-bullying statute. *Mazzo v. Town of Fairfield Board of Educ.*, No. CV 126031781S, 2013 WL 4872203 (Conn. Super. Ct. 8/20/13).

A. Bullying Claims

1. Negligence

◆   A New Hampshire student was punched in the face during a fight on her school bus. The driver reported the fight, and the principal met with the student the next day. She asked the principal not to report the incident to her mother, but the principal said he would have to do so. Despite a school policy requiring notification to parents of any student involved in a reported bullying incident, the principal did not tell the parent about the fight. Later, the student reported receiving threats on social media from a classmate. When the principal learned of this, he went to the cafeteria and told the classmate to see him after lunch. A fight broke out, resulting in injuries to the student and an emergency room visit. When the principal met her mother in the emergency room, he told her for the first time about the bus incident and threats. In a state court, the student's parent sued the school district, seeking damages for violation of the reporting requirements of state law and the district's anti-bullying policy. She noted state law requires each school district to have a policy containing a procedure for notifying the parents of all students involved in a reported bullying incident within 48 hours. The court dismissed the case, finding the negligence claim based on the failure to notify the parent of alleged bullying was barred by state law immunity.

On appeal, the Supreme Court of New Hampshire rejected the parent's claim that the principal had a common law duty to protect and supervise her child. In addition, the state law declared that it created no private right of action. Another provision of state law provided for immunity from suit from any civil liability for good-faith conduct arising from the reporting, investigation, findings, recommended response or implementation of a response under state law. No law imposed on schools an "overarching duty to protect and supervise in all instances and against all harms." Any duty of schools to exercise supervisory responsibility over students was limited. **The court declined the parent's invitation to extend the duty of reasonable supervision over students to create a new duty to report bullying.** There was no statutory duty to inform parents of generalized threats at school and no common-law duty to notify parents of third-party threats. As a result, the court held for the district. It also declined the parent's invitation to find a constitutional violation. *Gauthier v. Manchester School Dist., SAU #37*, 168 N.H. 143, 123 A.3d 1016 (N.H. 2015).

Courts have found no liability for harm that is "sudden" or "without warning" and have held that schools and staff members are not liable for injuries that are unforeseeable. Schools are not considered the "insurers of student safety," and state immunity laws offer school districts and their employees immunity unless there is some intentional misconduct, deliberate indifference or other gross departure from professional standards.

For example, **New York courts have held there is no school liability for injuries caused by sudden, impulsive acts that are not preceded by prior misconduct**. In *Mirand v. City of New York*, 84 N.Y. 44, 637 N.E.2d 263 (N.Y. 1994), the state's highest court held a school is liable for student-on-student violence only if it had "specific, prior knowledge of the danger that caused the injury." A student's acts must have been foreseeable by the district to impose liability. If an assault occurs so suddenly that it could not be prevented by any amount of supervision, there is no school liability.

Mirand and many other courts have held prior unrelated incidents of student discipline do not put a school on notice of a specific threat of danger requiring supervision. While schools have a duty to supervise students, "this duty does not make schools insurers of the safety of their students, for they cannot be reasonably expected to continuously supervise and control all movements and activities of students."

◆ A Kansas seventh-grader reported students made fun of his "lazy eye" and his height. A classmate pushed him, put him in a headlock and threw him to the ground. After the classmate threatened the student with a knife, police were called. The school district suspended the classmate out-of-school and required him to report to the office upon arrival at school. He was also sent to a classroom at lunch time. But another classmate then began threatening the student. As the two were in a bus-loading area after school, the classmate hit the student and fractured his jaw. The student was removed from the school by his mother, and she filed a state court lawsuit against the school district, bullies and their parents. In pretrial activity, the family settled the claims against the bullies and their parents. The principal sought judgment based on the Paul D. Coverdell Teacher Protection Act of 2001.

The Coverdell Act is a No Child Left Behind Act provision immunizing teachers from liability for taking "reasonable actions to maintain order, discipline, and an appropriate educational environment." The family conceded the principal was entitled to Coverdell Act immunity, and the court awarded him judgment. It also held for the school district, and appeal reached the state court of appeals. In assessing the lower court judgment, the court noted the district had received immunity based on *respondeat superior* principles. *Respondeat superior* allows employers to be held liable for harm caused by employee negligence within the scope of employment. **But the**

Coverdell Act only immunizes teachers, administrators and other school employees. No language in the act immunizes a school district as an entity. Moreover, the court held the district could not claim immunity under the doctrine of *respondeat superior*. As the principal had received judgment on Coverdell Act grounds, there had been no legal or factual determination regarding negligence. Since the district had an independent duty to reasonably protect students from harm, liability was not imputed to it based on employee negligence. As the trial court should not have held for the district based on *respondeat superior* principles and adoptive immunity, the case was returned to the lower court for more activity. *Sanchez v. Unified School Dist. 469*, 50 Kan.App.2d 1185, 339 P.3d 399 (Kan. Ct. App. 2014), (Kan. Review Denied, 7/22/15).

◆   Soon after a student's family moved from Georgia to New Jersey, she encountered problems in her classroom. During her fourth-grade year, her mother reported that classmates had spit on the student, hit her, kicked her and confronted her physically. The school called meetings at which the parents and students discussed the reports and appropriate behavior. More incidents were reported the next year. Most reports came from the mother, and the school could not verify many of them. The student said she felt the misconduct was directed toward her mother's obesity and her aunt's disability. She was placed in a new school but had difficulty with her peers there. An escort plan was formulated to ensure the student's safety and to separate her from girls who were making her feel uncomfortable. Near this time, the family spent time in a shelter and began counseling sessions. The student was diagnosed with adjustment disorder, enuresis and trichotillomania. Her mother sued the school board, superintendent and others in a federal court for violations of the Constitution and the New Jersey Law Against Discrimination (LAD). In pretrial activity, the court explained that the state Anti-Bullying Act required each school district to adopt a policy prohibiting harassment, intimidation or bullying.

Although the act required schools to have procedures for investigating such reports, the law created no private cause of action and did not create or alter any state law tort liability. A number of incidents were investigated by a school anti-bullying specialist, but no evidence or witnesses were found. As for the LAD claim, the court found no reasonable jury could find there had been bullying based on gender. The family had reported bullying by both male and female students, and nothing indicated the bullying was due to the student's sex. Although the mother asserted discrimination on the basis of being from the South, the court held this did not support a claim for national origin discrimination. As there was no evidence of discrimination based on a protected status, the court dismissed the LAD claim. School officials were entitled to qualified immunity. The court held for the board and officials. *Thomas v. East Orange Board of Educ.*, 998 F.Supp.2d 338 (D.N.J. 2014).

◆   An Illinois student said peers subjected him to verbal and physical abuse at school for an extended time. He said he was punched and pushed by other students and that he told school officials many times about bullying. After the student claimed to have been beaten up outside his classroom by peers, he sued the school district in a state court for negligence, asserting it failed to provide him with a safe environment. The court dismissed the case, finding the district had immunity under the Illinois Local Governmental and Governmental Tort Immunity Act. Appeal went before the Appellate Court of Illinois. It noted the trial court's finding that dealing with student bullying was a discretionary decision for which the Tort Immunity Act provided absolute immunity. The court explained that the act protected local entities and employees from liability arising from government operations. Immunity was a legislative choice to prevent the diversion of public funds from their intended purposes to pay out claims. A public employee in a policy-making position or exercising discretion was not liable for any injury resulting from an act or omission in determining policy. The court held this meant there was an absolute grant of immunity from liability for public entities. Under prior state cases, a principal had broad discretion in handling bullying cases and was entitled to discretionary immunity under the Tort Immunity Act.

A bullying policy could provide a school district with discretion to determine whether bullying had occurred, what consequences would result and any remedial actions. Since a school's handling of bullying incidents fit within the definition of a "discretionary act" under the Tort Immunity Act, the court held for the school district. *Malinksi v. Grayslake Community High School Dist. 127*, No. 2012-CA-002178-MR, 2014 IL App. (2d) 130685-U (Ill. Ct. App. 2/14/14).

◆   An Illinois parent claimed three classmates bullied her daughter from kindergarten through grade four. She asked the principal to reassign her child to a different classroom. The parent later said the principal declined the request. Later in the school year, the parent met with the district superintendent and principal to discuss the bullying problem. She also sought to arrange a meeting that would include parents of the other girls and police. After an incident in which the student said the girls trapped her in a school lavatory and threatened her, the parent called the police. She again called the principal, who promised appropriate disciplinary action. A second police report was made after the student said one of the girls again threatened her in a lavatory. An investigating officer spoke to the parents of the other girls, who stated they had never been told previously that their children were bullying the student. After the parent was denied a meeting with police, school administrators and a teacher, the parent sued the school district and administrators in a state court for negligence. The case was dismissed, and the parent appealed to the Appellate Court of Illinois.

On appeal, the court explained that government employees may qualify for immunity under the Illinois Tort Immunity Act if their jobs require determination of policy or the exercise of discretion. Under the parent's theory, the district's anti-bullying policy required administrators to respond to reported bullying without any exercise of discretion. But the court explained that **school administrators balance competing interests when handling bullying cases**. As maintaining the anti-bullying policy called for the broad exercise of discretion, the court held immunity was correctly granted under the Tort Immunity Act. While expressing sympathy for the parent's claims, the court held the administrators were entitled to immunity from any liability. It affirmed the lower court's judgment. *Hascall v. Williams*, 996 N.E.2d 1168 (Ill. App. Ct. 2013).

◆   While in a high school hallway, a Washington student was fatally shot by a student with disabilities. The victim's family sued the school district in a state court, arguing the disabled student's behavior and medical records indicated he was a risk to others. It was asserted that the district negligently failed to maintain a safe environment. In trial court proceedings, evidence was produced that the disabled student had paranoid schizophrenia and tried to commit suicide two years before the shooting. His doctors noted he heard voices at the time of the shooting and claimed to get into fights with people he did not know. After hospitalization, the disabled student underwent 11 months of outpatient mental health care and received anti-psychotic medication. Since his condition had been found to be stable on medication, the outpatient services were terminated. There was no evidence that the disabled student had previously committed any assaults. In pretrial activity, the court rejected the estate's theories of liability. After the court denied the estate's request to reconsider dismissal, the estate appealed.

On appeal, the Court of Appeals of Washington held that **school districts must exercise reasonable care when supervising students. But the duty to exercise reasonable care extends only to foreseeable risks of harm.** Although the court agreed with the estate that foreseeability is normally a jury question, it found nothing in school or medical records indicating the disabled student presented a risk of harm to anyone at school. Since there was no indication that he might try to harm someone, the court found the shooting was not foreseeable to the district. The court found the estate's arguments ignored state and federal antidiscrimination laws and school district obligations to serve the disabled student. As the district did not have evidence that he would act violently, the court affirmed the judgment for the school district. *Kok v. Tacoma School Dist. No. 10*, 177 Wash.App. 1016 (Wash. Ct. App. 2013). (Wash. Review Denied, 6/4/14).

◆   A 14-year-old Iowa student was considered vulnerable and functioned at a third-grade level. She was rarely without direct supervision, and her teachers usually took precautions beyond what school policy required. A special education teacher saw her spending time with a 19-year-old special education student. Although she saw them touching and kissing, she assumed they had an age-appropriate relationship. On a day when the student's mother allowed the student to ride the bus home from school with a friend, the student skipped her last class. She then left school with the friend, met the 19-year-old student and went to still another student's house.

The 19-year-old then took the student to the garage and raped her. After the mother learned of the rape, she sued the school district in a state court for negligence. After a jury trial, the court denied motions by the district. The jury returned a verdict of $500,000 for the student, reducing it by 30% based on her own fault. When the case reached the Supreme Court of Iowa, it held the scope of liability was for a jury to decide. Generally, tort law limits liability to the physical harm resulting from the risks that make an actor's conduct a tort in the first place. Questions about the scope of liability were fact-intensive. As there was no "bright-line rule" to resolve such questions, the court held the issue was left to the judgment and common sense of the jury. In the court's opinion, there was sufficient evidence in this case to generate a jury question on the issue of whether the student's injuries were among the potential harms that made the school district's conduct a tort. The court rejected the district's argument that **the off-campus location of the assault and the fact that it took place after school hours disposed of the case**. As a result, the court held for the student. *Mitchell v. Cedar Rapids Community School Dist.*, 832 N.W.2d 689 (Iowa 2013).

◆ A federal district court dismissed an action by a deceased student's family against a Utah school district that sought to hold school officials liable for his suicide death based on failure to address harassment and bullying. Although the family claimed school administrators knew of the harassment and bullying and failed to act, the court found the family did not file an action until more than a year after his death. **A state-law notice of claim requirement thus barred the action.** *Hancock v. North Sanpete School Dist.*, No. 2:12-cv-00072, 2012 WL 3060118 (D. Utah 7/25/12).

◆ A Tennessee student claimed a classmate began threatening and harassing him. He complained about the bullying to an assistant school principal and the principal, and his father also reported it to teachers and school officials. But the next school year, the bully paid a friend $5 to hurt the student. The attack was carried out at school, and the student was severely beaten. In a state court action against the bully, friend, their parents and the board of education, the court found the board 25% at fault for the student's injuries. It found the bully, his friend and their parents jointly and severally liable for the remaining 75% of fault. But the court held the board had state-law immunity. As a result, the board was dismissed from the case and the judgment was modified to hold the bully, his friend and their parents liable for a damage award in excess of $50,000. On appeal, the Court of Appeals of Tennessee explained that state law immunized the conduct of government employees who performed discretionary functions. Policy-making and planning-level acts were thus entitled to immunity.

The court agreed with the student that school officials did not follow the board's disciplinary procedures and policies. Implementing a policy is operational, not discretionary, so immunity was removed. Administrators did not follow the board policy on bullying and harassment. No complaint manager was assigned to investigate, and school disciplinary guidelines were not followed. As the trial court held, **the school was on notice of possible injury to the student**. All the defending parties played a role in the harm, so the court held them equally liable. *Moore v. Houston County Board of Educ.*, 358 S.W.3d 612 (Tenn. Ct. App. 2011), appeal denied 1/13/12.

◆   A West Virginia high school student created a MySpace.com web page that ridiculed a classmate. She opened the page to about 100 MySpace "friends," and some of them added vulgar criticisms of the classmate. The classmate filed a harassment complaint with the school, which found the student had created a "hate website" in violation of a school policy against harassment, bullying and intimidation. She was suspended for five days and excluded from school social activities for 90 days. In a federal court, the student sued the school district for speech rights and due process violations. After the court held for the district, the student appealed. In upholding the discipline, the court found that bullying is a major concern in schools, leading to student depression and even thoughts of suicide. **The court held "schools have a duty to protect their students from harassment and bullying in the school environment."** It was foreseeable that the student's conduct would reach the school via computers or other devices. The nexus between the speech and school pedagogical interests justified discipline. The court held speech originating outside of school "but directed at persons in school and received by and acted on by them was in fact in-school speech." *Kowalski v. Berkeley County Schools*, 652 F.3d 565 (4th Cir. 2011).

◆   Two female students in Idaho reported that two males were planning a Columbine-style attack at school. The principal confronted one of the male students, who said he was "going to have a school shooting" on a specified date. The two male students were warned about their threatening conduct, and they agreed not to make further statements. But one month later, the students were accused of threatening to shoot guns at a school dance. Two years after these incidents, one of the male students wrote threatening notes that were viewed by his locker partner. Although the threats were brought to the attention of the school resource officer and a vice principal, they were "dismissed." The same month as the notes were found, the student and a male accomplice murdered a female student at the house of her friend. When her parents sued the school district in a state trial court, it was found that **the district owed no duty to protect the student off school grounds and after school hours**. On appeal, the Supreme Court of Idaho found nothing in the record that the district knew one of the male students would commit a murder based on information received about him some 30 months earlier. As the murder was not foreseeable, the district had no duty to prevent it. *Stoddart v. Pocatello School Dist. #25*, 239 P.3d 784 (Idaho 2010).

2. Constitutional Claims

Federal constitutional liability for school entities based on peer bullying is limited by precedents such as *DeShaney v. Winnebago County Dep't of Social Services*, 489 U.S. 189 (1989). In *DeShaney*, the U.S. Supreme Court held there must be a "special relationship" between a state agency and a victim of private violence for a constitutional duty to exist. While no federal law prohibits bullying, the federal government has targeted peer bullying by holding bullying prevention summits and joining other federal agencies in the Federal Partners in Bullying Prevention Steering Committee. A "Dear Colleague" letter by the U.S. Department of Education's Office for Civil Rights details federal expectations for confronting bullies in schools. See *http://www2.ed.gov/about/offices/list/ocr/letters/colleague-201010.html.*

◆   An Indiana student said she was relentlessly bullied by classmates as early as grade three. She said the bullying became more physical and vicious when she entered grade six. The student said other girls threw basketballs at her head, tripped her and ignored her during practice. She said this conduct escalated even further during her seventh- and eighth-grade school years. The student claimed school officials intervened only twice and that some staff members joined the bullying or were complicit in misconduct. During the student's eighth-grade school year, she said other basketball team members taunted her and called her names to the point that she called her mother to pick her up from school. The mother then yelled at the bullies. Later, the student's father and grandfather confronted the bullies, leading to a call to police. Eventually, the principal banned the father and grandfather from the school. The family sued the school district in a federal court, asserting equal protection and due process violations as well as municipal liability and state law claims. The court held for the district, and the parents appealed.

On appeal, the U.S. Court of Appeals, Seventh Circuit, explained that **the Due Process Clause of the Fourteenth Amendment does not impose an affirmative obligation on states to ensure those interests are not harmed through other means**. The court held the clause does not guarantee minimal levels of safety and security. In this case, it was not shown that teachers and coaches instigated, created or increased bullying of the student at school. Nor did the record support the student's contention that inaction or ineffective responses to her reports increased the danger. While she claimed school staff participated in bullying incidents, the court found the actions were not sufficiently egregious to create liability. An equal protection claim failed due to a similar lack of evidence. Since the student could not demonstrate any violation of her constitutional rights, the court held she could not proceed with the case. *D.S. v. East Porter County School Corp.*, 799 F.3d 793 (7th Cir. 2015).

◆   A Texas parent said her child experienced many years of bullying at his school and that school officials did not respond to repeated complaints. She said her child was shoved into walls, pushed, kicked and spat upon and that school officials increased the danger by punishing him for defending himself and not imposing any punishment on the perpetrators. In a federal court, the mother sued the school district and principal, asserting constitutional violations and state tort claims. The court dismissed the tort claims with permission for the family to refile them in a state court. It then held the federal claims were not viable. Appeal reached the Fifth Circuit.

The court explained that to state a constitutional claim against a Texas agency, a party must show an official policymaker has violated a constitutional right and was the moving force behind the violation. Texas law was clear that a school district's board was the final policymaker in school liability cases. But the mother did not mention an official policy, arguing only that there was a widespread district custom of tolerating bullying. She claimed the majority of the district's board of trustees knew of or approved of their employees' actions in a way that established an official district custom or policy. But the court held the mother did not assert sufficient facts to show an official policy. Moreover, the Fifth Circuit has repeatedly refused to recognize a "state-created danger" theory as a basis for constitutional rights protection. As the complaint did not assert enough facts to show a policy or custom of tolerating bullying, the court held for the district and principal. *G.M. v. Shelton*, 595 Fed.Appx. 262 (5th Cir. 2014).

The U.S. Supreme Court later denied the parent's request to review the Fifth Circuit's decision. *G.M. v. Aledo Independent School Dist.*, No. 14-1070, 135 S.Ct. 2830 (cert. denied, 2015).

◆   Pennsylvania parents said their children were bullied and injured at their middle school. They said that despite notice, the school district did not respond. In fact, the parents claimed school officials criticized and belittled them to deflect their responsibility to stop the misconduct. The parents sued the school district and officials in a federal court, asserting constitutional violations and a number of state law claims. The court dismissed the case, and appeal reached the Third Circuit. First, the court dispensed with a claim that officials had retaliated against the families. The court held allegations of inaction were insufficient to maintain a constitutional claim. As the parents did not plead any retaliatory action by the school district, the trial court correctly dismissed the First Amendment claim. Their claims based on violation of due process rights were also properly dismissed. The families did not assert any affirmative acts by the district but only argued that it did not act to prevent bullying by the classmates. To recover for a constitutional violation, **any deprivation of rights must be attributable to a state actor and not a private actor such as a bully**. As the actions at issue were attributed to students and not the district, there was no due process violation. *Monn v. Gettysburg Area School Dist.*, 553 Fed.Appx. 120 (3d Cir. 2014).

◆   A North Carolina high school senior attacked a freshman with a box cutter in a school hallway, injuring her face, neck and scalp. A teacher/coach intervened almost immediately. After the attack, the senior pled guilty to assault and no contest to a weapons possession charge. She received a suspended sentence and was placed on supervised probation.

After an investigation, the principal suspended the freshman for 10 days. She attended a half-day school schedule for the rest of the school year. Meanwhile, the senior was suspended for the rest of the school year. In a state court lawsuit, the freshman's parent claimed the school board violated her child's right to the opportunity for an education free from psychological abuse and harm. After a hearing, the court dismissed both the negligence and constitutional claims on the basis of state law immunity. On appeal, the Court of Appeals of North Carolina noted the state supreme court has held that no state constitutional claim could be made other than for matters directly related to public school educational opportunities. **Public school students had no constitutional right to recover damages from an education board for injuries resulting from a negligent failure to supervise public school employees.** Similarly, the court held there was no right under the state constitution for a student to recover damages from a board of education for injuries resulting from a negligent failure to remain aware of and supervise the conduct of other public school students. While the court held the student was permitted to raise a constitutional claim, it held for the board, finding no actions by the board affecting the nature, extent and quality of the educational opportunities made available to public school students. *Mack v. Board of Educ. of Public Schools of Robeson County*, 748 S.E.2d 774 (N.C. Ct. App. 2013).

◆   An Oklahoma student who was often ill and absent from school said others ridiculed and threatened her. A psychotherapist diagnosed her with depression, and her mother homeschooled her for several weeks. When she returned to public school, her mother gave the school nurse ibuprofen and Aleve to administer for headaches. During the school year, the mother claimed that nurses denied her child medication or delayed giving it when it was needed. Incidents of bullying by peers increased, and the family's house was vandalized. Some Internet postings were claimed to be cyberbullying. The school issued detentions and counseled the students about some misconduct. But the mother felt they should have been suspended, and she eventually removed her child from school due to depression and a suicide attempt. The family moved so the student could attend a new school.

The parent sued the district and officials – including the superintendent and principal – in a federal court. In pretrial activity, the court dismissed the claims against the district and state tort claims against the school employees. According to the parent, school staff members had a constitutional duty to protect the student based on a "special relationship." She claimed the actions by school staff to deny or delay her access to medication prevented her from caring for herself, rendering her vulnerable. The court found no legal authority for a claim that public school students have a special relationship with their teachers or other school employees. Staff members did not create a danger or increase the student's vulnerability, so no constitutional claims could be made against them. **State actors are liable only for their own acts, not those of third parties.** In any event, qualified immunity protected the staff members. *Reyna v. Independent School Dist. No. 1, Oklahoma County, Oklahoma*, Nos. CIV–09–1223–D, CJ–2009–9583, 2012 WL 1023526 (W.D. Okla. 3/27/12).

◆   After a Texas middle school student committed suicide, his mother claimed he was the victim of constant bullying by other students at school. She sued the school district in a federal court, asserting that no one protected him from harm at his school. In pretrial activity, the court refused to dismiss claims filed under Title IX of the Education Amendments of 1972 and the Due Process Clause of the Fourteenth Amendment. A few weeks later, the U.S. Court of Appeals, Fifth Circuit, decided *Doe v. Covington County School Board*, 675 F.3d 849 (5th Cir. 2012). Upon reviewing *Doe*, the court agreed with the district that reconsideration of a judgment was appropriate.

    As a general matter, a state's failure to protect an individual against private violence does not constitute a due process violation. While the mother argued the failure to enforce anti-bullying policies violated her son's due process rights, the court held *Doe* barred such a ruling in the absence of a special relationship. An alternative argument, based on the school's "culture that condoned bullying," which increased the danger posed to the child during the school day, also failed. *Estate of Brown v. Cypress Fairbanks Independent School Dist.*, 863 F.Supp.2d 632 (S.D. Tex. 2012).

B. Threatening and Bullying Speech

    Students accused of bullying often assert that school discipline based on their speech and other conduct would violate a First Amendment right to free speech. In making this argument, they typically rely on *Tinker v. Des Moines Independent Community School Dist.*, 393 U.S. 503 (1969). Under *Tinker*, student speech may be regulated by school officials only if they could reasonably forecast substantial disruption or material interference with school activities, or if the speech would infringe upon the rights of others.

◆   While off campus and without using any school resources, a Mississippi student posted a recording containing profanity and threatening language regarding two teacher/coaches on his publicly accessible Facebook profile page. He later posted it on YouTube. When school officials were told of the posted recording, the student was removed from school pending a disciplinary committee hearing. At his hearing, the student said he did not report any conduct by the coaches because he felt any reports would have been ignored. He claimed the "students all have Facebook" and would hear his voice. Finding the recordings constituted harassment and intimidation of the teachers in violation of the school's policy and state law, the committee recommended a seven-day suspension from school and a six-week placement in the county's alternative school. By the time his case reached a federal court, the alternative placement had nearly ended and the request for an order was denied as moot. Three months later, the court granted the board's request for judgment. In 2014, a three-judge panel of the Fifth Circuit Court of Appeals held the board violated the student's rights.

A majority of the judges of the Fifth Circuit agreed to rehear the case and issued a new order for the board. This time, the court found "this incredibly profane and vulgar rap recording had at least four instances of threatening, harassing and intimidating language against the two coaches." While students do not forfeit their rights under *Tinker v. Des Moines Independent Community School Dist.*, this chapter, **the court held the First Amendment "does not provide students absolute rights to such freedoms."** After reviewing many post-*Tinker* cases, the court rejected the argument that *Tinker* is limited to speech within the confines of a school. The internet, cell phones, smartphones and social media did not exist when *Tinker* was decided. Off-campus communications might reference events at a school or involve members of the school community, yet can be accessed anywhere by anyone at any time. The court held school officials need to react quickly and efficiently when threats, intimidation and harassment are directed to the school community. In this case, the conduct could be forecast to cause a substantial disruption. Threats, harassment and intimidation of teachers disrupted the school's mission and could not be permitted. *Bell v. Itawamba County School Board*, 799 F.3d 379 (5th Cir. 2015).

◆ An Ohio student said peers at her schools harassed and bullied her throughout her middle and high school career. She reported routine abusive statements by peers who called her a "dirty Jew" and said she would "rot in Hell" because she did not believe in Christ. She was hit, tripped and shoved in school halls. On one occasion, the student was stabbed in the leg with a pencil. The family reported daily harassment on a school bus, but the bus driver never disciplined the harassers or filed a report. The student reported being assaulted in a school choir room. She was taken to a hospital and had to use crutches for several weeks. But verbal and online harassment continued. After four years of harassment, the student's mother removed her from her school and sued the district and school officials in a federal court.

Appeal reached the U.S. Court of Appeals, Sixth Circuit, which found the complaint adequately stated school officials had knowledge of the misconduct. **While the officials were entitled to immunity for a federal due process claim based on a state-created danger theory, the court held they did not have immunity regarding the equal protection and state law claims.** In the court's view, the conduct described by the family would have emboldened bullies by giving them "license to act with impunity." Officials could not be "shielded from liability where they took meager steps they knew to be ineffective to address severe and pervasive harassment that went on for years." As a result, the court held the equal protection and state law claims would go forward in further court proceedings. *Shively v. Green Local School Dist. Board of Educ.*, 579 Fed.Appx. 348 (6th Cir. 2014).

◆   An Oregon student was assigned a C grade, which prompted his mother to ground him for part of the upcoming summer break. The student made a series of Facebook comments about the teacher, saying she was "the worst teacher ever" and calling her names. In response to a friend's comment, the student wrote "Ya haha she needs to be shot." Within 24 hours, the student's mother instructed him to delete the entire post, which he did. The postings were made with a home computer on a day when school was not in session. Six weeks after the postings, the parent of another student placed a printout of the Facebook postings in the principal's mail. After the principal questioned the student, she suspended him in school for three and one-half days. The parent objected and sued the school district in a federal court for First Amendment and due process violations. The court referred the case to a federal magistrate judge, who recommended dismissing the due process claim but ruling for the student on the First Amendment claim. In considering the recommendation, the court found Ninth Circuit authority declaring that **schools may take disciplinary action in response to off-campus speech that presents "an identifiable threat of school violence."**

The court agreed with the magistrate judge that the student's postings did not meet the "material and substantial" impact rule from *Tinker v. Des Moines Community Unit School Dist.*, 393 U.S. 503 (1969). While the teacher reported feeling "scared, nervous and upset," the court found there was no threat to her safety in this case. In the court's view, there was no showing that the student's postings materially and substantially interfered with school discipline. In fact, the student did not intend the comments to reach school. No students missed school, and the teacher did not miss work. Significantly, the court found the school took no action indicating that it considered the postings to be a threat. The principal simply had the student sit in the office for over three school days. As a result, the court adopted the magistrate judge's report to find a speech rights violation. It agreed with the school district that there had been no due process violation. *Burge v. Colton School Dist. 53*, No. 3:14-00605-ST, 2015 WL 1757161 (D. Or. 4/17/15).

◆   From off-campus locations, a Nevada student sent friends a series of increasingly violent and threatening instant messages. He invoked the image of the Virginia Tech massacre, boasting he could "get 50+ people / and not one bullet would be wasted." Friends grew concerned when he sent messages about a school shooting to take place on April 20. This is Hitler's date of birth and the date of the Columbine shootings. Some of the student's friends told a coach about the threats, and the principal was notified. Police interviewed the friends and viewed the online messages. They questioned the student in the principal's office. After a hearing, the school board voted to expel the student for 90 days. He sued the board for constitutional rights violations. A federal court held for the board, and the student appealed.

The U.S. Court of Appeals, Ninth Circuit, held that courts had to balance the speech rights of students against the need to provide a safe school environment. In doing so, the courts were "not to react in favor of either." The idea was to strike an appropriate balance between safety and speech rights. In this case, the court held school officials did not violate the student's rights. The nature of the threats was "alarming and explosive." For this reason, the court held **officials did not have to wait for an actual disruption to materialize before acting**. As it was reasonable for the officials to interpret the student's messages as a safety risk and a substantial disruption, there was no speech rights violation. The court held the student had adequate warning from a student handbook that he faced discipline for making threatening statements. There was no due process violation, and the judgment for the school district was affirmed. *Wynar v. Jefferson County Board of School Commissioners*, 728 F.3d 1062 (9th Cir. 2013).

◆   A Nevada student-athlete made off-campus tweets about his coaches. According to the student, his Twitter account settings made his tweets private. School administrators gained access to the account from a third party and initiated discipline against him for cyberbullying. An appeal panel reassigned the student to another high school. In a federal court, the student and his father sought a preliminary order to return him to the school he had formerly attended. In assessing the speech rights claim, the court examined the tweets, which repeatedly referenced coaches and administrators in a disparaging and profane manner. One of the tweets stated that a coach should be repeatedly sodomized. Others implied similar conduct. According to the court, **only the tweet that explicitly referred to sodomy was considered obscene and unprotected**. It held other tweets reviling the coaching staff had stated a preliminary case for a speech rights violation, and it refused to dismiss this claim. Although the student contended he had a privacy interest in his tweets that was constitutionally protected, the court held he had no reasonable expectation of privacy in them.

The court dismissed his equal protection and due process claims as meritless. Finding no validity to a federal race discrimination claim and tort claims, the court dismissed them. But it refused to dismiss claims for defamation and conspiracy. These claims, as well as the First Amendment claim, would require further consideration. *Roasio v. Clark County School Dist.*, No. 2:13-CV-362 JCM (PAL), 2013 WL 3679375 (D. Nev. 7/3/13).

◆   Pennsylvania sisters claimed they were repeatedly threatened, assaulted and racially intimidated by another student and her friend at their high school, by phone and the Internet. Eventually, the other student was put on probation and ordered to have no contact with one sister. She was adjudicated delinquent, and no-contact orders from the juvenile court were provided to the school. Despite the court orders, the other student boarded the sisters' bus and threatened one sister. That evening, she elbowed the other sister in the throat at a school football game. After the incidents were reported, officials told the sisters they could not guarantee their safety. Officials asked the parents to consider moving the sisters to another school, and they soon did so. In a federal court, the sisters sued the school district and assistant principal, claiming due process violations. It dismissed the case, and the sisters appealed to the U.S. Court of Appeals, Third Circuit.

On appeal, the court held **the Due Process Clause did not create an affirmative duty by a state to protect a person from other persons**. A narrow exception applied if a "special relationship" existed between a state and a person who is taken into custody against his or her will. But this exception had only been applied to prisoners or involuntarily committed individuals. A school's authority over a child during the school day did not implicate the type of physical custody to create a "special relationship." Nor did knowledge of the risks created by the other student's presence create a duty. While the school's response might have been as "inadequate as it was unfair," the court held the school did not authorize the other student to bully the sisters. There was also no reason to apply the "state-created danger" theory of constitutional liability, as there was no affirmative act by the school district. Finding no constitutional duty to prevent the bullying, the court held for the district. *Morrow v. Balaski*, 719 F.3d 160 (3d Cir. 2013).

◆   A New York fifth-grader responded to a science assignment by writing "Blow up the school with the teachers in it" on his paper. He was suspended for one day in-school and for five days out-of-school, as the principal found the picture had frightened a girl in the class. Although the student claimed he was just kidding, the school board upheld the discipline. A federal court dismissed the family's First Amendment violations lawsuit, and his parents appealed to the U.S. Court of Appeals, First Circuit. It observed that the threat had been drawn in crayon and that no prior events indicated the student was a danger. More proceedings were needed to determine whether the student had caused a foreseeable risk of material and substantial disruption. When the case returned to the district court, evidence of prior incidents was introduced about the student. He had previously drawn a picture of a person firing a gun and wrote "one day I shot 4 people each of them got four blows + they were dead." And in fourth grade, the student wrote a story about "a big wind that destroyed every school in America."

Based on this evidence, the court held for the school district. When the case returned to the Second Circuit, it held student rights are not coextensive with the rights of adults in other settings. Student speech may be curtailed by administrators if "the speech will materially and substantially interfere with the requirements of appropriate discipline." Significantly, the court held "this test does not require school administrators to prove that actual disruption occurred or that substantial disruption was inevitable." In fact, an "actual disruption standard would be absurd." In this case, school officials could reasonably foresee that the drawing could create substantial school disruption. **Administrators needed to react quickly and decisively to address threats of violence in schools.** As for the parent' claim that the punishment was excessive, the court found that was for school officials to determine. *Cuff v. Valley Cent. School Dist.*, 677 F.3d 109 (2d Cir. 2012).

C. Hazing and Locker Room Incidents

Hazing was traditionally seen at higher education institutions, but some incidents have occurred in secondary schools. A plaintiff in a hazing case must show that the school was aware of the hazing before liability may be imposed on the school. Ordinary negligence principles may apply, but school liability may also depend on state law definitions.

Kathleen Conn, Ph.D., J.D., LL.M., Associate Professor for the Division of Education and Human Services at Neumann University says schools should take the following steps to address athletic team hazing:

* Increase bus and locker room supervision
* Have a district anti-hazing policy at the high school and middle school levels
* Recognize sexualized hazing as sexual violence and address it as such, and
* Ensure coaches do not approve, participate in or turn a blind eye to hazing.

◆ A high school senior who was disciplined for severely hazing and sexually harassing a teammate on an overnight wrestling trip had no viable due process claims against his school district, according to the U.S. Court of Appeals, Ninth Circuit. The student admitted hazing and degrading the teammate by taping him to a table, exposing his genitals, spanking him, placing him in a hotel hallway while still taped to the table, taking pictures of him and urinating on him. **A lower court had found the student received adequate notice and a hearing regarding his exclusion from school.** A semester suspension for this "vile" conduct was upheld. *Borovac v. Churchill County School Dist.*, 621 Fed.Appx. 479 (9th Cir. 2015).

◆ Texas parents said their 13-year-old son committed suicide after being repeatedly bullied at school. They said much of the misconduct took place in the school locker room. Among their claims was that members of the football team stripped the student, tied him up and put him in a trash can. Students called him "fag," "queer" and "homo," and one student videotaped the attack. The parents said the video was then put on YouTube. Shortly after this incident, the student committed suicide. According to the parents, school officials knew of the bullying but were deliberately indifferent to it.

In a federal court, the parents asserted the school had policies against bullying, but officials ignored them. The court dismissed the case. On appeal, the Fifth Circuit Court of Appeals held the complaint asserted widespread harassment by peers. In addition to the videotaped incident, it was alleged that football players accosted the student in the locker room many times. There were charges that boys took off his underwear while a teacher observed them. As a result, the court reversed the judgment on a Title IX claim and returned it to the district court. **The court held the removal of a person's underwear without consent on numerous**

occasions would constitute pervasive sexual harassment. But the parents could not pursue their equal protection claim, which had been properly dismissed. *Carmichael v. Galbraith*, 574 Fed.Appx. 286 (5th Cir. 2014).

◆   A Texas student complained that classmates pushed him down in his gym class and kicked him while he was on the floor. He claimed a coach told him he was not fit for athletics because he was fat. The student's mother sued the coach, school district and officials for negligence and violation of the student's constitutional rights. After a state court dismissed the case, the parent appealed to the Court of Appeals of Texas. She brought claims for failure to properly train employees and peer harassment, among others. The court held there is generally no constitutional duty of the state to protect people from the acts of others. Exceptions exist when there is a special relationship between a state agency and a citizen or where the state has increased the danger of harm. Where a "state-created danger" is alleged, there can be no liability unless it is shown that state actors used their authority to place a citizen in a dangerous place that did not otherwise exist.

The court held the claims in this case were not specific enough and did not allege personal involvement by school officials in creating a constitutional deprivation. Moreover, the parent did not show a causal link between official conduct and any constitutional violation. Since the federal claims were insufficient to assert any due process or equal protection violation, the court held they were properly dismissed. It further found the Texas Tort Claims Act immunizes professional school employees from personal liability unless there has been the use of excessive force resulting in bodily injury. Since the student was not injured by the coach, the state law claims failed. *Fike v. Miller*, 437 S.W.3d 640 (Tex. Ct. App. 2014).

◆   An Indiana high school basketball team manager said four senior team members harassed him constantly in the school locker room. He said the seniors taunted him with sexual comments, "flashed" him and grabbed his genitals. He said they "gooched him," a term used for anal penetration with fingers, either directly or through clothing. During a school bus trip, the student claimed some seniors called him to the back of the bus, held him down and anally penetrated him. A parent reported the incident a few weeks later, and some of the seniors were expelled. In a federal court, the student asserted Title IX violations and other claims. The court found a same-sex harassment claim may survive under Title IX based on gender stereotyping. Although the court held there had been severe and objectively offensive harassment that denied the student educational opportunities, it found the school acted almost immediately upon learning about the bus incident.

Actual notice of harassment is required for school liability to exist under Title IX. The student claimed that the coaches and school must have known about the sexual assaults because they had been occurring in the basketball program for years. But the court dismissed the Title IX claim as unsupported by admissible evidence. While the court found no merit to the student's constitutional claims, it agreed to consider his state tort law claims in further proceedings. When the student appealed the federal claims to the Seventh Circuit, it affirmed the judgment. In the court's view, **the school district could not have violated Title IX or other federal laws because there was no evidence it actually knew about the misconduct until it had ended**. This was just before the school began investigating the parent's report. As a result, the school district was entitled to judgment on the federal claims. *Davis v. Carmel Clay Schools*, 570 Fed.Appx. 602 (7th Cir. 2014).

◆ Members of a Michigan middle school basketball team engaged in locker room horseplay that escalated during the course of the season. Eighth-graders on the team victimized seventh-grade team members in "games" with sexually violent overtones. One involved "turning off all the lights in the locker room, then 'humping and gyrating on the seventh graders.'" Eventually, some eighth-graders grabbed a seventh-grader, forced him to the floor, "pulled his pants down and anally penetrated him with a marker." The incidents were not met with a speedy response by school administrators, and the seventh-graders soon stopped going to the school. In a federal court, the seventh-graders sued the board of education for sexual harassment and assault by the eighth-graders. A jury returned twin $100,000 verdicts for the seventh-graders on their Title IX claims. Appeal reached the U.S. Court of Appeals, Sixth Circuit. It held **a jury could have reasonably viewed the marker incident as "not just horseplay gone awry, but rather as a serious incident of sexual assault."** A jury could have reasonably expected the school would impose more punishment than 11-day school suspensions and a month of team suspension on the eighth-graders. *Mathis v. Wayne County Board of Educ.*, 496 Fed.Appx. 513 (6th Cir. 2012).

◆ According to an Ohio state court complaint filed by parents of a student with Down syndrome, their child was sexually assaulted due to "an extreme lack of teacher oversight" in her classroom. They claimed the school knew that one of her attackers had a history of psychological issues relating to abuse and assault. According to the complaint, teachers were reckless in placing students in the class and in monitoring class activities. It was alleged that staff did not even notice when students disappeared from class.

A state trial court held for the school district and employees. On appeal, the Court of Appeals of Ohio held the attackers' conduct was not "hazing" under state law. Although the parents claimed the trial court had improperly dismissed claims under a state anti-hazing statute, the court found no error. **"Hazing" applied to an initiation into a student organization.** A prior Ohio case restricted the term "student organization" to voluntary membership in a group and not an entire student body. The part of the lower court decision regarding the hazing statute was affirmed. School districts were protected by a general grant of immunity by state law, unless an exception applied. But a claim that the student was sexually assaulted under circumstances of recklessness and "an extreme lack of teacher oversight" was sufficient to establish potential liability by school employees, and the trial court should not have dismissed the claim. *E.F. v. Oberlin City School Dist.*, No. 09CA009640, 2010 WL 1227703 (Ohio Ct. App. 3/31/10).

◆   An Ohio student claimed two older students invited him to a "jazz band meeting" early in a school year. He followed them into a lavatory, where he was punched and kicked by a group of students. The student said he received numerous bruises and neck and back injuries, and was threatened with more beatings. He sued the board and school officials in a state court, asserting the school board and administration knew of and tolerated a "Freshman Beating Day." The court held for the board and administrators, and the student appealed. State law authorized civil actions against student organizations, schools and school employees, if the school knew or should have known of hazing and made no reasonable attempt to prevent it. The Court of Appeals of Ohio held "student organization" meant a specific organization, not an entire student body. The "jazz band meeting" reference did not make the beating an initiation into a student organization. "Initiation" implied voluntary membership and consent by the victim to be hazed. The student did not agree to be beaten and would probably not have entered the lavatory had he known it was planned. **The court held that even if the school officials were aware of and tolerated "Freshman Friday," the beating did not constitute "hazing" under state law.** *Duitch v. Canton City Schools*, 157 Ohio App.3d 80, 809 N.E.2d 62 (Ohio Ct. App. 2004).

D. Legislative Responses

California legislators amended a law to require the state education department to assess whether school districts have provided certificated employees information on existing school site and community resources related to the support of lesbian, gay, bisexual, transgender and questioning pupils. School site resources include peer support or affinity clubs and organizations, safe spaces for LGBTQ pupils, counseling services and training to support these pupils. The state's Safe Place to Learn Act requires the department to monitor and review local district policies to assess whether they comply with state requirements to prohibit discrimination, harassment and bullying. California 2015-16 Regular Session, Ch. 562, A.B. No. 827. Education Code Section 234.1.

A **Montana** law promotes safe schools by prohibiting bullying of students and clarifying means of redress for victims. "Bullying" means harassment, intimidation, hazing, or threatening, insulting, or demeaning gestures or physical contact, including any intentional written, verbal, or electronic communication or threat directed against a student that is persistent, severe, or repeated. To meet the statutory definition of bullying, conduct must cause a student physical harm, damage a student's property, or place a student in reasonable fear of harm. In addition, bullying is conduct that creates a hostile environment by interfering with or denying a student's access to an educational opportunity or benefit; or that substantially and materially disrupts the orderly operation of a school. "Bullying" includes retaliation against a victim or witness who reports information about an act of bullying and includes athletic hazing. Bullying of a public K–12 student by another student or an employee is prohibited, and a person alleging a violation of the law may seek redress under any available civil or criminal law. Montana 2015 Session Laws, Regular Session, Ch. 253 H.B. No. 284.

In 2015, **Montana** legislators enacted a Suicide Awareness and Prevention Training Act that requires the office of public instruction to provide guidance and assistance to schools on youth suicide awareness and training materials. Annual training on youth suicide awareness and prevention is recommended for each school district employee who works directly with students. At least two hours of awareness and prevention training for school employees is recommended every five years. Montana 2015 Session Laws, Regular Session, Ch. 351 H.B. No. 374.

Minnesota amended its laws in 2014 to make bullying or cyberbullying forms of "prohibited conduct." The law requires school districts to adopt written policies to prevent and prohibit student bullying. A district that does not adopt and implement a local policy will have to comply with a state model bullying policy. School district policies must establish research-based, developmentally appropriate best practices to address and deter bullying. Policies are to emphasize remedial responses to bullying reports and must be included in student handbooks with school policies.

Provisions of the law allow schools to address the skills and proficiencies of students with individualized education programs or Section 504 plans to address skills and proficiencies for avoiding prohibited conduct. The law specifies that it does not establish a private right of action or limit rights available under other civil or criminal laws, including the state Human Rights Act and speech provisions of the Constitution. Eighty-Eighth Minnesota Legislature, 2014 Regular Session, Ch. 160, H.F. No. 826. Minnesota Statutes Sections 121A.031, 121A.0311, 124D.10, 127A.052.

Michigan legislators enacted the Matt Epling Safe School Law, which added requirements for reporting school bullying and adds cyberbullying to existing provisions of state education law. The amended law requires the state education department to establish a form and procedure for school districts and public school academies to report bullying incidents on an annual basis and to make this data readily available to the public. Among the provisions of the amended law is a requirement that individuals who report acts of bullying are assured confidentiality in making such reports.

A provision of the law includes the term "cyberbullying" within the existing definition of the term "bullying." Cyberbullying means any electronic communication intended to harm one or more students by substantially interfering with educational benefits or opportunities by doing one of several listed acts. Acts that may constitute bullying include adversely affecting the ability of a student to participate in school programs or activities by placing the student in fear of harm or causing substantial emotional distress. Causing substantial disruption or substantial interference with the orderly operation of a school also meets this definition. Ninety-Seventh Michigan Legislature, Regular Session, Public Act No. 478 (S.B. 74). Michigan Compiled Laws, Section 380.131b.

A **Nevada** law provides for discipline against school employees who do not report bullying as required by law. The amended law declares that every area of a public school, its buses and grounds will be maintained as a safe and respectful learning environment. School administrators and personnel are authorized to take immediate action to protect a victim or target of bullying or cyber-bullying on the premises of a public school. Among the provisions of the law is the establishment of the Office for a Safe and Respectful Learning environment within the state Department of Education. Seventy-Eighth Nevada Legislature, 2015 Regular Session, Ch. 115, S.B. No. 504. Ch. 189, A.B. 112.

A 2014 **New Jersey** amendment requires school districts to incorporate instruction on the responsible use of social media into their technology education curriculums for students in grades 6-8. The requirement is a part of each school district's implementation of the state Core Curriculum Content Standards in Technology. Instruction shall provide students with information on: (1) the purpose and acceptable use of social media platforms; (2) social media behavior that ensures cyber safety, cyber security, and cyber ethics; and (3) potential negative consequences of failing to use various social media platforms responsibly, including cyberbullying. Two-Hundred Fifteenth New Jersey Legislature, 2d Annual Session, Ch. 257, Assembly No. 3292. Title 18a, New Jersey Statutes Section 35.4.27.

An **Oklahoma** law prohibiting students from assaulting education employees or attempting to harm them was amended in 2015 to declare that no education employee will be liable for the use of necessary and reasonable force to control and discipline a student. The amendment applies when a student is in school or in transit to or from school, or at a school-authorized function. Fifty-Fifth Oklahoma Legislature, 2015 First Regular Session, Ch. 15. S.B. 135, Oklahoma Statutes, Title 70, Section 6-149.7.

Oklahoma's School Protection Act imposes civil and criminal penalties on students who attempt to harm education employees or volunteers. Under a 2014 law, students in grades 6-12 who try to physically harm an education employee or volunteer at a school are subject to an out-of-school suspension. School employees who are injured due to an assault or battery in the performance of their duties are entitled to a leave of absence without loss of their leave benefits. Penalties under the act are in addition to and do not amend state Government Tort Claims Act remedies. Additional provisions of the School Protection Act prohibit people from making false accusations of criminal activity against education employees to law enforcement officers or school district officials. Adults who violate the false reporting provision are subject to misdemeanor convictions and fines, while those under 18 are subject to juvenile court proceedings. Fifty-Fourth Oklahoma Legislature, First Extraordinary Session 2013, Ch. 7 (H.B. 1009). Oklahoma Statutes Title 70, Sections 6-149.1, 6-149.2, 6-149.3, 6-149.4, 6-149.5, 6-149.6, 6-149.7, 6-149.8, 6-149.9.

A 2015 **Tennessee** amendment clarifies that a student may be suspended for off-campus criminal behavior that results in charges of an offense that would be a felony if a student was an adult. The student's presence in school must be found to pose a danger or threaten disruption. The amendment clarifies the power of school directors to expel a student when a criminal or juvenile complaint is issued for a violent felony. A school director may also send students to alternative schools. A student who is adjudicated delinquent or convicted of a violent felony may be expelled if it is found the student's continued presence would have a substantial detrimental effect on the school's general welfare. One-Hundred-Ninth Tennessee General Assembly, Ch. 501, H.B. 174. Tennessee Code Title 49, Ch. 6.

Connecticut legislators amended the state's school climate law in 2014 to provide for parental notification when a bullying incident is being investigated and to invite parents of students involved in bullying incidents to attend school meetings to prevent further bullying. Safe school climate plans must require each school's safe school climate specialist to promptly notify the parents of students involved in a bullying incident that an investigation has commenced. Safe school climate plans must further require that each school invite the parents or guardians of a student who commits any verified act of bullying to a meeting to discuss specific interventions by the school to prevent further acts of bullying. The law authorizes prevention and intervention strategies that may include culturally competent, school-based curriculums focusing on social-emotional learning, self-awareness and self-regulation. Interventions with a bullied child under the act may include referrals to a school counselor, psychologist or other appropriate social or mental health service, and periodic follow-up. Connecticut General Assembly, 2014 February Regular Session, P.A. No. 14-172, S.B. No. 106. Connecticut Statutes Section 10-222d.

An amended **Illinois** law requires each school board in the state to adopt a policy that declares teen dating violence unacceptable and prohibited. A district policy must state that each student has the right to a safe learning environment. Board policies must incorporate age-appropriate education about teen dating violence into training programs for students in grades 7-12 and school employees. District policies must establish procedures for employee responses to incidents of teen dating violence taking place at schools, on school grounds, at school-sponsored activities, or in school vehicles. Policies are to identify by job title the school officials who are responsible for receiving reports related to teen dating violence. Ninety-Eighth Illinois General Assembly, P.A. 98-190, H.B. 3379. Illinois Statutes Section 105-110/3.10.

New York's Dignity for All Students Act declares the state's policy to afford public school students an environment free of discrimination and harassment. Under the act, no student can be discriminated against on the basis of race, color, weight, national origin, ethnic group, religion, religious practice, disability, sexual orientation, gender or sex by school employees or students on school property or at school functions. The act defines "harassment" as "conduct, verbal threats, intimidation or abuse" based on one's "actual or perceived race, color, weight, national origin, ethnic group, religion, religious practice, disability, sexual orientation gender or sex."

"Harassment" includes the creation of a hostile environment by conduct or verbal threats, intimidation or abuse that unreasonably and substantially interferes with a student's educational performance, opportunities or benefits, or mental, emotional or physical well-being. Harassment may include conduct, threats, abuse or intimidation that reasonably causes students to fear for their own safety. School boards must create policies and guidelines to create a school environment free from bias and harassment. The amendment includes reporting requirements and guidelines for nondiscriminatory instructional and counseling methods, and it requires the state to provide model policies and other assistance to school districts.

II. THREATS AND VIOLENCE

In *Parmertor v. Chardon Local Schools*, this chapter, the court rejected claims that an Ohio school board's failure to implement added building security measures could be deemed a "physical defect" of a school for purposes of a claim to immunity. See Chapter Nine of this Volume Form III-9: School Violence Prevention and Intervention Checklist.

A. Students

◆ Families of the victims of a shooting rampage at a school in Chardon, Ohio, sued school officials in a state court, claiming there should be school liability. The families said the shooter attended an alternative school for at-risk students with serious academic or behavioral problems and was known to be mentally unstable and at high risk for committing more violent acts. In pretrial activity, the court granted state law immunity regarding negligence claims against the school district, board of education, members of the board, the alternative school where the shooter was a student, a county educational service center, and the school officials. But immunity was denied for claims asserting the officials acted recklessly and with conscious disregard for safety, and claims for malice and willful and wanton misconduct. When the case reached the state court of appeals, it explained that state law immunizes political subdivisions and their employees unless an exception applies.

According to the families, the board negligently failed to remedy a hazardous condition at the school and created a physical defect that at least in part caused the injuries. But the court instead found the injuries resulted from the deliberate actions of the shooter. It also rejected the families' argument that the individual board members acted with conscious disregard and malice in failing to properly warn victims and secure the grounds. On the other hand, the school officials were not entitled to immunity at this stage of the lawsuit regarding claims that they acted willfully, wantonly and with malice and conscious disregard for the victims. **These claims were based on a lack of adequate security despite warning of the need for additional measures.** The families said the shooter was "mentally unstable and at high risk for committing violent acts," making his attack foreseeable and preventable. Despite its very general allegations, the court found the complaint was sufficient to defeat the officials' claim to immunity. *Parmertor v. Chardon Local Schools*, 47 N.E.3d 942 (Ohio Ct. App. 2016).

◆ A Connecticut teacher claimed her elementary school administrators did not let teachers send disruptive students to the office and refused to discipline violent or disruptive students. She said the administrators refused to let teachers discipline students and did not protect those who were confronted with violent or disruptive students. After experiencing escalating violence at the school, the teacher said students assaulted her in a classroom and knocked her to the floor. She sued the school district in a state court, claiming school administrators acted willfully and maliciously. She said their conduct was extreme, outrageous and carried out with knowledge that it would cause her severe emotional distress. The court considered motions by the administrators to dismiss the case for failure to state viable claims.

The court explained that **employees who are injured during the course of their employment have a right to be compensated exclusively through workers' compensation and are generally barred from suing their employers for injuries**. To be exempt from workers' compensation coverage, the employee must either show the employer actually intended to injure the employee or that the employer intentionally created a dangerous condition that made the employee's injury substantially certain to occur. The court held the teacher failed to make either showing and did not assert facts supporting her claim that the administrators acted willfully or maliciously. A non-intervention policy in student discipline did not show willful, malicious, extreme or outrageous conduct. As the teacher did not show the administrators' conduct led to her injury, her claims were not exempt from the workers' compensation act. *Binkowski v. New Haven Board of Educ.*, No. NNH CV 1460500006S, 2015 WL 6405818 (Conn. Super. Ct. 9/30/15).

◆   A Michigan student tweeted threats to stab a classmate. The classmate reported this to a school counselor and assistant vice principal (AVP). The AVP then questioned the classmate and learned that the student had been bullying her. The AVP called the student's mother and asked to meet with her. Later, the mother claimed the AVP issued a suspension by phone. The next day, the AVP met with the student, her mother and brother. She told them some students had told her the student brought a knife to school, and she suspended the student. Family members met with the superintendent. He advised them of the evidence, then stated he would recommend expulsion. The board refused to allow the student's brother to attend the hearing, as she had asked for a closed meeting. After a hearing, the board voted to expel the student. She sued the school district, board members and administrators in a federal court. The court held for the district and officials.

On appeal, the U.S. Court of Appeals, Sixth Circuit, held there was no due process violation. **Students who are a continuing danger may be immediately removed from school.** The student received enough explanation of the charges to prepare her defense. As for the expulsion hearing, the court found she had another opportunity to hear the charges and present evidence. All told, she had three opportunities to tell her story. At the hearing, the student's father read the same prepared statement which the brother intended to read. There was no evidence that the brother had anything more to add. Rejecting all the student's arguments, the court held for the school district. *C.Y. v. Lakeview Public Schools*, 557 Fed.Appx. 426 (6th Cir. 2014).

◆   A Florida student reported being attacked by another student with a history of school discipline, bullying, fighting and class disruption. She said the attacker was in possession of a blade prior to the attack and should have been serving an in-school suspension (ISS) on the day of the attack. As a result of the incident, the student suffered a broken leg. In a state court action against the board, the family of the injured student submitted four theories of negligence. One was the theory that the board was negligent for not placing the attacking student in ISS on the scheduled day. A jury agreed with this theory and with the theory that the board negligently supervised the attacker just before the assault took place. On appeal, the board argued the trial court committed an error by excluding testimony by a third party that a racial slur may have prompted the incident. But the court noted no student, administrator, teacher or other student heard a slur. It found any such evidence "amounted to no more than improperly stacked inferences."

Next, the court held the board was foreclosed from arguing that the jury should not have been able to hold it liable for failing to place the attacker in ISS under sovereign immunity principles. The court held the board could not now challenge the jury's alternative basis for liability – that negligent supervision of the attacker resulted in harm to the student. The court found the board's current argument was different from its initial defenses that it had no duty to the student and enjoyed sovereign immunity. As **negligent**

supervision was an accepted basis for school liability, and the court found "plentiful evidence" to support the verdict, it held for the student. *Duval County School Board v. Buchanan*, 131 So.3d 821 (Fla. Dist. Ct. App. 2014).

◆   A Mississippi student with a mental disability was placed in a regular classroom for part of each school day. According to a classmate, the student had a "documented history of emotional outbursts and misbehavior." She said that on two occasions, the student threatened her. She said that on the second occasion, he grabbed her, held her head against a wall and rubbed a cleaning wipe into her eye. In a federal court, the classmate's mother said school officials violated her child's due process rights by failing to immediately remove the student from the classroom when they learned of his violent propensities. The court held for the school district, and appeal reached the Fifth Circuit. In *Doe v. Covington County School Dist.*, 675 F.3d 849 (5th Cir. 2012), this chapter, the Fifth Circuit refused to adopt the state-created danger theory in a case involving a school's failure to protect a child from being signed out from her school by an unauthorized adult. In affirming the judgment for the school district and officials, the court noted language from *Doe* declaring that **to create any opportunity for school liability, "the school must be aware of an immediate danger to a specific and identifiable student."** The court found the classmate was only one of many who "faced a generalized risk resulting from the school's attempt to integrate a mentally disabled child into a normal school environment." It affirmed the judgment for school officials. *Dixon v. Alcorn County School Dist.*, 499 Fed.Appx. 364 (5th Cir. 2012).

◆   While in his high school's student center, a New York student told some of his classmates and a teacher that he was "going to just blow this place up." After discussing the statements, school administrators were unsure about the seriousness of the risk, and they called the student's parents and the police. The student was suspended for five days and charged with insubordinate, disorderly, violent, disruptive conduct and violation of the school code. Following a manifestation determination at which no connection was found between the student's behavior and his disability, the school board held a hearing and recommended suspension for 25 more days.

After the district superintendent and board adopted the recommended discipline, the student appealed. The state commissioner of education approved the board's action, and appeal reached the New York Supreme Court, Appellate Division. The court explained that the relevant inquiry was whether his conduct might reasonably have led school authorities to forecast substantial disruption of or material interference with school activities. In this case, the student had declared to several others that he was going to blow up the school. In the court's opinion, these **statements on school property made it reasonably foreseeable that there would be a substantial disruption**. Although the administrators were not sure whether the threat was serious or not, the court found this irrelevant. The statement prompted a call to the police. In addition, the student had compounded the threat of substantial disruption by making his declaration to classmates who might try to copy or escalate the threat. Since school officials could reasonably conclude that the student's statements would substantially disrupt the school, their decision to suspend him did not violate his speech rights. The commissioner's decision upholding the suspension was affirmed. *Saad-El-Din v. Steiner*, 953 N.Y.S.2d 326 (N.Y. App. Div. 2012).

◆   A Michigan law specifies that if a student in grade six or above assaults another student, the school board "shall suspend or expel the pupil from the school district for up to 180 school days." A school board had a policy to enforce this provision. After a student assaulted a classmate, a school investigation determined his actions were intentional and not a manifestation of his disability. He was suspended for 180 days. After the school board upheld the discipline, the case reached the Court of Appeals of Michigan. **The court described the assault as an "extreme bullying incident."** It explained that school officials have wide discretion in creating rules to maintain order. Adequate notice of a 180-day suspension was provided based on the state law and school board policies. Moreover, the handbook allowed adjustment of the term of a suspension based on the circumstances. Since there was no arbitrary or capricious conduct by the board, the court affirmed the discipline. *Stansky v. Gwinn Area Community Schools*, No. 305287, 2012 WL 5290301 (Mich. Ct. App. 10/25/12).

◆   An Illinois student with autism kicked, punched and bit his teacher. He was suspended, but not expelled. When the student reached grade three, the teacher asked to be reassigned, but the principal declined her request. An IEP team recommended transferring him to a therapeutic day school. But the parents and their attorney resisted, and the student was again placed in a supported general education setting for grade four. He had a behavioral support plan and a solitary room or "office" where he could go when his behavior became a problem. Late in the school year, the teacher encountered him in an agitated state. She said he picked up a chair and swung it at her.

As a result, the teacher hit her head on a white board and her neck on a chalk ledge. She later filed a claim for workers' compensation benefits. The student was suspended and placed in an alternative school after the incident. The teacher then sued the school district and school administrators in a federal court. The case reached the U.S. Court of Appeals, Seventh Circuit, which held that only state action that "shocks the conscience" may give rise to a due process violation. No conduct that was shocking to the conscience was found in this case. In a 1986 case, the court held the **"due process clause does not assure safe working conditions for public employees."** While the administrators' actions "may well have been short-sighted, flawed, negligent, and tortious," there was no constitutional violation. *Jackson v. Indian Prairie School Dist. 204*, 653 F.3d 647 (7th Cir. 2011).

◆   After being expelled from their high school for fighting two other students, two South Carolina brothers appealed to the district superintendent and the school board. When the decisions were upheld, they did not appeal to a court. Nearly two years later, the family sued the school district in the state court system, claiming due process violations. The court held for the district, finding the students' decision not to appeal their expulsions to a court was a failure to exhaust administrative remedies. The state court of appeals reversed the decision. Appeal reached the Supreme Court of South Carolina, which found the students received all the process they were due.

Under *Goss v. Lopez*, 419 U.S. 565 (1975), **a public school student facing a short-term suspension only needs to receive notice of the charges being brought and an opportunity to explain his or her side of the story**. As expulsion is a more serious disciplinary action than a short-term suspension, the South Carolina court found an accused student deserves greater procedures and protections when facing expulsion. Section 59-63-240 of the state code specifies that parents must be notified in writing of the time and place for a hearing in expulsion cases. At a hearing, parents have statutory rights to have counsel present and to present evidence and question witnesses. In this case, the family chose not to have counsel at the initial hearing and did not exercise the right to present evidence or question witnesses. Finding the state law protections were constitutionally sufficient, the court reinstated the trial court's decision. *Stinney v. Sumter School Dist. 17*, 391 S.C. 547, 707 S.E.2d 397 (S.C. 2011).

◆   During a physical education class, an Ohio student was threatened by a girl and responded "I'm sick and tired of you threatening me. If you're going to beat me up, then just do it already." On this basis, the school suspended both girls for three days. An Ohio court modified the decision. It held the student's behavior did not amount to a threat of physical harm and was not an "assault" in violation of the relevant student handbook provision. As a result, the penalty was reduced to a Saturday detention. On appeal, the state court of appeals agreed with the lower court that the student did not commit an "assault." According to the court, the relevant handbook provision "first and foremost requires an unlawful threat to injure another person." But it held the student never made any threat. Despite a school associate principal's position that the student committed an assault by "offering to fight with somebody," the court found she had only told the other girl to stop threatening her. Since **none of the student's statements was an "assault,"** it was not error to modify her suspension. *Cisek v. Nordonia Hills Board of Educ.*, Case No. CV 2009 10 7363, 2011 WL 806518 (Ohio Ct. App. 3/9/11).

◆   North Carolina school staff members tried to break up a fight between two students in the cafeteria. One of the students admitted hitting a teacher about 20 seconds after being separated from the other student. An assistant principal interviewed the students, staff members and witnesses. Police also conducted an investigation. The student was charged as a juvenile with assault on a school employee and disorderly conduct, and the other student was charged as an adult with a misdemeanor. The school board suspended the student for 10 days for violating four school board policies, including one providing for a long-term suspension for assaulting a school employee.

After the suspension was imposed under North Carolina law, the student received a number of hearings where he was represented by an attorney, and the long-term suspension was upheld. Appeal reached the Court of Appeals of North Carolina. It appeared to the court that the student had an opportunity to learn the nature of his offense and respond to the charges. He received two hearings, which included an "exhaustive fact-finding inquiry" by the school board. While the student asserted self-defense, he had admitted a delay of 20 seconds from the end of the fight to the time he hit the teacher. No witnesses supported his claim of self-defense. State law required imposing a long-term suspension for violating the policy against assaulting school employees. **Protecting school employees is a goal of school discipline, so the court upheld the suspension.** *Watson-Green v. Wake County Board of Educ.*, 700 S.E.2d 249 (N.C. Ct. App. 2010).

◆ A North Carolina school decided a ninth-grader should attend an alternative school pending a risk assessment based on threats to harm himself and others. A school counselor recommended a psychological evaluation of the student, but the parents resisted. An in-school suspension (ISS) was imposed after classmates said the student tried to cut or stab himself and threatened violence. He remained in ISS for the rest of the school year and was assigned to an alternative learning center (ALC) pending completion of a risk assessment. A panel found the assignment to the ALC was not disciplinary in nature. It found a reasonable basis to believe the student was a danger to himself or others and upheld the decision to place him in the ALC until he underwent a risk assessment. He sued the board in a state court for constitutional violations, but the court affirmed the ALC assignment. On appeal, the state court of appeals held **students who were recommended for alternative or ALC placements as an alternative to suspension were entitled to a hearing before the district superintendent**. The student was suspended for refusal to submit to a risk assessment, and the court found the ALC assignment for the same behavior was an "alternative to suspension" as described in a district policy. Since an ALC assignment would be reflected in the student's cumulative record, the court held he was entitled to a hearing. *Rone v. Winston-Salem/Forsyth County Board of Educ.*, 701 S.E.2d 284 (N.C. Ct. App. 2010).

◆ Two female students in Idaho reported that two males were planning a Columbine-style attack at school. The principal confronted one of the male students, who said he was "going to have a school shooting" on a specified date. The two male students were warned about their threatening conduct, and they agreed not to make further statements. But one month later, the students were accused of threatening to shoot guns at a school dance. Two years after these incidents, one of the male students wrote threatening notes that were viewed by his locker partner. Although the threats were brought to the attention of the school resource officer and a vice principal, they were "dismissed." The same month as the notes were found, the student and a male accomplice murdered a female student at the house of her friend. When her parents sued the school district in a state trial court, it was found that the district owed no duty to protect the student off school grounds and after school hours. On appeal, the Supreme Court of Idaho affirmed the judgment. Nothing in the record convinced the court that the district knew that one of the male students would commit a murder based on information received about him some 30 months earlier. **As the murder was not foreseeable, the district had no duty to prevent it.** *Stoddart v. Pocatello School Dist. #25*, 239 P.3d 784 (Idaho 2010).

B. School Employees

◆   A 42-year-old Indiana teacher began exchanging personal emails with a 17-year-old student via his school email. Soon, he texted the student naked pictures of himself and began sending her graphic, sexual propositions. The two kissed in the teacher's classroom, but she declined his invitation to go to his house. When the school learned of the relationship, it reviewed the teacher's school emails. On the same day, he was pulled out of class and suspended. The school called the police and child protective services. The teacher was forced to resign. Due to gossiping by other students, the student finished the school year at an alternative school. She sued the school district and teacher in a federal court. In pretrial activity, the court found **the school responded promptly when it learned of the inappropriate relationship**.

The court found the student pointed to no authority that the school had a duty (or that it was even a best practice) to read every email going through its server. As a result, her claim under Title IX of the 1972 Education Amendments was dismissed. Next, the court held the student failed to describe any unconstitutional system-wide policy or practice. Her constitutional claims were subject to dismissal because the district lacked notice of the teacher's actions. There was no evidence that the school did not adequately train staff members. Due to the failure by the parties to present arguments on an equal protection claim against the teacher, the claim would be resolved at a trial. There was also insufficient information before the court to dismiss an invasion of privacy/illegal seizure claim at this stage of the case. As for the state law claims against the teacher, the court found a jury might find for the student. He had sent her nude pictures of himself, arranged private time during which she would be required to be with him, and knew of her vulnerability based on her emails and knowledge of her parents' divorce. While the school was no longer a party, the remaining claims against the teacher would go forward. *Doe v. Crown Point School Corp.*, No. 2:12-cv-00264-PPS, 2015 WL 5038093 (N.D. Ind. 8/26/15).

◆   An Alabama band teacher was fired for leaving a pistol in his locked office. He admitted it was his gun and said he had accidentally left it in the band room office while he accompanied the band to a competition in Georgia. At a board hearing, the teacher argued his excellent record justified a lesser penalty. But the board voted for termination based on violation of its weapons policy. A hearing officer later found the teacher violated the board's policy and that the board had authority to discharge him. While finding the teacher's exemplary service record justified a lesser penalty than termination, the hearing officer declined to reduce the sanction. He felt the Alabama Students First Act of 2011 did not authorize him to modify a school board's decision. After a state appeals court upheld the decision, the case reached the Supreme Court of Alabama. According to the court, the Students First Act removed fact-finding duties from hearing officers and vested education boards with this role. But the standard of review was the same as under prior laws governing teacher discipline and dismissal.

The court held a deferential arbitrary-and-capricious standard of review applied to teacher termination challenges under the Students First Act. This standard furthered the objective of eliminating costly, cumbersome and counterproductive legal challenges to routine personnel decisions. But unlike the appeals court, **the state supreme court held the arbitrary-and-capricious standard permitted a hearing officer to impose a lesser penalty than a board of education**, if the hearing officer found the sanction imposed by the board was arbitrary and capricious. As a result, the court held the case would be returned to the hearing officer with instructions to review the sanction that had been imposed by the board of education under the arbitrary-and-capricious standard of review. *Lambert v. Escambia County Board of Educ.*, No. 1130071, 2015 WL 5086453 (Ala. 8/28/15).

◆   A New Jersey teacher accused of touching two middle school students was unable to proceed with a federal malicious prosecution case after his criminal charges were dismissed. Following a student's report, the teacher was suspended, arrested and kept in police custody. After the charges were dismissed, he sued police and school officials. When the case reached the U.S. Court of Appeals, Third Circuit, it agreed with the trial court that **the officials took action based on probable cause of child endangerment by the teacher**. This was sufficient to dispose of his claims against the officials. *Schirmer v. Penkethman*, 553 Fed.Appx. 268 (3d Cir. 2014).

◆   Maryland's highest court agreed with criminal prosecutors that intimate (but not sexually explicit) letters from a paraeducator to an eight-year-old student supported the paraeducator's sexual abuse conviction. The Court of Appeals of Maryland held there was sexual abuse despite the lack of sexual contact. In a prior case, the court had held **child sexual abuse includes failure to act to prevent molestation or exploitation when it is reasonably possible to do so**. Based on the totality of the letters and evidence that the two had hugged and held hands, the court found the child was exploited under the Maryland Child Sexual Abuse Statute. In affirming a prison sentence of 13 years, the court found sufficient evidence to support the conviction. It held "sexual abuse" was not limited to specified acts of incest, rape, sexual offense, sodomy and other practices listed in the statute. The court found the statute was not impermissibly vague and held the broad statutory language struck a careful compromise between the need for specificity and the desire of legislators to craft a law to "target the ever-shifting manner in which some people will target and abuse children." *Walker v. State of Maryland*, 432 Md. 587, 69 A.3d 1066 (Md. 2013).

◆   Three Colorado students who were subjected to inappropriate conduct by a former teacher at their high school lost their appeal against their school district and administration. The students claimed the teacher sent them explicit texts, sought nude pictures and solicited sexual relations with them. While the court allowed claims against the teacher to proceed, it held the case could not proceed against the district or administrators who did not know of the teacher's conduct. **A single state law claim for failure to report child abuse was allowed to proceed against a school security guard and coach who knew of an incident of sexual conduct between the teacher and one student.** In a brief order, the U.S. Court of Appeals, Tenth Circuit, affirmed the judgment. *Doe v. Boulder Valley School Dist. No. RE-2*, 523 Fed.Appx. 514 (10th Cir. 2013).

◆   A California student claimed a school counselor engaged him in sexual conduct. He filed a state court negligence action against the school district, counselor and others that reached the state supreme court. It held that although districts and their employees are not "insurers of the physical safety of students, California law has long imposed on school authorities a duty to supervise at all times the conduct of the children on the school grounds and to enforce those rules and regulations necessary to their protection." Lack of supervision or ineffective supervision may constitute a "lack of ordinary care" in cases alleging lack of student supervision, and a district is liable for injuries caused by such negligence. **Previous California decisions had found that a school district and its employees have a "special relationship" with students.** In *Dailey v. Los Angeles Unified School Dist.*, 2 Cal.3d 741, 87 Cal.Rptr. 376 (1970), the court held school personnel may be individually held liable for the negligent failure to protect students. The court held administrators have the responsibility of taking reasonable measures to guard students against harassment or abuse from foreseeable sources, including teachers or counselors. Administrators could be held liable for employee misconduct based on a "special relationship" theory. But even if an administrator was liable, the court found the greater share of fault would likely lie with the counselor herself. The case was returned to the lower courts for further consideration. *C.A. v. William S. Hart Union High School Dist.*, 138 Cal.Rptr.3d 1, 270 P.3d 699 (Cal. 2012).

◆   A Kentucky teacher sent many inappropriate letters to a colleague, then threatened her with "increasing danger." After investigating, the school principal reprimanded the teacher and authorized his transfer to another school. The teacher signed a memorandum (MOU) requiring him to stop communicating with the colleague. Three years later, he emailed the colleague about a meeting of the Louisville Area Chemistry Alliance (LACA). The principal reprimanded him for violating the MOU. The reprimand instructed him to have no more communication with the colleague and permanently barred him from LACA meetings. In a federal court, the teacher sued the school board and officials for constitutional violations. The court held for the board and officials, but the U.S. Court of Appeals, Sixth Circuit, reversed the ban on attending LACA meetings. It affirmed the rest of the judgment for the board and officials.

In later proceedings, the lower court entered an order preventing the board from barring the teacher from LACA meetings. But it dismissed the claims against school officials. The teacher appealed to the Sixth Circuit, which held his association with the LACA was protected by the First Amendment, and that the district's ban was overly broad. As the board had "no tenable explanation for such a sweeping and everlasting prohibition," the board was properly denied judgment. In developing a reprimand, the principal and a district human resources director did not follow any simple procedure or standard policy. **Since they had used their discretion, the court held qualified immunity applied.** The principal and director were not final policymakers, and so could not create school board liability. *Baar v. Jefferson County Board of Educ.*, 476 Fed.Appx. 621 (6th Cir. 2012).

C. Parents

In *Doe v. Virginia Dep't of State Police*, below, the U.S. Court of Appeals, Sixth Circuit, rejected a parent's argument that a state law sex offender requirement violated her constitutional rights. In doing so, the court relied on *Connecticut Dep't of Public Safety v. Doe*, 538 U.S. 1 (2003). In that case, the U.S. Supreme Court held a state's decision to publish registry information on sex offenders was not a denial of due process, even if the offender could prove he was not currently dangerous.

◆   A Mississippi student had an ongoing conflict with another girl about a boy. At school, she received a threatening text message from the other girl's mother. Police were called, and both students were interviewed. Within a few weeks, the mother of the other girl drove in front of the student's car on a street near the high school. She and her daughter then attacked and injured the student. In a state court, the student's family asserted claims under the Mississippi Tort Claims Act. It was claimed that the district breached a duty of supervision to avoid assaults and to provide a safe school. The court denied the school board's request for immunity, and appeal went before the Supreme Court of Mississippi. It explained that to prevail in a negligence case, a party has to establish there was a duty owed by the defending party.

State law created a duty to use ordinary care to minimize foreseeable risks. The lower court had misplaced its reliance on this provision to deny immunity to the board. State law required school staff to maintain and control discipline over students while they were at school. But the incident occurred off school grounds and after the students had been dismissed.

The street in front of the school was not "school property" under state law, as the student urged. **State law did not impose a duty on schools to provide a safe environment to students who had been dismissed from school and were off school property.** This claim had been properly dismissed. The student argued that the school handbook created a duty to notify law enforcement of threats. But the court found the handbook was not in the record and had not been reviewed by the trial court. As a result, this claim was returned to the trial court for more consideration. *Moss Point School Dist. v. Stennis*, 132 So.3d 1047 (Miss. 2014).

◆ A Virginia parent was convicted of carnal knowledge of a minor in 1993. As required by law, she registered on the state Sex Offender and Crimes Against Minors Registry. A 2008 amendment to state law reclassified the parent's crime as a "sexually violent offense." As there was no procedure for sexually violent offenders to remove their names from the registry, she would "now remain on the registry for life." Sexually violent offenders could not go on school property or daycare centers, so she was barred from churches offering on-site daycare. The parent challenged the law in a federal court, which denied her petition.

Appeal reached the U.S. Court of Appeals, Fourth Circuit, which held that since the parent had not yet petitioned a state court or her school board for access, any injury was hypothetical. As for her constitutional claims, the court held failure to follow the law's procedures made the effect of the law unclear. Since the parent had been reclassified by the state police superintendent as a sexually violent offender and placed on the state registry, she had standing to pursue a claim against him. But this proved to be irrelevant, as the court found *Connecticut Dep't of Public Safety v. Doe*, 538 U.S. 1 (2003), foreclosed the claim. In that case, the U.S. Supreme Court held **a state's decision to publish registry information on sex offenders was not a denial of due process, even if the offender could prove he or she was not currently dangerous**. As a result, the court affirmed the judgment against the parent. *Doe v. Virginia Dep't of State Police*, 713 F.3d 745 (4th Cir. 2013).

◆ A Mississippi parent argued with a middle school principal about a student disciplinary matter. Tensions escalated, and when the principal told the parent to leave his office, he called him a "coward." The principal called the police, and the parent was charged with creating a public disturbance. Police escorted him to a court, and a judge barred him from appearing on county school property. Later, the charges were dropped. In a federal court action against the school district and principal, the parent asserted First

Amendment violations and unlawful seizure in violation of the Fourth Amendment. The court refused to dismiss many of the claims prior to a trial. In holding that the parent could pursue a speech claim against the principal, the court found that criticism of public officials "lies at the very core of that speech protected by the First Amendment." It found the parent had been "seized" within the meaning of the Fourth Amendment when the police told him of a warrant and requested that he come to the police station. Although the court found the principal would have to defend his actions in further proceedings, it held **a government entity may not be held liable for constitutional rights violations unless the violation was due to an official policy**. As a result, the court held the claims against the school district could not proceed. *Cash v. Lee County School Dist.*, No. 1:11-CV-00154-SA-DAS, 2012 WL 6737540 (N.D. Miss. 12/28/12).

◆ A Michigan teacher claimed a parent became upset during a disciplinary hearing and hit her in the stomach before leaving with his son. She was pregnant at the time, and a student witness heard her scream. The teacher reported the incident to police, and the parent was prosecuted on a charge of assault with intent to do great bodily harm. A jury found the parent not guilty of the criminal charge, and he sued the teacher and school district in a state court for malicious prosecution, infliction of emotional distress and defamation. After the court dismissed the action, the parent appealed. The Court of Appeals of Michigan noted that the parent had been criminally charged by the county prosecutor, not the teacher. **There is an important state policy of encouraging citizens to report possible crimes.**

According to the court, a person who has no active role in initiating a criminal prosecution cannot be held liable for malicious prosecution. The teacher was not accused of lying to authorities, and she did not institute the charges. As she made a full and fair disclosure of the incident and the prosecutor recommended the action, no malicious prosecution claim against her could succeed. **A person needs only reasonable grounds of suspicion of a person's guilt to file a report with authorities.** And the prosecutor had conducted an independent investigation of the incident based on the teacher's account, which was corroborated by a student witness. Governmental immunity protected the school district, the teacher and another staff member from liability in this case. Since information available to the prosecutor would cause a reasonable person to believe the parent was guilty and there was no evidence of false testimony by the teacher, the court affirmed the judgment. *Bradley v. Detroit Public Schools*, No. 292749, 2011 WL 255274 (Mich. Ct. App. 1/27/11).

◆ After a sex offender entered a Texas school and exposed himself to a child, the district implemented a regulation requiring every visitor to produce a state-issued photo identification as a condition of entering secure areas where students were present. Under the regulation, pictures were taken of visitor identification cards but no other information was taken. The system enabled schools to check visitor names and birth dates to determine if they were listed on national registered sex-offender databases. A parent refused to allow her child's school to either scan her driver's license or permit manual entry of her information. As a result, she was denied access to areas of the school. She and her husband sued, challenging the policy as a violation of their constitutional rights. A federal court held for the district, and the Fifth Circuit affirmed. **The regulation addressed a compelling state interest and was not overly intrusive.** The system took only the minimal information needed to determine sex offender status. *Meadows v. Lake Travis Independent School Dist.*, 397 Fed.Appx. 1 (5th Cir. 2010).

◆   A Louisiana father gave his children's middle school documentation that he had their sole "provisional custody." He claimed that they could only be released to him. School policy allowed only the persons listed on a check out form to sign a student out of school. When the children's mother appeared at their school prior to a holiday break, the principal telephoned the father. He stated that under no circumstances could they be released to her, and that he would come to the school. But when the father arrived at school 20 minutes later, the principal had already released the children to the mother. The father sued the school board, principal and insurer. After the case was dismissed, the state court of appeal held that the father's claims for out-of-pocket expenses could proceed if the school officials owed him a duty to refrain from allowing the mother to check the children out of school. **Schools have a "duty to make the appropriate supervisory decisions concerning a student's departure from campus during regular school hours."** As the father asserted violation of the policy on checking out students and claimed the sole authority to do so, the principal had violated the policy and her duty to the children and father. *Peters v. Allen Parish School Board*, 996 So.2d 1230 (La. Ct. App. 2008).

D. Others

◆   A federal court upheld significant parts of New York's SAFE Act, which was enacted in response to the 2012 Sandy Hook Elementary School mass shootings. It upheld the act's regulation of "assault weapons" and large-capacity gun magazines, finding it furthered the interest in public safety and did not violate the Second Amendment. The court upheld a requirement for ammunition sales to take place "face-to-face" to prevent Internet sales. It also upheld the act's ban on military-style gun features. But the state did not justify a prohibition on the possession of gun magazines with more than seven rounds of ammunition. Also struck down was the act's reference to muzzle "breaks" and the regulation of semiautomatic pistols that were a "version of an automatic rifle, shotgun or firearm."

On appeal, the U.S. Court of Appeals, Second Circuit, consolidated the case with a challenge to similar legislation enacted by the Connecticut legislature in response to the 2012 Sandy Hook Elementary School mass shootings. The court held core provisions of the laws prohibiting possession of semiautomatic assault weapons and large-capacity magazines did not violate the Second Amendment, and that the challenged provisions were not void for vagueness. But a New York provision regulating load limits and Connecticut's prohibition on one particular Remington non-semiautomatic weapon infringed upon Second Amendment rights. The court otherwise affirmed the judgments upholding the prohibition of semiautomatic assault weapons and large-capacity magazines and invalidating a New York provision limiting load capacity to seven rounds. *New York State Rifle and Pistol Ass'n, Inc. v. Cuomo*, 804 F.3d 242 (2d Cir. 2015).

◆ A 2007 legislative amendment placed private contractor employees under the scope of Florida Statutes Section 1012.467. This required criminal background screening for non-instructional contractors. Those who were found to have been convicted of child abuse and certain other charges were disqualified from access to public school grounds when students were present. The statute defined the term "convicted" to include a no contest plea. An employee of a private contractor underwent a level-two criminal background screen as required by the new law and was notified that he would no longer have access to school property due to a 1996 no contest plea to a child abuse charge. As he had to work on school property when students were present in order to perform his job duties, the contractor fired him. A state court enjoined the board from barring him from school property. The board appealed to a state district court of appeal.

On appeal, the court held the statute changed the nature of a no contest plea. It held a "substantive, vested right" is in turn an "immediate right of present enjoyment, or a fixed right of future enjoyment," and not a mere expectation. In this case, the trial court had improperly referred to the employee's loss of a job and his "right" to come on school property. **The school board never terminated the relationship or demanded that the contractor fire him, and he had no vested right to go on school grounds.** Since the employee failed to show the school board had divested him of any right of present enjoyment or a present fixed right of future enjoyment, the court reversed the judgment of the trial court. *School Board of Miami-Dade County, Florida v. Carralero*, 992 So.2d 353 (Fla. Dist. Ct. App. 2008).

◆ A Virginia court convicted a man of taking indecent liberties with a child in his custody. Upon his release from a brief period of imprisonment, he registered as a sex offender and completed his term of probation. After a hearing, a state court considered the man's application to go onto school property to observe his stepson's activities, and to pick him up, drop him off and go to school conferences. The court granted him conditional rights to be on school property and terminated his duty to re-register every 90 days as a sex offender. The Commonwealth of Virginia, city school board and its superintendent of schools appealed to the Supreme Court of Virginia.

According to the Commonwealth, Virginia Code Section 18.2-370(B) granted school boards authority to determine whether to allow a convicted sex offender to enter onto school property. After noting that Section 18.2-370.5 prohibited convicted violent sex offenders from entering public school grounds in most circumstances, the court held the law gave circuit, juvenile and domestic relations courts the authority to remove this statutory ban. It held "decisions regarding the safety and welfare of students are manifestly a part of the supervisory authority granted the school boards under Article VIII." Allowing the offender a right to enter school property related to the education of his stepson, and not the public safety. Instead, the Commonwealth correctly argued that a court had supervision over a violent sex offender on probation or a suspended sentence. **Once a court lifted the statutory ban on sex offenders from entering school property, the school board would be permitted to exercise its supervisory authority under the state constitution.** The court reversed the judgment and returned the case to the circuit court for it to decide whether and under what circumstances the statutory ban from school property on the offender might be lifted. *Comwlth. v. Doe*, 278 Va. 223, 682 S.E.2d 906 (Va. 2009).

III. STALKING AND HARASSMENT

A. Gender

1. Harassment

In the mid-1980s, courts began recognizing sexual harassment as a form of sex discrimination that violates federal law. Sexual harassment and assault may create school liability for failing to comply with Title IX of the Education Amendments of 1972, the Equal Protection Clause of the Fourteenth Amendment, and other federal laws. Failure to prevent sexual harassment and assault also gives rise to state law tort claims.

To avoid liability under Title IX, educators must comply with the basic regulatory requirements of federal law. Schools must publish a notice of non-discrimination and name the particular laws involved. They should explain what kind of conduct these laws prohibit, state that the school will enforce them and describe what the penalty will be. Legal commentators have observed that many victims of peer bullying and harassment do not know how or where to report such misconduct. Schools must appoint a Title IX coordinator and conspicuously post information on how and where to report misconduct. The nationally known law firm of Hogan Lovells has devised the following checklist to help prevent student harassment claims.

☑ **CHECKLIST –** *Harassment Prevention*

☐ Foster an atmosphere of mutual respect among faculty, staff and students.

☐ Have clear policies on prohibited conduct.

☐ Set clear boundaries of acceptable behavior for students and employees.

☐ Make sure teachers, staff, students and parents are aware of policies and expectations.

☐ Make clear who is available to **welcome** concerns and complaints about such issues.

☐ Encourage staff and students to speak up about inappropriate behavior whenever it occurs.

☐ Intervene early to monitor and correct potentially problematic behaviors: sexual or gender-based teasing; inappropriate jokes about sex; "casual" comments of a sexual nature; or any unwelcome touching.

Thorough investigation of harassment reports is another key to avoiding school liability in Title IX cases. Here are Hogan Lovells' suggestions:

☑ CHECKLIST – *Harassment Investigation*

☐ Develop a timeline for the investigation to ensure that it is completed properly.

☐ Develop a plan for the investigation.

☐ Determine the type of harassment that may be present.

☐ Determine what facts are necessary to show the type of harassment.

☐ Determine potential witnesses that need to be interviewed.

☐ Determine what, if any, documents need to be reviewed.

☐ Draft possible questions for each interview.

☐ Conduct interview of complainant and witnesses.

☐ Consider using a team approach.

☐ Use open-ended questions.

☐ Ask the complainant and/or parents what they would like done.

☐ Ask questions that establish a foundation for the incidents, such as who was there, where each incident took place and when each incident took place.

☐ Tell the witness that the investigation is ongoing and that no decision will be made until all witnesses and relevant information have been considered.

☐ Ask questions that elicit facts – not perceptions.

☐ Ask if there are any other witnesses.

☐ Take notes.

☐ Analyze all relevant information.

☐ Communicate the results, but be careful of privacy rights.

The checklist information above is copyrighted by Hogan Lovells (formerly Hogan & Hartson) and the National School Boards Association (NSBA). See *http://www.nsba.org/* and *http://www.hoganlovells.com/*.

2. Peer Harassment Case Law

In *Doe v. Board of Educ. of Prince George's County*, this chapter, the Fourth Circuit Court of Appeals relied on venerable federal guidance interpreting the "deliberate indifference" standard of liability applied by the courts in cases arising under Title IX of the Education Amendments of 1972. The guidance was cited in *Davis v. Monroe County Board of Educ.*, 526 U.S. 629 (1999), the leading school case on peer sexual harassment.

Title IX prohibits sex discrimination by recipients of federal funding. In *Davis*, the Supreme Court held schools could be liable under Title IX for student-on-student harassment. To prevail in a Title IX case, students must show (1) sexual harassment by peers; (2) deliberate indifference by school officials with "actual knowledge" of the harassment; and (3) harassment so severe, pervasive and objectively offensive it deprived the student of access to educational opportunities. **In order for school liability to exist, there must have been deliberate indifference by school officials to known acts of peer sexual harassment, where the school's response is clearly unreasonable under the circumstances.** A teacher's knowledge of peer harassment may create "actual knowledge" that may trigger school liability.

In *Fitzgerald v. Barnstable School Committee*, 555 U.S. 246, 129 S.Ct. 788, 172 L.Ed.2d 582 (2009), the Supreme Court held Title IX does not bar gender discrimination claims against schools under 42 U.S.C. § 1983. Section 1983 is a post-Civil War statute that creates no rights, but is a vehicle to enforce rights created by other federal laws and the Constitution. Because the *Fitzgerald* case has the potential to expand school liability in peer sexual harassment cases, educators must be willing to investigate all harassment claims and intervene promptly in a manner that is reasonably calculated to remedy misconduct.

◆ A Mississippi high school student was sexually assaulted by a male student who pushed her into a vacant school bus and forced her to perform oral sex. Later, her father sued the school district for negligence claims including inadequate school security and failure to warn his daughter of the male's history of sexual misconduct. The parties engaged in the pretrial information-gathering process known as "discovery" for a period of over a year and a half. During discovery, the male's history of criminal and delinquent misconduct was revealed. Prior to his transfer to the student's school, he had committed five instances of inappropriate touching of females and sexual battery against a 12-year-old girl. He had been arrested and placed under a no-contact order. Asserting discretionary-function immunity, the district moved for pretrial judgment. The court granted the district's motion, and the case reached the Supreme Court of Mississippi.

In *Brantley v. City of Horne Lake*, 152 So.3d 1106 (Miss. 2014), the court held state law immunity was no longer limited to decisions involving policy considerations. Under *Brantley*, courts were to first determine whether the governmental function at issue was considered "discretionary" or "ministerial." Next, a court was to examine any narrower duty associated with the activity at issue to determine whether a statute, regulation or binding directive rendered a duty "ministerial." To defeat discretionary-function immunity, the student would have to show an act done in furtherance of a broad discretionary function "also furthered a more narrow function or duty which is made ministerial by another specific statute, ordinance, or regulation promulgated pursuant to lawful authority." Since the court's rules for assessing discretionary-function immunity had changed greatly during the pretrial stages of this case, the court returned the case to the trial court for review under *Brantley*. **In returning the case to the lower court, the supreme court held the school district did not waive its immunity.** *Doe v. Rankin County School Dist.*, 189 So.3d 616 (Miss. 2015).

◆ Parents of a bilingual special education child who was sexually assaulted in a school lavatory could pursue negligence claims against Connecticut school officials for allowing students to go to the lavatory unsupervised. According to a state court complaint filed by the student's parents, a teacher repeatedly chose a certain classmate to accompany the student during non-lunchtime lavatory breaks. They claimed the classmate sexually assaulted their child on more than one occasion. Further, the parents claimed that allowing special education students to leave a classroom unattended was unsafe and that the teacher ignored their child's request that the classmate not be permitted to go with him. The school officials sought a judgment based on immunity for discretionary conduct.

The court explained that for a negligence action to survive pretrial dismissal, there must be evidence that a legal duty was breached. Next, the injured party must have suffered an injury that was caused by an allegedly negligent party. If a duty is found to exist, the injured party must show the defending party did not exercise reasonable care under the circumstances and caused the injury. It must be shown that without the defendant's negligence, the injury would not have occurred and that the negligence more likely than not caused the injury. Concluding that a fair and reasonable mind could find the sexual assaults would not have taken place if the teacher had refused to allow the classmate to accompany the student to the lavatory, the court refused to dismiss the case. Evidence was presented that the student did not want to go to the lavatory with the classmate. Although the teacher claimed state law immunity because her decisions involved discretion and judgment, the court found a factual issue existed regarding whether there was a school policy or directive in place creating a ministerial duty in this case. As a result, the court denied the officials' claim to immunity. *Doe v. New Haven Board of Educ.*, No. NNHCV105033148S, 2015 WL 6144099 (Conn. Super. Ct. 9/18/15).

◆ A Maryland student said he was bullied and teased by a classmate and other students. Despite several reported incidents, the two students were placed in the same classroom the next school year. The student continued to report harassment, including an incident in which the classmate tried to climb into his lavatory stall while his pants were down. In response, the student was offered a lavatory escort. During the school year, the classmate was told that further complaints would be grounds for a suspension. Meanwhile, the student's mother discovered text messages from her son to the classmate and found explicit photos sent by the classmate. She reported this to the police. When questioned by a detective, the student revealed that the classmate had forced him into sexual activity in the school library and a school lavatory. He had not previously told his parents of these incidents.

The classmate said the contact was consensual, and the student also told the detective he had consented to it. In a federal court, the student's family sued the board for violating Title IX. The court held for the board, and the family appealed to the U.S. Court of Appeals, Fourth Circuit. As the lower court had found, the school responded to all of the incidents once they were reported. **The students were separated to the extent possible in class, and procedures to protect the student were implemented for lavatory use.** These measures were held sufficient. As the Fourth Circuit found the school's response to the reports was not clearly unreasonable, the board prevailed on the Title IX claim. Liability for negligence and gross negligence could not be based on a theory that the classmate's behavior should have been seen as an escalating pattern. As a result, the board of education prevailed on all the student's claims. *Doe v. Board of Educ. of Prince George's County*, 605 Fed.Appx. 159 (4th Cir. 2015).

◆ A Louisiana student's classmates reported her for engaging in sexual conduct on a school bus while en route to a class field trip. A disciplinary administrator held a hearing at which he informed those present of the charges and evidence. At the end of the hearing, he transferred the student to another school for three months. Although the parent sought review by the school board, the board failed to set up a hearing. In a federal court, the parent charged the board with violating her constitutional rights, as well as those of her daughter. The court held for the board and administrator, and the parent appealed to the U.S. Court of Appeals, Fifth Circuit. It rejected a claim that the administrator had formulated his decision prior to the hearing. **State law did not require the board to review the administrator's decision because the student was not expelled.** As the lower court found, the administrator could not be liable for defamation. A negligent supervision claim against the board was properly dismissed as untimely, and the court held for the board and administrator. *Robinson v. St. Tammany Parish Public School System*, 569 Fed.Appx. 303 (5th Cir. 2014).

◆ A Connecticut student reported frequent bullying and harassment by a classmate. During the student's sophomore year, he said there were times when the bullying and harassment would stop when a male vice principal "clamped down on them." But the student claimed that the classmate continued saying anti-gay epithets. When the student complained to the male vice principal, he was told that the school resource officer would be "on alert" for trouble. The classmate was then suspended for two days.

After the classmate returned to school, he followed the student out of the cafeteria and assaulted him in a school hallway. In a state court negligence action against the classmate, vice principals, board of education and others, the student asserted there was a duty by the officials and government entities to protect him from known bullying. The court rejected a claim by the school's female vice principal that she had no duty to protect the student. It found both vice principals were responsible for monitoring the student body. A school policy required staff to "be particularly alert to possible situations, circumstances or events which might include bullying." **The ultimate test for the existence of a duty to use care was found in the foreseeability that harm might result if reasonable care was not exercised.** Although the court agreed with the board that the acts involved in this case were discretionary, it denied their claim to immunity. It found there were genuine issues of fact involving the question of whether the student was an "identifiable victim" and whether he faced imminent harm. As a result, the court denied the school board's motion for pretrial judgment. *Straiton v. New Milford Board of Educ.*, No. DBD CV 10 6003255S, 2012 WL 1218160 (Conn. Super. Ct. 3/13/12).

◆ A California shop teacher lent a metal shop key to a student. According to the student's former girlfriend, the student sexually assaulted her at knifepoint in the shop. She sued the student, his parents, the school district and the shop teacher in a state court. Among the claims was negligent supervision. A state superior court held for the district and shop teacher, and the former girlfriend appealed. She claimed the teacher knew the student sometimes brought a Swiss Army Knife with screwdrivers, pliers and a knife to school. The court found the student used the tool for farm chores and did not use it during the assault. According to the former girlfriend, he had been caught with a knife on campus before but had not been disciplined. The district noted there had not been a sexual assault on the campus for over 25 years. The teacher had known the student since infancy and had a relationship of trust with him. There was also evidence that it was common for teachers at the school to give students keys. School records indicated no prior assaults by the student, and he had no history of behavior issues or mental disability. The tool played no part in the incident, and the student had concealed it at school. **As nothing indicated to the school district or the teacher that the student would sexually assault anyone at school, the court upheld findings by the lower court that the assault was unforeseeable.** It held for the district. *Sheaffer v. Scott Valley Union School Dist.*, No. C069156, 2012 WL 6059248 (Cal. Ct. App. 12/6/12).

◆ A California school district operated a free after-school program on a school playground. Between 200 and 300 children participated, with two adults typically present to supervise them. One day, only one supervisor was present to watch over 113 participants. A second-grade girl was led by an older girl to an unlocked shed on campus that was off-limits to program participants. The older girl forced a boy to have sexual contact with the second-grader. Both the boy and the second-grader later said the girl held them against their wills and threatened to hit them. The second-grader's mother sued the school district for negligent supervision, claiming the district and employees knew for some time that some of the children had been kissing and engaging in other inappropriate activity. The case reached the state court of appeal, which noted that the after-school program was voluntary. A question remained regarding whether the absence of a supervisor from her post contributed to the injury. As a result, the case required more fact-finding. **If the supervisor allowed dangerous conduct to go on, liability could be imposed.** *J.H. v. Los Angeles Unified School Dist.*, 183 Cal.App.4th 123, 107 Cal.Rptr.3d 182 (Cal. Ct. App. 2010).

3. Harassment by School Employees

◆ A Minnesota middle school coach lent his cell phone to a 14-year-old girl to call her parents for a ride home. She later retrieved his number from her home phone caller ID and began texting him explicit messages on her cell phone. Eventually, they had sexual contact in the school weight room. Another student's parent learned of the explicit text messages and called the student's mother. The day the school learned of the relationship, the police were called and the coach was arrested. The district fired him, and he pled guilty to criminal charges. The parents sued the coach and school district in a state court for vicarious liability, negligence, negligent supervision and other claims. The court held for the school district, and the student appealed.

On appeal, the state court of appeals held the school district was entitled to immunity. There was no dispute that the coach did not act on behalf of the district in the performance of duties lawfully assigned by a competent authority. The court agreed with the school district that state law creates a general rule of immunity from vicarious liability for torts committed by state employees, unless committed within the scope of office or employment. Next, the court rejected the student's claim that the district should be held liable because "red flags" made sexual abuse by the coach foreseeable. To succeed on a negligence or negligent supervision claim, the student had to show there was some risk of foreseeable harm. The incidents cited by the student did not include any sexual conduct. She said she yelled at the coach during a football practice and shouted "Chris, I love you" at another. Like the lower court, the court of appeals found none of the incidents similar to (or indicative of) sexual abuse in a manner that put the district on notice of any inappropriate relationship. **Finding the red flags gave no objectively reasonable indication of a specific danger of sexual abuse, the court held the abuse was not foreseeable** and ruled for the district. *Doe 175 v. Columbia Heights School Dist., ISD No. 13*, 873 N.W.2d 352 (Minn. Ct. App. 2016).

◆   A 14-year-old California student gained a second chance to hold the Los Angeles Unified School District (LAUSD) liable for negligence based on sexual abuse by a former teacher who invited her to be friends on a social networking site. After she turned 14, the two had sex many times. A friend of the student reported the relationship to another employee at the school, who made a report. As a result, the teacher was arrested. He pled no contest to one of the charges and served prison time. In a state court, the student sued LAUSD for several negligence-based claims. After a two-week trial, a jury returned a verdict for LAUSD. The student then appealed to the state court of appeal, which held the trial court's instructions had improperly required the student to show the teacher had a "dangerous propensity to sexually abuse minors." California Civil Jury Instructions only required the student to prove the teacher had the potential to sexually abuse minors in order to establish a claim for negligent hiring, supervision or retention.

Next, the court held the student was not required to show the teacher was unfit because he had committed prior acts of misconduct. It found several facts indicated he had the potential to sexually abuse minors. He hugged female students, talked to them about his personal life, rearranged his classroom and laid on a table near two female students. Next, the court agreed with the student that the lower court had erroneously allowed LAUSD to admit evidence of her prior sexual history in order to measure the damages she was claiming for emotional distress. While this evidence was only supposed to shed light on her damages, the court found it had been discussed throughout the trial. It had also been improper for the lower court to instruct the jury to apply comparative fault principles. Since the teacher had acted in a criminal manner, the student could not have consented to sexual misconduct and could not be apportioned any part of the damages. The court explained that **"the law puts the burden on the adult to avoid the sexual relationship."** Since the jury instructions harmed the student, the court returned the case to the trial court for a new trial. *S.M. v. Los Angeles Unified School Dist.*, 250 Cal.App.4th 543 (Cal. Ct. App. 2015).

◆   Washington's highest court refused to review a lower court decision that upheld a $1.425 million jury verdict based on the sexual assault of a child by a driver on her school bus. The court held there were sufficient facts that the driver had previously abused other kindergarten girls on district buses and had child pornography. Moreover, **expert trial testimony had established the district could have taken certain measures that would have prevented the abuse**. *Gutierrez v. Olympia School Dist.*, No. 91306-4, 183 Wash.2d 1004 (Wash. review denied, 6/3/15).

◆   A wheelchair-bound student was denied U.S. Supreme Court review of lower court decisions denying him relief under the Rehabilitation Act for claims based on a sexual assault committed by a school employee. According to the student, an aide who was assigned to help him molested him in a school lavatory. In pretrial activity before a federal court, the family settled its claims against the aide. After the court held for the school district on the remaining claims, the family appealed to the U.S. Court of Appeals, Fifth Circuit. In the court's view, the facts did not support any of the claims. Two employees accompanied the student to the vast majority of his lavatory visits, and there was no showing of intentional discrimination. In addition, he did not show the denial of a free appropriate public education under federal special education law. Any flaws in his IEPs did not result in the loss of an educational opportunity. As a result, the court held for the school district. *Estrada v. San Antonio Independent School Dist.*, No. 14-648, 135 S.Ct. 1408 (cert. denied 2/23/15).

◆ Three high school soccer players from two Florida families said male junior varsity coaches created a hostile environment through misconduct and sexual comments. Their parents complained to the school board and a federal agency, and the girls then sued the board for violating Title IX. They said they were dismissed from the school soccer team and threatened with a transfer to another high school. The girls also claimed the soccer coaches threatened to sue their parents for defamation. The girls' case was settled.

In a separate federal case, the parents sued the board, asserting a pattern of retaliation against them and their children. A female teacher whose daughter participated in the school soccer program joined the case. She asserted the board retaliated against her by delaying her tenure for a year and not hiring her for a position she sought. **Since Title IX covers only federal funding recipients and does not allow for individual liability, the coaches were not named in the action.** Only one of the coaches was let go – the others remained in the school district. The court held the parents did not present enough evidence to show retaliation by the school board. It rejected the parents' theory that the board sought to transfer their children as a form of retaliation. No transfer was ever made and the issue only arose based on a report that one of the families was living outside the school's attendance boundaries. Finally, the court found the teacher did not show any retaliation in the delay of tenure or denial of the job she sought. Since the evidence strongly supported the school board's position, the court held in its favor. *Bigge v. Dist. School Board of Citrus County, Florida*, No. 5:13-cv-49-Oc-10PRL, 2015 WL 641657 (M.D. Fla. 3/13/15).

◆ A Texas high school counselor's daughter attended an after-school mariachi program instructed by a paraprofessional. The counselor saw text messages on her daughter's phone from the paraprofessional. In one text, the daughter asked the paraprofessional a sexually explicit question. He did not respond to it but disclosed personal information to her and sent her a picture of himself without a shirt. The counselor and her husband met with the paraprofessional and his wife. They agreed that except for music, all communications between the paraprofessional and the daughter would end.

Neither the counselor nor a colleague who also saw the texts reported them to law enforcement, child protective services or school administrators.

Later, a school employee reported the incident to school administrators and then to child protective services. Both the counselor and the colleague were placed on leave for failing to report the text messages. The counselor was allowed to resign, but her colleague was only given a written reprimand. The board found good cause existed for terminating the counselor's contract. After the state commissioner of education affirmed the decision, appeal reached the Court of Appeals of Texas. The court found a school district policy subjected employees to discipline for the failure to make a required report. The court disagreed with the hearing officer's finding that the counselor did not have to make a report due to her uncertainty. Neither district policy nor state law limited the reporting requirement to situations where a teacher had an actual, subjective belief that abuse or neglect had occurred. **As the board and commissioner later found, a report must be made if there is sufficient reason to believe abuse may occur in the future.** As the evidence supported the conclusion that the counselor's inaction placed students at risk and there was good cause for contract termination, the court held for the district. *Judson Independent School Dist. v. Ruiz*, No. 04-13-00706-CV, 2015 WL 1501758 (Tex. Ct. App. 3/31/15).

◆   A Georgia teacher called, emailed and wrote to an eighth-grade student. His parents met with the school principal at least twice and reported the continuing communications. But they told the principal they "did not think anything was going on" between the two. It was later learned that the teacher had performed oral sex on the student at least five times during the summer before his eighth-grade year. She pled guilty to criminal child molestation charges and was sentenced to prison. The parents sued the school district in a federal court for violating Title IX. The court found no evidence that the principal knew of sexual harassment by the teacher and held for the district. On appeal, the U.S. Court of Appeals, Eleventh Circuit, stated that the principal was a person with authority to take corrective measure in response to actual notice of sexual harassment under Title IX.

In a previous case, the court had found that lesser forms of harassment may provide actual notice of sexually violent conduct. But in this case, the court found it clear that **the principal was never put on notice of a single act of sexual harassment by the teacher**. The court rejected the parents' claim that reports of repeated texting and other contacts put school officials on notice of harassment. It appeared to the court that the principal knew the teacher's conduct was "inappropriate, devoid of professionalism, and reeked of immaturity." But in the court's estimation, her known conduct was not of a sexual nature and could not have put the principal on notice of sexual harassment, defeating the Title IX claim. *J.F.K. v. Troup County School Dist.*, 678 F.3d 1254 (11th Cir. 2012).

◆   A 26-year-old Wisconsin teacher brought a 14-year-old student to her apartment. She later admitted kissing him for 15 to 20 minutes, while he asserted there was also some additional touching. When the student's mother discovered some text messages they had sent, she transferred him to a private school. The teacher was fired and pleaded guilty to fourth-degree sexual assault charges. The mother then sued the school district in a federal district court under Title IX. The court held for the district, and the family appealed to the U.S. Court of Appeals, Seventh Circuit. It explained the liability standard for sexual harassment by school staff members was announced in *Gebser v. Lago Vista Independent School Dist.*, this chapter. **Seventh Circuit case law required proof of "actual knowledge of misconduct, not just actual knowledge of the risk of misconduct"** in order to impose Title IX liability. In this case, the teacher had denied the encounter with the student when the principal questioned her. Later, the district superintendent continued investigating. As soon as the mother made a report, the school took prompt action. Suspicions of an improper relationship between the student and teacher did not make the true nature of the relationship "obvious" or a "known risk." In holding for the board, the court noted "judges must be sensitive to the effect on education of heavy-handed judicial intrusion into school disciplinary issues." It dismissed the federal claims and a state court claim as well. *Doe v. St. Francis School Dist.*, 694 F.3d 869 (7th Cir. 2012).

◆ A North Dakota high school student claimed a custodial supervisor sexually harassed and touched her while she worked for a school district, and twice put her in a "chokehold." However, she did not inform any school official about either incident. Some time later, the student claimed the supervisor told her to "bend over," while he was behind her, then pushed her by the neck. The student told her mother about the third incident, and the mother reported it to the building principal. According to the mother, the principal only responded "well, that's just how Gary is, rough." Although a district policy designated the building principal as the person to receive sexual harassment reports, the principal instructed the mother to report to the district superintendent. She did not make a report. Later, the student said the supervisor put his hands in her pants and pulled her toward him. This time, the mother made a report to the district superintendent. In response, the superintendent ordered the supervisor to have no contact with the student and to participate in an improvement plan.

Two years later, the student sued the district in a state court for negligence, assault and battery. A two-year state statute of limitations barred the assault and battery claims, and the court dismissed them. It found the supervisor's conduct was not foreseeable and held the negligent supervision and retention claims were barred by the state Workforce Safety and Insurance Act. On appeal, the Supreme Court of North Dakota held that while employee actions against employers are typically barred by the exclusive remedy provisions of the act, certain exceptions are included in the law. In this case, the student did not seek workers' compensation benefits for her injuries. According to the court, the essence of her action was not to recover for her physical injuries, but for non-physical injuries. It held the district did not show the student suffered any injury that was compensable under the workers' compensation act, so the act did not bar recovery in this case. **The court found sufficient evidence of negligent supervision for the student to proceed with that claim, as the district had failed to address the supervisor's misconduct after it was reported.** *Richard v. Washburn Public Schools*, 809 N.W.2d 288 (N.D. 2011).

◆ In 1998, the U.S. Supreme Court examined the liability of school districts for sexual harassment of students by teachers and other staff under Title IX. The case has become one of the most important legal precedents for courts attempting to analyze school liability based on harassment of students by staff members. The case involved a Texas student who had a sexual relationship with a teacher. The Court rejected the liability standard advocated by the student and by the U.S. government, which resembled *respondeat superior* liability under Title VII. Title IX contains an administrative enforcement mechanism that assumes actual notice has been provided to officials prior to the imposition of enforcement remedies. **An award of damages would be inappropriate in a Title IX case unless an official with the authority to address the discrimination failed to act despite actual knowledge of it, in a manner amounting to deliberate indifference to discrimination.** Here, there was insufficient evidence that a school official should have known about the relationship to impose Title IX liability. Accordingly, the school district could not be held liable for the teacher's misconduct. *Gebser v. Lago Vista Independent School Dist.*, 524 U.S. 274, 118 S.Ct. 1989, 141 L.Ed.2d 277 (1998).

4. Non-Student Harassment and Assault Cases

◆ A Mississippi adult was able to sign a young child out of school by falsely indicating he was her parent six different times. He then sexually molested her and returned her to school. After the child's parents learned of this, they sued the school district in a federal court. Among their claims was that the school's check-out policy violated the Constitution by allowing employees to release a child without first verifying the signer's identity or authority to sign out the child. A federal court held constitutional liability was foreclosed under the U.S. Supreme Court's decision in *DeShaney v. Winnebago County Dep't of Social Services*, 489 U.S. 189 (1989).

Appeal reached the Fifth Circuit, where a three-judge panel held for the family. But a majority of judges of the Fifth Circuit voted to rehear the case and found a constitutional claim could proceed only if the district had a duty to protect the student from a private party. This required a special relationship between the student and district. But state compulsory attendance laws did not create a special relationship between schools and their students. The court held **public schools have no special relationship with students that would require protection from harm by private actors such as the adult in this case**. The parents raised other arguments, but the court rejected them. It held the student's young age was not a relevant factor under the special relationship analysis. Carelessness by school employees did not mean they knew that the adult was unauthorized to sign out the child. And the parents did not claim the district was deliberately indifferent to a known danger. The court held for the district. *Doe v. Covington County School Dist.*, 675 F.3d 849 (5th Cir. 2012).

◆ A Nebraska elementary school policy required visitors to check in at the main office. An intruder entered and was confronted by a teacher. She asked him if she could help him, but he ignored her. Two other teachers also noticed him, and one directed him to a restroom. Although she told him to report to the office after he was finished, he instead went to another restroom where he sexually assaulted a five-year-old student. The student's mother sued the school district in a state court for negligence. After finding the district's security plan was adequate, the court held for the district. Appeal reached the Supreme Court of Nebraska, which stated that under prior law, the foreseeability of a particular injury was part of the inquiry into whether an entity had a legal duty to the injured party. But the court found that approach required a court to decide legal questions "uniquely rooted in the facts and circumstances of a particular case." In any negligence case, the legal duty of a party was to conform to the standard of conduct. By contrast, foreseeability questions depended upon the unique facts of each case.

The court held foreseeability is not part of the analysis of duty, as this transforms a factual inquiry into a legal issue. It also expands the authority of judges at the expense of juries. The court found this improper, as **foreseeability questions involve common sense, common experience, and the application of community standards and behavioral norms**. These areas have long been understood to be within the province of a jury, and not a judge. Under the court's decision, a jury would have to determine, based on the facts of each case, whether or not the evidence established a breach of duty. **School districts owe their students a duty of reasonable care, as the duty of teachers to supervise and protect their students is well-established.** But the question of whether the assault in this case was reasonably foreseeable involved a fact-specific inquiry for a jury to determine. As the teachers had permitted the intruder to evade them, reasonable minds could differ as to whether the assault was foreseeable. It had thus been improper for the lower court to award pretrial judgment to the district. The case was returned to the lower court for further proceedings. *A.W. v. Lancaster County School Dist. 0001*, 784 N.W.2d 907 (Neb. 2010).

◆ A Texas State University student was leaving a campus library one night at around 11:00 p.m. when an unknown person sexually assaulted her at knifepoint. She said the attacker dragged her under a dark stairwell of a campus building. The student sued Texas State and others, in a state district court, alleging it was negligent. She asserted the security on campus was inadequate because Texas State employees had "negligently implemented the campus safety policies." Texas State also was negligent, the student said, in its use or misuse of the lighting in the area where she was attacked and its use of security boxes on campus. The student contended she got hurt because Texas State did not use ordinary care to keep the campus safe, properly lit, and free from criminal trespassers. Furthermore, she said, the university failed to inspect the property for dangerous conditions or to warn the student of any such defect. The district court granted a motion to dismiss, and the student appealed to the Court of Appeals of Texas.

The court explained that under the Texas Tort Claims Act, state entities can waive governmental immunity only under limited circumstances. Section 101.021(2) of the act provides a state governmental unit is liable for personal injury if, as a private person, it would be liable according to Texas law. **The student failed to establish immunity was waived because she did not show a connection between the alleged defect and her injuries. The court found the actions of the student's attacker, not the allegedly defective lights, were what caused her to be harmed.** It rejected the student's argument that governmental immunity was waived. As the negligent implementation of a security policy does not waive governmental immunity, the judgment was affirmed. *Dimas v. Texas State Univ. System*, 201 S.W.3d 260 (Tex. Ct. App. 2006).

5. Stalking

◆ A Western Kentucky University student died three days after she was assaulted, raped and set on fire in her dormitory room. Two men who were not residents of the dorm were later charged in the case. The student's estate filed negligence claims in a state court against the university, a foundation that operated the dormitory, and university officials. The court dismissed the case, and the state court of appeals affirmed the decision to dismiss the claims against the university and the officials. But it reversed the decision to dismiss the claims filed against the foundation. On appeal, the Supreme Court of Kentucky explained that governmental immunity extends to state agencies that perform governmental functions, but does not extend to agencies which are not created to perform a governmental function.

Officials of state agencies can also be entitled to immunity if the agency itself is immune to suit. Applying these principles, the court held the university had immunity. It rejected the argument that the operation of the dorm was a proprietary rather than a discretionary function. **The university operated the dorm as part of its statutory duty to provide college instruction. As such, its operation of the dorm was not proprietary, and it was entitled to immunity.** Because the claims against the university were barred by immunity, the court held the claims against the officials in their official capacities were barred. The foundation was entitled to immunity because it acted as an alter ego of the university and derived immunity status through it. The decision to grant immunity to the university and officials was affirmed, and the decision to deny immunity to the foundation was reversed. *Autry v. Western Kentucky Univ.*, 219 S.W.3d 713 (Ky. 2007).

◆ A Connecticut university student contacted a female student in a chat room. He made several attempts to date her, but she rejected his advances. Despite the rejections, the student continued to pursue her, appearing uninvited at her dormitory room and presenting her with gifts. The student then sent an email to a professor expressing an "excessive interest" in the female classmate. The professor was disturbed by the email and reported the student to a community standards specialist at the university. After interviewing the student, the classmate and the professor, the specialist instructed the student he was to have no further contact with the classmate.

About a month later, the student offered to pay the classmate's friend to spy on her. A disciplinary hearing was held by the university, after which an administrative hearing officer concluded the student had stalked the classmate. The officer suspended the student from the university for a period of 15 months. The student filed an unsuccessful internal appeal, then sued the university in state court requesting reinstatement as a full-time student. The court denied the student's request. He would be entitled to the requested injunction only if he could show the suspension proceeding failed to meet due process requirements. The student failed to make this showing. **He could not prove a violation of any substantive due process right, because there is no fundamental right to attend college.** Nor was there any violation of the student's procedural due process rights. He received notice of the charges against him, and neither the form nor content of the notice prejudiced his ability to defend the charges. Because the student failed to show he was denied due process with respect to the university's procedures, the court denied his request for preliminary relief. *Danso v. Univ. of Connecticut*, 919 A.2d 1100 (Conn. Super. Ct. 2007).

◆ A New York college student was assaulted at knifepoint in her dorm room. At the time of the attack, the college had a security policy that required all outer doors to its residential halls be locked 24 hours a day. An exception was that during office hours, a "breezeway" entrance remained open to allow students to enter from the open quadrangle created by the four other student dorms. The policy also required those visiting a dorm to register with personnel stationed at resident hall lobby desks. Despite the policies, students held and even propped open doors to the resident halls so people could enter without registering. The student sued the college in a federal district court, alleging it was negligent. The court dismissed the complaint, and the student appealed. The U.S. Court of Appeals, Second Circuit, disagreed with the district court's conclusion that the attack was unforeseeable because of the low history of on-campus crime. In each of the previous five years, there had been significant events and a security reporting firm reported there were other undocumented assaults on campus. **A jury could readily have found the college administration had been alerted to the presence of more crime than it publicly reported.** The district court's analysis of foreseeability was flawed, because it assumed that only actual prior crimes could put the college on notice of the risk of future crimes. The security firm had repeatedly raised security concerns with the college. **While the attack was foreseeable, the district court reasonably found that the student did not establish a causal connection between negligence by the college and the attack.** Because the attacker was never caught or identified, she did not prove he was a resident of the dorm. While New York law did not require the student to identify her assailant, she had to provide some evidence that he was an intruder. As she failed to do so, the judgment for the college was affirmed. *Williams v. Utica College of Syracuse Univ.*, 453 F.3d 112 (2d Cir. 2006).

◆   A Massachusetts high school student sodomized a six-year-old and was charged with various felonies. His school principal obtained a police report describing the student's description of the incident as "a joke." The principal suspended the student, finding he posed a threat to the safety, security and welfare of students at the high school. School officials notified the student's parents by letter of the disciplinary action, and they appealed to the superintendent of schools. After a hearing, the superintendent upheld the suspension, and the parents sought a preliminary order from a state superior court. The court denied the request for preliminary relief but later reversed the suspension, finding the superintendent's action was an abuse of discretion.

According to the court, Massachusetts General Laws Chapter 71, § 37H 1/2 requires more than criminal charges alone to justify a student suspension. On appeal, the Massachusetts Supreme Judicial Court observed that Section 37H 1/2 authorizes the suspension of students who have been charged with felonies. School administrators must provide students written notice and a hearing before any suspension takes effect. As the trial court had found, a felony charge against a student is an insufficient basis for suspension. **There must be a finding that the student's continued presence in school would have a substantial detrimental effect** on the general welfare of the school. **The superintendent's decision was within his discretion because it was fully supported by the evidence.** The principal was permitted to draw inferences from the nature of the crime and the student's lack of remorse. Given the seriousness of the charges, the principal reasonably found a danger that the student would attempt similar behavior at school. As the superintendent acted within his discretion by suspending the student, the court reversed the decision. *Doe v. Superintendent of Schools of Stoughton*, 437 Mass. 1, 767 N.E.2d 1054 (Mass. 2002).

B. Sexual Orientation and Gender Identity

Transgender student rights moved to the forefront of K-12 education law during 2016. A case involving a Virginia student with gender dysphoria was appealed to the U.S. Supreme Court, which denied his request to use school lavatories according to his gender preference, pending further court review. *Gloucester County School Board v. G.G.*, No. 16A52, 2016 WL 4131636 (U.S. 8/3/16). See Chapter Nine of this Volume for Form III-7: Gender Support Plan and Form III-8: Gender Transition Plan.

In *L.W. v. Toms River Regional Schools Board of Educ.*, 189 N.J. 381, 915 A.2d 535 (N.J. 2007), **the Supreme Court of New Jersey recognized a cause of action against school districts for student-on-student harassment based on perceived sexual orientation**. Liability would be imposed for peer harassment only if a district failed to reasonably address harassment and the district knew or should have known about it.

In *Romer v. Evans*, 517 U.S. 620 (1996), the U.S. Supreme Court held that sexual orientation discrimination violates the Establishment Clause. In *Oncale v. Sundowner Offshore Services, Inc.*, 523 U.S. 75 (1998), the Court held same-sex harassment may violate Title VII of the Civil Rights Act of 1964. In addition, many state human rights acts establish sexual orientation as a protected class of persons. But the U.S. Court of Appeals, Eighth Circuit, has held that bullying or harassment that is not based on a student's gender does not create liability under Title IX. Instead, it held that under Title IX, the "acts of discrimination" must be "on the basis of sex."

In *Donovan v. Poway Unified School Dist.*, 167 Cal.App.4th 567, 84 Cal.Rptr.3d 285 (Cal. Ct. App. 2008), a California court observed that school administrators are better situated than courts to address peer sexual harassment. Administrators can take affirmative steps to combat racism, sexism and other forms of bias which courts cannot. And administrative actions are typically resolved more quickly than lawsuits.

◆ A Maine child who was born male was later diagnosed with gender dysphoria. An educational plan, modeled after a Section 504 plan, was devised to address the student's gender identity. The team agreed the student would be called "Susan." A counselor emphasized the need for Susan to use the girls' lavatory starting in grade five, and the team agreed. A male student followed Susan into the girls' lavatory to show he also had this right. After a controversy and media coverage, the school discontinued Susan's use of the girls' lavatory. For the rest of grade five, Susan used a unisex faculty lavatory. The family filed a complaint with the state human rights commission. The commission found there had been discrimination and joined the family in a suit against the school district. The case reached the Supreme Judicial Court of Maine. It noted the state Human Rights Act made it unlawful to discriminate against individuals, or to withhold or deny equal enjoyment of public accommodations based on sexual orientation.

While the state Sanitary Facilities Law required schools to offer clean toilets that were separated by sex, the court found the law did not offer any guidance about gender identity. By contrast, the Human Rights Act had the intent of ensuring access to opportunities and public accommodation. Schools had to maintain separate lavatories for each sex, but the court found the Sanitary Facilities Law did not dictate a discriminatory result. Since the Sanitary Facilities Law did not mandate the way transgender students should use sex-separated facilities, the court held each school was left with the responsibility of creating its own policies concerning the use of public accommodations. School policies had to comply with the human rights act. **The court held treating the student differently from others based on transgender status was discrimination forbidden by the Human Rights Act.** *Doe v. Regional School Unit 26*, 86 A.3d 600 (Me. 2014).

◆   A California student threatened to commit suicide in grade six. But when he met with a school counselor he said things were better. School employees heard no more reports of suicidal thoughts about the student. After the student's seventh-grade school year, his mother observed him to be "generally happy and positive." But he became upset about being bullied at school. The student told a friend about committing suicide, but she did not feel he was going to do it. While the student appeared to be generally happy in grade eight, his mother took him out of school due to bullying.

After the student committed suicide at home on a weekend, the mother sued the school district. In pretrial activity, a federal court looked for a connection between the school district's conduct and the suicide. Suicide was historically viewed as an intervening event that broke the chain of causation and precluded tort liability. But the court found expert testimony required it to examine whether the school district's conduct was the legal cause of an "uncontrollable impulse" to commit suicide. In allowing the uncontrollable impulse claim to proceed, the court noted medical literature discussing a connection between bullying based on sexual orientation and suicidal ideation. But the court dismissed the remaining claims. **No case law imposed a duty on a school district to prevent suicide.** Even the parent conceded that she never thought her son was suicidal. *Walsh v. Tehachapi Unified School Dist.*, 997 F.Supp.2d 1071 (E.D. Cal. 2014).

◆   Two Illinois students wore shirts to school saying "My Day of Silence, Straight Alliance" on the front, and "Be Happy, Not Gay" on the back. A school official crossed out "Not Gay" based on a school rule forbidding derogatory comments referring to race, ethnicity, religion, gender, sexual orientation or disability. The students sued school officials in a federal district court, asserting First Amendment violations. The court denied their request for a preliminary order allowing them to wear the T-shirts, and they appealed. The U.S. Court of Appeals, Seventh Circuit, found the school was not trying to ban student discussion of public issues. It only sought to prohibit derogatory comments about sensitive personal characteristics. **The court found it foreseeable that the high school environment would deteriorate if negative comments were made by students on either side of the debate.** It held the students were not entitled to a preliminary order suspending the school rule. However, the slogan was only a play on words that was not derogatory or demeaning. Since the message was not targeted toward anyone and was "only tepidly negative," the students could wear the shirts on a preliminary basis.

After the case returned to the district court, a preliminary order was issued permitting the students to wear the shirts. A permanent order was entered, and they were awarded $25 each for infringement of their rights. The case returned to the Seventh Circuit, which agreed with the students that any evidence of harassment of homosexual students at the school was negligible. **Federal court precedents make it clear that speech cannot be stifled just because it offends others.** So the fact that homosexual students and their sympathizers harassed one of the shirt-wearing students was not a permissible ground for banning the shirts. The court found the damages awarded were justified and did not "exaggerate the harm" to either student. *Zamecnik v. Indian Prairie School Dist. # 204*, 636 F.3d 874 (7th Cir. 2011).

◆   An Arkansas student was widely ridiculed by classmates. He reported pushing, shoving, name-calling, and being falsely called a homosexual. He withdrew from school in tenth grade and sued the school district in a federal court for sexual harassment in violation of Title IX. At trial, school officials and classmates claimed the misconduct did not violate Title IX because it was not gender-based. A jury was told that to win, the student had to show he was harassed "on the basis of sex" in a manner so severe, pervasive, and objectively offensive that it deprived him of access to educational benefits or opportunities. He further had to show that the district knew of the harassment but was deliberately indifferent to it. The jury held for the officials, and the student appealed. On appeal, the Eighth Circuit Court of Appeals held the jury instructions reflected Title IX's "on the basis of sex" requirement and correctly summarized Supreme Court precedents.

The court rejected the student's argument that it would be enough under Title IX that peers called him names and spread rumors to "debase his masculinity." In *Davis v. Monroe County Board of Educ.*, this chapter, the Supreme Court held that **to be actionable, harassment must be gender-oriented conduct amounting to more than "simple acts of teasing and name-calling."** There was no authority supporting the student's claim that the use of sex-based language in rumors or name-calling proved sex-based discrimination. As a result, the court held for the school officials. *Wolfe v. Fayetteville, Arkansas School Dist.*, 648 F.3d 860 (8th Cir. 2011).

C. Race and National Origin

Title VI of the Civil Rights Act of 1964 prohibits race discrimination in any program that receives federal funds. Many discrimination complaints allege violations of Title VI, the Equal Protection Clause, and analogous state law provisions. Courts require proof of intentional discrimination in Title VI cases. School officials may be held liable for violating Title VI if they are deliberately indifferent to clearly established student rights. Courts frequently analyze race-based peer harassment cases under the liability standard described in *Davis v. Monroe County Board of Educ.*, this chapter.

◆   Three African-American sisters reported repeated racial harassment by classmates at their Texas schools, including frequent use of the "N-word." One of the sisters found a noose near her car in a school parking lot with a note disparaging African-Americans. When she reported this to the school, police were called and an investigation was begun. All three sisters reported being targeted for racial slurs and epithets. They were sometimes drawn into fights with white students, which resulted in discipline for students of both races. One sister reported that the school athletic director admonished her for violating a school rule by wearing streaks of burgundy in her hair.

One of the sisters became involved in a bullying incident with white students. Based on these and other incidents, the family filed a grievance with the district's board of trustees. School employees were then required to attend trainings on discrimination, harassment and bullying, and students had to attend a special school assembly. Ultimately, two sisters withdrew from the school district. The family sued the district, softball coach and athletic director in a federal court for civil rights violations. The court held for the district and officials, and the family appealed to the Fifth Circuit. In the court's view, the repeated use of the N-word and the noose incident demonstrated severe, pervasive and objectively offensive peer harassment. Moreover, the harassment deprived the sisters of access to educational opportunities or benefits. But the court held the family did not show the school was deliberately indifferent to the harassment. **Some action was taken in response to almost all the reported incidents.** Training was provided, and the sisters were allowed various safety accommodations. School officials cooperated with police and FBI investigations, and students who called the sisters names were suspended for misconduct. The court held the school district did not commit an equal protection violation. School officials did not violate the sisters' rights by enforcing district hair color and school team rules. As a result, the court held for the district and officials. *Fennell v. Marion Independent School Dist.*, 804 F.3d 398 (5th Cir. 2015).

◆ Washington parents withdrew their consent to their child's special education program shortly after moving into a new school district. During his first two months in the new district, the parents said his teacher and a co-principal blamed him for classroom incidents in which a classmate made cruel and racial remarks. The parents said the school blamed their child for other incidents and improperly decided not to question important student witnesses. When the child wrote two "disturbing essays" describing incidents in which the classmate was violently harmed, nobody told the parents. After the district investigated, information about one of the essays appeared in the report. As soon as the parents saw it, they asked for an immediate transfer of their son. They filed a complaint against the school district, and their case reached the state court of appeals. It held the district did not follow proper investigation procedures by neglecting to interview all the students in the work group. The co-principal could not explain her feeling that the child's disability would affect his ability to hear a racial epithet. The essays were not shared with the parents, and the school did not take into account the discrepancy between his grades in social studies class and his other classes. In fact, the court found the school refused to consider any scenario in which the child was not to blame for conflicts with the classmate. The court found the school district did not appropriately discipline the classmate, despite his history of serious behavior problems.

The court found the parents showed the harassment was severe, pervasive and objectively offensive and deprived their child of access to educational opportunities or benefits. He was repeatedly humiliated and reduced to tears in front of his peers. In ruling for the student, **the court held school districts have a duty to promptly investigate harassment and take prompt and effective steps calculated to end it**. Finding the district acted with deliberate indifference to the reports of harassment, the court held there was a violation of state law. *Mercer Island School Dist. v. Office of Superintendent of Public Instruction*, 186 Wash.App. 939, 347 P.3d 924 (Wash. Ct. App. 2015). Washington review denied 12/2/15.

◆ According to the parent of a six-year-old Virginia student, peers targeted him for threats and theft. She said he was mocked for not fighting back and repeatedly called "gay" "nigger," "bitch" and "motherfucker." She reported this to the vice principal, who spoke with one offending student. The mother said that a few weeks later, the same student again called her son names in front of other classmates. She said the school administration then failed to act. Within a week, the parent withdrew her son from the school. Only then did a school bullying specialist call her. She filed a federal lawsuit, but the court dismissed it. On appeal, the Fourth Circuit held a claim filed under Title IX required additional consideration. But the Title VI claim failed. In a 1992 case, the U.S. Supreme Court held no private action for damages is authorized by Title VI unless intentional discrimination is alleged. **The parent's failure to allege intentional conduct by the school was fatal to the Title VI claim.** She only sought to hold the school board liable for the response of administrators to peer harassment based on race. Although the parent claimed the school's response was dilatory and inadequate, the court found the school had only days to respond to her complaint just before a spring break. Since the Title VI claim failed, that part of the judgment was affirmed. *M.D. v. School Board of City of Richmond*, 560 Fed.Appx. 199 (4th Cir. 2014).

◆ A high school in northern California had a history of gang and race-related violence. In 2009, the school recognized Cinco de Mayo in a "spirit of cultural appreciation." But the event prompted threats among students of different ethnic backgrounds. Some students hung a makeshift U.S. flag and chanted "USA." During the 2009 incident, a school assistant principal (AP) had to intervene when a student threatened others who had raised the U.S. flag. A student who had worn U.S. flag clothing to school on Cinco de Mayo in 2009 was among several students who again sought to display the flag on Cinco de Mayo 2010. In response to rumors of a confrontation between students of different ethnic backgrounds, the AP told the student he should turn the shirt inside out or risk his own safety. The student and another student who went home with an excused absence joined their parents in a federal court action against the school district, principal and AP.

The case reached the Ninth Circuit Court of Appeals, which found other recent federal appeals court cases have held that schools may prohibit speech that might reasonably lead school officials to forecast substantial disruption of (or material interference with) school activities. **Many federal cases have held school officials need not wait for actual disruption before acting. "In fact, they have a duty to prevent the occurrence of disturbances."** The administrators in this case were faced with a threat of school disruption and impending violence, and the court found the AP was entitled to judgment on the speech rights claim. Since the lower court had correctly held for the AP, the court affirmed the judgment. *Dariano v. Morgan Hill Unified School Dist.*, 745 F.3d 354 (9th Cir. 2014).

◆   Missouri twin high school students created a website with racist, bullying speech. School administrators linked the twins to the site and suspended them for 10 days. After two hearings, the district suspended the twins for 180 days, allowing them to enroll in a public academy. The twins sued the school district in a federal court and sought a preliminary order to lift the suspensions. At a hearing, they said the postings were satirical, not serious, and they denied being racists. School witnesses claimed the website caused substantial disruption at the school. Numerous attempts were made at school to access the site, and teachers said that their students were distracted or upset. Media representatives had come to the school, and two teachers stated that the incident ranked among the most disruptive events of their careers. Although the court issued the order sought by the twins, it found the website had caused considerable disturbance and disruption. In addition, the court found the site was "targeted at" the school. Appeal went before the U.S. Court of Appeals, Eighth Circuit. It held that in prior federal court decisions, *Tinker v. Des Moines Independent Community School Dist.*, **this chapter, had been applied to off-campus student speech** when it was reasonably foreseeable that the speech would reach the school community and cause a substantial disruption. As the postings had caused substantial school disruption, the court reversed the lower court's contrary order for the students. *S.J.W. v. Lee's Summit R-7 School Dist.*, 696 F.3d 771 (8th Cir. 2012).

◆   A part-white, part-Latino student moved to an overwhelmingly white New York school district. Students began threatening him and repeatedly calling him "nigger." During the rest of the student's high school career, he continued to report incidents of racial harassment and taunting, some of which involved physical contact, death threats and a reference to lynching. The family attorney, and later the local human rights commission and the local NAACP affiliate, suggested a "shadow" to accompany the student while he was at school. These entities also sought to implement racial sensitivity programs in the district. Although these services were offered for free, the district declined them. A district compliance officer, who was supposed to investigate Title IX violations, did not respond to complaints. The student's mother made the choice to allow him to accept a special education diploma rather than to attend school further.

The student sued the school district in a federal court for race discrimination. A jury found the district violated Title VI and awarded the student $1.25 million. After the court reduced the damages to $1 million, appeal went to the U.S. Court of Appeals, Second Circuit. Applying *Davis v. Monroe County Board of Educ.*, this chapter, the court held **official action was "deliberately indifferent" under either Title IX or Title VI if it was "clearly unreasonable in light of the known circumstances."** A reasonable juror could find the harassment met Title VI liability standards, as it was "severe, pervasive, and objectively offensive." Peers "taunted, harassed, menaced and physically assaulted" the student, called him "nigger" nearly every day, and threatened him with death. Staff members reported many incidents to the principal, and the mother contacted school administrators 30 to 50 times. Other reports were lodged by the human rights commission, the NAACP, and the police. While the school district was not required to eliminate all the harassment, it ignored many signals that more action was necessary. The decision for the student was affirmed. *Zeno v. Pine Plains Cent. School Dist.*, 702 F.3d 655 (2d Cir. 2012).

D. Disability

According to a 2015 report by the U.S. Department of Education, Office for Civil Rights (OCR), complaints about disability harassment and bullying represented the largest percentage of complaints within the agency's oversight during 2013-14. OCR jurisdiction includes compliance with federal laws prohibiting race, gender, national origin and disability discrimination. See the report at *http://www2.ed.gov/about/reports/ annual/ocr/report-to-president-and-secretary-of-education-2013-14.pdf.*

◆ The parents of a New York student with a learning disability complained to her school that bullying of the child occurred almost every day of a school year. When the committee on special education (CSE) met to discuss her placement for the next school year, the parents claimed the principal said a CSE meeting was an inappropriate place to discuss bullying. When the case reached a federal court, it held schools are required to investigate promptly and respond appropriately when they learn that disability harassment may have occurred. It also held free appropriate public education protections apply to bullying cases. The court applied the "deliberate indifference" approach from sexual harassment cases under Title IX of the 1972 Education Amendments and *Davis v. Monroe County Board of Educ.*, 526 U.S. 629 (1999). It held **"a school must take prompt and appropriate action" in response to bullying incidents, and take appropriate steps to prevent future incidents**. This duty existed regardless of whether the conduct was covered in an anti-bullying policy and regardless of whether a student had complained. *T.K. and S.K. v. Dep't of Educ. of City of New York*, 779 F.Supp.2d 289 (E.D.N.Y. 2011).

When the case returned to administrative levels, a hearing officer found bullying had occurred but the child was not significantly restricted in her educational opportunities. The case returned to the federal court, which held that when a school responds to bullying, its actions must be prompt and appropriate. **Evidence of past bullying and prior implementation of IEPs was important in determining if the student was provided a free appropriate public education (FAPE).** In this case, the court found the bullying of the child created a substantial probability that it would severely restrict her educational opportunities if left unaddressed. **The court found a school should convene an IEP team as part of its response to peer bullying.** Since the child was not offered a FAPE, the parents were entitled to be reimbursed for their private placement costs. *T.K. v. Dep't of Educ. of City of New York*, 32 F.Supp.3d 405 (E.D.N.Y. 2014).

On appeal, the U.S. Court of Appeals, Second Circuit Court, held bullying may substantially interfere with a child's learning opportunities. The court held **the school department denied the student a FAPE by refusing to discuss bullying at IEP meetings, despite reasonable concerns by the parents**. Since the persistent refusal to discuss bullying in the IEP process significantly impeded the parents' participation rights, the court upheld a decision to award them their private school tuition costs for a full school year. *T.K. and S.K. v. New York City Dep't of Educ.*, 810 F.3d 869 (2d Cir. 2016).

◆   A Massachusetts student faced physical and developmental challenges attributed to his premature birth at 27 weeks. He was very small for his age and had attentional and executive function disorders. Among his symptoms were inappropriate social behavior, poor impulse control and issues with problem-solving. A Section 504 plan called for counseling, supervision and monitoring of peer conduct to protect him from abuse. According to the student's parent, he was regularly bullied and abused by peers based on his social behavior, small stature, Jewish ethnicity and religion, perceived sexual orientation and symptoms of his disorders. The parent claimed peers mocked him, expressed a desire to kill him, made snide comments about the Holocaust and used social media to suggest he was gay. Stating the misconduct included attacks and physical assault, the parent sued the school district and several officials in a federal court for claims based on bullying, harassment, retaliation and violations of constitutional and state law rights.

In her complaint, the parent accused teachers and school administrators of engaging in abusive conduct. She asserted they did not protect her child from peer abuse. In pretrial activity, the court held the parent did not comply with the presentation requirements of the state Tort Claims Act. For this reason, all of the negligence claims had to be dismissed. Because the parent did not file a due process hearing request, the court dismissed her federal disability law claims. Next, the court found no due process violation. While the parent said the school district violated her son's right to associate with peers by allowing bullying to occur, the court held a claim based on interference with personal relationships did not apply to social relationships. The same was true of a state freedom of association claim under Massachusetts law. Not enough factual support was included in the complaint for the parent to proceed with many other federal claims. But the court granted her an opportunity to refile her papers to include additional facts. It found a plausible retaliation claim existed under Section 504 of the Rehabilitation Act. She could also amend her complaint to attempt to prove an equal protection violation. **A claim under Title VI of the Civil Rights Act of 1964 based on religious and ethnic harassment was dismissed for failure to show severe, pervasive religious or ethnic-based harassment.** But the parent could refile the Title VI claim against the school district. *Pollard v. Georgetown School Dist.*, 132 F.Supp.3d 208 (D. Mass. 2015).

◆   A Texas parent became concerned that a student with a disability who had sexually assaulted a girl and spent time in an alternative education program would be returned to his child's middle school. He insisted the returning student be moved to another school, but officials reassured him that others would be protected. In December of the school year, the disabled student and another male were accused of "T-bagging everybody." The child of the complaining parent said the boys "hung their crotches in students' faces and humped them." He also reported that the disabled student teased and taunted his child many other times. A school assistant principal and the principal investigated the charges and put the disabled student and his friend on in-school suspension. After interviewing over 50 students, administrators recommended sending the disabled student and his friend to a disciplinary alternative educational placement. The complaining child's parent withdrew his son from the school and sued the school district for harassment in violation of Title IX of the 1972 Education Amendments.

After a federal district court dismissed the case, the parent appealed to the Fifth Circuit Court of Appeals. The court held that school liability for peer sexual harassment under Title IX requires proof that the school district had actual knowledge of the harassment. It must be shown that the harassment was "so severe, pervasive, and objectively offensive" that it barred a victim's access to an educational opportunity, and that the school district remained deliberately indifferent to the harassment. In this case, the lower court had found the school district had no knowledge of the harassment until the "T-bagging" was reported. Student witnesses said the conduct took place when teachers were not looking. **When administrators learned of the problem, they took prompt investigative and remedial action.** After confirming the misconduct, the offending students were disciplined and eventually transferred. **Since the court found the district had no actual knowledge of harassment, it found no Title IX violation.** *Kelly v. Allen Independent School Dist.*, 602 Fed.Appx. 949 (5th Cir. 2015).

◆   Alabama parents of a student with disabilities who committed suicide sought to impose liability for her death on school officials. They claimed officials knew about peer harassment and bullying but failed to address it. A federal court rejected the parents' theory that any school employee named in the lawsuit had authority to take corrective action to end peer harassment. While the bullying alleged in this case was severe, the court rejected the family's claim that the bullying was so open and obvious that anyone at the school would know about it. Only actual knowledge of peer harassment could trigger school liability under Title IX of the 1972 Education Amendments. Of the three identified school employees who might have some knowledge of misconduct, only the assistant principal had the ability to take corrective measures in response to bullying complaints. But the parents did not prove he knew of the bullying or had even heard about it. **Since the parents could not show an "appropriate person" with the authority to act to end the bullying had actual knowledge of any misconduct, the court held for the board of education.** *Moore v. Chilton County Board of Educ.*, 1 F.Supp.3d 1281 (M.D. Ala. 2014).

◆   A California parent claimed his son was repeatedly abused, beaten and kicked by peers because of his disabilities and his non-native English speaker status. The parents made two written incident reports detailing attacks on their son and identifying the assailants. But they claimed school officials did not act and suggested only that he change classrooms to avoid the perpetrators. In a California superior court, the father sought a special order against the school district. In pretrial activity, the father asserted that the district had failed to adopt or implement a comprehensive safety plan that met the requirements of California Education Code Section 32282.

The court dismissed the case, holding the parent did not have standing to pursue it. On appeal, the state court of appeal held **the case involved a well-identified public interest in maintaining a school system that was free of the destructive influence of discrimination, harassment and bullying**. State legislators enacted interrelated statutes to protect students from discrimination and harassment based on race, gender, sexual orientation or disability. California public schools had an affirmative duty to combat racism, sexism and other forms of bias. A code provision required school districts to have comprehensive safety plans. For these reasons, the court held the father had standing to pursue the case both as a parent and a state taxpayer. There was a "manifest public interest in enforcing the antibullying statutes and no urgent competing interests which outweighed that public interest." *Hector F. v. El Centro Elementary School Dist.*, 227 Cal.App.4th 331,173 Cal.Rptr.3d 413 (Cal. Ct. App. 2014).

◆   The family of a Georgia high school student with Asperger's syndrome could not recover damages from his school district after he committed suicide. According to the family, the student was repeatedly bullied at school before he died. A federal court held that in hindsight, the school should have done more to address disability harassment. **But it held the family did not meet the "deliberate indifference" liability standard** under the U.S. Constitution and federal laws including Rehabilitation Act Section 504. On appeal, the U.S. Court of Appeals, Eleventh Circuit, noted that "deliberate indifference is an exacting standard" under which administrators are held liable only if their response (or lack of one) is found "clearly unreasonable in light of the known circumstances." As this standard was not met, the court held for the school district. *Long v. Murray County School Dist.*, 522 Fed.Appx. 576 (11th Cir. 2013).

◆ A Pennsylvania student with bipolar disorder began having mood changes during grade eight. She had an excessive desire to sleep and trouble maintaining relationships with her school peers. She became self-destructive, cut herself and attempted suicide. When the student entered high school, her boyfriend told classmates about her condition. One of these classmates was a cousin of the student, who began calling her names and threatening her.

After beginning her junior and senior years in her regular high school, the student had problems with other students, and she left school for homebound instruction. She sued her former district and school officials in a federal court for disability discrimination. In the court's view, the student did not qualify for protection under federal disability laws. It held that "the genesis of the harassment was conflicts about boys." On appeal, the U.S. Court of Appeals, Third Circuit, held that proof of a discrimination claim under federal law requires a student to establish she has a disability, is "otherwise qualified" to participate in a school's program, and was discriminated against based on a disability. While the student's bipolar disorder was a mental or physical impairment, the court held **she did not demonstrate that her limitations substantially limited her ability to interact with others, care for herself, concentrate on school work or sleep**. No information was provided regarding the frequency, severity or permanency of the student's symptoms. This prevented the court from finding that she was significantly restricted in a major life activity. For this reason, she was not considered an individual with a disability under federal law definitions. Since the lower court had correctly found the student was not substantially limited in a major life activity, the court affirmed the judgment for the school district. *Weidow v. Scranton School Dist.*, 460 Fed.Appx. 181 (3d Cir. 2012).

◆ A Michigan special education student believed a classmate was his girlfriend. He shoved her into a locker because he saw her talking to another boy and later demanded that she perform oral sex on him. At a school basketball game, the student made obscene gestures at the classmate and her stepfather told him to stay away from her. The stepfather wrote to administrators about the incident and the attempt to solicit sex. In response, the school formed a 30-day plan to constantly supervise the student. Seven weeks after the supervisory period passed, the student sexually assaulted the classmate at school. Later, the school board voted to expel him.

In a federal court action, the classmate said the student's history of misconduct put school officials on notice of a risk of harm. But she did not assert that any prior misconduct included sexual harassment, and the court held for the school district and officials. On appeal, the U.S. Court of Appeals, Sixth Circuit, held harassment must take place in a context subject to a school's control in order to impose liability. Victims of peer harassment lack rights to make particular remedial demands. The court held the incidents in this case did not amount to severe, pervasive and objectively offensive conduct. **The classmate could not rely on incidents involving other victims to meet the "severe and pervasive" part of the Title IX liability analysis.** When the school district learned of the harassment, it imposed a supervision plan. The district's response to the assault was "prompt, reasonable, and not deliberately indifferent." Constant supervision of the student was not required. No authority supported the argument that activity at other schools or off campus was relevant to a Title IX claim, as the district had no control over it. As the district was not deliberately indifferent to peer harassment, the court held in its favor. *Pahssen v. Merrill Community School Dist.*, 668 F.3d 356 (6th Cir. 2012).

◆ New York parents claimed teachers and school administrators did not intervene when classmates subjected their autistic child to daily name-calling, abusive language and violent conduct. A teacher was alleged to be present during some of the incidents. In a federal court complaint against the school district and several teachers, administrators and staff members, the student claimed peers called him a "fucking retard," "asshole," "faggot" and "bitch." According to the parents, nobody took effective measures to deter the harassment or discipline the harassers. In pretrial activity, the court refused to dismiss the disability harassment claims. It used the standard of liability from sexual harassment cases under Title IX and *Davis v. Monroe County Board of Educ.*, this chapter. Since the student claimed he was regularly harassed and bullied and that officials took no meaningful action, **the court held he could pursue the harassment-based Section 504 claims.** The court found no evidence of anti-male bias, and it dismissed claims under Title IX and the Equal Protection Clause. But the student could pursue claims against the district for negligent hiring and negligent supervision, violation of the state civil rights act, and discrimination. *Preston v. Hilton Cent. School Dist.*, 876 F.Supp.2d 235 (W.D.N.Y. 2012).

◆ Parents of a Maryland child with autism claimed their child was attacked at school by a male student and suffered black eyes and a swollen lip. It was claimed that the same student had previously attacked the child. The parents claimed they told school officials and a teacher about the perpetrating student, but that he was allowed to sit in close proximity to their child shortly after the attack. At some point after the incident, the parents said their child was placed in a lower grade, taken off the academic "graduation" track and not afforded an opportunity to be educated in the least restrictive environment. The complaint did not say why or when the child's placement was changed. A federal district court held that the family's failure to request an administrative due process hearing was fatal to their claims under the IDEA and Section 504. **Tort-like damages are inconsistent with the IDEA, which exists to assure the provision of a free appropriate public education** (FAPE). As the court found no facts to support the remaining claims, it dismissed them. *Wright v. Carroll County Board of Educ.*, Civ. No.11-cv-3103, 2012 WL 1901380 (D. Md. 5/24/12).

◆ A New York student with an individualized education program (IEP) and behavior problems was removed from his parents' home at age three for neglect and possible abuse, then hospitalized for severe aggression, but he had no record of sexual aggression. During a two-year stay in a psychiatric center, the student continued to have behavior problems. Upon being released, he was placed in a community residence and began attending school under an IEP. After being placed with foster parents, the student entered another year of public school under an IEP. Later, the student exposed himself to a kindergartner and forced her to touch him while they were on a school bus. The child's mother sued the school district. The case reached the Court of Appeals of New York, which explained that **school districts are liable for foreseeable injuries that are caused by the absence of adequate supervision. Unanticipated acts by third parties, such as the student in this case, do not create school liability unless the school had some notice of prior similar conduct**. According to the court, the sexual assault in this case was not foreseeable. While the student had a history of severe behavioral issues, there had been no such conduct for over two years. Since his hospitalization, he had not displayed aggression. As the student's past conduct did not indicate sexually aggressive behavior that would give the school district specific knowledge or notice of similar conduct, a judgment for the district was affirmed. *Brandy B. v. Eden Cent. School Dist.*, 15 N.Y.3d 297 (N.Y. 2010).

IV. USE OF TECHNOLOGY

A. Internet and Cyberbullying

◆ A Texas student claimed classmates were bullying her and school officials did nothing when she reported it. An assistant principal (AP) called her into his office to discuss the circulation of lewd pictures of the student and a friend off campus. After the meeting with the AP, the student was transferred to a district alternative learning academy for 30 days. A provision in the district student code of conduct prohibited "sexting" and cyberbullying by students either on or off school property. In a federal court, the student sought to stop the transfer. She added claims related to the bullying she reported. First, the court rejected her claim that relevant terms in the student code of conduct were too vague to satisfy constitutional requirements. It held terms such as "abusive," "obscene," "sexually oriented," "sexting" and "substantial disruption" were sufficiently clear that a student of ordinary intelligence would know what conduct was prohibited.

Schools do not have to spell out in detail what is meant by "obscene" or "sexually oriented." High school students undoubtedly understood the ban on such conduct. There was no merit to the due process claims. Fifth Circuit authority held students had no constitutionally protected interest in halting a disciplinary transfer to an alternative school. Next, the court found the student's negligence claims against the district, AP and the school principal were barred by state law immunity. **Nor could liability be imposed on school officials for failing to report bullying to child protection authorities or not developing a policy governing reports of child abuse or neglect.** A speech rights violation claim against the AP and principal failed, and the court held for the school district on all of the student's other claims. *S.N.B. v. Pearland Independent School Dist.*, No. 3:13-CV-441, 2014 WL 2207864 (S.D. Tex. 5/28/14).

◆   Three Colorado students who were subjected to inappropriate conduct by a former teacher at their high school were denied an appeal to review their claims against their school district and administration. According to their federal court complaint, the teacher sent the students explicit texts, sought nude pictures and tried to solicit sexual relations with them. **While the court allowed claims against the teacher to proceed, it held the case could not proceed against the district or administrators**, who did not know about the teacher's conduct. A single state law claim for failure to report child abuse was allowed to proceed against a school security guard and coach who knew about an incident of sexual conduct between the teacher and one student. In a brief order, the U.S. Court of Appeals, Tenth Circuit, affirmed the judgment. *Doe v. Boulder Valley School Dist. No. RE-2*, 523 Fed.Appx. 514 (10th Cir. 2013).

◆   A Tennessee student and classmate argued with each other about a boy they liked. After the classmate called a friend to let her know she was with the boy, the student tweeted to the friend that she would help the friend shoot the classmate. The classmate's mother took the tweets seriously and reported them to the school. According to the student, the school resource officer yelled at her angrily during a 30-minute meeting. She tearfully told him she was just joking and didn't mean to hurt the classmate. After the principal assigned the student to 45 days in an alternative school, the mother requested a disciplinary hearing. The school reduced the discipline to 10 days, but the family sued the school district in a federal court. **The court held schools may categorically prohibit vulgar, lewd, indecent or offensive speech.** Schools may also censor school-sponsored student speech in a manner consistent with pedagogical concerns. In other cases, school officials may only regulate student speech that would substantially and materially interfere with school work or discipline under *Tinker v. Des Moines Independent Community School Dist.*, 393 U.S. 503 (1969). **In this**

case, the court found the tweet had little to do with school. No school computers were used, and the message was not directed toward the school.

Significantly, the court found no disruption of school activities or any impact on the school environment. As a result, the court held the student could proceed with her First Amendment claim. But the court held that when a student is suspended for 10 days or less, a school need only offer minimal procedures. In this case, the student was told she was in trouble about the tweets. In her meeting with the resource officer, she did not deny them. The court dismissed her due process and other federal claims. *Nixon v. Hardin County Board of Educ.*, 988 F.Supp.2d 826 (W.D. Tenn. 2013).

◆ Jessica Logan committed suicide in 2008, shortly after graduating from an Ohio high school. Her family attributed her suicide to her anguish over the "sexting" of a nude photo of her among other high school students. In a federal action, it was asserted that high school students were circulating the nude photo with their cell phones. When the student reported the activity to a counselor, the counselor referred her to the high school resource officer. The resource officer agreed to speak to the other students, and he asked them to delete the photo from their cell phones. Later, Jessica appeared on a television broadcast about sexting. She claimed the harassment increased after the broadcast. She committed suicide. Her parents sued her school district, school officials, the resource officer and his municipal employer in a federal court. The school district argued that it could not be held liable because neither the student nor anyone acting on her behalf made a sexual harassment report. The court held **there is no constitutional duty of government actors to protect individuals against private parties such as the harassing students in this case**. As there was no evidence that the resource officer acted unreasonably, he was entitled to qualified immunity. There was also no viable claim against his municipal employer for failing to train or supervise him. *Logan v. Sycamore Community School Board of Educ.*, 780 F.Supp.2d 594 (S.D. Ohio 2011).

In a later order, the court found other courts have **held appropriate persons for reporting under Title IX of the Education Amendments of 1972 "do not need to be aware of the exact details of a plaintiff's experience to have notice, as long as they 'reasonably could have responded with remedial measures.'"** Since evidence indicated that school officials knew of the harassment, the mother could proceed with her Title IX claim. *Logan v. Sycamore Community School Board of Educ.*, No. 1:09-CV-00885 (S.D. Ohio 6/5/12). After the court's order of June 5, 2012, the lawsuit was settled for $220,000, including attorneys' fees.

◆ A Mississippi student admitted having a key logger program demonstration disk, and after an investigation, he was suspended for possessing software that damaged the school computer system. The student's mother was a school employee. After the superintendent recommended placing the student in an alternative school for 45 days, he learned that personal data on teachers might have been compromised when the student used his mother's computer. She was reassigned and soon discharged. The student and his mother sued the school district for speech and due process violations, and related claims. After a federal court held for the district, the family appealed. The U.S. Court of Appeals, Fifth Circuit, stated that a state's extension of the right to an education is protected by the Fourteenth Amendment and cannot be withheld absent fair procedures. **A student's transfer to an alternative education program does not deny access to public education, and such an assignment does not violate the Fourteenth Amendment.** The student and his parents had opportunities to meet with school officials, and he had "multiple opportunities" to tell his side of the story. As the court found he received notice and a chance to explain himself, no due process rights were violated. Finding no merit to the mother's First Amendment claims, the court held for the school district. *Harris v. Pontotoc County School Dist.*, 635 F.3d 685 (5th Cir. 2011).

◆ A New Hampshire principal and teacher received sexually explicit messages and reported them to the police. Both messages were traced to a student who attended their school. She admitted opening an email account on a computer at home, then sending both messages. After a hearing, the board voted to suspend the student for 34 days for violating several student handbook rules. These included the board's use policy for school computer systems, the behavior and discipline code and the anti-harassment policy.

Appeal went to the state education board, and a hearing officer upheld the suspension. On appeal to the Supreme Court of New Hampshire, the parents argued the 34-day suspension violated state law and the rules of the state board. They also claimed the district violated its own rules for long-term suspensions. The court rejected the parents' claims regarding state law and state board rules violations. **State law authorized suspensions of up to 10 days for gross misconduct or for neglect or refusal to conform to reasonable school rules.** A school board could expel a student for a variety of enumerated reasons. State and local boards had authority to create rules and policies regarding student conduct and discipline. But the court held that a suspension of 34 days was improper due to the school board's failure to comply with the limits of its own school policy. As the policy limited long-term suspensions to between 11 and 20 school days, the court affirmed the part of the judgment pertaining to the state law violations, but vacated the decision that would have permitted a suspension of over 20 days. *Appeal of Keelin B.*, 162. N.H. 38, 27 A.3d 689 (N.H. 2011).

B. Cell Phones and Other Electronic Communication

◆ A Texas high school counselor learned of explicit texts between her daughter – a freshman at the school – and a paraprofessional who worked in the daughter's after-school music program. The counselor and her husband met with the paraprofessional and his wife. But the counselor and a colleague did not report the texts to law enforcement officers, child protective services or school administrators. Another staff member reported the texts. Police, child protective services and the school district investigated the case. The counselor and her colleague were placed on leave for failing to report the texts. The colleague was reprimanded, but the district proposed terminating the counselor. A hearing examiner found the counselor violated a school policy requiring her to report child abuse in accordance with state law. But the hearing examiner found she did not feel abuse occurred, and he held the board lacked good cause to dismiss her.

The board considered these findings but decided to terminate the counselor's contract. After the state commissioner of education affirmed the decision, appeal reached the Court of Appeals of Texas. It found failure to make a required report subjected an employee to discipline, including employment termination. The court disagreed with the hearing officer's finding that the counselor did not have to report the texts. Neither the district policy nor state law limited the reporting requirement to situations when a teacher actually believed abuse or neglect had occurred. As the board found, a report must be made if there is sufficient reason to believe future abuse may occur. The counselor's actions indicated she feared future abuse. The paraprofessional continued working at the school, and the delay in reporting his conduct endangered other students. **A school board had the power to decide whether a violation was good cause for employment termination.** The court rejected the counselor's claim that her discipline was arbitrary and capricious, despite the slight discipline issued to her colleague. When child safety was at risk, a court would not overturn discipline due to such a disparity. *Judson Independent School Dist. v. Ruiz,* No. 04-13-00706-CV, 2015 WL 1501758 (Tex. Ct. App. 3/31/15).

◆ An investigation of sexting by students was begun in Tunkhannock, Pennsylvania schools after officials found photos of nude and semi-nude female students on cell phones. Officials learned that male students had been trading the images over their cell phones. The district attorney investigated and made a public statement to the media that possession of inappropriate images of minors could justify criminal prosecution for possession or distribution of child pornography. Teens suspected of "sexting" were then presented with a choice of either attending an education program or facing child pornography charges. As part of the education program, female students were asked to write a report explaining "why you are here," "what you did," "why it was wrong," and related issues. Several parents brought a federal court action to halt the proceeding. They said the threat of prosecution came in retaliation for their refusal to attend the education program. The court granted them preliminary relief, and appeal went before the U.S. Court of Appeals, Third Circuit.

The court noted that parents have a due process right to raise their children without undue state interference. **The government cannot coerce parents to accept official ideas of morality and gender roles.** While the district attorney could offer the education program voluntarily, he could not coerce attendance by threatening prosecution. It appeared that the district attorney's motive in bringing the prosecution was retaliatory and was not a good-faith effort to enforce the law. Ruling that a decision not to attend the program was constitutionally protected, the court upheld the preliminary order. *Miller v. Mitchell*, 598 F.3d 139 (3d Cir. 2010).

◆   An Arkansas coach texted frequently with female students. He agreed to stop it after parents complained, but continued making suggestive comments. A student told the superintendent that her ninth-grade cousin "might have a crush" on the coach and often left classes to visit him in the gym. The student told the ninth-grader's mother of these suspicions, and she approached the principal to discuss it. The cousin offered more information and identified staff members who allegedly knew of inappropriate conduct. According to the mother, the principal promised to investigate. Soon the coach was accused of texting "OMG you look good today" to a student. Due to this report and other concerns, the district made preparations to nonrenew the coach's contract. When students reported details of sexual contact between the coach and ninth-grader, the coach was arrested. He was eventually prosecuted and sentenced to 10 years in prison.

A federal court dismissed the students' claims against the district and most of the officials, but the principal was denied immunity. On appeal, the U.S. Court of Appeals, Eighth Circuit, found the principal could be liable for constitutional violations if she knew of the coach's conduct but failed to take remedial action in a manner that caused injury. The court held **the coach's texts did not provide the principal with "actual notice of sexual abuse."** Inappropriate comments alone did not alert her to a possible sexual relationship. School administrators investigated each report they received, and at the relevant time they lacked any evidence of improper contact. The court held "a student's familiar behavior with a teacher or even an 'excessive amount of time' spent with a teacher, without more, does not automatically give rise to a reasonable inference of sexual abuse." It reversed the order denying immunity to the principal and held the district was not liable under Title IX. *Doe v. Flaherty*, 623 F.3d 577 (8th Cir. 2010).

◆   Maryland law officers charged a 26-year-old teacher with sex crimes after a 17-year-old student at his high school reported their sexually oriented text, telephone and instant message communications. The teacher had emailed the student sexually explicit pictures of himself. She came to his classroom, where he exposed his penis to her. A few weeks later, the student reported the teacher's conduct, and police persuaded her to place a one-party consent call to him. In the course of the call, the teacher admitted exposing himself. Police then obtained a search warrant for his residence, vehicle, cell phone and computers. A state court denied his motion to suppress evidence found through the warrant. A jury found him guilty of sexual abuse of a minor, indecent exposure and telephone misuse. The teacher appealed to the Court of Special Appeals of Maryland, which held that the search warrant application identified reasonable grounds to believe that evidence of crime could be found in his house. **Enough evidence was present to reasonably infer that the teacher used home computers to communicate with students** and that this evidence remained in the house. As a result, the court affirmed the judgment. *Ellis v. State of Maryland*, 185 Md.App. 522, 971 A.2d 379 (Md. Ct. Spec. App. 2009).

◆ New York City school rules forbade students from bringing cell phones into public schools without authorization from principals. A state court held that any enforcement system focusing on the use, rather than possession, of cell phones would require teachers to observe and enforce the ban. Teachers would become involved in confronting students and punishment decisions. For that reason, the board had a rational basis for a complete ban. The involvement of teachers in enforcing the cell phone ban would take time from their teaching mission and increase the perception of teachers as adversaries to students. Each principal could address specific situations by allowing students to carry cell phones when there was a special need for it.

The court rejected claims by parents who asserted a right to be able to communicate with their children while they were at school. It held that "the department has a rational interest in having its teachers and staff devote their time to educating students and not waging a 'war' against cell phones." **The court found the use of cell phones for cheating, sexual harassment, prank calls and intimidation was a threat to order in the schools.** *Price v. New York City Board of Educ.*, 51 A.D.3d 277, 855 N.Y.S.2d 530 (N.Y. App. Div. 2008).

C. Surveillance

☑ CHECKLIST – *Practice Tips For School Video Surveillance*

Sara C. Clark, Deputy Director of Legal Services for the Ohio School Boards Association, has the following suggestions for school surveillance:

☐ Install surveillance cameras only in locations where people would not have a reasonable expectation of privacy, such as hallways, lunch rooms and parking lots.
☐ Notify staff, parents, students and others in the community that surveillance cameras are present and in use.
☐ Post signs in the areas where cameras are in use. Include a notice in staff and student handbooks.
☐ Narrowly limit the time and scope of taping.
☐ Establish procedures for maintaining and viewing records.

The checklist is copyrighted by the National School Boards Association.

◆ A Utah student became involved in a fight with other students outside a classroom at their middle school. His parent asked the school for all digital video of the area during the relevant time. His request was made under the state Government Records Access and Management Act (GRAMA). The district responded that disclosure of the video was governed by the Family Educational Rights and Privacy Act (FERPA). The school district explained that since FERPA governed the video, the parent would have to obtain the written consent of the parents of all students depicted in order to see it. After the school district refused to change its position, the parent filed a state court action against the district. After reviewing the video records, the court found other students were clearly identifiable. It found FERPA governed the request and held the district had properly denied the parent's request for unrestricted access to the records.

After learning the images of the other students could be blocked out for about $120, the court held the parent could have a copy of the video records with the images of other students blocked out at his expense. He instead appealed to the Court of Appeals of Utah, which held **a surveillance recording is an "education record" under FERPA. Unless there is written consent by parents, FERPA prohibits the release of education records that are maintained by an educational agency.** The court held the FERPA term "education record" applied to all records, files, documents and other materials containing information directly related to a student that were maintained by an educational agency. As FERPA applied, the court held the school district had correctly insisted that the parent obtain consent from all other parents before disclosing anything. Next, the court found the GRAMA was applicable to the extent consistent with FERPA. The state law allowed the district to provide the parent with a copy of the video record, with the images of students other than his own son blocked. State law provided that a government entity could charge a fee for providing a record in a requested form. As a result, it was appropriate to require the parent to pay the district for the cost of blocking out student identities. *Bryner v. Canyons School Dist.*, 351 P.3d 852 (Utah Ct. App. 2015).

◆ A West Virginia student said he was hurt by another student in what he called a "choking game" intended to restrict blood flow and experience a high. Administrators investigated and deemed the incident "horseplay." The student sued the school district in the state court system for negligent supervision. After a state circuit court held for the school board, the student appealed to the Supreme Court of Appeals of West Virginia. Among his claims was that the board failed to provide enough supervision in the cafeteria. The court found evidence that two or three teachers were in the cafeteria at the time of the incident. While the student claimed a "choking game" had been going on in the school for decades and was well known, the court instead looked to the student accused of doing the choking. It found he had no history of violence and had no known issues with the student. No evidence indicated school employees had actual knowledge of a "choking game." **The court rejected a claim that an employee should have been constantly monitoring the 16 cameras positioned in the high school throughout the school day.** It was not feasible for school employees to see what every student was doing in the cafeteria or hallways at every moment of the school day. In the court's view, the student did not show the hallways were inadequately supervised. *Glaspell v. Taylor County Board of Educ.*, No. 14-0175, 2014 WL 5546480 (W.Va. 11/3/14).

◆   A Texas school district announced a pilot program requiring students to wear ID badges with radio frequency identification chips to track their whereabouts on campus. Badges would also be used as multi-purpose "smart cards" to check out library books, buy food at the cafeteria and buy tickets for school events. A student's parent claimed the chip was "the mark of the beast" and declared that tracking his daughter at school would "condemn us to hell." A district administrator offered to let the student wear an ID card without a tracking chip. But the parent rejected this and other efforts by the district to compromise and filed a lawsuit. When the case came before a federal court, it noted the parent's conflicting statements and found he had been "pushing for dissolution of the entire ... pilot program."

The court rejected a religious free exercise challenge, finding the policy was neutral and generally applicable to all students. The rule served many purposes that had nothing to do with religion. **The court found the district had a legitimate need to easily identify students for safety, security, attendance and state-funding reasons.** A smart ID badge rule was a rational way to meet that need. The student could not show that wearing an ID badge without a tracking chip substantially burdened the free exercise of her religion. She had worn a badge with no tracking chip for years in other district schools. While the family asserted speech, equal protection, and due process claims, and added a claim for violation of the Texas Religious Freedom and Restoration Act, the court dismissed the action. *A.H. v. Northside Independent School Dist.*, 916 F.Supp.2d 757 (W.D. Tex. 2013).

◆   A Pennsylvania student discovered webcam photos and screenshots of himself on a school laptop. The school district agreed to disable the security tracking software on the laptop, but the student and others pursued a federal district court case. The court prohibited the district and its agents from remotely activating webcams on laptop computers issued to students. Under the court order, the school district could not remotely capture screenshots of laptops, except for maintenance, repairs or trouble-shooting. The district could use an alternate means to track lost, stolen or missing laptops.

A global positioning system or other anti-theft device that did not permit the activation of webcams or capture screenshots was permitted. The order prevented the district from accessing any student-created files on laptops, such as emails, instant messages, Internet use logs and web-browsing histories. Under the court order, the district was required to adopt official policies governing the use, distribution and maintenance of student laptops. It was further required to issue regulations for student privacy on laptops and to train staff on the oversight and enforcement of the policies. Under the order, the district would have to provide students and parents an opportunity to view images already taken from webcams. Such images were to be destroyed when the process was completed. *Robbins v. Lower Merion School Dist.*, No. 10-665, 2010 WL 1976869 (E.D. Pa. 5/14/10).

◆   Based on a review of surveillance camera video, some Washington school employees identified a former student as the person who broke into a junior high school and damaged it. After police arrested him and charged him with criminal conduct related to the break-in, a fingerprint analysis showed he was not the offender. By the time the fingerprint analysis exonerated him, the former student had spent 19 days in jail. He sued the school district in a state court for malicious prosecution. It found the district could not be liable, as it did not initiate the prosecution. On appeal, the Court of Appeals of Washington found malicious prosecution actions are not favored. It is in society's best interest to take steps to arrest offenders. **According to the court, a citizen acting in good faith should not face damages if the accused party is not ultimately convicted.** The court held the former student did not prove a malicious prosecution claim. He had to show more "evil intent." The conclusory statement that school staff "had it in for him" did not show hostility or ill will. As a result, the judgment for the school district was affirmed. *Hubbard v. Eastmont School Dist. No. 206*, 152 Wash. App. 1040 (Wash. Ct. App. 2009).

V.   TRANSPORTATION

This section has cases about potential liability in transportation cases. See Chapter Nine for Form III-10: Sample Statement to the Media: School Bus Accident (150). For steps key personnel should take in the event of a bus accident, see Form III-1 in Chapter Nine. For a sample parent letter to be sent in the event of a bus accident, see Form III-2 in Chapter Nine.

◆   An Illinois high school freshman left an after-school event called the International Fair and walked to a McDonald's a block from campus on the other side of a 12-lane road. While trying to return to school, the student was struck and injured by a moving vehicle. In a state court, the student's parent sued the school district for willful and wanton failure to supervise her child. She sought damages and charged the district with voluntarily undertaking the responsibility to supervise the streets and intersections near the high school by hiring crossing guards, traffic control officers and police during certain after-school events at the high school. After the court dismissed the complaint, appeal went before the Appellate Court of Illinois.

On appeal, the court held the state Tort Immunity Act bars liability unless there is a duty to provide supervision imposed by common law or statute. Liability cannot be imposed against a local public entity unless the entity or an employee fails to provide supervision in a manner that is found "willful and wanton." Under the parent's theory, the school district was liable for failing to use due care in performing a voluntary undertaking. But the court held she did not show which intersections around the school were assigned crossing guards or how frequently they were used at after-school events. As she did not support her claim that the school used crossing guards for after-school events, her voluntary undertaking theory failed. **After-school events are optional, and without facts showing the school had a closed-campus policy for after-school events, the parent could not proceed with her case.** *Renkiewicz v. Township High School Dist. 211*, No. 1-15-0989, 2016 IL App (1st) 150989-U (Ill. App. Ct. 1/22/16).

◆ A Maryland student died after being hit by a car as she crossed a busy highway to try to catch a school bus. Her family later sued the school board for negligence. The case came before a jury, where the family produced evidence that the school board was supposed to have bus stops on both sides of the busy highway where the accident took place, but did not. A jury found the board was negligent and awarded over $90 million to the family.

The court granted the board's motion notwithstanding the verdict, and the family appealed to the state court of special appeals. It found a state regulation required the board to have a bus stop on both sides of the four-lane highway. For this reason, the board owed the student a duty of care. Next, the court held the student's failure to use a crosswalk did not make her contributorily negligent as a matter of law. The lower court should have let the jury decide this matter. The board had to show the existence and nature of its insurance coverage, and its coverage limits. If the board was self-insured or part of a pool, it had immunity for damages over $100,000. If the board had private insurance with limits above $100,000, the verdict was to be reduced to the amount of the policy limit. If the board had no insurance at all, the verdict could not be reduced. Last, **the court rejected the lower court's findings that the verdict was shocking to the conscience and had to be reduced by $20,000 received by the family in a settlement from the driver**. There could be no reduction based on the settlement, because the driver did not admit negligence. The court returned the case to the lower court for a hearing. *Davis v. Board of Educ. for Prince George's County*, 222 Md.App. 246, 112 A.3d 1035 (Md. Ct. Spec. App. 2015).

◆ A Pennsylvania student suffered a crushed pelvis and amputation of one leg when a school district-owned bus accelerated out of control onto a sidewalk and struck her. In a state court action for negligence, the district admitted the bus driver caused the accident and that it was liable. Although the district had $11 million in insurance coverage, it argued recovery was limited to $500,000 by the state Political Subdivision Tort Claims Act.

After a four-day trial, a jury returned a verdict of over $14 million against the school district. The court granted the district's motion to reduce the verdict to $500,000. Arguing that the statutory cap on damages was unconstitutional on several grounds, the family appealed. Before the state high court, the family argued the damage cap violated equal protection principles and unfairly reduced the verdict by over 96%. The court held **Pennsylvania's decision to allow tort recovery and then subject it to a liability cap involved questions of policy best addressed by the state General Assembly**. In addition, the court found the family did not show any state classification violated the principles of equal protection. Next, the court rejected claims based on three state constitutional provisions. It found the General Assembly acted within its constitutional authority when providing for limits to tort claims. Despite the tragic facts of the case, the court refused to overturn its prior decisions and held for the school district. *Zauflik v. Pennsbury School Dist.*, 104 A.3d 1096 (Pa. 2014).

◆ A Georgia student was hit by a car when trying to cross a road at his usual bus stop. Visibility was reduced by heavy fog, and the car failed to yield for the stopped bus. In a state court negligence action, the parties made a pretrial stipulation that the bus driver was immune from personal liability for performing a discretionary function in the scope of her employment and acting without malice. It was further stipulated that the district had waived immunity to the extent of its $1 million commercial liability insurance coverage. The district then hired a new attorney and argued for immunity. The court instead found the district waived sovereign immunity to the extent of the insurance it had purchased. The school district appealed to the Court of Appeals of Georgia. It held the state legislature created a two-tier scheme by which local governments were deemed to have waived immunity. Under tier one, school districts waived immunity up to prescribed limits for incidents involving motor vehicles, regardless of insurance. Tier two provided for a waiver to the extent a local entity purchased liability insurance that was greater than the prescribed limits set forth in tier one. Since the school district in this case had purchased liability insurance greater than the amount prescribed in tier one, it had waived sovereign immunity to the extent of the insurance coverage it purchased.

The court rejected the district's argument that the General Assembly intended to exclude school districts from the waiver provision. **Immunity was waived to the extent of the district's insurance coverage.** As the parent did not appeal the part of the trial court order pertaining to the bus driver, the driver was relieved of any personal liability. *Tift County School Dist. v. Martinez*, 331 Ga.App. 423, 717 S.E.2d 117 (Ga. Ct. App. 2015).

◆ Nebraska's highest court held a county could not be held liable for a school bus accident based on its failure to have a traffic sign inspection policy. The case involved a collision between a pickup truck and a school bus at a rural blind intersection. At the intersection, a stop sign facing the truck was missing. An injured motorist sued the county and a property owner in a state district court, which found both of the drivers negligent.

But the court also found the county liable, finding it would have discovered the sign was missing if it had regularly inspected signs. **Appeal reached the state supreme court, which held the trial court was wrong to find the lack of an inspection policy was a legal cause of the accident.** The court reversed the part of the judgment finding the county liable and returned the case to the trial court for a reallocation of liability between the pickup driver and the school district. *Hall v. County of Lancaster*, 287 Neb. 969, 846 N.W.2d 107 (Neb. 2014).

◆ A New York sixth-grader had attention deficit disorder, attention deficit hyperactivity disorder and a mild mental disability. She crossed a busy road to try to catch her bus after the driver missed her stop. The student was then struck by another vehicle and seriously injured. In a state court negligence action, the court held the student's status as a special needs child imposed an expanded duty on the district. Appeal reached the New York Court of Appeals, which held **a school had no duty to prevent injury to a student released from a bus in a safe and anticipated manner**. But it held a school breached a duty if it released a child without supervision into a foreseeably hazardous setting it helped to create. Evidence showed the student had walked onto the highway and was not in the district's custody when she was struck. Finally, the court found no special duty was owed to the student by virtue of her IEP or "the special busing services" afforded her in the IEP. In fact, the IEP only directed the district to transport her to and from school. Rejecting the parent's other arguments, the court held for the school district. *Williams v. Weatherstone*, 22 N.Y.3d 384 (N.Y. 2014).

◆ An 11-year-old Arizona charter school student was struck and injured by a truck in the crosswalk of a busy intersection as she rode her bicycle home from school. The intersection had traffic lights and crosswalks but no crossing guards. The student's parents sued the school for negligence in a state court. In pretrial activity, the court held the school had no duty to protect the student as she traveled to or from its campus. The parents appealed to the Court of Appeals of Arizona, which stated that **as a general rule, an educational institution had no duty to supervise students going to or from their homes**. Arizona law recognized that if a school voluntarily offered protection at a street crossing, a duty of care was then imposed on that conduct. Although a school may create a duty for itself by an affirmative act, the court found no such act in this case. It held the school did not owe the student any duty of care to protect her while she went home.

Instead, the court found the student had left the school's custody at the relevant time. Since the charter school did not have custody of the student at the time, the court held it had no protective obligation to her and lacked any student-school relationship when she was hit. Rejecting all the parents' other arguments, the court held for the charter school. *Monroe v. Basis School, Inc.*, 234 Ariz. 155, 318 P.3d 871 (Ariz. Ct. App. 2014).

◆   West Virginia's Supreme Court upheld the dismissal of a school bus driver who left her bus running to use the lavatory while students were onboard. In a brief memorandum decision, the court noted **the bus driver had violated a state law against leaving a bus while it was still running**. The driver admitted she did not have to leave the bus running despite her urgent need to use the lavatory. As a result, employment termination was appropriate. *Hale v. Board of Educ. of Lewis County, West Virginia*, No. 13–0469, 2014 WL 350892 (W.Va. 1/31/14).

◆   A Washington middle school student was hurt when a car hit her as she crossed a street in front of a neighboring elementary school. A supervising adult traffic monitor had dismissed the crosswalk patrol seven minutes before the accident. In a state court, the student's guardian filed a personal injury action against the driver and school district. The court held the school district had no duty at the time of the incident. On appeal to the Washington Court of Appeals, the court found schools have a duty to protect students in their custody from reasonably foreseeable harm. While the guardian argued the school district had a common law duty to station patrols or monitors at designated crosswalks, the court found no support for this theory in a case involving a middle-school student crossing the street in front of an elementary school. **State laws and rules about school patrols set forth only "suggested procedures," not the times a patrol should be on duty.** As the lower court had correctly held for the district, the judgment was affirmed. *Brady v. Reinert*, 175 Wash.App. 1074 (Wash. Ct. App. 2013).

◆   An Indiana high school student was struck and injured by a school bus as he bicycled to school. According to records of the bus transportation service that served the student's school district, the driver left the bus terminal about 10 minutes late on the morning of the collision. In a state court, the student's family sued the driver and transportation service for negligence. The student argued the contract between the school district and transportation service "called for money back guarantees when a driver is late," making the contract relevant to his theory that the driver was running late and was negligent. At the close of the trial, the student's attorneys asked the jury to return a $35 million verdict. Instead, the jury awarded the student $5.2 million, reduced by the amount of his own negligence, which was found to be 25%. On appeal, the state court of appeals found no merit to the bus service's claim that there had been unfair trial tactics or an unfair trial.

The court also rejected arguments that the trial court made incorrect rulings of evidence. The driver admitted that she could be penalized for lateness. The court rejected a claim that the verdict was the result of a "runaway jury." **The reduction for comparative negligence indicated the jury had exercised discretion.** Since there was evidence to support the $3.9 million damage award, the court left it intact. *Reed v. Bethel*, 2 N.E.3d 98 (Ind. Ct. App. 2014).

◆   A Louisiana high school student was struck and killed by a school bus as she fought with another student near their school. In a state court action for negligence, the student's mother said school employees did not supervise students, failed to timely respond to the fight and did not adequately staff the area. Eight school board employees avoided liability by asserting that no cause of action existed against them under Louisiana Statutes Section 17:439(A). This section precluded claims against school employees based on "any statement made or action taken" within the course and scope of an employee's duties and within specific guidelines for employee behavior set by a school board. As for the bus driver, the trial court held there could be no direct claim against him under Section 17:439(D). Appeal reached the Supreme Court of Louisiana. It held that persons are liable for acts of omission and acts of commission under Civil Code Article 2315. The court reversed the decision regarding school employees other than the drivers. A determination had to be made regarding whether their statements or actions were covered under Section 17:439(A). A lower court had correctly held the driver was subject to a direct action to the extent of his insurance or self-insurance. **The case was returned to the court of appeal to consider whether employee statements or actions were "within the course and scope" of their duties** and whether they were within specific guidelines for employee behavior established by the board. *Credit v. Richland Parish School Board*, 85 So.3d 669 (La. 2012).

◆   A Florida parent who claimed her child was inappropriately touched by another student on a school bus did not state sufficiently definite facts to pursue a lawsuit against her school board and principal. A federal district court dismissed the parent's claims under the U.S. Constitution for failing to state a claim. It also dismissed her state law claims but allowed her to pursue them in the state court system. The parent then appealed to the U.S. Court of Appeals, Eleventh Circuit. The court affirmed the lower court's ruling that she did not state a claim with regard to alleged lying, harassment and bias. The parent contradicted her claim that school officials failed to address her report that a male student had improperly touched her daughter by admitting that school officials had taken action after her report. A vice principal had met with the male student and prohibited all males from sitting with females on the school bus. A report had been made to the state child protection agency. **Schools do not generally have the required level of control over students to have a constitutional duty to protect them from third parties.** As the parent identified no district policy or custom that deprived her daughter of her federal rights, the court affirmed the judgment for the board. *Porter v. Duval County School Board*, 406 Fed.Appx. 460 (11th Cir. 2010).

◆   A nine-year-old North Carolina student was seated on a school bus next to another student who was poking holes in paper with a pencil. The driver told the other student to put the pencil away and told the student to turn around in the seat and stay out of the aisle. When the bus went over a dip in the road, the driver heard a scream. The student's left eye was punctured by the other student's pencil, causing a serious injury. In a State Tort Claims Act proceeding before the North Carolina Industrial Commission, the student's parents claimed the bus driver's failure to supervise the other student was the cause of the eye injury. The commission found the student's injuries resulted from the driver's negligence and awarded the student $150,000 in damages. The state court of appeals upheld the award. **Evidence supported the commission's finding that the driver had a duty of care to enforce school safety policies but failed to do so.** And this failure was the legal cause of the student's eye injury. *Lucas v. Rockingham County Schools*, 692 S.E.2d 890 (N.C. Ct. App. 2010).

◆   An Ohio kindergartner was left on a school bus during her first day of school. According to the parents, the bus driver drove away from the child's stop even though one parent was waiting there and became hysterical. They stated that the driver did not inspect the bus at the conclusion of her route, and the child later awoke alone in a dark school bus garage. In the parents' state court action for personal injury, the district sought dismissal based on sovereign immunity. It argued that any injury to the student did not occur as the result of the "operation" of a school bus. After the court denied the motion, the district appealed. The state court of appeals explained that in *Doe v. Marlington Local School Dist. Board of Educ.*, the Ohio Supreme Court held **a state law exception to immunity for negligent operation of a motor vehicle pertained only to negligence in driving or otherwise causing a vehicle to be moved**. In this case, the driver was operating the bus, not supervising the conduct of any students. Since the evidence supported the lower court's decision, the court affirmed the judgment. *Swain v. Cleveland Metropolitan School Dist.*, No. 94553, 2010 WL 3722280 (Ohio Ct. App. 9/23/10).

VI. STUDENT SAFETY

See Chapter Nine of this volume for new Form VI-14: Quiz: 10 Playground Safety Questions. In *Estate of C.A. v. Castro*, this chapter, the U.S. Court of Appeals, Fifth Circuit, rejected arguments to recognize the "state-created danger" theory under the Due Process Clause of the Fourteenth Amendment. It followed its decision in *Doe v. Covington County School Dist.*, 675 F.3d 849 (5th Cir. 2012), this chapter. But federal courts in Pennsylvania and Oklahoma have allowed students and their families to pursue state-created danger claims.

◆   A Wyoming school district sold a building to a community group. The locks were changed, and the community group began using the building. A child attended a basketball game at the building and played with others on a stage area. He was crushed and killed instantly when a heavy lunchroom bench fell on him. The bench had been leaned against a wall in a storage room adjacent to the stage. It was not known when the bench was propped there or who did it. In a state court action, the child's estate sued the school district, town and county for wrongful death. When the district sought to be dismissed, the court held the district did not breach a duty of care and did not cause the child's death. On appeal, the Supreme Court of Wyoming found the lower court had based its decision on a finding that no school employee had placed the bench against the wall. But factual issues remained that were appropriate to present to a jury. **Pretrial dismissal in negligence cases is proper only when the facts are undisputed.**

The court agreed with the estate that nothing showed the district had ever warned the community group of the dangerous condition created by the improperly placed bench. Finding reasonable jurors could reach different conclusions on the question of whether the district breached a duty of reasonable care and caused the accident, the court reversed the judgment. *Amos v. Lincoln County School Dist. No. 2*, 2015 WY 115 (Wyo. 2015).

◆ A Florida student had been twice disciplined out of school. A week after the second incident, the student threw an eight-pound book at a male classmate's head, fracturing his eye socket. Although the teacher was standing in front of the class at the time and was only a few feet away, it was later agreed that the book-throwing was spontaneous and could not have been prevented. In a state court, the classmate sued the student's family and the school district for his injuries. Among the claims was one for negligent supervision. The student's family settled the claim with the classmate, but the negligence claim against the district was heard by a jury.

Acknowledging that the teacher did no wrong, the classmate asserted the principal had been negligent for not disseminating the student's prior disciplinary record to the teacher. **The court explained that student disciplinary records are educational records that are subject to federally protected privacy rights.** While federal law allows school officials to decide which of its employees have a "legitimate educational interest" in access to disciplinary records, the court held this did not create a legal duty to make disciplinary reports available to teachers. Federal law entrusts school officials with discretion to determine which employees may have a legitimate educational interest in protected student data. The student's prior disciplinary record did not indicate a history of assault or behavior problems. Instead, the court held the case involved an instantaneous event in which the teacher had no chance to intervene. In sum, the court found no evidence of negligent supervision. The school district's legal duty was to properly supervise students, not to disseminate student disciplinary records. As a result, the court held for the school district. *School Board of Miami-Dade County, Florida v. Martinez-Oller*, 167 So.3d 451 (Fla. Dist. Ct. App. 2015).

◆   New York parents filed separate federal cases in which they sought declarations that a state law and rule permitting the temporary exclusion from public schools of students from state immunization requirements violated the Constitution. After the cases were consolidated, one parent testified that she objected to the law not only due to her religion, but because she believed vaccination could kill her daughter by putting her into anaphylactic shock. When questioned, the parent could not say which Catholic tenet prohibited vaccination. She cited medical reasons for objecting, but a federal magistrate judge denied her request. The court adopted the magistrate judge's recommendation to deny the families relief.

On appeal, the U.S. Court of Appeals, Second Circuit, held any due process claim was foreclosed by *Jacobson v. Comwlth. of Massachusetts*, 197 U.S. 11 (1905). In that case, the Supreme Court held mandatory vaccination was within a state's police power. Moreover, in *Zucht v. King*, 260 U.S. 176 (1922), **the Supreme Court rejected a claim that individual constitutional liberties could overcome a state's judgment that mandatory vaccination is in the interest of the whole population**. The court explained that the right to practice religion freely did not include liberty to expose the community or a child to communicable disease, ill health or death. In fact, the court explained, a state could constitutionally require all children to be vaccinated in order to attend a public school. Since the state had the power to bar children from school altogether, the court held New York's more limited action of temporarily excluding students during an outbreak of vaccine-preventable disease was clearly constitutional. A judgment for various state government agencies was affirmed. *Phillips v. City of New York*, 775 F.3d 538 (2d Cir. 2015).

◆   A Florida student said she was attacked by a classmate with a long history of discipline, bullying, fighting and class disruption. She said the attacker was in possession of a blade prior to the attack and should have been serving an in-school suspension (ISS). In a state court action against the board, the student submitted four theories of negligence. One was the theory that the board was negligent for not placing the attacking student in ISS on the scheduled day. It was claimed this allowed the attacker to be on the playground at the time of the injury. A jury agreed and found the board negligently supervised the attacker. The board appealed to a Florida District Court of Appeal, which found the board's current argument was different from its initial defenses that it had no duty to the student and was protected by immunity. It had limited the appeal to other liability theories. **As negligent supervision was an accepted basis for school liability, and the evidence supported the verdict, the student prevailed.** *Duval County School Board v. Buchanan*, 131 So.3d 821 (Fla. Dist. Ct. App. 2014).

◆   Before arriving at school to help prepare for a school prom, an Oklahoma student drank alcohol. When a staff member smelled alcohol on him, she reported it to the superintendent, who obtained the student's admission that he had consumed alcohol before coming to school. But the parents were not called, as required by state law and a school policy. Instead, the superintendent told the student to go home with two other students. At some point after leaving school, the student grew distraught. He left the other students in another vehicle and later died in a one-vehicle rollover accident. His parents sued the school district and superintendent for constitutional rights violations and negligence. A federal court found enough facts to allow the negligence claim to proceed against the school district. **The district owed the student a duty of care, as he was on school grounds and participating in a school function at the time of the superintendent's questioning.** Although the court refused to dismiss a negligence claim against the district, it found no liability under the state-created danger theory. While the superintendent may have made poor choices, the court found nothing outrageous or conscience-shocking about his conduct. As a result, the constitutional claim failed and the superintendent was dismissed from the case. *Kerns v. Independent School Dist. No. 31 of Ottawa County*, 44 F.Supp.3d 1110 (N.D. Okla. 2014).

◆   Indiana's highest court held a principal's four-hour delay in reporting the rape of a student in a school lavatory triggered liability for a misdemeanor. During the delay, the court found the principal was neither reporting nor investigating the rape. It found he was instead "ignoring the issue." He spent two hours interviewing candidates for an open position. After the superintendent told the principal to contact the appropriate child protection agency, he did so. The perpetrator admitted the rape and made a guilty plea, and the investigation shifted to the principal. The state charged the principal with failure to report the incident. He was tried and convicted.

The principal filed a lawsuit that reached the state supreme court. It found the state had proven **the principal had reason to believe the student was a victim of child abuse or neglect**. The student was a rape victim, and by virtue of her prior designation as a ward of the county, she was "a person who needed care, treatment or rehabilitation" that was unlikely to be provided or accepted without the coercive intervention of a court. The principal knowingly failed to make an immediate report to a child protection agency or police. While he argued "immediate" was a vague term allowing up to 24 hours to make a report, the court disagreed. It had no sympathy for the principal's four-hour delay, noting he had dropped the matter for a routine interview. The principal admitted to investigators that he had not read relevant reporting policies. He and his staff held the mistaken view that an allegation of a rape by another minor could not be child abuse. The court commented that the principal was not entitled to take time to "assess and reflect" about a report, as he did not need a high level of certainty to do so. Mandated reporters had to identify and report the facts within their knowledge. As a result, the principal's conviction and sentence were upheld. *Smith v. State of Indiana*, 8 N.E.3d 668 (Ind. 2014).

◆ New Jersey's Supreme Court held a school principal was not liable for injuries to a pedestrian who cut across public school grounds on a Saturday and was attacked by a dog. According to the pedestrian, the dog had previously slipped out of its leash and accosted other passersby. She said the principal had called animal protection officials at least one other time when a dog was loose while school was in session. In the pedestrian's state court action, she advanced claims against the school district, principal, dog owner and the owner of the property where the dog had been leashed. After the claims against the dog owner and property owner were dismissed for failure to prosecute them, the court rejected arguments by the pedestrian that the principal and school district had a duty to prevent future attacks. She said the dog was a known danger on school property. The court held for the school district and principal, but a state appellate division court disagreed.

On appeal, the pedestrian argued the principal was on notice of the risk of an attack because he had received a report that the dog had attacked two others nine days before her injury. He had also reported dogs to the animal control unit of the police when dogs were observed at school during school hours. According to the pedestrian, the school district should also be held liable in this case because the principal knew that a vicious dog created a dangerous condition on school grounds. The court explained that proving a negligence claim depends upon the finding of a duty of care that the party being sued owes to the party bringing the lawsuit. Once a duty is found to exist, liability follows if there is a breach of the duty that causes injury and damages. In this case, **neither the principal nor the school board had any control over the dog or the activities on neighboring property**. Once the school day ended, the principal could not monitor school grounds. There was also no relationship between the school and the pedestrian. Finally, the court found no public interest in imposing a duty on school personnel to protect persons with no relationship to a school from attacks by neighborhood dogs. Since there was no duty of care to protect the pedestrian in this case, the court held for the principal and school district. *Robinson v. Vivirito*, 217 N.J. 199, 86 A.3d 119 (N.J. 2014).

◆ The U.S. Court of Appeals, Fifth Circuit, held a Texas school district and administrators were not liable to the estate of a student who drowned in a school pool. The parents sued the school district, principal and other officials in a federal court, asserting constitutional rights violations based on a state-created danger theory. The court held for the school district and officials, and the parents appealed to the Fifth Circuit. On appeal, the parents argued their son's death occurred despite the school's knowledge of an obvious danger of unsupervised use of the swimming pool. The court noted that the parents' claims arose under the Due Process Clause of the Fourteenth Amendment. Although they urged liability under the "state-created danger theory," the court explained that it had already refused to recognize the theory. State actors such as the school officials in this case were entitled to qualified immunity so long as their conduct did not violate clearly established constitutional rights of which a reasonable person would have known. In this case, **the family was unable to identify a constitutional violation because the state-created danger theory was invalid**. Even had they shown a constitutional violation, the court held they would still be unable to show such a right was clearly established at the relevant time. *Estate of C.A. v. Castro*, 547 Fed.Appx. 621 (5th Cir. 2013).

◆   After a shooting at a Detroit high school, the families of the victims said that a recent merger of the high school with another school had increased a risk of violence due to gang rivalries. In a federal court, the families sued the shooter and his accomplices for assault and battery. They added claims against the school district, high school principal and security officers for gross negligence, constitutional violations and public nuisance. The court entered judgments totalling $8 million in damages against each of the shooters for assault and battery. But it dismissed the school system from the case. Before the U.S. Court of Appeals, Sixth Circuit, the families claimed the merger of the high schools resulted in a state-created danger of increased violence due to the known gang presence. **The court explained that there is no constitutional requirement for the government to protect life, liberty and property of citizens against private actors such as the shooters in this case.** To create liability, an affirmative government act must present a special danger to an individual whom the government has placed at risk. In the court's view, neither the merging of the high schools nor the breaking up of a fight prior to the shootings satisfied the "affirmative act element of the state-created danger claim." As the tort claims were barred by state law immunity, the court held for the school district and employees. *Walker v. Detroit Public School Dist.*, 535 Fed.Appx. 461 (6th Cir. 2013).

◆   A Texas student missed his school bus twice during his first week of kindergarten. Later in the month, school officials required him to sign a disciplinary form due to bus misbehavior, even though he could not read and no parent was present. After an investigation by the school district and subsequent hearings, the district's board denied the parent's grievance. On appeal, a state administrative law judge held the Texas education commissioner had no authority to hear federal law questions and that the parent did not claim violations of state law. A state trial court affirmed the commissioner's order, and appeal reached the Court of Appeals of Texas. It noted the commissioner's power to review school board actions was limited to actions or decisions by a school board that violated the school laws of the state or a provision of an employment contract. The court found the parent did not show any violation of Chapter 26 of the Texas Education Code.

The parent did not show the district neglected to adopt a grievance process for parental complaints. At most, he showed an inaccurate investigation of his son's bus incidents and failure to accurately follow its local grievance policy. **The court found no merit to the parent's claim that the commissioner had power over claims regarding the creation of**

an unsafe learning environment. A state code provision regarding safe and disciplined school campus environments contained only "a mission statement." Because federal claims arising under the Paul D. Coverdell Teacher Protection Act and the Family Educational Rights and Privacy Act were outside the commissioner's authority, the case had been properly dismissed. *Maiden v. Texas Educ. Agency*, No. 03-09-00681-CV, 2011 WL 1744963 (Tex. Ct. App. 5/6/11).

◆   An 11-year-old New York student fell from a banister at school while unsupervised and suffered serious injuries. When his parents sued the district for negligence, it asserted that he had assumed the risk of harm by engaging in horseplay when he slid down the banister. The case reached the Court of Appeals of New York, which found that assumption of risk is typically raised in cases involving athletic and recreational activities. Allowing the defense here would have unfortunate consequences. **If the student's injury was attributable to his own conduct, this could be handled by allocating comparative fault.** The court returned the case to a lower court for more proceedings. *Trupia v. Lake George Cent. School Dist.*, 927 N.E.2d 547 (N.Y. 2010).

◆   A New Hampshire student with learning disabilities was having problems at his middle school. During his seventh-grade year, a teacher's aide overheard him say he "wanted to blow his brains out." A guidance counselor called the student's mother and had the student sign a contract for safety, but she took no other action. Several weeks later, the mother claimed that a special education teacher made a false and knowing attempt to impose discipline on her son. The next day, the student was reported to the vice principal and suspended. After the suspension, the student returned home and hanged himself. The mother sued the school administrative unit, a teacher and the guidance counselor for negligence, infliction of emotional distress and wrongful death. A state trial court dismissed the case, and later the Supreme Court of New Hampshire affirmed this decision. It rejected the mother's claim that the counselor and administrative unit had a special duty to prevent the suicide and that the counselor voluntarily assumed a duty to prevent it. **There was no intentional or malicious conduct in this case that might create a duty to prevent the suicide.** *Mikell v. School Administrative Unit #33*, 972 A.2d 1050 (N.H. 2009).

CHAPTER FOUR

Campus Law Enforcement

I. SEARCH AND SEIZURE

A. The *New Jersey v. T.L.O.* Standard

The Fourth Amendment to the U.S. Constitution protects individuals from unreasonable searches and seizures. The Fourth Amendment states:

"The right of the people to be secure in their persons, houses, papers and effects, against unreasonable searches and seizures, shall not be violated, and no Warrants shall issue, but upon probable cause, supported by Oath or affirmation, and particularly describing the place to be searched, and the persons or things to be seized."

Underlying all search and seizure cases in the criminal context is the "exclusionary rule," which allows a suspect to exclude from consideration any evidence that is seized in violation of the Fourth Amendment.

165

The Fourth Amendment's warrant and probable cause standard does not typically apply to school officials who search students suspected of violating a law or school rules. Instead, the courts apply a "reasonableness" standard, by which the legality of a school search depends upon its reasonableness under all the circumstances. In *New Jersey v. T.L.O.*, this chapter, the Supreme Court held school searches are "administrative searches" as they do not result in criminal prosecution and loss of liberty. The "special need" beyond law enforcement that justifies relieving school administrators from the burden of obtaining warrants is the need to protect student safety. In *T.L.O.*, the Court held: 1) a search by school officials need only be reasonable at its inception, and 2) its scope may not exceed what is necessary under the circumstances.

For example, a teacher who smells marijuana odor wafting from a student would be reasonable in believing that there was some rules violation, satisfying the first requirement that the search be "reasonable at its inception." After the student is sent to the office, an administrator or liaison officer then asks the student if he has marijuana in his possession and asks him to turn out his pockets. This kind of search is regarded as "not intrusive" and satisfies the second *T.L.O.* consideration by "not exceeding what is necessary under the circumstances." By contrast, a highly intrusive "strip search" would go beyond what would be reasonable in this case.

◆   In the *T.L.O.* case, a teacher at a New Jersey high school found two girls smoking in a school lavatory in violation of school rules. She brought them to the assistant vice principal's office, where one of the girls admitted to smoking in the lavatory. However, the other girl denied even being a smoker. The assistant vice principal then asked the latter girl to come to his private office, where he opened her purse and found a pack of cigarettes. As he reached for them, he noticed rolling papers and decided to thoroughly search the entire purse. He found marijuana, a pipe, empty plastic bags, a substantial number of one dollar bills and a list of "people who owe me money." The matter was then turned over to the police. A juvenile court hearing was held, and the girl was adjudicated delinquent. She appealed the juvenile court's determination, contending that her constitutional rights had been violated by the search of her purse. She argued that the evidence against her should have been excluded from the juvenile court proceeding.

The U.S. Supreme Court held that the search did not violate the Fourth Amendment's prohibition on unreasonable searches and seizures. Stated the Court: "The legality of a search of a student should depend simply on the reasonableness, under all the circumstances, of the search." Two considerations are relevant in determining the reasonableness of a search. First, **the search must be justified initially by reasonable suspicion of a violation**. Second, **the scope and conduct of the search must be reasonably related to the circumstances which gave rise to the search, and school officials must take into account the student's age, sex and the nature of the offense**. The Court upheld the search of the student in this case because the initial search for cigarettes was supported by reasonable suspicion. The discovery of rolling papers then justified the further searching of the purse, since such papers are commonly used to roll marijuana cigarettes. The Court affirmed the delinquency adjudication, ruling the "reasonableness" standard was met by school officials in these circumstances, and the evidence was properly obtained. *New Jersey v. T.L.O.*, 469 U.S. 325, 105 S.Ct. 733, 83 L.Ed.2d 720 (1985).

◆ Based upon an anonymous tip that a student had a gun at school, a Florida assistant principal brought him to a conference room. A search of his book bag yielded a loaded semiautomatic handgun. In a juvenile court proceeding, the student sought to exclude the gun from evidence, arguing the search violated the Fourth Amendment. After a trial, the court imposed a 15-day detention and probation. Appeal reached a Florida District Court of Appeal, which held that generally, **an anonymous tip must have sufficient detail and information that could be independently verified by police to establish a level of reliability**. On the other hand, some circumstances justify protective searches based on a threat of extraordinary danger. Courts have recognized that schools are an area where a person's reasonable expectation of privacy is reduced. For this reason, public school officials are held to a standard of reasonable suspicion, rather than probable cause. In the court's view, the search in this case was reasonable. There were reasonable indicia of reliability to the tip, which accurately identified the student by name and his school. Given the student's reduced expectation of privacy, the moderate intrusiveness of the search, the gravity of the threat, and the reduced level of reliability necessary to justify a protective search, the court held the decision to search the book bag was reasonable. *K.P. v. State of Florida*, 129 So.3d 1121 (Fla. Dist. Ct. App. 2013).

◆ An Oregon principal learned that a student had either called or texted a classmate that he would bring a gun to school and shoot her. Upon learning this, the principal called a deputy sheriff and the student's mother. While awaiting the deputy and mother, the principal searched the student's locker. After finding no gun there, he escorted the student to the office and confiscated his backpack. When the student denied making the threats, the principal continued to question him and searched his backpack, where a .45 caliber semiautomatic handgun and ammunition were found. The deputy confiscated the gun, placed the student in handcuffs and read him his criminal rights. In a juvenile court, the student sought to exclude the handgun and ammunition from the evidence. He argued the principal lacked reasonable suspicion to believe a weapon was in the backpack. In denying the student's motion, the court held the principal had relied on specific facts indicating a threat. It also held the search was not overly intrusive. On appeal, the court held a student can be searched without a warrant or probable cause when a school official reasonably suspects, based on specific and articulable facts, that the student possesses something that poses an immediate threat. In this case, the principal reasonably suspected the backpack could hold a weapon, and he did not know whether the student had the gun on his person, in the backpack, or at another place in school. The court held that **when school officials perceive an immediate threat to school safety, they must be able to take prompt, reasonable steps to address it**. As there was a real threat to safety in this case, the court held the search was reasonable. *State v. A.J.C.*, 254 Or. App. 717 (Or. Ct. App. 2013).

◆   Four California police officers learned from a high school principal that a student had told a classmate he would "shoot up" the school. He was said to be a victim of bullying and had been absent from school for two days. Concerned that the student was a threat, the police went to his house. When they arrived, they knocked on the door but received no response. Nobody answered the home telephone, and the student's mother hung up her cell phone after a police sergeant identified himself and said he was waiting outside. Soon, the student and his mother came outside and learned that the officers wanted to discuss the threats. The student responded, "I can't believe you're here for that." When the sergeant asked to come inside the house to talk, the mother refused. He asked her if there were any guns in the house, and she went inside. Fearing they were in danger, the officers entered the house. Ultimately, they concluded the report about the student was false.

Later, the family sued the officers for Fourth Amendment violations. Appeal reached the U.S. Supreme Court, which found none of its prior decisions had found a Fourth Amendment violation on facts comparable to those present in this case. The Court held **a reasonable police officer could read the Court's prior decisions as allowing their entry into a residence if there was a reasonable basis to believe there was an imminent threat of violence**. As a result, the Court found a lower court had correctly held the officers had an objectively reasonable basis for their actions. This included the mother's initial failure to answer the door or the phone, hanging up the cell phone on the sergeant, refusing to answer questions, and running into the house. *Ryburn v. Huff*, 132 S.Ct. 987, 181 L.Ed.2d 966 (U.S. 2012).

B. Electronic Devices and Social Media

◆   A Mississippi freshman cheerleader argued with a senior cheerleading captain while the squad visited a TV station. Later, off school grounds and without using school computers, the freshman posted threats against the captain on social media. When the captain reported this, the advisor lectured the squad and then asked all squad members for their Facebook user names and passwords so she could inspect their accounts. After checking the freshman's Facebook account, the advisor suspended her from the squad for two weeks. When the freshman was not invited to join the cheer squad the next school year, she claimed others bullied her and that she suffered anxiety and depression. In a federal court, she sued the school district, advisor, principal, superintendent and others. Appeal reached the U.S. Court of Appeals, Fifth Circuit, which held that qualified immunity shields government officials from having to pay damages unless the injured party shows a violation of a right that is clearly established at the time of the violation. The contours of the right must be sufficiently clear that every reasonable official would understand it. As for the demand for Facebook passwords and account information, the court found it was not clearly established in 2007 (at the time of the incident) that this violated federal law.

At the time of the advisor's request for student social media information, no precedent held the Fourth Amendment proscribed her actions. Since school officials acting in 2007 had no fair warning that they could not access social network accounts upon receiving information of online threats among students concerning school activities at a school function, the lower court should not have denied qualified immunity to the school officials on the privacy violation claim. Similarly, **the court held that as of 2007, no case law placed officials on notice that punishing a student based on her Facebook messages would violate the First Amendment**. *Jackson v. Ladner*, 626 Fed.Appx. 80 (5th Cir. 2015).

◆   A 14-year-old New Mexico seventh-grader refused multiple requests by her teacher to turn over her phone. The teacher stopped class and an administrator took the student to the office. There, the student ignored repeated requests to give up her phone, even after the school resource officer (SRO) intervened. The SRO told her she was in violation of school rules and a state law by texting in class and refusing to turn over her phone. After the student ignored his repeated requests to give up her phone, he placed her under arrest, handcuffed her and brought her to a juvenile detention center. In a federal court, the student's parent sued the SRO and school district. The court found evidence that the student had ignored her teacher and refused to stop texting in class. Her refusal to follow instructions required the teacher to stop class and seek help from the administration and eventually the SRO.

Since there was evidence that the SRO had probable cause to arrest the student, he was entitled to qualified immunity for the claim of wrongful arrest. There was no evidence that he used greater force than he needed, defeating the student's excessive force claim. As for the use of handcuffs, **the court found "handcuffing is appropriate in nearly every situation where an arrest is authorized."** The fact that the student was a minor did not change this. In any event, the SRO's use of force was minimal. In the court's view, it was not unreasonable for an SRO to seize contraband from a student. Removing a phone that visibly protruded from a pocket was not unconstitutional. As it was not clear that the SRO lacked probable cause to arrest the student, or that he committed any violation of state law or used excessive force, he would have immunity from liability. *G.M. v. Casalduc*, 982 F.Supp.2d 1235 (D.N.M. 2013) (10th Cir. appeal dismissed 6/6/14).

◆   Virginia high school administrators received two reports from parents that a male student had been smoking marijuana on a school bus. Later in the day, the assistant principal brought the student to the office and told him to empty his pockets. The assistant principal patted him down and searched his backpack, shoes and pockets. The school's associate principal searched the student's belongings, including a Vaseline jar, a sandwich wrapper and cell phone. No marijuana was found, and the student was sent back to class.

Later, the student and his family sued the administrators and school board in a federal court. First, the court held the receipt of information from two parents concerning a student smoking marijuana on a bus justified a search. Patting him down and searching his belongings was held reasonable. The search took place in the privacy of an administrative office and was not intrusive. Since drugs could have been found in a Vaseline jar or a sandwich wrapper, the court found it had been reasonable to search them. But the court held the administrator's search of the cell phone was not reasonable. **The search of the cell phone was not reasonably related to the objective of finding evidence of drug use on the school bus.** In addition, the court denied the associate principal's request for qualified immunity. Since she did not link her search of the cell phone to the purpose of a search for illegal drugs, she would not have immunity in the lawsuit. *Gallimore v. Henrico County School Board*, 38 F.Supp.3d 721 (E.D. Va. 2014).

◆   A federal court held a Nevada student who made vulgar off-campus tweets about his high school basketball coaches lacked a privacy expectation in his social media comments. School administrators had accessed his tweets on the account of one of his "followers," so the court held the tweets were being disseminated to the public. While only Twitter "followers" could read private tweets, the court held a person who sent private tweets was still disseminating postings and information to the public. In fact, the court found the student's Twitter privacy settings were irrelevant to the case.

While only Twitter "followers" could read private tweets, **the court held a person who sent private tweets was still disseminating postings and information to the public**. A 1978 U.S. Supreme Court criminal case held that if a person shares information with a third party, he or she takes a risk that the third party may then provide it to the government. According to the court, **a person using Twitter takes the risk that friends will turn information over to the government**. Another federal court had held that when Facebook privacy settings allowed postings by friends, the government may access them through a cooperating "friend" without violating the Constitution. In addition to dismissing the student's Fourth Amendment claim, the court dismissed his equal protection and due process claims as meritless. *Roasio v. Clark County School Dist.*, No. 2:13-CV-362 JCM (PAL), 2013 WL 3679375 (D. Nev. 7/3/13).

◆   In separate criminal cases, two adult criminal suspects claimed their Fourth Amendment rights against unreasonable searches and seizure were violated when police officers examined the contents of their cell phones after their arrests. When their appeals reached the U.S. Supreme Court, it explained that police are typically required to obtain a warrant to meet the constitutional "reasonableness" standard. Prior case law established that police may search a detainee for weapons that may be used to resist arrest. By contrast, a leading Supreme Court case held an extensive, warrantless search of a home was unnecessary to protect the safety of the police officers or to preserve evidence of a crime. In the Court's view, the risks identified in prior detention cases were not present when officers seized cell phones from criminal detainees. Cell phones held vast quantities of personal data. Searching them did not resemble the typically brief search of a suspect.

The Court refused to allow warrantless police searches of cell phones. It issued a sharp admonition to police seeking to view the contents of a suspect's cell phone: "Our answer to the question of what police must do before searching a cell phone seized incident to an arrest is accordingly simple – get a warrant." In ruling for both suspects, the Court held a cell phone search would typically reveal more than the search of a house. It recognized that "fact-specific threats may justify a warrantless search of cell phone data" if a specific risk of exigent circumstances was present. *Riley v. California*, 134 S.Ct. 2473, 189 L.Ed.2d 430 (U.S. 2014).

◆   The U.S. Court of Appeals, Sixth Circuit, held "using a cell phone on school grounds does not automatically trigger an essentially unlimited right enabling a school official to search any content stored on the phone." The court stated that even if checking a student's messages on the cell phone was justified by a need to determine if he was contemplating harm to himself or others, any search was subject to the two-part analysis for all school searches. It had to be tailored to the nature of the violation and related to the objectives of the search. In the court's opinion, the viewing of the student's cell phone text messages was unreasonable. **General knowledge of drug abuse or depressive tendencies was not enough to enable such a search.** Since the school district did not show that a search of the phone would reveal evidence of criminal activity, the court found the search was not justified at its inception and violated his rights. *G.C. v. Owensboro Public Schools*, 711 F.3d 623 (6th Cir. 2013).

◆   A Georgia high school student violated a ban on electronic communication devices by bringing an iPod and cell phone to class. After confiscating the iPod and putting it in a drawer, the teacher left the room, and a classmate took it from the drawer. When the teacher returned, he found the iPod missing and asked who had taken it. After no student admitted having the iPod, all of them were told to open their book bags, turn out their pockets and untuck their shirts. A classmate later confided the identity of the iPod taker to the assistant principal. He avoided confronting the iPod taker to protect the identity of the informer. Although the identity of the iPod taker was already known, the secretary told a student to remove her pants and underwear. The student sued the teacher, district and others in a federal court. In *Thomas v. Roberts*, 261 F.3d 1160 (11th Cir. 2001), the Eleventh Circuit considered a strip search of Georgia fifth-graders for $26 in missing cash. *Roberts* **put schools on notice that a strip search for non-dangerous contraband violates the Fourth Amendment. Officials lacked individualized suspicion that the student had the iPod.** As the search was not based on individualized suspicion that the student had an iPod, a jury could find a Fourth Amendment violation. But as the assistant principal was not a "final policymaker" for the district, there could be no district liability. *Foster v. Raspberry*, 652 F.Supp.2d 1342 (M.D. Ga. 2009).

◆   A Pennsylvania student had his cell phone on, in violation of a school policy. When a teacher confiscated the phone, a text message appeared on its screen from another student requesting marijuana. The teacher and an assistant principal then called nine students listed in the cell phone's directory to see if their phones were turned on in violation of school policy. They accessed the student's text messages and voice mail and used the phone's instant messaging feature. The student sued the teacher, assistant principal, superintendent and school district in a federal district court. It held the superintendent could not assert absolute immunity for his statements to the press. The teacher and assistant principal also had no immunity for the invasion of privacy claims. The court agreed with the family that **accessing the phone directory, voice mail and text messages, and use of the phone to call persons listed in the directory amounted to a "search or seizure" under the Fourth Amendment**. The court found no basis for the "search," as it was not done to find evidence of wrongdoing by the student, but instead to obtain evidence of possible misconduct by others. As a result, it held the Fourth Amendment claims would proceed. *Klump v. Nazareth Area School Dist.*, 425 F.Supp.2d 622 (E.D. Pa. 2006).

C. Strip Searches

The leading case in this area is *Safford Unified School Dist. #1 v. Redding*, this chapter. In it, the Supreme Court disapproved of an Arizona school's decision to ask a 13-year-old student to pull down her underwear and expose her breasts and pelvic area based on another student's statement that she was distributing pills at school. Although refraining from the term "strip search," the Court found the search "categorically distinct, requiring distinct elements of justification on the part of school authorities for going beyond a search of outer clothing and belongings." Further, the Court held "the suspicion failed to match the degree of intrusion."

◆   Santa Fe Public Schools contracted with a private company for security at high school proms. Four female students said security guards subjected them to intrusive pat-down searches as they tried to enter the 2011 prom. Two of them said security guards pulled their dresses up and felt their bare legs. They said the security guards (all females) touched their bras, ran fingers down their dresses and patted down their back sides. In a federal court, the students sued the security company, school district, school board, principal and others. Finding the searches were likely unconstitutional, the court issued an order prohibiting the school district from performing pat-down searches without reasonable suspicion. It also dismissed the claims against the principal. **Less intrusive searching, such as with visual inspection or the use of magnetic wands, would be allowed.** The court ordered the company's guards to undergo instruction by the federal Transportation Safety Administration. The school district was ordered to stop conducting pat-down searches of every student "as a first approach." **Security officers were to use a graduated approach similar to those used by airport security guards.** Only after such an approach, and when reasonable grounds existed, could security guards use pat-down searches.

Months later, the court issued an order finding the "highly invasive" pat-down searches were attributable to a district search protocol. The fact that a private security firm was performing the searches did not absolve the district from liability. There was sufficient evidence and an ample basis for a jury to find a district custom and practice caused a violation of student rights. In the court's view, a reasonable jury could find the school district's practice of suspicionless pat-down searches arose from training or supervision that was deliberately indifferent to student rights. But the court found the evidence was largely circumstantial. In further court activity, the district would be entitled to attack the factual inferences being made by the students. *Herrera v. Santa Fe Public Schools*, 41 F.Supp.3d 1188 (D.N.M. 2014).

◆   A Kansas student was accused by a classmate of placing marijuana in her bra while at school. After being brought to the school office, she consented to be patted down and to have her shoes and backpack searched. After the school resource officer found nothing, an assistant principal told her she would have to search her bra based on the classmate's report. Two female school officials then instructed the student to lift up her shirt and pull her bra from her body, exposing her breasts. No drugs or paraphernalia were found. Within a few weeks, the student "disenrolled from the school" and she later sued the school district. A federal court found no evidence of an unconstitutional policy or custom that would create district liability. The court expressed concern about the failure of school administrators to corroborate the classmate's tip as well as the manner of the search. But it held **the student did not identify any prior cases discussing whether a student informant's tip created "reasonable suspicion" for a school search**. Federal case law did not clearly establish whether a student's tip created reasonable suspicion to search another student's bra. The *Safford* case did not establish that the conduct in this case violated the Fourth Amendment. Having dismissed the federal claims, the court held the state law claims should be heard by a state court. *S.S. v. Turner Unified School Dist. #202*, No. 12-CV-0246-CM, 2012 WL 6561525 (D. Kan. 12/14/12).

◆   An Arizona assistant middle school principal questioned a 13-year-old student about knives, lighters and a cigarette found in her planner. When the student denied owning any of the contraband, the assistant principal questioned her about prescription-strength ibuprofen pills and an over-the-counter painkiller. After the student denied knowing about the pills, the assistant principal told her he had received a report from a male student that she was giving pills to others at school. She denied this and allowed the assistant principal to search her belongings. He found no contraband there but told female staff members to further search the student in the nurse's office. An administrative assistant and school nurse asked the student to remove her jacket, socks, shoes, pants and T-shirt. They then instructed her to pull her bra to the side and shake it. Finally, the two staff members told the student to pull out the elastic of her underpants. No pills were found.

The student's mother sued the school district for Fourth Amendment violations. The case reached the U.S. Supreme Court, which held the male student's report created enough suspicion to justify searching the student's backpack and outer clothes. But asking her to pull away her underwear and expose her breasts and pelvic area made the search "categorically distinct, requiring distinct elements of justification on the part of school authorities for going beyond a search of outer clothing and belongings." Further, "the suspicion failed to match the degree of intrusion." The Court stated "the *T.L.O.* concern to limit a school search to reasonable scope requires the support of reasonable suspicion of danger or of resort to underwear for hiding evidence of wrongdoing before a search can reasonably make the quantum leap from outer clothes and backpacks to exposure of intimate parts." **Despite the violation, this legal area was not so well established as to deprive school officials of immunity.** *Safford Unified School Dist. #1 v. Redding*, 557 U.S. 364, 129 S.Ct. 2633, 174 L.Ed.2d 354 (2009).

◆   Two students in an Ohio high school nursing class reported missing cash, a credit card and gift cards. The other 15 or 16 students in the class were taken to the first aid room, where their purses, books, shoes, socks and pockets were searched. After a search of each student's locker, staff members received a report that an unidentified student was hiding the missing items in her bra. The school director then instructed a female instructor to search the students in the lavatory. Eleven students sued the school district, instructors and other school officials in a federal court for violating their Fourth Amendment rights. The court denied the officials' request for qualified immunity. On appeal, the U.S. Court of Appeals, Sixth Circuit, affirmed the judgment, and the officials appealed to the U.S. Supreme Court. It returned the case to the Sixth Circuit in view of its decision in *Safford Unified School Dist. #1 v. Redding*, above. The Sixth Circuit held there must be "reasonable grounds for suspecting that the search will turn up evidence that the student has violated or is violating either the law or the rules of the school." **A student handbook policy did not create consent to conduct the strip searches, as the district argued.**

There was no waiver of privacy expectations, as some students did not even know about the policy. The court held "students have a significant privacy interest in their unclothed bodies." The severity of the school's need in this case was held "slight." A search for money served a much less important interest than a search for drugs or weapons. The court found the search was unlikely to uncover any evidence and violated the students' rights. As a result, it again denied the officials immunity. *Knisley v. Pike County Joint Vocational School Dist.*, 604 F.3d 977 (6th Cir. 2010).

D. Recent Search and Seizure Cases

◆ A young Florida student saw three older students in a school lavatory "examining" a handgun. He told his teacher that the student holding the gun was a tall, thin African-American with a dark complexion and a "low afro" haircut. He wore a red shirt and "skinny jeans," and was carrying a book bag with a cartoon character or "some type of bling" on it. The teacher advised the principal and school police officer of the description, and the principal emailed teachers to be on the lookout for someone with this description. The principal and officer then walked through the hallways to locate the student with the gun. The suspect student happened to be in the first classroom checked by the officer and principal. The student admitted having a gun and was charged with three offenses. In juvenile proceedings, he moved to suppress the gun and his statements from the evidence, claiming the school officials had no reasonable suspicion for the search. After denying the motion, the court found the suspect student delinquent on all three counts.

The student then appealed to a Florida District Court of Appeal. On appeal, the court explained that **a search may be unreasonable under the circumstances if it is based on a "generalized description" of a suspect that could apply to a large number of innocent people** in the area. But in this case, the court found the description given by the younger student was very specific. He provided details about height, weight, race and skin tone, and he described the approximate age, haircut, clothing and decorations on his book bag. Moreover, the informant was not anonymous. The court found school officials acted reasonably given the grave danger posed by an armed student on campus and the relaxed constitutional standards for school searches. As a result, the judgment was affirmed. *R.M. v. State of Florida*, 129 So.3d 1157 (Fla. Dist. Ct. App. 2014).

◆ Based upon an anonymous tip, a Florida assistant principal removed a student from class and brought him to a conference room. A search of the student's book bag by a school resource officer yielded a loaded, semiautomatic handgun. In a juvenile court proceeding, the student sought to exclude the gun from evidence, arguing the search violated the Fourth Amendment. After a trial, the court imposed a 15-day detention and one year of probation. Appeal reached a Florida District Court of Appeal, which held that tips from informants had to be examined for "indicia of reliability."

Generally, an anonymous tip must have sufficient detail and information that could be independently verified by police to establish a level of reliability. On the other hand, the U.S. Supreme Court had found some circumstances justify protective searches based on a threat of extraordinary danger. Since a person's reasonable expectation of privacy is reduced at a public school, school officials are held to a standard of reasonable suspicion. In the court's view, the search in this case was reasonable. **No reasonable person would contest that the government had a substantial interest in protecting students from gun violence.** The court found the search was no more intrusive than an airport search. Given the student's reduced expectation of privacy, the moderate intrusiveness of the search, the gravity of the threat, and the reduced level of reliability necessary to justify a protective search, the court held the search of the book bag was reasonable. *K.P. v. State of Florida*, 129 So.3d 1157 (Fla. Dist. Ct. App. 2013).

◆   In conjunction with law enforcement officials, a Missouri school district permitted police dogs to sniff student lockers, desks, backpacks and other items that were not in a student's possession. School personnel decided a drug detection search was necessary to address a drug problem in district schools. Searches were held in all of the district's high schools. A student claimed he fully zipped his backpack when he and others were told to leave the classroom for the search. He later said he "felt like the pockets of his backpack had been unzipped and stuff." On this basis, his parents sued the school district, along with school and sheriff's officials in a federal court.

During pretrial activity, the court held for the district and officials, finding their procedures were reasonable. On appeal, the Eighth Circuit noted that the Fourth Amendment demands that a seizure of property be reasonable. What is reasonable depends upon the context. In the court's opinion, the student was not harmed by being briefly separated from his possessions. **A drug dog search was found "minimally intrusive," and the court had previously found them to be an effective means to form individualized suspicion** for further, more intrusive searches. In addition, the court found the district showed an immediate need for a drug dog search based on substantial evidence of a drug problem in the school district. As the lower court had found, the claims against the school officials repeated the claims against the district and had been properly dismissed as redundant. *Burlison v. Springfield Public Schools*, 708 F.3d 1034 (8th Cir. 2013).

◆   A California student who was searched because he was in a school hallway without a hall pass avoided a juvenile court sentence because the campus aide who detained him could not articulate a reason for performing the search. The Court of Appeal of California held that under ordinary circumstances, a search of a student by a school official must be justified at its inception, reasonably related to the objectives of the search, and not excessively intrusive. In a prior case, *In re Lisa G.*, 125 Cal.App.4th 801 (Cal. Ct. App. 2004), the court of appeal held that disruptive behavior alone did not justify the search of a student. In that case, a teacher failed to articulate a reasonable suspicion of misconduct by a student that was sufficient to justify searching the student's purse. Similarly, in this case, the aide was unable to explain a reasonable suspicion that searching the student would reveal evidence of a crime or violation of a school rule. In the court's view, **"a suspicion that a student was tardy or truant from class, without more, provides no reasonable basis for conducting a search of any kind."** As a result, it found the evidence seized in this case was inadmissible and should have been suppressed. The judgment was reversed. *In re Diego C.*, No. B232230, 2011 WL 6740151 (Cal. Ct. App. 12/29/11).

◆   A California student attended a class, left campus, and then returned to school. An assistant principal learned the student had left and called him to the office. There, the student was asked to empty his pockets based on a school policy subjecting students to searches when they returned to campus after being "out-of-bounds." A plastic bag containing 44 ecstasy pills was found, and a state juvenile court petition was filed against the student for possession of a controlled substance. He sought to suppress the pills from evidence on the theory that the policy of searching all students who leave and return to campus during the day was unlawful. After the court held the school's policy was constitutional, the student admitted possessing a controlled substance and was placed on probation. On appeal, the California Court of Appeal held the state constitution recognized rights of students and staff to attend safe, secure and peaceful campuses. School officials do not investigate violations of criminal law and "must be permitted to exercise their broad supervisory and disciplinary powers, without worrying that every encounter with a student will be converted into an opportunity for constitutional review." The policy supported safe schools. The search was done without touching the student, who was only asked to empty his pockets. **As the court found the search consistent with the special need to keep a safe school environment, it found no constitutional violation.** *In re Sean A.*, 191 Cal.App.4th 182 (Cal. Ct. App. 2010).

◆   A Minnesota special education cooperative provided federal Setting IV programs for students with disabilities from six different school districts. Many of the students had serious behavior problems. Each of the programs required the searching of students daily upon arrival. A federal district court held the daily searches of disabled students at these segregated facilities violated the Fourth Amendment's prohibition on unreasonable searches and seizures. The court found the cooperative's programs were educational and not punitive in nature. This distinguished the case from *C.N.H. v. Florida*, 927 So.2d 1 (Fla. Dist. Ct. App. 2006), where a Florida district court of appeal approved of daily pat-down searches at an alternative school where students attended by court order and in lieu of confinement. In the Minnesota case, the students did not attend school in lieu of detention. **A policy of daily, suspicionless searches was unconstitutional under the circumstances.** A jury would have to decide whether daily searches over a course of years was "highly offensive" under state law principles. *Hough v. Shakopee Public Schools*, 608 F.Supp.2d 1087 (D. Minn. 2009).

E. State Supreme Court Cases

In *J.P. v. Millard Public Schools*, below, the Supreme Court of Nebraska held school officials could not lawfully conduct an off-campus search of a student's vehicle. It rejected the argument that driving to and from school created "a nexus to the school" that justified the search. For a search to be reasonable, the court held the district needed the authority to perform a search in the first place. A Pennsylvania court had reached this conclusion in *Comwlth. v. Williams*, 749 A.2d 957 (Pa. Super. Ct. 2000).

◆   After arriving at his school, a Nebraska student left the building to retrieve items from his truck, which he had parked on a street off campus. When the student returned, an assistant principal told him to empty his backpack and pockets. Finding no contraband, the assistant principal told the student he would search the truck. In an off-campus search, drug pipes, papers, cigarettes and lighters were found in the truck. After a hearing and administrative appeals, the student was suspended for 19 days. A state trial court held the school board violated the Fourth Amendment and improperly charged him under a student handbook provision by searching his truck, since it had been parked off campus.

Appeal reached the Supreme Court of Nebraska. Noting school districts only have the powers granted to them by the legislature, the court found the Nebraska Student Discipline Act was limited to conduct "on school property, in school vehicles, or at school-sponsored activities." The court found no right of school officials to conduct off-campus searches that were unrelated to school-sponsored activities. Although the school board argued that driving to school is a school-sponsored activity that has a "nexus" to the school, the court found this claim of authority was too broad. Instead, the court held school authority "was not intended to overlap the authority of law enforcement officers to enforce order on the public streets." **A school district did not have implied authority to conduct an off-campus search of a student's vehicle.** In this case, school officials had all the information they needed to impose school discipline when the student returned to the building. The court commented that if they suspected there was contraband in the truck, they should have notified law enforcement authorities. *J.P. v. Millard Public Schools*, 285 Neb. 890, 830 N.W.2d 453 (Neb. 2013).

◆   A North Dakota school resource officer learned about possible drug use by students a short distance from school, and a security guard was assigned to patrol the area. Two students evaded the guard, who returned to campus and told the resource officer he had "smelled something funny." When the officer followed the students in a patrol car, they walked away. The officer told the principal of their evasive behavior and said he suspected drug activity. The principal questioned one student. He emptied his pockets, which contained a pipe and synthetic marijuana. In criminal proceedings, a state court convicted the student of felony charges. On appeal, the state supreme court held the "reasonable suspicion" standard applies when school officials initiate a search or when police involvement is minimal. **The reasonable suspicion standard applied when a school resource officer acted on his or her own initiative or at the direction of other school officials to further educational goals.** The court found the relevant factors supported applying the reasonable suspicion standard in this case. The resource officer did not initiate the investigation. He notified the principal of his observations and let him decide how to handle the situation. The officer had only a small role in the questioning and worked with and at the direction of the principal. Applying the "reasonableness standard," the court held the search was justified at its inception and not excessively intrusive. It upheld the student's conviction. *State v. Alaniz*, 815 N.W.2d 234 (N.D. 2012).

◆ A New Hampshire school parking lot monitor observed a student walking away from the school. Three school employees caught up with the student as he crossed a field about 200 yards from the building. He said he did not feel well. The employees persuaded him to return to school, where they searched him under a policy applying to any student who returned to school after leaving an assigned area. An assistant principal asked the student if he "had anything on him that he shouldn't have on school property." The student handed over a small bag of marijuana he had hidden inside a sock. In juvenile proceedings, a New Hampshire family court denied his motion to exclude the marijuana from evidence. On appeal, the Supreme Court of New Hampshire found no distinction between a "search" and the treatment of the student in this case. According to the court, **courts and schools are to consider a child's age, school record, the extent of the problem to which the search was directed, the exigencies at the time, the probative value and reliability of information justifying the search, and prior experiences with the student**. Consideration of these factors did not support the state's claim that the search was "justified at its inception." There was no record of a drug problem at the school, and no administrator had any prior disciplinary experiences with the student. Since the search was not justified at its inception, it was held unreasonable under the state constitution. *In re Anthony F.*, 163 N.H. 163, 37 A.3d 429 (N.H. 2012).

◆ A Connecticut school policy allowed police to make unannounced searches on school property with drug-sniffing dogs even without warrants or suspicion of any crime. The policy recited that its inclusion in the student and/or parent handbook was the only notice required to advertise searches. A high school student was arrested as a result of contraband found during a sweep conducted according to the policy. His parents filed a state court lawsuit against the school board. After a hearing, the court found a policy of warrantless and suspicionless drug-dog sweeps on school property without notice to parents did not violate any constitutional rights. It held **the use of drug-sniffing dogs was not a "search" under the Fourth Amendment**, since "students do not have a reasonable expectation of privacy in the odor or 'aroma' emanating from their unattended lockers" and vehicles. Arguing that the trial court should have reviewed the case under the state constitution, the parents appealed. But when the case reached the Supreme Court of Connecticut, they acknowledged their son had graduated from high school. Since he was no longer subject to the policy, **the case was held moot, and the appeal was dismissed**. *Burbank v. Board of Educ. of Town of Canton*, 299 Conn. 833, 11 A.3d 658 (Conn. 2011).

◆   An Oregon student was called to the office and told that an anonymous witness saw him trying to sell drugs. After speaking to his mother, the student agreed to turn his pockets inside out. Marijuana, plastic bags and a pipe were found, and he admitted he had tried to sell marijuana. In juvenile court proceedings, the student claimed any evidence seized by school officials should be excluded from trial because there was no probable cause for a search. Finding probable cause was unnecessary, the juvenile court held the search was lawful. It also concluded that the student was delinquent. Appeal reached the Supreme Court of Oregon. It discussed Article I, Section 9, of the Oregon Constitution, which prohibits unreasonable searches or seizures. The court held school searches are different from law enforcement searches. Only searches involving safety concerns justify a departure from the "warrant and probable cause" requirement. When school officials perceive an immediate threat to safety, they need the ability to take prompt, reasonable steps.

   School officials have wide latitude to take safety precautions when they have reasonable suspicion based on specific and articulable facts that an individual poses a threat to safety or possesses an item posing such a threat. "Reasonable suspicion" applies to searches for drugs on school property. Since officials reasonably suspected that the student had illegal drugs at the time of the search and that he intended to sell them at school, the judgment was affirmed. *State ex rel. Juvenile Dep't of Clackamas County v. M.A.D.*, 348 Or. 381, 233 P.3d 437 (Or. 2010).

◆   A New Jersey assistant principal (AP) received a report that a high school student was under the influence of drugs. After being taken to the AP's office and interviewed, the student denied any wrongdoing. A search of his pockets yielded three white capsules. The AP searched his car and denied his request to call home. The search yielded contraband, including a bag containing what appeared to be illegal drugs. A school resource officer arrested the student, who waived his right to remain silent and admitted that the contraband was his. In juvenile court proceedings, he moved to suppress evidence seized from his car as a violation of his right to be free from unreasonable searches and seizures. Based on a finding that the AP's search of the car was reasonably related to a suspicion that the student had drugs and posed a danger to the school, the trial court denied the student's motion.

   Appeal reached the Supreme Court of New Jersey, which explained that under *New Jersey v. T.L.O.*, this chapter, the school setting required some easing of police search standards in view of the need to maintain school discipline and safety. The court found no reason to avoid the *T.L.O.* standard in vehicle cases, as "the school setting calls for protections geared toward the safety of students." **The court was not convinced by the student's claim to a greater expectation of privacy in his car than he might have in a locker or purse.** A "reasonable grounds" standard applied to the search of a student's car on school property by school authorities. Based on a classmate's statements, the student's apparent drug use, his statements and his possession of pills, it was reasonable for the AP to extend the search to the student's car. As a result, the court affirmed the judgment. *State v. Best*, 201 N.J. 100, 987 A.2d 605 (N.J. 2010).

◆ An Arkansas teacher confiscated a student's cell phone as he was using it in violation of a school rule. Although his parents demanded the return of the phone, it remained in the school office for two weeks, as required by a district policy. It was then returned, but the family sued the teacher and principal in a state court for trespass and taking property without due process of law. The court held for the district, and appeal reached the Supreme Court of Arkansas. On appeal, the parents claimed the Arkansas Code did not authorize the confiscation. The court explained that the section pertained only to the suspension or dismissal of students from public schools. **State law declared that school policies were to "prescribe minimum and maximum penalties, including students' suspension or dismissal from school."** Arkansas school boards have broad discretion to direct school operations, and "courts have no power to interfere with such boards in the exercise of that discretion unless there is a clear abuse of it." The court refused to interfere with the board's decision about the best way to enforce its policy. The family did not cite any authority defining a property right to have a cell phone at school. As a result, the judgment for school officials was affirmed. *Koch v. Adams*, 361 S.W.3d 817 (Ark. 2010).

F. Police Participation and *Miranda* Warnings

1. *Miranda* Warnings

The Fifth Amendment forbids the government from compelling a person to testify against him or herself in a criminal case. In *Miranda v. Arizona*, 384 U.S. 436 (1966), the U.S. Supreme Court announced the now familiar constitutional rights advisory known as the "*Miranda*" warning.

Under *Miranda*, a criminal suspect who is in police custody "must be warned that he has a right to remain silent, that any statement he does make may be used as evidence against him, and that he has a right to the presence of an attorney, either retained or appointed." Police must advise criminal suspects of their rights whenever there is a "custodial interrogation."

When police take a student into custody for questioning, the student must be advised of his or her Fifth and Sixth Amendment rights. The Supreme Court of Pennsylvania has held school police officers are to be considered the same as municipal police. But courts in Texas, Rhode Island,

New Jersey, Massachusetts, Florida and California have held school officials need not issue *Miranda* warnings when questioning students about rules violations. In *State v. Antonio T.*, this chapter, the Supreme Court of New Mexico held that while a school official may insist that a child answer questions relating to school disciplinary proceedings, any statement elicited by the official cannot be used against the child in a delinquency proceeding, unless the child has made a knowing, intelligent and voluntary waiver of rights. The court held its ruling should not be construed to require administrators to advise children of their criminal rights in order to use such statements in school disciplinary proceedings.

◆   A Mississippi municipal police officer came to a high school to investigate damage to a security camera. Security footage captured the image of a juvenile who attended the school. The juvenile depicted on the security footage said another student was also involved in the incident. The officer then arrested the other student and charged him with malicious mischief. Neither the vice principal nor the officer called his parents. The vice principal repeatedly asked the student if he was involved in vandalizing the camera. The officer handcuffed the student and juvenile and escorted them out of school. The student was charged with a misdemeanor and ordered to pay $40 in restitution for the damage. In a federal court, the student and his parents sued the city, chief of police, arresting officer and the vice principal for civil rights violations. The court explained that an action based on an unlawful conviction or sentencing depends upon proof that a conviction or sentencing was reversed or invalidated.

In this case, a youth court had ordered the student to pay restitution and he admitted being present when the camera was vandalized. **Since the officer had probable cause to arrest the student, there was no "unlawful seizure."** Parents have no constitutional right to be notified and present during an investigation or questioning of children under *Edmonds v. Oktibbeha County, Mississippi*, 675 F.3d 911 (5th Cir. 2012). The parents said the police acted in concert with the school by routinely questioning students without probable cause. But the court held they did not show any officers were ever told to make unlawful arrests. The court held the city, police chief and officer were entitled to judgment. Although the school district and vice principal failed to join the motion for dismissal, the court held they would be granted judgment unless there was a timely objection filed by the family. *Bryant v. City of Ripley, Mississippi*, Civ. No. 3:12 CV37-B-A, 2015 WL 686032 (N.D. Miss. 2/18/15).

◆   New Mexico teachers noticed a student was acting drunk and referred him to the assistant principal (AP). She questioned him in the presence of a school resource officer (SRO). The student admitted bringing alcohol to school and then drinking it. At the AP's request, the SRO gave the student a breath test, which tested positive. Only then did the SRO advise the student of his right to remain silent. The student declined to answer the SRO's questions about his possession of alcohol. In a state court, the student was charged with a delinquent act. He asked the court to suppress statements he made to the AP because they were elicited without a knowing, intelligent and voluntary waiver of his right to remain silent. The court denied the student's motion, and appeal reached the Supreme Court of New Mexico.

The court found that under a state law, a child suspected of committing a delinquent act cannot be questioned without a constitutional rights advisory. **In order to proceed with questioning, a child had to knowingly, intelligently and voluntarily waive his or her rights.** If this right was violated, the child's statement was excluded from court proceedings. The court held that the state law was not confined to law enforcement officers. As a result of the legislature's broad language, the requirement of a knowing, intelligent and voluntary waiver of a child's constitutional rights applied to the statements elicited by the AP. There was a difference between questioning a child for school disciplinary matters and questioning based on criminal suspicion. While the AP could compel answers from the student and use them for school discipline, the court held they could not be used in court proceedings without showing compliance with the statute. The state did not show the student had been advised of his right to remain silent, nor did it show the necessary statutory waiver. As state law barred the admissibility of the statements, the court held for the student. *State v. Antonio T.*, 352 F.3d 1172 (N.M. 2015).

◆   A Kentucky principal investigated a report that a student had unlawfully entered school and stolen money from a classroom. He told the student to "tell the truth," and said that a police officer was in the building. The student then admitted being involved in the burglary. After the confession, the principal walked the student to his office. There, the officer read the student his *Miranda* advisory and questioned the student in the presence of the principal and a juvenile justice officer. The student repeatedly stated "I don't want to tell on myself." But he eventually admitted he was involved in the theft. In juvenile proceedings, the student sought to suppress his statements.

The court held the student was not in police custody when he admitted being involved in the burglary. On appeal, the state court of appeals held that while police must issue *Miranda* warnings when they question a suspect in custody, the requirement generally does not apply to school administrators. **As principals are not trained or equipped to perform police investigations, they do not issue *Miranda* warnings.** But when a principal acted in concert with the police, a different rule applied. The principal in this case was not acting in concert with police when he began the questioning, since he was investigating a school matter. But because the police officer repeatedly questioned the student while he was in custody after he said he did not want to answer questions, the court held the confession could not be used as evidence in juvenile court. *A.K.M. v. Comwlth. of Kentucky*, No. 2012-CA-001190-DG, 2014 WL 3887910 (Ky. Ct. App. 2014).

◆   After a narcotics detector dog ran through a California school, a 15-year-old student was sent to the office. A school resource officer ordered her to sit down, but she refused. She said the officer handcuffed her and "slammed her to the ground." The student claimed the 240-pound officer kept his weight on her and refused to let her get up. When paramedics arrived, the student said she had a "swollen and blooded face, carpet burns on her arms, and a broken clavicle bone." She claimed the officer had placed a hood over her head and that her hands remained painfully handcuffed behind her. In a federal court, the student said school employees, including the assistant principal, were in the room when the officer apprehended her but did not intervene. Among her charges were use of excessive force and battery by the officer. After finding the school district had Eleventh Amendment immunity, the court held **there was no authority for a claim that failure by school officials to intercede against police or school resource officers violated clearly established federal rights**. But the court held the student could proceed with a negligence claim against a school employee who was claimed to be in the room when the resource officer acted. The court dismissed all the other claims. *Tasia R. v. Grossmont Union High School Dist.*, No. 13cv2874, 2014 WL 3734475 (S.D. Cal. 7/28/14).

◆   A Minneapolis school security officer and a school resource officer (SRO) approached students in the school cafeteria in response to a report that they were out of control. A 19-year-old student with disabilities said the security officer used a racial epithet and that he told the officer "he wouldn't be doing all of that, all of that without the badge." After the students left the cafeteria, the security officer and SRO told a teacher they wanted to speak to the student in her office. An associate educator who was outside the office said she heard the student yelling and swearing at the officers and that he refused to follow their directions. She said "the next thing I remember is one of the officers had him in a neck restraint," and that one officer said "night, night," or "good night." The student accused the security officer of lifting him out of a chair. He said he struggled to get out of a choke hold as the SRO encouraged the officer to "put him to sleep." The student blacked out. The SRO later denied saying anything like "night night." In a federal court, the student sued the city, security officer and SRO for civil rights violations.

In view of the highly conflicting accounts of the incident, the court held a reasonable jury could find the officers had no basis for requiring him to meet with them. **The court also found a jury could reasonably find the SRO encouraged the security officer when using a choke hold, or at least should have intervened but did not.** In further court proceedings, the officers would not enjoy qualified immunity. The court held a reasonable officer should have known a choke hold on a student was inappropriate under the circumstances and that a reasonable officer would have known to intervene and stop a colleague from applying a choke hold when such a restraint was unprovoked. *Thomas v. Barze*, 57 F.3d 1040 (D. Minn. 2014).

◆ A uniformed school resource officer removed a 13-year-old North Carolina seventh-grader from class to question him about break-ins in his neighborhood. A police investigator, an assistant principal and a school intern were also present. Neither the officers nor any school administrators called the student's guardian prior to questioning the student, and nobody told him he was free to leave the room. After the student denied any wrongdoing, an assistant principal urged him to "do the right thing." The resource officer told the student "this thing is going to court," and threatened him with juvenile detention. The student then admitted he had committed the crimes. Only then did the officer inform him he could refuse to answer the questions and that he was free to leave the room. After offering further details, the student wrote a statement at the officer's request. After juvenile petitions were filed against the student, his public defender moved to exclude the statements and evidence obtained from the school interview.

Finding the student was not "in custody" of the police at the time of the interrogation, the juvenile court found him delinquent. Appeal reached the U.S. Supreme Court, which held a duty to issue a *Miranda* warning arises if there has been such a restriction on a person's freedom as to render him or her in police "custody." Whether a suspect is in custody depends on the circumstances, and whether a reasonable person would feel at liberty to end the questioning and leave. According to the Supreme Court, a child's age and the school setting were relevant to the *Miranda* analysis. If the age of a child suspect was known to the officer at the time of questioning, or would have been objectively apparent to a reasonable officer, the Court held **consideration of age was consistent with the *Miranda* custody analysis**. The Court reversed the judgment and returned the case to a state court to determine if the student was in police custody at the time of the questioning. *J.D.B. v. North Carolina*, 131 S.Ct. 2394, 180 L.Ed.2d 310 (U.S. 2011).

◆ An anonymous informant told Wisconsin school officials that a student had drugs at school. He consented to the search of his person, book bag and locker by a school liaison officer and a municipal police officer. When no drugs were found, an assistant principal searched the student's car and found marijuana, a pipe, Oxycontin and cash. She turned over these items to the police, who arrested the student and took him to the police station, where he received his criminal rights warnings, known as "*Miranda* rights." Prior to trial, the student sought to exclude evidence seized from his car and any statements he made during the investigation. He claimed he was "in custody" of the police at the time he was questioned in the parking lot. If this was the case, it was necessary to read him his *Miranda* rights at that time. The court denied the student's motions to suppress his statements and the evidence seized from his car. On appeal, the Court of Appeals of Wisconsin found *Miranda* **warnings are only required when a person is in police "custody."** Whether a person is in custody depends upon the circumstances. Formal arrest, restraint on freedom of movement, or interrogation that is likely to elicit an incriminating response are examples of "custody" for *Miranda* purposes. Here, while the student was "escorted" to his car by police, an assistant principal was still in control of the investigation, including the search of the car. As a reasonable person would not have considered himself to be in "custody" at the time, the student was not entitled to have his *Miranda* rights read to him in the parking lot. The court also found the search was reasonable under the circumstances. *State of Wisconsin v. Schloegel*, 769 N.W.2d 130 (Wis. Ct. App. 2009).

◆ A Tennessee student told a school resource officer that marijuana found in his truck belonged to him. As they returned to the school building, the student also admitted he had left school to smoke marijuana with a friend that morning. The resource officer took the student to juvenile court and charged him. The student later moved to suppress his statements on grounds that she did not inform him of his *Miranda* rights prior to questioning. The juvenile court denied the student's motion, finding the student was not in police custody at the time. On appeal, **the Supreme Court of Tennessee held that the student was not confined for questioning, and he was not in police "custody."** Thus, his incriminating statements had been properly admitted into evidence. However, since *New Jersey v. T.L.O.* was decided, there has been an increased presence of law enforcement officers in public schools. Municipalities have "blended" the traditional duties of school officials and law officers to protect the safety of students and teachers. Based on the resource officer's duties, a new trial would be held to find whether the search required probable cause or reasonable suspicion. *R.D.S. v. State of Tennessee*, 245 S.W.3d 356 (Tenn. 2008).

2. Liability Issues

In *Chavez v. Martinez*, 538 U.S. 760 (2003), the Supreme Court held courts cannot award damages against police investigators who wrongly induce suspects to provide incriminating information unless it is actually used in a criminal prosecution. Until compelled statements are used in a criminal case, there is no potential violation of the Fifth Amendment.

◆ A seven-year-old New Mexico child with autism weighed 50 pounds and stood just over four feet tall. He had a behavior intervention plan (BIP), but it did not include a physical restraint strategy. For two hours, the child disrupted his class and did not respond to interventions. Calls were made to the parents, but the father refused to come to school because he was busy at work. After locking himself in the school nurse's lavatory, the child ran out and into the cafeteria. A security officer reached the child's mother by phone, and she agreed to come to the school. She consented to the restraint of her child. After kicking the officer, the child sat on the floor with his legs crossed. But while waiting for his mother, he started playing with a rubber band and disregarded the officer's instructions to put it down. The child shot the officer with the rubber band twice. She then stepped on the rubber band, and he started to kick her. After the child disregarded the officer's further instructions, she placed him in handcuffs. When the mother arrived, she demanded removal of the handcuffs and took pictures with her cell phone.

The parents sued the school district in a federal court for violating the Americans with Disabilities Act. Finding no discrimination or denial of a reasonable accommodation, the court held for the school district. On appeal, the U.S. Court of Appeals, Tenth Circuit, found no evidence that the district or its staff took action against the child based on a disability. He had been handcuffed based on his misconduct, not "by reason of his disability." The court rejected a claim that the child's behavior was a manifestation of his disability. It refused to imply a manifestation simply because he had a BIP. Next, the court found no proof that the child was excluded from district services or benefits, or had otherwise been discriminated against on the basis of a disability. No authority suggested a 15-minute interruption of a disabled child's school day was a denial of benefits. Nothing convinced the court that the district knew any lack of training was likely to harm the child's rights. **The court noted the mother had given the officer permission to restrain her child without mentioning particular limits on the type of restraint.** Finding all the claims failed, the court held for the school district. *J.V. v. Albuquerque Public Schools*, 813 F.3d 1289 (10th Cir. 2016).

◆ A nine-year-old Utah student stole an iPad from his school. The principal saw him with it and tried to take it away. The student struggled with the principal and he hit, bit and head-butted other school employees. After the student's grandmother arrived at the school, he began to calm down, and the employees released him. When a police officer arrived at the school, the student was seated in a hallway. The officer told him "we can do this the easy way by you talking to me, or we can do this the difficult way or hard way by you not talking to me." The officer then grabbed the student by the arm and pulled him up. Witnesses stated that the student grabbed the officer's arm. She responded by putting the student in a "twist-lock," which involved twisting his hand to place tension on his arm. The officer then pushed him against the wall and handcuffed him. The officer escorted the student to the office and cited him for theft. Later, the grandmother sued the city and police officer in a federal court for constitutional rights violations.

During pretrial activity, the court found no evidence that the officer immediately placed the student in a twist-lock. It was found that the student grabbed the officer first. Under the circumstances, the court held the use of a twist-lock restraint was objectively reasonable. Appeal went before the U.S. Court of Appeals, Tenth Circuit, which found the grandmother herself had made a statement that the student grabbed at the officer before she applied a twist-lock. Every other witness to the event stated the child had grabbed the officer first. During pretrial activity, the officer denied using excessive force and said the student had grabbed her gun. In finding a twist-lock was not a constitutional violation under these circumstances, the court commented that **the Fourth Amendment does not require the police to use the least intrusive means of detention**. It was reasonable for the officer to try to de-escalate the situation and command the student's compliance with a twist-lock. As the lower court held, there was no constitutional violation. *Hawker v. Sandy City Corp.*, 591 Fed.Appx. 669 (10th Cir. 2014).

◆   An 11-year-old California student forgot his medication for attention deficit hyperactivity disorder. He became unresponsive on the school playground. Due to fears that he would try to leave campus, a teacher called the police. When the officers arrived, she told them that the student was a "runner" who had forgotten his medication. The officers handcuffed the student and put him in a squad car. As his parents were out of town, the officers brought him to his uncle's business. In a federal court, the student's parent alleged state and federal civil rights claims. The family settled its claims against the teacher and school district. A jury found the city and officers were not liable for excessive force and unlawful seizure. The judge found the verdict "inconsistent and incomplete." Further instructions to the jury failed to clarify the inconsistency, and appeal reached the Ninth Circuit.

The Ninth Circuit found no violation of clearly established law and held the officers had qualified immunity regarding both federal claims. But since the judge's instructions to the jury and later attempts at clarification were potentially misleading, the court found there had to be a new trial. Months later, the majority of judges of the Ninth Circuit decided to reconsider the decision. It then issued a new decision finding the chief and the police officer were entitled to qualified immunity on the unlawful seizure claim. But the court held **the officers did not have immunity for an excessive force claim based on keeping the student in handcuffs for 40 minutes**. In denying immunity for the excessive force claim, the court found the student "was doing nothing more than sitting quietly and resolutely in the school playground." *C.B. v. City of Sonora*, 769 F.3d 1005 (9th Cir. 2014).

◆   A Delaware school resource officer (SRO) interrogated an eight-year-old student in a room with a classmate who was accused of bullying. The SRO used the student to elicit a confession of school misconduct from the classmate. The SRO carried a gun, handcuffs and other police equipment. After the incident, the student's parents sued the SRO and other officials. When the case reached the Supreme Court of Delaware, it held the Fourth Amendment was implicated because a reasonable eight-year-old in the student's position would not have felt free to leave the room. This was a "seizure" for Fourth Amendment purposes. Next, the court noted the SRO had said he was 99% sure the student was not involved in the reported bullying incident. He did not contact the student's mother or any school official for permission to question the student. The court found the SRO's reason for questioning was suspect. It was reasonable to infer that the SRO brought the student to the interview room to compel the bully's confession.

According to the court, **the fact that the SRO "shamed" the bully into confessing supported a finding that his seizure of the student was unreasonable**. There was evidence that the student was so upset that he could not return to school for the rest of the year. For this reason, the court held he could proceed with a claim for infliction of emotional distress. His false arrest claim was also viable. On the other hand, the court found no merit to a claim for battery. It returned the case to the lower court for further review of the Fourth Amendment, infliction of emotional distress and false imprisonment claims. *Hunt v. State of Delaware*, 69 A.3d 360 (Del. 2013).

◆ A Washington school resource officer arrested a student after he observed him with a bag of marijuana. The dean of students "took a passive role" during the arrest. As they waited for a patrol car, the officer noticed the student's backpack was padlocked. When the student refused to give him the key, the officer handcuffed and searched him. He found the key to the padlock, opened the backpack, and found a BB pistol inside. In juvenile court proceedings, the BB gun was used as evidence, and the student was convicted of carrying a gun and possessing marijuana at school. On appeal, the state supreme court found educators have a substantial interest in maintaining discipline that often requires swift action. At the time of the backpack search, the officer had already handcuffed the student. Because he was under control, the court found there was no need for swift action. **There is a fundamental difference between a resource officer and a school administrator, based on the objectives of their searches.** Due to overwhelming indicia of police action, the court held the officer needed a warrant to search the backpack. Finding the search was unlawful, the court held the BB gun could not be used as evidence. *State v. Jamar Billy DeShawn Meneese*, 174 Wash.2d 937, 282 P.3d 83 (Wash. 2012).

◆ An Oregon state child protective services worker and a deputy sheriff interviewed an elementary student at her school without a warrant or the consent of her parents, based on suspicion that her father had sexually abused her. At some point, the student said she had been abused, and her father was charged criminally. But a jury failed to reach a verdict, and the charges were dismissed. Years later, the student's mother sued the social worker and deputy sheriff in a federal court for failing to obtain a warrant in violation of the Fourth Amendment. The court held the officials violated the Constitution, but granted their request for qualified immunity. When the case reached the Supreme Court, it held **public officials had a right to appeal decisions that found their conduct violated the Constitution**. This was true even if they were entitled to immunity and would not have to pay monetary damages. An official who was entitled to immunity still had an interest in appealing from an adverse decision in order to "gain clearance to engage in the conduct in the future." Fear of constitutional liability should not unduly inhibit officials in the discharge of their duties. But the student was now nearly 18 and had moved to Florida. As she would never again be interviewed by child protection officials, the case was now moot. *Camreta v. Greene*, 563 U.S. 692, 131 S.Ct. 2020, 179 L.Ed.2d 1118 (2011).

II. DISCIPLINE ISSUES

A. Weapons Possession

This section considers recent case law on student discipline for school code violations and crimes. For new student discipline forms, please see Chapter Nine: Form IV-1: Sample Parent Letter Following Weapons Incident; and Form IV-2: Student Knife Contract.

◆ Minnesota school officials conducted a random search of a high school with a drug-sniffing dog. After the dog alerted on a student's locker, a school liaison officer searched the locker and found a purse containing a three-inch hunting knife. The student said she put the knife in her purse after helping with chores on a friend's farm but later forgot about it. At a school board hearing, witnesses testified that the student was an outstanding scholar who participated in sports and mentoring programs. But the board voted to expel her for the last six weeks of the school year. The state commissioner of education affirmed the decision, and the student appealed to the state court of appeals. It found the state Pupil Fair Dismissal Act (PFDA) permits expulsions for willful conduct by a student. The court agreed with the student that she did not commit a willful violation of the board's weapons policy. It held the PFDA requires not just a violation of a school policy, but awareness by the student of the policy and a deliberate, conscious, intentional choice to violate the policy. She did not willfully violate the school policy by bringing the knife to school and not disclosing that the knife was in her locker after the lockdown and search began.

Appeal reached the Supreme Court of Minnesota. It held the PFDA requires a student to know of a school policy and make a deliberate, intentional decision to violate that policy before the student may be dismissed under the "willful violation" provision of the act. **In sum, the court found the school board did not explain how the student's accidental bringing of the knife to school constituted a willful violation of the school district's weapons policy.** As a result, the court found the board's decision was not supported by substantial evidence. Last, the court affirmed the lower court's decision that the record lacked substantial evidence that the student exposed anyone to actual or probable harm. *In re Expulsion of A.D. From United South Cent. Public Schools No. 2134*, No. A14-1587, 2016 WL 4126377 (Minn. 8/3/16).

◆ A California campus safety officer entered a classroom to ask a student about a stolen iPod. After the suspect denied knowing anything, the officer searched the bags of all students present. A small folding knife was found in a student's handbag, and it was turned over to the police. School administrators suspended the student pending an expulsion. In a federal court, she sued the security officer, principal, an assistant principal and the school district. In pretrial activity, the court found **there was reasonable suspicion that the stolen iPod was in the possession of a student in the**

classroom. After the officer determined the original suspect did not have the item, the court held it was reasonable for him to conduct a limited search of other students in the classroom. The search was not intrusive, as the officer did not touch the student. Since case law did not put him on notice that the search for the iPod was prohibited, the court held he had qualified immunity. Among the student's many civil rights claims was that retaliation and reprisals by school administrators precluded her from gaining higher education financing, leading to economic damages in excess of $1 million. But the court found her assertions conclusory and without sufficient factual detail. **School officials did not violate the Constitution by giving the knife to the police.** A review of the complaint indicated only that her grades had fallen, and an administrator ordered her to pick up some trash that she had not dropped. As a result, the court held the case should be dismissed. *Gallardo v. Hanford Joint Union School Dist.*, No. 1:12-cv-01612 GSA, 2015 WL 641657 (E.D. Cal. 2/13/15).

◆   A Michigan high school freshman had conflicts with a classmate. On a school day, she tweeted "stab stab stab. Going to stab stab stab you today to see your insides, ya ya ya." The classmate told an assistant vice principal (AVP) about the tweets. After investigating, the AVP obtained a written statement from another student who said the student had told her she planned to stab the classmate with a knife she had in a binder. The AVP called the student's mother. The next day, the AVP met with the student and her family. She told them of the charges without revealing the statements. The AVP suspended the student, and the board later met to consider expulsion. The student requested a closed session where she answered questions and submitted a statement from her psychologist. The board then voted for expulsion. The student sued the school district, board members and administrators in a federal court. The case reached the U.S. Court of Appeals, Sixth Circuit, where the parent argued the suspension exceeded 10 days because the AVP made the suspension during their phone conversation.

The court found that even if the AVP had suspended the student by phone, there was no due process violation. **Students who are a continuing danger may be immediately removed from school.** The court found there had been no due process violation, regardless of whether the student had received witness statements. She received an adequate explanation of their contents to prepare her defense. All told, the student had received three opportunities to tell her story, hear the charges against her and present evidence. Rejecting all her other arguments, the court held for the school district. *C.Y. v. Lakeview Public Schools*, 557 Fed.Appx. 426 (6th Cir. 2014).

◆   A 14-year-old California charter school student with attention deficit hyperactivity disorder (ADHD) brought a knife to his charter school and threatened others with it. He was dismissed from the school. In a state superior court, the student sought a special order (called a writ) declaring that the board did not provide him with a hearing as required by state Code of Civil Procedure Section 1094.5. He also said his knife did not meet applicable state education code definitions. The court denied the student's petition, finding the dismissal was proper based on his conduct. On appeal, the Court of Appeal of California rejected an argument that the knife was too short to meet a definition under state Education Code Section 48915.

According to the student, a "knife" had to meet each of the various descriptions in Section 48915. In the court's opinion, the characteristics described in Section 48915 were listed in the alternative. Proof of the court's interpretation could be found in the listing of both folding and fixed blades in the law. As the knife met Section 48915 definitions, the court held the student could not rely on the section to claim he was not in possession of a knife. Next, the court rejected the student's argument that the board order had to be set aside since it did not include any findings. Significantly, the court held the student was not entitled to an evidentiary hearing. There was a difference between a dismissal by a charter school and an expulsion under the education code. As charter schools were generally exempt from the laws governing school districts, **the court held state Education Code Section 48918 hearing requirements were inapplicable**. A charter school dismissal did not implicate the same concerns as a public school expulsion. A dismissed charter school student could immediately enroll in another school. In fact, a letter to the parent from the charter school had advised her to enroll him in another school and had attached his transcripts to facilitate this effort. As the student was not entitled to a hearing, the court affirmed the judgment. *Scott B. v. Board of Trustees of Orange County High School of Arts*, 217 Cal.App.4th 117, 158 Cal.Rptr.3d 173 (Cal. Ct. App. 2013).

◆ Illinois high school administrators received a bomb threat that later proved false. After an investigation, a student admitted that a friend had asked him to write the threatening note. Administrators suspended him for 10 days. At an expulsion hearing, the school relied on statements from other students that had been obtained by the principal during her investigation. As a result, the only testimony supporting the expulsion was hearsay. Over objection by the student's attorney, the board admitted the statements and expelled the student from school and school activities for two calendar years. The student's parent sued the school district and several officials for due process violations. A federal court held that to satisfy the Due Process Clause of the Fourteenth Amendment, **"the expulsion procedure must provide the student with a meaningful opportunity to be heard."** Expulsion procedures need not resemble a trial, as students need only have notice of the charges, the time of the hearing, and a full opportunity to be heard. In this case, the student was notified of the charges and informed of the time of his hearing. He did not present any witnesses and did not ask that any students attend. Under the circumstances, there was no due process violation. *Werner v. Board of Educ. of Pope County Community Unit School Dist. No. 1*, No. 11-cv-1095-JPG, 2012 WL 3562619 (S.D. Ill. 8/16/12).

◆   A Wisconsin student who was expelled for bringing a knife to school continued to use a weight room at the school and pick up friends in his car. A teacher saw him in the weight room and told him to leave. The student became confrontational, swore and punched a locker. Officials notified him that he could no longer enter school property. When the student later drove onto school grounds, a police officer cited him for trespassing. In a federal court, he asserted constitutional rights violations, including interference with his right to travel. The court held the student had no right to enter school property. On appeal to the U.S. Court of Appeals, Seventh Circuit, the student claimed the district violated his due process rights by banning him from school property without notice and an opportunity to be heard. But the court noted that when the ban was enacted, he was attending a private school. **A former student could be constitutionally banned from school as a "non-student" without notice or a hearing.** *Hannemann v. Southern Door County School Dist.*, 673 F.3d 746 (7th Cir. 2012).

◆   A South Dakota student fought with another student and brought a knife to school. An IEP team found his misconduct was not a manifestation of his learning disability. After missing four days of school, he was placed in an alternative setting. His grandmother asked for a board hearing but was told that was not possible because the student was no longer suspended. In his alternative placement, he received two hours of instruction four days a week instead of his usual 30 hours per week. A due process request was filed, and it eventually reached the U.S. Court of Appeals, Eighth Circuit.

In the court's view, the student had been suspended for only four days. The assistant principal had explained the charges and given him an opportunity to respond. **As suspensions of 10 days or less trigger only minimal due process protection, due process had been satisfied.** The IEP team could have placed the student in an interim alternative educational setting if it had chosen. A federal law provision allows an IEP team to unilaterally remove a student to an interim alternative educational setting for up to 45 school days without holding a manifestation hearing based on weapons possession. The provision, found at 20 U.S.C. Section 1415(k), also applies to the sale, use or possession of drugs at school, and to cases involving infliction of serious bodily injury while at school, on school grounds, or at a school event. The team could place him in an alternative educational setting with parental consent. This is what occurred, as the grandmother agreed to the change. Federal law stated that IEP teams determine any interim alternative educational placement. Once the IEP team changed the student's placement with the grandmother's consent, the team, not the school board, "became the decision-maker authorized to change his placement" under 34 C.F.R. Part 300.530(d)(5). As the school district did not violate the student's rights, the judgment was reversed. *Doe v. Todd County School Dist.*, 625 F.3d 459 (8th Cir. 2010).

◆   After a Mississippi student reportedly sold drugs on campus, the school principal searched his backpack and found an item described as either a nail file or a knife. A school district appeals committee voted to expel the student after a hearing, and the school board later met to review the case. At his hearing, the student was permitted to argue that the item was a nail file. But since the item was unavailable for inspection, the board assigned to the superintendent the decision of determining whether it was a prohibited item. He decided it was a knife. The board upheld the expulsion, and the student was placed in an alternative school. Within weeks, he was accused of possessing marijuana. Another appeals committee accepted an expulsion recommendation, and the student filed a lawsuit. A Mississippi chancery court reversed the board's decision, finding the expulsion was arbitrary and capricious, unsupported by substantial evidence and in violation of the student's due process rights. The student appealed, and the Supreme Court of Mississippi found a reasonable basis for the board to find that the item was a knife and not a nail file. The Mississippi Code did not require the school board to physically examine the weapon. **As the student was permitted to speak on his own behalf before the appeals committee, due process was satisfied.** The court reinstated the board's decision. *Hinds County School Dist. Board of Trustees v. D.L.B.*, 10 So.3d 387 (Miss. 2008).

B. Possession of Drugs and Alcohol

◆   A California high school student was sent to detention at least 14 times for tardiness and other offenses. At a disciplinary meeting, he admitted smoking marijuana before coming to school. A school administrator found he was a danger to persons or property or threatened to disrupt the instructional process. She ordered his transfer to a continuation school for the rest of the school year. The student's appeal later reached the Court of Appeal of California. It held state law provided for involuntary transfers to continuation schools "only when other means fail to bring about pupil improvement." But the word "only" was not synonymous with "all," and the court rejected the argument that "all" other means of correction had to be exhausted before an involuntary student transfer. While the student had a fundamental interest in a public school education, the court found this interest was not at stake in an involuntary transfer case.

   In contrast to an expulsion or suspension, the court found involuntary transfer to a continuation school did not deny access to public education. The court held the disciplinary meeting complied with state law requirements by offering the student and his parents a chance to inspect and challenge documentary evidence, question witnesses and present evidence. *Nathan G. v. Clovis Unified School Dist.*, 224 Cal.App.4th 1393, 169 Cal.Rptr.3d 588 (Cal. Ct. App. 2014).

◆   A California school administrator suggested a "sting operation" to trap a 14-year-old student suspected of selling drugs at school. Administrators agreed to a plan that involved arranging for a 12-year-old student to buy drugs from the 14-year-old. But they did not contact the student's parents or law enforcement officials. A school administrator gave the 12-year-old a marked $5 bill and after several attempts, the student was able to buy some marijuana from the older student. Later, the 12-year-old student's parents sued the school district and officials in a state court. A trial was held at which testimony revealed the 12-year-old was still in fear of retaliation by the seller. A jury found he had severe emotional distress due to the conduct of administrators. The jury awarded him $1 million for past and future noneconomic losses, plus $15,250 for tutoring and other economic losses.

On appeal, the Court of Appeal of California rejected the school district's argument that misconduct by the family's lawyer justified a new trial. Even if the lawyer's statements had been improper, the court found they were unlikely to have any effect on the verdict. **In the court's view, there was sufficient evidence to support the damage award.** A psychologist who examined the student found he had post-traumatic stress disorder. The court explained that the standard for reversing a jury award required a showing that the jury was inflamed by passion or prejudice so as to "shock the conscience." There was no such showing of this here. A comparison of awards from other cases was of no value, and the court upheld the jury verdict for the student. *Roe v. Los Angeles Unified School Dist.*, No. B240654, 2013 WL 6451773 (Cal. Ct. App. 12/9/13).

◆   A Massachusetts high school principal claimed a student was somehow involved in an on-campus marijuana sale. He did not disclose the informants to the student's parent. Claiming he had "direct evidence," the principal advised the father he "had no choice" but immediate expulsion. At a hearing, the student did not answer questions, and the superintendent did not present any witnesses or other evidence. She later upheld the expulsion. In a state court action against the superintendent, a judge proposed allowing the student to return to school conditionally, with random drug testing at the family's expense and other conditions including completion of homework. He also required that the student eat together with his family at least three times per week. On appeal, the Supreme Judicial Court of Massachusetts held **the judge did not consider the proper standards for preliminary relief**. He failed to evaluate the facts and did not analyze the student's likelihood of success on his constitutional challenge. As the judge did not evaluate the superintendent's decision and had fashioned his own remedy, the preliminary order was vacated, and the case was returned to the trial court for reconsideration before a new judge. *Doe v. Superintendent of Schools of Weston*, 461 Mass. 159, 959 N.E.2d 403 (Mass. 2011).

When the case returned to the trial court, it held for the school system. **A state appeals court held the student had no viable due process claims.** He did not contest statements by a school nurse and other students, and his silence justified a negative inference. Later, the supreme judicial court refused to hear another appeal. *Doe v. Superintendent of Schools of Weston*, 467 Mass. 1103, 3 N.E.3d 81 (Table) (Mass. appeal denied 1/14/14).

◆   An Ohio school resource officer reported drug activity at school that implicated a student. A search of the student's locker revealed nothing. The assistant principal (AP) questioned the student, and she admitted she had received marijuana from another student at school. The AP notified the student of the school's intent to suspend her for a drug offense and general misconduct. When the student was interviewed, she was not accompanied by a counselor, teacher, parent or other individual, as required by a school handbook provision for questioning by school officials or staff "as part of a police investigation." A hearing was then held, and she was notified that she was expelled for the remaining 55 days of the school year. Claiming that the lack of a representative during questioning was a due process violation, the student appealed to a state court. It noted that the assistant principal knew of a companion police investigation when he interviewed the student. As a result, the court agreed with the student that she had been denied her right to be accompanied during her interview as stated in the student handbook.

On appeal, the Court of Appeals of Ohio found the student was notified of the school's intention to suspend her and was provided with the reasons for this. When meeting with the AP, the student was provided with the constitutional minimum notice and opportunity to challenge the reasons for her suspension. It was clear to the court that the school had met the constitutional and statutory minimums for due process. In addition, the court found no violation of the handbook provision. **Although a school resource officer had turned over evidence to municipal police, the court found this did not convert the assistant principal's questioning into an interrogation done "as part of a police investigation."** As the handbook provision did not apply to the questioning in this case, the court held for the board of education. *Sellars v. Dublin City School Dist. Board of Educ.*, No. 12AP-1007, 2013 -Ohio- 3367 (Ohio Ct. App. 8/1/13).

◆   A New Jersey board of education approved a rule permitting revocation of student extracurricular participation rights based on off-campus misconduct. The rule encouraged students to maintain good grades and abide by all school rules. Extracurricular activities participants were required to refrain from using, possessing or distributing any alcoholic beverage or drugs both on and off school grounds during the season or activity in which the students participated. A student objected to the rule and filed a petition with the state commissioner of education to invalidate it. Appeal reached the New Jersey Superior Court, Appellate Division.

The court found a board's authority to regulate off-campus student conduct is carefully circumscribed by state regulations. Section 6:A:16-7.6 of the state code permitted the discipline of students for off-campus conduct only when reasonably necessary for the safety, security and well-being of students and staff. To be subject to regulation, the off-campus conduct at issue has to materially and substantially interfere with the requirements of appropriate discipline in the operation of the school. The board's regulation exceeded its authority by encompassing too many potential conduct violations that did not meet the requirements of Section 6A:16-7.6. While the board cited the state's Anti-Bullying Bill of Rights Act as evidence of a legislative intent to allow school districts to regulate off-campus conduct, the court disagreed. **In defining harassment, intimidation or bullying, the act reaffirmed the requirement that there be a connection between the misconduct and school activities.** The court held for the student. *G.D.M. v. Board of Educ. of Ramapo Indian Hills Regional High School Dist.*, 427 N.J.Super. 246, 48 A.3d 378 (N.J. Super. Ct. App. Div. 2012).

◆   A whiskey bottle fell out of a Louisiana student's backpack and broke on the floor of his classroom. He told a disciplinary administrator he did not know the bottle was in his backpack and later gave the same account to the police. After the student was arrested for under-age alcohol possession, the school's student council president reported to the school that the whiskey bottle belonged to him and that he had put it in the student's backpack without telling him. The disciplinary administrator did not share this information with other school officials. After the student met informally with administrators, an expulsion and alternative placement for five months was recommended. At a hearing, the student called the student council president to give his account. A board member doubted this account, and the board voted 9-2 to expel the student. Instead of going to the alternative school assignment, he elected to obtain a GED. He sued the board in a state court for tort liability. The court found the disciplinary administrator's failure to tell other school officials the student council president's story tainted the disciplinary process. It held the board had a duty to ensure the correct application of its own policies, and it awarded the student $50,000.

On appeal to the Supreme Court of Louisiana, the board argued that, regardless of what administrators did, the board never deprived the student of due process. He received a hearing and was allowed to present evidence and argue on his own behalf. **While administrators did not properly review the evidence, the court found the student was not denied due process at the board hearing**, where his version of the facts was rejected. As the court held he did not show the board violated his due process rights, the judgment was reversed. *Christy v. McCalla*, 79 So.3d 293 (5th Cir. 2011).

◆   Texas school officials found a small amount of alcohol in a vehicle parked on school property. Under the school district's zero-tolerance policy, the student who had driven the vehicle to school had to be placed in an alternative school. After several hearings, an alternative school assignment was upheld. According to the district superintendent, the student would have been allowed to avoid the placement had he presented evidence to support his claim that he did not know there was any alcohol in his vehicle.

The student sued the school district and officials in a state court for due process violations. The case reached the Court of Appeals of Texas. It held the student did not show the zero-tolerance policy was unconstitutional as it was applied to him. It noted that zero-tolerance policies "have promoted consistency over rationality." Strict adherence to a zero-tolerance policy, without consideration of a student's state of mind, "would appear to run afoul of substantive due process notions." But **there was no due process violation in this case, because the superintendent offered the student a chance to show he did not know about the alcohol**. As the district provided him "an escape mechanism in lieu of strict application of the zero-tolerance policy," his challenge failed. *Hinterlong v. Arlington Independent School Dist.*, No. 2-09-050-CV, 2010 WL 522641 (Tex. Ct. App. 2/11/10).

◆   Several people told a Florida middle school principal that a student had been drinking alcohol with a friend at home the day before. Upon interviewing the student, the principal learned that the two girls drank alcohol before school. A sibling of the student had then taken them to school. A child study committee met and found the student was under the influence of alcohol at school. After a hearing, the school board expelled the student for substantially disrupting the orderly conduct of the school and for gross misconduct in violation of a school policy against drinking alcohol. On appeal, a Florida District Court of Appeal found **Florida law and the school's own policy limited the board's power to punish students for conduct occurring on school grounds or during school-provided transportation**. In this case, the consumption of alcohol occurred at the student's residence about 45 minutes before school began. As she argued, the board could not punish her for drinking alcohol at home.

There was no evidence that the student was under the influence of alcohol at school or that she behaved in an impaired manner. Since the court found no evidence that the student disrupted the learning environment despite her ingestion of alcohol, she could not be expelled under the school policy. As a result, the court vacated the school board's decision. *A.B.E. v. School Board of Brevard County*, 33 So.3d 795 (Fla. Dist. Ct. App. 2010).

◆   Alabama high school staff members noticed a student smelled of alcohol at a school prom. A Breathalyzer test showed his blood-alcohol level was between .001 and .006. A disciplinary committee held a hearing and found no evidence of alcohol possession at the prom. The student was also not "under the influence of alcohol to the extent that he would have been guilty of ... criminal offenses." Based on findings that he drank alcohol on the day of the prom, the board suspended him and sent him to an alternative school. The reason stated was being under the influence of alcohol at the prom in violation of a school handbook provision. In a juvenile court hearing, the court found the term "use" from the school policy meant "to ingest alcohol while on school property or at any other school function." As there was no evidence that the student had "used" alcohol on school property or at a school function, the court held he did not violate the policy. Appeal reached the Court of Civil Appeals of Alabama.

Rules governing student conduct had to be sufficiently definite to provide them reasonable notice that they must conform their conduct

to the expected requirements. In this case, the school had applied a student handbook provision to students who used alcohol shortly before going to the prom. A policy that did not notify the student of possible consequences for arriving at the prom after drinking alcohol deprived him of due process. The court affirmed the juvenile court's decision reinstating him to school. *Monroe County Board of Educ. v. K.B.*, 62 So.3d 513 (Ala. Civ. Ct. App. 2010).

C. Employees

◆   An Alabama band teacher was fired for leaving a pistol in his locked office. He admitted it was his gun and said he had accidentally left it in the band room office while he accompanied the band to a competition in Georgia. At a board hearing, the teacher argued his excellent record justified a lesser penalty. But the board voted for termination based on violation of its weapons policy. A hearing officer later found the teacher violated the board's policy and that the board had authority to discharge him. While finding the teacher's exemplary service record justified a lesser penalty than termination, the hearing officer declined to reduce the sanction. He felt the state Students First Act of 2011 did not authorize him to modify a school board's decision. After the state court of civil appeals upheld the decision, the case reached the Supreme Court of Alabama.

According to the court, the Students First Act removed fact-finding duties from hearing officers and vested education boards with this role. But the standard of review was the same as under prior teacher discipline and dismissal laws. The court held a deferential arbitrary-and-capricious standard of review applied to termination challenges under the Students First Act. This standard furthered the objective of eliminating costly, cumbersome and counterproductive legal challenges to routine personnel decisions. Unlike the appeals court, the supreme court held the arbitrary-and-capricious standard permitted a hearing officer to impose a lesser penalty than a board of education, if the officer found the sanction imposed by the board was arbitrary and capricious. As a result, **the court returned the case to the hearing officer with instructions to review the sanction that had been imposed by the board of education under the arbitrary-and-capricious standard of review**. *Lambert v. Escambia County Board of Educ.*, No. 1130071, 2015 WL 5086453 (Ala. 8/28/15).

◆   Nevada police arrested a teacher at his home for marijuana possession. He maintained the substance was for medical purposes, but he pleaded guilty to an offense and was placed on probation. His employing school district began dismissal proceedings based on immorality, conviction of a felony involving moral turpitude, and any cause that constituted grounds for license revocation. The teacher's application for unemployment benefits was denied by the state employment security division (ESD) based on his guilty plea. The ESD found the school district had discharged him for "workplace misconduct," which disqualified him from eligibility for benefits. After an unsuccessful petition to a trial court, the teacher appealed to the Supreme Court of Nevada. The court found the teacher had not been convicted in his criminal proceedings. Instead, the proceedings were put on hold to allow him to complete his probationary period and avoid the entry of a conviction. Section 453.3363(4) of the state code specified that a discharge and dismissal of this type was not a conviction for purposes of employment, civil rights or any statute or license, or for any other purpose.

When the ESD denied benefits to the teacher, he was midway through his probationary period, so a dismissal and discharge of the criminal case had yet to occur. Moreover, the court held an employer could not use a guilty plea to establish misconduct-based grounds for termination for the purpose of denying unemployment compensation during a probationary period. The school district had relied on the guilty plea as grounds for both terminating his employment and establishing that it was misconduct-based, making him ineligible for benefits. In addition, the school district had changed its stated grounds for termination upon the teacher's entry of a guilty plea. Its amended notice of termination recited that he had been actually convicted for possession of a controlled substance in violation of state law. **The school district had improperly equated the teacher's guilty plea with a felony conviction, and the court found further review by the ESD was necessary.** An employee's termination, even if based on misconduct, did not necessarily require disqualification under the Nevada unemployment compensation law. The ESD would have to determine whether the school district proved the teacher had committed disqualifying misconduct. In doing so, it would not be able to consider the guilty plea. *Hohenstein v. Nevada Employment Security Division*, 346 P.3d 365 (Nev. 2015).

◆ A New York court reinstated an order to dismiss a teacher who entered a courthouse in possession of heroin. After the teacher's arrest, the incident received widespread negative publicity and the New York City Department of Education sought his dismissal. An arbitrator found dismissal was appropriate, but a state trial court vacated the award. When the case reached the state appellate division, it held **the dismissal of a teacher for heroin possession could not be considered irrational, against public policy or an abuse of the arbitrator's power**. The court reinstated his dismissal. *Esteban v. New York City Dep't of Educ.*, 131 A.D.3d 880, 17 N.Y.S.3d 21 (N.Y. App. Div. 2015).

◆ A Massachusetts court affirmed the denial of unemployment benefits to a cook who was fired for repeatedly refusing to submit to a drug/alcohol test. Although the cook denied being under the influence of alcohol or drugs, two school officials observed evidence of slurred speech, inability to control her limbs and incoherent rambling. In addition, the cook had a prior record of poor attendance and threatening behavior toward students. The court rejected the cook's arguments that she was undergoing a "stress attack" and that she did not understand her contract required her to undergo drug and alcohol testing. *Dottin v. City of Cambridge*, 87 Mass.App.Ct. 1103, 2015 WL 264108 (Mass. App. Ct. 1/22/15).

◆   A New York school bus driver tested positive for marijuana. She had no prior violations in 10 years with her school district. In disregard of a collective bargaining agreement (CBA) provision calling for progressive discipline, the school board decided to fire the driver. In an arbitration matter, the arbitrator found the board violated the CBA. He ordered her reinstated, although she would receive no back pay. This amounted to a six-month unpaid suspension. In addition, the award imposed follow-up drug and alcohol testing, evaluation by a substance professional and other conditions. The board appealed to the state court system, seeking to vacate the part of the arbitration award that reinstated the driver. When the case reached the state appellate division, the court found the CBA specified progressive discipline, except in the most serious cases. No "zero tolerance policy concerning positive drug tests" was referenced in the CBA, as the board maintained. Instead, the CBA controlled the relationship between the parties. The court held the arbitrator could have reasonably found the board violated the CBA by imposing discharge as if it were mandatory.

The court confirmed the arbitration award. Appeal then reached the New York Court of Appeals. It noted there were only three narrow grounds for vacating arbitration awards. A court could vacate an arbitration award if it violated a public policy, if it was irrational, or if it clearly exceeded a specifically enumerated limitation of the arbitrator's power. But the court found none of those conditions applied in this case. There was no abuse of arbitrator powers, as he determined that the agreement of the parties did not require termination in this case. In the court's opinion, **reinstatement under the conditions of the arbitration award was an appropriate outcome that did not violate public policy**. As a result, the judgment was affirmed. *Shenendehowa Cent. School Dist. Board of Educ. v. Civil Service Employees Ass'n*, 20 N.Y.3d 1026 (N.Y. 2013).

◆   The Urbana (Illinois) School District hired a teacher who had worked for McLean County (Illinois) schools. At an Urbana elementary school, he sexually abused two students. Parents of the victims sued the teacher, both districts and school officials. They said McLean administrators knew the teacher abused children after gaining their trust through "sexual grooming" behavior. McLean officials were accused of failing to record incidents, investigate reports or timely report abuse as mandated by law. The parents claimed the teacher left McLean under a severance agreement that intentionally concealed his abuses and falsely indicated he had worked a full school year. A court found no duty based on willful and wanton conduct and dismissed the case. Appeal reached the Supreme Court of Illinois.

In the court's opinion, a duty was owed to the parents based on McLean's misstatement about the teacher's work history on an employment verification form. Urbana officials were not told that the teacher was twice removed from his classroom for discipline and had left his job during the school year. **The court held misrepresentations of misconduct created a duty based on the relationship between the parties and supported the willful and wanton conduct claims.** And the parents showed injury was reasonably foreseeable and likely. By falsely stating the teacher had taught for the full school year, McLean implied that his severance had been routine. Urbana officials had no reason to suspect he had left due to misconduct. Courts in California, New Mexico and Texas have found injuries were reasonably foreseeable based on similar facts. As injury was foreseeable and any "burden" of truthfully filling out employment forms was slight, the parents could pursue willful and wanton misconduct claims. *Doe-3 v. McLean County Unit Dist. No. 5 Board of Directors*, 973 N.E.2d 880 (Ill. 2012).

◆ A North Carolina high school student accused her band teacher of making many sexual advances and inducing her into having sex with him. He was eventually arrested and pleaded guilty to taking indecent liberties with a child. In a state court, the student sued the board of education for negligent hiring, supervision and retention. She added emotional distress and state constitutional violations claims. The court dismissed the negligence and emotional distress claims, but it refused to dismiss the constitutional claims. On appeal, the Court of Appeals of North Carolina noted the lower court had based its constitutional rulings on *Craig v. New Hanover City Board of Educ.*, 363 N.C. 334, 687 S.E.2d 351 (N.C. 2009). In *Craig*, the state supreme court had stated that the existence of common law claims that were barred by governmental immunity did not also bar a party from asserting any available constitutional claims. But **the court held there was no state constitutional right to recover damages from local boards for injuries based on negligent supervision of employees**. As the student did not state a viable claim under the state constitution, she could not recover damages, and the judgment was reversed. *Doe v. Charlotte-Mecklenburg Board of Educ.*, 731 S.E.2d 245 (N.C. Ct. App. 2012).

◆ An Alaska teacher arrived late to school and appeared intoxicated. Her principal sent her to an assessment program for alcohol testing. After her blood alcohol level was found to be 0.155, she was assigned to a treatment program. But the teacher violated program rules. She was allowed to sign a "last-chance agreement," but she violated it as well. After the treatment program discharged the teacher, the district initiated termination proceedings. Upon the advice of a union representative, she resigned. The teacher secretly recorded a telephone conversation with a district human resources director in which the director said that the teacher would be ineligible for rehiring. But he added "you wouldn't have anything negative on your record if you were to apply somewhere else." The teacher resigned.

Later, the school district refused to provide a recommendation sought by the teacher for another district. In a state court, she sued the district for disability discrimination, breach of contract and related claims. A trial court held for the school district, and appeal reached the state supreme court. It found the director's promise in the resignation agreement "covered anything negative." As the teacher raised the possibility that the comments violated the agreement, the court reinstated the contract claim. But the court held **the district's refusal to provide a recommendation to other school districts did not violate the resignation agreement**. The trial court would have to reconsider whether the district had immunity. The director's statements could be an implied waiver of the district's right to disclose information about her. But the teacher could not prevail on her disability discrimination claim. The school district stated a legitimate, nondiscriminatory reason for discharging her. Upon learning that she had alcoholism, the district offered her rehabilitation assistance. She was threatened with firing only after she violated the last chance agreement. *Boyko v. Anchorage School Dist.*, 268 P.3d 1097 (Alaska 2012).

◆ Alabama's highest court refused to review a lower court decision allowing a school board to suspend a special education coordinator for possessing marijuana at school. Her daughter had placed the marijuana in her car without her knowledge. Although the employee was not charged with a crime, the board suspended her without pay for 90 days. She appealed, and a hearing officer found she did not intend to have an illegal substance at school. On appeal, the Court of Civil Appeals of Alabama held **the state's new Students First Act required the hearing officer to apply the board's zero-tolerance policy against drug possession on campus**. Since he did not, the court reversed the judgment. *Chilton County Board of Educ. v. Cahalane*, 117 So.3d 363 (Ala. Civ. App. 2012).

◆ Mississippi first-grade students reported that their teacher was lying on her classroom floor with her eyes closed. An assistant superintendent instructed her to undergo a drug test pursuant to district policy. After initially refusing a test, she agreed to take one, and it indicated she had used opiates. She also admitted taking Xanax and Ambien, resulting in notice that she would be dismissed for refusing to take the drug test and for neglect of duty and insubordination. At a hearing, the school board voted for employment termination, based on the teacher's own testimony of a positive drug test and statements by other teachers. Appeal reached the Supreme Court of Mississippi. A district policy defined "reasonable suspicion" as a belief that an employee was using or had used drugs or alcohol. Reasonable suspicion was based on "abnormal conduct or erratic behavior while at work, absenteeism, tardiness or deterioration in work performance."
    The court held state law committed the entire matter to the discretion of the school board. Under this standard, the decision was not arbitrary and capricious. District policy stated the consequences for those who refused to take a drug test upon request. The board had relied on the policy's clear language when it discharged the employee, and the court found its decision was well-reasoned. Since the board had the prerogative

to select the appropriate punishment, the court upheld the decision. *Smith County School Dist. v. Barnes*, 90 So.3d 63 (Miss. 2012).

III. TRUANCY, JUVENILE JUSTICE AND CHILD PROTECTION

A. Truancy

Students have argued that failure by school officials to enforce truancy policies should result in school liability for off-campus injuries. But in *Collette v. Tolleson Unified School Dist. No. 214*, 203 Ariz. 359, 54 P.3d 828 (Ariz. Ct. App. 2002), the court held a school district had no duty to prevent students from leaving campus. Similarly, the Supreme Court of Florida has held that a school's general duty to supervise students does not create a duty to supervise the movements of all students at all times.

◆   Alabama's Juvenile Justice Act required the Alabama State Board of Education (ASBE) to publish a definition of the term "truancy." The term was one of several for which a juvenile court could declare a child in need of supervision. An ASBE rule declared that a student with seven unexcused absences within a school year was "truant" for the purposes of a juvenile petition. However, a provision of the ASBE rule allowed any local education agency to adopt a policy more rigorous than the state policy. Two local boards of education established policies that permitted the filing of a truancy petition if a student had only five instances of truancy. After attendance officers for the local boards filed truancy petitions against two students for habitual truancy, the students challenged the ability of the boards to create policies defining truancy to include a child with less than seven unexcused absences in a school year. Although the students had only six unexcused absences each, the court found both had committed truancy and were in need of state supervision, treatment, rehabilitation, care and protection. The students were placed on probation for six months and ordered to perform 25 hours each of community services. They appealed to the Court of Civil Appeals of Alabama, which consolidated the cases.

The court found no evidence that either student had been absent without an excuse for seven days, and thus no support for finding them habitually truant from school. In the court's view, the legislature had clearly delegated the task of defining the term "habitually truant from school" to the ASBE. **No statutory language authorized the ASBE to delegate the duty of defining "habitually truant from school" to local education boards.** As there was no evidence that the students had violated state law, they could not be found in need of supervision. *K.L.M. v. State of Alabama*, Nos. 2130911, 2130966, 2015 WL 291854 (Ala. Ct. App. 1/23/15).

◆   A Wyoming student missed 36 days of school over four months. Thirty of the absences were unexcused and he was failing his classes. The student's mother did not respond to letters and personal visits from a state department of family services (DFS) social worker, and the county filed a juvenile petition alleging the student was a neglected child. At an initial hearing, the mother appeared and denied the charges. The court ordered the student to remain in her custody under DFS supervision and to complete a summer education program. At a later hearing, the court charged the mother with a misdemeanor for neglecting the student by failing to provide an adequate education. On appeal, the mother argued the juvenile court had improperly applied child protection laws instead of the state compulsory attendance laws. Under this theory, the mother argued the school had to give her notice and counseling before the case could be referred to a prosecutor.

The Supreme Court of Wyoming held the compulsory education laws did not apply in this case. Instead, the case arose under state child protective services statutes. As the state argued, **the DFS and prosecuting attorney fully complied with the child protective services statutes in this juvenile neglect proceeding**. State compulsory attendance laws addressed the duties and did not govern DFS cases. In this case, the mother received proper notice and an opportunity to be heard under the child protection statutes. Since the mandatory requirements of the state compulsory attendance laws did not depend on school district counseling or written notices to a parent concerning unexcused absences, the court held for the state. *In re JM*, 2014 WY 114, 334 P.3d 568 (Wyo. 2014).

◆ Massachusetts high school officials assigned a student to Saturday school for repeated tardiness. He was then suspended for failing to attend Saturday school. In a state court, the student claimed his due process rights were violated by this detention. The court held for the school officials, and appeal reached the Court of Appeals of Massachusetts. It found no violation of his state or federal due process rights. Instead, the court described the Saturday school assignment as "relatively minor punishment" for violation of school disciplinary rules set forth in the student handbook.

The punishment was held "directly, clearly and rationally related to the offense." Next, **the court found no merit to a claim that the discipline violated fundamental family rights to personal privacy and illegally interfered with parental rights and prerogatives**. A claim that punishment invaded privacy rights by demanding a "specific" reason for tardiness was held "specious." It was sufficient that the student handbook required a reason for the tardiness. There was no due process violation, as the Saturday assignments complied with the student handbook. The student received a thorough explanation of the charges and an opportunity to be heard. As the disciplinary process had been conducted with basic fairness, the court held for the town. *Doe v. Town of Weston*, 85 Mass.App.Ct. 1102, 3 N.E.3d 616 (Table), 2014 WL 695743 (Mass. Ct. App. 2/6/14).

◆ A Nebraska student missed 48.14 school days during a school year. A school guidance director sent her family letters explaining that state law banned more than five absences per quarter or 20 days in a school year for any reason. The school requested medical records to assess whether the absences were excused by a serious illness. Records showed the student had been sick, but two statements indicated she was to return to school. No meeting was ever held among the parents and school officials to discuss an attendance plan. But the school referred the case to the county attorney, who filed a petition for habitual truancy from school. A juvenile court found the student was habitually truant. On appeal, the Supreme Court of Nebraska noted that state law permitted a school attendance officer to make a report to the county attorney if a child was absent more than 20 days per year, even if the absences were excused. **Noncompliance with the compulsory education statutes without first being excused by a school established truancy and created juvenile court jurisdiction.** The student's noncompliance with the compulsory education statutes had been proven.

The court found evidence to overcome the student's claim that her due process rights had been violated. The school sent her family many letters before taking action, and the county attorney's office also wrote to the family regarding possible prosecution. Like the trial court, the supreme court rejected the student's argument that the school had to provide the services described in the compulsory education statutes before she could be found truant. **The court rejected the student's claim that juvenile court authority was premised on school compliance with Nebraska compulsory attendance statutes.** Since compulsory attendance laws imposed no preconditions on juvenile court jurisdiction, the district did not have to comply with the services described in the laws before the proceeding was initiated. As a result, the court held for the state. *In re Interest of Samantha C.*, 287 Neb. 644, 843 N.W.3d 665 (Neb. App. 2014).

◆　Two male Mississippi students tried to sexually assault a female student when she left an after-school track practice to use a lavatory in the girls' locker room. On the next day, the school principal advised the parents of the offending students that each would be immediately suspended and that he would recommend their expulsion for a year. Prior to their disciplinary hearings before the school board, the male students obtained temporary restraining orders from a youth court that ordered their return to school.

At a hearing, the board expelled the male students for a calendar year. A week later, the youth court granted a motion by two of the students for re-enrollment. Relying on Section 43-21-621 of the code, the court held the actions did not fit any of the statutory categories permitting expulsion. Appeal reached the Supreme Court of Mississippi, which held the case was governed by Mississippi Code Section 43-21-621. This section permitted a youth court to order the enrollment or re-enrollment of any "compulsory-school-age child in schools, and further order appropriate educational services." But the students were over 17, and thus not of "compulsory-school-age." In addition, the same code section forbade the re-enrollment of a student who had been suspended or expelled by a public school for offenses including weapons possession or "involving a threat to the safety of other persons, or for the commission of a violent act." The section authorized the superintendent to assign students to alternative school programs. Ultimately, the court agreed with the school board that the youth court exceeded its authority by ordering the re-enrollment of the students. **If the board had found evidence that a sexual assault had occurred, this was "without a doubt, a violent act."** *Lauderdale County School Board v. Brown*, 106 So.3d 807 (Miss. 2013).

◆   A group of Pennsylvania students who claimed their school district unlawfully sought and retained truancy fines could proceed with a federal court class action lawsuit against the district. According to the students, the district issued at least 1,489 truancy citations against more than 700 parents and students. While state law limited fines for truancy violations to $300 against the parents of a child violating the state compulsory attendance law, **the students claimed the district sought and retained at least $107,000 in illegal fines**. This included 340 fines greater than the statutory maximum, some of which exceeded $900. A federal court found the students satisfied all the requirements for representing all those in the school district whose rights might have been similarly violated. *Rivera v. Lebanon School Dist.*, No. 1:11-cv-147, 2012 WL 2504926 (M.D. Pa. 6/28/12).

◆   A Washington school district notified a student's family that the student would be reported to a truancy court due to his poor school attendance. His father then participated in county court truancy review proceedings. At a hearing, the court ordered the student to attend school. In a separate action in federal district court, the family asserted civil rights violations as a result of the state truancy proceedings. In a federal suit against school and county officials, the family sought an order clearing the student's record of truancy and contempt findings, compensation of over $3 million, and other relief. In the court's opinion, there was an insufficient factual basis for any liability.

According to the court, a single instance or action by a municipal employee was insufficient to meet the liability standard for constitutional rights violations in cases filed under 42 U.S.C. § 1983. There could be no liability under Section 1983 based on an employment relationship. **Simple dissatisfaction with the truancy hearings and the "sentiment that constitutional violations occurred" were insufficient to support a Section 1983 claim.** As no municipal policy or custom was implicated in this case, the court held for the county and district. *Blevins v. County of Mason*, No. 3:12-cv-05451 RBL, 2012 WL 3815568 (W.D. Wash. 9/4/12).

◆   A Washington juvenile court found a middle school student truant. At her hearing, she was not represented by a lawyer. She kept missing school and at a contempt hearing held three weeks later, a court commissioner found her in contempt and ordered her to perform 10 hours of volunteer work. Over the next year, the student remained in contempt and appeared in juvenile court several times. Various orders were made requiring her to write papers, try an alternative school, spend time in detention at home with a monitor, or obtain therapy. Each of the orders failed to obtain the student's compliance. Over a year after the initial truancy hearing, her lawyer moved to set aside the finding of truancy, claiming she should have had an attorney appointed for her at the initial hearing. The case reached the Supreme Court of Washington, which found state law permitted initial truancy hearings without requiring the parties to be represented by legal counsel. It was significant that a contempt sanction could not be imposed at an initial truancy hearing. Only a contempt petition created the possibility that a juvenile court could deprive the student of her liberty.

As the truancy order issued at an initial hearing did not deprive the student of physical liberty, the court held she had no due process right to be represented by counsel at that point. The purpose of the compulsory school attendance and admission statute was to protect a child's right to an education. No private interest was affected by the initial truancy hearing that would trigger due process protection. While a child should be afforded an appointed counsel at a contempt hearing, the court held there was no such right at an initial truancy hearing. The court held the state law was not unconstitutional. *Bellevue School Dist. v. E.S.*, 171 Wash.2d 695, 257 P.3d 570 (Wash. 2011).

◆   A Maryland student was absent 74 days during the 2006-07 school year. State prosecutors filed an adult truancy petition against her parent for violating the state compulsory attendance act. The parent claimed that the student usually arrived at school on a regular basis. But the student admitted that once at school, she often cut her classes and was "hanging out" in school hallways. The parent asserted that after her child was at school, she was in the care and custody of school officials. The trial judge expressed disbelief at the parent for failing to ask her child about missing classes and found her "involved in" the child's truancy. After the court upheld the petition and placed the parent on probation, she appealed to the Court of Appeals of Maryland, the state's highest court. The lower court had found the parent's testimony both "incomprehensible" and incredible. As it was error for the trial court judge to make an inference that the opposite of her testimony must be true, the parent was entitled to a new trial. Once the daughter entered the school building, her custody shifted to the school.

The compulsory attendance law did not make clear that criminal liability would be imposed on a parent whose child cut classes. While children were at school, their parents transferred power to act as their guardians to school officials. In order to find that the parent violated the compulsory attendance law at a new trial, there had to be "proof beyond a reasonable doubt" that her child did not attend school. Evidence that the student was not in her homeroom when attendance was taken would be sufficient to establish that she did not attend school on that day. *In re Gloria H.*, 410 Md. 562, 979 A.2d 710 (Md. 2009).

◆   A California student and three others walked out of their middle school with the intent of participating in protests against pending immigration reform measures. The middle school vice principal allegedly threatened them harshly with discipline upon their return, calling them "dumb, dumb and dumber" and warning them of the possible legal consequences of their truancy. He also allegedly threatened them with a $250 fine and juvenile sentencing, but this did not occur. After returning home on the day of the discipline, the student committed suicide, leaving a note that stated "I killed myself because I have too many problems. ... Tell my teachers they're the best and tell [the vice principal] he is a mother f#@(-)ker." The student's estate sued the school district, vice principal and others for constitutional and state law violations in a federal court. The case reached the U.S. Court of Appeals, Ninth Circuit. It held **no First Amendment retaliation claim could be based on threats of discipline if it was based on a lawful consequence that was never administered**. The policy of disciplining truancy violated no First Amendment rights, even if the students sought to leave for expressive purposes. Further, the vice principal's words were not a form of corporal punishment, and nothing indicated that he had a retaliatory or discriminatory motive. Finally, since the suicide was not foreseeable, the estate failed to show negligence. The court affirmed the judgment. *Corales v. Bennett*, 567 F.3d 554 (9th Cir. 2009).

◆   The parents of an Iowa student who was arrested and detained in a juvenile detention center could not claim any monetary damages from her school district. The state court of appeals affirmed a trial court decision ruling that **the district had no duty to notify parents that their daughter had been arrested**. There was no deprivation of any parental rights, and the parents had no standing to assert a claim based on their child's due process rights. Many attempts were made by staff to contact them after the student was detained. *Simmons v. Sioux City Community School Dist.*, 743 N.W.2d 872 (Table) (Iowa Ct. App. 2007).

B. Special Education Students

A federal regulation at 34 C.F.R. Part 300.535(a) explains that special education protections do not shield students who commit crimes or juvenile offenses from law enforcement efforts. No federal law prohibits an agency from reporting a crime committed by a child with a disability to appropriate authorities or prevents state law enforcement and judicial authorities from exercising their responsibilities with regard to the application of federal and state law to crimes committed by a child with a disability.

◆   A California student pleaded guilty to misdemeanor theft and marijuana charges and was placed on probation. Within four months, he was charged with five sexual offenses against his nine-year-old niece. The student's probation was revoked, and he admitted to one count of lewd conduct. The next year, he was found unsupervised in the presence of children under 13. After admitting failure to enter a treatment program, the student was ordered to juvenile detention for 77 days and then to his mother's custody under supervision. But his probation was revoked due to absences or tardiness at school and other counts. Following revocation of his probation, the student was ordered into a "level A" placement. On appeal, the Court of Appeal of California held the student had forfeited his claim that he had special needs because he failed to show he had an IEP.

While a report regarding his sexual crimes stated he had once had an IEP, his mother said he received passing grades and was "not a special education student." Despite evidence that the student had a specific learning disability, a later study reported his only identified educational need was English as a Second Language. At his juvenile disposition, the court found no IEP had been established. As a result, **the court had found the student was not an individual with special needs**. But the student correctly argued that the juvenile court should not have ordered him to pay $20 for each drug test. The costs of required testing cannot be made a condition of probation. *In re Jose G.*, No. C076503, 2015 WL 3814292 (Cal. Ct. App. 6/19/15).

◆ A sixth-grade Philadelphia student died from an asthma attack. According to a complaint against her school district, her teacher, principal and other staff knew of her chronic asthma. On the morning of the student's death, she told her teacher she was having trouble breathing. The teacher responded that no nurse was on duty and that she "should be calm." Although her condition worsened, the complaint alleged that nobody contacted emergency medical aid or took her to the hospital. Instead, it was asserted that she was kept at school despite having reported that she could not breathe. Later in the day, the student was driven home and then immediately taken to a hospital. On the way, she suffered a respiratory arrest. Emergency workers and hospital staff were unable to revive the student. Later, a medical examiner declared her cause of death to be acute exacerbation of asthma. In pretrial activity, the court refused to dismiss claims against the school district. **There was evidence that the student was kept at school and denied medical care or permission to take medication.** As an intentional violation of rights was asserted, the court denied the school district's request for a pretrial ruling. A claim for deprivation of life and liberty was also not dismissed, as facts were alleged to support a state-created danger claim. Since willful misconduct was alleged, the court denied the district's request for state law immunity. *Estate of Massey v. City of Philadelphia*, 118 F.Supp.3d 679 (E.D. Pa. 2015).

◆ A New York student with autism and other disabilities attended a public high school at age 19. A teacher asked her about a mark on her face. She said her brother had thrown something at her, and the teacher sent her to the school social worker. Police were called, and the student told a municipal officer that her brother had assaulted her. Although the brother was charged with third-degree assault, the charges were ultimately dismissed. Later, the parent sued the school district, teacher, social worker and others for constitutional and state law violations. A federal court dismissed the constitutional claims against the school district, since the case implicated no official policy or custom. There was no duty by school district officials to intercede to prevent an "unconstitutional seizure and interrogation." **The court found no authority to suggest that an interview of a possible child abuse victim at school violates the Fourth Amendment**, at least where there was no removal of the child from the parents' custody. In any event, qualified immunity was available to school officials. There was no merit to the due process claims. The court held in-school interrogation of a child without parental consent did not infringe on the parent's rights to care, custody and control of her daughter. While the parent claimed school officials did not comply with state abuse reporting requirements, the court held them inapplicable, as the student was 19. Since the complaint did "not come close to stating a violation" of rights, the federal claims were dismissed. The family could refile the state claims in a state court. *K.D. v. White Plains School Dist.*, 921 F.Supp.2d 197 (S.D.N.Y. 2013).

◆ A Missouri student with a learning disability tried to bring a knife to his charter school. He was arrested and admitted to a psychiatric hospital. After the school expelled him, his mother enrolled him in a public school. The superintendent knew of the knife incident and his hospitalization, but didn't inform staff members, and the IEP did not refer to the knife incident. About a year later, the student attacked a classmate with a box cutter and sliced his neck open. The victim sued the superintendent for negligence, but the Supreme Court of Missouri granted him immunity under the Coverdell Act. **The superintendent did not have to provide notice of the student's criminal conduct because the student was not attending district schools at the time of the incident.** Moreover, his IEP made no mention of potentially violent behavior. *Dydell v. Taylor*, 332 S.W.3d 848 (Mo. 2011).

C. Child Protection

◆ A teacher at the preschool of a three-year-old Ohio child observed that his eye was bloodshot. When she asked what happened, he said "nothing." He later said he fell. Under better light, the teacher noticed red marks on the child's face. A lead teacher lifted the child's shirt and saw more injuries. After further questioning, the child identified his mother's boyfriend as the perpetrator. The next day, a social worker took the child and his 18-month-old sister from their grandparents' home. A physician discovered other bruises and injuries suggesting child abuse. The sister had black eyes, a swollen hand, and a large burn on her face. Two of her pigtails had been ripped out of her hair at the roots. A grand jury later indicted the boyfriend on five counts of felonious assault. At his trial, the prosecution introduced some of the child's statements to teachers as evidence of guilt. The court found the child incompetent to testify. But it allowed his statements to the teachers to come into evidence, finding they were sufficiently trustworthy.

A jury found the boyfriend guilty on all but one of the counts, and he was sentenced to 28 years in prison. He obtained reversal by higher courts in the state court system. On appeal, the U.S. Supreme Court found the case implicated the Confrontation Clause of the Sixth Amendment to the U.S. Constitution. The clause excludes testimonial statements of witnesses who do not testify at a criminal trial, unless the witness is unavailable at trial and the accused had a prior opportunity for cross-examination. According to the state of Ohio, the child's statements were not testimonial and should be allowed as evidence. The Court agreed, ruling that in an ongoing emergency, the primary purpose of questioning was not to create a record for trial. In such cases, statements were outside the scope of the Sixth Amendment. In this case, **the child's statements were not made with the primary purpose of creating evidence for the prosecution**. Instead, the Court held the child's statements took place during an ongoing emergency investigation. Finding the teachers' objective was to protect the child, the Court found no constitutional violation and held his statements had been properly used as evidence. *Ohio v. Clark*, 135 S.Ct. 2173 (U.S. 2015).

◆   An Ohio school administrator told teachers to document comments by a 17-year-old student. One of the teachers noted that during a classroom discussion about menstruation and hygiene, the student said her "dad puts her tampons in her and it really hurts her." The teacher also noted the student said "sometimes she and her dad lick each other on the faces and necks" and "her whole family hangs around the house naked sometimes."

In addition, the teacher wrote the child told her "her Dad put her cream on her vagina for her." Despite knowledge of these and other strange comments, the administrator told the teachers not to report them. When the administrator finally made a report to child protection authorities, she added irrelevant information about the father, describing him as "unkempt," "creepy" and obsessed about a boyfriend for his daughter. A criminal investigation of the father was dropped, and he sued the director and other officials in a federal court. When the case reached the U.S. Court of Appeals, Sixth Circuit, it found the administrator's report was motivated at least in part by his protected conduct. A child abuse report that was made for a partly retaliatory motive could be grounds for liability, even if there was some evidence of a reasonable basis to suspect child abuse or neglect. Since the court found a reasonable official in the administrator's position would have understood that she violated the parent's right to be free from retaliation for exercising his constitutional rights, the court held she had no immunity in the case. *Wenk v. O'Reilly*, 783 F.3d 585 (6th Cir. 2015).

◆   A Minnesota parent withheld food from her child and required her to do "written assignments" for hours after school as punishment. The parent received county funding for personal care assistants (PCAs) to care for the child. After school staff members reported suspected abuse to the county, child protection authorities removed the child from the parent's home. A 12-day trial produced evidence that the parent installed cameras in her child's bedroom and used the PCAs to monitor her at all times. She installed an alarm to alert her if the child tried to use the bathroom at night. The child's food intake was closely controlled at home and school. Although she did not like bologna sandwiches, the parent sometimes limited her food intake to them, leading to malnourishment. After the trial, the court found the parent guilty of felony child neglect, continuing through the child's 18th birthday. In addition, the court imposed a sentence for criminal neglect of a vulnerable adult and gross-misdemeanor malicious punishment of a child.

The parent appealed to the state court of appeals, which found support for the neglect findings. There was evidence that the parent deprived the child of food by locking a freezer and monitoring the kitchen via video cameras. She denied food as punishment, and staff observed that the child was often hungry. **A physician testified that providing a bologna sandwich for three daily meals did not meet basic nutritional needs.** The child weighed 96 pounds, was malnourished and had an abnormal absence of menstruation. As a result, the court found sufficient evidence to support convictions of neglect based on food deprivation. Next, the court found support for the conviction for malicious punishment of a child. It found the parent sometimes required the child to write from around 3:30 p.m. until 7:30 p.m. This conduct occurred over the course of seven years. As the "written assignments" caused her emotional harm, the court affirmed the conviction for malicious punishment. *State of Minnesota v. Hinrichs*, No. A14-1895, 2015 WL 9942227 (Minn. Ct. App. 2/1/16).

◆ A teacher who claimed she was dismissed in retaliation for reporting bullying at her school could not pursue an action based on violation of a Massachusetts state law prohibiting employment retaliation against mandated reporters who file good-faith reports under the statute. **The state court of appeals held the law does not apply where there is no evidence of abuse or neglect by a "caretaker."** Since the bullies reported by the teacher in this case were not "caretakers" but were students, the statutory protections she sought did not apply. *Rosseel v. Fay School*, No. 14-P-1278, 41 N.E.3d 331 (Table) (Mass. App. Ct. 12/3/15).

IV. GANGS AND CAMPUS INTRUDERS

A. Civil Cases

◆ A Georgia school resource officer (SRO) confronted three students who were loitering in a school hallway and told them to come with him to the school office. A student became defiant and profane and shoved the SRO when he tried to handcuff him. Another SRO then arrived, and the officers took the student to the floor and handcuffed him. After being brought to the school office, the student continued his combative, loud, and profane behavior. He disparaged and threatened an SRO before being taken to a youth detention center for three days. A school administrator later advised the parents that the student was not suspended and could return to school after his release from juvenile detention. After the student returned to school, the board held an expulsion hearing. At his hearing, the student said he hit the SRO in self-defense. But the hearing officer found he violated the student code. Before the board of education, the student asserted violation of a state code provision requiring a school disciplinary hearing within 10 days of a suspension. Adopting the hearing officer's findings, the board modified the discipline by finding the disciplinary action "complete" as of the date of its decision. Appeal reached the Court of Appeals of Georgia.

The court noted that at the school disciplinary hearing, the student said he acted in self-defense. But he was not suspended before his disciplinary hearing. He was instead told he could return to school upon release from detention. **According to the court, law enforcement and juvenile officers could not cause a school "suspension."** This defeated the claim that his school hearing was not held within 10 days of a "suspension" and was untimely. There was "more than sufficient evidence" in this case that the student had cursed and repeatedly refused to follow the SRO's directions. As the evidence justified a suspension, the court held for the board. **State law permitted school administrators to report student criminal action to a law enforcement agency or officer for investigation.** *Fulton County Board of Educ. v. D.R.H.*, 325 Ga.App. 53, 752 S.E.2d 103 (Ga. 2013).

◆   After a Kentucky child was picked up from school by an unauthorized individual, the parent sued the education board and superintendent for negligence. The case reached the Court of Appeals of Kentucky, which stated that immunity applied to the board if it was performing a "governmental function." Here, the board's after-school pick-up and drop-off policy directly furthered the education of students, which was a governmental function. So the board was entitled to immunity. According to the parent, the superintendent did not investigate, take disciplinary action or enact policies to prevent future incidents. But the court held these alleged failures did not strip the superintendent of immunity. **Nothing in the complaint alleged any failure by the superintendent to exercise personal discretion, in good faith and within the scope of his authority.** Both the school board and superintendent were entitled to immunity. *Breathitt County Board of Educ. v. Combs*, No. 2009-CA-000607-MR, 2010 WL 3515747 (Ky. Ct. App. 9/10/10).

◆   A Minnesota kindergartner said that he did not want to go outside with his class for recess. He stayed in a supervised detention room in the school office, but an aide instructed him to use a lavatory down the hallway instead of the one in the detention area. While in the lavatory, the kindergartner was sexually assaulted by a recent high school graduate who had been inside the school several times in the days before the assault. He entered the school through a side door without signing in and obtaining a visitor badge. The kindergartner's mother sued the school district for negligent supervision and failure to have and enforce a specific policy on school security. A court denied pretrial judgment on the negligent supervision claim, and the Court of Appeals of Minnesota agreed that a trial was required on that issue. The aide had let the kindergartner go unaccompanied to a restroom outside a detention room equipped with its own lavatory, and the graduate somehow got in the school building without signing in and wearing a badge. But the school district was entitled to immunity for not having a specific policy to protect elementary children from intruders. **These decisions took place at the planning level and involved the evaluation of financial, political, economic and social factors.** *Doe v. Independent School Dist. No. 2154*, No. A09-2235, 2010 WL 3545585 (Minn. Ct. App. 9/14/10).

◆　Gang activities at a West Virginia high school escalated when a gang leader was arrested for shooting a police officer. Gang members verbally assaulted the faculty and staff at school, and fights and disturbances became prevalent. The principal advised staff members that the slogan "Free A-Train" was banned. A student wrote "Free A-Train" on his hands several times and was suspended for 10 days. He sued the school board in a federal district court for speech rights violations. The court held schools may ban gang-related clothing if evidence indicates a potentially disruptive gang presence and gang-related disturbances. Recent federal cases suggest schools may regulate expression if they can reasonably forecast material and substantial disruption at school. This defeated the student's claim that speech must lead to an actual disruption before school administrators may suppress it. As students and parents had expressed fear over the use of the slogan, administrators could reasonably forecast that allowing the student to keep displaying it may have exacerbated the tensions and increased these fears. **The court held the "distraction from classes or intimidation from passive displays of support may serve as the basis of a disruption,"** and found no speech rights violation. *Brown v. Cabell County Board of Educ.*, 714 F.Supp.2d 587 (S.D. W.Va. 2010).

◆　Nine North Carolina students sued the Durham Public School System, asserting a "wholesale challenge" to its disciplinary process. They claimed that they were disciplined more severely than white students for less serious offenses. In addition, the students claimed that the board's anti-gang policy was unconstitutionally vague. A state trial court dismissed the action, and the students appealed. The Court of Appeals of North Carolina held that most of the claims had been properly dismissed, as each individual student failed to allege a claim for relief against each individual official. But the lower court would have to reconsider a due process claim brought on behalf of a now-deceased student who had been suspended for 13 days. His mother claimed that the superintendent of schools misled her and backdated correspondence to make a long-term suspension appear to be a short-term suspension. The trial court was also to reconsider a challenge to the school board's anti-gang policy. On appeal, the Supreme Court of North Carolina held the student had an adequate remedy under state law. So he could not sue the board for due process violations. Here, two **North Carolina statutes allowed any student who was suspended in excess of 10 school days to appeal to the education board, and then to a state court**. The court did not consider the gang policy issue, which was to return to the trial court. *Copper v. Denlinger*, 688 S.E.2d 426 (N.C. 2010).

◆   A California student was attacked by eight males while he walked past the school gymnasium. A second student was assaulted by three others while approaching a school exit. Both students suffered substantial injuries, and their guardian sued the school district in a state court for negligence. She also asserted violation of a mandatory duty to supervise students found in California Government Code Section 815.6 and California Education Code Section 44807. The guardian claimed the officials were indifferent to reports of threats against the students, and that daily brawls and rampant gang activity were seen at the school. The court held for the district and officials.

The guardian appealed to the Court of Appeal of California. The court noted superior court findings that **the guardian did not show the assaults would not have occurred had the officials increased their security measures**. In premises liability cases, the person seeking damages must produce "non-speculative evidence" and show a causal link between the injury and the failure to provide adequate security measures. The guardian failed to show the officials caused the injuries to the students arising from the third-party attacks. She did not show it was more probable than not that additional security precautions would have prevented the attacks. Similarly, the guardian was unable to prove the breach of a mandatory duty to protect the students. The court affirmed the judgment for the district and officials. *Castaneda v. Inglewood Unified School Dist.*, No. B198829, 2008 WL 2720631 (Cal. Ct. App. 7/14/08) (Unpublished).

B. Criminal Proceedings

In *Edmonds v. Oktibbeha County, Mississippi*, 675 F.3d 911 (5th Cir. 2012), the U.S. Court of Appeals, Fifth Circuit, held **parents have no constitutional right to be notified and present during an investigation or questioning of their children by police officers**.

A 2015 Tennessee state law amendment clarifies that a student may be suspended for off-campus criminal behavior that results in charges of an offense that would be a felony if a student was an adult. The student's presence in school must be found to pose a danger or threaten disruption. The amendment clarifies the power of school directors to expel a student when a criminal or juvenile complaint is issued for a violent felony. A school director may also send students to alternative schools. A student who is adjudicated delinquent or convicted of a violent felony may be expelled if it is found the student's continued presence would have a substantial detrimental effect on the school's general welfare. One-Hundred-Ninth Tennessee General Assembly, Ch. 501, H.B. 174.Tennessee Code Title 49.

◆   A Louisiana security guard wanded a student at her school with a metal detector. The search revealed a concealed knife, razor blade and can of mace on her person. Police were summoned, and they arrested the student and confiscated the items. In a juvenile court, charges were filed against the student for illegally carrying a weapon. The court found the student guilty of the charges. She was placed on probation with special conditions for six months. On appeal to the Court of Appeal of Louisiana, the student claimed she could not be convicted under a state law prohibiting the carrying of a firearm or dangerous weapon onto school property. She said the law required possession of a firearm or a dangerous weapon and so did not apply to the carrying of a knife, razor blade or a can of mace to school.

According the student, the state's argument would criminalize the carrying of pocket knives and other everyday "school supplies" to school. The court found that while pocket knives and utility blades had innocent uses, these items could not be dismissed as "standard school supplies." **The court found the concealment of items on the student's person suggested that she foresaw using them as weapons.** As a result, the evidence was sufficient to support the juvenile delinquency charges. *State of Louisiana In the Interest of R.D.*, 158 So.3d 936 (La. Ct. App. 2015).

◆   An intruder entered an office at a Missouri university, saying he wanted to enroll. He acted strangely when he met with a professor. When a university assistant asked him to leave, he slammed the door to the office. The assistant hit a panic button to summon security, and the intruder ran out of the building. He went to the psychology professor, apologized to her and left a written marriage proposal on her desk. When security personnel found the intruder, he told them he was from Homeland Security and said the university had failed a test because he was able to drive onto the campus. As he became more and more agitated, his comments became increasingly bizarre, and police arrested him for trespassing. The intruder told police he had explosives in his truck, which was parked on university property. The campus was evacuated, and a bomb squad was called. After a thorough search that included the use of a robot, no explosives were found.

The intruder was charged in a state court with making a terroristic threat. A jury found him guilty and sentenced him to three years in jail. On appeal, the Court of Appeals of Missouri rejected the argument that the statute did not apply to false reports of explosives. **The threat involved a "condition involving danger to life," which is an element of the crime.** As the evidence was sufficient to show the intruder consciously disregarded a substantial risk of causing the evacuation of the university, his conviction was affirmed. *State v. Tanis*, 247 S.W.3d 610 (Mo. Ct. App. 2008).

◆   A Kansas municipal police officer confronted a jogger whose dog was running loose on school grounds. The jogger was placing items from the trunk of her parked car into an athletic bag on the ground next to her car at the time. When the officer looked down, he saw a handgun case in the athletic bag. After questioning the jogger, the officer recovered a 9 mm handgun from her and informed her that it was illegal to have a firearm on school property. The gun was not loaded, and the magazine clip was empty.

The jogger stated she did not have any ammunition in her possession. A state court considered a criminal charge of possessing a firearm on school property in violation of Kansas law. The court held that since school was not in session at the time of the offense, the jogger should be acquitted of the charge. The state appealed to the Court of Appeals of Kansas, which noted that trial courts are not permitted to inquire into legislative intent, unless there is ambiguity or lack of clarity. In this case, state law declared that possession of a firearm by any person (other than a law enforcement officer) on any school property or grounds was a criminal offense. No exception applied to this case. **The court held that whether school was in session was irrelevant to the outcome of this case.** If the jogger's argument was correct, a sniper arriving on school grounds would not violate state law until a student actually arrived on school property or if classes were in session. As a result, the court reversed the judgment. *State of Kansas v. Toler,* 41 Kan.App.2d 986, 206 P.3d 548 (Kan. Ct. App. 2009).

◆   A Florida statute makes it unlawful for any person to enter a "school safety zone" without legitimate business or authorization at the school from one hour prior to the start of school until one hour after the end of school. The statute allowed those with authorization or legitimate business at a school to remain in a school zone. A state district court of appeal upheld trespassing and resisting arrest charges against a Miami-area high school student who was spotted walking away from the campus of a school he did not attend. The court held the student did not show that those seeking to engage in protected speech or assemblies could not receive "authorization." He did not show that persons who had received notices barring them from school safety zones have any First Amendment rights to return to a school safety zone. **The law was clearly intended to protect children, which is a compelling government interest.** The court affirmed the order declaring the student a juvenile delinquent. *J.L.S. v. State,* 947 So.2d 641 (Fla. Dist. Ct. App. 2007). The Supreme Court of Florida let the decision stand in *J.L.S. v. State,* 958 So.2d 919 (Fla. 2007).

CHAPTER FIVE

Employment

I. HIRING PRACTICES

A huge part of school safety depends on having competent and trustworthy staff – and that starts with good hiring practices.

Take background checks, for example. They are acknowledged to be so important that an increasing number of states and localities require them even for school volunteers. Some have started running them for all visitors to school.

Where job applicants are concerned, the requirement for background checks may be out of your hands. You may simply have to follow the state laws, collective bargaining agreements or other rules that dictate the procedure. But one area that may be within your discretion is checking an applicant's references.

Few people enjoy making the calls to check references, but it's an important step toward having a safe school. And like a failure to run background checks, a failure to check references for an employee that later goes south and hurts someone can come back to haunt a district, diocese, HR department, school or administrator by way of a lawsuit.

The injured parties may bring a negligent hiring suit to claim that running the background check or talking to references could have revealed an important reason not to hire the applicant.

A. Negligent Hiring

◆ A student's mother claimed a school security guard groomed her daughter for a sexual relationship and ultimately impregnated the girl. The mother alleged the security guard's conduct permanently destroyed her relationship with her daughter. She sued the school district to recover damages on her own behalf, not her daughter's. Among other things, she accused the district of negligently hiring him. The trial court dismissed the claim, finding the district owed a duty to protect only a student from negligent hires, not a parent. But a Washington state appeals court reversed the dismissal. Under Washington law, **an employer's duty to exercise care in hiring was owed to "foreseeable victims" of its negligence**. The appeals court allowed the claim because "it is possible to conceive of facts under which it would be foreseeable to the District that if [the security guard] was engaging in sexual conduct with a student, that conduct might harm the parent's relationship with the student." *Evans v. Tacoma School Dist. No. 10*, No. 47612-6-II, 2016 WL 3853744 (Wash. Ct. App. 7/12/16).

◆ Just after his January hire, a new assistant principal pulled a 16- or 17-year-old special ed student out of class to talk to her about a bullying problem she'd reported. When he ran into her a few days later, they exchanged phone numbers. He texted her that day. That night, he picked her up at home and drove her to a hotel, where they had sex. The sexual relationship continued, and he sometimes pulled her out of class, prompting classmates to roll their eyes and call her a "whore" and a "home-wrecker." In April, teachers told the principal they suspected an improper relationship, but the student denied it, as did other students the principal questioned. But after a different student reported the relationship to a school resource officer in September, the police investigated and arrested the assistant principal. The student and her mother then sued the superintendent and principal for negligent hiring in violation of Pennsylvania law. They alleged school officials didn't adequately check his background so didn't discover he'd pled guilty to a disorderly conduct offense of inducing a minor to buy alcohol. While **that was a different offense, the court found "it does indicate a history of targeting minors"** so found it suggested the school defendants negligently hired him. However, the court dismissed the claim, finding the student and her mother didn't allege the malice or willful misconduct required to strip the defendants of their state-law immunity from negligence claims. *M.S. ex rel. Hall v. Susquehanna Township School Dist.*, 43 F.Supp.3d 412 (M.D. Pa. 2014).

◆ The mother of an eight-year-old Louisiana student dropped her daughter off at around 7:20 a.m. for the school breakfast, which was to be served at 7:30. A janitor stopped the student on the way in and told her that a teacher wanted to see her. He led her to an upstairs classroom, put a towel over her head, told her to bare one foot and touched her with a part of his body that wasn't his hand. She reported the incident despite his warning not to, and her mother sued the school board for vicarious liability and negligence in its retention/supervision of the janitor. A court granted pretrial judgment to the school board, but the court of appeal reversed, finding issues of fact that required a trial. However, the court did state that **the board could not be liable for negligent hiring of the janitor because it performed a background check on him and found no criminal record**. *Booth v. Orleans Parish School Board*, 49 So.3d 919 (La. Ct. App. 2010).

◆   An Indiana high school teacher had a sexual relationship with a student during her freshman and sophomore years. When the school discovered this two years after the fact, it promptly suspended the teacher, who later pleaded guilty to sexual battery and resigned. The student's parents sued the district for negligent hiring. A federal court ruled against them, and the Seventh Circuit affirmed. Although the parents asserted he'd assaulted two former students prior to his hire – marrying one of them – the school never learned of those relationships. It received positive references from the teacher's previous employer and interviewed him several times. He also possessed a valid teaching license and was not on a list of known sex offenders. And there was no indication that the former student he married had been in a sexual relationship with him while he was her teacher. Thus, **the school's thorough hiring procedures protected it from the claim of negligent hiring**. *Hansen v. Board of Trustees of Hamilton Southeastern School Corp.*, 551 F.3d 599 (7th Cir. 2008).

◆   A Tennessee school district hired a school cafeteria worker as a cheerleading sponsor. Although she did not have a teaching certificate, she supervised the cheerleading squad for two and a half years without incident. She attended cheerleading camps, and she obtained training and assistance from a previous squad sponsor. One day, while the sponsor left to attend to other duties, the cheerleading squad warmed up for a pep rally. A cheerleader broke her arm when she landed on the ground while attempting to perform a "basket toss" maneuver. She sued the school board and the sponsor for negligent hiring and negligent supervision. The school board claimed immunity under the state's tort liability act. A trial court found that the board was not entitled to immunity, but it granted pretrial judgment to the defendants. The Tennessee Court of Appeals reversed in part. It held that **the school board could not be liable for negligent hiring because there was no causal connection between the sponsor's lack of experience and the injury**. The injured cheerleader failed to show that the sponsor's experience was inadequate or fell below an established standard of care. However, there was a question of fact regarding the negligent supervision issue. This required a trial. *Britt v. Maury County Board of Educ.*, No. M2006-01921-COA-R3-CV, 2008 WL 4427190 (Tenn. Ct. App. 9/29/08).

B. Background Checks

◆   After child porn was found on a special-needs teaching aide's computer, the principal identified a "non-verbal and almost non-communicative" student in one image. The aide was convicted of offenses related to secretly viewing or recording another person without consent, and the child's parents sued the district for negligence. The principal testified she'd contacted his previous employers. Under Arizona law, **a public employer had immunity for claims based on an employee's felony unless it knew about the employee's propensity to commit the crime**. After the parents discovered a prior employer had fired him for touching a patient's vagina and telling her "she felt moist[,]" they claimed the propensity exception applied. They argued the principal should be deemed to know why the previous employer fired the aide, thus informed of his criminal propensity. But the trial court granted the district summary judgment, and an appeals court affirmed, finding the exception only applied if the district actually knew of his criminal propensity. The parents didn't show it did. *Gallagher v. Tucson Unified School Dist.*, 349 P.3d 228 (Ariz. Ct. App. 2015).

◆ A man lost his job after the New York City Department of Education (DOE) refused to certify him as a school bus driver. His application disclosed he'd been convicted of two drug-related felonies 16 years prior and three misdemeanor thefts – the most recent 13 years ago when he was 41. He explained the crimes were related to a drug addiction he'd since overcome. DOE denied his application, deciding **the seriousness of his crimes and the mature age when he committed them made him unsuitable to have authority over children in the largely "unsupervised environment of a school bus."** He sued, alleging the district violated a state law banning unfair discrimination based on past criminal convictions. The trial court found in his favor, but an appeals court reversed – and the state's highest court affirmed. The law didn't create an entitlement to licensure or employment, and it included a safety exception. To overturn the denial, the bus driver had to show the district's decision was arbitrary or capricious. He couldn't. *Dempsey v. New York City Dep't of Educ.*, 33 N.E.3d 485 (N.Y. 2015).

◆ A Florida teacher applied for a high school teaching job using the district's paper application process. He was offered a position even though he had disclosed two prior DUI convictions. He rejected the offer and taught elsewhere. Two years later, after his application with the district expired, he reapplied using the district's new electronic application process. This time he failed to disclose his DUIs. Again he was offered a job. However, when the district conducted a criminal background check, it discovered the teacher's criminal record. Without revealing any specifics, the district's human resources (HR) director notified the principal and a vice principal that the teacher's application was not accurate. The HR director disqualified the teacher and rescinded the job offer. A school district committee reconsidered hiring the teacher, but **required proof of treatment to fulfill obligations under its safe and drug-free workplace policy**. He submitted proof of treatment the day after another teacher was hired. When he sued for disability discrimination, the Florida District Court of Appeal ruled against him. It held that the district's policy was neutral and that he failed to prove discrimination. *St. Johns County School Dist. v. O'Brien*, 973 So.2d 535 (Fla. Dist. Ct. App. 2007).

◆ A charter school freshman claimed the dean of students sexually assaulted her on campus during school hours. She sued the school on multiple grounds, including negligence. A state court granted the school judgment, finding it was entitled to immunity and the dean's conduct was outside the scope of his employment. The court of appeals affirmed. The school ran a criminal background check before hiring the dean. It revealed an arrest for insurance fraud but no criminal convictions. Importantly, **the criminal background check didn't reveal he'd ever been arrested for or convicted of criminal sexual conduct**. As the dean's conduct wasn't foreseeable, the ruling in the school's favor was proper. *Wilson ex rel. Wilson v. Detroit School of Industrial Arts*, No. 265508, 2006 WL 1237033 (Mich. Ct. App. 5/9/06).

II. POST-HIRING ISSUES

Under most state laws, employers can be held liable for negligent supervision or retention if the employer knows or should have known of an employee's unfitness and doesn't act – such as by investigating, discharging or reassigning the employee.

Public employers, like school districts, can often be held liable for an employee's negligence while acting within the scope of his or her employment. But if an employee is exercising discretion with respect to school safety and not acting in bad faith, maliciously or with a conscious indifference to the rights of others, the employee will probably be entitled to state-law immunity from suit.

A. Immunity

◆ An assistant principal found contraband, including knives and a cigarette, in an Arizona middle school student's day planner. The student denied that the contraband was hers and also denied distributing drugs to fellow students, but agreed to let him search her belongings. He searched her backpack and found nothing. He then had an administrative assistant take her to the nurse's office, where the nurse and administrative assistant made her strip to her underwear, then asked her to pull her bra out and shake it, and to pull out the elastic on her underpants, exposing her breasts and pelvic area to some degree. They found nothing. She and her mother sued for Fourth Amendment violations, and the case reached the U.S. Supreme Court. The Court held that the strip search violated the Fourth Amendment because the assistant principal did not have sufficient suspicion to justify its extent. However, **the law was not clearly established at the time of the search**. Thus, the assistant principal, the administrative assistant and the nurse were entitled to qualified immunity. Only the district could be liable for the Fourth Amendment violation. *Safford Unified School Dist. No. 1 v. Redding*, 557 U.S. 364, 129 S.Ct. 2633, 174 L.Ed.2d 354 (2009).

◆ High school administrators heard rumors a 16-year-old special ed student with a disciplinary record of sexually harassing girls was asking girl students to have sex with him in a school bathroom. They investigated but couldn't substantiate the rumors. When a 14-year-old girl told a teacher's aide he'd just asked her to have sex with him in a bathroom, the aide suggested she go along with it just long enough for them to catch him in the act and end the harassment. The two say they ran the plan by an assistant principal. She seemed "disinterested" and didn't OK the plan or tell them not to do it. The girl went into the bathroom with the boy. By the time the aide got teachers to check on the bathroom, he'd raped her. The girl's guardian sued the school board and school staff for claims that included negligent/wanton hiring, training and supervision. An Alabama federal judge granted most of the defendants judgment without a trial, finding them protected by state law immunity. But the Eleventh Circuit affirmed the judge's decision that the assistant principal was not entitled to immunity. Alabama public employees were not entitled to immunity if they acted beyond their authority. Based on the student's story, the assistant principal ratified the plan by not stopping it. Under regulations adopted by the board of education for dealing with students' sexual harassment complaints, **using one student as bait to catch another student committing sexual harassment went beyond an assistant principal's authority**. The Eleventh Circuit reversed the judge's decision that the aide was entitled to immunity on the student's tort of outrage claim. Using the girl as bait was likely to – and did – cause her emotional distress, and carrying out the plan was extreme and outrageous conduct. *Hill v. Cundiff*, 797 F.3d 948 (11th Cir. 2015).

◆ After a Delaware fourth-grade class watched a movie on a 32-inch screen TV perched atop a four-to-five-foot-tall rolling cart, the teacher told a student to move the cart to the back of the room. As she was pushing it, the TV's cord got tangled in the cart's wheels. The TV fell, striking the student's head and knocking her down. The student's mother sued district defendants, including the teacher, for personal injury. The trial court found the suit blocked by the state's immunity statute. The Delaware State Tort Claims Act provides all state political subdivisions, including school districts and their employees, immunity for discretionary acts performed in good faith and without gross negligence. The student's mother claimed the teacher was grossly negligent to have a student move the TV cart. Instead, the court found that allowing a student to assist in a classroom task does not constitute gross negligence: "a gross deviation from the standard of conduct that a reasonable person would observe." At most, the teacher was negligent. As **gross negligence was required to overcome the teacher's immunity to a personal injury claim**, the trial court granted the district's request to dismiss the case. *Morales v. Family Foundations Academy, Inc. School*, No. N12C-03-176 JRJ, 2013 WL 3337798 (Del. Super. Ct. 6/11/13).

◆   A North Carolina teacher was accused of allowing a teacher's aide to regularly force-feed and abuse a severely disabled student in her classroom. The aide allegedly yelled at the student, force-fed him to the point of choking, used abusive language, violently jerked his head and pulled his hair, and intimidated him with a stuffed toy because she knew it terrified him. After the student was hospitalized, his parents sued the teacher, the district and various officials. The teacher sought immunity, which a trial court denied. Subsequently, the North Carolina Court of Appeals affirmed that decision, noting that the teacher did not meet the test for public official immunity because her position was not "created by statute." Further, the complaint alleged that the teacher knew of and might have witnessed the abuse, and yet never intervened on the student's behalf. And the abuse violated clearly established constitutional rights of which the teacher should have known. *Farrell v. Transylvania County Board of Educ.*, 682 S.E.2d 224 (N.C. Ct. App. 2009).

◆   A Tennessee high school principal decided to temporarily deny a female student access to a weightlifting class in the last semester before graduation. The class was scheduled to include about 30 males and one other female. Students were required to "spot" one another, requiring some physical contact. **The principal consulted with the weightlifting teacher and decided to remove the girls from the class for "safety and liability reasons," fearing a possible sexual assault.** A school official confirmed that the school would not permit enrollment of one or two girls in a class with all male students and a male teacher. After a state attorney notified the director of schools about a possible Title IX violation and informed the principal that the students could not be removed from class because of their gender, the principal allowed the students to return to class. The other student chose not to return, and the student who did return missed only three days of class and earned an A. However, she claimed that the incident caused her great stress and sued for constitutional rights violations.

A federal court granted the board's motion to dismiss the case, and the Sixth Circuit affirmed. Here, the principal was not executing an official board policy at the time he ordered the student's removal, and he was not acting as a board policymaker. The board had no role in the decision to remove the student from class, and it took immediate corrective action as soon as the director of schools learned about the incident. *Phillips v. Anderson County Board of Educ.*, 259 Fed.Appx. 842 (6th Cir. 2008).

◆   An Ohio student attacked another student after gym class. The victim's parents sued the school district, claiming it knew of the attacker's history of assaulting students, yet did not take the necessary precautions to protect other students from him. **A trial court held that the district was immune, noting that it did not act with malice, in bad faith or recklessly.** It also found that **the teacher's supervision at the time of the attack was not even negligent**. The Ohio Court of Appeals affirmed. Although the student aggressor was disruptive at times, there were no indications that he was terrorizing other students. The fact that he had been in a juvenile detention center several times was not enough to put the school on notice that he was likely to attack another student. *Aratari v. Leetonia Exempt Village School Dist.*, No. 06 CO 11, 2007 WL 969402 (Ohio Ct. App. 3/26/07).

◆ On the last day of the school year for an Alabama elementary school, various teachers and coaches were called into the guidance counselor's office and asked to sit in the chair facing the guidance counselor's desk. As each teacher sat in the chair, the chair slowly reclined in the back, causing the front part to slant upward. As each teacher sat in this "sinking" chair, the guidance counselor and the other teachers present would laugh. The teachers would then summon another staff member on whom they could play the practical joke.

A coach who was summoned to the office and instructed to sit in the chair did so, at which point the chair reclined under her. She reinjured her back, upon which she had undergone several surgical procedures. She sued the principal (one of the first people duped by the "sinking chair"), the guidance counselor and others for negligence, wantonness, conspiracy, and failure to warn. A trial court granted judgment as a matter of law for the defendants, and the coach appealed.

The Court of Civil Appeals of Alabama noted that the principal was responsible for safety on the school campus. She knew of the condition of the chair, because she had sat in it earlier. She testified that she never viewed the chair as a safety problem. She left shortly after the joke was played on her and was absent from the school when the guidance counselor asked the coach to sit in the chair. The court determined that **the principal was exercising her judgment regarding school safety and concluded that she was entitled to state-agent immunity on the coach's claims of negligence and wantonness**. There was no evidence of a conspiracy, nor did the other teachers present have a duty to warn the coach about the sinking chair. The only person with potential liability to the coach was the guidance counselor, who brought the chair to school. *Bayles v. Marriott*, 816 So.2d 38 (Ala. Civ. App. 2001).

B. Safety Policies

◆ A vocational agriculture teacher had a 15 feet by 20 feet classroom that opened onto a 40 feet by 60 feet workshop that had tools and heavy machinery. He was teaching younger students in the classroom when three seniors unexpectedly ask to take their final early. The teacher left the younger students unattended while he set up laptops in the workshop for the seniors' exam. It took longer than expected, but **he was only gone six minutes. That was still long enough for a student to put a "sleeper hold" on two students, choking them.** One, a special needs student, briefly lost consciousness. The teacher was unaware of the misbehavior. Students later reported it out of concern for the special needs student. The principal reviewed surveillance video from the classroom, and then the superintendent initiated termination proceedings. The board fired the teacher for good and just cause, but a trial court overturned the dismissal. An appeals court affirmed. **The board alleged the teacher had a pattern of willfully ignoring district policy, but admitted they'd never warned him about it.** The courts found the evidence suggested other things – like the layout of his class space – were responsible for his purported misbehavior. Also, the student who misbehaved took "advantage of a small window of opportunity" to "engage in serious misconduct" while the teacher attended "to other tasks directly related to his teaching responsibilities[.]" None of this added up to good and just cause to fire him. *Badertscher v. Liberty-Benton School Dist. Board of Educ.*, 29 N.E.3d 1034 (Ohio Ct. App. 2015).

◆   For more than two years, teachers picketed in front of a middle school at morning drop-off. They were protesting the district's failure to reach a contract with their union. When rain was forecast for a planned protest, teachers voted to park in front of the school that morning and display their picket signs in the car windows. They left room for dropped-off students to reach the sidewalk but not for parents to pull up to the curb as usual. Parents had to let children out in the middle of the street in the rain, and traffic backed up in both directions. Parents called the school about the traffic jam, and the principal called the police. The traffic snarl also made at least 16 teachers late that day. The picketing teachers were charged with misconduct. Two – one fined $500 and the other fined $1,000 – appealed to a court. Participating in a peaceful union protest is protected from retaliation under the First Amendment. The teachers alleged a violation of their speech rights. A trial court found the discipline was legal. The teachers appealed, and an appeals court reversed. The district appealed, and New York's highest court reversed again, upholding the discipline because the way the teachers engaged in their protected speech rights, "interfered with the safety of students[.]" The court found **the teachers' speech rights "were outweighed by the District's interests in maintaining an orderly, safe school[.]"** *Santer v. Board of Educ. of East Meadow Union Free School Dist.*, 13 N.E.3d 1028 (N.Y. 2014).

◆   A fired New Jersey school bus driver filed a bias charge with the state civil rights agency to allege his termination was discriminatory. The board of education agreed to settle his claim. As part of the settlement, the board agreed to reinstate him. He went back to work. Two months later, **the supervisor of security rode along on an afternoon run and heard a school bus full of students "shriek in fear"** because a railroad crossing gate had come down on top of the bus while its back end was still on the tracks. The driver ignored it when the vehicle ahead of him pulled up to give him room to clear the tracks. The bus remained on one set of tracks while a commuter train sped past on the next set, so close it made the bus rock. Something similar happened on the morning run five days later. Meanwhile, the board was getting calls and letters from parents complaining about the driver and worried about their children's safety. The board fired the bus driver for unsatisfactory performance, and the driver sued the board for breaching their settlement agreement. The court granted the board judgment. The bus driver appealed, but the appeals court affirmed, finding: **"[T]he Board's first responsibility was the safety and welfare of the children in the district,"** and it had reasonable grounds to question the driver's safety – including "uncontradicted evidence of two life-endangering incidents." The board didn't breach the settlement agreement by firing the bus driver under these circumstances. *Valos v. Garfield Board of Educ.*, No. A-3313-12T2, 2014 WL 4355637 (N.J. Super. Ct. App. Div. 4/9/14).

◆ A front office employee at a Georgia high school was approached by a man who claimed to be a student's uncle. She failed to ask for identification or verify that the man was allowed to check out the student. In fact, only the student's parents were allowed to check her out of class early. When the student arrived at the office, the man told her that her mother had sent him to pick her up. He then took her to his daughter's house and molested her. The student's parents sued the principal and the employee in their individual capacities. The defendants sought immunity, but the Georgia Court of Appeals granted it only to the principal. **The employee had a mandatory duty to verify that the man had the right to sign the student out of school and failed to do so.** As a result, the lawsuit against her could proceed. A jury would have to decide whether the molestation was a reasonably foreseeable consequence of her failure to follow the rules. *Cotton v. Smith*, 714 S.E.2d 55 (Ga. Ct. App. 2011).

◆ A Pennsylvania student was sexually assaulted by a driver's education teacher during a solo lesson. When she complained, the district suspended the teacher, but the principal sent out letters asking people to contribute to the teacher's defense and stating that he thought the student was lying. After the teacher was reinstated, the student left school and sued the district, claiming that it ignored the teacher's misbehavior for years before the incident, making it possible for him to assault her. She asserted that the teacher hadn't even been disciplined after asking a student if he could see her pierced nipple. The district sought to have the case dismissed, but a federal court allowed parts of the lawsuit to continue. The student had alleged a custom of inadequate training for employees who are likely to respond to incidents of sexual harassment. The district also allegedly had a custom of ignoring or downplaying reports of harassment, and had a custom of suppressing specific complaints of harassment against the teacher. Finally, **the school district had a custom of allowing the teacher to take students out for driving lessons alone, in violation of official school district policy**. As a result, the student's lawsuit against the district could proceed with respect to those claims. *E.N. v. Susquehanna Township School Dist.*, No. 1:09-CV-1727, 2010 WL 4853700 (M.D. Pa. 11/23/10).

◆   A New York special education teacher noted a student's progressively disruptive behavior and aggression toward classmates, and initiated a "Type Three referral" to remove him from her classroom. This process could take as long as 60 days. Forty-one days later, the student attacked a classmate. The teacher intervened to protect the classmate, and she sustained injuries. She sued the city of New York for negligence. Although a jury awarded her $512,465 for her injuries, the Court of Appeals reversed the award. It found that **the district did not have a special relationship with the teacher such that it owed her an increased duty of care**. Her supervisors' vaguely worded assurances that they were working on removing the student from her class did not give rise to a reasonable reliance on her part that could result in liability. *Dinardo v. City of New York*, 921 N.E.2d 585 (N.Y. 2009).

◆   A Louisiana special education teacher noted that a student began making a sound he typically made before self-injurious episodes. When he starting hitting himself on the head, she called the PE coach, two paraprofessionals and the principal. She was pushed into a wall while trying to keep a mat under the 185-pound student to prevent injury. During the 45-minute struggle, she was twisting and sliding the entire time. However, she was not hit, knocked down or bitten by the student. When she sustained injuries to her hand, she nevertheless sought "assault pay" from the board. A court granted pretrial judgment to the board, but the court of appeal reversed, noting that there was a question of fact as to whether the teacher's injuries were a result of an assault by the student. **If the student intended to harm her during the episode, she would be entitled to assault pay.** The case required a trial. *Miller v. St. Tammany Parish School Board*, No. 2008 CA 2582, 2009 WL 3135208 (La. Ct. App. 9/11/09).

◆   In 2005, an Oregon school district adopted a policy that any employee having a firearm in school or at a school event would face discipline up to and including termination. A teacher in one of the district's schools had an ex-husband whom she feared might turn violent. She sought to bring a handgun to school, asserting that she was licensed to carry a concealed weapon and that she needed it for self-defense. The district's human resources department warned her that she could be fired for bringing the gun to school, and she sued. She claimed that the policy was illegal because Oregon law states that only the legislature can "regulate" firearms or pass ordinances concerning them. A court dismissed her claim, holding that the law didn't apply to workplace policies, and the Oregon Court of Appeals affirmed that decision. It noted that the state law was only intended to prevent cities and counties from creating a patchwork of conflicting laws concerning firearms, and that it wasn't intended to reach as far as internal employment policies. *Doe v. Medford School Dist. 549C*, 221 P.3d 787 (Or. Ct. App. 2009).

◆   A West Virginia county board of education implemented a random drug testing policy for all safety-sensitive employees, which included teachers. Three teachers and their union sued to block the new provisions from taking effect, claiming that the random testing would violate their Fourth Amendment right to be free of unreasonable search and seizure. A federal court granted a preliminary injunction prohibiting the board from enforcing the policy. **The board failed to show that there was a special need for the suspicionless searches.** In addition, the teachers did not hold safety-sensitive positions as that term has been defined by the Supreme Court. Thus, they did not have a reduced expectation of privacy. Finally, the risk of harm from not testing was more speculative than real. *American Federation of Teachers-West Virginia, AFL-CIO v. Kanawha County Board of Educ.*, 592 F.Supp.2d 883 (S.D. W. Va. 2009).

◆   A nine-year-old New Jersey student was dismissed from school on an early-dismissal day, walked off school grounds without an adult, and was struck by a car a few blocks from school over two hours later. The accident paralyzed him from the neck down.

The school district had a four-page policy memorandum titled "Pupil Safety" that addressed a wide range of student safety topics, including supervision of students at dismissal time. The memorandum stated that "[t]he chief school administrator shall seek the cooperation of parents/guardians to prevent any children [from] being unsupervised on school property during lunch hour and during morning arrival and afternoon dismissal times." The memorandum did not, however, outline how dismissal supervision would be administered by the schools.

Instead, the school adhered to a practice that all school personnel supervise dismissal. On a typical school day, the school's 500 students were dismissed at 2:50 p.m. Teachers escorted the students from their classrooms to designated exits at the sounding of the school bell, and the teachers remained at their designated duty stations to ensure that the children left the school premises. According to the principal, all school personnel – including teachers, teachers' aides, and security personnel – supervised dismissal to ensure that the children left school before the adults. The principal personally supervised early-dismissal days to "make sure that there were no children whose parents did not pick them up."

The student and his family sued, alleging that the school district and principal breached their duty of reasonable supervision. They also claimed they did not have advance notice of the early-dismissal day. The case reached the Supreme Court of New Jersey, which held that schools in New Jersey must exercise a duty of reasonable care for supervising students' safety at dismissal. **The duty requires school districts to create a reasonable dismissal supervision policy, provide suitable notice to parents of that policy, and effectively comply with the policy and subsequent and appropriate parental requests concerning dismissal.**

The court remanded the matter to the trial court for further proceedings. *Jerkins v. Anderson*, 922 A.2d 1279 (N.J. 2007).

C. Fitness for Duty

◆ A 36-year-old high school English teacher in New York began buying guns around the same time he had online conversations with a friend who worked as a psychic medium. The teacher told her he thought the government was controlling the weather and said he wanted to shoot down one of the planes "that sprays chemicals through the sky[.]" A "female friend" of his then anonymously called the FBI, which alerted local law enforcement. They began to monitor him online and at school. Soon after, **he instant-messaged the psychic medium that he believed the government had controlled the mind of the Newtown Elementary School shooter**, but a bigger problem was the "entities that came to this planet in order to try to control us ... I'm working on deprogramming myself ... that has been the nightmare of my life."

After he intimated he might have a secret mission to remove evil people from power during "a civil war in America," the police stopped him on his way home from a trip to the gun store and involuntarily committed him. His refusal to cooperate with the psych evaluation the district required prompted a charge of misconduct/conduct unbecoming a teacher. The district also charged him with incompetence to work as a teacher due to mental illness. After an eight-day hearing, the district discharged him.

He sued the district, the police and other local officials, claiming they conspired to retaliate against him for his exercise of constitutionally protected speech. The court dismissed the claim, finding **his speech wasn't protected as it constituted true threats** and didn't address matters of public concern. Also, the district could reasonably predict it would cause a disruption at work that potentially outweighed the value of his speech, and he was fired because of the potential disruption, not in retaliation for his speech. The court found that if his speech had become known while he was still a teacher, it "would have caused substantial (and well-justified) disruption that far exceeded the value of plaintiff's delusional, paranoid and far-fetched conspiracy theories." It dismissed the suit. *Heller v. Bedford Cent. School Dist.*, 144 F.Supp.3d 596 (S.D.N.Y. 2015).

◆ A tenured second-grade teacher in New Jersey used a motorized wheelchair and crutches. He was put on administrative leave based on allegations of conduct unbecoming a teacher. Among other offenses, **he allegedly urinated into a bottle in front of students and had them take the bottle to the bathroom to empty it**. He was also accused of urinating in and around the trash can in his classroom with students nearby. An administrative law judge (ALJ) found the district proved 14 of 17 charges brought against him. The commissioner of education adopted the ALJ's recommendation to revoke his tenure and remove him as a teacher. He appealed, but a court affirmed. Under New Jersey law, a tenured teacher could only be dismissed for "inefficiency, incapacity, unbecoming conduct, or other just cause." **Unbecoming conduct was defined as conduct that tended to destroy respect for government employees and confidence in the operation of public services.** The court found the commissioner had a more than sufficient reason to remove the teacher. As the ALJ found, even if he couldn't make it to a bathroom – which wasn't credibly proved – he didn't report what he'd done and make sure the trash can in his classroom was cleaned. *In re Tuitt*, Dep't of Educ. No. 307-10/11, 2014 WL 10208983 (N.J. Super. Ct. App. Div. 8/10/15).

◆ While an elementary school custodian was telling the principal about her problems with the head custodian, she mentioned she'd previously considered suicide. The principal called the school resource officer, who called the police. Officers arrived and took the custodian to a crisis center. She was placed on unpaid leave and told she couldn't return to work until she'd completed a fitness-for-duty evaluation with a psychiatrist. After the doctor decided she was disabled by disorders that included depression, she was placed on an extended leave. Though her own psychiatrist cleared her to return to work about four months later, the district required her to be cleared by its psychiatrist – but then waived the requirement and let her come back to work at a different elementary school. She sued the district, **alleging it violated the Americans with Disabilities Act by requiring a fitness-for-duty evaluation before she returned to work**. A Florida federal judge found it didn't, writing, "Employers may require a medical evaluation to assess an employee's fitness to return to work after a health-related absence." *Rodriguez v. School Board of Hillsborough County, Florida*, 60 F.Supp.3d 1273 (M.D. Fla. 2014).

◆ A high school physics teacher taught a math and physics class for struggling students. Many had behavioral issues or were diagnosed with attention deficit disorder or other learning-related conditions. To engage them, the teacher developed a less authoritarian, more collaborative teaching style. That meant students were more familiar with him than with other teachers. One day in class, a 17-year-old girl said she wasn't happy with her grade and asked if she could pay for a better grade. A male student responded, "You mean short of sexual favors?" The teacher joked, "Yes, that is the only thing that would be accepted." The students laughed. He added, "Don't be ridiculous," and said the only thing that would improve her grade was better work. He offered her extra help after school. When she arrived to take him up on the offer, he was helping another female student. **The student again asked to pay for a better grade. He replied she already knew "the only thing that I would accept is a sexual favor."** She laughed, but the other student reported the teacher's remark. He was put on administrative leave, investigated for sexual harassment, and ultimately fired for conduct unbecoming a teacher. The teacher appealed, and the matter went to arbitration. The arbitrator found that despite the teacher's intent, the remarks were objectively inappropriate and made a student uncomfortable enough to complain – so violated the school's sexual harassment policy and created a hostile educational environment. Even so, the arbitrator reinstated him, finding that was in the best interest of district students, given 11 years of strong performance weighed against a comparatively minor isolated incident. A court affirmed the arbitration award, but Massachusetts' highest court vacated it, finding the arbitrator didn't have the authority under the state's teacher's statute to reinstate the teacher. That law required the arbitrator to assess conduct that jeopardized students' safety or self-esteem primarily in light of the pupils' interest in a safe learning environment. **The arbitrator's error was in letting "pupils' interest in the academic success of their school to override their interest in a safe, supportive classroom environment."** The court found that ran contrary to the law's stated purpose "and the high standards of behavior the public expects from its teachers." *School Committee of Lexington v. Zagaeski*, 12 N.E.3d 384 (Mass. 2014).

◆ A Kentucky high school's SRO took two boys to the principal after classmates overheard them talking about a bomb and saw they had a map. The principal determined they had been discussing a video game. A few days later, on the same day as the school shooting in Newtown, Connecticut, the Spanish teacher dictated a letter to a student and told the student to sign his own name. It claimed a student had twice brought weapons to school and had "plotted a map of bomb and gun attack sites around the school area" but wasn't disciplined. **The letter asked if the superintendent was "afraid to enforce school rules[.]"** The superintendent met with police and then closed the high school and middle school to search for weapons. None were found. Final exams scheduled for that day were postponed. The lost day was made up on a day the rest of the district had off. After police discovered the Spanish teacher wrote the letter, **the superintendent fired her for insubordination and conduct unbecoming a teacher**. The teacher sued, alleging violation of her free speech rights. She asked for a court order to reinstate her employment pending the resolution of her lawsuit. The court refused, finding she wasn't likely to win her suit. Assuming the teacher was speaking as a private citizen on a matter of public concern, the district's interest in promoting the efficiency of its educational services outweighed any speech rights she had in the letter. She mailed the letter the day after Newtown shooting, and the day the school reopened, attendance was down by 10%. Also, closing the schools affected around 900 students and their families. This, plus the rescheduled exams and make-up day, meant she significantly impeded school operations. As the court found her speech wasn't protected, she wasn't likely to win her case. *Pacheco v. Waldrop*, No. 5:13-cv-00044-TBR, 2013 WL 2581016 (W.D. Ky. 6/11/13).

◆   A New York teacher exchanged emails and instant messages with a student, at one point telling him that the lines of their relationship were becoming blurred and that she was confused. The student reported the conversations to the principal, and the teacher entered therapy to cope with the situation. Later, the student found postings made by the teacher under an alias on a public website, in which she acknowledged her desire to be physically close to him and kiss him. She was suspended pending termination, but a hearing officer determined that **she had shown remorse and entered therapy, making termination too harsh a penalty**. Instead, she was suspended for 90 days and transferred to a different school. The New York Supreme Court, Appellate Division, upheld that decision. *City School Dist. of City of New York v. McGraham*, 905 N.Y.S.2d 86 (N.Y. App. Div. 2010).

◆   A Tennessee school district investigated a tenured teacher who was alleged to have kissed a student in class and written notes professing love for students. The district suspended the teacher (first with pay, then without pay), placed him on probation and forced him to take sensitivity training. Other students told investigators that the teacher had hugged them and told them that he loved them. He challenged the suspension, but the Tennessee Court of Appeals upheld it. While the teacher's unprofessional conduct was not a statutory ground for dismissal under the state's Tenured Teachers Act, **his unprofessional conduct was harmful to student learning and therefore justified the suspension**. *Taylor v. Clarksville Montgomery County School System*, No. M2009-02116-COA-R3-CV, 2010 WL 3245281 (Tenn. Ct. App. 8/17/10).

◆   A Delaware school district charged a teacher with four incidents of misconduct and/or immorality, including "selling" grades to students for cash, sleeping during the work day and swearing in front of students at a school football game. The most serious charge against the teacher was that he asked one of his students for a ride to a dangerous area to purchase drugs. At the time, the teacher's driving privileges were suspended due to a DUI conviction. A hearing officer found the teacher's statements inconsistent and incredible, while grade book evidence supported the charges that the teacher raised students' grades in exchange for amounts of $10 and $30. The hearing officer recommended discharge, and the Supreme Court of Delaware upheld the termination. The teacher's claim that the board had relied on "stale" evidence failed because the board was permitted to hear all evidence that could conceivably shed light on the controversy. And board procedures met minimum standards for due process. *Bethel v. Board of Educ. of Capital School Dist.*, 985 A.2d 389 (Table) (Del. 2009).

◆   A nontenured Connecticut teacher posted a profile on MySpace to keep in contact with students. A school counselor learned of the profile and was disturbed by what she saw – pictures of naked men and inappropriate comments posted near student pictures. She complained to the teacher, who took down the profile and created another one that was very similar. The district then notified the teacher that it would not be renewing his contract. It granted him a formal hearing, but affirmed its decision not to renew his contract. When he sued the district for violating his First and Fourteenth Amendment rights, he lost. A federal court held that his nonrenewal apparently resulted from his interactions with students. **His conduct as a whole was disruptive to school activities and indicated a potentially unprofessional rapport with students.** *Spanierman v. Hughes*, 576 F.Supp.2d 292 (D. Conn. 2008).

◆   A Maryland vice principal summoned a student to his office to discuss alleged harassment by the student. The vice principal claimed that he showed a knife to the student – a knife that a smaller student had brought to school after being picked on – and asked how he would feel if a student he had harassed brought a knife to school. However, **the student claimed that the vice principal brandished the knife directly in front of him**. He sued the vice principal for assault. The vice principal asked the school board to supply him with legal counsel, but the school board refused. The vice principal obtained an attorney under his insurance policy, and a jury ruled that he did not assault the student. His insurer then sought reimbursement for his defense costs. The Court of Appeals of Maryland held that the school board was required to provide legal counsel to the vice principal, and thus had to reimburse the insurer for the defense costs. Since the vice principal claimed that he acted in the scope of his employment and without malice, the school board had a duty to defend him. *Board of Educ. of Worcester County v. Horace Mann Insurance Co.*, 969 A.2d 305 (Md. 2009).

◆   A Pennsylvania classroom assistant worked with a special education teacher. One day, she did not feel well and left the classroom for about 45 minutes. She was discovered in a restroom stall, unconscious, choking and struggling to breathe. The police were called, and they found a Fentanyl patch on her back that had caused an overdose. She was charged with disorderly conduct and possession of a controlled substance. After she was suspended without pay and recommended for discharge, she filed a grievance. An arbitrator determined she could be fired only for just cause and that, **while her behavior had been foolish and irresponsible, it was not so grossly offensive to the morals of the community that it rose to the level of immorality**. It was the only incident of its kind in 23 years of service. A court and an appeals court overturned the arbitrator's decision, but the Pennsylvania Supreme Court held that the courts should have followed the deferential "essence test" to overturn arbitration awards only where there is no foundation for them or where they did not flow from a collective bargaining agreement. The court returned the case to the trial court for a determination of whether public policy precluded the award. *Westmoreland Intermediate Unit #7 v. Westmoreland Intermediate Unit #7 Classroom Assistants Educ. Support Personnel Ass'n PSEA/NEA*, 939 A.2d 855 (Pa. 2007).

◆ A West Virginia teacher, who was also the head football coach at his high school, beat his son with a belt after the son was disciplined for making inappropriate comments in front of his class. When staff members learned of the beating, they contacted the state department of health and human resources, which removed the son and two of his siblings from the house. The teacher was charged with felony child abuse and entered a plea of misdemeanor domestic battery. He also underwent counseling and a psychiatric evaluation, after which the school board rejected the superintendent's recommendation that the teacher be dismissed. A psychologist determined that the teacher presented no greater risk to his students than any other teacher, and he was allowed to return to the classroom. The state's Professional Practices Panel then determined the teacher's license should be suspended for four years. The teacher appealed to the Supreme Court of Appeals of West Virginia, which agreed with him that **the four-year suspension of his certificate was not based on unfitness to teach**. The state superintendent failed to show a nexus between the teacher's home conduct and the duties he had to perform as a teacher. He exhibited no cruel behavior to his students or the staff, and he was not unfit to teach. *Powell v. Paine*, 655 S.E.2d 204 (W. Va. 2007).

◆ A Mississippi high school teacher with no history of sexually harassing students began a sexually inappropriate relationship with a student, though both he and the student denied that sexual intercourse ever occurred. A rumor circulated about the relationship, but the principal detected no sign of it. He confronted the teacher, who vehemently denied there was any inappropriate relationship. However, the truth eventually came out in some discarded love letters and some impassioned emails. The student's family sued the school district for negligent hiring and retention, among other claims. A court ruled for the school district, and the Court of Appeals of Mississippi affirmed. Here, **the school district did not have either actual or constructive notice of the inappropriate relationship between the student and teacher, as required to establish a claim for negligent hiring or retention**. The teacher had no prior history of wrongdoing, and many of his contacts with the student were under the guise of innocence, such as his tutoring of the student and her babysitting of his child. *Doe ex rel. Doe v. Pontotoc County School Dist.*, 957 So.2d 410 (Miss. Ct. App. 2007).

◆ A tenured high school teacher in New York received several unsatisfactory evaluations and claimed that he was also denied certain benefits and opportunities. He sought an accommodation for dust and pollen allergies, which the school claimed it provided. He then sent letters to the assistant principal, calling her "Mein Fuhrer," and referring to her as a "snooperviser." He also referred to himself as "an indentured subject of her sick experiment." Fearing he represented a threat to the safety of staff and students, the school reassigned him to administrative work at another high school and required a psychological evaluation. Pending the results, his photograph was given to school safety officers and custodial staff who worked in his old high school building during evenings and weekends to ensure that he would not enter the building. He was determined to be fit for duty and was returned to the classroom without any loss of pay or benefits. He then sued for discrimination under state and federal law. A federal court granted pretrial judgment to the defendants. Here, the school provided an accommodation that met the requirements listed in the Board of Education Accommodation. He merely found them unsatisfactory. Further, **the reassignment was a temporary measure taken to ensure the safety of students and staff, and he was transferred back to a teaching position once the evaluation found him fit for duty**. *Krinsky v. Abrams*, No. 01 CV 5052(SLT)(LB), 2007 WL 1541369 (E.D.N.Y. 5/25/07).

D. Failure to Train

◆ A freshman boy in Nevada kept missing his sixth-period class. In May, he had sexual relations with his English teacher. Police at the school found out about it the next day and took him to an office to question him – and left a window open. Other students overheard. When the teacher was arrested later that day, students put two and two together. The following year, he claimed another teacher gave him a hard time and accused him of putting her friend out of work. He tried to kill himself. His parents placed him in a private school in another state and sued the school district. Although other claims were allowed to continue against the district, a Nevada federal judge dismissed the parents' claim that the district negligently failed to train the teacher that abused him. Under Nevada law, the district didn't have immunity for negligent acts committed in bad faith – but **the parents failed to provide any facts to back up their claims** that the teacher had a reputation of flirting with male students, the district knew about it but failed to stop her or that it knew the student was spending his sixth periods with the teacher and turned a blind eye. Without such facts, their claim couldn't stand, so the court dismissed it. *Doe v. Clark County School Dist.*, No. 2:15-cv-00793-APG-GWF, 2016 WL 4432683 (D. Nev. 8/18/16).

◆ Special ed aides went to elementary school administrators to complain about the teacher of a class of multi-handicapped students. The teacher allegedly screamed at children (sometimes, "I hate you!"); ignored their basic needs; and incited escalating behaviors by throwing their property in the trash, walling them off behind dividers, and taking their food. She made a child who used a walker crawl to the bathroom, made another child stand in front of the class for extended periods, and knocked a table into another child's mouth. A principal responded to the aides' concerns by saying that "she went to college for this; she knows what she's doing[.]" Finally, the school librarian – who also complained with no result – called the police. After investigating, they decided not to prosecute the teacher or the school district. She was allowed to resign with severance pay and a positive reference. No school administrator was reprimanded for not reporting the abuse. Parents only discovered the complaints about the teacher after a citizen activist's work got the records of the investigation released. Five of her former students and their parents brought a Section 1983 claim to allege the district was liable for violating the childrens' substantive due process and equal protection rights as well as their rights to be free of unreasonable seizures. The district objected it couldn't be sued under this section, but the court decided it could be based on an allegation that **the district failed to train administrators to identify potential abuse of students, appropriately report it and inform parents of the allegations**. *H.M. v. Board of Educ. of the Kings Local School Dist.*, 117 F.Supp.3d 992 (S.D. Ohio 2015).

◆   A woman that a kindergarten teacher had never met announced she was there to take a child out of school. The teacher asked for the woman's ID and verification that the woman was allowed to do so. The woman refused to provide any documentation, but the teacher released the child to her anyway. The woman went on to brutally sexually abuse the child, severely injuring her, before abandoning her in a playground, where the child was found by a sanitation worker before dawn on a January morning. Among other claims, the child's mother brought a Section 1983 *Monell* claim against Philadelphia's school district and its school reform commission. The mother alleged their failure to train the teacher on policies about releasing students amounted to deliberate indifference to the kindergartner's rights. The court refused to dismiss the claim, finding the mother alleged the district defendants were **aware of the risk of child abduction yet didn't train and supervise staff on its policy that preK-8 students were never to be released to adults who weren't properly identified** and checked against school records – and that this was what caused the alleged violation of the child's Fourteenth Amendment due process right to bodily integrity. *L.R. v. School Dist. of Philadelphia*, 60 F.Supp.3d 584 (E.D. Pa. 2014).

◆   A Florida teacher knew that other students had been taunting a 13-year-old girl who had texted sexually suggestive pictures of herself to a boy. The teacher saw what looked like self-inflicted cuts on the student's legs and sent her to the office. The school's social worker had the student sign a "no-harm contract," promising not to kill herself, but didn't notify the student's parents as required by school policy. **After the student killed herself at home the next day, the parents sued the school board for negligence, alleging that it failed to properly train the social worker.** The school board sought to have the case dismissed, but a judge refused to do so. Although the parents couldn't claim a constitutional violation, they could pursue their negligence claims. *Witsell v. School Board of Hillsborough County*, 2011 WL 2457877 (M.D. Fla. 6/20/11).

III. SCHOOL SECURITY OFFICERS

At schools in many states, school security officers are an integral component of an overall plan to maintain safety.

◆   An African-American security officer at a New Jersey high school had an unblemished work record when the school board hired its first districtwide director of security. The new director assigned him to work outside in harsh winter weather, disciplined him for a dress code violation, overly monitored him, reprimanded him for being away from his post and finally transferred him to a less prestigious middle school. He sued the district for racial discrimination under Title VII, but the court found he failed to state a valid claim. The Third Circuit agreed. He didn't show he suffered an adverse employment action: a significant change in employment status like not being hired, being fired or passed over for promotion, being reassigned with significantly different responsibilities or suffering a significant drop in benefits. While he did make much less in overtime in his new position, there were changes to overtime that impacted all the officers. Also, he couldn't show racial bias. The director explained he transferred an Hispanic officer to the high school because of the growing number of Spanish speakers there and sent the officer to the middle school because **he was needed to accommodate the physical demands of the disabled students and because he was an "excellent de-escalator."** *Stewart v. Union County Board of Educ.*, No. 15-3970, 2016 WL 3743181 (3d Cir. 7/13/16) (Unreported).

◆   The security department at a California high school received a call regarding vandalism on campus. Three campus security officers responded, while a peace officer with the unified school district drove his patrol car around the perimeter of the campus. The three campus security officers encountered a group of students, and one officer ordered a student with whom he'd had many conversations in the past to stop running. The student instead continued to flee, stopping only when the peace officer encountered him after he exited the campus. After the student was convicted of willfully resisting a public officer in the discharge of his duties, he appealed, asserting that campus security officers were not "public officers" under the law. A state court ruled that campus security officers are public officers, but the California Court of Appeal reversed the conviction, holding that campus security officers are not public officers. On further appeal, the California Supreme Court reversed the court of appeal, holding that **school security officers are "public officers."** A public officer is understood to include a variety of public officials and employees who perform law enforcement related duties in connection with their employment. *In re M.M.*, 278 P.3d 1221 (Cal. 2012).

◆ **A school security officer in Tennessee used gory photos in a scared-straight presentation to highlight the dangers of drunk driving.** He tried to ensure that none of the students would see pictures of dead relatives by checking names, asking teachers about students with potential issues, telling students they didn't have to look at the photos (which were placed in an envelope with the victims' names on the outside), and warning them about the nature of the accident and the names of the victims. Despite these precautions, a student saw a picture of her father. She didn't use her father's last name and knew him by his nickname rather than his given name. She and her mother sued the city for negligent infliction of emotional distress, and a judge awarded them nearly $67,000. However, the Tennessee Court of Appeals reversed, holding that the security officer didn't breach his duty to the students and that he'd taken reasonable steps to prevent such traumatic harm. *Marla H. v. Knox County*, 361 S.W.3d 518 (Tenn. Ct. App. 2011).

◆ A security guard with a private company worked at a junior high school in New York. When a student fight broke out on campus, he intervened and ended up sustaining injuries. He brought a lawsuit against the school district, claiming negligent supervision, but a court ruled in favor of the district. An appellate division court affirmed, noting that **the district owed no legal duty of protection to the security guard**. The duty to supervise students was intended to prevent injuries to other students, not to adult security guards. *Stinson v. Roosevelt U.F.S.D.*, 877 N.Y.S.2d 400 (N.Y. App. Div. 2009).

◆ A high school safety officer's daughter, who attended the school where she worked, got into an altercation with another student outside the school. The altercation resulted in the filing of charges against the safety officer's daughter. A day later, the safety officer called the other student's mother, claiming that she did so at the direction of the assistant principal for security. She asked the mother to come to the school to participate in a mediation. **The mother alleged that the safety officer threatened her on the phone, telling her that if she cared about her daughter's safety, she would drop the charges.** Based on the alleged threat, the safety officer was charged with aggravated harassment. After she was convicted, she appealed. A New York appellate division court upheld the conviction, noting that the lower court permissibly discredited her testimony that she never made the threat. *People v. Wilson*, 872 N.Y.S.2d 124 (N.Y. App. Div. 2009).

◆ A New York school security officer became involved in an altercation with an honors student who entered the school before the start of scheduled classes. When the security officer asked the student to leave the building, the student refused to do so. The incident escalated, and the officer arrested the student. As the officer prepared to escort the student from the building, the principal asked the officer to take the student through a back entrance to save her the embarrassment of passing through the front entrance, where hundreds of students were waiting to enter. After the officer denied the principal's repeated requests to take the student out the back door, the principal physically blocked the main entrance to the school. **The security officer then attempted to arrest the principal, who flailed his arms and kicked the officer to avoid being handcuffed.** Eventually, the principal was charged with one count of resisting arrest and one count of obstruction of governmental administration. The principal asked to have the charges dismissed, and a court agreed to do so. The principal had a solid performance history, and his conduct did not threaten the safety of the officer or the school community. His request to take the student out the back entrance was reasonable. *People v. Federman*, 852 N.Y.S.2d 748 (N.Y. City Crim. Ct. 2008).

IV. EMPLOYEE PREPAREDNESS AND RESPONSE

Coordinating employee responsibilities with respect to crisis prevention and response is critical. One way to aid in forming an effective team among school employees is to conduct a staff skills inventory that matches individual employees with particular areas of experience and/or expertise. For a form that can be used to conduct such a skills inventory, see Form I-1 in Chapter Nine.

◆   A divorced couple's parenting plan required the father to tell the school when the mother had his permission to pick their son. He hadn't notified the school on a day the mother and her new husband arrived to pick him up. Forced to wait while the school secretary repeatedly tried to contact the father, the stepfather got impatient. The secretary overheard him tell the boy that if the doctor confirmed the stepfather had cancer at his appointment "next Tuesday ... **I'm going to come back in here with an AK-47 ... kill everybody in here and then kill myself.**" The secretary asked the principal if they should call 911. She said no, concerned about "causing a scene" that would upset children at a science club meeting. But a police-officer friend of a teacher later took a statement from the principal and got a warrant for the stepfather's arrest. A jury later convicted him of disorderly conduct and attempted terrorism, but the attempted terrorism conviction was reversed on appeal. The state's law required the fear of bodily injury to be "imminent." The stepfather's threat about "next Tuesday" didn't meet that standard. So the appeals court returned the case to the lower court for sentencing only on the disorderly conduct conviction. *State v. Watts*, No. M2013-02750-CCA-R3-CD, 2015 WL 3863242 (Tenn. Crim. App. 6/23/15).

◆   A Pennsylvania teacher confiscated a student's knife. He informed the principal and his program's director, but he didn't think their response went far enough. He emailed them three days later to complain about their response. Shortly thereafter, he confiscated brass knuckles from a student.

After he became irate at a staff meeting and swore at another teacher, he was suspended for eight days, but a union arbitrator later overturned the discipline. He wrote to the state's school safety center to report unsafe classroom conditions, and later sued the principal and the program director for **violating his free speech rights by retaliating against him for speaking out about school safety**. A federal court granted pretrial judgment against him. Here, it was one of his duties to ensure school safety, so he wasn't speaking as a citizen when he complained, but rather as an employee. *Ankney v. Wakefield*, 2012 WL 2339683 (W.D. Pa. 6/19/12).

◆ An Alabama special education teacher sustained injuries when a student whom she had repeatedly reported as violent attacked the principal in the office and while doing so bit her, knocked her down and kicked her in the head. She sued the school district for violating her Fourteenth Amendment rights by failing to remove the student from school and by **failing to train her to handle him, despite knowing of his propensity for violence**. She claimed that this amounted to deliberate indifference to her safety. The district sought to have the case dismissed, and a federal court agreed that the case ought to be dismissed. The teacher failed to show that the district's policies amounted to deliberate indifference so as to reach the level of a constitutional violation. And this was not a case of a state actor inflicting injury on the teacher, but rather a private individual. As a result, the court dismissed the case. *May v. Mobile County Public School System*, No. 09-00625-NS-C, 2010 WL 3039181 (S.D. Ala. 7/13/10).

◆ On September 15, 1999, New Jersey's governor declared a state of emergency due to the approach of Hurricane Floyd. However, in Rutherford, New Jersey, less than an inch of rain fell that day, and school officials didn't cancel after-school football practice. After the practice, a 16-year-old student got a ride home from a teammate's sister. About a half-mile from the field, the driver lost control of the car on a curve and struck a tree. The student, who was sitting unrestrained in the rear passenger seat, suffered severe head injuries and sued the school district for negligence, asserting that it should have canceled the practice because of the hurricane warnings and that it shouldn't have let him go him with the teammate's sister, given the weather. A court ruled for the district, and the Superior Court of New Jersey, Appellate Division, affirmed. Here, most of the severe weather from the hurricane arrived the following day rather than the day in question. Because of the absence of extraordinary weather conditions, **the district's employees did not breach a duty of care to the student by not canceling the practice due to the impending hurricane**; nor did they breach a duty of care by allowing the teammate's sister to drive him home. *Pluchino v. Borough of Rutherford*, 2010 WL 335041 (N.J. Super. Ct. App. Div. 2/1/10).

◆ A custodian in Washington received a call from her supervisor asking her to report to work early to replace a distraught co-worker. The supervisor offered no further explanation. When the custodian arrived at school, the district superintendent repeatedly directed her to clean up the scene of a student's suicide. However, a law enforcement officer told her not to touch anything. She also learned of the possibility that the deceased student had left a bomb in the building. She was ordered to accompany the principal on a search for the bomb and was later given permission to clean up the suicide site. However, when she picked up a book bag, she was told to drop it. The book bag apparently contained a pipe bomb, which was detonated on a school field. The superintendent told her to make it look as though nothing had happened at the site. She finished her work at 4:15 a.m., at which point she was distraught and physically ill.

She had to return to the school by 8:00 a.m. to hand out cookies and coffee as counselors assisted students and staff. For the next several days, she had to clean up candles and cards left by students at the scene of the suicide. Later, she sued the school district and superintendent for infliction of emotional distress. A state court held that workers' compensation was her exclusive remedy, but the Washington Court of Appeals reversed. It held that **her post-traumatic stress disorder resulted from the performance of her duties over several days**. Thus, her injury was excluded from the workers' compensation act's definition of an occupational disease. Her lawsuit could continue. *Rothwell v. Nine Mile Falls School Dist.*, 206 P.3d 347 (Wash. Ct. App. 2009).

◆   An Ohio high school principal convened a meeting with senior staff members to discuss the subject of testing during a week when state educational tests were being administered at the school. While the meeting was in progress, the principal was informed that a female student had been assaulted and forced to perform sex acts on a number of male students. She was also told that another male student had videotaped part of the assault. She did not call the police or the department of children services. Instead, she set up a meeting for the following morning to discuss the assault. She also failed to report the sexual assault as her supervisor instructed her to do. She left at 4 p.m. to take care of some personal business without leaving anyone in charge. Nor did she assign anyone to meet with the police officers who had been summoned to the school by the victim's father. The board of education fired her, and she challenged the termination.

The Ohio Court of Appeals upheld the decision to fire her, noting that she violated state law by failing to report the sexual assault. Further, her failure to follow her supervisor's order to report the assault also justified her discharge. **She was not relieved of her duty to contact law enforcement just because the victim's father had called the police.** And her failure to handle the situation immediately was further evidence that she had been properly fired. *Crenshaw v. Columbus City School Dist. Board of Educ.*, No. 07AP-883, 2008 WL 802708 (Ohio Ct. App. 3/27/08).

CHAPTER SIX

Extracurricular Activities

I. AFTER-SCHOOL PROGRAMS

Schools can no longer throw open their doors so that neighborhood children can use their facilities after the school day ends. Nor can they rely on minimal supervision for after-school programs. Threats to security and student safety mean they must now devise plans for how to safely engage students after the school day ends.

Some well-recognized means of decreasing risk are:

- reducing the number of open doors
- concentrating after-school activities in limited areas

- assigning trained personnel to supervise activities rather than relying on custodians
- developing emergency/crisis preparedness training, and
- if contracting with an outside entity to run a program, building into the contract security requirements that must be followed.

A. Negligent Supervision

◆ Two ninth-graders slipped into a locker room during football practice and urinated all over a tenth-grader's gym locker. His father sued the school board, alleging negligent supervision. The Louisiana Court of Appeal upheld a judgment in favor of the school board, noting that there was no evidence that the coaches weren't properly supervising students at the time of the incident. **No one at the school had any notice that misbehavior might occur in the locker room because such an incident had never occurred before.** *Creekbaum v. Livingston Parish School Board*, 80 So.3d 771 (La. Ct. App. 2011).

◆ A California school district created an unstructured "open playground" for students who couldn't be picked up right away after school. Allegedly as few as two adults were responsible for overseeing up to 300 students. One seven-year-old student who stayed after school in the program was asked by another student to join a "kissing club" in an unlocked shed. She went to the shed, where a boy stuck his tongue in her mouth, which upset her so much that she left. Two days later, the student who had recruited her informed her that she had to come back to the club, which she did out of fear. At this meeting, the recruiter forced her to pull down her pants and the same boy then took off his pants and rubbed against her from behind. She later told a fifth-grader, who told the playground supervisor, who called the student's mother, who brought in the police.

In the lawsuit that followed, the school asserted that it didn't have a duty of care to children who participated in voluntary after-school programs. A court agreed, but the California Court of Appeal reversed, holding that a trial was needed to determine if the lack of supervision was responsible for the student's injury and if the injury was foreseeable. Here, **the after-school program, despite its voluntary nature, created a special relationship between the school district and the program participants**. And the student had a right to reasonable protection while in the program. *J.H. v. Los Angeles Unified School Dist.*, 107 Cal.Rptr.3d 182 (Cal. Ct. App. 2010).

◆ A Connecticut elementary student participated in an after-school program run by the town of New Milford. While hanging on a basketball rim installed seven feet above the ground, he fell onto the concrete surface below and sustained injuries. He sued the town and the employees who had been supervising the program for negligence. After examining the "imminent harm" exception to discretionary act immunity, the Superior

Court of Connecticut ruled in favor of the town. The imminent harm exception test requires three things: (1) an imminent harm; (2) an identifiable victim; and (3) a public official to whom it is apparent that his or her conduct is likely to subject that victim to that harm. Here, the supervisors testified that no one else had ever been hurt after dropping from the rim. Nor was hanging on the rim a prohibited activity. **Since there was no apparent risk of injury to the student, the town and employees were entitled to immunity.** *Zaborowski v. Town of New Milford*, No. LL1CV054002368S, 2007 WL 1413911 (Conn. Super. Ct. 4/24/07).

◆   The parents of a child injured on a school playground sued the after-school program providers, alleging negligent supervision. The child was injured when he slipped and fell while engaged in normal play on a "monkey-bars" apparatus in a schoolyard during an after-school program. Two supervisors employed by the defendants were approximately 15 feet away from the child when they saw him fall. At least one other supervisor was within the same complex of playground equipment, and two additional adult volunteers were assigned to supervise the group of 25 to 30 children of which the child was a member. The case reached the New York Supreme Court, Appellate Division, which noted that the child was not engaged in any rough or inappropriate play prior to the accident and that **the defendants were not on notice of any horseplay or defective condition so as to warrant closer supervision or intervention**. Accordingly, the degree of supervision afforded by the defendants was reasonable and adequate under the circumstances, and the child's injury was not proximately caused by a lack of supervision. The lawsuit was dismissed. *Berdecia v. City of New York*, 289 A.D.2d 354, 735 N.Y.S.2d 554 (N.Y. App. Div. 2001).

B. Duty to Protect Students

◆   A 14-year-old student injured his hand while playing basketball during an after-school program. **His hand hit a metal cage a foot away from the backboard, and the tip of a finger stuck there.** He sued the school to recover for his injuries. A court awarded him over $1 million in past and future damages (for the next 40 years). The Supreme Court, Appellate Division, upheld the finding of liability, noting that the student had not assumed the risk of such an injury. However, the damage award was excessive. The court offered the student $300,000 in damages or a new trial limited to determining an appropriate amount. *Robinson v. New York City Dep't of Educ.*, 94 A.D.3d 428 (N.Y. App. Div. 2012).

◆   A New York middle school student disobeyed his mother's instructions to attend an after-school program. Instead, he went to a park after school and fell from a swing, breaking his leg. He sued the after-school program, claiming a failure to adequately supervise. A trial court ruled against him, and the New York Supreme Court, Appellate Division, affirmed. A school's duty to supervise students is coextensive with its custody and control over them. Here,

**the student got hurt while he was beyond the after-school program's
authority**. Neither the program nor the school was responsible for his injuries.
Even though the program failed to notify the student's mother that the student
did not show up that day, that failure did not cause the child's injuries. *Fotiadis
v. City of New York*, 853 N.Y.S.2d 591 (N.Y. App. Div. 2008).

◆   A California school opened its campus at 7:00 a.m., but trouble spots,
such as restrooms, were unsupervised before 7:45 a.m. School administrators
knew that one eighth-grade special education student was usually dropped
off at 7:15 a.m. A classmate who also had disabilities teased and ridiculed the
student daily before classes began. The student sometimes went to the office
to escape this, and he complained to the staff. He was told to stay away from
the classmate, even after he told the vice principal this did not work. The
classmate twice isolated the student and sexually assaulted him. The district
learned of the incidents and expelled the classmate, who was also arrested.
The student was hospitalized with depression, and he attempted suicide. He
sued the school district and the classmate's family. A jury trial resulted in a
verdict of over $2.5 million for the student, and the district appealed.

The Court of Appeal of California observed that **school districts have
a well-established duty to supervise students at all times while on school
grounds. This duty included supervision during recess and before or
after school.** The district was liable for injuries resulting from the failure of
school staff to use ordinary care to protect students. The district unlocked its
gates at 7:00 a.m. each day, but did not provide supervision until 7:45 a.m.
It could have simply precluded students from arriving early or kept them in
particular areas of the school. The district's claim to immunity failed
because there was no exercise of discretion by the principal, and evidence
that he knew of the classmate's violent behavior. The damage award was
not excessive, and the court affirmed the judgment. *M.W. v. Panama Buena
Union School Dist.*, 1 Cal. Rptr. 3d 673 (Cal. Ct. App. 2003).

◆   The family of a New York student brought a lawsuit against the board of
education, seeking to recover damages for injuries the student allegedly
sustained when, upon being pushed by a schoolmate, he fell down a
staircase at a public school during an after-school program run by the
YMCA of Greater New York. There was no handrail on the right side of the
staircase where the student was walking. The supreme court denied the
board's motion for pretrial judgment and the Supreme Court, Appellate
Division, affirmed.

The testimony of the student at a hearing and at his deposition
demonstrated that he tried to grab the handrail on the opposite side of the
stairs to stop his fall, but could not reach it. The unchallenged statement of
the family's expert **engineer demonstrated that the absence of a handrail
on the right side of the staircase was a violation of the applicable
building code**. Thus, there were triable issues of fact as to whether the
absence of the handrail was a proximate cause of the student's injuries and

whether the fact that he was pushed by a fellow student severed any nexus (connection) between the city's alleged negligence in the design of the staircase and his injuries. The case required a trial. *Ocasio v. Board of Educ. of City of New York*, 35 A.D.3d 825, 827 N.Y.S.2d 265 (N.Y. App. Div. 2006).

II. FIELD TRIPS AND OFF-CAMPUS ACTIVITIES

Field trips provide a dual challenge to schools. First, they must ensure the safety of their students off school grounds, in settings where outside influences are not as easily controllable.

Second, they must ensure the safety of the general public from reasonably foreseeable acts of violence or horseplay by students. This latter concern, while slight for many schools (especially elementary schools), can be a real problem for others.

Increased supervision presents the single easiest solution, especially the usage of parent volunteers to assist with oversight. But this also presents a problem: how to verify that parent volunteers are not a threat. Background checks are the best insurance policy against threats to students.

Some schools charge parents to conduct background checks; others impose a fee for all students for field trips, a part of which can be used to conduct the background checks. For a sample field trip permission slip, see Form VI-3 in Chapter Nine. A sample questionnaire for chaperones can be found at Form VI-1, and a sample of chaperone guidelines can be found at Form VI-2 in Chapter Nine.

◆   Graduates of a Washington high school arranged for kegs of beer for a party at an off-campus location and without adult supervision. During the party, three graduates confronted a junior, who was the only underclassman there. One of the graduates hit the junior on the forehead with a heavy beer mug. Although the wound appeared minor, the junior collapsed and fell into a coma four months later. Four years after that, the junior died, and **his estate sued the graduates who had purchased the beer** as well as the graduates who confronted the junior and the beer distributor who made the kegs available. The Court of Appeals of Washington ultimately ruled that only the junior's assailants could be liable for his death. It refused to recognize an inherent propensity for violence at teenage keg parties so as to broaden liability to others. *Cameron v. Murray*, 214 P.3d 150 (Wash. Ct. App. 2009).

◆   During a school-sponsored field trip, a Nevada student found a knife on the floor of the bus and turned it in to the bus driver. Another student admitted that the knife was his. He was allowed to participate in the field trip, but the next day, a school vice principal suspended him for 10 days pending expulsion. The vice principal drafted a letter to the student explaining the district's weapons policy and detailing the violation. A school district disciplinary panel conducted a hearing at which the charges against the student were read, and a school police liaison officer testified for the district. The student claimed that he brought the knife along accidentally, and his parents asserted that he was not a disciplinary problem. However, the panel recommended expulsion for the remaining weeks of the school year.

The school board met in a closed session, without the family, and accepted the recommendation for expulsion. Afterward, the family sued in a federal court, claiming that the district had not given the student adequate due process prior to expelling him. The court determined that **the disciplinary hearing met the heightened requirements for expulsion proceedings**. The school board did not need to conduct another hearing with the student. Accordingly, the student received all the due process to which he was entitled. And his admission that the knife was his also made another hearing unnecessary. *Hardie v. Churchill County School Dist.*, No. 3:07-CV-310-RAM, 2009 WL 875486 (D. Nev. 3/30/09).

A. Negligent Supervision

1. Duty of Care

◆ Staff at a private high school in Florida intercepted end-of-year party invitations with a faintly visible liquor bottle in the background. The principal announced that he intended to stop by the party and also talked with the host's parents to ensure that they would be home to chaperone. He arrived at the party around 4:00 p.m., confirmed that the host's mother was there, and left. About forty-five minutes later, two students who had gotten someone else to obtain alcohol for them left the party. They were drunk and crashed their car into a tree. One student died; the other became a quadriplegic. He and his parents sued the school and its archdiocese for negligence, **asserting that the principal, by undertaking to check on the party, had a duty to act with reasonable care**, and that he breached that duty. A jury found the school defendants 25% at fault, but the Florida District Court of Appeal reversed. First, the private school's contract with students clearly stated that the school wasn't liable for events not officially sanctioned. Second, the accident occurred outside school hours at a non-school activity. The court refused to punish the school for the principal's good deed of checking up on the students. *Archbishop Coleman F. Carroll High School, Inc. v. Maynoldi*, 30 So.3d 533 (Fla. Dist. Ct. App. 2010).

◆ After being released from school on a rainy day, a 12-year-old New York student used a cell phone to call his mother, who was parked across the street. Although there was a stop sign, crosswalk and crossing guard at one intersection, and a stop light and crosswalk at the other, the student crossed in the middle of the street at his mother's direction. He was hit by a car and sustained injuries. His mother sued the school district for negligence in dismissing the student in an area it knew was hazardous. The New York Supreme Court, Appellate Division, dismissed the case, noting that schools are not insurers of student safety. **Schools' custodial duty of care for students ends when the students pass out of their "orbit of authority."** Here, the student was hurt while off school property and under the control of his mother, and there was no indication that the school had created a special hazard. *Vernali v. Harrison Cent. School Dist.*, 857 N.Y.S.2d 699 (N.Y. App. Div. 2008).

◆ An eleventh-grade Florida student left school without authorization along with four classmates after first period to go out for breakfast. She got into a classmate's car and was killed when he ran into a pair of trees at high speed. Her father sued the school board, claiming it could have prevented the accident by following its policy regarding habitual truancy. The policy required principals to report habitually truant students to the school board and state department of highway safety and motor vehicles. It also called for the filing of a truancy petition or a "child in need of services" petition. These steps were not taken for the student because she had not accumulated at least 15 absences in a 90-day period so as to be categorized as habitually truant. After the trial court ruled for the school board, the Florida District Court of Appeal affirmed. **The school was not obligated to supervise students while they were engaged in off-campus activities unrelated to school.** Further, the school could not be held liable for injuries suffered by students who violate school attendance policies. *Kazanjian v. School Board of Palm Beach County*, 967 So.2d 259 (Fla. Dist. Ct. App. 2007).

◆ Approximately 200 eighth-grade students from a middle school in Texas went on a field trip to an athletic club, where the activities included swimming. No lifeguards were hired. Sometime during the day, an eighth-grader drowned in the swimming pool. His family sued the district and various employees under 42 U.S.C. § 1983. The district employees sought pretrial judgment, asserting that they were entitled to immunity for their actions. The trial court disagreed, and the employees appealed to the Texas Court of Appeals.

The claims here included allegations that the school district employees committed constitutional violations because they failed to properly supervise and/or discipline the student on the field trip. The court held that the school district employees were acting within the scope of their discretionary authority at the time of the incident. Further, **there was no special relationship to create a constitutional duty on the part of the employees to safeguard the student against potential harm during the field trip**. The employees should have been granted pretrial judgment. The appellate court reversed the lower court's decision. *Leo v. Trevino*, 285 S.W.3d 470 (Tex. Ct. App. 2006).

◆ An Arkansas student attended a band competition in Atlanta with his school band. He became ill after arriving and missed the entire competition while remaining in his hotel room. Shortly after the student returned home, his mother took him to a medical center. However, he suffered a cardiac arrest and died the next day. The death was attributed to undiagnosed diabetes. The mother sued the school district and officials in a federal district court for negligence and deliberate indifference to her son's medical needs. The court dismissed her federal constitutional claims. It held federal jurisdiction should be rejected in cases that involved common law torts incidentally involving action by a government employee. The mother appealed to the U.S. Court of Appeals, Eighth Circuit. The court echoed the district court's opinion, noting that "the Due Process Clause of the Fourteenth Amendment is not a 'font of tort law.'" Neither the text nor the history of the clause indicated state entities must guarantee minimal safety and security to individuals. The Due Process Clause generally does not confer affirmative rights to government aid, even if this may be necessary to secure individual life, liberty or property interests.

A state assumes a constitutional duty to protect an individual's safety only when it has restrained the individual's liberty through incarceration, institutionalization or some other form of restraint that renders the individual incapable of self-care. The district court had correctly dismissed the due process claim against the school district, because there was no district policy of violating student constitutional rights. There was also no evidence that the band director had restrained the student's ability to care for himself. **School officials have no duty to care for students who participate in voluntary school-related activities such as school band trips.** There was no claim that the student could not leave the band activity at any time, and his family was not prevented from arranging for him to leave Atlanta. The court found no evidence that the student's "voluntary participation evolved into an involuntary commitment" during the trip. While a tort remedy might still be available in the state courts, the judgment for the school district on the mother's federal claims was affirmed. *Lee v. Pine Bluff School Dist.*, 472 F.3d 1026 (8th Cir. 2007).

2. Harmful Acts of Others

◆ A student on a field trip to the National Zoo in Washington claimed that he was assaulted, kicked, and beaten by five male students who were on a school field trip with their private, non-profit school chartered under District of Columbia law for at-risk youths. **He alleged that at the time of the attack, the students were unsupervised.** He also alleged that he suffered a concussion and injuries to multiple areas of his body. He sued the school, alleging negligent supervision. The school sought to dismiss the case, arguing that it owed the victimized student no duty to provide a constant watch over its students during a school field trip in order to prevent an unforeseeable act of violence. The injured student argued that the school did owe him a duty of care and cited to the Restatement of Torts (2d) § 319:

One who takes charge of a third person whom he knows or should know to be likely to cause bodily harm to others if not controlled is under a duty to exercise reasonable care to control the third person to prevent him from doing such harm.

The court permitted the injured student to maintain his negligence claim on the ground that the school had a duty to make reasonable efforts to protect members of the public from its students during the field trip. **A school's duty to supervise its students to guard against foreseeable harm does not disappear on field trips.** So if the injured student could show that the school should have known his attackers had a propensity for violence, the school could be liable. *Thomas v. City Lights School*, 124 F.Supp.2d 707 (D.D.C. 2000).

◆   A New York student's sixth-grade class, along with five other fifth- and sixth-grade classes, attended a drug awareness fair at a park near their school. Sponsored by the board of education and the police department, the fair permitted students to walk through the park on their own and participate in program activities that interested them. Seven teachers and four or five aides supervised the group. A student received permission to get lunch at a nearby pizzeria, but she did not return from lunch by the time her teacher decided to return to school. The teacher looked for her but did not inform any teachers or police officers providing security at the fair that he could not locate her. The student had left the park to walk home after she failed to find her classmates. On the way home, she was raped by a junior high school student and his friend. She sued the board of education for her injuries.

A jury ruled in her favor and awarded her $2,250,000 in damages, but the Supreme Court, Appellate Division, reversed. The case then reached the Court of Appeals, New York's highest court, which held that a rational jury could have determined, as the jury in this case did, that the foreseeable result of the danger created by the school's alleged lack of supervision was an injury such as occurred here. The jury permissibly determined that **the rape was the foreseeable result of a danger created by the school's failure to adequately supervise the student**. Thus, the board was liable for the student's injuries. *Bell v. Board of Educ. of the City of New York*, 687 N.E.2d 1325 (N.Y. 1997).

◆   A Washington high school sponsored a "Workday" event, in which community members donated $15 for three hours of student work to raise funds for a student association. A student's mother agreed to let her daughter split and stack firewood with a classmate's father. She learned on the day of the event that the classmate's father planned to have the students split logs with a hydraulic log splitter. The mother cautioned the student, but apparently did not turn in a parental permission slip to perform the work. While the students were operating the log splitter, they were distracted by a car, and the student lost three fingers.

The student sued the school district and classmate's father for negligence. The court found the student's mother had consented to the activity and awarded judgment to the school district. The student appealed. The Court of Appeals of Washington stated that schools are not insurers of student safety, but are liable for foreseeable wrongful acts of third parties. **Liability may result if a school supervises and exercises control over extracurricular activities.** As the student was in the district's custody, it owed her a duty of reasonable care. A jury could have found the district should have taken appropriate steps to find out what was planned for each workday location and identify any obvious safety problems. The student had presented enough evidence to receive a jury trial to decide whether her mother's consent superseded the district's duty. The court reversed and remanded the case for a trial. *Travis v. Bohannon*, 115 P.3d 342 (Wash. Ct. App. 2005).

B. School Policies – Permission

◆ Kansas' highest court determined an injured student's travel was authorized, so he was entitled to reimbursement from the school's insurance company. Several soccer players traveled to an away game in a teammate's car. They were in an accident. One teen suffered injuries that required round-the-clock care. The school purchased an insurance policy to cover injuries sustained by athletes, as well as "covered travel" to and from sanctioned events. But the claim was denied. The student's mom sued the school and its insurance company. The school said the ride to the game wasn't "authorized travel" by the school as the student chose to forgo the team bus and ride with a teammate. The school pointed to a permission slip signed by the injured boy's dad that allowed him, among other things, to "ride with other players to games." The case reached the state supreme court, which rejected the school's argument. The court held that **by "employing permission slips from parents," the school "created and sanctioned" this system of informal transportation**. The court found the student was injured during authorized travel and could be reimbursed, so the case was remanded. *Rodriguez v. Unified School Dist. No. 500*, 351 P.3d 1243 (Kan. 2015).

◆ The summer before her senior year, an Illinois student went on two school-sponsored trips to China. She was told repeatedly that alcohol was forbidden, and she signed a contract to that effect. She and other students were caught drinking during the second trip. When she returned home, her principal suspended her for 10 days. She sought a preliminary injunction to stop the suspension and only served three days because she graduated before the case came to trial. When her lawsuit challenging the suspension came before a judge, the court ruled that her procedural due process rights had been met because **she had been informed of the charges and given an opportunity to respond to them**. *Sabol v. Walter Payton College Preparatory High School*, 804 F.Supp.2d 747 (N.D. Ill. 2011).

◆ A sixth-grade student with asthma went on a field trip to a district-operated science camp. When she suffered an attack, camp counselors gave the student her inhaler and performed CPR on her until paramedics arrived. However, she died as she was being airlifted to a hospital. Her parents sued the district that operated the science camp for negligently failing to provide adequate medical staff and for misrepresenting the level of medical staffing that would be available. The case reached the California Court of Appeal, which held that the district was entitled to immunity under the state education code. **Any person on a school field trip or excursion is deemed to have waived all claims against the school district**, charter school or the state for injury, accident, illness or death occurring "during or by reason of the field trip or excursion." The parents' lawsuit failed. *Sanchez v. San Diego County Office of Educ.*, 182 Cal.App.4th 1580, 106 Cal.Rptr.3d 750 (Cal. Ct. App. 2010).

◆   A group of Ohio students attended a school-sponsored student exchange program in Germany. Before the trip, a teacher explained to students that they would stay with a "host family" for two weeks. They would have some supervised field trips, but would spend a great deal of time with host families without any direct supervision by school staff or the host school. While in Germany, a number of students drank alcohol with their "host parents." They were of legal drinking age in Germany and believed they were permitted to drink without supervision. Upon returning home, the school suspended the students for three to five days for violating student code prohibitions on consuming or possessing alcohol while in the school's control and custody. The students asked for a hearing before the school board, arguing the teacher had "verbally created an exception to the school's code of conduct regarding the consumption of alcohol." Students and parents understood the exception as allowing the parents and host parents to determine whether students could drink alcohol. The board overturned the suspensions but required the students to perform community service.

An Ohio trial court vacated the discipline, and the board appealed to the Court of Appeals of Ohio. The court stated that **Ohio law gives school districts the authority to devise codes of conduct, adopt a policy for suspension, expulsion and removal of students, and to specify the types of misconduct resulting in discipline**. There was undisputed evidence that the teacher had "engrafted an exception on the disciplinary code's provisions concerning alcohol consumption." Only the teacher and another employee had testified that the "exception" required direct supervision of host parents for any student drinking. The exception was not written. The students and parents had all stated their understanding of the policy allowed parents and host parents to determine the circumstances for alcohol consumption by students. The court upheld the trial court's decision to vacate any discipline. *Brosch v. Mariemont City School Dist. Board of Educ.*, No. C-050283, 2006 WL 250947 (Ohio Ct. App. 2/3/06).

◆   Minnesota students attending an auto shop class were bused to a body shop for class instruction. En route, the teacher observed a student holding a knife that was passed to him from a classmate. When the bus arrived at the body shop, the teacher called a school coordinator to report the knife. The coordinator and principal decided each student should be searched, and the principal called a school liaison officer. Before the search began, the classmate voluntarily handed over the knife. The liaison officer found a collapsible baton in the student's pocket, and he was charged with violating a state law prohibiting possession of a dangerous weapon on school property. The district brought an expulsion proceeding against the student, who sued for civil rights violations.

The case reached the Eighth Circuit, which stated that school and municipal officers are entitled to qualified immunity when their conduct does not violate clearly established federal statutory or constitutional rights of which a reasonable officer would have knowledge. While law officers are normally required to have probable cause of wrongdoing to support a search or seizure of persons or property, the more lenient standard of "reasonable suspicion" applies to searches and seizures in the context of public schools. School administrators initiated the search, and one of them played a substantial role in it. **The fact that the search took place off school grounds did not call for imposing the stricter probable cause standard.** The liaison officer's conduct was reasonable, as he did not know whether other students might also have weapons. He had reasonable grounds to believe that the student possessed a knife and was not required to use the least intrusive means of performing a search. As the search was justified and reasonable in scope, the officer was entitled to immunity. *Shade v. City of Farmington, Minnesota*, 309 F.3d 1054 (8th Cir. 2002).

◆ A teacher employed by the Kansas State School for the Deaf (KSSD) asked an assistant football coach to recruit players to help him improve property he owned. The project involved moving discarded railroad ties that weighed 150 pounds. The school's head teacher turned down a written request for a field trip to the property, but later signed the request form. Two students and the assistant football coach accompanied the teacher to the property. When the teacher left to prepare lunch, one of the students was struck and killed by a train. KSSD's board ruled the teacher's conduct did not reflect high standards of professional conduct, especially for the safety needs of deaf students. A KSSD investigation committee adopted a motion terminating the teacher's employment for jeopardizing the health and safety of students, failing to exercise appropriate professional judgment, failing to comply with school policies, and failing to conduct himself "in a manner reflecting positively on the school." However, a KSSD hearing committee held for the teacher, finding the board did not prove he displayed a lack of professional judgment.

The case reached the Kansas Supreme Court, which **upheld the hearing committee's finding that no school policy or student safety regulations applied to the case. The board showed no evidence of a loss of confidence in the teacher**, as the testimony of members of the deaf community was "all to the contrary." While the teacher did not inform parents about the nature of the field trip, this was the head teacher's duty. There was evidence that the practice of taking railroad ties from railroad property was common and not inappropriate. The court refused to reweigh the evidence or substitute its judgment for that of the committee. *Kansas State Board of Educ. v. Marsh*, 50 P.3d 9 (Kan. 2002).

III. ATHLETIC EVENTS

Student-athletes assume the risks incidental to sports participation and, absent a showing of gross negligence or intentional conduct by a coach, league or school, may not recover damages for their injuries.

A. Participants

1. Duty of Care

State laws require a showing that the school or its staff acted recklessly or intentionally to overcome the defense of governmental immunity.

◆ A New York appeals court refused to dismiss the negligence claim of a student-athlete who was injured before football coaches arrived for practice. The football players' horseplay got out of hand when they used a blocking sled to hurl each other through the air. A 15-year-old fractured both wrists as he landed. He and his mother filed a negligence claim, but the court dismissed the case, saying the football player "assumed the risk of injury." On appeal, the boy's mom argued **this wasn't a typical sports injury, where her son assumed the risk by participating, because "using the blocking sled to catapult each other into the air" wasn't part of the game**. And the coach wasn't on the field at the time, the mother pointed out, which she said showed the students weren't properly supervised. The court said more info was needed to determine whether the level of supervision was appropriate, so the case had to move forward. *Duffy v. Long Beach City School Dist.*, 22 N.Y.S.3d 88 (N.Y. App. Div. 2015).

◆ An Iowa jury decided a school fumbled its response to a football player's head injuries, so the former athlete was awarded nearly $1 million. The student played football on his school's team. He had a pre-existing medical condition: abnormally formed blood vessels in his brain. He suffered a head injury but was allowed to keep playing and practicing, which caused internal bleeding in his brain. Then he needed surgery to remove a blood clot near the brainstem. His permanent injuries resulted in a mobility impairment. A negligence suit alleged the district and the school nurse failed to notify the football coaches about the student's potential concussion or brain injury and follow up with the student's grandmother, his guardian, to make sure he was seen by a doctor.

The student received $140,000 for past medical expenses and $850,000 in additional damages for pain, suffering, loss of future earnings and loss of mind and body. But **the jury stopped short of awarding punitive damages, saying the evidence didn't show "willful and wanton" disregard**. *K.R.S. v. Beford Community School Dist.*, No. 4:13CV00147, 2015 WL 3745161 (S.D. Iowa 5/11/15).

◆ In New York, a cheerleader was injured while attempting a stunt at practice. The move required the girl to stand on another cheerleader's shoulders. But she fell during the stunt. She sued the district, claiming the school was negligent because it did not provide proper supervision while she attempted the stunt. The trial court refused to grant the school judgment without a trial, but on appeal, the appellate court reversed. Under New York law, **a student assumes the inherent risks of an extracurricular activity by participating**. And because falling is an obvious risk associated with cheerleading, the claim failed. *Kristina D. v. Nesaquake Middle School*, 98 A.D.3d 600 (N.Y. App. Div. 2012).

◆ An Iowa high school basketball player elbowed an opposing player in the head during a game and was immediately ejected. The other player went to the bench briefly, but then returned to the game, though he played poorly from that point on. His family sued the school district and the player, seeking damages of more than $1.5 million. The case reached the Iowa Supreme Court, which dismissed the claim against the district, noting that **the battery by the player was not reasonably foreseeable, as was required for the district to be held liable for breaching a duty of care**. The student's prior conduct, although aggressive, did not put the district on notice that he was a dangerous person. The court did uphold, however, a damage award against the student for $23,000. *Brokaw v. Winfield-Mt. Union Community School Dist.*, 788 N.W.2d 386 (Iowa 2010).

◆ A 13-year-old student on his junior high school basketball team blacked out at a Monday practice. His mother told the coach that he was only allowed to walk through plays – and could not do anything strenuous. But at the Wednesday practice, the coach made the whole team, including the student, perform a running drill. After the student collapsed and died, his parents sued the school district for wrongful death. The district asserted that the student knew better than to perform a running drill in his condition; thus, his contributory negligence prevented the parents from recovering money damages. However, the Supreme Court of Indiana disagreed. It noted that **children 7 to 14 years old are generally too young to be held responsible for their own injuries** because they lack the maturity to foresee harm and take steps to prevent it. The only way to rebut the presumption that a 7- to 14-year-old is not responsible for his injuries is to show that the child had the "mental capacity, intelligence and experience" to be accountable for himself. Since that was not the case here, the parents were entitled to recover from the district. *Clay City Consolidated School Dist. v. Timberman*, 918 N.E.2d 292 (Ind. 2009).

◆ A Louisiana cheerleader – the "flyer" on her squad – suffered injuries when she was lifted up by an untrained recruit who held onto her feet tightly even though he should have left her feet free in case she needed to jump. When she fell, she landed on her back and sustained herniated discs that left her with chronic pain. She sued the school district for her injuries, and **a jury found the district negligent for allowing the untrained recruit to participate in the difficult stunt**. It awarded her more than $274,000. However, the judge reduced the amount by one-fourth, ruling that she was a quarter to blame because she didn't fall the right way. The Louisiana Court of Appeal reversed the judge's decision and gave her the full jury award. She did not breach a duty to fall a certain way when the stunt went bad. *Comeaux v. Acadia Parish School Board*, 13 So.3d 252 (La. Ct. App. 2009).

◆ A member of a high school track team in Pennsylvania sustained injuries when a teammate hit her in the leg with a javelin during practice. She sued the district and the coaches for negligence, and she also asserted that her due process rights had been violated. The defendants sought to have the case dismissed, and a federal court agreed to do so. First, it found no due process violation because **the district had proper policies in place to deal with injuries**. And even if the district failed to comply with those policies, that was not sufficient to support a due process claim. Further, the district did not have a special relationship with her such that it owed her an increased duty of care. Finally, the district did not create the danger that resulted in her injuries. It was the teammate's decision to throw the javelin that caused the harm. *Leonard v. Owen J. Roberts School Dist.*, No. 08-2016, 2009 WL 603160 (E.D. Pa. 3/5/09).

◆ A junior high school wrestling coach in Pennsylvania instructed a 152-pound wrestler to grapple with a 240-pound teammate during a practice. They were to simulate competitive conditions, and the coach paired them up because there was no suitable partner for the heavier wrestler. The smaller wrestler injured his leg when his teammate fell on it. He sued the coach and his school district for violating his liberty interests under the Constitution. A federal court ruled against him, but the Third Circuit allowed his lawsuit against the coach to proceed. There was evidence that the coach acted with "deliberate indifference" to his constitutional rights. Under the state's interscholastic athletic association rules, students were not permitted to move more than one weight class from their own. Here, **the teammate who caused the injury was three weight classes above the injured student**. However, the lawsuit against the school district could not proceed because the coach did not make policy for the district, and the student failed to show that the district had a policy or custom of violating students' federal rights. *Patrick v. Great Valley School Dist.*, 296 Fed.Appx. 258 (3d Cir. 2008).

◆   A California community college student played on a visiting baseball team in a preseason game against a host college. The host team's pitcher hit him in the head with a pitch, cracking his batting helmet. The student claimed he was intentionally hit in retaliation for a pitch thrown by his teammate at a batter from the host team in the previous inning. After being hit, the student staggered, felt dizzy, and was in pain. His manager told him to go to first base. The student did so, but complained to his first-base coach, who told him to stay in the game. Soon after that, the student was told to sit on the bench. He claimed no one tended to his injuries. The student sued the host college for breaching its duty of care by failing to supervise or control its pitcher and failing to provide umpires or medical care. The court dismissed the case, but the state court of appeal reversed. The Supreme Court of California held that Section 831.7 of the California Government Code did not extend to injuries suffered during supervised school sports.

Section 831.7 was intended to be a premises liability provision for public entities. **In sports, the doctrine of assumption of risk precludes any liability for injuries deemed "inherent in a sport."** The college did not fail to adequately supervise and control the pitcher. Being hit by a pitch is an inherent risk of baseball. Colleges are not liable for the actions of their student-athletes during competition. The failure to provide umpires did not increase risks inherent in the game. The student's own coaches, not the host college, had the responsibility to remove him from the game for medical attention. *Avila v. Citrus Community College Dist.*, 38 Cal.4th 148, 41 Cal.Rptr. 299, 131 P.3d 383 (Cal. 2006).

◆   A Louisiana freshman football player injured his back in a weight training session. His physician diagnosed him with a lumbar strain and dehydrated disc, and gave him a medical excuse excluding him from football for one week with instructions for "no weightlifting, squats or power cleans." The coaching staff interpreted the weightlifting limitation to be for only one week, and a coach instructed the student to do a particular lift. He did the lift and suffered severe back pain. The student was diagnosed with a disc protrusion and a herniated disc. He lost interest in school, failed classes and transferred to an alternative school. The student sued the school board for personal injury. A state trial court awarded him less than $7,500 for medical expenses, but awarded him $275,500 for pain and suffering, future medical expenses and loss of enjoyment of life.

The school board appealed to a Louisiana Circuit Court of Appeal, which reviewed testimony that the student continued to experience severe back pain and often could not sleep. **The evidence supported the trial court's finding that he had been severely injured and would experience recurring pain that would limit his daily activities indefinitely.** The trial court did not commit error in awarding the student damages for pain and suffering. The court affirmed the damage award for loss of enjoyment of life, based on evidence that the student lost the opportunity to play varsity baseball and football. There was further evidence he suffered depression and emotional anguish. *Day v. Ouachita Parish School Board*, 823 So.2d 1039 (La. Ct. App. 2002).

◆ A Maryland high school junior was the first female football player in her county's history. She participated in weightlifting, strength-training exercises and contact drills. In the first scrimmage with another team, the student was tackled while carrying the football and suffered multiple internal injuries. Three years later, the student and her mother sued the school board, claiming it had a duty to warn them of the risk of serious, disabling and catastrophic injuries.

A Maryland trial court granted the board's motion for summary judgment, finding no such duty to warn of the risk of varsity football participation. The student and her mother appealed to the Court of Special Appeals of Maryland. There they argued the lower court had erroneously held the board had no duty to warn of catastrophic risks and that the student had assumed the risk of injury by participating. **The court found no case from any jurisdiction holding that a school board had a duty to warn varsity high school football players that severe injuries might result.** The dangers of varsity football participation were self-evident, and there was no duty to warn of such an obvious danger. The court, therefore, affirmed the order for summary judgment in favor of the school board. *Hammond v. Board of Educ. of Carroll County*, 639 A.2d 223 (Md. Ct. Spec. App. 1994).

2. Governmental Immunity

The doctrine of governmental immunity (sometimes called discretionary or official immunity) precludes school or individual liability when employees are performing "discretionary duties" within the scope of their employment. By contrast, employees performing "ministerial duties" are unprotected by immunity, as are those who do not act in the scope of their employment.

◆ An Oklahoma court refused to grant immunity on the negligence claim of a student who broke his neck during a pep rally practice. A student volunteered to participate in a pep rally cheer. At a practice supervised by school staffers, he and a friend attempted a two-man somersault. But the stunt went wrong. The teen suffered a broken neck that required hospitalization and surgeries. He sued, claiming negligence. When the court dismissed the claim, the student appealed, saying the district was liable under the theory of *respondeat superior*. In other words, he said the district was responsible for its employees' negligent conduct. To determine if the district could be held liable under this theory, the court had to decide whether immunity applied. It looked at whether the district had adopted a policy to allow the pep rally and practice, whether the employees who supervised the practice had the authority to make discretionary judgment calls, and if not, whether questions existed about how their duties were carried out during the pep rally practice. The court said the first prong was met for immunity. **But it couldn't determine whether the staffers were given discretion to make judgment calls – or whether a policy outlined how coaches must make decisions for the pep rallies and practices.** Questions existed, so immunity wasn't appropriate, the court explained. The ruling was reversed, and the case was remanded for further proceedings. *Hasenfratz v. Ponca City Independent School Dist.*, 358 P.3d 964 (Okla. Ct. App. 2015).

◆   The Third Circuit excused a Pennsylvania cheerleading coach from a lawsuit, finding she was entitled to immunity. After the squad saw the "twist down cradle" stunt at a competition, they wanted to learn it. The stunt called for four "base" cheerleaders to launch a "flyer" into the air, where she does a twist before landing in the bases' waiting arms. The coach waited seven months until she thought the squad was ready. Then she had another high school's cheerleader – an assistant coach for a middle school squad – demonstrate and help teach the stunt. The squad used a large room with a concrete floor for practice. Its carpeting had little, if any, padding. The day the squad started to learn the stunt, six to eight spotters plus four base cheerleaders were ready to catch the flyer. She overshot all of them. Landing badly, she struck her head on the floor and suffered a severe injury. The injured cheerleader sued the district and the coach, alleging they violated her substantive due process right to bodily integrity. A federal judge granted the district judgment without a trial. But it ruled the coach had to stand trial, as she wasn't immune to the claim. The coach appealed, and the Third Circuit reversed. School officials have qualified immunity if sued for violation of a constitutional right that wasn't clearly established at the time. The cheerleader argued that national cheering organizations' safety standards require padded floor mats, so the coach's "deliberate indifference" constituted a violation of her right to bodily integrity. But the Third Circuit found this wasn't clearly established, as **no court decisions would've informed "a reasonable person in [the coach's] position that failure to take certain precautions in a high school cheerleading practice** would amount to a constitutional violation" – so the court ruled the claim couldn't proceed. *Hinterberger v. Iroquois School Dist.*, 548 Fed.Appx. 50 (3d Cir. 2013).

◆   While lifting weights, two football teammates quarreled over the CD they were listening to. They started pushing each other, and teammates intervened to separate them. One began walking away, while teammates held the other one back. The coach then asked them if they wanted to settle it. The student being held back said he did, and the coach said, "OK." At that point, the formerly restrained student violently attacked the other one, causing injuries. When the student sued the coach for his injuries, the Michigan Court of Appeals ruled that **the coach was not the proximate cause of the injuries**, and thus he was entitled to immunity. He did not commit gross negligence, and the other student's assault was the most direct cause of the harm. *Gray v. Cry*, No. 07-717218-NO, 2011 WL 4375074 (Mich. Ct. App. 9/20/11).

◆ Two years after a highly publicized hazing incident involving football players at a New Mexico high school, a football player at another New Mexico high school was subjected to hazing by seniors. The seniors threw him to the floor, then physically and sexually battered him. He and his mother sued various officials, including the coaching staff, the principal and the superintendent, for negligence. The officials sought to have the case dismissed on immunity grounds, but a federal court allowed the lawsuit to proceed. Here, **they knew about the hazing at the other school and yet took no action to prevent hazing at the student's school**. *C.H. v. Los Lunas Schools Board of Educ.*, 852 F.Supp.2d 1344 (D.N.M. 2012).

◆ An Illinois school district operated a summer football camp. Coaches instructed camp participants to run from a locker room to the practice field. One student tripped over a grass-concealed shot-put bumper along the route and sustained injuries. His mother sued the school district for negligence, seeking $50,000. A state court granted recreational immunity to the district, but the Appellate Court of Illinois reversed. There was a question as to whether the camp was educational in nature, which would nullify the recreational immunity provisions of state law. The case required a trial. *Peters v. Herrin Community School Dist. No. 4*, 928 N.E.2d 1258 (Ill. App. Ct. 2010).

◆ A 17-year-old student suffered heatstroke during football practice at his Mississippi high school on a hot August day. After he collapsed, emergency responders were unable to revive him. Upon his death, his family sued the school district for negligence, and the case reached the Supreme Court of Mississippi, which ruled that **the district was entitled to immunity**. The Mississippi Tort Claims Act provides immunity to state and political subdivisions whose employees act in the course and scope of their employment and exercise discretion. Here, the coaches were exercising discretion in the way they conducted their practices. *Covington County School Dist. v. Magee*, 29 So.3d 1 (Miss. 2010).

◆ A Delaware school district agreed to let its facilities be used by a charitable organization that wanted to conduct a cheerleading competition. During the event, a man fell off the bleachers, which did not have guard rails installed. He sued the organization and the district for his injuries, and the school district asserted that it was entitled to immunity. The Superior Court of Delaware noted that the organization had agreed to indemnify the district for any damages resulting from a judgment against it. **The court then found some evidence that school employees, without justification, deliberately chose not to install safety devices** and thus created a known risk. As a result, an issue of fact remained that required a trial. If the district was grossly negligent in electing not to install guard rails, the organization would have to pay the man for his injuries. But the district would not have to pay. *Boyle v. Christiana School Dist. Board of Educ.*, No. 07C-07-248 JAP, 2009 WL 4653832 (Del. Super. Ct. 11/30/09).

◆ A Georgia high school student participated in a voluntary workout session for the football team. The next morning, he collapsed and died. His parents sued the school system, school officials and several coaches, asserting that their son had been subjected to an "intense and unreasonable practice." They claimed the coaches failed to give their son enough to drink and ignored signs that he was becoming dehydrated. They also stated that the coaches failed to attend to their son until after a team meeting, even though he had collapsed during drills. They maintained that the coaches violated their son's substantive due process rights. A federal court dismissed all the defendants except three coaches, who appealed. The Eleventh Circuit held that **the coaches were entitled to qualified immunity because their conduct did not rise to a "conscience-shocking" level**. The parents made no allegation that the coaches intended to harm their son. Thus, they failed to prove a constitutional violation. *Davis v. Carter*, 555 F.3d 979 (11th Cir. 2009).

◆ A 14-year-old Minnesota student participated in a community education gymnastics program sponsored by a local school district. She performed a difficult vault known as a Tsukahara vault, which she had performed many times previously. This time she under-rotated and landed on her knees. She told a coach she would try it again, but that she would need assistance. However, when she attempted it a second time, no assistance was provided. The second time, she also under-rotated and landed on her head. She sued the school district for negligence. The district sought to have the lawsuit dismissed on grounds of immunity, but a trial court refused to do so. The Minnesota Court of Appeals reversed the lower court and granted immunity to the district. **The state's recreational use statute generally bars claims based on injuries sustained on government property that is intended for recreational use.** And no exception applied to the statute in this case. *Goetz v. Independent School Dist. No. 625*, No. A08-0254, 2009 WL 22270 (Minn. Ct. App. 1/6/09).

◆ In an effort to improve security, a Tennessee school board approved the installation of video surveillance equipment throughout one of its middle schools. The assistant principal decided to place cameras in the boys' and girls' locker rooms. Images were displayed on a computer in the assistant principal's office. They could also be accessed through a remote Internet connection. **When the assistant principal learned that the cameras were videotaping areas where students routinely dressed, he recommended to the principal that the cameras be moved, but no changes were made.**

After a visiting girls' basketball team noticed the camera and complained, the principal assured the coach that the camera was not operational, although in fact it was. The next day, the locker room cameras were removed. Thirty-four students then sued for a violation of their privacy rights. The principal, assistant principal, director of schools and school board members claimed immunity. The Sixth Circuit Court of Appeals held that the board members and the director were entitled to immunity because their roles in placing the cameras were too indirect to make them liable. However, the principal and assistant principal were not immune. They violated a clearly established constitutional right to privacy at the time of the videotaping. *Brannum v. Overton County School Board*, 516 F.3d 489 (6th Cir. 2008).

◆   An Ohio student injured his forehead and wrist during a pole vault at a high school track meet. He landed on improper padding near the landing pad. The padding was later identified as in violation of National Federation of State High School Associations rules. The student sued the school district, coach and other officials for negligence. The court awarded pretrial judgment to the district and school officials, but the Court of Appeals of Ohio held that the trial court had improperly granted immunity under the state recreational user statute. The student was not a "recreational user." The student did not assume the risk of being provided inadequate safety equipment for pole vaulting. The sponsor of a sporting event has a duty not to increase the risk of harm over and above any inherent risks of the sport.

While the Ohio Political Subdivision Tort Liability Act generally grants immunity to government entities, an exception applies when an injury was caused by employee negligence occurring on school grounds in connection with a governmental function. The court rejected the district's claim to immunity. The Tort Liability Act protects employees unless they act with a malicious purpose, in bad faith, or in a wanton or reckless manner. **The track coach was entitled to immunity, because there was no evidence he acted with malice, bad faith or reckless or wanton conduct.** The court affirmed the judgment in the coach's favor, but held the action could proceed against the school district. *Henney v. Shelby City School Dist.*, No. 2005 CA 0064, 2006 WL 747475 (Ohio Ct. App. 3/23/06).

◆   A Maine high school wrestling team ran timed drills in school hallways as part of its warm-up routine. A wrestler was seriously injured after being bumped into a window by a teammate during a drill. The school had no policy prohibiting athletic training in school hallways at the time. The student sued the school district in a state court for personal injury, asserting officials negligently allowed the team to competitively race through the hallways. The court held the district and officials were protected by discretionary immunity. The student appealed to the Maine Supreme Judicial Court, which stated that **governmental entities are generally entitled to absolute immunity from suit for any tort action for damages**. One of four state law exceptions to this rule imposes liability on government entities for the negligent operation of a public building.

The court held that allowing relay races in the school hallway was not the "operation of a public building." The focus of this case was the manner in which the team was required to run through the halls, not the operation of a high school building. To impose liability under the "public building" exception to immunity, the claim must implicate the physical structure of the building. Decisions, such as wrestling team rules, focused on the supervision of students, not the maintenance or operation of the building. **Since the failure to prohibit racing in the halls was not related to the operation of a public building, the district and officials were protected by discretionary immunity.** *Lightfoot v. School Administrative Dist. No. 35*, 816 A.2d 63 (Me. 2003).

◆ A Kansas school football team held its first practice on an August day when the temperature reached 83 degrees by 8:00 a.m. Players practiced from then until 12:50 p.m. with a 45-minute break at 10:15 and five-minute water breaks every 20 minutes. The team then began circuit conditioning. Players spent four minutes at various stations, then rested for two minutes before rotating to another. A student reported feeling ill after completing the first two stations. An assistant coach instructed him to drink some water, which he did. He asked to sit out further drills and was told again to get water. As the team left practice, the student collapsed and was taken to a hospital, where he died the next day. His estate sued the school district and head coach for negligence. A state court granted the estate's motion to prevent the district and coach from relying on the "recreational use" exception to the Kansas Tort Claims Act (KTCA), which precludes liability for injury claims arising from the use of any public property used for recreational purposes, except in cases of gross and wanton negligence.

The district and coach appealed to the state supreme court, which observed the trial court did not take into account the KTCA's legitimate purpose to encourage construction of public recreational facilities. The court found a rational basis for distinguishing between injuries occurring on public recreational property and those occurring elsewhere. The trial court committed error by refusing to apply the discretionary function exception to the KTCA. **The discretionary function exception protects government entities and employees from claims based on the exercise of discretion or the failure to exercise it.** The recreational use exception eliminated any liability for ordinary negligence and barred all the claims. The court reversed and remanded the case for a determination of whether the district or coach acted with gross or wanton negligence. *Barrett v. Unified School Dist. No. 259*, 32 P.3d 1156 (Kan. 2001).

3. Assumption of Risk and Waiver

Many courts have determined that when a participant has assumed the risks of playing sports, a school district should not be held liable for injuries.

One way to guard against liability is through the use of releases. Cases involving parental releases are uncommon, but the Supreme Judicial Court of Massachusetts upheld the use of one in *Sharon v. City of Newton,* below.

◆ **A New York wrestler contracted herpes simplex I and believed he caught it from a wrestler at another school.** He sued his school, the other school and the other student for personal injury. A state court refused to dismiss the case, but the Supreme Court, Appellate Division, threw the case out. It noted that communicable diseases are an inherent danger of the sport and that students' participation is seen as an agreement to accept the obvious risks associated with wrestling. Even the student's own expert witness acknowledged that the possibility of contracting herpes and other communicable diseases from wrestling was well known. *Farrell v. Hochhauser,* 65 A.D.3d 663 (N.Y. 2009).

◆ A Massachusetts school district required a signed parental release for all students seeking to participate in extracurricular activities. For four years, the father of a high school cheerleader signed a release form before each season. During her fourth year, she was injured during a practice. When the cheerleader reached age 18, she sued the city in a state superior court for negligence and negligent hiring, and retention of the cheerleading coach. The court awarded summary judgment to the city on the basis of the parental release, agreeing that **the father had forever released the city from any and all actions and claims**.

The cheerleader appealed to the Massachusetts Supreme Judicial Court, asserting the release was invalid. The court held the trial court properly allowed the city to amend its answer by asserting release. **Enforcement of a parental release was consistent with Massachusetts law and public policy.** There was undisputed evidence that the father read and understood the release before signing it, and that the form was not misleading, since it required two signatures and clearly ensured parental permission was granted. It was not contrary to public policy to require parents to sign releases as a condition for student participation in extracurricular activities. The father had signed the release because he wanted the student to benefit from cheerleading. The court found that to hold the release unenforceable would expose public schools to financial costs and risks that would lead to the reduction of extracurricular activities. *Sharon v. City of Newton,* 437 Mass. 99, 769 N.E.2d 738 (Mass. 2002).

◆ Indiana parents received a new trial in a lawsuit based on the death of their son from heatstroke after a school football practice. The release forms they signed did not specifically waive claims based on negligence. The student, who weighed over 250 pounds, had "dry heaves" early in a morning practice session. He stopped his activity for a minute, then told two coaches he felt better. The student ate lunch during a team rest period and kept it down. He spent time lying on the locker room floor. The head coach asked the student how he felt, and the student again said he was OK. Near the end of the afternoon session, the student told a coach he did not feel well. The coach told him to get water, but he soon collapsed. The coaches took him to the locker room and placed him in a cool shower. The student lost consciousness, and the coaches called for an ambulance. He died at a hospital the following day.

The student's parents sued the school district for negligence. A jury returned a verdict for the school district. The parents appealed to the Court of Appeals of Indiana, which noted that **the release forms signed by the parents and students did not refer to "negligence."** Thus, the district was not effectively released from negligence claims. The trial court should have granted the parents' request for a jury instruction stating they had not released the district from negligence. The court reversed and remanded the case for a new trial. *Stowers v. Clinton Cent. School Corp.*, 855 N.E.2d 739 (Ind. Ct. App. 2006).

◆   A New York student participated on his high school wrestling team and was instructed before a match to wrestle an opponent in the next higher weight class. The student agreed to do so and was injured when the opponent hit his jaw during a take-down maneuver. The student voluntarily continued participating in the match after a medical time-out. He later filed a personal injury lawsuit against the school district in a New York trial court, which denied the district's dismissal motion. On appeal, the New York Supreme Court, Appellate Division, stated that **the student had assumed the risk of incurring a blow to the jaw and the injury was reasonably foreseeable in a wrestling match**. There was evidence that the size of the opponent had not caused the injury and that the student was aware of the risks involved in wrestling. The district's duty of care was limited to protecting the student from unassumed, concealed or unreasonable risks. The trial court judgment was reversed. *Edelson v. Uniondale Union Free School Dist.*, 631 N.Y.S.2d 391 (N.Y. App. Div. 1995).

B. Spectators, Employees and Parents

◆   Having decided a federal claim could not proceed, a Georgia federal court refused to hear a coach's state-law claims and dismissed his suit. Georgia high schools Warren County and Hancock Central were football rivals. Early in the 2011 football season, Warren fired its head coach and Hancock hired the coach as an assistant. The coach said his new team saw that year's game against Warren as a chance to "get even" for the way he was treated by his former team. A week before the game, football players from both teams got into such a heated altercation that police put one boy in handcuffs. Over the next week, the players and other students exchanged taunting text messages. The matchup was Hancock's homecoming game. Twelve officers were scheduled for security, but only four officers were at the game. Hancock lost 21-2. After their loss, Hancock players taunted the Warren team. A fight broke out. Cops rushed forward with pepper spray, and the coach tried to stop a Hancock athlete from hitting a Warren player. The Hancock athlete turned and attacked, hitting the coach in the face and head with a helmet. He suffered a "blow out" of the bones around one eye, requiring multiple surgeries and metal plates. He also needed extensive treatment in a brain injury rehabilitation program. The injuries have permanently impaired his ability to work. He sued Hancock's school district in federal court. Along with state-law claims, the coach alleged a breach of his substantive Fourteenth Amendment right to bodily integrity by failing to protect him. He said the district hired only four off-duty deputy sheriffs and knew they had no crowd-control experience. The court dismissed the claim, finding **the acts didn't "shock the conscience" in the constitutional sense**. With no federal claims remaining, the federal court dismissed the suit. *Daniel v. Hancock County School Dist.*, No. 5:13-CV-390 (CAR), 2014 WL 1813712 (M.D. Ga. 5/7/14).

◆   A New York school hosted a charity football game played by two other schools. A student who was a member of the hosting school's football team attended the charity event as a spectator. During halftime, the student went into the locker room to get gear from his locker. The locker room was being used by one of the visiting teams playing in the charity game. There, the student got into an argument with the visiting team's coach and head-butted him. Defending their coach, the team jumped the student. He suffered injuries he claimed were permanent. The student sued multiple parties for personal injury, including the city of New York and its department of education. He claimed the defendants breached their duty to provide for students' safety. But the court ruled that the defendants have no duty to protect students from injuries by a third party unless the school had a special relationship with the student. **The school wasn't liable because it had no reasonable warning the attack might occur and the attack happened "in a matter of seconds" – too fast for an onlooker to step in.** So the claim failed. *Chavis v. City of New York*, No. 101909/11, 2013 WL 3388643 (N.Y. Sup. Ct. 6/28/13).

◆   The mother of a New Jersey high school football player claimed that she tripped in a hole by the football field while leaving a game. She injured her ankle and sued the school for her injuries. A court granted pretrial judgment to the school, and the superior court, appellate division, affirmed that decision. **The woman failed to prove that the hole existed.** The school's athletic director described the area where she fell as "grassy." And though she maintained that there was a hole and produced photos of the area, there was no definitive proof that the hole even existed. *Pazos v. Borough of Sayreville*, 2010 WL 3257800 (N.J. Super. Ct. App. Div. 8/17/10).

◆   An Illinois man took his son to the local high school's batting cage to throw batting practice for him. He sat on a bucket behind a screen to throw pitches. One ball hit back by his son struck the screen, passed through the mesh, and struck him in the face, causing injury. He sued the school, alleging that it was willful and wanton in providing defective equipment. However, the Appellate Court of Illinois ruled against him, noting that **no one had seen the defect in the screen, including the man himself**. Therefore, the school couldn't have been willful and wanton in providing defective equipment because no one saw a defect. *Vilardo v. Barrington Community School Dist. 220*, 941 N.E.2d 257 (Ill. App. Ct. 2010).

◆ A Louisiana child sustained injuries when she fell while on the bleachers at a high school football game. Her parents claimed the fall was caused by a lack of adequate traction guards on the bleachers, and they sued the school board. A school custodial supervisor, however, testified that he saw the child being chased just before she fell. He also testified that the girl's family did nothing to stop her while she ran along the bleachers. A court ruled for the school board, and the Louisiana Court of Appeal affirmed. **It found no evidence that the bleachers were defective** or that there had been prior similar incidents in the area where the fall had occurred. *Mason v. Monroe City School Board*, 996 So.2d 377 (La. Ct. App. 2008).

◆ A physical education teacher at a New York high school adjusted a volleyball net that had been set up improperly by another teacher. As she stepped back from the base that supported the net, the teacher fell and twisted her ankle. She sued the board of education to recover for her injuries, and the board sought pretrial judgment. The New York Supreme Court, Appellate Division, granted the motion. It noted that **the duty to provide a safe workplace does not obligate an employer to remove hazards that typically come with the job**. Nor are employers required to protect employees from conditions or defects that are open and obvious. The teacher was hurt while performing a task that was inherent in her employment. In addition, the condition that caused the fall was open and obvious. Accordingly, the teacher could not recover damages for her injuries. *Monahan v. New York City Dep't of Educ.*, 851 N.Y.S. 2d 586 (N.Y. App. Div. 2008).

◆ A West Virginia spectator slipped and fell on ice and snow on school grounds while going to a high school basketball game. On the day of the injury, the superintendent of schools cancelled all classes in county schools because of a major snow storm. But the high school principal and athletic director decided not to cancel the game. The spectator sued the board, arguing it was negligent to hold the basketball game on a day when the entire school system was closed. The school board claimed immunity under the state Governmental Tort Claims and Insurance Reform Act. The Supreme Court of Appeals of West Virginia ruled that the school board was entitled to immunity. **The court rejected the spectator's argument that the decision to hold the basketball game was an affirmative act that was not immunized.** While the act of holding the game may have encouraged her to venture out into the snow, it did not cause the conditions at the school. The Tort Claims and Insurance Reform Act provided immunity for losses or claims resulting from snow or ice on public ways caused by the weather. *Porter v. Grant County Board of Educ.*, 633 S.E.2d 38 (W.Va. 2006).

◆ A spectator at a high school football game in New York was stabbed during a fight that occurred on school grounds following the game. The spectator sued the school district and school officials in a New York trial court. The court held for the spectator, and the school appealed to a New York appellate division court. The spectator claimed the school was negligent when it failed to properly supervise the crowd. The court disagreed, holding **the district could not be found negligent because it did not have a duty to supervise non-student spectators at the game**. The court reversed the judgment and held for the district. *Jerideau v. Huntingdon Union Free School Dist.*, 21 A.D.3d 992, 801 N.Y.S.2d 394 (N.Y. App. Div. 2005).

IV. OTHER SCHOOL ACTIVITIES

Courts have held schools liable for injuries during school-sponsored events that resulted from the failure to provide a reasonably safe environment, failure to warn participants of known hazards (or to remove known dangers), failure to properly instruct participants in the activity, and failure to provide supervision adequate during age-appropriate school events, such as plays, dances, musicals and more. For a sample student behavior contract at school dances, see Form VI-11.

A. Physical Education Class Accidents

1. Duty of Care

Courts have held that schools and staff members are not liable for injuries that are unforeseeable. It has long been recognized that schools are not the insurers of student safety. The fact that each student is not personally supervised at all times does not itself constitute grounds for liability.

◆ Wyoming's supreme court rejected the negligence claim of a student who slipped and fell in a school locker room. The student took a swimming class for her PE course. When she fell in the locker room, she injured her back. She needed three surgeries. She sued the school for negligence, claiming it failed to maintain the shower facilities in a reasonably safe condition. Her suit alleged the shower drains were backed up and flooded into the dressing area. After a trial, the court granted judgment for the school. The student appealed to the state supreme court, which upheld the ruling. **The plumber – a 16-year veteran of the district – testified that he'd only needed to "snake" the drain on one occasion, and the head custodian testified about the daily, monthly and yearly cleaning**

routines. The evidence didn't support the claim that the area was not properly maintained. So her claim failed. *Halvorson v. Sweetwater County School Dist.,* 342 P.3d 395 (Wyo. 2015).

◆   A New York appeals court refused to dismiss the negligence claim of a student who alleged he was injured because a PE teacher got too competitive during a game. After splitting the class into two teams to play floor hockey, the teacher played on one of the teams. The student was injured when he tried to block the teacher's shot. The blade of the teacher's stick hit the student's hand. According to the student, the teacher took a "slap shot" – probably a rules violation, though the decision doesn't say this. The teacher denied taking a slap shot. He also claimed the student was running up behind him when the stick hit his hand. New York schools can be held liable for foreseeable injuries caused by not adequately supervising students. The student sued the district for personal injury. His suit was initially dismissed, but an appeals court reversed the dismissal. It held **proceedings were needed to decide if the teacher negligently supervised the game** and if his negligence caused the student's injury. *Godoy v. Cent. Islip Union Free School Dist.,* 985 N.Y.S.2d 732 (N. Y. App. Div. 2014).

◆   A New York appeals court reversed a ruling to dismiss the suit of a student who was injured in gym class. The PE teacher told the class to walk backward fast. One girl asked to be excused from the exercise, saying her ankle hurt and felt unstable. The teacher denied her request to be excused. So the girl obeyed, but she fell while walking backward and was seriously hurt. Her family sued New York City's school district for personal injury, claiming the girl had been negligently supervised. The district asked the court to grant it judgment without a trial. It did and dismissed the lawsuit. But the family appealed, and the appeals court reversed. New York **schools have a duty to supervise students with the same degree of care as a "reasonably prudent parent."** Schools can be held liable for injuries that are foreseeably caused by their failure to do so. The appeals court decided a trial was needed to determine whether this school was negligent – as it's arguably foreseeable that a child with a weak and painful ankle could suffer a fall and an injury if forced to walk backward fast. The appeals court decided the trial court was wrong to dismiss the suit, so it sent the case back to the lower court for further proceedings. *Anastasiya M. v. New York City Board of Educ.,* 976 N.Y.S.2d 202 (N.Y. App. Div. 2013).

◆   An Illinois student was hurt while adjusting a volleyball net, presumably at her gym teacher's instruction. She did so by turning a crank attached to a "collar" wrapped around a pole. The collar bore the warning: "DO NOT OVERTIGHTEN – MAY CAUSE SERIOUS INJURIES[.]" As the student turned the crank, either it or the collar broke and struck her face. She sued the district for personal injury. But Illinois districts are immune to injury claims related to recreational facilities unless staff caused the injury by "willful or wanton conduct" – meaning they meant to hurt the student or were deliberately indifferent to it. The student didn't make this showing, so the trial court dismissed her claim. She appealed, arguing the warning label proved that the school knew using the equipment was likely to hurt her – and was deliberately indifferent to the risk. The appellate court disagreed with her and affirmed the trial court ruling. **Warning labels make a product safer by telling the user how to avoid injury, the court explained.** *Leja v. Community Unit School Dist. 300*, 979 N.E.2d 573 (Ill. App. Ct. 2012).

◆   A New York fourth-grader fell off the balance bar during a physical education class. She climbed back on the bar, fell off again, climbed up again and fell a third time, injuring her ankle. A fellow student then ran over to the teacher to tell him about it. The student's parents sued the district for negligent supervision, and the district sought pretrial judgment. Both a trial court and the Supreme Court, Appellate Division, held that a trial was required. Here, the teacher admitted that both the balance beam station and the rope climbing station required extra supervision. Therefore, a question of fact existed as to whether the district was negligent in supervising the student and whether its alleged negligence caused the student's injury. **The student's three falls, plus the fact that a student had to run to get the teacher, suggested that the teacher failed to provide the extra supervision he knew was needed.** *Talyanna S. v. Mount Vernon City School Dist.*, 948 N.Y.S. 2d 103 (N.Y. App. Div. 2012).

◆   New York high school students were playing floor hockey in a PE class when one student accidentally hurt another with his stick. The injured student sued the school district, alleging negligent supervision, and the district sought pretrial judgment. Although the trial court denied the motion, an appellate division court ruled that the district needn't go to trial on the student's claims. Here, **the injury wasn't foreseeable and it happened so fast that there was no way to avert it by closer supervision**. *Odekirk v. Bellmore-Merrick Cent. School Dist.*, 70 A.D.3d 910 (N.Y. 2010).

◆   A New Jersey PE student sustained injuries to her nose when a classmate hit her with a hockey stick during a floor hockey game. She required surgery, then sued the district, the gym teacher and the classmate to recover for her injuries. A court dismissed her claims, and the appellate division affirmed. It noted that even though gym class was mandatory and not voluntary, **she had to prove more than simple negligence by the classmate**; she had to show that he acted recklessly or intentionally when he hurt her. This she failed to do. Further, since she suffered no permanent injury, she could not pursue a claim for non-economic damages against the district. *Saracino v. Toms River Regional High School East*, 2009 WL 3460680 (N.J. Super. Ct. App. Div. 10/20/09).

◆ While playing freeze tag during a physical education class, a New York fourth-grader was knocked to the ground by a classmate. As he tried to get up, another classmate tripped over him and he fell, hitting his face on the floor. He suffered serious injuries to two permanent teeth. His father sued the school district for negligent supervision, claiming that the teacher and the teacher's aide were talking to each other when the accident happened. He asserted that the teachers should have intervened sooner and prevented the second child from tripping over his son. The New York Supreme Court, Appellate Division, ruled against him, noting that **school districts are not insurers of student safety**. The fact that the teacher and the aide did not see the accident happen failed to establish negligent supervision. The father could not show that more supervision would have prevented the injury, which appeared to result from a spontaneous and accidental collision. There was also no prior history of rough play, and the teacher-student ratio was adequate. *Doyle v. Binghamton City School Dist.*, 874 N.Y.S.2d 607 (N.Y. App. Div. 2009).

◆ A New York student, while participating in a game of dodgeball during gym class, stepped backward and tripped over a schoolmate's foot. The student and her mother sued the school district for her injuries, claiming the teacher failed to adequately supervise the class. The district sought pretrial judgment, which a trial court denied. An appellate division court, however, found for the district. **The accident happened so quickly that it could not have been avoided by even the most intense supervision.** Accordingly, the district was not liable. *Knightner v. William Floyd Union Free School Dist.*, 857 N.Y.S.2d 726 (N.Y. App. Div. 2008).

◆ A New York student was injured in phys ed class while participating in a game of "tape ball." The game was played in the school gymnasium and involved the use of bases that were placed on the floor. One of the bases slipped when the child stepped on it. He fell and sustained injuries. His mother sued the school district, claiming the student was hurt because it failed to adequately supervise the class and failed to provide proper equipment. A trial court denied the school district's motion for pretrial judgment, and the district appealed. The Supreme Court, Appellate Division, reversed. The parent failed to prove that the district was aware of a danger and breached its duty of care in a way that caused the injury. **The physical education teacher was present during the entire class period, and closer supervision would not have prevented the fall.** The school district only had to exercise the same degree of care "as a parent of ordinary prudence" in comparable circumstances, and it did so. *Milbrand v. Kenmore-Town of Tonawanda Union Free School Dist.*, 853 N.Y.S.2d 809 (N.Y. App. Div. 2008).

◆ An autistic Kentucky student attended a gym class that was twice the size of a typical class and was staffed by two teachers. After the class began, the para-educator, who was assigned to assist him and other special education students in the class, lost sight of him and began to search the gym. She noticed an open door and searched the area outside the gym, but failed to spot the student. The student's mother and the police were notified, the search was expanded, and the student was eventually found three hours later about three blocks away. He was dirty and unclothed, but there were no signs he had been sexually assaulted. He was examined at a hospital and released. His father said the boy did not suffer any physical or emotional harm as a result of the incident, but his mother claimed she suffered an emotional injury. The family sued the school district for constitutional rights violations, but a federal court dismissed the case. **Public education is not a constitutionally protected right, and compulsory attendance laws do not create a constitutional obligation on the part of schools to maintain a safe environment.** Any claim for negligence would have to be made in state court. *A.P. v. Fayette County Public Schools*, No. 5:06-247-JMH, 2008 WL 215397 (E.D. Ky. 1/24/08).

◆ A New York student hurt his ankle during a soccer game in gym class when another student kicked him. He and his father sued the board of education and the city to recover for his injuries. They alleged that the injuries resulted from negligent supervision. A trial court refused to dismiss the case, but the New York Supreme Court, Appellate Division, did so. It explained that **the school could be held liable only if the injury was foreseeable and was caused by a lack of supervision**. Here, the student had admitted that the kick was an accident, and it happened so suddenly that it could not have been prevented by closer or increased supervision. Therefore, the school was not liable. *Paca v. City of New York*, 858 N.Y.S.2d 772 (N.Y. App. Div. 2008).

◆ A 14-year-old eighth-grader in Ohio obtained his gym teacher's permission to retrieve his prescription inhaler from his locker. Minutes later, another teacher found the student unconscious and not breathing on the locker room floor. Despite the administration of medical treatment, he died. The school board maintained a policy requiring parents or guardians to bring prescription medications to the school office. Students were not allowed to bring medicine to school themselves, but the school principal let students carry inhalers once they were at school. The student's estate sued the school board in the state court system for wrongful death. The jury found for the school board, and the estate appealed. The Court of Appeals of Ohio found that the district could not be liable because the student's death was not foreseeable. A physician had testified that the death of a student previously recognized as having only "mild asthma" was "one in a million." **According to the physician, not even medical professionals could have foreseen the death.** *Spencer v. Lakeview School Dist.*, No. 2005-T-0083, 2006 WL 1816452 (Ohio Ct. App. 6/30/06).

◆ A 16-year-old Louisiana student who weighed 327 pounds collapsed and began having seizures during a physical education class. The class was conducted by a substitute art teacher in a gym that was not air-conditioned. The temperature was at least 90 degrees. The student collapsed after playing basketball for 20 minutes and died at a hospital. The substitute teacher had played in the game instead of monitoring students. The student's parent sued the board and its insurer in a state court for wrongful death, and the court awarded her $500,000.

The Court of Appeal of Louisiana found no error in trial court findings that the board breached its duty to exercise reasonable care and supervision. The lower court was also entitled to hear the testimony of a physical education professor and allow medical testimony as reliable. The court held teachers have a duty to exercise reasonable care and supervision over students in their custody, and to avoid exposing them to an unreasonable risk of injury. **As physical education classes may involve dangerous activities, due care must be used in them to minimize the risk of student injury.** *James v. Jackson*, 898 So.2d 596 (La. Ct. App. 2005). The state supreme court denied the board's appeal. *James v. Jackson*, 902 So.2d 1005 (La. 2005).

◆ A New York student was playing football in a physical education class when a classmate threw a football tee that hit her in the eye. A state trial court denied the school district's motion for summary judgment, and the district appealed. A state appellate division court held school districts have a duty to adequately supervise and instruct students, and are liable for foreseeable injuries proximately caused by their negligence. However, **school districts are not insurers of student safety and will not be held liable for every spontaneous, thoughtless or careless act by which one student injures another**. The degree of care required is what a reasonably prudent parent would exercise under similar circumstances. The court found the teacher had not instructed students on how to properly handle the tee and never told them not to throw it. The evidence differed as to whether the students had previously thrown the tee or had seen the teacher throw it. In affirming the judgment for the student, the court held a trial court must determine if the injury causing conduct was reasonably foreseeable and preventable. *Oakes v. Massena Cent. School Dist.*, 19 A.D.3d 981, 797 N.Y.S.2d 640 (N.Y. App. Div. 2005).

◆ Three Louisiana students assaulted a classmate in their locker room after a PE class, causing serious injuries. The classmate sued the school board, the parents of the students and their insurers in a Louisiana court for personal injuries. A jury found the students were not at fault, and the court found the board 100% at fault. It held the coach caused the injuries by failing to supervise the students. According to the court, an atmosphere of roughhousing and lack of supervision invited the attack, and the board failed to conform to the required standard of care. On appeal, the court apportioned 70% of the fault to the board and 30% to one of the students.

The state supreme court held school boards have a duty of reasonable supervision over students. Boards are not insurers of student safety, and constant supervision of all students is not required. **To hold a school board liable for negligence, it must be shown that a risk of unreasonable injury was foreseeable and could have been prevented with the required degree of supervision.** In this case, the attack happened suddenly and without warning. Because it was unforeseeable to the classmate himself, there was no way for the coach to foresee and prevent it. The trial court had erroneously imposed liability on the board independent of the students. As the incident could not have been prevented with a reasonable degree of supervision, the court reversed the judgment. *Wallmuth v. Rapides Parish School Board*, 813 So.2d 341 (La. 2002).

◆   Arkansas parents claimed their son's school district did not administer his Ritalin prescription for five consecutive school days, despite knowledge that failure to do so placed him in jeopardy of physical and psychological injury. The student fell from a slide on school grounds and fractured his right wrist. The parents sued the district in the state court system for outrageous conduct causing injury. The court dismissed the case, and the parents appealed. The state court of appeals held the parents could not prevail unless they showed the district intended to inflict emotional distress on the student. They had to demonstrate extreme and outrageous conduct by the district, and to prove its conduct caused emotional distress so severe that no reasonable person could endure it. **The court found no evidence of knowledge by the district that failure to administer the student's medication would result in emotional distress.** The parents did not show his suffering was so great that no reasonable person could be expected to endure it. The court affirmed the judgment for the district. *Foote v. Pine Bluff School Dist.*, No. CA 02-806, 2003 WL 1827282 (Ark. Ct. App. 4/9/03).

2. Governmental Immunity

◆   Colorado school officials were not entitled to immunity after a child was injured on the playground. The nine-year-old broke her arm and wrist when she fell from a zip line. After her parents learned that two other students had also been hurt on the equipment, they filed a tort claim. The court tossed the claim, and the parents appealed. They argued the district created a dangerous condition because "no matter how well designed, maintained or constructed, the zip line at issue [was] inherently dangerous." **The court looked at the history of two other children being hurt on the same playground structure and said that more info was needed.** It reversed the immunity ruling for the school and remanded the case for further proceedings. *Loveland v. Saint Vrain Valley School Dist.*, No. 14CA1888, 2015 WL 5607645 (Colo. Ct. App. 11/24/15).

◆ An 11-year-old Missouri student, while skipping rope during PE class, fell and hit her head against a cinder block wall. She was taken to the nurse's office. The nurse gave her an ice pack for her head and made sure her pupils were dilating, then called her mother to pick her up and wrote a note explaining that she had suffered a minor head injury. The note instructed her mother to wake her at midnight, which the mother did. The next morning, the student stayed in bed. At 10:30, she was unresponsive. Paramedics failed to revive her. Her mother sued the district, the superintendent, the principal, the nurse and the teachers involved. A court dismissed the defendants, but the court of appeals reversed in part, finding that **the nurse was not entitled to official immunity, nor were the teachers**. Only if they had discretion in treating head injuries would they be entitled to immunity. A trial was required on that issue. *Nguyen v. Grain Valley R-5 School Dist.*, 353 S.W.3d 725 (Mo. Ct. App. 2011).

◆ An Ohio middle school included a weeklong roller-skating course in its PE program. It required students to bring signed permission slips to participate. A student who was inexperienced at roller skating grew tired of being the only student in the "safe zone" for beginners and moved to the general skating area. A classmate lost his balance and fell. His skate hit the student's leg, breaking it. When the student sued the school board and the teachers, the court ruled against him, holding that the defendants were immune to the lawsuit. **The student failed to show that the gym floor was too slippery for roller skating and thus defective.** *Simmons v. Yingling*, No. CA2010-11-117, 2011 WL 3567083 (Ohio Ct. App. 8/15/11).

◆ A Wisconsin physical education teacher divided a class into two groups to practice golf. One group practiced driving while the other group practiced chipping. The teacher instructed the drivers to stand in line while waiting to hit and not to swing their clubs in the waiting area. While she was working with the chippers, the drivers practiced about 40 to 50 feet away. A student in the drivers' group was hit in the face by a club swung by a classmate. He sued the district in a state circuit court for personal injuries, but the case was dismissed.

The state court of appeals held Wis. Stat. § 893.80(4) bars actions against government entities and employees for acts done in the exercise of legislative, judicial and similar functions. The law allowed liability for the negligent performance of ministerial duties. Ministerial duties were "absolute, certain and imperative," leaving nothing for judgment or discretion. The teacher had a ministerial duty to conduct and supervise her class in a particular manner. **Her decision to provide students with safety instructions was discretionary and did not subject the district to liability.** The court affirmed the judgment, finding the danger created by swinging golf clubs was not so obvious and predictable as to be a compelling or known danger. *Livingston v. Wausau Underwriters Insurance Co.*, 260 Wis.2d 602, 658 N.W.2d 88 (Table) (Wis. Ct. App. 2003), review denied, 266 Wis.2d 62, 671 N.W.2d 849 (Table) (Wis. 2003).

◆   An Alabama purchasing foreman drafted bid specifications and made recommendations to his school board on bids for movable bleachers for a high school. After the board contracted for the bleachers, the foreman's office issued purchase orders, and the bleachers were installed. A student was severely injured when the bleachers collapsed on him as he and a classmate tried to close them at their teacher's request. The student sued the district and school officials, including the purchasing foreman, for negligent inspection and maintenance of the bleachers. The trial court entered pretrial judgment for all the officials except the foreman, and he appealed.

The Alabama Supreme Court considered the foreman's claim to state-agent immunity based on the discretionary nature of his activities. The student argued the foreman did not deserve immunity, as he was not engaged in discretionary functions. The court held the question of immunity was not properly addressed in the framework of discretionary or ministerial functions. Instead, it had devised an analysis based on categories of state-agent functions under which government employees are immune from liability in the exercise of judgment. One category was the negotiation of contracts, so the foreman was entitled to summary judgment for the claims that he had failed to properly evaluate bids for the bleachers and inspect them after installation. However, the court found **the act of passing along a maintenance brochure to other employees did not require judgment. The foreman was not entitled to state agent immunity** with respect to this claim, and the case was remanded for further proceedings. *Ex Parte Hudson*, 866 So.2d 1115 (Ala. 2003).

◆   Students in an Illinois physical education class had to run laps or rollerblade around a wooden gym floor. Rollerbladers paid a $7 fee to use rollerblades with "experimental" toe brakes, and they were not furnished with helmets, gloves or shin, elbow and knee guards. A student who chose to rollerblade fell and broke two bones in his right leg. He sued the school district in a state court for negligence, and willful and wanton failure to provide safety equipment. The court held the district was entitled to immunity under Sections 2-201 and 3-108(a) of the state governmental tort immunity act, which affords immunity to government entities and their employees for failing to supervise students except in cases of willful and wanton misconduct. The state appellate court reversed the judgment, and the district appealed to the Supreme Court of Illinois.

The supreme court observed that the immunity act did not create duties for government entities, but accorded them certain immunities based on specific government functions. The district's failure to provide necessary equipment did not involve supervision. The tort immunity act shielded any decision by district employees that involved a determination of policy or the exercise of discretion. **"Policy decisions" were those requiring the balancing of competing interests so that a government entity had to make a "judgment call." The court agreed with the school district that its decision not to provide safety equipment was discretionary and thus entitled to immunity.** *Arteman v. Clinton Community Unit School Dist. No. 15*, 763 N.E.2d 756 (Ill. 2002).

B. Plays, Dances, Music and More

◆ A New York appeals court refused to dismiss a personal injury claim filed by the mother of a child who was injured during recess. An eight-year-old fell from the monkey bars during recess at her elementary school. She suffered unspecified injuries. Her mom sued to recover for personal injuries, and the district asked the court to dismiss the claim. The court refused to toss the case, and the district appealed. On appeal, the court explained **the district could've gotten the case dismissed – if it had provided conclusive evidence that showed the child had been adequately supervised by a teacher or other staffer at the time of her fall, or the ground cover underneath the monkey bars was maintained in a reasonably safe condition**. But the school didn't make either showing, so a trial is needed, the court held. *Pochat v. Monroe Woodbury Cent. School Dist.*, 23 N.Y.S.3d 301 (N.Y. App. Div. 2016).

◆ A California appeals court revived the negligence claim of a student who was injured at a break-dancing practice for a talent show. A group of students practiced the routine in the mornings before school. A teacher agreed to let the group practice in his classroom. He frequently left the classroom for short periods during the practices to make copies, use the restroom and make phone calls. While the teacher was out of the classroom, a 14-year-old was seriously injured after classmates urged him to try to flip. He filed a personal injury suit. The court found the district did not have a duty to protect the boy from the inherent risks of break-dancing. It granted judgment to the school. But the appellate court said **the real issue was whether the teacher's decision – allowing middle school students to engage in a potentially risky activity, break-dancing, in his classroom without supervision – created legal liability, especially since the assistant principal had testified that he'd instituted a "no flip" policy**. The court pointed out the teacher broke school rules, as he left the room without getting another teacher to supervise or telling the group to stop dancing until he returned, and he never told the students they couldn't do flips. The court said a reasonable jury "could find this lack of supervision proximately caused [the boy's] injuries." Or, the court added, it could find the district didn't take adequate steps to enforce the "no flip" policy the assistant principal said was in place. Summary judgment wasn't appropriate. The ruling was reversed, and the case was remanded. *Jimenez v. Roseville City School Dist.*, 247 Cal.App.4th 594 (Cal. Ct. App. 2016).

◆   A New York appeals court affirmed a ruling that a school was not liable for a playground injury during recess. The plaintiff in this case was knocked to the ground by a fellow student who was running backward while attempting to catch a football. Afterward, the angry mom filed a negligence claim. The court granted judgment to the school, and the mother appealed. The appellate court affirmed the ruling for the school, as **it showed teachers were present to monitor the students, the children who were playing football had been told to stay on their side of the yard and the unanticipated spontaneous act of another child – colliding into the victim – was the proximate cause of the incident**. The ruling for the school was affirmed. *Chung v. New York City Board of Educ.*, 136 A.D.3d 608 (N.Y. App. Div. 2016).

◆   An Iowa appeals court refused to grant a new trial for a student who was injured in shop class. He was operating a table saw in his woodworking class when a piece of wood kicked back from the blade and hit him in the stomach. As he leaned forward, his left hand came in contact with the blade. It severed two fingers and severely injured two more. He sued for negligence. As part of pretrial activity, he had to list all of the damages he claimed as a result of the injury. After a four-day trial, the jury awarded the boy $28,578 for past medical expenses and $31,421 for future medical expenses. But the jury stopped short of awarding damages for loss of earning capacity. It also found the boy was 45% responsible for the injury. He appealed the verdict and asked for a new trial, claiming the jury was wrong to find "zero value for his loss of earning capacity." He insisted a reasonable juror should've concluded that the loss of one hand would have an effect on his earning potential in some manner. He pointed to an expert that testified he'd lose – over the course of his work life – around $500,000. The court rejected the argument, explaining that **a jury "is free to accept or reject any testimony."** The court affirmed the jury's decision. *T.D. II v. Des Moines Independent Community School Dist.*, No. 14-2166, 2016 WL 351516 (Iowa Ct. App. 1/27/16).

◆   School officials did not have a duty to protect a student who was hit by a car as he crossed an off-campus street as he left an after-school event, an Illinois appellate court held. The student attended an event on campus. As he was leaving, he crossed a six-lane highway. He was struck by a car and suffered injuries. His mother sued for damages, alleging negligence based on willful and wanton conduct. The court granted judgment to the school. On appeal, the mother said the school violated its duty to protect her son. To recover damages based on willful and wanton conduct, she had to show the school had a duty to protect her son, it breached that duty and the breach was the proximate cause of the injuries. She argued the school voluntarily assumed a duty to supervise students because it had provided crossing guards for prior unnamed after-school events. The court rejected her argument, as **she did not include facts about which intersections around** the school had previously been assigned crossing guards, the history or frequency of using crossing guards during after-school events and whether the intersection where her son's accident occurred had ever been one of the locations that had crossing guards during prior events. The mother failed to establish the school had a duty to protect her son, so the court affirmed the decision to dismiss her negligence claim. *Renkiewicz v. Township High School Dist. 211,* No. 1-15-0989, 2016 WL 363193 (Ill. App. Ct. 1/22/16).

◆ The Eleventh Circuit affirmed a Florida ruling that held a pre-prom Breathalyzer did not violate students' constitutional rights. Seniors who purchased tickets for the prom were required to sign a contract stating the district's zero-tolerance policy for drugs and alcohol. It also warned that they could be subjected to a breath test. Approximately 37 students arrived at the prom on a rented party bus between 10:15 and 10:30 p.m. The school dean told the students they couldn't enter the prom until the bus had been inspected. When a police officer asked for permission to search the bus, the driver gave his consent. The officer searched the bus and found an empty champagne bottle. The driver told the officer it belonged to the students. But when asked, none of the students confessed ownership of the bottle. The students were told they'd have to take and pass a Breathalyzer test before they'd be allowed to enter the prom. By the time the tests were administered, the prom had ended. Several students sued the district and the police department, claiming violations of their rights under the Fourth Amendment. The court tossed the claim, and the students appealed. The court rejected the illegal search claims, explaining the U.S. Supreme Court has already held "a third-party's consent is valid if he has mutual use of the property." The driver's consent made the search legal. The court also held the school had reasonable suspicion to administer the Breathalyzer tests – as an empty bottle was found on the bus. And the driver said it belonged to the kids. Further, **the breath tests were OK because they weren't "excessively intrusive ... the test merely required students to exhale,"** the court ruled. Examining the illegal seizure claim, the court held the time frame was reasonable – as administering 37 breath tests took time. The students failed to state valid claims, so the ruling to dismiss the case was affirmed. *Ziegler v. Martin County School Dist.,* No. 2;14-cv-14221-DDM (11th Cir. 7/28/16).

◆ A school could not be held liable for an injury that was caused by a design flaw in school equipment, a Michigan appeals court held. In 2011, a student fell off the back of the chorus risers and injured her head and neck. She was not the first student to fall off of the risers. After she fell, the school ordered and installed a railing on the back of the risers. The student filed a personal injury suit, alleging negligence. The court granted pretrial judgment to the school, and the student appealed.

As a general rule, public schools are entitled to immunity in personal injury cases – but exceptions apply. One is the public buildings exception. The student said this one applied in her case. The school argued the exception didn't apply because:

* the risers were fixtures rather than a part of the building, and
* it didn't fail to maintain or repair a dangerous condition.

The court agreed the school didn't fail to maintain or repair a dangerous condition. The student argued the school failed to repair a dangerous condition, as it knew students had fallen off the risers but didn't install the railing to prevent her injury. The court rejected the argument, explaining that in *Renny v. Michigan Dep't of Transportation*, the U.S. Supreme Court held the public building exception does not impose liability for a design defect. Essentially, the lack of a railing to prevent falls was a defect in the design of the risers, the court found. If a railing had been installed on the risers and the school removed it, the argument would have merit, the court explained. Because **the school could not be held liable for a flaw in a product's design**, the exception did not apply. So the school was entitled to governmental immunity. *Williams v. Grand Ledge High School*, No. 13-000163-NO, 2015 WL 3980517 (Mich. Ct. App. 6/30/15).

◆　The Fifth Circuit refused to find a school constitutionally liable for a student's drowning death on campus. A physics class went to the school pool to conduct buoyancy experiments. They made boats out of cardboard and duct tape and then sailed them in the shallow end of the pool. The teacher told them to stay out of the water when not testing their boats. But after the experiment, some kids jumped in and swam a lap. Minutes later, one student was spotted lying at the bottom of the pool. They pulled him out and called paramedics, but he died. His parents sued his principal and physics teacher, alleging they violated their son's Fourteenth Amendment right to life. A Texas federal judge granted the school defendants judgment without a trial. The parents appealed to the Fifth Circuit, but it affirmed. Public school officials have "qualified immunity" to such suits, meaning there is no liability unless they violated a clearly established federal legal right. The U.S. Supreme Court has explained that **the purpose of the immunity rule is to give government employees "breathing room to make reasonable but mistaken judgments about open legal questions."** The parents didn't show the school defendants violated a clearly established constitutional right. To do so, they would've had to show "reasonable teachers and school officials were on notice that designing and executing a high school science experiment involving a pool violated the constitutional right to life of any student that may drown." That wasn't the case, so school officials were immune to this suit – and the federal judge was right to dismiss it. *Estate of C.A. v. Castro*, 547 Fed.Appx. 621 (5th Cir. 2013).

◆　A Wisconsin student with brittle bone disease and poor balance attended class under an IEP that called for her to be released from class separately from other students so that she wouldn't have to be in the hallways with them between classes – thereby reducing her chance for injuries. Despite that, she fell in a school hallway walking between classes and sustained injuries. **Her parents sued the district for negligence, but the Wisconsin Court of Appeals ruled against them**, noting that the district was entitled to immunity. The IEP did not impose a ministerial duty (which would mean no immunity) on school employees because it did not eliminate discretion (which meant immunity was available). For example, the IEP didn't state whether the student should be released from class early or late. *Edwards v. Baraboo School Dist.*, 803 N.W.2d 868 (Table) (Wis. Ct. App. 2011).

◆   A 15-year-old North Dakota student got badly hurt practicing a bike stunt in the auditorium for a "Sixties day" event scheduled as part of a history class. He sued the district and the teacher to recover for his injuries, and a jury decided that **the district was 30% at fault, while the student was 70% at fault**. As a result, the student was not entitled to receive anything. On appeal, the Supreme Court of North Dakota upheld that determination. Neither the student nor his parents could recover 30% of his costs from the district. *M.M. v. Fargo Public School Dist. No. 1*, 815 N.W.2d 273 (N.D. 2012).

◆   During recess, a New York third-grader passed by a fire pole that students were sliding down while another student slid down the pole. The other student barreled into him and he sustained injuries. His father sued the district for negligent supervision, and the district sought pretrial judgment, asserting that it wasn't negligent and, even if it was, any negligence was incidental to the injury and not a cause. The Supreme Court, Appellate division, held that **there were questions about whether the district properly instructed students on how to use the playground equipment** and whether it provided a proper surface. Also, there was a question as to whether the student sliding down the pole was playing tag at the time in violation of school rules. A trial was required. *Dworzanski v. Niagara-Wheatfield Cent. School Dist.*, 89 A.D.3d 1378 (N.Y. Sup. Ct. A.D. 2011).

◆   A New York second-grader sustained injuries when he was pushed down a slide by a fellow student during lunch recess, who then slid down on top of him. He sued the school district for money damages, alleging negligent supervision. The case reached the Supreme Court, Appellate Division, which ruled against him. Here, **the school provided adequate playground supervision**, and that level of supervision had not caused the student's injuries. *Benavides v. Uniondale Union Free School Dist.*, 95 A.D.3d 809 (N.Y. Sup. Ct. App. Div. 2012).

◆   A Utah high school decided to perform the play "Oklahoma." The school's drama teacher wanted to enhance the sound effects during the performance by using a gun that would fire blanks. A vice principal approved the request provided that an adult brought the weapon, kept it under control at all times and was the only person to fire it. However, the drama teacher did not ensure that the rules were followed, and a student fired the gun during rehearsals and the play's performances. The drama teacher apparently knew that the student was doing so. One day, prior to a performance, the student shot himself with a blank and died. His parents sued, alleging violations of the student's substantive and procedural due process rights. The school, the vice principal and the drama teacher sought to have the case dismissed, but a federal court dismissed only the school and the vice principal from the lawsuit. **The drama teacher may have acted in conscious disregard for the serious risks to the student, so the lawsuit against him was allowed to continue.** *Thayer v. Washington County School Dist.*, 781 F.Supp.2d 1264 (D. Utah 2011).

◆ A Connecticut student attended an eighth-grade graduation dance at a private facility. During the evening, a glass goblet fell to the floor and broke, leaving pieces of glass on the floor. A student shed her shoes while walking from her table to the dance floor and severely cut her foot on a shard of glass. She sued the school board and two teachers who chaperoned the event, alleging negligent supervision. A state court ruled that the school board was entitled to immunity, and the Supreme Court of Connecticut agreed. Here, **the school board's decision to sponsor the graduation dance was a discretionary decision that entitled it to immunity**. Further, the dance wasn't held at the school, attendance wasn't mandatory, and the student voluntarily took off her shoes. Thus, no extra duty of care was imposed on the school board to offset its claim to immunity. *Coe v. Board of Educ. of Town of Watertown*, 19 A.3d 640 (Conn. 2011).

◆ An Ohio student played in the marching band. One day, while they were practicing in a parking lot, a school maintenance employee asked the marching band director if he could mow the lawn in an area near where the marching band was practicing. School policy dictated that employees were not to mow in the vicinity of students, and when they mowed without a bag, they were supposed to use the manufacturer's discharge chute. The director told the maintenance employee he could mow near the marching band. However, the employee took the bag off the mower and did not install the discharge chute. A piece of metal ejected by the lawn mower struck a student in the head and cut an artery, causing him to lose consciousness and suffer some paralysis to his face. His family sued the school district, which sought immunity.

The Ohio Court of Appeals noted that school districts are generally entitled to immunity unless employees act in a "wanton or reckless" way. Here, the family alleged that the band director and the employee acted recklessly so as to disallow immunity. The court agreed that **the maintenance employee might have acted recklessly by failing to use the discharge chute**. However, the family failed to show that the band director acted recklessly or wantonly by allowing the employee to mow near the parking lot. Thus, the director was entitled to immunity, but the maintenance employee was not. *DeMartino v. Poland Local School Dist.*, No. 10 MA 19, 2011 WL 1118480 (Ohio Ct. App. 3/24/11).

V. TEACHER BEHAVIOR OUTSIDE OF SCHOOL

Although teachers have the freedom to do as they like off school grounds while not on duty, they cannot break the law or engage in behavior that could be construed as harmful to students.

A. Inappropriate Relations With Students

◆   An Arkansas high school girls basketball coach sent inappropriate text messages to a number of students, including "are you drunk yet?" to a student who had obtained a public intoxication ticket, and "OMG you look good today" to another student. A school investigation found no other problems, but the school prepared to non-renew his contract at the end of the school year. Later, the coach entered into a sexual relationship with a ninth-grader. He was sentenced to 10 years in prison, with six years suspended. The ninth-grader's parents sued the principal and school officials under Title IX and 42 U.S.C. § 1983, asserting constitutional violations. The case reached the Eighth Circuit, which held that the principal and school officials were entitled to immunity because **the inappropriate text messages by the coach did not alert them to the sexual abuse that followed**. The principal and school officials had investigated following the text messages and found no evidence of improper physical contact. *Doe v. Flaherty*, 623 F.3d 577 (8th Cir. 2010).

◆   A Delaware elementary school teacher encountered a 17-year-old former student when she came to the school to pick up a younger sibling. The teacher later called her and offered to help her with her homework. After a time, **he became romantically involved, eventually engaging in a sexual relationship with the student**. The student told a friend, who told her parent, who reported it to the state police. The teacher was charged with fourth degree sexual rape because of the student's age and his position of trust, authority or supervision over her. However, the charge was later dropped. Shortly thereafter, the school board notified the teacher that it intended to fire him based on immorality and/or misconduct. After he was fired, the teacher appealed, asserting that he had not been criminally convicted, that the student no longer attended district schools, and that his positive employment evaluations indicated he was still able to teach. The Supreme Court of Delaware ruled against him, noting that he could be fired for immorality and that he had compromised his position of trust and his status as a role model. *Lehto v. Board of Educ. of Caesar Rodney School Dist.*, 962 A.2d 222 (Del. 2008).

◆   An Oklahoma student claimed that she was subjected to sexual harassment, advances and molestation by her music teacher when she was 15 years old. She claimed that he first kissed her in the school bus barn, and then began touching her inappropriately at least once a week, although the two never had sexual intercourse. When her parents learned of the inappropriate relationship, they contacted the school, which immediately suspended the teacher. He resigned shortly thereafter. The student sued the school district and the teacher under 42 U.S.C. § 1983 and Title IX. She asserted that the district had knowledge of the teacher's inappropriate behavior based on statements her boyfriend made to an assistant principal about the teacher and another student. The district moved for pretrial judgment, **claiming it never had actual notice that the teacher was acting inappropriately**. It showed that the boyfriend had admitted lying about the teacher having an inappropriate relationship with the other student. The court ruled for the school district, finding no evidence that it was deliberately indifferent to the inappropriate relationship between the teacher and the student. However, the student's lawsuit against the teacher under 42 U.S.C. § 1983 could proceed. *S.R. v. Hilldale Independent School Dist. No. I-29 of Muskogee County, Oklahoma*, No. CIV-07-335-RAW, 2008 WL 2185420 (E.D. Okla. 5/23/08).

◆   An 18-year-old Idaho student began flirting with a teacher. She confessed her feelings for him to another staff member, and the school conducted an investigation. Both the student and the teacher denied any impropriety. A month later, the teacher and student had sexual intercourse. She did not admit this until the end of the school year. The teacher resigned, and the student sued not only him but also the school district and various school officials, asserting claims of negligent supervision and violations of Title IX. Before a jury, the student presented evidence of post-traumatic stress disorder (PTSD) and other psychological harm. However, she offered no medical records, cost estimates or other statistics on damages. The school district offered testimony from a psychologist who stated that her emotional problems were triggered by the lawsuit itself and not by the sexual relationship.

The jury found that the school district was liable for negligent supervision, but that the student failed to prove she was entitled to damages. It, therefore, awarded her none. On appeal, the Supreme Court of Idaho held that a reasonable jury could have found **the student proved no damages. Even her own experts disagreed as to her condition**, with one finding she did not have PTSD. It seemed that the litigation brought about the psychological difficulties by focusing the student on her experience, memories and trauma. The district's expert also believed the student pursued the lawsuit to comply with her family's request. The district did not have to pay for the negligent supervision of the teacher. *Hei v. Holzer*, 181 P.3d 489 (Idaho 2008).

◆ A Maryland high school teacher gave a 14-year-old student who had a crush on him a ride home. On the way, he took her to his house to play pool and allegedly had consensual sexual intercourse with her. After he was convicted of child abuse and sexual offenses, he appealed. The Court of Special Appeals of Maryland ruled that consensual sexual intercourse could constitute child abuse under Maryland law. The court stated that because a parent impliedly consents to a teacher taking all reasonable measures to assure the safe return of his or her child from school, including personally driving that child home; because the teacher assumed that responsibility when he agreed to drive the child home; because the events leading up to this unfortunate occurrence were set in motion on school property; and because, at the time of the offense, there had been no temporal break in the teacher and student relationship that existed between the teacher and the victim, the court upheld his conviction.

The Court of Appeals of Maryland affirmed. It rejected the teacher's argument that once he was with a student off school grounds, for a non-school-related activity, the implied consent rationale was inapplicable and that once he was no longer acting as a teacher, he did not have a responsibility to supervise the student, so could not be convicted of child abuse.

It was uncontested that the act of sexual intercourse by an adult with a 14-year-old girl qualified as "abuse" under the statute. **Although the teacher was neither a parent nor household or family member of the victim, he had "responsibility for the supervision" of the victim at the time of the alleged misconduct.** The evidence was sufficient to support the conviction. *Anderson v. State*, 372 Md. 285, 812 A.2d 1016 (Md. 2002).

◆ A Georgia teacher socialized with a troubled student's family, befriending his mother and promising to "look after" both him and his sister. An assistant school superintendent received an anonymous email during the school year, accusing the teacher of having inappropriate relationships with a list of students who had graduated or dropped out of school. She learned of a similar complaint against the teacher three years earlier, but the student involved in that incident vehemently denied anything inappropriate. The assistant superintendent warned the teacher, both orally and in writing, to avoid any appearance of impropriety with students and situations where she would be alone with male students. Vehicles owned by the teacher and the troubled student were later seen parked together in some woods. The superintendent promptly notified the school board and the police, and asked the state Professional Standards Commission (PSC) to investigate the incident. She told the school principal to monitor the two, prevent unnecessary contact between them and to report suspicious behavior to her. The teacher resigned and surrendered her teaching certificate after a substitute teacher discovered a note written by the student that threatened to expose their relationship if she did not comply with certain demands. The parents sued the district in a federal court for Title IX and civil rights violations under 42 U.S.C. § 1983. The court awarded pretrial judgment to the district, and the parents appealed.

The U.S. Court of Appeals, Eleventh Circuit, held that the parents could not demonstrate school officials acted with deliberate indifference at any time. They responded to each report of misconduct by investigating the charges and interviewing relevant persons. The officials consistently monitored the teacher and warned her about her interaction with students. They requested a PSC investigation after they received the first report specifically linking the teacher and student, monitored her and confronted her when the explicit note was discovered. In light of the many corrective measures taken by district officials, the court held they were not deliberately indifferent. **A district is not deliberately indifferent because the measures it takes are ultimately ineffective in stopping the harassment.** The court affirmed the judgment for the district. *Sauls v. Pierce County School Dist.*, 399 F.3d 1279 (11th Cir. 2005).

◆ New York twins claimed their history teacher sexually harassed them. One of them claimed the teacher confided to her about his personal life. According to one of the twins, a school psychologist dismissed her report about the teacher and implied the relationship between her and the teacher was a good one. The psychologist later dismissed reports by the twins' mother and one of the twins. The psychologist did not investigate or report the teacher's conduct, which included improper touching and the giving of gifts and cards. Many incidents occurred before the principal met with the teacher and told him he was to have no more contact with the twins than he would with any other student. The following summer, the teacher spoke with one of the twins several times on her cell phone and left her a romantic message. Their parents gave the recorded message to the principal. The school reassigned the teacher the next day and told him not to report to the high school until further notice. The twins sued the school district in a federal district court for sexual harassment in violation of Title IX. The court held that even though the case did not involve allegations of an official policy of sex discrimination, there could be district liability for sexual harassment under Title IX. **The twins only had to show "an official of the school district – who at a minimum has authority to institute corrective measures on the district's behalf – had actual notice of, and was deliberately indifferent to, the teacher's misconduct."** The court rejected the district's claim that the principal had no actual notice that the teacher was harassing the twins until he heard the phone message. It denied the district's motion for summary judgment. *Tesoriero v. Syosset Cent. School Dist.*, 382 F.Supp.2d 387 (E.D.N.Y. 2005).

◆ A 14-year-old Illinois student gave birth to a child in 1986. Blood tests indicated a 99.99% probability that the assistant principal of her junior high school was the child's father. The school district dismissed him under Section 24-12 of the Illinois School Code. Almost two years later, the assistant principal was acquitted of aggravated criminal sexual assault. The student's paternity action was closed shortly after the acquittal based on "lack of activity." A hearing officer reversed the school board's action dismissing the assistant principal in 1991, finding the district did not prove he had sexual contact with the student. A state court affirmed the assistant principal's reinstatement, as did the Appellate Court of Illinois. In 1997, the paternity case was reopened and a court ordered him to pay child support. The state superintendent of education notified the assistant principal of an action to suspend his teaching and administrative certificates for immoral conduct. A hearing officer upheld the action under Section 21-23 of the state school code.

The case reached the Appellate Court of Illinois, which held that the action to suspend the assistant principal's certificates was not barred by the district's effort to dismiss him years earlier. The Section 24-12 employment dismissal and Section 21-23 certificate suspension proceedings were distinct and were brought by different entities. **The assistant principal's acquittal from criminal charges did not prevent the state superintendent from suspending his certificates. The code required the superintendent to suspend a holder's certificate for conviction of specified sex or narcotics offenses.** *Hayes v. State Teacher Certification Board*, 359 Ill.App.3d 1153, 835 N.E.2d 146 (Ill. App. Ct. 2005). The Supreme Court of Illinois denied further appeal.

B. Drugs and Alcohol

◆ A Tennessee county school board decided to conduct random drug screens after a second teacher in seven years was arrested on drug charges. The board hired a private company to perform the drug screens. Four teachers and their union sued, asserting that the random drug testing violated the Fourth Amendment, and a federal court agreed. **Although teachers are highly responsible for the safety of others, making random drug screening generally permissible, the way the policy was implemented violated the law.** First, the policy didn't give teachers enough information about which drugs were being tested. It gave scientific names, but not brand names. And second, the way the policy was implemented allowed a company employee to separate out a sample into two containers (in case retesting was necessary) in front of other employees. This violated employees' privacy rights. *Smith County Educ. Ass'n v. Smith County Board of Educ.*, 781 F.Supp.2d 604 (M.D. Tenn. 2011).

◆ A California teacher received her third DUI and was placed on home detention for 30 days, but she was also allowed to teach her class during that time while wearing an ankle bracelet. Two years later, the state commission on teacher credentialing suspended her credential for 60 days. She challenged the suspension, but the state court of appeal upheld it, finding that **her drinking and driving, while off school grounds and away from children, provided enough evidence of her unfitness to teach** so as to justify the suspension. *Broney v. California Comm'n on Teacher Credentialing*, 108 Cal.Rptr.3d 832 (Cal. Ct. App. 2010).

◆ An Oregon teacher was dismissed by her school district for "immorality" and "neglect of duty" after a police search and ensuing events brought to light evidence that her husband had been using their jointly owned home to grow and sell marijuana and that the teacher was aware of that. The teacher appealed to the Fair Dismissal Appeals Board, which reversed the dismissal and ordered her reinstated. The district sought review before the Oregon Court of Appeals.

The court of appeals noted that the teacher's job responsibilities included instruction and extracurricular participation in the district's anti-drug program. Here, the teacher did essentially nothing to deter her husband's use of their home for illegal drug activities. Her workshop training gave clear notice that off-duty personal drug involvement was contrary to a teacher's role in connection with the anti-drug instructional program. **She had a duty to prevent her home from being used for marijuana sales regardless of how that act might upset her occasionally violent husband.** The appeals board should have focused on the propriety of her conduct in the light of her responsibilities to the district and her students. The court reversed and remanded the case to the appeals board for reconsideration. *Jefferson County School Dist. No. 509-J v. Fair Dismissal Appeals Board*, 102 Or. App. 83, 793 P.2d 888 (Or. Ct. App. 1990).

◆ A South Carolina teacher was arrested for possessing crack cocaine in 1988, but authorities dismissed his case. In 2000, the teacher was arrested "in his car in a well-known drug area" while his passenger attempted to buy crack. Charges against the teacher were dropped when the passenger pled guilty. After the 2000 incident, the teacher was placed on administrative leave, pending an investigation. The superintendent advised him by letter that his contract was being terminated. At his school board hearing, the superintendent said the termination was based solely on the teacher's unfitness and not on negative publicity. The board upheld the discharge. A state court held that being arrested but not convicted for two criminal charges was not substantial evidence of unfitness to teach. It reversed the board's decision, but the state court of appeals reinstated the board action. It found substantial evidence of the teacher's unfitness to teach, based on the arrests, his dishonesty, the publicity surrounding the 2000 arrest, and the negative response it caused in the community.

The Supreme Court of South Carolina held that the appeals court committed error by failing to confine its decision to the grounds stated in the order terminating his employment. **Two drug arrests, 12 years apart, neither resulting in charges, did not support a finding of unfitness to teach.** This was especially true when the district did not contend the teacher ever used, possessed or sold illegal drugs. The teacher was entitled to reinstatement with back pay and benefits from the date of his suspension. *Shell v. Richland County School Dist. One*, 362 S.C. 408, 608 S.E.2d 428 (S.C. 2005).

◆   A Texas teacher checked out a district vehicle to drive to a soccer clinic. Before picking up a colleague who was going to the clinic, the teacher stopped at a dry cleaner and then a grocery store, where he purchased beer and other items. A witness reported seeing him leaving the store with beer and getting into the vehicle. The teacher admitted buying beer while using the vehicle when the school principal confronted him about it. He submitted his resignation after being formally reprimanded, but he later changed his mind and rescinded it. The superintendent recommended not renewing his contract, and the school board voted for non-renewal after a hearing. The state education commissioner affirmed the decision, finding substantial evidence that the teacher was "in the course and scope of his employment while he was in possession of alcohol."

A Texas district court affirmed the decision, and the teacher appealed to the state court of appeals, arguing he was on a personal side trip to run errands when he bought beer. The court held the commissioner's decision had to be affirmed unless it was arbitrary and capricious. **A court could not substitute its judgment for the commissioner's and could only review it to determine if it was supported by substantial evidence.** The teacher had admitted his error and stated buying beer "was a dumb thing to do." He also stated to the board he was acting within the scope of his duties to attend the soccer clinic. The teacher agreed it was reasonable to assume he was acting for the school when the school day began. As the commissioner's decision was supported by substantial evidence, the court affirmed it. *Simpson v. Alanis*, No. 08-03-00110-CV, 2004 WL 309297 (Tex. Ct. App. 2/19/04).

C. Assault

◆   After an Iowa student gave his football coach the finger, the coach put his hands on the student to escort him off the bus. The student said he was "thrown down the aisle." Seeing bruises on their son, his parents called the police, who charged the coach with assault. Then the state licensing board charged the coach with "student abuse." **At the hearing, the coach's previous written reprimands were examined. They included instances of the coach duct-taping droopy trousers to one student and grabbing another and ripping his shirt for calling the coach an "idiot."** The board revoked his teaching license for 90 days and his PE and coaching endorsements for good. The coach appealed to the state supreme court, which found the decision was supported by the evidence. *Christiansen v. Iowa Board of Educ. Examiners*, 831 N.W.2d 179 (Iowa 2013).

◆   First-graders in a California school sued their district and three others, alleging that they hired the substitute teacher who molested them even though they knew of his misconduct at prior schools. One of the prior hiring districts sought to be dismissed from the case, asserting that it could not be liable for the future molestation of the students in the current district. The court of appeal agreed with the district that **it could not be liable for future assaults at a different school district**. The reason there could be no liability was because the earlier district was never a "custodian" of the molested students in this case. So even if the district violated the state's Child Abuse and Neglect Reporting Act, it was not liable for the molestation. *P.S. v. San Bernardino City Unified School Dist.*, 94 Cal.Rptr.3d 788 (Cal. Ct. App. 2009).

◆ A Pennsylvania school district IT employee also served as an assistant coach for the girls' softball teams. He became friends with a student's family, but the mother grew suspicious when she noticed calls from her daughter to the employee at odd hours. She went to the head coach, who went to the principal who, along with the head coach, met with the parents and the student's sister. The family told the coach and principal that they suspected an inappropriate sexual relationship. **The principal told the employee to stay away from team members and that same day, the superintendent gave the employee the option of being fired or resigning.** He resigned. Ten months later, he was charged with sexual offenses against the student. The family then sued the district under 42 U.S.C. § 1983, alleging violations of the student's Fourteenth Amendment rights, but a federal court found no evidence that district officials knew about the sexual abuse or were deliberately indifferent to it. Here, the district conducted a background check on the employee before hiring him, had a written sexual harassment policy in place, and acted promptly to force the employee's resignation when confronted with evidence that he was behaving inappropriately with the student. *Maier v. Canon McMillan School Dist.*, No. 08-0154, 2009 WL 2591098 (W.D. Pa. 8/20/09).

◆ An Oregon teacher served a school district for 19 years with no disciplinary problems. Her husband left her, moved in with his girlfriend, and sought a divorce. The teacher drove to the girlfriend's house and had an argument with her husband. She attempted suicide by taking prescription medications, then rammed her vehicle into her husband's vehicle and damaged the house. She voluntarily committed herself for psychiatric treatment. The incident was reported in local newspapers. Law officials charged her with four crimes, three of which were dropped via plea bargain. She pleaded no contest to a criminal mischief charge, which provided for dismissal with no charges if she completed her term of probation. The school board voted to dismiss the teacher after a hearing, and she appealed to the Oregon Fair Dismissal Appeals Board (FDAB).

An FDAB hearing panel heard testimony from a psychologist who said the teacher's conduct was isolated and unlikely to reoccur. The board had previously let two teachers return to work after suicide attempts, and another had returned after entering into a diversion agreement for domestic violence charges. The FDAB panel found the dismissal had been "unreasonable" under ORS § 342.905. The board overreacted to an isolated incident and had to reinstate the teacher. The Court of Appeals of Oregon reversed the panel's decision, and the teacher appealed. **The Supreme Court of Oregon stated that contract teachers may be dismissed only for immorality or neglect of duty.** The FDAB was authorized to determine whether actions by school boards were "unreasonable" or "clearly an excessive remedy." In the context of the statute, "unreasonable" meant "acting without rational or logical justification" for an action. The FDAB panel failed to apply this interpretation, and its decision did not provide a rational connection between the facts and the conclusion. The court returned the case to the panel for further action. *Bergerson v. Salem-Keizer School Dist.*, 341 Or. 401, 144 P.3d 918 (Or. 2006).

◆   After a Pennsylvania teacher pled guilty to simple assault of his wife, the state education department filed a notice of charges and a motion with the state Professional Standards and Practices Commission to revoke his professional teaching certification. The notice informed the teacher that simple assault was a crime involving moral turpitude, requiring revocation. The teacher admitted the assault, but he contended he had pled guilty to avoid embarrassment to himself and his family. He asserted his actions were unrelated to moral turpitude but were the result of his wife's attempt to gain an advantage in divorce proceedings. The commission revoked the teacher's license without a hearing, finding that simple assault was within the state code's definition of "moral turpitude."

The teacher appealed to the Commonwealth Court of Pennsylvania, arguing that the commission denied him due process by refusing to give him a hearing. The court held that a teaching certificate is a property right entitled to due process protection. The court agreed with the teacher that **simple assault is not necessarily a crime involving moral turpitude**. It found the state code and cases defining the term "crime of moral turpitude" required the assailant to have a "reprehensible state of mind." At minimum, a crime of moral turpitude required knowledge of private impropriety or the potential for social disruption. Crimes involving dishonesty, such as fraud, theft by deception, and specific intent drug-trafficking offenses were crimes of moral turpitude. By contrast, the statutory definition of "simple assault" included negligence. A person could lack a "reprehensible state of mind" when engaged in a fight or scuffle by mutual consent. While many forms of simple assault, including spousal battery, were abhorrent, a simple assault was not always a crime of moral turpitude. The commission had erroneously revoked the teacher's certification without a hearing. The court reversed and remanded the case. *Bowalick v. Comwlth. of Pennsylvania*, 840 A.2d 519 (Pa. Commw. Ct. 2004).

D. Other Off-Duty Conduct

◆   A Michigan teacher attended a bachelor/bachelorette party and engaged in a simulated act of oral sex on a mannequin. Someone photographed her without her knowledge and posted the photos on a website without her consent. Two years later, students at her school accessed the photos until they were removed. The school board suspended and then fired the teacher for engaging in lewd behavior contrary to the moral values of the educational and school community. She appealed, and the state tenure commission found no professional misconduct and ordered her reinstatement. The Court of Appeals of Michigan upheld that decision, noting that **her conduct was not only off-duty, but lawful and not involving children**. And it did not have an adverse effect on the educational process. *Land v. L'Anse Creuse Public School Board of Educ.*, No. 288612, 2010 WL 2135356 (Mich. Ct. App. 5/27/10).

CHAPTER SEVEN

Health Issues

I. ALLERGIES

A. Food Allergies

1. Generally

All foods have the potential to cause an allergic reaction, and sometimes even a very small amount is all that is needed. Seven foods – peanuts, tree nuts, milk, egg, soy, wheat and fish – account for the vast majority of all food allergies. Of these, peanuts, tree nuts, eggs and milk most commonly cause problems for children, and the majority of severe and fatal reactions involve peanuts and tree nuts. Food allergies can be managed, but they are not curable.

Millions of Americans have food allergies, and food allergies in American children have increased significantly since 1997, according to a study by the Centers for Disease Control (CDC). In addition, the CDC reported a drastic increase in the number of hospital admissions related to children's food allergies, which indicates children's reactions to the allergens are becoming more severe.

Allergies are diseases that cause the immune systems of affected individuals to overreact to substances known as allergens. In people with food allergies, the immune system identifies a specific protein in a food as a potentially harmful substance. The immune system responds to the perceived threat by producing an allergic antibody to the food. This response triggers the release of what are known as chemical mediators, such as histamine. The release of the mediators can cause inflammatory reactions in the skin, the respiratory system, the gastrointestinal system, and the cardiovascular system. A potentially life-threatening condition called anaphylaxis occurs when these inflammatory reactions occur in more than one of these systems. Approximately 30,000 episodes of anaphylactic shock and an average of 200 deaths caused by the episodes occur in the U.S. each year – primarily in children, according to the National Institute of Allergy and Infectious Disease. Common symptoms of anaphylaxis include hives, vomiting, itching, swelling, coughing, dizziness, and difficulty swallowing.

Students who have food allergies should have an action plan to indicate how school officials should manage an allergic reaction that may progress to anaphylaxis. The action plan should indicate whether emergency treatment with an EpiPen or EpiPen Junior is required. EpiPen is an auto-injector that administers adrenaline and is available by prescription only. EpiPens should be stored properly and securely, but they should also be readily available. EpiPens should be accessible to school officials. Decisions regarding whether students should be allowed to carry their own EpiPens should be made on a case-by-case basis and according to the district's policies.

EpiPens should be stored in temperatures ranging from 68 degrees to 77 degrees. They should not be refrigerated, and they should not be exposed to light or extreme heat.

Two red flags indicate that an EpiPen should be replaced, even if it has not reached its expiration date. Specifically, an EpiPen should be discarded if it has solid particles in it or if it has a pink or brown tint.

In 2016, the Food and Drug Administration (FDA) issued new instructions for proper use of the EpiPen and other epinephrine devices. In a nutshell, you should:

- Hold the leg firmly in place. Reports of lacerations and embedded needles prompted this change. Many kids kick when receiving an injection, and holding the leg steady reduces the chances of injury.
- Hold the injector firmly in place for a count of three seconds. Count slowly. This is down from the previous 10-second guideline.
- See a doctor for signs of infection at the injection site, like persistent redness, warmth, swelling and tenderness. Avoid injecting a child in the behind – as it is more likely to get infected. Always inject in the outer thigh – through clothing if necessary.

In November of 2013, President Barack Obama signed into law the School Access to Emergency Epinephrine Act. This law encourages states to adopt laws that require schools to keep epinephrine auto-injectors on hand.

The law gives more grant preference to schools in states that:

- require schools to stock the auto-injectors
- allow students to self-administer medication for anaphylactic reactions (and asthmatic reactions), and
- submit a statement providing that the state's "Good Samaritan" laws adequately protect staffers who administer epinephrine to a student who is reasonably believed to be having an anaphylactic reaction.

Legislative action taken in Michigan was likely a response to the passage of this federal legislation. Effective on the first day of the 2014-15 school year, state law required all schools in the state to have at least two EpiPens in every school – and two staffers who know how to use them.

Children with food allergies present difficult challenges for school administrators and parents. Once a student is identified as having a food allergy, steps must be taken to ensure that the student can completely avoid the food while at school. Families, schools and students all have responsibilities when it comes to managing food allergies. See Form VII-18 in Chapter Nine for a Food Allergy Action Plan.

- It is the **family's** responsibility to notify the school of the existence of the student's food allergies and to work with the school to develop an effective management plan. It is also the responsibility of the family to teach the child to self-manage the food allergy to the maximum extent possible and to provide any required medications.
- **Schools** should form teams, consisting of the student's teacher, the school's principal, the school's nurse, food service personnel and other key personnel to work with the student and the family to develop an effective management plan. It is advisable to adopt and enforce a policy barring eating on school buses, except to accommodate legitimate special needs. Schools would also benefit by providing training and education to staff regarding food allergies and practicing emergency drill responses to food allergy reactions.
- **Students** with allergies should be instructed not to exchange food with others and not to eat anything with unknown ingredients. In addition, allergic students should be instructed to notify an adult immediately if they ingest something they believe might cause an allergic reaction.

Constant monitoring is crucial, as problems can arise in unforeseeable ways. Here's an example: High school student Joshua Hickson was charged with assault after he smeared peanut butter on the forehead of a student with a peanut allergy. Hickson was suspended from school and charged with misdemeanor assault, which is punishable by up to a year in jail and a $5,000 fine.

A multi-faceted approach to keeping allergic students safe is preferable. For example, Tim Henson, principal of a South Carolina elementary school, took all of the following steps:

- school sent letters to parents discussing food allergies and outlining what was permitted and what was not
- staffers talked to students about rules pertaining to nut-free tables that were set up in the cafeteria, and
- administrators talked to lunchroom employees, who completed special training regarding specifics such as cross-contamination and the proper way to clean nut-free tables.

In 2013, the Centers for Disease Control (CDC) issued guidelines for managing food allergies in schools. The CDC says schools should manage food allergies on a daily basis, prepare for food allergy emergencies and provide staff training on food allergies. The guidance is available online at *http://www.cdc.gov/healthyyouth/foodallergies/pdf/13_243135_A_Food_Al lergy_Web_508.pdf.*

Harvard Medical School Professor Dr. Nicholas Christakis advises school officials not to overreact to food allergies by implementing a school-wide ban on nuts. The "disproportionate response" may contribute to an increased sensitization of children to nuts, he asserts, citing a study that reported children who were exposed to peanuts at a young age apparently had fewer allergies to peanuts than children who were exposed at a later age.

As in any other situation involving student safety, communication is a crucial element in keeping students with food allergies safe. Electronic media, such as a school's website, can be an effective communication tool. For example, in response to a student's allergy to AXE body spray, a high school principal in Pennsylvania posted a notice on his school's website. The notice appealed to students and parents to show concern for the student's health by refraining from using the spray at school.

For an example of a letter to parents explaining that a child in the class has a food allergy, see Form VII-1 in Chapter Nine. For a sample letter informing substitute teachers that a child in the class has a food allergy, see Form VII-2 in Chapter Nine.

2. Legal Decisions

◆ The IDEA does not entitle a student with severe food allergies to be accompanied throughout the school day by an individual who is trained in CPR and the Heimlich maneuver, so the Fourth Circuit affirmed a Maryland court ruling to dismiss the claim. A first-grade student suffered several disabilities – including severe food allergies. A one-to-one aide was assigned to the boy. The school implemented an IEP for the student, which stipulated in the event that the student choked, the assigned aide should call 911 and have trained staff perform the Heimlich maneuver. The parents weren't happy with that section of the IEP. They wanted an assigned aide who was trained in CPR and the Heimlich maneuver by their son's side at all times throughout the school day. The parents filed a due process complaint, saying the school failed to provide their son with a FAPE as required by the IDEA. The ALJ found the school satisfied the requirements of the IDEA, and the parents sued. A Maryland court upheld the ALJ's ruling, explaining "reasonableness is something less than perfection, and as found by [the ALJ], the measures that defendant has put in place provide adequate protection." The Fourth Circuit affirmed the dismissal, noting **the ALJ didn't have to consider what the school "could have done; rather, it is required to look at whether the [school's] actions were appropriate"** under the law. *SE.H. v. Board of Educ. of Anne Arundel Co. Public Schools*, 647 Fed.Appx. 242 (4th Cir. 2016).

◆ A Tennessee federal judge refused to dismiss retaliation claims filed by the parents of a girl with allergies. The child suffered from severe peanut allergies. The school teamed up with the girl's allergist and pediatrician and created a plan to address her allergies. Later, her parents raised concerns about how the plan was implemented. Afterward, they claimed the principal became angry, as if their child's health and safety was a "nuisance." Then the principal allegedly retaliated against them by reporting to child protective services they emotionally abused their daughter and by requiring the mother to "check in" at the office because she passed out flyers in her daughter's class. The parents sued, alleging retaliation in violation of the ADA, Section 504 of the Rehabilitation Act and the First Amendment. The court refused to grant judgment without a trial. **Many facts, specifically those regarding the principal's motives behind his actions, were in dispute.** More info was needed, so summary judgment wasn't appropriate. *C.G. v. Cheatham County Board of Educ.,* No. 3-14-2309, 2016 WL 1366671 (M.D. Tenn. 4/6/16).

◆ Virginia's highest court held that school officials' statements to the media were misleading and aimed at the mother of a student who died at school from an anaphylactic reaction. The mother sued, alleging six school officials made malicious statements about her to divert public anger about the school's failure to follow the student's allergy plan. She sought damages for defamation. In 2012, the student died at school as a result of an allergic reaction to peanuts. Prior to the student's death:

* her mother had informed the school of the girl's allergy
* the school was given a copy of the anaphylaxis plan signed by the student's pediatrician, and
* her mother brought an EpiPen to school for an emergency. The nurse told her to take it home, as the school stocked EpiPens.

After the student ate the peanut, she reported "bumps" and "scratching" in her throat. But she was not given medication as the plan directed. Her death received widespread attention from local, national and international media. Both mother and child were named in the articles, and several school officials were quoted. The complaint showed a common theme in 13 public statements: School officials implied the mother failed to work with the school to prevent her daughter's death.

Virginia law recognizes a claim for defamation by inference, implication or insinuation. The long legal battle went all the way to the state supreme court, which held implication was present. **The school officials' statements were clearly "aimed directly [at the mother] and no other person,"** the state's highest court held. It remanded the case for further proceedings consistent with its ruling. *Pendleton v. Newsome,* 772 S.E.2d 759 (Va. 2015).

◆ A school proposed to accommodate a student with a nut allergy by providing that he would eat only food brought from home and would sit at a nut-free table in the cafeteria. His parents objected because the student would be eating alone. The child's doctor asked the school to seat the child at a rectangular table with a two-foot buffer between him and classmates who also had nut-free lunches. However, the school only had round lunch tables. The parents withdrew the student from school and asked for a due process hearing. A hearing officer determined that the school met its obligation to accommodate the student, and a federal court agreed. **The proposed accommodations were reasonable,** and the parents did not show that the school officials were deliberately indifferent to the student's rights.

T.F. v. Fox Chapel Area School Dist., No. 12cv1666, 2013 WL 5936411
(W.D. Pa. 11/5/13).

◆ A nine-year-old student with allergies to many foods and substances
began to have trouble breathing after finishing lunch at school. A school
nurse injected the student with EpiPens, but he died two days later. His
parents suspected that the student's reaction was triggered by his exposure
to blueberries during a classroom lesson on the morning of the event. They
sued the student's school, the city department of education and the school
nurse, among others. They alleged that the defendants negligently allowed
the student to be exposed to a substance to which he was allergic and then
failed to properly respond to his symptoms. The court held that the
department of education met its obligations by formulating a proper
individualized education program for the student. In addition, the school
provided adequate supervision; typically there were about 10 children in the
student's class and four supervising adults. Further, **the nurse did not
depart from good and accepted nursing and professional practice**,
especially since blueberries were not included on the list of known allergens
for the child and the parents never proved what triggered the student's
reaction. *Begley v. City of New York*, 111 A.D.3d 5 (N.Y. App. Div. 2013).

◆ The parents of a child with an allergy to nuts sued an elementary school
principal and others, claiming the defendants failed to consider the
possibility of excluding nut products from the school and forced the child to
eat his lunch in an office away from all the other children. The lawsuit
accused the defendants of failing to make any reasonable accommodations
for the child. **It also claimed the child's school served peanut butter
cookies to all students and caused the child to suffer an allergic
reaction, even though it knew he was allergic to peanuts.** The court
dismissed the parents' claim for negligent infliction of emotional distress
because they did not respond to the defendants' motion to dismiss it. The
court also dismissed a claim for violation of 42 U.S.C. § 1983, a conspiracy
claim under 42 U.S.C. § 1985, a claim under 42 U.S.C. § 1986, a claim of
intentional infliction of emotional distress, and a state civil rights claim with
leave to amend. Finally, it denied a defense motion to dismiss a slander
claim, which was based on the allegation that district defendants distributed
false statements about the child to his classmates. *McCue v. South Fork
Union School Dist.*, No. CV-F-10-233 OWW/DLB, 2010 WL 2089524
(E.D. Cal. 5/21/10).

◆ Residents of New York enrolled their child in a New Jersey nonprofit
school that catered to developmentally atypical children. The child had
severe food allergies and was accompanied by a private nurse at all times. He
was instructed to eat only food that was supplied by his parents. The child
died, allegedly after he was exposed to substances at the school and suffered
an allergic reaction. The parents sued the school in a New York court, seeking

monetary damages for personal injuries and wrongful death. The parents claimed that the school failed to exercise reasonable care of the child while the child was under its direction and control. The school filed a motion for summary judgment, arguing that it was immune from liability under a New Jersey statute that generally barred claims for damages against nonprofit corporations. The parents opposed the motion on the grounds that New York law did not recognize the principle of charitable immunity. The court held that the New Jersey law of charitable immunity did not apply because it offended the public policy of New York. The parents showed that sufficient contacts existed between them, the injury and New York, and they also showed that **application of the New Jersey charitable immunity statute would violate a "fundamental principle of justice."** The parents lived in New York, and the child's tuition at the New Jersey school was paid by the New York City Board of Education. Further, New York had an interest in protecting its citizens from "unfair and anachronistic foreign statutes," and the state of New York had first rejected the concept of charitable immunity nearly 50 years earlier. The school's motion for summary judgment was denied. *Begley v. City of New York*, 836 N.Y.S.2d 496 (N.Y. Sup. Ct. 2007).

◆ A child broke out in splotches and hives while at a daycare facility. Following the incident, the child's doctor determined the child was allergic to peanuts and peanut derivatives. The child then suffered a second allergic reaction at the daycare facility, after which the facility refused to provide further daycare services to her. The child's mother then sued the facility under the Americans with Disabilities Act (ADA) and state law, claiming discrimination on the basis of disability. A district court granted summary judgment in favor of the daycare facility, and the parent appealed. The appeals court upheld the district court's determination on the basis that the child did not have a "disability" as that term is defined in the ADA. Although the child's allergy was a physical impairment, it did not substantially limit her ability to eat or breathe. **The child's doctor stated that the child's allergy impacted her life only "a little bit," and the record did not show she was restricted from eating any other kind of food.** Nor did the parent show that the child was disabled under the ADA because she had a record of a disability or was regarded by the school as disabled. Finally, the court rejected the state-law claim because the child was not disabled under the state law. *Land v. Baptist Medical Center*, 164 F.3d 423 (8th Cir. 1999).

◆ A student with an allergy to peanuts went on a field trip with his elementary school class. The district's food staff, the boy's teacher, two school nurses and several parent volunteers all were aware that the child was allergic to peanuts. Nonetheless, the child was given a snack lunch that included peanut-based foods. The child reported feeling sick after he ate a peanut-based cookie. Trip chaperones did not want to curtail the activities of the other children on the trip, so they placed the student on the school bus to wait. His condition worsened, and he later died after being taken to a hospital by car. After the student's parents entered into a settlement agreement with the school district regarding the incident, a newspaper sought the release under a public disclosure act of an investigator's notes, an investigator's hand-drawn map, conference notes by counsel for the district, and counsel's report to an insurer. A trial court ruled that the records were not subject to disclosure because they were attorney work product and attorney-client privileged material. The newspaper appealed. The appeal court affirmed the determination that the records were not subject to disclosure. **The documents were attorney work product and were further protected by attorney-client privilege.** The public disclosure act's provisions relating to open government did not outweigh the countervailing interest in insulating confidential pretrial communications from public inspection. Finally, the district did not waive its privilege to keep the information private when it made selected disclosures of information to the public and the student's family. The trial court's decision was affirmed. *Soter v. Cowles Publishing Co.*, 130 P.3d 840 (Wash. Ct. App. 2006). On appeal, the Supreme Court of Washington affirmed the appeals court's decision. *Soter v. Cowles Publishing Co.*, 174 P.3d 60 (Wash. 2007).

B. Other Allergies

1. Generally

School officials need to be aware that a range of allergies other than food-related allergies may affect the school environment, as shown by the following cases.

2. Legal Decisions

◆ A Washington federal judge refused to dismiss discrimination claims of a student with diabetes. A student had a severe case of diabetes, and her blood sugar had to be monitored every two hours. Her mother asked for an accommodation – a qualified school nurse – to monitor the student's blood level throughout the day. Her mom said the accommodation would help the child learn to become more independent – a goal listed in her IEP – as she entered first grade. Instead of granting the accommodation, the school said the child would be transferred to a nearby school that could handle the accommodation – but the transfer had to take place in two days. The mother rejected the district's accommodation offer, citing concerns about the abrupt change. She sued, seeking damages for alleged violations of the ADA and Section 504 of the Rehabilitation Act. The school asked the court to dismiss the claims. It refused. The girl's mother had to show the school intentionally discriminated against the child on the basis of her disability. She did, as email documentation showed the school knew about the disability and failed to provide accommodations. The court said a reasonable jury could find the school was deliberately indifferent because it didn't act to address the child's needs. **The court pointed out the transfer accommodation could've been a reasonable one – if the school had allotted more than two days for the**

transition. It didn't, so the claim had to proceed. *Snell v. North Thurston School Dist.*, No. C13-5786RBL, 2015 WL 6396092 (W.D. Wash. 10/21/15).

◆   A student with allergies to certain body sprays, perfumes, colognes, laundry detergents, fabric softeners and scented lotions alleged that his high school violated Title II of the Americans with Disabilities Act by refusing to implement a written policy against spraying perfumes at school. The student did not know which specific scents triggered reactions, how much of a particular fragrance was needed to trigger a reaction, or what the severity of any given reaction would be. The school offered several accommodations, including allowing the student to park in a different area and enter the school through a different door, allowing the student to leave class early, allowing the student to arrive at a different time, and exploring whether the student could wear a mask. **The court ruled for the school, finding it took sufficient steps to accommodate the student's condition.** Moreover, the student did not show that the written policy he sought would have been effective. *Zandi v. JVB Fort Wayne Community Schools*, No. 1:10-CV-395-JVB, 2012 WL 4472006 (N.D. Ind. 9/27/12).

◆   The parent of a two-year-old enrolled the child at a nursery school where teachers used powdered latex gloves to change children's diapers. The parent, who had an allergy to latex, asked the teachers at the school to use non-powdered latex gloves. She also asked her son's teacher to use non-latex gloves, and she offered to provide them. When the parent spoke to the head administrator at the school about switching to non-powdered gloves, the administrator initially told the parent he would look into it. The parent also had her physician send the administrator a letter explaining her allergy. Despite the request and the letter, the administrator allegedly later told the parent he was not willing to switch to another type of gloves. However, he did tell staff members not to use latex gloves when changing the diaper of the parent's child. After the parent provided the administrator with a letter discussing her rights under the law, the administrator asked the parent to withdraw the child from the school. The parent removed the child from the school and later sued it, claiming it violated a county human rights code by discriminating against her based on her latex allergy. A jury found in her favor and awarded $1,683 in economic damages and $5,000 in non-economic damages. It also awarded $22,800 in attorneys' fees. The trial court entered judgment on the verdict, and the school appealed. The appeals court reversed the lower court's judgment in favor of the parent because she did not show that her latex allergy was a disability under the law. However, the state's highest court reversed the appeals court's decision and held that **it was for a jury to decide whether the parent's latex allergy was a "handicap" within the meaning of the law** at issue. Since the evidence was sufficient for the jury to conclude the parent had a "handicap," the judgment favoring her was restored. *Meade v. Shangri-La Limited Partnership*, 36 A.3d 483 (Md. 2012).

◆ A parent of two students sued a city, a board of education and several individual defendants, claiming the defendants' failure to properly maintain public school buildings caused the students to become disabled. The parent asserted that the defendants' failure to properly maintain a middle school caused it to sustain water damage that led to mold and bacterial growth and high levels of moisture in the indoor air. She also claimed that the defendants' failure to properly maintain a high school resulted in asbestos problems, leaks and poor ventilation. **The parent said that conditions at the schools caused one of the students to suffer irreversible lung disease and the other to suffer allergies and asthma.** She claimed that the students were eligible for special education services and that the defendants wrongfully failed to provide them. The parent's suit against the defendants raised several claims, including federal claims under the Individuals with Disabilities Education Act, Section 504 of the Rehabilitation Act and the Americans with Disabilities Act. The parent also filed several state law claims. The defendants filed a motion to dismiss the case, and the parent filed a motion to remand the case to state court. The court granted the motion to dismiss several of the claims raised by the parent because the parent failed to exhaust her administrative remedies under the Individuals with Disabilities Education Act. It also declined to exercise supplemental jurisdiction over some remaining state law claims. The court remanded remaining state law claims to a state court. *Avoletta v. City of Torrington*, No. 3:07CV841 (AHN), 2008 WL 905882 (D. Conn. 3/31/08).

◆ A student with a latex allergy broke out in hives after he was given a latex ball to play with at school. His representatives sued the school district, accusing it of failing to prevent him from sustaining injury by failing to convey his special needs to teachers and aides. The representatives also raised claims under the Individuals with Disabilities Education Act and the Americans with Disabilities Act. After the school district removed the case to federal court, the representatives filed a motion to remand it back to state court. The court granted the motion to remand. **The theories of relief advanced by the student's representatives were based solely on state tort law.** Because no claim in the case arose under federal law, the court granted the motion to remand the case. *Reuther v. Shiloh School Dist. No. 85*, No. 07-cv-689-JPG, 2008 WL 191195 (S.D. Ill. 1/18/08).

◆ A village resident installed an outdoor wood-burning furnace adjacent to his garage and approximately 50 feet from the elementary wing of a local school. The resident used the furnace to provide heat for his home. Teachers, school employees and parents of students complained about the smell of smoke in the school cafeteria and some classrooms. After a school official advised the county department of health that teachers and students had allergies to wood smoke and were becoming ill from it, the health department ordered the resident to stop using the furnace. The resident sued the school district, the county and others, claiming they violated the

Constitution by depriving him the right to use his property without due process of law. He also claimed an equal protection violation, alleging no enforcement actions were taken against others whose use of wood-burning furnaces caused smoke to enter the school. The court granted summary judgment against the resident. The resident failed to prove an equal protection violation because he did not identify any other resident who used wood for heating fuel. Even if he had, the equal protection claim would fail because the smoke created a respiratory hazard. The resident's due process claim failed as well, because **he did not have a constitutionally protected property interest in heating his home with wood**. The defendants' motions for summary judgment were granted. *Tallman v. County of Chautauqua*, No. 05-CV-02769A(Sr), 2007 WL 4276825 (W.D.N.Y. 12/3/07).

◆   The parents of a sixth-grade student sued the student's school principal and others under the Americans with Disabilities Act, the Rehabilitation Act and state law, claiming they failed to accommodate the student's allergic reactions to environmental factors at her school. The parents claimed the student was hypersensitive to phenol, which can be present in vapors emitted by cleaning agents or paints. The defendants filed a motion to exclude the expert testimony of the student's primary treating physician, who concluded the student was hypersensitive to environmental phenol even though the student was unable to complete a test to determine whether the hypersensitivity existed. The court granted the motion to exclude the expert's testimony. **The expert's conclusion that the student was hypersensitive to phenol was an inference that was not based on adequate scientific data, testing or methodology.** As a result, it was unreliable and was not a proper subject for expert testimony. *Kropp v. Maine School Administrative Union #44*, 471 F.Supp.2d 175 (D. Me. 2007).

◆   The parents of an eighth-grade student with multiple chemical sensitivities protested a school board's plan to use pesticides on school playing fields. The board approved the plan, and the parents asked the student's gym teacher to keep her inside while fields were sprayed. The student was assigned to begin ninth grade at a high school that was located across the street from a working farm. During the summer before the student's ninth-grade year, the student's parents asked the school district for a Section 504 Service Agreement that would permit the student to fulfill her gym requirement at a location away from the school. In addition, **they asked that the school not be sprayed with pesticides, and they asked for a transfer to a school that was located in a more urban area**. The school proposed a service agreement that excused the student from participating in outdoor PE activities and offered a transfer to the urban high school. The parents objected to the proposed agreement for several reasons. Among other things, they wanted to substitute gym class with dance, and they stated there was no guarantee that balls used indoors had no pesticides on them. After the school proposed modified agreements, the parents withdrew their request for a service agreement but continued to seek accommodations for the student. The school district submitted the matter for a due process hearing, and the hearing officer found the district offered a reasonable agreement. The school reversed the transfer offer. The parents withdrew the student and sued the district under the Rehabilitation Act, the Americans with Disabilities Act, and 42 U.S.C. § 1983. **They claimed that the district's attempt to enter into a service agreement was an abuse of process and violated their due process rights.** The court granted the defendants' motion for summary judgment. There was no evidence that the district used process in any way not intended as proper use when it sought a due process hearing. The court also rejected the claim that the parents' civil rights were violated because they were forced into a Section 504 service agreement. To prove that the plan violated their due process rights, the parents were required to show actions on the part of the school district that "shocked the conscience." They failed to do so. The parents also failed to show that the district retaliated against them for exercising their First Amendment rights by intensifying the use of pesticides, forcing them into a service agreement or stigmatizing the student as disabled, and that claim was also time-barred. Finally, the court rejected claims of emotional distress and conspiracy. *Sutton v. West Chester Area School Dist.*, No. Civ.A. 03-3061, 2004 WL 999144 (E.D. Pa. 5/4/04).

◆   The parent of an 11-year-old sixth-grade student with an allergy to scents demanded that school officials provide the student a scent-free environment. In response to the demand, the school implemented a voluntary scent-free classroom for the student. The parent spoke to the student's teachers, classmates and their parents regarding the student's condition, and the teachers and classmates voluntarily refrained from wearing scents. However, the student was exposed to scents at school on three occasions. On one occasion, a school administrator who was wearing a scent left the student's classroom. On a second occasion, a substitute teacher wore a fragrance. The student was sent to the library. The student was also sent to the library on a third occasion when a classmate wore cologne. The parent continued to request a mandatory scent-free environment, but the school refused to provide one. School officials said a mandatory scent-free environment policy would be impossible to enforce and would conflict with the rights of other students and teachers. When the student's physician informed school officials that the student required a scent-free classroom, the school informed the parent that the student would no longer be allowed to attend because it could not provide a scent-free environment. **The parent then sued the school, claiming that it discriminated against the student on the basis of disability in violation of the Rehabilitation Act.** The parent filed a motion for injunctive relief. The court denied the motion and entered judgment for the school and other defendants. The school met its duty to provide the student with a minor adjustment when it provided a voluntary scent-free classroom. It would not be reasonable to require the school to enforce a mandatory scent-free policy. The student attended several different classrooms and also spent time in the school gymnasium and church, and **it would be unduly burdensome to require the school to implement a mandatory scent-free policy**. The court also found that the school was not required to provide a written contingency plan in the event the student was exposed to scents, and it rejected a claim of retaliation. *Hunt v. St. Peter School*, 963 F.Supp. 843 (W.D. Mo. 1997).

II. DIABETES

A. Symptoms and Management

Diabetes is an incurable, chronic disease that is characterized by an inability to properly produce or use insulin, which is a hormone that converts food into energy. Lack of insulin causes blood glucose to rise to an abnormally high level, resulting in a condition called hyperglycemia. When this happens, the body may excrete blood glucose in the urine, causing it to lose its main fuel source.

There are two main types of diabetes. Individuals with Type 1 diabetes, which often afflicts school-age children, are unable to produce insulin and must receive insulin on a daily basis. Type 2 diabetes involves an inability to utilize insulin that the body produces. It can be controlled with insulin, oral medications or both.

Management of diabetes involves maintaining proper blood glucose control, a task which requires constant vigilance. Careful monitoring is imperative, and administration of insulin therapy is often required.

Controlling blood glucose levels is often a difficult balancing act. If not enough insulin is given, the individual's blood glucose level will rise to an unacceptable level. But administration of too much insulin can cause a dangerous condition called hypoglycemia, or low blood glucose. According to the U.S. Department of Health and Human Services, hypoglycemia presents a greater danger to school-age students than hyperglycemia. Some of the symptoms of hypoglycemia, as noted by the U.S. Department of Health and Human Services, include the following:

- shakiness
- sweating
- hunger
- pale appearance
- blurred vision
- sleepiness
- dizziness
- confusion
- disorientation
- lack of coordination
- irritability or nervousness

- change in personality
- inability to concentrate
- weakness
- lethargy
- changes in behavior

In severe cases, there may be an inability to swallow, seizure or convulsions, or loss of consciousness.

Because it is a relatively common disease among school-age children, many, if not most, schools will have a student or students with diabetes enrolled. School personnel play a key role in helping students manage the condition.

In New York, South Jefferson School District implemented on-site virtual clinics for students who have diabetes. Each school building in the district was equipped with a computer and a webcam. School nurses used the equipment to communicate with medical personnel at a diabetes center about students' blood glucose test results. School nurses could also download student data and coordinate meetings between students and the diabetes control center. The meetings took only 10 to 15 minutes, but they improved lab test results. In addition, the number of urgent calls relating to the diabetic students was significantly reduced.

For a sample diabetes management plan, see Form VII-3 in Chapter Nine.

B. Legal Decisions

◆   The Sixth Circuit rejected the attempts of a Kentucky family to collect damages based on alleged disability discrimination. The student was diagnosed with Type-1 diabetes when he was four. He had to take insulin injections and needed to monitor his sugar throughout the day. During kindergarten enrollment, his parents explained his medical needs. After several meetings, the district determined he needed to be enrolled at an elementary school with a full-time nurse on staff. His parents disagreed with the placement – they wanted him to be enrolled in a school closer to home. By the time he reached the second grade, he was independently using an insulin pump, so the district agreed to transfer the boy to the school of the parent's choosing. But in the middle of the transfer, the parents moved out of the district and filed a disability discrimination suit that sought damages. To win damages, the parents had to show that the school was "deliberately indifferent" to their son's federally protected rights. But that wasn't the case, the court explained, as the school didn't ignore the boy's request for help. "Rather, **the parents simply disagreed ... as to whether a nurse was necessary to provide" medical care**, the court held. So the child wasn't entitled to damages. *R.K. v. Board of Educ. of Scott County, Kentucky*, 637 Fed.Appx. 922 (6th Cir. 2016).

◆   The parent of a seventh-grade student with Title I diabetes sued a city, city agencies and city officials. In the lawsuit, the parent accused the defendants of violating the Rehabilitation Act and the Americans with

Disabilities Act by denying her request to heat the child's food at school. The parent claimed that the school was required to heat the child's food because the child would skip lunch if his food was not heated. The court rejected her claim, finding that **the child's school provided adequate accommodations by offering lunch menu options and monitoring the child's blood glucose level**. Heating the student's food may have helped him adjust to his disability, but the school was required to provide only meaningful access and not preferred arrangements. The laws relied upon by the parent did not require optimal accommodations, and it was undisputed that hot food is not essential to effective management of diabetes. *Moody v. NYC Dep't of Educ.*, 513 Fed. Appx. 95 (2d Cir. 2013).

◆   The Americans Nurses' Association and other trade organizations representing registered and school nurses sued to challenge a state department of education's decision to authorize public school employees other than nurses to administer insulin to students with diabetes. The plaintiffs in the case sought declaratory relief and a writ of mandate. A lower court ruled in favor of the associations, finding that state law did not authorize unlicensed school personnel to administer insulin. On appeal, the state's highest court reversed the lower court's decision. The appeals court determined that **state law did not ban school personnel other than licensed health care providers from administering insulin to students with diabetes**. In addition, it decided that advisory statements recommending administration only by licensed professionals were not entitled to deference. *American Nurses Ass'n v. Torlakson*, 304 P.3d 1038 (Cal. 2013).

◆   The mother of a second-grade student became dissatisfied with the way her daughter's school was handling her diabetes. The mother informed the school nurse that she wanted the nurse to give the student insulin shots whenever her blood sugar tested higher than a specified level. The nurse told the mother that written authorization from a physician was required, but the mother never provided the authorization. The nurse later asked the student what she ate at home every day. She also called the student's doctor to ask what she should do if the student's blood sugar level showed a shot was needed and she could not reach the mother. Then, an anonymous caller filed a complaint against the mother with a governmental department of job and family services for medically neglecting the child. The mother later sued the school district and others, alleging that the district violated her right to privacy by asking the student what she ate at home and allegedly filing the anonymous complaint of alleged medical neglect. She also filed a retaliation claim against the school superintendent based on the superintendent's alleged role in filing the neglect complaint against her. The court granted summary judgment against the motion. It rejected her privacy claim because **she did not present authority to support the proposition that she had a fundamental liberty interest in information relating to her management**

of her child's diabetes. In addition, the mother failed to produce evidence showing that the district or any of the other defendants had ever revealed the student's medical records to anyone. *Jenkins v. Board of Educ.*, 463 F.Supp.2d 747 (S.D. Ohio 2006). On appeal, the Sixth Circuit reversed the lower court's ruling with respect to the retaliation claim because factual issues existed as to that claim. *Jenkins v. Rock Hill Local School Dist.*, 513 F.3d 580 (6th Cir. 2008).

◆ A child with Type I diabetes was accepted for admission into a preschool program. The child's status as a diabetic was disclosed at the time of the initial interview. A month before the child was to start attending the preschool, his mother informed the preschool's owner that the child had been fitted with an insulin pump. The mother showed two teachers at the preschool how the pump operated. The mother claimed that the owner withdrew the child's acceptance on the day of the meeting. She sued, claiming discrimination. A trial court found that the school was a place of public accommodation under the state law and that the claim was not preempted by the Individuals with Disabilities Education Act. However, it ruled for the school because the law did not obligate the school to provide reasonable accommodations in connection with the child's care. Both sides appealed, and the appeals court affirmed in part and reversed in part. It affirmed the conclusions that the school was a place of public accommodation under the state law and that the claim was not preempted by the Individuals with Disabilities Education Act. **However, it held that the lower court erred when it concluded that the state law against discrimination did not obligate places of public accommodations to provide reasonable accommodations to individuals with disabilities.** Regulations implementing the statute indicated that the provision of reasonable accommodations was required, and the law was to be construed broadly. In addition, federal precedent under the Americans with Disabilities Act, which requires places of public accommodation to provide reasonable accommodations, was relevant. The court was unable to determine whether the school had breached its duty to provide a reasonable accommodation. So further proceedings were needed. *Ellison v. Creative Learning Center*, 893 A.2d 12 (N.J. Super. Ct. App. Div. 2006).

◆ A board of education posted a job opening for a classroom aide. State law defined the position as an aide who had completed a state-approved training program, held a high school diploma, or received a general educational development certificate. It did not include additional requirements. When the board posted the opening, it added the requirement that the successful candidate must be licensed as a practical nurse. The board added this requirement because the successful applicant would serve the needs of two diabetic students. Both students were considered "brittle" diabetics. One received insulin through an insulin pump, and the other received insulin injections. The board hired an individual who was licensed as a practical nurse. Two unsuccessful applicants, who were not licensed as practical nurses, filed grievances with a state grievance board. **They claimed that the board wrongfully expanded the statutory qualifications of the aide position by requiring the successful candidate to be licensed as a practical nurse.** The grievance board granted the grievances, finding that only a school nurse could administer the required care based on the students' specialized health needs. A lower court affirmed, and the board appealed. The appeals court held that the board of education permissibly added practical nurse licensure as a qualification for the position. It was within the discretion of the school board to hire an applicant who possessed the additional qualification of licensure as a practical nurse. The decision of the lower court was reversed. *Board of Educ. of the County of Randolph v. Scott*, 617 S.E.2d 478 (W. Va. 2005).

◆   The parents of a seventh-grade student with diabetes alleged that a school district and school officials violated the Individuals with Disabilities Education Act (IDEA) and Americans with Disabilities Act by failing to recognize that their daughter was a student with a disability and by failing to accommodate her condition. The parents claimed that the defendants denied the student extra time to complete assignments. They also alleged that they ridiculed her in front of other students based on her disability and displayed animosity toward her. The court ruled against the parents because they failed to exhaust administrative procedures and remedies under the IDEA. Exhaustion of administrative remedies is generally required before a party can proceed to court with an IDEA claim. Exhaustion is excused when it would be futile or fail to provide relief, or when an agency has adopted a policy or pursued a practice that violates the law. The parents argued that exhaustion was not required because the monetary relief they sought could not be granted at the administrative level. However, **a plaintiff seeking monetary damages must exhaust administrative remedies even though money damages may be unavailable under the IDEA or through the administrative process**. In this case, the plaintiffs alleged injuries that could be redressed, at least partially, via the IDEA's administrative procedures. Therefore, they were required to exhaust administrative remedies before filing a court claim. The court granted the defense motion for summary judgment. *Eads v. Unified School Dist. No. 289*, 184 F.Supp.2d 1122 (D. Kan. 2002).

◆   While a high school pep band was returning to school after a basketball game, a student asked the band instructor if the bus could stop so he could use a restroom. The student claimed the instructor failed to respond three times. Other students began to tease the student, and the bus driver deliberately pumped the brakes to jar the bus and aid in the teasing of the student. The student used a profanity while demanding that the instructor let him off the bus. Before he was able to get off, the student wet himself. The next day, the instructor told the student he would not be allowed to participate in the pep band for the next game and that he might be removed from the pep band. The student was given a one-day out-of-school suspension for using profanity on the bus, and the principal later ordered him to serve three days of detention. A short time later, the student was diagnosed as having diabetes and post-traumatic stress disorder (PTSD). His parents sued the instructor, the principal and the school district, claiming that they triggered or accelerated the student's development of diabetes and caused his PTSD. After the student's physician testified that the added stress created by the bus incident "could have" contributed to the student's development of diabetes, a trial court granted summary judgment against the parents on the ground that the harm to the student was not foreseeable. The parents appealed. **The appeals court affirmed the trial court's decision because the parents failed to present enough evidence of a causal connection between the actions of the defendants and the student's injuries.** The physician's testimony was admissible only if it was based on an opinion that it was more likely than not that the defendants' conduct caused the student's injuries. The physician's testimony that the stress of the bus incident could have caused the student's injuries did not meet this standard. The trial court's decision was affirmed. *Hinkle v. Shepherd School Dist. #37*, 93 P.3d 1239 (Mont. 2004).

III. ASTHMA

A. Symptoms and Management

Asthma is a chronic inflammation of the airways. It can leave students or teachers who suffer from it feeling tired, wheezing, suffering a persistent cough or even struggling to breathe.

Without asthma, our bodies do a very good job of filtering out things like smoke, dust and mold. They get stopped before they reach our lungs by getting trapped in phlegm so they can be coughed or sneezed away.

In people with asthma, the bronchial airways become inflamed by an over-reaction to irritants. The airways swell or become blocked, making it difficult for air to reach the lungs. This over-reaction could have several causes, but the overwhelming number of children with asthma – as many as 80% – also suffer from allergies. Other causes of asthma attacks include viruses and airborne irritants.

According to the Asthma and Allergy Foundation of America, 36,000 students miss school because of asthma – that's 36,000 students missing school because of asthma *every day*.

The American Lung Association says asthma comes first on the list of chronic illnesses that keep children out of school.

Asthma is also high on the list of things that send children to the hospital. In 2004, more than 640,000 children under age 15 visited emergency rooms because of their asthma.

Most serious of all, students occasionally die from asthma attacks – and the condition is affecting more students than ever.

The Centers for Disease Control and Prevention (CDC) has estimated 7 million children have asthma.

When it comes to treatment, the news is mixed. We're doing a good job of treating childhood asthma – when there's access to medicine. On the plus side, the CDC report, *The State of Childhood Asthma, United States, 1980 – 2005*, showed a direct correlation between the drop in death rates from juvenile asthma and increased medical treatment. But it also found a disproportionate number of African-American children dying from asthma. Experts say many of these deaths were avoidable. They were apparently caused by under-medication.

Which brings us to the most basic point about your school and asthma: Asthma can't be cured, but it can be controlled. And there are many things schools can do to help.

The American Lung Association defines controlling asthma as taking steps to reduce its frequency and severity in order to lessen its interference with asthmatics' everyday life. From your perspective, you not only want to keep all your students physically safe, you also want to do everything you can to make sure they're learning. A student who is worrying if the chest-tightness she's feeling is the first sign of an attack, or a student who is finding it hard to breathe, is too distracted to pay attention in class or concentrate on homework.

One crucial step in controlling asthma is to eliminate the common triggers for asthma attacks. In its publication *Asthma & Physical Activity in the School*, the National Heart, Lung and Blood Institute has identified the following as common triggers:

- exercise, especially in cold weather
- upper respiratory infections, such as head colds or the flu
- laughing or crying hard
- allergens, such as mold, dust and animal dander, and
- irritants, such as tobacco smoke, chemical fumes and chalk dust.

B. Controlling Asthma's Impact at School

There are many ways to make your school environment a place where asthmatics can breathe freely. These include:

- eliminating dust, dust mites and other allergens by keeping rugs, padded furniture, stuffed animals and cushions out of classrooms
- making sure classroom surfaces are kept clear so that janitors can wipe and mop them
- impressing on staff that using highly scented personal products – including laundry detergents and fabric softeners – could make it harder for some students to breathe
- keeping animals out of school
- maintaining a smoke-free environment, and
- having the right air filters – and keeping them clean.

For a checklist on how your school's doing, see Form VII-28: How

Asthma-Friendly is Your School? in Chapter Nine.

There also are several things that staff should be on the alert for when it comes to students and asthma. For example:

- Persistent coughing. The American Lung Association has stated that coughing is the most common symptom of asthma. Coughing can be a sign that an asthmatic child may be in distress. In children not diagnosed with asthma, it could be a sign that they should be evaluated for it.
- Children who experience lots of respiratory infections also should be evaluated.
- Since exercise can be a trigger, gym teachers and playground monitors need to be especially vigilant – particularly when the air is cold.
- Emotion also can play a role in the onset and severity of asthma attacks. Adults can help by staying calm, themselves.

In the CDC's *Strategies for Addressing Asthma Within a Coordinated School Health Program*, a six-part plan of attack is suggested:

1. **Establish management and support systems for asthma-friendly schools.** These include identifying asthmatic students, setting up effective home-school-health provider communication, and assigning a person to coordinate asthma-control efforts.
2. **Provide appropriate school health and mental health services for students with asthma.** For example: following students' own asthma action plans or else a standard emergency protocol for students without individualized plans.
3. **Provide asthma education and awareness programs for students and school staff.** This could include teaching everyone asthma-control basics as well as providing quit-smoking support programs for staff.
4. **Provide a safe and healthy school environment to reduce asthma triggers.** In addition to strategies similar to those discussed above, the CDC encourages schools to use integrated pest management techniques.
5. **Provide safe, enjoyable physical education and activity opportunities for students with asthma.** Students should be encouraged to participate fully when well, but some asthmatics need preventative medication before participation. Immediate emergency access to medication also should be available.
6. **Coordinate school, family, and community efforts to better manage asthma symptoms and reduce school absences among students with asthma.** One thing schools can do is ask for parents' permission for the school health staff and the student's doctor to share health information. They also can get involved with asthma-control initiatives in the wider community.

Schools have been rising to the challenge to help control the impact of asthma on their students in other ways.

Some schools have obtained special equipment to make sure children can get necessary treatment at school.

One piece of equipment some schools consider vital is a peak-flow meter. This is a handheld device that measures how well people can move air out of their lungs.

Another piece of equipment is a nebulizer, a device that turns asthma medication into a fine mist that can be breathed in to penetrate deeply into the lungs. Some states have laws requiring nebulizers in schools.

Schools have also been educating themselves on the subject to better help their students. One excellent free resource you might want to check out is the American Lung Association's *Back to School with Asthma Toolkit*, available at *lung.org*.

In addition to learning about asthma, reducing triggers, training staff and having the right equipment, the following cases illustrate that a quick and appropriate response to a student asthma attack is absolutely necessary. See Forms VII-12 and VII-13 in Chapter Nine for parent and physician letters regarding asthma.

C. Legal Decisions

1. Asthma-Related Deaths

◆   A Pennsylvania federal judge refused to dismiss claims filed by the estate of a student who died from an asthma attack at school. School officials knew the sixth-grader had asthma and took medicine to treat her symptoms. One day, the student complained to her teacher about breathing problems. No nurse was on duty, so the teacher told the student to "be calm." School policy prohibited the use of medicine "without the supervision of a nurse." The girl's condition worsened, but no medical attention was sought. After school ended, the girl's mother drove her to a hospital. There, she died from "an acute exacerbation of asthma," doctors said. The girl's estate sued, alleging constitutional violations. **The court said a reasonable jury could find the school violated the girl's rights – as school defendants may have "acted affirmatively to [the girl's] detriment by maintaining a policy ... of not permitting students to use prescription medication without a nurse on duty."** The court refused to grant qualified immunity to the principal and district. *Estate of Massey v. City of Philadelphia*, 118 F.Supp.3d 679 (E.D. Pa. 2015).

◆   Because the evidence supported the jury's verdict that a district's negligence did not cause an asthmatic student's death, a Washington Appeals court affirmed the verdict for the school. A student had both asthma and life-threatening allergies. The school had a doctor-prescribed inhaler on the premises for her in case of an asthma attack. It also had her doctor-prescribed EpiPen for an allergic emergency. One day she had trouble breathing and said she felt sick. The staff at the school's health room were familiar with her medical conditions. They decided she was having an asthma attack, so treated her with the inhaler. They tried it again when she didn't get better and then called 911. The school nurse had prepared an emergency health care plan for the student, but staff didn't look at it that morning. They also didn't call the school nurse. The student lost consciousness before the ambulance arrived. Staff didn't perform CPR, and the girl died. An autopsy attributed the death to asthma. The family sued the school district, its school health clerk, and the school nurse for wrongful death. The family claimed the district defendants were responsible for her death because they didn't administer the EpiPen or give her CPR. At trial, expert testimony established the girl probably would have survived if staff had administered the EpiPen before she lost consciousness or administered CPR after she did. The epinephrine posed no real threat of side effects, and an asthma attack could qualify as a medical emergency. The jury decided the school defendants were negligent but their negligence didn't cause the girl's death. The family appealed, but the appeals court affirmed. To find against the school defendants, the jury had to decide their negligence proximately caused the student's death. It didn't. And because the jury could have found staff might not have administered the EpiPen or performed CPR even if they consulted the emergency plan or contacted a school nurse, the verdict didn't go against the evidence – so the appeals court affirmed it. *Mears v. Bethel School Dist.*, No. 403, No. 43121-1-II, 2014 WL 3933555 (Wash. Ct. App. 8/12/14).

◆ A California appeals court found the state's field-trip immunity law meant neither district could be sued over the death of one district's asthmatic student at another district's outdoor "camp."

The school district San Diego County Office of Education (SDCOE) owned and operated "Camp Fox" at the base of Palomar Mountain. The camp provided science-related programs to students. Its staff were all SDCOE employees.

Sixth-grader Virginia Sanchez from the McCabe Union School District went to Camp Fox for a voluntary five-day field trip with her class. While there, she had an asthma attack. Staff gave Virginia her inhaler and performed CPR until paramedics arrived, but she died.

Virginia's parents sued SDCOE for negligence. The trial court awarded SDCOE summary judgment, finding it immune under state law. The parents appealed, but the appellate court affirmed.

State law provided immunity to "the district, a charter school, or the State of California" for a student's "injury, accident, illness or death" while on a field trip. The parents claimed this immunity was only for the school district the student attended, so it could sue SDCOE. The court disagreed, finding the statute covered both districts – so blocked the parents' lawsuit entirely. *Sanchez v. San Diego County Office of Educ.*, 182 Cal.App.4th 1580 (Cal. Ct. App. 2010).

◆ At the start of an academic year, the mother of a five-year-old kindergarten student with asthma gave the school nurse asthma medication and an inhaler. She also provided an authorization and a pediatrician's directive regarding use of the inhaler, and she gave the nurse a separate authorization for an allergy medication.

The child began coughing in class, and the nurse gave him inhaler medication and determined he was breathing, alert and not in distress. The child's mother was notified, and she picked him up from the school. The nurse suggested the mother take the child to his pediatrician. But when the child became ill during the ride, she drove home and went inside to dial 911. The child died shortly after emergency personnel took him to the hospital.

The mother sued the school district and others, claiming the nurse was negligently hired and committed malpractice. The trial court denied a summary judgment motion filed by the district and nurse. They appealed. The appeals court reversed. **The child's mother did not show the defendants breached a legal duty owed to her or the child.** The mother removed the control of district employees. Also, she decided to take him home rather than to the doctor, as the nurse had suggested. *Williams v. Hempstead School Dist.*, 850 N.Y.S.2d 459 (N.Y. App. Div. 2007).

◆ The mother of a third-grader who died from an asthma attack at school could sue a teacher for violating his right not to be deprived of life without due process of law. There was evidence her actions led to his death.

When an asthmatic student started the third grade, his mother told the school he'd been treated in an emergency room at least 10 times and that not treating his symptoms immediately could put his life at risk.

The school developed an individualized education program that called for him to use his inhaler before exercise and when suffering symptoms; for his mother to be called promptly about any asthma-related incident; and for the school to perform CPR and call emergency services if he stopped breathing.

In late September, the student told his teacher he felt tired and was having trouble breathing. Instead of administering his inhaler, she told him to rest with his head on the desk. There was a phone in the room, but she didn't call for medical help or let him call his mother. About 15 minutes later, a classmate saw he wasn't breathing and had turned purple. His teacher sent a student to tell the office this. No school official tried to administer his inhaler or perform CPR, but someone did eventually call for emergency help. Medics weren't able to revive him, and he died in the hospital.

The mother sued the teacher, alleging she had violated the student's Fourteenth Amendment rights, and the court allowed the suit to go forward.

Under the state-created danger doctrine, a public school teacher can have a constitutional duty to protect a student if the court finds that:
• the harm was foreseeable
• the student was a foreseeable victim of it
• the teacher's actions were bad enough to "shock the conscience," and

- the teacher used classroom authority in a way that created the danger or made it worse.

Here, **the mother demonstrated that the school understood her son could die if his symptoms weren't promptly and properly treated** – so the harm and victim were both foreseeable. Also, the court said refusing to let an asthmatic child seek medical help was conscience-shocking. Finally, if the mother could show that the teacher refused to let her son call her for help, a Fourteenth Amendment violation could be shown. *Taylor v. Altoona Area School Dist.*, 513 F.Supp.2d 540 (W.D. Pa. 2007).

◆   An appeals court affirmed a verdict for a school district in a wrongful death suit brought by parents of a student found dead in a locker room shortly after his teacher gave him permission to go there to use his inhaler.

During gym class, a 14-year-old with a history of mild asthma asked his gym teacher for permission to go get his prescription inhaler from the locker room. The teacher said he could. Between five and 15 minutes later, the teacher found the student lying on the locker room floor with the inhaler in hand. The boy wasn't breathing and was later pronounced dead.

The boy's parents sued the school district for wrongful death. **The main issue at trial was if the school was negligent not to supervise the boy when he went to the locker room to get his inhaler.** If the court found it foreseeable the student was likely to die without supervision while he retrieved and used his inhaler, it would have found the school negligent.

But the Ohio trial court did not find the lack of supervision likely to lead to the student's death. First, the father testified it was normal for the boy to get and use his inhaler without adult supervision. Second, there was expert testimony the likelihood of this kind of death from only mild asthma was "one in a million." The parents appealed, but the appellate court affirmed the verdict for the school. *Spencer v. Lakeview School Dist.*, No. 2005-T-0083, 2006 WL 1816452 (Ohio App. Ct. 6/30/06).

◆   The New Mexico Supreme Court decided parents could sue a school district for wrongful death after a substitute gym teacher ignored an asthmatic student's request to stop exercising and then administrators responded inadequately to her ensuing asthma attack.

A 14-year-old special ed student's IEP said she was asthmatic. Her parents gave the school permission to get her emergency medical help without contacting them first. They also told her gym teacher exercise could trigger an attack. The gym teacher agreed to let her rest instead of participating if she felt an attack coming on. The day the gym class had a substitute teacher, the student asked for permission to rest, but the sub said no. The student began to have trouble breathing. Others saw her face was red, and she was crying as she struggled to keep up with the class. The student used her inhaler after gym, but collapsed at her desk as her next class began. The teacher called the front office and then tried to administer the student's inhaler. A school secretary with some nursing training arrived, checked the student's vital signs and asked the office to call 911 – but the call wasn't made. Instead, staff put the student in a wheelchair and wheeled her into the hall. Seeing her there, a school police officer called 911. By that time, it was 15 minutes after the start of her asthma attack. When medical personnel arrived, the student had stopped breathing and couldn't be revived. Her parents sued the school district for wrongful death, but a trial court and then an appeals court found the district was immune to the suit. The parents appealed to the New Mexico Supreme Court. It reversed, allowing the parents' wrongful death suit to go forward. An exception to the state's immunity law OK'd school districts to be sued for negligence in operating or maintaining a building. The supreme court found **the school's failure to follow its safety procedures for a special needs student was similar to failing to follow procedures for a fire drill**. It failed to follow its procedures by ignoring the student's IEP, not administering CPR and not calling 911 immediately. Immunity also wasn't proper here because the school knew the student was asthmatic, but an employee forced her to keep exercising in spite of her visible distress – so the school actively participated in causing the asthma attack. *Upton v. Clovis Municipal School Dist.*, 141 P.3d 1259 (N.M. 2006).

◆ An appeals court reapportioned the blame for a student's asthma-related death – finding a school counselor, not the principal, mainly responsible.

At a school event, a high school senior began to have an asthma attack. Her eighth-grade sister asked a security guard to call 911. Instead, he used a walkie-talkie to call the principal, who said to call the student's parents.

The walk to the office to use the phone aggravated the student's condition. When they got there, the guard and the sister were holding her up. The sister told a counselor to call 911 because the student was having an asthma attack. He told the sister to call her mother to ask if she would pay for the ambulance.

The sister had to wait for a phone and then couldn't reach her mother.

The student's condition deteriorated. The counselor fanned her and tried to help her use her medication and then tried taking her outside for fresh air. When the sister got back, the student told her, "I'm not going to make it." The sister called 911. About 10 minutes later, the counselor called 911, too. The student lost consciousness, and the school called 911 again.

The ambulance arrived around 50 minutes after the onset of the asthma attack. The student was pronounced dead at the hospital.

The student's sister and mother sued the school board, principal and counselor for negligence. The case was tried before a jury. **The court determined the failure to immediately call for emergency medical help was a cause-in-fact of the student's death.** It apportioned the blame for this as: 50% to the principal, 30% to the counselor and 20% to the school board. It awarded the family well over $1 million in damages. The school defendants appealed.

The appellate court affirmed the school's responsibility for the student's death, but reduced the damages by about $170,000 – leaving the award at just about $1 million.

The appellate court also determined the counselor bore the largest portion of the blame. Unlike the principal, he saw the seriousness of the student's condition. The court decided the principal was 30% to blame because he should have followed up on the report from the security guard and made sure someone called 911. The court found the counselor was 50% responsible. His failure to respond reasonably to a student in obvious distress created an immediate and fatal risk to her. *Declouet v. Orleans Parish School Board*, 715 So.2d 69 (La. Ct. App. 1998).

2. Other Asthma Cases

◆   A teacher who alleged school construction caused her asthma could bring disability bias claims against the school board, but not a claim of negligent failure to provide her a safe working environment.

A school board divided an elementary school art classroom in half by putting in a new wall. This left the room with poor ventilation, as there were no operable windows, exterior doors or air conditioning.

The art teacher complained about water damage to the ceiling tiles as well as strong construction odors from paints, sealants and adhesives. Ultimately, the students' art classes were moved elsewhere, but the teacher had to be in the room twice a day to load and unload art supplies. **She said the exposure to construction odors, dust and mold left her with asthma.**

The teacher went on medical leave in October. She filed a workers' comp claim in December – and says a school-board-requested medical exam confirmed conditions in the classroom caused her asthma.

The board installed an air filter, and she returned to work in January – but had a severe asthma attack after workers removed the skylight in the room while she was teaching, releasing dust and particles.

The teacher's doctor removed her from work for the rest of the year. She returned for the following school year, but discovered the air filter in her classroom had been recycled from a school since demolished due to mold problems. She says it was replaced by a poor-quality filter.

Her doctor removed her from work for the next school year, and she was diagnosed with multiple myeloma, an environmentally induced disease.

The teacher sued the board of education and others, alleging multiple claims. The school defendants asked the judge to dismiss her suit.

The judge found the defendants had state-law immunity with respect to the teacher's claim that the town and board negligently failed to provide her a safe working environment – so dismissed it.

But the judge found her claims under the Rehabilitation Act could go forward. They alleged the school board discriminated against her and retaliated against her by failing to accommodate her disability. *Gallagher v. Town of Fairfield*, No. 3:10-cv-1270 (CFD), 2011 WL 3563160 (D. Conn. 8/15/11).

◆   A school board was ordered to pay $130,000 to a disabled student who was hospitalized for six months after an asthma attack that could have been prevented if the school had followed its policies.

Under a middle school's policy, critical student health information was supposed to be collected from enrollment forms, entered into computer records, red-flagged and copied to the student's teachers. The policy also required setting up individualized education program (IEP) meetings for transferring special ed students as soon as possible – preferably within two weeks. The student had mental retardation and qualified for special education, but a school social worker didn't come to his home to get his IEP information until mid-October.

The mother told the social worker the student had severe breathing problems and said the school should call 911 if he had trouble breathing at school. The student's enrollment forms clearly stated he had asthma, and his mother gave the school a doctor's note to allow him to use his inhaler at school. But the mother didn't include this information on the student's PE health form or write any response to the form's request to list any reason the student should sit out PE or have a modified gym program.

In late October, a classmate saw the student stop while doing laps in PE class. When he clutched his chest, she asked if he needed his inhaler. He nodded. She ran to tell the PE teacher, but the teacher told both children to keep running. The teacher later said he hadn't been told the student had asthma and mental retardation. Later that day, the mother picked up the student because he was ill.

When the breathing treatments his mother tried at home didn't work, she called an ambulance. The student spent the next six months in the hospital. A doctor stated his health crisis was caused by overexertion in PE class and failure to use his inhaler.

The student's mother sued the school board under the Tennessee Governmental Tort Liability Act. The court held for the student. The school board appealed, but the appellate court affirmed.

Under the act, governmental entities could be held liable for student injuries caused by staff members' "operational" acts – but not by their "discretionary" acts. Generally, "operational acts" are actions taken pursuant to an established order or policy, while "discretionary acts" are acts involving planning or policy-making.

The court noted the board already had policies in place to notify teachers about a student's health problems. **But the policy wasn't followed, so the judge found the board negligent for not following its own policies.** The appellate court also upheld the apportionment of the blame and its damages award. The lower court judge decided the mother was 20% at fault because she didn't provide information on the PE health form. The rest of the fault was apportioned to the school board. It was ordered to pay the student $130,000, the highest amount allowed under the act. *Small v. Shelby County Schools*, No. W2007-00045-COA-R3-CV, 2008 WL 360925 (Tenn. Ct. App. 2/12/08).

IV. MRSA INFECTION

A. Background

Methicillin-resistant staphylococcus aureus, more commonly referred to as MRSA, is a type of staph bacteria that is resistant to certain antibiotics. MRSA infection has been identified in hospital patients since the 1960s, and the overwhelming majority of cases continue to be associated with healthcare. However, MRSA infection has made its way into other community-based settings, including schools. Within the school setting, members of athletic teams are at a higher risk of contracting MRSA infection, especially if they participate in a contact sport such as wrestling or football. Despite the rise in incidence rates, MRSA infection is both preventable and treatable.

An October 2007 study released by the Centers for Disease Control and Prevention (CDC) reported the results of the agency's population-based surveillance for MRSA infection in nine geographic areas between July 2004 and December 2005. The study, which tracked nearly 9,000 cases, showed that MRSA infection affects particular populations disproportionately. Specifically, the study reported a significantly higher incidence rate among people age 65 or older. In addition, the incidence rate among African-Americans was about double the rate among others, and it was slightly higher among males.

The study also identified risk factors for MRSA infection. Among the most common were a history of hospitalization, a history of surgery, and long-term-care residence.

The CDC has identified the following five factors, which it refers to as the "5 C's," that increase the risk of the spread of MRSA infection:
- **Crowding**
- frequent skin-to-skin **Contact**
- **Compromised** skin (i.e., cuts or abrasions)
- **Contaminated** items and surfaces, and
- lack of **Cleanliness**.

B. Diagnosis and Treatment

MRSA infection occurs when staph bacteria, which sometimes are carried on the skin or in the nose of healthy people as well as in people who already are infected, enter a break in the skin of another person via skin-to-skin contact or a shared item such as a towel or piece of athletic equipment. The entry of the bacteria causes a skin infection that is characterized by symptoms such as pimples, rashes, boils, and impetigo. MRSA also can cause more serious infection, such as pneumonia and bloodstream infection. Symptoms of more serious infection include fever, swelling, headache and fatigue.

MRSA is definitively diagnosed via laboratory testing that specifically identifies the bacteria at the root of the infection. Laboratory testing helps healthcare professionals decide whether treatment with antibiotics will be required and, if so, which antibiotics to administer.

The specific course of treatment for MRSA infection varies depending on a number of factors, including the severity of the illness and the site of the infection. Treatment of MRSA infections typically includes keeping the infected area clean and dry. Infected individuals must also wash their hands after caring for the infected area and properly dispose of bandages. Treatment also may involve drainage of pus and the administration of antibiotics. If more severe infections occur, such as pneumonia or bloodstream infections, additional measures must be taken. However, such complications are rare in healthy people who contract MRSA infections.

MRSA can be difficult to treat, according to the CDC. Usually, it is resistant only to penicillin and other similar drugs. However, the CDC reported that of 824 samples, an alarming 10% were resistant to several stronger antibiotics.

C. Prevention

1. Generally

There are many steps schools should take to prevent the occurrence of MRSA infection among students. Perhaps the best way for schools to prevent MRSA infection is to encourage the practice of good hygiene. This involves frequent hand-washing with soap and water or use of an alcohol-based hand sanitizer. Encouraging good skin care is another way to prevent the spread of MRSA infection. Cuts, scrapes and other breaks in the skin must be kept clean and covered with a bandage, and contact with other people's bandages and wounds must be avoided. Students also should be instructed not to share personal items, such as towels, toothbrushes, razors or water bottles. Schools also should establish cleaning procedures for surfaces that regularly come into contact with people's skin, such as sinks, showers and toilets. These surfaces, which also include light switches, door handles, handrails, tables and desks, should be cleaned with a disinfectant on a routine basis. Access to sinks, soaps and clean towels should be ensured, and bar soaps should not be used. Gloves should be worn when handling dirty laundry or caring for wounds.

Schools now have the option of installing antimicrobial lockers, which are designed to minimize the spread of disease-causing microbes. These lockers feature a powder-coated finish that protects against bacteria, mold, yeast and mildew for up to 20 years. To see an example, visit *www.aPlusWhs.com*.

2. Athletic Programs

Because MRSA infection occurs more frequently in student-athletes than it does in other members of the student population, special additional steps should be taken with respect to school athletic programs. These include the following:

☑ **CHECKLIST – *Avoiding MRSA Infection***

☐ Athletic equipment is disinfected between uses.
☐ Uniforms, towels and other items are laundered using hot water and detergent for washing and the hottest available setting for drying.
☐ Athletes shower with a non-hand soap and water immediately after participating in contact sports and use a dry clean towel.
☐ Athletic equipment and towels are not shared.
☐ Students avoid contact with other students' wounds or any items that have been in contact with the wounds.
☐ Antibiotics and ointments are not to be shared.
☐ Students avoid common hot tubs or whirlpools, especially if they have a break in the skin.
☐ Students do not share water bottles.
☐ Cuts and scrapes are kept clean and covered.

Sports equipment and athletic areas should be disinfected at least weekly. High-use equipment, such as wrestling mats, should be disinfected prior to each practice and several times a day during tournaments.

D. Response

1. Generally

In most cases, MRSA infection does not necessitate school closure. There are situations, such as the occurrence of an outbreak, where consultation with public health officials with respect to this issue would be appropriate. When a MRSA infection occurs, the school should disinfect surfaces that are likely to come into contact with infected areas of the skin that are not properly covered. MRSA can be removed from the school environment by cleaning facilities with disinfectants. The Environmental Protection Agency has compiled a 25-page list of cleaning products that are effective against MRSA. To view the list, go to *http://epa.gov/oppad001/ chemregindex.htm.*

When a case of infection occurs, the school nurse and physician should decide whether students, parents and staff should be notified. The CDC advises that it usually is not necessary to inform the entire school community in the case of a single MRSA infection. A MRSA-infected student should not be barred from attending school unless exclusion is directed by a treating physician. Infected students should be instructed to cover the wound and clean their hands frequently. For a sample notice to parents regarding MRSA in general, see Form VII-4 in Chapter Nine.

2. Athletic Programs

Some additional specific measures can be taken when a student-athlete contracts a MRSA infection. It is not necessary to test all team members for MRSA infection whenever a single student-athlete contracts a MRSA infection. However, it is helpful to take these steps:

- Prohibit student-athletes with MRSA infections from using whirlpools or hot tubs.
- Regularly clean all sports equipment and athletic areas that might come in contact with the wound.
- Place coverings over tables used to provide treatment.
- If disposable items come in contact with the infected site, dispose of them separately.
- Stress the importance of washing hands frequently.
- Make sure the student-athlete keeps the infected area covered at all times.
- Instruct the student-athlete to shower and wash clothes regularly.
- Use gloves to treat broken skin and discard them before treating another student-athlete.

E. Legal Decisions

◆ A 13-year-old student was admitted to a hospital for treatment of a MRSA infection. Over a period of 47 days, the student received treatment that included nine surgeries. The student's mother spoke to the principal of the school and other school officials about the possibility of home-schooling for the student. The mother was told that no teacher would go to the student's home for homeschooling because the student had MRSA. School officials also told the mother that the student's sister and two cousins, who attended a different school, needed to be picked up from school at once because they had been in close contact with the infected student. The school officials further informed the mother that none of the children would be permitted to return to school until they had received a "clean bill of health from a physician." The sister and cousins did not have any symptoms of MRSA, and they did not have a doctor. The student's doctor provided his school with informational literature about MRSA, including information indicating that children should not be excluded from school due to MRSA infection. School officials continued to ban the student, his sister and his cousins from school, and they were not provided any homeschooling services. The children's mothers sued the schools' principals and the district superintendent, claiming they violated the students' constitutional rights to due process and equal protection. The court denied a defense motion to dismiss the case. **Some process is required before a child is excluded from school, and the parents alleged that school officials banned their children from school without properly investigating whether allowing them to attend would pose an**

unreasonable risk of harm. As to the substantive due process claims, which were based on the allegation that the school officials abused their power by arbitrarily banning the students from school, the court said the allegations supported an inference that the officials acted arbitrarily and irrationally. The equal protection claims, which were based on the charge that other students with contagious diseases were not banned from school, were not dismissed. It was too soon in the case to conclude that the parents would be unable to show that other students with contagious diseases were allowed to stay in school and that school officials lacked a good reason to make the distinction. *King-Cowser v. School Dist. 149*, No. 07 C 6551, 2008 WL 4104354 (N.D. Ill. 8/25/08).

V. MENTAL HEALTH

A. Emotional Problems vs. Mental Illness

The World Health Organization's definition of mental health is: "a state of well-being in which every individual realizes his or her own potential, can cope with the normal stresses of life, can work productively and fruitfully, and is able to make a contribution to her or his community."

At your school, students in this state of well-being are able to concentrate in class and while doing their homework. They get along well with others and are active members of your school community – whether that's singing in the choir, playing on the basketball team, painting scenery for the school play or attending Chess Club meetings.

The opposite is likely to be true for students with mental health issues. They might be having trouble keeping up scholastically. They also might be talking back to teachers or getting into fights with other students. Or – if they're depressed – it may be hard to get any response from them at all. Students with mental health issues also are more likely to hurt themselves with a weapon or by self-medicating with drugs, cigarettes, alcohol and other substances.

While there is a big difference between transitory emotional problems and serious mental illness, students need help with both.

You might find it easier to relate to the problems caused by transitory emotional problems because you've experienced them yourself. The capacity to cope with the big ups and downs of life increases with life experience – which is why young students need adults' help. This help could be anything from referring the matter to the school's counseling office to deciding a formal evaluation or an outside referral is required.

Alternatively, the best help available for a student struggling with a life issue might be an informal heart-to-heart with someone trusted – maybe the student's coach or music teacher.

The Centers for Disease Control and Prevention (CDC) has posted two online brochures that provide this kind of basic emotional guidance for students at *www.bt.cdc.gov/preparedness/mind*. One brochure is aimed at middle school students, and the other is intended for high school students. Titled, *Maintain a Healthy State of Mind*, the advice was compiled with the intention of helping children cope with disaster. But it's also useful for dealing with other emotional challenges – such as losing a pet or a loved one, or coping with serious illness.

This guidance doesn't wave any magic wands – there are some things only time can heal. But in the meantime, it can help students to know they are normal if they are reacting to a serious emotional blow by:

- feeling shock, numbness and disbelief
- having a hard time thinking clearly
- having trouble focusing on school, friends and family
- eating too much or too little
- having trouble sleeping
- experiencing bad dreams and nightmares
- crying more
- acting moodier, and
- wanting to either be alone or be surrounded by people more than usual.

If the problems connected to helping students with difficult (but transitory) emotional problems can seem daunting, the problems posed by students with mental illness might feel paralyzing.

One thing that helps is that there are mechanisms in place to deal with these serious conditions in the procedures related to the Individuals with Disabilities Education Act, Section 504 of the Rehabilitation Act, the Americans with Disabilities Act and state laws that address the rights of students with disabilities. For an emergency information form for students with autism, see Form VII-20 in Chapter Nine.

Because the Sandy Hook Elementary School intruder suffered from Asperger's syndrome, the tragedy opened up national conversations on the importance of students and mental health issues.

Due to the newfound interest in the topic, the CDC released the most comprehensive mental health study ever compiled. (The report is at *www.cdc.gov/mmwr/preview/mmwrhtml/su6202a1.htm?s_cid=su6202a1_w.*)

It outlines the number of U.S. children between the ages of three and 17 who have specific mental health disorders. To compile this comprehensive report, the CDC teamed up with three key federal partners:

- Substance Abuse and Mental Health Services Administration
- National Institute of Mental Health, and
- Health Resources and Services Administration.

In "Mental Health Surveillance Among Children – United States, 2005-2011," the data provides information on mental disorders, including:

- ADHD
- disruptive behavioral disorders (such as oppositional defiant disorder and conduct disorder)

- autism spectrum disorders, and
- mood and anxiety disorders (including depression, substance abuse disorders and Tourette syndrome).

The study found children between the ages of three and 17 had:

- ADHD (6.8%)
- Behavioral or conduct problems (3.5%)
- Anxiety (3%)
- Depression (2.1%)
- Autism spectrum disorders (1.1%), and
- Tourette syndrome (.02%).

The study also found:

- ADHD was the most prevalent current diagnosis among children between the ages of three and 17.
- Boys were more likely than girls to have ADHD, behavioral or conduct problems, autism spectrum disorders, Tourette syndrome and cigarette dependence.
- Adolescent boys between the ages of 12 and 17 are more likely than girls in the same age bracket to die from suicide.
- Adolescent girls between the ages of 12 and 17 are more likely than boys in the same age bracket to suffer from depression and/or abuse alcohol.

Since 2009, the United States Preventative Task Force has recommended a routine medical screening for depression for all teenagers. They said depression was too common – and too frequently undetected and untreated – to justify screening only kids in high-risk groups.

We know from the research that some groups of students are more at risk than others. Boys are more likely to have significant emotional or behavioral problems than girls, and students between the ages 15 and 17 represent the age group that is most at risk.

Not surprisingly, a 2009 survey of 5,000-plus children found a strong link between experiencing racism and having mental health problems. Compared to children who didn't report racism, Hispanic children who did were more than three times as likely to suffer depression. African-American children were twice as likely. There was also a heightened incidence of ADHD, oppositional disorder and conduct disorder among the children who'd experienced this discrimination.

Another common stressor is test anxiety – which some think has been kicked into overdrive by the No Child Left Behind Act requirements. The increase in standardized testing has caused stress and anxiety for many students – but there are some indications it's especially bad for first generation Asian-American students with parents who stress high academic achievement.

We also know poverty has a markedly negative impact on students' mental and emotional well-being. Only 4% of children from well-off households were found to have serious mental health issues, but this percentage rose to 5% in homes where money was tight, and then up to 7% for children from families that were living below the poverty line. These numbers have especially serious implications now, given the impact of the economic downturn on so many families.

Although most people associate student mental illness with school violence, this connection is not always present. As pointed out in the June 2007 Report to the President on Issues Raised by the Virginia Tech Tragedy, most people who are violent do not have a mental illness, and most people with a mental illness are not violent.

And as the CDC's Choose Respect initiative makes clear, violence is less likely to be a symptom of mental illness than it is to be rooted in denigrating attitudes caused by ignorance or a lack of empathy. Choose Respect is aimed at 11- to 14-year-olds. Its mission is to challenge harmful beliefs that lead to dating violence and thus eliminate the health problems that go with it, such as:

- injuries that send 8% of boys and 9% of girls to the emergency room after dates
- binge drinking
- suicide attempts
- unwanted pregnancies
- STDs and HIV infections, and
- poor self-esteem.

More information about this initiative is available at *cdc.gov/ chooserespect*.

Apart from the fact that the stereotypical connection between violence and mental illness is often absent, mental illness should be de-linked from school violence also because mental illness already bears enough of a social stigma – and too many students don't seek help for that reason.

B. Violent Students and Privacy Laws

While most people with mental illness aren't violent, the university student who committed the deadliest school shooting in U.S. history was. The young man who killed 32 people at Virginia Tech in April 2006 suffered from depression and an anxiety disorder called selective mutism.

In middle and high school, he received help under a special education plan. When his middle school teachers noticed he was writing about killing himself and other people in 1999 after the Columbine shootings, he was treated by a psychiatrist.

The fact that the student's university wasn't alerted to these red flags by his records led the governor-appointed Virginia Tech Review Panel to conclude that the state's mental health laws were flawed. Complicating the issue, the panel also found there was widespread confusion about sharing records among schools. Even when it came to students likely to harm themselves or others, schools weren't sure what information they could release to other schools without violating state and federal privacy laws.

Similarly, the Report to the President on Issues Raised by the Virginia Tech Tragedy found that schools were so worried about violating student privacy – or being sued for doing so – that they were likely to share less information about serious potential problems than the law actually allowed.

It is important to be aware of the fact that some state laws and regulations have stricter privacy requirements for student records than the federal Family Educational Rights and Privacy Act (FERPA) and the privacy rule of the Health Insurance Portability and Accountability Act. That said, one result of the Report to the President was the creation of new guides to help schools and parents better understand FERPA's requirements. They are available at *ed.gov/policy/gen/guid/fpco/ferpa/safeschools*.

This FERPA guidance for elementary and secondary schools specifies that:

- Schools don't need permission in an emergency to release "education records" to parties like law enforcement, public health officials or medical personnel if the release will protect anyone's health or safety.

- Guidance posted at *rems.ed.gov* in 2010 also reminds administrators who release info under this FERPA exception to make a note of the disclosure in the student's education records. The note should include: the info that was disclosed, the parties who received it and the threat that prompted the disclosure. The note should be made as soon as reasonably possible.

- The *ed.gov* guidance also spells it out that school officials don't need permission to pass along their personal observations about a student to the proper authorities. For example, if a teacher overhears a student making a threat, she can report it to the police.

- The school employees who serve as the school's "law enforcement unit" – responsible for calling the police when the school suspects a crime – might keep its own records, such as investigation logs. These are not "education records" subject to FERPA, so no permission is needed to disclose them. But the Department of Education suggests avoiding any confusion by keeping these documents separate from "education records."

- Tapes of students recorded by security cameras maintained by the "law enforcement unit" are also not "education records" subject to FERPA. Because of this, the Department of Education suggests schools that haven't designated a "law enforcement unit" should do so and assign the unit this responsibility.

- Schools have to notify parents every year about FERPA rights. In this notification, the school has to let parents know which office or school official serves as its "law enforcement unit." The Department of Education has suggested one way to go about this, which you can see if you turn to its Model Notification of FERPA Rights (Form VII-5 in Chapter Nine).

- In your notification to parents, you should list "law enforcement unit" personnel employed by the school as "school officials" with a "legitimate educational interest." This will mean they can access protected student records – but also that they are bound by the same FERPA restrictions as other school officials concerning "education records."

- You can send all "education records" to a transfer school or postsecondary institution a student plans to attend without parents' permission – so long as you have stated on your notification to parents that you make these disclosures to other schools. If you haven't stated this, you have to make a reasonable attempt to notify the parent of the disclosure (unless the parent asked you to send the records, of course). Also, if asked, you have to provide the parents a copy of the information you disclosed as well as provide them the opportunity for a hearing on the matter.

See Chapter Nine for Form II-17 explaining exactly what does – and does not – constitute an "education record."

Finally, although the responsibility for any judgment call remains yours, you can email the Department of Education's Family Policy Compliance Office at *FERPA@Ed.Gov* for a fast reply on a routine question. You can write to them for "a more formal response" at:

Family Policy Compliance Office
U.S. Department of Education
400 Maryland Avenue, SW
Washington, DC 20202-8520

Many perpetrators of school shootings, including the one whose attack prompted the FERPA guidance above, have ended the rampage by killing themselves.

The Bureau of Justice Statistics' *Indicators of School Crime and Safety 2010* points out "[v]iolent deaths at school are rare but tragic events" – with 15 homicides and 7 suicides at school for the year the report covered (July 1, 2008 to June 30, 2009). You can download this report at *nces.ed.gov/pubs2011/2011002.pdf.*

But while a violent death *at school* is a relatively rare occurrence, the numbers are much higher when it comes to off-campus suicides among those ages 10 to 24 – and this is of increasing concern not only to school officials but also to lawmakers because the evidence increasingly links young people's suicides to things that have happened at school.

C. Self-Injury

Self-injury habits start younger than most people might think, according to a 2012 study published in *Pediatrics*.

Researchers at the University of Denver and Rutgers University teamed up to conduct the study in Colorado and New Jersey.

Participating students in both locations shared similar reports about their behavior. Third-graders between the ages of 7 and 9 revealed:

- 8% admitted they'd intentionally hurt themselves by cutting, burning or poking their skin with sharp objects.
- Nearly two-thirds of those students said they'd intentionally hurt themselves more than once.

Other findings include:

- 4% of sixth-graders self-injured their bodies, and
- about 13% of ninth-graders developed the habit.

Some students claim self-injuring helps them cope with emotional stressors, such as family issues, bullying and difficulty in school.

To reduce physical pain, the body releases endorphins, which are basically "feel-good hormones." Some researchers believe this naturally occurring endorphin release may explain why students "feel better" after hurting themselves.

Self-injury is often difficult to spot because most students keep wounds hidden, according to the Mayo Clinic. Warning signs that may indicate self-injury include students who:

- have fresh wounds or scars, such as from burns or cuts
- keep sharp objects on hand
- spend a lot of time alone
- wear long sleeves and pants – even in hot weather, and
- claim to have frequent accidents or mishaps.

The full study is available at *bit.ly/cutting555*.

D. Suicide Prevention

In 2010, the CDC reported a study by its scientists (published in the online edition of the *Journal of Pediatrics*) showed a connection between kids getting bullied and an increase in their suicidal thoughts and behaviors.

The CDC also reported suicide is the third leading cause of death for 10- to 24-year-olds, with boys overwhelmingly more at risk than girls. Boys account for 83% of the suicides for that age group.

But it was a girl's suicide after bullying that grabbed the most press attention in 2010 – partly because of the community's unusually legalistic response to the tragedy. First, in a highly unusual move, the district attorney filed criminal charges against the students who allegedly bullied Massachusetts student-suicide Phoebe Prince. Second, the state quickly enacted an anti-bullying law in response to two student suicides (one of them Prince's).

Many states have also decided they need to do more to prevent such tragedies. Colorado, Georgia, Mississippi and New Hampshire passed anti-bullying legislation in 2010, and Kentucky law began to require middle schools and high schools to provide suicide prevention information to students – and training on suicide prevention techniques to educators.

The suicide of college student Tyler Clementi prompted New Jersey to enact "The Anti-Bullying Bill of Rights" in 2011, amending its existing anti-bullying law. Now considered the toughest law in the country, it also contains a suicide-prevention component.

The federal government also provided some extra help to schools trying to put the pieces together after student suicides.

Grants awarded by the U.S. Department of Education's Office of Safe and Drug-Free Schools include Project School Emergency Response to Violence (SERV) awards. The funds they provide are intended to pay for resources districts need to recover from traumatic events and make affected schools safe places for students again.

In 2011, Project SERV awards included:

- $50,000 to Millard Public Schools in Omaha, Nebraska, to provide counseling and added security after a student shot and killed a vice principal who'd suspended him and then committed suicide after fleeing the school, and

- $46,484 to Vermont's Chittenden East Supervisory Union, which has 10 schools, following its fifth student suicide in a year; he shot himself in the head in a school bathroom. The area is extremely rural, and about a third of the population – less than 15,000 – are younger than 25. The money will be used for counseling as well as training to help parents and teachers recognize the signs of suicide.

If you're looking for ideas for suicide-prevention at your school, you might want to check out "The Youth Suicide Prevention School-Based Guide" at: *theguide.fmhi.usf.edu.*

Student suicides highlight the need for schools to help students with transitory emotional problems. Many students who consider suicide (or actually commit it) are suffering an "unbearable" problem that could be made bearable with the right kind of help from an adult. For suggestions about ways to deal with a student that you believe may be suicidal, see Form VII-6 in Chapter Nine.

Suicide risks for depressed students can start earlier than expected, according to a 2012 study published in the *Journal of Adolescent Health.* Collecting data on suicide attempts from 883 students who suffered from depression, researchers found:

- more than 40% of students who attempted to commit suicide first tried before high school, and

- the rate of suicide attempts rose sharply around the age of 12, or sixth grade, and continued to increase through the ninth grade.

Researchers concluded that mental health programs may need to start in elementary and middle school.

A student suicide is a traumatic event not only for the student's family but for his school community as well. For suggestions about how to announce a student suicide to the school, see Form VII-7 in Chapter Nine.

Whether or not the cause was suicide, any time a student dies it is a significant event in the life of the school that needs to be dealt with appropriately and with respect. For suggestions about making an announcement to let students know a classmate has died, see Form VII-8 in Chapter Nine. An alternate notification statement is available on Form VII-19.

For model letters to provide more details to students or their parents after such an event, see Form VII-9 and Form VII-10 in Chapter Nine.

When a student does commit suicide, grieving parents may try to make sense of the tragedy by blaming the school for things the school did or did not do to prevent it. But as you will see from the cases summarized below, only very rarely will a court agree with the parents that the school had a duty to prevent the suicide.

In one of these decisions, the judge pointed out: "Attempted suicide by school-age children is no slight matter; but it has no single cause and no infallible solution [. ...] Different schools will react differently, depending upon resources, available information, and the judgment of school and public health authorities, who may fear making a bad situation worse. Absent a showing that the school affirmatively caused a suicide, the primary responsibility for safeguarding children from this danger, as from most others, is that of their parents; and even they, with direct control and intimate knowledge, are often helpless." *Hasenfus v. LaJeunesse*, 175 F.3d 68 (1st Cir. 1999).

E. Legal Decisions

1. Liability for Student Suicide

a. Constitutional Claims

◆   A school could not be held liable for the suicide attempt of a student who was bullied about her eating disorders, a New York federal judge held. The student suffered from anorexia and bulimia. She was allegedly bullied by classmates about her weight and eating disorders for approximately 18 months. She and her parents said they complained to school officials many times, but they failed to take steps to stop the bullying. The girl attempted to commit suicide by drug overdose. Her parents transferred her to a different school and filed a lawsuit, alleging a violation of the Equal Protection Clause. The court dismissed the claim, as **weight and disability are not vulnerable classes under the Equal Protection Clause** – and since the complaint didn't allege a class-of-one claim, the plaintiffs failed to state a valid claim, the court held. *Terrill v. Windham-Ashland-Jewel Cent. School Dist.*, No. 1:15-CV-0615 (GTS/DJS), 2016 WL 1275048 (N.D.N.Y. 3/31/16).

◆   After a high school student with Asperger's Syndrome killed himself, his parents sued, alleging the district and principal violated his "liberty right to be free from psychological and bodily abuse" by not training staff to protect him from bullying – but a Georgia federal judge dismissed the case.

Seventeen-year-old Tyler Long hanged himself at home, leaving a note saying "This World [*sic*] will be a better place without me." He had Asperger's syndrome, and Tyler's friends and parents said he'd been bullied at school because of it.

After his death, students wrote "we will not miss you" and "it was your own fault" on school walls – and some wore nooses at school.

Tyler's parents sued his principal and the district, alleging they breached Tyler's substantive due process right to be free from abuse.

The judge dismissed the case, finding **school defendants didn't have a constitutional duty to protect Tyler from other students**.

The Due Process Clause protects citizens from government officials' abuse of power. Apart from a few narrow exceptions, it *doesn't* require the government to protect citizens from each other.

Under Eleventh Circuit law binding on this Georgia federal court, the government had a duty to protect a citizen from other citizens if it had the victim in custody. Courts had found jail constituted custody, but not school.

A narrow exception existed when a government official caused harm by conduct that was "arbitrary or conscience shocking in a constitutional sense." That standard could be met by excessive corporal punishment at school. The parents claimed it was met by school defendants' failure to train staff to protect the student despite knowing he had a disability and was being bullied – but that was negligence or deliberate indifference at most.

As the parents' substantive due process claim didn't meet the required legal standard, the judge dismissed it. *Long v. Murray County School Dist.*, No. 4:10-CV-00015-HLM, 2012 WL 2277836 (N.D. Ga. 5/21/12).

◆   A Texas federal judge dismissed a suit brought by parents that alleged school officials breached the substantive-due-process and equal protection rights of a student who committed suicide.

Thirteen-year-old Jon Carmichael was bullied nearly every day at school. The day before he killed himself, students videotaped themselves stripping Jon naked, tying him up and then stuffing him into a trash can.

Jon's parents sued school officials, claiming they violated Jon's rights, but the judge dismissed their suit.

The parents claimed school officials breached Jon's substantive due process "right to life and bodily integrity" – but the judge dismissed the claim because Due Process Clause generally doesn't require the government to protect citizens from other citizens.

School officials hadn't "confined" Jon in a way that left him unable to protect himself, and the Fifth Circuit – with jurisdiction over this Texas federal court – hadn't adopted the state-created danger theory. Under it, a school can be held liable if it creates or increases the danger to a student.

The parents alleged officials discriminated against Jon as a male because they passed off the bullying by saying "boys will be boys " – but to state an equal protection claim, they had to show school officials applied policies differently when a girl was the victim or when the bully and victim weren't the same sex. As the parents' claims failed, the judge dismissed the case. *Estate of Carmichael v. Galbraith*, No. 3:11-CV-0622-D, 2012 WL 13568 (N.D. Tex. 1/4/12).

◆   A California federal judge refused to dismiss equal protection claims based on a principal's and assistant principal's failure to investigate and discipline the bullying of an openly gay student.

After Seth Walsh came out as gay in the sixth grade, classmates called him "pansy" and "sissy," pushed him into lockers and suggested he kill himself. His mother reported this. **The principal said classmates "in a perfect world" wouldn't harass Seth**, but these students were at a difficult age and the principal couldn't change attitudes they learned at home.

When Seth was in the seventh grade, the bullying became more widespread, sexually explicit and confrontational. The principal and vice principal saw it, and Seth's mother reported it, but the administrators took no steps to stop it. At some point, the vice principal suggested the solution to the problem was for Seth to leave school.

In September of Seth's eighth-grade year, the day after other students threatened and assaulted him, Seth hanged himself at home.

Seth's mother sued the district and district officials, alleging multiple claims. The school defendants asked the judge to dismiss her suit. The judge dismissed some claims, but not her equal protection claim against the principal and vice principal.

The principals argued the mother couldn't make this claim as she hadn't shown they responded differently to harassment claims made by non-homosexuals. The judge found she didn't have to at this stage of the case.

To make her equal protection claim at this stage, Seth's mother only had to show Seth was discriminated against due to his membership in an identifiable class. She did by showing Walsh suffered pervasive harassment as a homosexual and that neither administrator took disciplinary action – instead only saying he wouldn't be discriminated against in a perfect world or that the solution to a student being harassed at school was for the student to leave the school. *Walsh v. Tehachupi Unified School Dist.*, 827 F.Supp.2d 1107 (E.D. Cal. 2011).

◆   An Ohio federal judge found that "however tragic and unfair [it] may seem," a school had no constitutional duty to protect a student from student-on-student bullying – or from killing himself because of it.

Eric Mohat committed suicide at age 17. His parents claimed he was driven to it by constant bullying and harassment that school officials were aware of but did nothing about.

His parents sued the school district, alleging they were deprived of their substantive due process rights to familial association, a liberty interest under the Fourteenth Amendment's Due Process Clause.

Generally, the Constitution doesn't require public school officials to protect a citizen's life, liberty or property interests against "the invasions of private actors" – such as the students who harassed Eric.

One exception to this rule is the state-created danger exception, but the court found the exception didn't apply in this case because school officials didn't take *affirmative action* that increased the danger to the student.

The parents alleged the school's failure to step in when other students bullied Eric contributed to or caused his suicide. But this was an alleged failure to act rather than an affirmative act.

The court wrote that "although parents should be able to expect that their children will be kept reasonably safe when under the school's supervision, the school had no constitutional duty to take affirmative action to protect Eric from harm imposed by other students through bullying[.]" *Mohat v. Mentor Exempted Village School Dist. Board of Educ.*, No. 1:09 CV 688, 2011 WL 2174671 (N.D. Ohio 6/1/11).

◆ A Texas federal judge dismissed a suit that claimed a school district violated a student's rights by not doing more to prevent her suicide attempt.

High school staff confiscated a note from the student that prompted the principal to call her mother to advise she get counseling for the girl.

A year later, the student spent a week at a psychiatric treatment facility. Not long after her release, she was arrested for shoplifting.

The day after her arrest, her mother went to school. She told the school secretary about the arrest and asked to be called if "anything happened[.]"

In English class, the student told a friend she was going to kill herself. The friend told the teacher, and the teacher sent the student to a counselor. The mother later claimed the counselor was so busy she simply sent the student to her next class without telling anyone else about her suicide threat.

The student was excused from her next class to go to the bathroom. There, she tried to kill herself. The attempt was unsuccessful but allegedly left her with a permanent injury.

Her mother sued the district and several individuals under Section 1983 of the U.S. Code. She alleged they violated the student's rights by not adopting a suicide prevention program and not taking steps to prevent her suicide attempt.

The school defendants asked the judge to dismiss the suit. He did.

To violate Section 1983, either a school official must commit "deliberate conduct" that makes the official "the 'moving force' behind the injury" or else the district must create a "special relationship" with the student – such as by making a specific promise to keep him or her safe.

Unlike most jurisdictions, the Fifth Circuit doesn't recognize a "state-created danger" ground for liability – which can make a district liable if it increased the danger to the student.

The court found **this suit only alleged negligence** – not a valid claim of a constitutional violation under Section 1983. So the court dismissed it. *Hejny v. Grand Saline Independent School Dist.*, No. 2-10-cv-50-TJW, 2010 WL 2521007 (E.D. Tex. 6/17/10).

◆ The mother of a boy who committed suicide after his guidance counselor determined he was not suicidal could not hold the counselor or the school district responsible for his death.

A 16-year-old boy passed a note to his ex-girlfriend after he found out she was dating someone new. He wrote the news "almost made me want to go kill myself," which worried her, so she took the note to a counselor.

The boy's guidance counselor called him into her office. The counselor told him his friends were worried about him and asked if he was having girl trouble. He said he'd been upset about a girl two months ago but was no longer upset. Asked if he had plans to hurt himself or would ever do so, he said, "definitely not." The counselor also asked him "forward thinking" questions and heard he had future plans. She asked if anything else was upsetting him and he said no. Believing he was not at risk, the counselor did not contact the school psychologist or the boy's mother.

A few days later, the student returned to ask the counselor if a blond girl had given her a note he'd written. The counselor said she couldn't tell him that. The boy said he'd thought she'd say that and didn't seem upset.

That night, the boy and his mother had an argument. Later that night, he hanged himself.

The deceased student's mother sued the district and the counselor, **arguing they violated his constitutional right not to be deprived of life without due process of law because the counselor did not prevent his death by reporting he was suicidal**.

Generally, public schools cannot be held responsible for acts of violence committed by non-school-personnel. But there is an exception to that rule if the school created the danger that harmed the student.

The mother could not succeed on her state-created danger claim because she could not show:

* it was foreseeable the student would kill himself if the counselor didn't report she'd screened him for suicidal ideation
* the counselor's behavior was bad enough to shock the conscience
* the student was a member of a group likely to commit suicide because of this behavior, and
* the counselor used her authority in a way that put the student in danger or put him at more risk than if she hadn't acted at all.

When the case reached the Third U.S. Circuit Court of Appeals, it found no one – including the student's mother – had considered him suicidal. It also did not consider the language in the note to be a clear cry for help and found the counselor had responded to the situation quickly and appropriately. *Sanford v. Stiles*, 456 F.3d 298 (3d Cir. 2006).

◆ A school did not have the responsibility to protect a student from committing suicide even though the student could be considered emotionally fragile and there had been a rash of suicides at the school in previous months.

A female student was raped when she was 13 years old and then had the trauma of testifying against her rapist in court. Less than a year later, the student was out on the school softball field with her gym class when several of her classmates began harassing her about the rape and her decision to testify. The student became upset. She shouted obscenities and threatened to hurt them. The gym teacher broke this up and told the student to go back to the locker room. There, the student tried to hang herself.

Classmates found her and called for emergency help. The student did not die, but she went into a coma. She ultimately emerged from the coma but was left with permanent impairments.

In the three months before this incident, seven students at that middle school had attempted suicide. Several of the attempts had happened at school or school events, and the student knew at least two of the students.

The student's parents sued the board of education and the gym teacher, alleging they violated the student's right to substantive due process. The trial court dismissed the case. The parents appealed, but the First U.S. Circuit Court of Appeals affirmed.

The parents argued the school had a duty to protect the student because it knew she'd been raped the year before and other students had attempted suicide. But this was not enough for the school to recognize her as part of an identifiable group of students at risk for committing suicide. Also, the gym teacher's actions were not bad enough to shock the conscience, another prerequisite to a finding of a constitutional violation. He only reprimanded a 14-year-old for misbehavior and sent her out of class. *Hasenfus v. LaJeunesse*, 175 F.3d 68 (1st Cir. 1999).

b. Negligence Issues

◆ An Illinois district wasn't liable for the death of a student in an elementary school restroom, a state appellate court held. The student and his class lined up in a third-floor hallway to go to PE. The teacher realized the student wasn't in line but took the class downstairs to the gym. Then the teacher checked his mail and went to look for the boy. By the time the teacher returned to the third floor, the student had been found in a restroom. He was hanging by his collar on the hook of a stall door. He died the next day, and his death was ruled a suicide.

His mother filed a wrongful death suit, claiming the district was negligent and its actions amounted to "willful and wanton" misconduct. The claim was tossed. The state's tort law doesn't allow negligence-based claims for failure to supervise an activity on public property. The court let his mother refile. In the amended complaint, the mom added information about her son's mental health issues, dating back to 2007. Her complaint alleged the school knew but failed to provide proper IEP and Section 504 plans to help keep her son safe. The school asked the court to dismiss that claim, saying the suicide wasn't foreseeable. The court did – noting the mother didn't show the school owed the boy a special duty. A second amended complaint alleged the school knew about a "hanging game" that students played in the bathroom. This claim was also dismissed, as it failed to show the school was the proximate cause of the suicide.

His mother appealed to the state appellate court, which held **the evidence didn't support her allegations**. So the ruling for the school was proper. *Marshall v. Evanston Skokie School Dist.* 65, No. 1–13–1654, 2015 WL 1442040 (Ill. App. Ct. 3/2/15).

◆ The Fifth Circuit reversed a Texas federal judge's decision that parents of a bullied student who committed suicide didn't provide evidence of the severe, pervasive sexual harassment needed for a valid Title IX claim. The student's parents said other boys bullied their son in the locker room in front of a teacher several times – including forcibly pulling off his underwear. Days before the student committed suicide, football team members attacked him in the locker room. They called him "fag," "queer" and "homo" as they stripped him, tied him up and put him in a trash can. Other students watched. One uploaded a video of the attack to YouTube. To sue the district under Title IX for deliberate indifference to student-on-student sexual harassment, the boy's parents had to show the harassment was severe and pervasive. The federal judge dismissed the claim. But **the Fifth Circuit reversed, as "[t]he removal of a person's underwear without consent on numerous occasions plausibly constitutes pervasive harassment of a sexual character."** It reversed the dismissal of the parents' Title IX claim. *Carmichael v. Galbraith*, 574 Fed.Appx. 286 (5th Cir. 2014).

◆ A New York court refused to dismiss the personal injury claim of a mother whose son committed suicide after being bullied. The student and his mother made multiple reports to school officials about the bullying. But the bullies were never disciplined. In 2010, the student came home from school and killed himself.

His mother sued the city and the district for negligence. She asked the court to award her damages for her son's personal injuries as well as for the emotional injuries and financial expenses his suicide caused her. The court dismissed her suit against the city, as it's well established that New York City isn't liable for its school district's negligence. The court also dismissed the claims for the injuries caused by the suicide. Under New York law, the district can't be held liable for the suicide because the student wasn't in school custody at the time.

But the court held a trial was needed on the district's liability for the personal injuries the student allegedly suffered at school before his death because he was on school premises when the alleged bullying took place. While the school took steps to combat bullying – talking to classes about misusing the word "gay," putting up posters and passing out brochures on harassment and how to report it – **the school didn't discipline the students who allegedly harassed the alleged victim in this case**. So the court refused to dismiss the mother's negligent supervision claim. *Elissa v. City of New York*, 990 N.Y.S.2d 780 (N.Y. Sup. Ct. 2014).

◆ Montana's highest court affirmed a ruling that a school wasn't liable for a student-athlete's suicide. The 17-year-old senior had racked up a long disciplinary record for things like talking back, theft, fighting and skipping school. After a school counselor saw him "putting a can of chew in his pocket," the principal, superintendent, and athletic director explained to the teen that having tobacco at school had triggered a school suspension – plus a 60-day suspension from sports under the athletic department's policy. The student was on the varsity wrestling team. He became very upset when he realized the sports suspension meant he would miss the state tournament. Later that day, he committed suicide while at home. His mother sued the town, the school and the superintendent, saying her son died due to their negligence. The trial court granted the school defendants judgment without a trial. His mother appealed to the state supreme court, but it affirmed. The rule in Montana is: No one but the suicide victim is responsible for his or her death. The court was willing to consider an exception based on foreseeability, but it found the exception didn't apply. In this case, **the student didn't tell anyone he felt suicidal or reacted to prior disciplinary punishments by threatening or attempting suicide**. The court said that if a student responds to discipline by getting suicidal – but the school has no reason to know about it – the school is not liable for an ensuing tragedy. *Gourneau v. Hamill*, No. DA 13-0210, 2013 WL 5634125 (Mont. 10/15/13).

◆   Delaware's highest court found school officials may be liable for failing to warn a suicidal student's family – even though the student killed himself at home. The court held that the school's inaction could be "negligence per se" – a legal doctrine that deems conduct negligent because it violated a law or regulation. The doctrine was relevant in this case because a state regulation requires schools to try to contact parents or guardians immediately if students are "clearly dangerous to themselves." A student told his school's behavior interventionist (BI) that his friend had tried to kill himself. The BI called the suicidal student into her office, where the boy admitted he had tried to take his own life. They talked for about four hours before the BI felt the student was OK. Then the boy was sent to class. The BI was a contract employee, so she emailed school staff to explain how she'd handled the incident and asked if she needed to do anything else. No one called the boy's family. That night, the student hanged himself at home. **The boy's family sued, claiming the school was negligent.** The court granted the school judgment without a trial. But the high court reversed, finding more info was needed with respect to the negligence per se claim. It wrote the family can base this claim on "violations of the State Department of Education and the School District's mandatory requirements to notify a parent or guardian" if a student is suicidal. So the case was sent back to the trial court for further development. *Rogers v. Christina School Dist.*, No. 45, 2013 WL 3722554 (Del. 7/16/13).

◆   A Michigan appeals court held a principal was immune to a father's suit claiming his son committed suicide due to a principal's gross negligence in being unduly harsh when disciplining him.

The court also said the proximate cause of 16-year-old Stan Burland's death "was his decision to take his own life and not defendant's conduct earlier in the day."

According to the principal, another student's mother showed him text messages that implicated Stan in a drug deal. After investigating, the principal called Stan's father. The principal said he read Stan and his father some of the text messages, suspended Stan for 10 days, and said Stan could be expelled if he discovered Stan was involved in drug dealing.

In Stan's father's version – which the principal denied – the father said he arrived to find Stan crying. He claimed the principal behaved in a physically intimidating manner and said: Stan would be expelled, the police would be involved, and "[t]his is going to be big[.]"

Later that day, Stan committed suicide.

The father sued, alleging the principal's gross negligence was the proximate cause of the student's suicide. The judge granted the principal judgment without a trial, finding him immune to the suit. The father appealed, but the appellate court affirmed.

Under Michigan law, the principal had legal immunity to this suit because the alleged conduct the father objected to occurred when the principal was performing employment duties as a principal. Also, he acted within the scope of his authority, there was no evidence he acted maliciously or for an improper purpose, and his acts were "discretionary" (that is, requiring him to use his own judgment") rather than "ministerial" (that is, simply following the rules).

The appeals court affirmed summary judgment for the principal because he met the test for state law immunity and because the judge found the proximate cause of the student's death was the student's decision to commit suicide – not the principal's discipline *Burland v. French*, No. 305652, 2012 WL 2362442 (Mich. Ct. App. 6/21/12).

◆   A Connecticut judge found school staff's alleged failure to follow a suicide-prevention policy may have made a student's suicide foreseeable – so he refused to dismiss negligence claims against them.

The school system was required by state law to have a suicide-prevention policy. The policy required any "school employee who may have knowledge of a suicide threat" to report it to the principal. It also required them to immediately refer an at-risk student to emergency medical personnel, a school psychologist or a school social worker. The policy specifically said the student was not to be left alone or allowed to go home alone. Instead, he could only be released to a responsible adult.

Student Michael Girard was allegedly despondent over a breakup.

His mother and stepfather – the Caseys – alleged high school staff heard Michael say he was going to hurt or kill himself. They also said a counselor knew Michael was suicidal, but let him go home alone one morning.

He died at home that day of a methadone overdose at around 10:30 a.m.

The Caseys brought a negligence suit against the board of education plus the superintendent, the principal and the counselor in their official capacities. The school defendants asked the judge to strike the negligence claims against them. He refused.

The general rule in Connecticut is that only the person who commits suicide can be held legally responsible for it. This is partly based on the theory that the act can't be predicted. The court found that rule may not apply in this case because Michael's suicide may have been foreseeable.

The judge concluded "a student's suicide could be a foreseeable result of school staff's failure to follow the suicide prevention policy" – so he refused to dismiss the negligence claims. *Girard v. Putnam*, No. CV085002754-S, 2011 WL 783599 (Conn. Super. Ct. 1/28/11).

◆   The Ninth Circuit affirmed parents couldn't hold a school responsible for their son's suicide because they couldn't show a harsh lecture he got at school was the proximate cause of his decision to shoot himself.

Three California students left their middle school without permission to attend public protests against a law that would have made it illegal to help undocumented immigrants.

One of them was on juvenile court probation for bringing a knife to school. His mother later said he could have been sent to prison for three years for violating probation.

Back at school, the students were called to a vice principal's office. According to one of them, he pointed to the students, saying, "You guys are all dumb, dumb, and dumber." He lectured them about the possible consequences of truancy – including police involvement, a $250 fine and a juvenile hall sentence. He also said they couldn't participate in a year-end trip to Disneyland.

After school, the boy on probation told a classmate he was afraid his mother would be mad at him and worried about the fine and juvenile hall.

The mother was running errands that day, but called home. The boy told her what had happened, but not in a way that made her fear for his safety. When she got home, however, she found he'd shot himself.

The student left a suicide note telling his family he loved them and saying: "Tell my teachers [they're] the best" and tell the vice principal "he is a motherf#@ker."

The boy's parents sued the school district, the principal and the vice principal, arguing they'd negligently caused the boy's death. A California federal court found they hadn't. The parents appealed to the Ninth U.S. Circuit Court of Appeals, but it affirmed the judgment.

To make their case, **the parents had to show the vice principal's harsh lecture was the proximate cause of the boy's suicide**. They couldn't.

Between hearing the lecture and killing himself, the boy went to classes and then spoke with a classmate and his mother. He also wrote a detailed suicide note. The court said: "The record seems to show he had the opportunity to appreciate the nature of his actions."

Because the parents couldn't show a reasonably close connection between the harsh lecture and the boy's suicide, judgment for the school defendants was proper. *Corales v. Bennett*, 567 F.3d 554 (9th Cir. 2009).

◆   A student's bereaved family failed to establish that a teacher's negative remarks to the student, apparently echoed in his suicide note, were a substantial factor in causing his death – because there wasn't reliable evidence the teacher actually said them.

A 13-year-old eighth-grade boy struggled with his grades. His family made it a rule he couldn't go hunting if he didn't pass his classes.

When the boy got his fall mid-term grades, he saw he had failed every class except gym. He complained to his science teacher that this meant he wouldn't be able to go deer hunting.

The teacher said he told the boy he wouldn't be going anywhere – meaning he wouldn't be going hunting. But according to the family, another student later told them the teacher actually said, "Your life is going nowhere" and called the student one of the dumbest people he had ever taught. But the family couldn't identify the student they said told them this.

The next day, the boy shot himself after the rest of his family left the house. He left a note saying, "I relize (*sic*) my life is going noware (*sic*) fast so I decided that I don't need to live anymore."

A trustee acting on behalf of the boy's family brought a wrongful death suit against the school, arguing school staff had caused the boy's suicide. The court held **the school didn't have a legal duty to prevent the suicide because the school could not have foreseen it**. The trustee also argued the boy used the same words in his note that his science teacher allegedly spoke to him, which meant these spoken words were a substantial factor in causing the suicide. However, the evidence that the teacher actually said those words wasn't reliable. The trustee appealed, but the appellate court affirmed. *Jasperson v. Anoka-Hennepin Independent School Dist. No. 11*, 2007 WL 3153456 (Minn. Ct. App. 10/30/07).

◆   An English teacher didn't violate a state duty to report a student was suicidal – even though the student killed himself six months after turning in an essay about overcoming suicidal tendencies – because the essay discussed past (not present) suicidal ideation.

For the student's junior-year high school English class, he wrote an essay in April called "My Most Difficult Decision." In it, he stated he had overcome the urge to kill himself and that the trigger for that urge was gone, and he could enjoy life now. His teacher wrote him a note on the essay saying he was glad he was no longer suicidal, but to come talk to him if the urge to kill himself ever came back.

The student's family moved to another state for the student's senior year. That November, his mother told police the student was missing, she'd found a note in his room saying "I'm sorry," and he'd written "Goodbye" on his calendar over the day he'd disappeared. The family was also missing a rifle, but the student's mother told police she had no reason to believe he was suicidal.

Not long after, his body was found in the state his family had moved from. The deceased student's family sued the school district and his former English teacher, arguing they had failed to comply with their state law duty to warn if a teacher had direct knowledge a student had suicidal tendencies. The case reached the state supreme court, which found **there was no violation of the duty to warn because a student's suicidal tendencies had to be present rather than past in order to trigger it – and the student's essay discussed overcoming an urge to kill himself in the past**. *Carrier v. Lake Pend Oreille School Dist. No. 84*, 134 P.3d 655 (Idaho 2006).

c. Sexting-Related Cases

◆   An Ohio federal judge refused to dismiss Title IX and equal protection claims brought against a school board based on its response to students circulating a nude photo of a student who later killed herself.

In May of Jessica Logan's senior year, a counselor sent her to the school resource officer (SRO) after she reported her nude photo was being texted around the school. (A proceeding dismissing a claim against the SRO in this suit is reported later in this section.)

Jessica went on to appear on a TV show about sexting. Her identity was disguised, but her parents claimed people saw through the disguise. On the show, Jessica cried over harassment she was experiencing at school – which her parents say got even worse after the TV appearance.

Jessica killed herself that summer.

Her parents sued the school board and several school officials. The school defendants asked the court to grant them summary judgment. **The judge could decide the case without a trial only if the parties agreed on all the facts that could affect the legal outcome.** They didn't when it came to the Title IX and equal protection claims.

To make their Title IX sexual harassment claim, the parents had to show the harassment was severe enough to deprive Jessica of access to educational benefits or opportunities, district officials knew about the harassment, and the officials were deliberately indifferent to the harassment.

The parties disagreed about whether the school defendants knew the nude image of Jessica was circulating and students were harassing her because of it.

To win their equal protection challenge, the parents had to show a key policymaker for implementing the school's sexual harassment policy, such as the principal, treated Jessica's report of harassment differently than other students' reports of harassment. Again, the parties disagreed whether administrators knew Jessica was being harassed. As the parents and school defendants disagreed about key facts that could change the legal outcome of these claims, the judge refused to grant school defendants judgment without a trial. *Logan v. Sycamore Community School Board of Educ.*, No. 1:09-cv-00885, 2012 WL 2011037 (S.D. Ohio 6/5/12).

◆   A Florida federal judge held a school board wasn't constitutionally liable for a 13-year-old's suicide following a sexting incident. Though tragic, an isolated incident of a staff member failing to follow the suicide-prevention policy didn't rise to a constitutional offense.

Thirteen-year-old H.S.W. had texted a suggestive photo of herself to a boy, and other students were harassing her about it. A teacher noticed shallow cuts on H.S.W.'s thigh and sent her to the office to talk to a counselor.

The school board had a written policy on suicide prevention. It required staff members to notify a student's parents if the student appeared to be at risk of suicide.

In the office, a school social worker counseled H.S.W. and then signed a "no-harm contract" with her. In it, H.S.W. agreed not to "attempt suicide or die by suicide" and to call the social worker if she had suicidal thoughts again. **The counselor didn't notify the student's parents that their child was at risk of suicide.**

The next day, H.S.W. killed herself at home. Her parents found the no-harm contract H.S.W. had signed with the social worker. They sued the school board, alleging it had violated their and their daughter's Fourteenth Amendment substantive due process rights by failing to train the social worker in the suicide prevention policy.

A municipality could be liable for a constitutional violations if it failed to properly train staff and knew the failure to train amounted to a deliberate indifference to constitutional rights. However, a single incident of a breached right wasn't enough to support this claim.

The court found the parents couldn't hold the school board liable, while noting that the parents had alleged "an admittedly tragic but isolated incident in which a social worker failed to follow established protocol." *Witsell v. School Board of Hillsborough County*, No. 8:11-cv-781-T-23AEP, 2011 WL 2457877 (M.D. Fla. 6/20/11).

◆   A Kentucky federal judge dismissed a claim against a principal, finding she couldn't have prevented a student's suicide attempt. The male student attempted suicide after his girlfriend discovered he'd texted nude photos of himself to a male teacher.

A high school student sent nude photos to a math teacher who'd been tutoring him – and giving him backrubs, touching his legs, and exposing himself to the student at a YMCA.

One Saturday morning, **the student's girlfriend found the nude photos and texts on the student's phone**. They quarreled. He went home around 11:00 a.m. and attempted suicide.

Meanwhile, the girlfriend called a different teacher to report what she'd discovered. The teacher passed the information along to the principal via a voicemail he left on her home phone. She got the message late Saturday or early Sunday.

On Monday morning, the principal spoke to the girlfriend and then suspended the math teacher and called the police. The math teacher was later arrested and fired.

The student sued the principal. Among his charges, he alleged the principal committed the tort of outrage by not investigating and calling the police as soon as she got the voicemail. He said a call to his mother could have prevented his suicide attempt.

The judge dismissed this claim. The principal got the voicemail hours after the student's suicide attempt, so an immediate investigation couldn't have prevented it.

In addition, Kentucky cases didn't allow an outrage claim alongside a negligence claim based on the same allegations – unless the allegedly outrageous conduct was intended "to cause extreme emotional distress in the victim[.]" The student had brought negligence claims against the principal based on the same allegations and didn't show she was trying to cause him extreme emotional distress. *Cole v. Shadoan*, 782 F.Supp.2d 428 (E.D. Ky. 2011).

◆   Parents of a student who committed suicide didn't convince an Ohio federal judge that a school resource officer (SRO) increased the risk to their daughter's life by mishandling a sexting incident. Therefore, the judge dismissed the SRO from the lawsuit.

High school senior Jessica Logan texted a nude photo of herself to a male classmate. It wound up on several classmates' phones. They harassed her, and she went to the SRO.

The SRO confronted Logan's classmates, telling them to delete the photo and stop harassing her. He also asked a prosecutor if Logan could take legal action, but was told she had no case as she wasn't a minor.

The SRO told Logan a television reporter had contacted him, hoping to create awareness about the consequences of sexting by telling students' stories. With her parents' approval, Logan agreed to a televised interview, hoping to influence other girls not to sext. It aired with her appearance and identity concealed and her voice altered.

Logan's parents said she was subjected to increased harassment at school after the interview. Logan then killed herself.

Her parents sued the SRO, saying he increased the risk to Logan's life by encouraging her to be interviewed. The judge disagreed and dismissed the SRO from their lawsuit.

Government officials like police officers are immune from federal claims unless they violate clearly established rights a reasonable person could be expected to know about.

The SRO had no general constitutional duty to protect Logan's life. But her parents argued the state-created danger exception applied, saying he had a duty to protect her because he'd increased the risk to her life.

The judge disagreed, finding the claims weren't credible. The parents alleged the SRO encouraged Logan to be interviewed on TV – but the court found he only gave her the reporter's phone number. They also claimed the interview intensified her harassment at school – but no evidence supported that allegation. Though they claimed the SRO was deliberately indifferent to the danger he'd caused Logan, **the judge found the SRO acted in good faith to try to help the student**.

Finding the SRO was entitled to qualified immunity, the judge dismissed him from the case. *Logan v. Sycamore Community School Board of Educ.*, 780 F.Supp.2d 594 (S.D. Ohio 2011).

2. Other Mental Health Issues

◆   A Massachusetts federal judge refused to dismiss discrimination claims against a city and a district in a proposed class action lawsuit. The district operated a public day school separately from its neighborhood schools. About 230 K-12 students – all of whom have mental health disabilities – were enrolled in the day school. It offered limited extracurricular activities – especially compared to the neighborhood schools in the district. But students who attend the day school couldn't participate in programs at the neighborhood schools. One parent filed suit on behalf of his child and other students at the day school, alleging disability bias in violation of the ADA. **The suit claimed the children could be educated alongside their non-disabled peers in neighborhood schools if reasonable accommodations were made.** The father stated a valid *prima facie* claim, as the boy's disability was undisputed, and "since only students with mental health disabilities are enrolled at [the day school]," the father "adequately pled that the exclusion of [his son] from the neighborhood schools was by reason of his disability," the court held. So the claim had to proceed. *S.S. v. City of Springfield, Massachusetts*, 146 F.Supp.3d 414 (D. Mass. 2015).

◆   A New Jersey federal judge refused to dismiss claims that a school violated the ADA, Section 504 of the Rehabilitation Act and the First Amendment. A student had attention deficit disorder, and his IEP outlined that he frequently doodled in class and carried a sketchbook. Days after the shooting at Sandy Hook Elementary School, a teacher noticed a drawing in the notebook. It featured a glove with a flame coming out if it. Concerned, the teacher notified the vice principal. The principal simultaneously called the boy's mother and police, who arrived at the family home with fire officials, crisis responders and a bomb squad. They searched and found wires, chemicals and switches – materials that could be used to make a bomb. Turns out, it was later explained the boy had the items to complete an engineering homework assignment. Nonetheless, he was criminally charged and spent 17 days in a juvenile facility. Upon release, he was ordered to four months of house arrest with an ankle bracelet. The boy received home instruction – and the district began proceedings to expel him. After two days of criminal proceedings, a judge found the child was not guilty. Even so, the district refused to allow him to return to school for 16 months. He sued, alleging a laundry list of claims. The court held three claims could move forward. It refused to dismiss claims that the school violated the ADA, Section 504 of the Rehabilitation Act and the First

Amendment. **More info was needed to determine whether the school's response to the drawing was reasonable**, the court held. So the claims had to proceed. *K.J. v. Greater Egg Harbor Regional High School Dist. Board of Educ.*, No. 14-145(RBK/JS), 2015 WL 5039460 (D.N.J. 8/26/15).

◆   A North Carolina court ruled against a student who was sentenced to life without parole following a shooting. The student unsuccessfully argued that the jury wasn't properly instructed on the insanity defense.

On August 30, 2006, high school student Rafael Castillo shot and killed his father at home. He then drove to school, where he set off smoke bombs and shot two students.

When Castillo's gun jammed, **the school's resource officer (SRO) and a teacher told Castillo to put down his weapons**. He did, and the SRO arrested him.

Charges against Castillo included first-degree murder, discharging a gun on school property, and assault with a deadly weapon with intent to kill.

At trial, the jury considered whether he was not guilty by reason of insanity. Under North Carolina law, a jury could reach this conclusion if it determined Castillo had a "disease or deficiency of the mind" that so impaired him that he didn't know "the nature or quality of his act" or wasn't capable of knowing if it was right or wrong.

Castillo's defense attorney argued the boy believed God wanted him to "sacrifice" his father. He'd also written in his diary, "I might save some children from sin" – and told officers immediately after the shootings that he'd tried "to save those kids from sex, drugs, pornography, and abusive people" like his father. When his mother later visited him at a mental institution, he told her that he "did the right thing."

But there was also evidence Castillo had idolized the Columbine shooters. He'd visited Columbine with his mother and bought himself a black trench coat during the trip. He'd also tried to kill himself on the anniversary of the Columbine shootings.

Several experts testified Castillo couldn't tell right from wrong and that he thought he was getting messages from God. But a hospital psychiatrist testified Castillo was severely mentally ill but could tell right from wrong. **She testified that he'd idolized the Columbine shooters and wanted to share their notoriety.**

The jury found Castillo didn't qualify for the insanity defense. He was sentenced to life without possibility of parole.

Castillo appealed, arguing he was entitled to the defense. He claimed the judge had improperly instructed the jury. But the appeals court found no error. The judge's instructions tracked the language in the state's Pattern Jury Instructions. Also, if the judge had agreed to use the instructions requested by Castillo's attorney, it wouldn't have affected the outcome because it wouldn't have changed the question the jury had to answer: whether Castillo was "under a delusion that God commanded him to kill his father and carry out a school shooting[.]" *State v. Castillo*, 713 S.E.2d 190 (N.C. Ct. App. 2011).

◆   Parents couldn't simply sue a district over its refusal to decide a student with depression and anxiety qualified for special education. Before suing, they first had to "exhaust administrative remedies" via hearings.

An Ohio elementary school student's academic performance deteriorated. He began to have anger issues and exhibit "demonstrated explosive behavior." He also began to refuse to go to school and to make comments about committing suicide.

In March, his mother asked the district to conduct a Multi-Factored Evaluation (MFE) to assess the student for special education eligibility. She said the principal told her it was too late in the year to conduct an MFE.

Two months later, his mother gave the school guidance counselor a copy of a psychiatrist's report diagnosing the student with ADHD, Asperger's Disorder, anxiety disorder and severe depression. She again asked for an MFE. Administrators again denied her request.

The parents and the district continued to discuss the matter over the summer. **Less than a week before the start of the new school year, the school district refused to concede the student had a disability.**

The parents sued the district under the Individuals with Disabilities Education Act (IDEA), Section 504 of the Rehabilitation Act and the Americans with Disabilities Act. The district asked the federal judge to dismiss the suit because the parents couldn't sue over an IDEA issue under any law without first exhausting administrative remedies, as required under the IDEA, by completing every hearing and appeal required by the state's special education law.

The judge agreed with the district that the parents had to exhaust administrative remedies before going to court. He dismissed the case. *Doe v. Dublin City School Dist.*, No. 2:09-cv-738, 2010 WL 1434318 (S.D. Ohio 2010).

◆   The Seventh U.S. Circuit Court of Appeals reversed the dismissal of a teacher's claim that a school violated the ADA by refusing to accommodate her seasonal affective disorder by giving her a classroom with natural light.

After five successful years teaching kindergarten at a Wisconsin elementary school, a teacher asked to teach a first-grade class. The school agreed, but it assigned her to a classroom with no windows. The teacher told the principal she had seasonal affective disorder and would have trouble functioning in a room with no natural light.

The district refused to move her to a room with windows. The teacher began experiencing fatigue, anxiety, hypervigilance, tearfulness, racing thoughts and trouble organizing her thoughts. She started having panic attacks, uncontrollable crying jags and trouble eating. She began thinking about suicide, and she had serious trouble focusing on her job and her students. On Oct. 17, her doctors put her on medication and suggested she take a leave of absence for the remaining three months of the semester.

She was granted leave. She sent the district's workers' compensation claims representative a letter from her doctor. It clarified "the importance of

natural light for individuals with a history of this disorder" and said the
teacher's "current episode of depression was most likely directly related" to
being assigned to a classroom with no windows.

The district didn't reassign the teacher to a different room, and she
never returned to the elementary school. She started teaching at a university
the next year.

The teacher sued the district, alleging it violated the ADA by failing to
accommodate her disability. The judge dismissed the case, finding the
district had engaged in an interactive process with the teacher and "making
changes aimed at reducing her stress."

She appealed to the Seventh Circuit. It reversed. The teacher's case had
to go forward because she presented enough evidence for a judge or jury to
find she was a qualified person with a disability and the district knew of her
disability but didn't accommodate it.

The Seventh Circuit said cases involving accommodation requests for a
mental disability require extra information "because any necessary
accommodation is often nonobvious to the employer. Thus our cases have
consistently held that **disabled employees must make their employers
aware of any nonobvious, medically necessary accommodations with
corroborating evidence" from a doctor before the employer is required
to provide it**. Here, the teacher provided such information when her doctor
wrote to the workers' compensation representative to explain her condition.

Because the teacher provided the evidence needed for a judge or jury to
find she was legally entitled to the accommodation she'd requested, the
lower court was wrong to dismiss her case. *Ekstrand v. School Dist. of
Somerset*, 583 F.3d 972 (7th Cir. 2009). On remand to the lower federal
court, the district again asked for judgment without a trial. The judge found
the Seventh Circuit had considered the same facts and arguments the district
was making but found a trial was needed. So the judge denied the district's
request for judgment. *Ekstrand v. School Dist. of Somerset*, No. 08-cv-193-
bbc, 2010 WL 3123143 (W.D. Wis. 8/6/10).

◆ Discovering a student had been admitted to a mental hospital triggered
a school district's child find duty under the Individuals with Disabilities
Education Act to determine if she qualified for special education. Its failure
to do so entitled the student to tuition reimbursement.

The student had been attending a private school, but her parents
enrolled her in the local public school in Connecticut the summer before her
eleventh-grade year. The public school didn't know she'd been admitted to
a hospital after the private school's psychologist told her parents the student
had bulimia and was suicidal.

Then, just before the school year began, the student overdosed and was
admitted to a psychiatric hospital. A few days later, her mother gave the
public school's nurse the health assessment record the state required for
public school enrollment. It reported the student was taking antidepressants.
Not long after, the mother told the school the student was in a psychiatric

hospital and wouldn't be able to attend her first day of school. A few days later, her parents enrolled her in an intensive therapeutic program in Utah.

The public school apparently didn't notice her absence. Her parents received a mid-quarter progress report in October saying the student was making good progress in Algebra and was a pleasure to have in class. In November, the parents enrolled her in a therapeutic boarding school in Massachusetts.

In December, the public school in Connecticut wrote to tell her parents their daughter – who had never attended the school – was making good progress in U.S. history class. Later that month the student was admitted to another hospital. In January, her parents enrolled her in another program in Utah. Their attorney wrote to the school to ask it to evaluate the student for special education.

The district convened a "planning and placement team" (PPT) meeting. At it, one of the student's doctors said he believed she met the criteria for special education under the emotional disturbance category and thought she needed to be educated in a therapeutic boarding school.

The PPT refused to find she qualified for special ed. It also refused to reimburse the parents for her therapeutic school tuition.

The parents requested a due process hearing. The hearing officer found the district had violated its child find duty – and had sufficient information by the PPT meeting to have determined she was eligible for special ed under the emotional disturbance category. It ordered the district to reimburse the parents for her therapeutic school costs starting with the date the parents had notified the district of their intent to enroll the student there.

The district appealed, but the court affirmed.

To find a procedural violation of a district's child find obligation, the court had to find school officials "overlooked clear signs of a disability" or were "negligent in failing to order testing" or had "no rational justification for not deciding to evaluate." It did.

The court agreed **the district ignored a clear sign of a disability when the student's mother informed it that the student couldn't come to school because she'd been admitted to a psychiatric hospital** – especially coupled with the info provided on the health assessment form.

Because the district's "disregard of its Child Find obligations constituted a gross procedural violation," the court affirmed the hearing officer's decision to award the student compensatory education by ordering the district to pay for her tuition at a therapeutic private school. *Regional School Dist. No. 9 Board of Educ. v. Mr. and Mrs. M.*, No. 3:07-CV-01484 (WWE), 2009 WL 2514064 (D. Conn. 8/7/09).

◆ A school custodian diagnosed with post-traumatic stress syndrome caused by events surrounding a student's gruesome suicide at school was allowed to sue the school district for damages – her remedy wasn't limited to workers' comp.

A school custodian was called in to work early because a student had shot himself in the head in the main entrance of the high school. After the school superintendent ordered her to clean up the site, she overheard a police detective say the dead student's name. She'd known the boy and was so upset she had to take half an hour to compose herself.

When she returned, the police told her not to touch the site. Instead, the principal told her to go through the classrooms where the boy had attended classes that day to look for any bombs he might have left. She found none.

When she returned, she got the OK to clean the site. She found a book bag in the corner and was carrying it away when she was told to leave it, so she dropped it. Later, she found out a robot had carried it out of the building and watched as a bomb squad detonated a pipe bomb that had been in the book bag.

This shocked and frightened her, as no one had warned her the bag had belonged to the suicide victim – and she'd dropped it, not suspecting it might contain a bomb.

The superintendent told her to make it look like the suicide hadn't happened. **She was there cleaning – including soot from the bomb detonation as well as brain matter, bone bits and blood – until after 4:00 a.m.** She was told to come back by 8:00 a.m. She spent the day handing out cookies and coffee to students, staff and parents there for grief counseling as well as guarding the school gates. The custodian was also ordered to clean up the suicide site every night because other people left candles and cards there to honor the boy who'd died. She found removing these items extremely upsetting. Over the next few weeks, she experienced anxiety, sleeplessness, recurring nightmares and frequent crying. She was diagnosed with post-traumatic stress syndrome.

The custodian sued the school district alleging intentional and negligent infliction of emotional distress. The trial court dismissed the suit, deciding her only remedy was to file a claim under the state's worker's comp statute. She appealed, and the appellate court reversed.

Washington's Industrial Insurance Act provided the exclusive remedy for workers injured in the course of their employment – but the appellate court found it didn't apply here because the custodian's injuries didn't fit the act's definition for "injury."

The act defined an "injury" as "a sudden and tangible happening, of a traumatic nature, producing an immediate or prompt result[.]" That wasn't the case here, as the emotionally traumatic events the custodian suffered did not occur suddenly or have an immediate result. Also, her mental injury wasn't the result of any one or identifiable task ordered by the district.

Since her injury didn't fall under the definition of the state's worker's comp statute, she wasn't limited to that remedy. The appellate court found her emotional distress suit could go forward. *Rothwell v. Nine Mile Falls School Dist.*, 206 P.3d 347 (Wash. Ct. App. 2009).

◆   A school district violated the Individuals with Disabilities Education Act (IDEA) by failing to identify a student as eligible for special education and provide her services despite clear evidence of her severe and persistent depression.

The student began to exhibit behavioral and emotional problems at school in the eighth grade. The next year, she tried to kill herself by swallowing a bottle of aspirin. After a hospital pumped her stomach, it admitted her to the pediatric mental health unit for five days, ultimately diagnosing her with clinical depression. The students' parents informed the school of this.

The next year, when the first report cards were issued, the student's parents discovered her grades had nosedived and she'd been skipping a lot of school. Her mother contacted her daughter's teachers to ask for help, but most didn't respond.

The student's parents had her tested by a psychologist, then forwarded his report to the school. He suggested ADHD might be an issue, so the parents had the student tested by an expert in that field, who diagnosed her with ADHD and major depression.

A few months after the student's parents arranged for her to start therapy, she was hospitalized for 11 days. During this stay, staff determined the student had suffered from a major depressive disorder since she was 12.

The parents contacted the school to ask it to assess her for services under Section 504 of the Rehabilitation Act. They provided doctors' diagnoses and other information. But when school staff met with the parents, they only seemed interested in making sure the student passed into the next grade, not in addressing the problems behind her poor grades.

Ultimately, the school's failure to respond to what the parents saw as their child's real needs prompted them to enroll her in a private school. There, her mood and performance improved. A year later, they approached the school about special education, but had such a hard time getting answers that they hired an attorney. When a school team finally assessed the student, it determined she wasn't entitled to special ed services.

The parents asked for a due process hearing, but the hearing officer upheld the ineligibility determination and also ruled against the parents on their charge that the district had violated its child find duty by not identifying their daughter for a special ed assessment based on what it knew about her mental health diagnoses and school performance.

The parents appealed, and a federal court reversed. It held that the student was eligible for special ed on the basis of **an emotional disturbance, defined under the IDEA's regulations as "a condition exhibiting one or more of the following characteristics over a long period of time and to a marked degree that adversely affects a child's educational performance."** The listed characteristics include:

- being unable to learn
- difficulty forming or maintaining school relationships
- having inappropriate emotional responses
- being pervasively depressed, or
- having physical symptoms or fears associated with personal or school problems.

The hearing officer wrongfully found the student's emotional disturbance didn't impact her education enough to create a duty on the part of the school to evaluate her for special ed. The school was aware of her suicide attempt, treatment for depression, the diagnoses by mental health professionals and the student's deteriorating academic performance. The district violated its child find duty by not assessing her for services. It also incorrectly determined she wasn't eligible for services once it did perform an assessment. The court ordered the district to reimburse the parents for the student's private school tuition. *N.G. v. District of Columbia*, 556 F.Supp.2d 11 (D.D.C. 2008).

◆ A student wasn't eligible for special education on the basis of emotional disturbance because his depression wasn't pervasive and didn't adversely impact his academic performance.

The student made two suicide attempts as a high school freshman and was admitted twice to a facility that provided psychiatric treatment.

As a sophomore, he turned in homework to his teacher Mr. Kieffer in which he wrote that he was planning to take over the world and then "kill ... or something that won't get me in trouble ... all the teachers that gave me F's," adding: "fair warning, Mr. Keefer [*sic*]."

The district expelled the student for threatening a teacher and paid for him to attend an alternative school for students with behavioral problems.

The student's mother asked the district to assess him for special ed. At a meeting to discuss this, she said the school should have determined the student had a mental illness disability based on his suicide attempts and psychiatric treatments as a freshman.

But after evaluating him, the school determined he wasn't eligible for special ed. The mother asked for a due process hearing. The hearing centered on whether the student's condition was an emotional disturbance that adversely affected his academic performance as defined by the IDEA's regulations. The hearing officer decided it was and that the school had to provide him services.

The district appealed in federal court. By this time, the student was a junior, not receiving special ed, successfully carrying a full class load, no longer depressed and enjoying playing on a football team. The district asked for summary judgment, and the court granted it.

The evidence showed the student didn't have an "emotional disturbance" under the IDEA. His inappropriate behavior and emotional responses were isolated incidents, not exhibited over a long period of time and to a marked degree. Also, the fact that he'd received passing grades – two As, a B and a C – at the end of his freshman year indicated his problems hadn't adversely impacted his academic performance to the degree required for him to be eligible to receive services under the IDEA. *St. Joseph-Ogden Community High School Dist. No. 305 v. Janet W.*, No. 07-CV-2079, 2008 WL 170693 (C.D. Ill. 1/17/08).

VI. WEIGHT-RELATED ISSUES

A. Weight Management

To maintain a healthy weight, students need to balance the number of calories they consume with the number they burn. To create this balance, which fosters a healthy lifestyle, students need to engage in regular physical activity and make healthy food choices, advises the Centers for Disease Control and Prevention (CDC).

The body mass index (BMI) method is a typical way to screen children and adolescents for excess weight and obesity. BMI assesses weight in relation to height. More information about BMI – plus charts – is available at *www.cdc.gov/growthcharts*.

One touted advantage of using BMI to determine whether students are at a healthy weight is that the method is minimally invasive – which is important when dealing with a vulnerable population such as children. But while asking for students' weights or having them get on a scale does not physically invade their bodies, it might trigger a big emotional reaction.

School officials might want to remember how touchy the subject of personal body weight is in this culture.

Because of the possibility of an overwhelming emotional reaction (which can be closely followed by hurtful teasing as other students pick up on it) some sensitivity on the school's part might be called for when personal body weight is discussed.

Schools – and state legislatures – are getting more involved in health initiatives to combat the problem. This is because an unhealthy body weight poses serious health issues.

1. Obesity

"Obesity" means a person's body weight is much higher than considered healthy for a person of that height.

Children whose weight is above what is deemed a healthy range have been shown to be at greater risk of developing – or suffering more from – certain diseases and other health problems. These include:

- diabetes
- asthma
- liver problems
- gall stones
- acid reflux
- sleep apnea
- hypertension
- high blood pressure
- high cholesterol levels, and
- depression linked to self-esteem.

In addition to health problems, students who are overweight or consider themselves to be overweight are more likely to attempt suicide, according to a 2009 survey conducted by the *Journal of Adolescent Health*.

More than 14,000 high school students participated in the study, which examined the links between teen suicide attempts and body mass indexes. With results equal in boys and girls, the study determined suicide risk is higher for students who:

- are obese
- are overweight, and
- have perceived notions of being too heavy.

The number of overweight students between the ages of 12 and 19 has tripled in the previous two decades, according to the CDC. The percentage of overweight children jumped from between 5% and 6% to its current percentage of around 17% – more than one obese child among every six.

The leap is even greater in some individual groups. In the early 1970s, 4% of 6- to 11-year-old children were overweight. By the early 2000s, that percentage had more than quadrupled to 18%.

The Federal Interagency Forum on Child and Family Statistics also tracked the trend. Although its numbers are slightly different, it found that among children ages 6 to 17:

- 6% were overweight in 1976-1980
- 11% were overweight in 1988-1994, and
- 18% were overweight in 2003-2004.

The good news is the 2008 CDC announcement that this upward spiral seemed to have stopped in recent years, with the percentage holding steady at around 17%. The bad news is that this is an incredibly high number.

In practical terms, this percentage means that one in six students is at risk for other health problems.

The CDC has come up with tactics to make important changes in things schools can control, such as its curriculum and policies. A 10-point plan is available at *http://www.cdc.gov/healthyyouth/keystrategies/pdf/make-a-difference.pdf*.

Schools officials are coming up with their own strategies, too. For example, more and more elementary schools are deciding to eliminate birthday "treats" – if the treat is food. There are lots of creative ways to celebrate a child's birthday at school that have nothing to do with cupcakes, such as letting the student pick a story to read to the class.

A big concern is using food as a reward, according to a 2010 report, *Bridging the Gap*. In it, school administrators were asked, "Are teachers allowed to use food as a reward for good behavior?" They answered:

- Yes (30%)
- Yes, but it is discouraged (31%)
- No (39%).

Nearly one-third of teachers are free to use food as a reward without any resistance from school administrators, according to this survey. Physical activity, such as extra recess or a game, would be a better reward for good behavior, according to First Lady Michelle Obama's "Let's Move!" plan.

A disturbing trend reported by the CDC is that Type II diabetes – formerly called "adult onset diabetes," because that was typically when it started – has begun showing up in children and adolescents.

When onset occurs this early, the complications that go with the disease (such as kidney failure and cardiovascular disease) also set in much earlier.

Schools can help students lower this risk, according to a 2010 HEALTHY national study. More than 4,600 middle school students who were overweight participated in the study and took Type II diabetes "intervention" steps at school, such as:

• going to longer gym classes

• eating more nutritious lunches

• getting classroom education on signs and symptoms, and

• engaging in other school activities that promote a healthy lifestyle.

By the end of the study, the group had a 21% lower obesity rate than their non-participating counterparts.

And according to a 2008 *New York Times* investigation, children are also increasingly being prescribed medications for other obesity-related conditions – such as acid reflux, high blood pressure, high cholesterol – that, like Type II diabetes, were virtually unseen in children 20 years ago.

Another worrying finding is that, according to 2009 research, obese adolescents have the arteries you'd expect to find in people in their forties.

Even when obesity is not linked to a serious illness, overweight children are missing more days of school, according to a study published in a 2007 issue of the journal *Obesity*. Among the 1,000 fourth- and fifth-graders the study followed, the overweight children missed two days more of school a year than the average-weight students.

Another problem related to overweight students that virtually every school has to deal with is teasing and bullying. A 2004 study showed that overweight children are more likely to be bullied than normal-weight children. There is a huge social stigma attached to obesity in this country.

State legislatures are well aware of the problems. Recent laws include policies to make sure schools provide healthier food options for students – and restrict or keep trans fat out of school food.

Published in *Pediatrics*, a 2012 study found that laws restricting the sale of sugary snacks and drinks at school help students avoid excessive weight gain. Conducted over a three-year period, the study tracked weight changes of 6,300 students. It found that students living in states with laws restricting the availability of sugar gained 2.25 fewer pounds than their peers who were able to purchase sugary snacks and drinks at school.

When it comes to wider social problems that drive up the incidence of obesity – and over which schools obviously have no control – the Department of Agriculture offers help through the National School Lunch Program and the School Breakfast Program.

Obesity is obviously caused by too many calories in and not enough burned off. But other influences significantly impact students' body weight, including their physical environments, their cultures, their personal attitudes, whether their parents are immigrants and whether their families are prosperous or struggling financially.

There is a direct correlation between poverty and obesity. Fresh fruits and vegetables cost a lot more than fast food and are not nearly as filling. The original reason behind the South's tradition of fried foods was that adding fat was a way the poor could make a limited amount of food go farther. Deep frying makes food more filling so it can feed more people. A speaker at the 2007 Childhood Obesity Conference in Oklahoma put it this way: With a dollar, you can buy either 200 nutritious calories or 800 calories of junk. Given the soaring price of produce since then, a dollar is buying even fewer nutritious calories now.

Where children live can also have a huge impact on their weight. It is almost universally true that poor areas of towns are short on two health basics: stores that stock affordable fresh food, and safe outdoor places where children can ride bikes or run around and play.

One reason behind rising obesity rates for children could be an increase in poverty.

Catholic Charities, for example, reported in late 2007 that they had experienced a 60% rise in people receiving their food services between 2002 and 2006. These services include food banks, soup kitchens and congregate meals.

And a Department of Agriculture study released in November 2007 found that more than 35.5 million Americans – or 12% of the population, more than one in every nine people – reported having to go hungry in 2006 because they didn't have enough money to meet their basic needs. Of these 35.5 million people, 12.6 million were children. Since then, of course, we've experienced a worldwide recession and soaring unemployment numbers in the United States.

Schools cannot be expected to solve the problem of poverty, but they can help to fight off its nutritional impact on their students by making sure children participate in PE classes and by making sure eligible students take advantage of the U.S. Department of Agriculture's School Breakfast Program and National School Lunch Program.

But due to the social stigma associated with poverty, the very students who most need it may not want to be seen getting a free-or-reduced meal. Depending on how things are set up at your school – or ways you can change them – it may be possible to protect students' dignity *and* get healthy food into their bodies.

The U.S. Department of Agriculture chose Michigan for a pilot program that will provide free breakfast, lunch and snacks to all students in eligible schools.

If at least 40% of students' families qualify for public assistance, schools can participate in the program, which aims to reduce the negative stigma associated with getting free lunches.

Starting in the fall of 2011, all students in Detroit Public Schools will "walk through a lunch line and not have to pay. Low-income students will not be easily identifiable and will be less likely to skip meals," a school official pointed out.

Part of the Healthy, Hunger-Free Kids Act of 2010, the free lunch program will be available to schools in additional states in coming years, with the long-term goal of being nationwide in the 2014-15 school year.

A 2010 report from the Food Research and Action Center found that many students don't take advantage of breakfasts offered at school.

So California school officials considered why students would want to skip breakfast. They identified two key problems:

- some students preferred to spend free time in the mornings with their friends, and
- some students don't arrive at school early enough to wait in line and eat.

The schools started offering more than just the typical breakfast options. Cafeteria staff still served traditional breakfasts, but also started:

- serving breakfasts in classes
- making cart rounds in the halls, where students could grab a bagged morning meal, and
- offering "second-chance" breakfasts served to students during mid-morning study halls.

2. Eating Disorders

The National Eating Disorders Screening Program (NDESP) coordinated the first nationwide screening initiative for U.S. high school students in 2000. With more than 35,000 participants, the study revealed that 25% of girls and 11% of boys reported "disordered eating and weight control symptoms severe enough to warrant clinical evaluation," according to researchers. The study concluded that screening high school students for potential eating disorders may identify at-risk students. These students may benefit from early intervention, which would help prevent long-term health complications associated with anorexia and other eating disorders.

The NDESP is held annually during National Eating Disorders Awareness Week. More information about the program is available online at *www.mentalhealthscreenings.org*.

Students who have eating disorders usually have unrealistic fears about gaining weight and distorted perceptions about their bodies. They also tend to deny the seriousness of their illness.

Eating disorders are commonly divided into two categories: anorexia nervosa and bulimia nervosa. Many individuals exhibit symptoms from both anorexia and bulimia. The disorders can be overcome, but doing so is extremely difficult for students for two reasons:

1. Anorexia and bulimia aren't really about food. The disorders stem from a negative self-image. While onset can occur at any age, eating disorders are commonly triggered just before or during puberty. In practical terms, students are most likely to develop eating disorders

during puberty because that's a time when their bodies are changing, which can lead to self-doubt. Reflecting today's extreme "societal pressure to be thin," advertising and the media only make students' self-image problems worse, according to the National Alliance on Mental Illness (NAMI).

2. In previous years, more students who suffered from anorexia and bulimia often felt alone and isolated. But technology has enabled students from around the world to interact with others who also suffer from eating disorders. The Internet has thousands of underground websites dedicated to promoting and maintaining anorexic and bulimic lifestyles. Sufferers have personified the disorders, commonly calling anorexia "Ana" and bulimia "Mia." Some students with eating disorders even refer to "Ana" or "Mia" as their best friend. Because students communicate primarily via technology, this online support system to perpetuate the disorders makes intervention and treatment more challenging than ever. On the websites, sufferers share tips on how to trick others into thinking they are eating and how to avoid giving in to hunger pains. The pro-ana/pro-mia online community glorifies anorexia and bulimia, calling them lifestyle choices rather than disorders.

It is difficult to do so, but students can overcome their eating disorders. The following resources are available to schools to help educate students:

• Entering Adulthood: Looking at Body Image and Eating Disorders is age-appropriate material for high school students. It's available in a pdf file at *www.eric.ed.gov/PDFS/ED329840.pdf*.
• Dying to be Thin: PBS Video and Teaching Resources are available from the PBS at *www.pbs.org/wgbh/nova/thin/*.

People who suffer from anorexia refuse to eat enough to maintain a healthy minimum body weight, which is generally accepted to be within 15% of a person's recommended body weight. Students who have anorexia:

• are often preoccupied with food and dieting
• refuse to maintain a healthy body weight, and
• believe they look fat when they're actually very thin.

In addition, anorexic females experience amenorrhea, which is the absence of three consecutive menstrual cycles due to extreme weight loss.

They also complain about feeling cold when others are comfortable. This is a sign of hypothermia, which is caused by a drop in body temperature caused by excessive weight loss. Lanugo (very fine hair, such as on newborns) may grow on the face or body. Other visible body changes include brittle nails, thin hair and dry, yellow skin.

Anorexia is potentially life-threatening. Seriously underweight students who refuse to eat have been shown to be at greater risk of developing – or suffering more from – certain diseases and other health problems, such as:

• damage to vital organs (heart, kidneys, brain)
• low heart rate

- mild anemia
- low blood pressure
- irregular heart rhythms
- heart failure
- osteoporosis, and
- death by starvation.

A 2010 research study conducted by the National Alliance on Mental Illnesses (NAMI) found that anorexia nervosa has the highest mortality rate of all psychiatric illnesses. The majority who suffer from anorexia are female adolescents between the ages of 15 and 24. However, anorexia has also been diagnosed in girls as young as seven and boys.

When people suffer from anorexia, they often develop eating rituals. For example, they may cut food into tiny pieces or refuse to eat in front of others. Common excuses for not eating include:

- "I already ate."
- "I had a big breakfast/lunch."
- "I just brushed my teeth."

Having college-educated parents may increase high school girls' risks of developing eating disorders, according to a 2009 study published in the *American Journal of Epidemiology*.

Researchers tracked more than 13,000 girls and found several links between higher education, academic excellence and eating disorders.

Having college-educated parents doubles girls' risks of developing eating disorders. Additionally, the risk is increased six-fold among girls whose maternal grandmothers have college educations. And those rates go up even more if the girl is also a good student.

For example, 15-year-old students who earned the highest grades in the class were twice as likely to require hospitalization due to an eating disorder than the 15-year-old students with the lowest scores.

This study does not indicate that education leads to eating disorders, researchers say. Instead, the findings point to a group of students who may be at higher risk than their peers.

School officials and parents can watch for warning signs that students may need help. Potential signs of an eating disorder include:

- feeling an unattainable pressure to succeed
- ongoing, unexplained weight loss, and
- going to the restroom immediately after meals.

Teachers and school officials should be aware of red flags at school that might indicate anorexia. They should watch for students who:

- have lost a significant amount of weight
- become extraordinarily reclusive
- wear very baggy clothing (to hide excessive weight loss)
- wear lots of layers (to add bulk as well as to keep warm)
- huddle around near heat vents or radiators (to keep warm)
- skip meals or bring their own low calorie food, and

- exercise during lunchtime instead of eating.

Anorexic students have specific challenges at school. Teachers and school officials can help students by:

- allowing severely malnourished students to opt out of physical activity until health improves
- remembering that lunchtime and meals are stressful for students who have eating disorders, and
- offering alternative meal locations other than the cafeteria, if the student desires.

Anorexia can be triggered by internal factors. For example, anorexic behaviors might be triggered by a personality trait. One of the most common personality traits of anorexics is perfectionism. Because of this, it may take an anorexic student longer to complete tests. Teachers can help anorexic students perform to their academic potential by allowing them to have a warm drink or a blanket to reduce chills (a common side effect), which often cause students to be distracted from their assignments.

The disorder can also be triggered by external challenges, such as peer bullying – and that can cause legal hassles for school officials.

For example, a mother in Pennsylvania filed a lawsuit against Pittsburgh Public Schools, claiming school officials failed to stop five male classmates from bullying her daughter about her weight. The victim and the bullies were sent to the guidance counselor's office and the principal's office at least three times, according to the suit. The victim alleged that the bullying was "open and apparent."

The suit claimed the ongoing bullying the girl suffered triggered an eating disorder – which eventually required her to leave school to enter an inpatient anorexia nervosa program. Filed under Title IX, the lawsuit didn't have to prove bullying *caused* the student's anorexia. Instead, the girl's mother only had to show the school failed to protect her daughter, which caused her to miss school.

School officials asked for dismissal, but the court refused to grant it because the U.S. Supreme Court has already ruled that peer-on-peer harassment violates Title IX if the school doesn't stop the abuse, and as a result, the victim loses educational opportunities. *Mary V. v. Pittsburgh Public Schools*, No. CA 9-1082, 2010 WL 562909 (W.D. Pa. 2/17/10).

The district paid $55,000 to settle the claim.

People who suffer from bulimia binge and purge. Sufferers frequently eat unusually large amounts of food and immediately try to remove the ingested calories by inducing vomiting, taking laxatives and exercising excessively. Students with bulimia often:

- feel as if they can't control their eating behavior
- refuse to eat in public, but binge in private
- eat to the point of discomfort during binges
- use or abuse laxatives, dietary supplements and herbal remedies
- exercise obsessively, and

- worry and complain they are fat.

Most students who are bulimic maintain normal body weight or are slightly overweight, which makes it harder for school officials and parents to detect the problem. This is extremely dangerous because bulimic students face health risks including:

- amenorrhea
- abnormal bowel functioning
- damaged teeth and gums
- dehydration
- gastroesophageal reflux disorder
- irregular heart rhythms
- chronically inflamed or sore throat
- kidney problems from diuretic abuse
- swollen salivary glands in the cheeks
- sores, scar or calluses on knuckles or hands (from forced vomiting)
- depression, and
- anxiety.

The majority who suffer from bulimia are female adolescents and young adults who have been subjected to "teasing" about their appearance from family members and/or peers.

Binging and purging is done in secret, so many students who have bulimia successfully hide their disorder. Red flags that might indicate students are bulimic include:

- wearing very baggy clothing to hide weight fluctuation
- following erratic diets, such as eating only a certain color food
- making frequent trips to the restroom – especially after eating
- talking about food constantly
- bringing their own food in a purse or book bag, and
- avoiding the cafeteria (or other social eating environments).

Eating disorders are common among student-athletes. A recent study conducted by the ERCI found that more than one-third of female athletes reported attitudes and behaviors that put them in the "at risk" category for eating disorders.

Sports that require athletes to weigh in or maintain a certain size to stay competitive further increase students' risks. Examples include gymnastics, bodybuilding, diving, wrestling, track and field, figure skating and dance.

Paying attention to warning signs is the most important thing coaches can do to help students, according to Karin Kratina of the National Eating Disorders Association. The leading causes of death for students with eating disorders are suicide and cardiac arrest. School officials and coaches can help reduce athletes' vulnerability to eating disorders by:

- adopting a positive coaching style in favor of an authoritative one
- influencing and supporting teammates by displaying health attitudes about athletes' sizes and shapes, and

- emphasizing contribution and teamwork more than a win-at-all-cost competitive mind-set.

Female student-athletes who have eating disorders have additional health risks, such as the loss of menses – which leads to calcium and bone loss. This means female athletes are more prone to stress fractures of the bones, according to a study relating to the impact of eating disorders on women's health and athletic activity conducted by the University of Minnesota Tucker Center.

The U.S. Department of Health and Human Services compiled the following list of recommendations school officials can follow to promote healthy weight control for student-athletes:

1. Nutritional needs for growth and development must be placed above athletic considerations. Fluid or food deprivation should never be allowed. There is no substitute for a healthy diet consisting of a variety of foods from all food groups with enough energy (calories) to support growth, daily physical activities, and sports activities. Daily caloric intake for most athletes should consist of a minimum of 2000 calories. Athletes need to consume enough fluids to maintain proper hydration levels.

2. In sports for which weigh-ins are required, athletes' weights and body composition should be assessed once or twice per year. The most important assessment is obtained before the beginning of the sport season. This should include a determination of body fat and minimal allowable weight when the athlete is adequately hydrated. Weigh-ins for competition should be performed immediately before competition. Athletes should be permitted to compete in championship tournaments only at the weight class in which they have competed for most other athletic events that year.

3. Male high school athletes should not have less than 7% body fat. This minimal allowable body fat may be too low for some athletes and result in sub-optimal performance. Female athletes should consume enough energy (calories) and nutrients to meet their energy requirements and experience normal menses. There are no recommendations on body-fat percentages for female athletes.

4. A program for the purpose of gaining or losing weight should (a) be started early to permit a gradual weight gain or loss over a realistic time period, (b) permit a change of 1.5% or less of one's body weight per week, (c) permit the loss of weight to be fat loss and the gain of weight to be muscle mass, (d) be coupled with an appropriate training program (both strength and conditioning), and (e) incorporate a well-balanced diet with adequate energy (calories), carbohydrates, protein, and fat. After athletes obtain their desired weight, they should be encouraged to maintain a constant weight and avoid fluctuations. A weight-loss plan for athletic purposes should never be instituted before the ninth grade.

5. Any athlete who loses a significant amount of fluid during sports

participation should weigh in before and after practices, games, meets, and competitions. Each pound of weight loss should be replaced with one pint of fluid containing carbohydrates and electrolytes before the next practice or competition. Fluids should be available, and the drinking of fluids should be encouraged at all practices and competitions.

6. Weight loss accomplished by over-exercising; using rubber suits, steam baths, or saunas; prolonged fasting; fluid reduction; vomiting; or using anorexic drugs, laxatives, diuretics, diet pills, insulin, stimulants, nutritional supplements, or other legal or illegal drugs and/or nicotine should be prohibited at all ages.

7. Athletes who need to gain weight should consult their physician for resources on healthy weight gain and referral to a registered dietitian. They should be discouraged from gaining excessive weight, which may impair performance, increase the likelihood of heat illness, and increase the risk of developing complications from obesity.

8. Ergogenic aids and non-therapeutic use of supplements for weight management should be prohibited.

9. Young athletes should be involved in a total athletic program that includes acquisition of athletic skills and improvement in speed, flexibility, strength, and physical conditioning while maintaining good nutrition and normal hydration. This should be done under the supervision of a coach who stresses a positive attitude, character building, teamwork, and safety.

B. Nutrition

1. School Meals

The U.S. Department of Agriculture's School Breakfast Program and National School Lunch Program require schools to serve meals that are low in fat and provide a certain percentage of the Recommended Dietary Allowances of protein, Vitamin A, Vitamin C, iron, calcium and calories – one-third for school lunches and one-quarter for school breakfasts.

Poor nutrition, from which many children suffer, has a negative impact on brain development and school performance. The National PTA's website notes that children who eat meals served by the school meal programs:

• get more nutritious meals than children who do not, and
• show improved standardized test scores, attendance and class participation.

Another advantage of school meal programs is that they are based on parental income, so they are either free or available at a greatly reduced cost to children that really need them.

The CDC has announced a four-part plan intended to help schools teach students that wellness is a lifestyle. It suggests that schools:

1. establish a coordinated school health program that includes these eight

components:
- health education
- physical education
- counseling, psychological and social services
- health services
- nutrition services
- healthy school environment
- parent/community involvement, and
- staff wellness

2. establish a school health council to promote healthy eating and exercise
   - Since 2004, federal law has required all school districts participating in federally funded school meal programs to establish a local school wellness policy through a process that involves parents, students, school representatives, and the public. A school health council can meet that requirement.
3. assess existing health programs and suggest improvements
   - To help, the CDC provides a self-assessment and planning tool at *apps.nccd.cdc.gov/shi*.
4. improve the school's food and exercise policies
   - For example, schools can find ways to make cafeteria food both healthy and tasty and come up with ways to incorporate exercise into the school day.

In spite of the continued push to provide healthier school meals, about half of elementary students could still buy whole milk, sodas, sports drinks and sugary fruit drinks during the 2009-10 and 2010-11 school years, according to a study published online in the *Archives of Pediatrics & Adolescent Medicine.*

You might be wondering: How is that possible?

Students purchased the sugary drinks and whole milk at school in *a la carte* lines, snack bars and vending machines. Because healthy beverages are an essential part of a healthy diet, the Institute of Medicine recommends that – if schools have *a la carte* lines and vending machines – they should offer the following beverages only:
- 100% fruit or vegetable juice
- non-fat or 1% milk, and
- water.

In 2010, former governor of California Arnold Schwarzenegger signed SB 1413 into law. The legislation requires public schools in the state to provide students with access to fresh, free drinking water in food service areas during meal times at schools. The law took effect on Jan. 1, 2011.

To meet the new legal requirement, schools:
- gave students 8-ounce bottles of water with their meals, and
- supplied 5-gallon containers of bottled water and paper cups for students in the lunchroom.

And that's not the only change in California. Jamie Oliver's Food

Revolution convinced the Los Angeles Unified School District (LAUSD) to remove strawberry- and chocolate-flavored milk from school menus.

When students returned to school in the fall of 2011, they had "wholesome plain white milk with their meals instead of liquid candy," according to the Food Revolution website.

Oliver's battle with LAUSD was televised on the ABC show, *Jamie Oliver's Food Revolution*. On the show, Oliver orchestrated stunts, such as filling school buses with sugar to help viewers visualize unhealthy choices. But behind the scenes, Oliver worked with schools and parents to help share nutritional information about flavored milk. A downloadable Sweetened Milk Calculator and nutritional milk fact sheet is at *http://sn.im/milk444*.

While that's good news, other studies show there's still room for improvement in school nutrition. For example, in 2010, the Physicians Committee for Responsible Medicine (PCRM) analyzed lunch menus from 18 schools across the country.

The result? Schools are still serving meals that are too high in saturated fat and sodium, according to PCRM nutritionist Kathryn Strong.

After the analysis was complete, PCRM identified what it called the worst lunches to serve to students. Here are the top five worst school lunches:
- Beef and cheese nachos. Topping the list, this meal has too much sodium (1,500 mg) and fat (24 g).
- Meatloaf and potatoes packs unhealthy calories (472) and cholesterol (78 mg).
- Cheeseburgers, which often have more saturated fat than students should have in an entire meal.
- Grilled cheese sandwiches and cheese quesadillas (tied) are loaded with saturated fat (7 g) and sodium (nearly 1,000 mg).
- Pepperoni pizza. The average slice contains saturated fat (6 g) and its processed meat has also been shown to increase cancer risk.

Schools can help children develop healthier eating habits by offering:
- more fruits, vegetables, lean meats and whole grains
- less fat, and
- appropriate portion sizes.

Students may balk at the options, but schools can take steps to encourage students to eat healthier foods, according to research conducted at Cornell University. Smarter Lunchroom researchers found that students are more likely to choose healthy meals when schools:
- provide healthy "grab and go" options in the lunchroom
- offer fruits and veggies as "default" sides
- make a gradual switch to whole grains, and
- sell suggestively at the register, as in "Would you like to add an apple?"

Be prepared to think creatively, too. For example, school officials in Minnesota looked for ways to get students to at least try healthy options instead of just grabbing the typical go-to favorites, such as the ones listed above. But students weren't interested, so the staff stirred up some intrigue by holding a "coolest veggie" contest.

Cafeteria staffers passed out sample cups of veggies to students who were waiting in the lunch line. Four veggies were in the running: jicama sticks, portabella mushrooms, red peppers and pickled beets. After lunch, students filled out a survey to vote for their favorite. When the votes were tallied, jicama sticks was named the coolest veggie.

Getting students' input helped the school find out which healthy options students would eat. Jicama sticks remained one of the students' favorite veggies on the lunch menu for years.

School officials can do other things to promote healthy lunch choices – and doing so doesn't have to break the budget. In 2010, Smarter Lunchrooms suggested the following well-planned tweaks to the layout of school cafeterias to improve students' lunch choices:

- The cash register. Remember – convenience is key! Students stand in line waiting. What last-minute items of convenience will they add to their trays? Replace chips and other pre-packaged goodies with fresh fruit or 100% fruit juice.
- The menu. What's in a name? Turns out, plenty when it comes to food. One cafeteria reported a 28% increase in sales after "vegetable soup" was renamed "rich vegetable medley soup." Smarter Lunchrooms recommends three specific food labels: nostalgic, regional and descriptive. For example: Grandma's chicken noodle soup, real Boston baked beans and creamy corn chowder.
- Walls and tables. Get creative by adding brightly colored posters of healthy fruits and veggies – and nutritional info – on cafeteria walls. Add a "try it table" – use table tents to invite students who are waiting in line to sample healthy options.
- Display cases. Lighting affects the way students view their choices. Make sure healthy lunch options are visually appealing by using well-lit display cases. Place the healthiest options at students' eye levels.
- The web. More and more cafeterias are putting their menus on school websites. Students who plan their meals based on online menus usually stick to healthier food choices than students who make decisions on a whim – while they're waiting in line and starving. If you haven't posted your menu on the web yet, it might be a good time to consider going online.

The Healthy School Meals Act of 2010 was one of the catalysts behind school lunch reform. The legislation required key changes to be tested in a pilot program, which was an overwhelming success in Berkeley, California schools.

President Obama signed the Healthy, Hunger Free Act of 2010 on Dec. 13, 2010. The new legislation:

- improves access to federally funded school meals by using Medicaid data to automatically determine eligibility for students

- increases focus on nutrition and health by improving the quality of school meals, removing junk food from schools and strengthening wellness policies
- improves school lunch program management by providing training for school food service providers and improving recall procedures in school settings, and
- saves taxpayer money by eliminating a Supplemental Nutrition Assistance Program (SNAP) benefit.

Key provisions included a pilot program conducted by the USDA to improve students' nutrition and eating habits to the National School Lunch and Breakfast Programs. The pilot program included free daily breakfasts for all students and organic lunch options. Changes included:

- incorporating more plant-based products into school cafeterias. The USDA also provides training to employees about nutritional information and food preparation
- offering incentives for schools to provide healthy plant-based meals. If districts offer at least two-thirds of students plant-based entrees on the daily lunch menu, those schools will receive additional USDA funding – 25% of the districts' total commodity assistance. The additional funding can be used to purchase additional plant-based food, such as fresh or frozen produce, legumes and whole grains.
- removing non-dairy milk substitution restrictions. Due to an increase in the number of students who have food allergies and suffer from lactose intolerance, the School Lunch program will be permitted to offer a milk substitute, such as soy- , almond- or rice-based fluids. One key requirement to note: The substitute must meet USDA nutritional standards. Additionally, students are no longer required to have written permission to choose milk alternatives, and schools will be reimbursed for meals that include healthy milk substitutions.

In response to the Healthy, Hunger-Free Kids Act of 2010, the U.S. Department of Agriculture (USDA) proposed and finalized rules on school nutrition standards, which took effect at the start of the 2012-13 school year. Under the new standards, school meals must:

- provide students with twice the amount of fruits and veggies as previously offered
- contain only whole grains
- include only low-fat or fat-free milk
- stay with sodium limits, and
- fall between minimum and maximum calorie requirements.

The USDA provided schools with a sample "Before and After" lunch menu, available at *http://sn.im/usda551*.

In 2011, the USDA also replaced the familiar food pyramid. On the new website, recommendations are now illustrated on a dinner plate in an attempt to help students visualize portion sizes of a healthy meal.

ChooseMyPlate.gov includes:

- nutrition information
- interactive games for students
- lesson plans for teachers, and
- poster displays for classrooms.

Visit *http://choosemyplate.gov/kids/index.html* to access these free resources.

In 2010, First Lady Michelle Obama introduced "Let's Move!" an all-encompassing initiative designed to improve student health. The USDA's voluntary HealthierUS School Challenge was incorporated into "Let's Move!" and a monetary award was added to encourage school officials to create healthier environments by promoting healthy nutrition and physical activity.

The financial incentive improved participation, as 809 awards were doled out to schools in 37 states within the first seven months of incorporation into "Let's Move!" For more information, go to *www.fns.usda.gov/tn/healthierus/index.html*.

2. Education

Wellness initiatives are designed to foster healthy food choices at a young age and to create habits that last a lifetime. Doing so helps students reduce health risks and increase their quality of life. Also, as opposed to going on and off reduced-calorie diets, developing good eating and exercise habits helps students maintain a healthy weight while ensuring their bodies have the nutrients to grow into healthy adults.

A key element is educating students on the benefits of healthy choices. Talk about it. Promote it at your school.

For example, remind students that being healthy is a lifestyle. Every healthy thing they do today – such as eating an apple instead of a candy bar or taking the stairs instead of the elevator – will pay off tomorrow. Getting into healthy habits has a cumulative effect.

Many school districts are finding ways to incorporate healthy, hands-on lessons into the school curriculum. For example, middle school students in Missouri are learning how to grow their own herb and vegetable gardens during science classes.

School officials in Maine have taken a light-hearted approach to encourage young students to make healthy choices. Each March during National Nutrition Month, teachers dress up as fruits and vegetables. But they don't stop there. Dressed in rented watermelon, banana, broccoli and carrot costumes, teachers march in a special parade in the hallway while students cheer as their favorites march by.

School officials noted that the parade helps remove some of the students' negative ideas associated with fruits and vegetables. The annual event has encouraged more students to eat – or at least try – fruits and vegetables. When financial constraints threatened the parade, school officials found a way to save the program from the budget ax. They found they could borrow costumes for free from their state department of education, as long as they made reservations in advance.

School officials should also consider the products promoted when students participate in school fundraising efforts. Do students sell candy bars? Are other options available? In 2000, almost 70% of schools sold cookies, candy and other baked goods to raise money. That number dropped to just over 50% in 2006, according to a study conducted by the Department of Health for the City of Saint Louis. While the reduction is good, there's always room to improve on showing students how school lessons should be applied in real-life settings. Non-food items that can be sold during school fundraisers or used as rewards include:

- special school supplies
- homemade crafts
- gift certificates to local gyms or mini-golf courses, and
- discount coupons to local sporting goods stores.

C. Physical Activity

There are six national standards for physical education (PE) in U.S. schools.

1. development of motor/movement skills
2. knowledge and application of movement concepts
3. personal/social responsibility
4. regular participation in physical activity
5. development and maintenance of physical fitness, and
6. valuing physical activity.

Every student in the U.S. needs physical activity, whether it's in a formal PE program or free play at recess – and more students are getting it at school. According to a 2010 study conducted by the National Association for Sport and Physical Education (NASPE) most states mandate PE. Here's the breakdown:

- 43 states mandate PE in elementary schools (up from 36 in 2006)
- 40 states mandate PE in middle schools (up from 33 in 2006), and
- 46 states mandate it for high school students (up from 42 in 2006).

While that's an improvement, the study noted that most states still do not specify minimum requirements. The NASPE recommends that schools provide at least 150 minutes of PE instruction each week to elementary school students. Middle and high school students need more PE – at least 225 minutes per week, according to recommendations.

The study also found about half of schools allow PE exemptions and/or substitutions, which the NASPE calls loopholes that reduce the effectiveness of the mandates.

In 2010, 32 states let students substitute other physical activities for their required PE credits, up from 27 states in 2006. Common allowed substitutions include:

- JROTC (18 states)
- interscholastic sports (15 states)

- marching band (10 states), and
- cheerleading (10 states).

In 2010, 30 states allowed schools or districts to grant waivers or exemptions from PE requirements. That's up from 18 states in 2006. Common reasons schools grant PE exemptions for students include:

- health issues
- physical disabilities
- religious beliefs, and
- early graduation.

Here's proof that technology's everywhere: Currently 22 states allow students to earn required PE credits online. But fewer than half of those states (only 10) require online PE classes to be taught by state-certified physical education teachers.

Five states – Illinois, Iowa, Massachusetts, New Mexico and Vermont – were recognized as the most consistent because every K-12 student was required to take PE classes in 2010. Two – New Jersey and Rhode Island – required students in grades one through twelve to take PE classes in 2010.

First Lady Michelle Obama's "Let's Move!" is one of the latest initiatives to increase students' activity. The program challenges all students to earn a Presidential Active Lifestyle Award (PALA). To earn a PALA, students must document their active exercise – at least 60 minutes per day, five days a week, for six weeks. Students can register at *www.fitness.gov* and log their daily activity. At the end of six weeks, students will receive a certificate of recognition from the President. More importantly, they'll be building healthy habits and feeling better with a more active lifestyle.

VII. OTHER HEALTH ISSUES

◆ Protecting the privacy rights of a pregnant 15-year-old did not amount to insubordination, New Hampshire's highest court held. The student confessed to the guidance counselor that she wanted to get an abortion without telling her mother. **She refused to talk to her mom, saying she was worried about her safety.** Looking for advice, the counselor contacted an ACLU attorney, who said the student was entitled to privacy. The counselor urged the principal to contact the ACLU attorney. The principal refused. Two days later, the attorney reached out to the principal to discuss the issue. During that conversation, the principal disagreed with the attorney and told her that he was going to tell the student's mom. The attorney filed a petition for a temporary restraining order blocking the principal from contacting the student's mother about the pregnancy. The court granted the order.

Four months later, the counselor received a non-renewal notice due to insubordination and breach of student confidentiality. The local school board upheld the decision. The counselor sought review. Appeal reached the state board of education, which reversed the ruling and ordered the counselor to be reinstated. But it didn't address remedies like back pay.

The district appealed, and the counselor cross-appealed, saying she was entitled to remedies. The state supreme court found:

- district policy only required the counselor to discuss disagreements with the principal. She did, so she wasn't insubordinate, and
- talking to the attorney didn't violate the student's privacy rights, because a FERPA exception allows sharing info if it's necessary to "protect the health or safety of a student." The girl said she had safety concerns about telling her mom, so the exception applied.

The ruling to reinstate the guidance counselor was affirmed, and the case was remanded to determine whether she was entitled to remedies including back pay. *Appeal of Farmington School Dist.*, 138 A.3d 496 (N.H. 2016).

◆   An Ohio court refused to dismiss a claim that a middle school principal violated a student's privacy rights by contacting her healthcare provider to obtain her medical information. As the student was recovering from back surgery, the hospital prepared medical excuses and accommodation forms for the school. Her parents met with school officials to craft a Section 504 plan so the girl could return to school. After the meeting ended, the principal contacted the hospital without obtaining permission. At that time, he allegedly spoke to an administrative assistant at the hospital about the girl's medical condition and treatment, persuaded the administrative assistant to make changes to the hospital's paperwork and provided misleading information to the administrative assistant to induce the paperwork changes. The girl's parents sued the district, the board, the principal, the hospital and the administrative assistant. School defendants asked the court to dismiss the claims, saying they were entitled to immunity. The court dismissed the claims against the board and the district. But it refused to dismiss several claims against the principal, including improperly inducing the hospital employee to disclose nonpublic medical info, bad-faith conduct and invasion of privacy. The principal appealed, saying he was entitled to immunity. But **if proven true, the allegations could show the principal "may have attempted to supersede ... the protections to [the girl's] health and safety as duly advised by her own physician,"** the court explained. Further, determining whether conduct is "malicious, wanton, reckless or in bad faith are generally for jury to decide," the court held. The claims had to proceed. *Schaad v. Buckeye Valley Local School Dist. Board of Educ.*, No. 15-CAE 080063, 2016 WL 693546 (Ohio Ct. App. 2/12/16).

◆   A New Hampshire federal judge refused to order a district to provide a handler for a student's service dog. An eight-year-old nonverbal student suffered from seizures. His trained service dog alerted to seizures. The boy couldn't handle the dog for two reasons: He used a "gait belt" for balance, and he's nonverbal so he couldn't issue voice commands. Administrators

told the boy's parents that they had to provide a handler for the dog. They
sued and asked the court to order the school to pay an employee to handle
the dog. To get an injunction, the parents had to show – among other things
– that they were likely to win their claim. They didn't. The court noted that
the dog needed to be handled all day long – rather than just for short
intervals such as during short breaks to relieve itself. But the ADA
specifically says that public schools aren't required to care for or supervise
a service animal. The parents weren't likely to win their claim, so the
injunction was denied. *Riley v. School Administrative Unit #23,* No. 15-cv-
152-SM, 2016 WL 183525 (D.N.H. 1/14/16).

◆   School defendants were entitled to immunity in a lawsuit that claimed
a search crossed the line, a New York court held. A 14-year-old girl was
called to the nurse's office to meet with the nurse, the psychologist and the
social worker – all employees of the district. Someone reported that the girl
had been cutting herself. The nurse ordered the girl to lift her shirt to her
bra and pull her pants down to her ankles. No indication of self-harm was
found. Unconvinced, the social worker searched the girl's social media
accounts to see if photos showed signs of cutting. None did. The girl's mom
sued, alleging violations of the First Amendment. The school defendants
asked the court to dismiss the claim, saying they were entitled to immunity.
Not all searches are protected by the Fourth Amendment. Whether it applies
depends on the nature of the search, the court said. For example, if the
purpose of the search is to find evidence of a crime, then the Fourth
Amendment applies. But **the law's fuzzy on whether searches for
medical purposes are protected by the Fourth Amendment**. In this case,
both searches were made for medical reasons – to see if the girl had injured
herself, the court held. "Given the contradictory holdings from different
circuits," the court concluded that it was not clearly established that a search
for medical purposes would violate the student's Fourth Amendment rights.
So immunity was appropriate, the court determined. *Masciotta v. Clarkson
Cent. School Dist.*, 136 F.Supp.3d 527 (S.D.N.Y. 2015).

◆   A Pennsylvania federal judge refused to dismiss claims of a disabled
student who was expelled. The student had ADD and Dysthymic Disorder.
In 2011, he admitted he gave synthetic marijuana – known as "spice"– to a
classmate. At the time, spice was still legal but considered contraband, as
per school policy. He was recommended for expulsion. At the hearing, **the
board found the student guilty of possessing contraband at school**. He
was expelled for more than a year. His mom sued, alleging a laundry list of
claims. The judge tossed the majority but allowed two to continue. His
mother stated valid *prima facie* claims that the school violated:
•   the student's right to due process and discriminated against him
    based on his disability by failing to consider it during the expulsion
    hearing, and

- Section 504 of the Rehabilitation Act by failing to provide the student with the same protection received by other non-disabled students because the board didn't consider his disability at the hearing.

Because questions existed, the court held the claims could proceed. *K.A. v. Abington Heights School Dist.*, 2015 WL 1812821, No. 3:12-CV-2486 (M.D. Pa. 4/20/15).

◆ A school's policies on service dogs violated Title II of the Americans with Disabilities Act (ADA), a Florida federal court held. A student had cerebral palsy and seizures. His mother got a trained service dog for him. The district said it would allow the animal at school if the mother:

- paid for liability insurance to cover the dog and listed the district as an insured party, as per district policy
- provided documentation for the dog's vaccinations as per district's policy, which exceeded state-law requirements, and
- provided a handler for the dog.

The mother sued, claiming the district's policies violated the ADA and its failure to provide reasonable accommodations was discriminatory. At trial, the court looked at the district's policy alongside the Title II regs regarding service dogs. The court found the liability insurance requirement violated the ADA because those costs were "over and above what other students" pay for school fees, the vaccination requirement was discriminatory as it "exceeded state law regarding the regulation of dogs permitted at school," and the requirement for a separate handler violated the ADA, as the regs clearly "permit tethering [to a wheel chair] as handling."

The district argued the student couldn't act as the dog's handler because he couldn't take the dog outside alone. It noted schools aren't responsible for care and supervision of service dogs. The court rejected that argument, explaining "care and supervision" entails much more – feeding, training, grooming – than just relief breaks. **A reasonable accommodation would be to have a staffer go outside with the student and the dog**, the court explained. So the school had to allow the dog – and drop the tacked-on requirements. *Alboniga v. School Board of Broward County Florida*, No. 14-CIV-60085-BLOOM/Valle, 2015 WL 541751 (S.D. Fla. 2/10/15).

◆ Indiana's highest court ruled a school might've concealed info about a student death, so her parents' suit could go forward. The student had Down syndrome and had trouble eating. Her dining plan required the school to monitor her food intake and cut up her food. In 2009, the student choked after a paraprofessional failed to cut up her food. No one attempted CPR or the Heimlich maneuver. The nurse arrived 10 minutes later but was unable to clear the student's airway. That's when 911 was called. The student died three days later. Meanwhile, the cafeteria supervisor told staffers they'd be fired if they spoke to anyone about the incident.

Months later, a cafeteria worker told the student's parents "things were not done properly." They filed a notice of tort claim in January 2010 and filed suit about six months later. The state asked for judgment, saying the parents didn't file the notice of tort claim within 180 days. The case went all the way to the state supreme court. State law generally bars tort claims that aren't filed within 180 days. But an exception applies if the defendant:

- "has actual knowledge of a wrongful act and intentionally concealed it from the plaintiff," or
- took action that was "calculated to prevent inquiry or to mislead."

The court held **a reasonable jury could find the school covered up info about the student's death**. The exception applied, so the case was remanded. *Lyons v. Richmond Community School Corporation*, 19 N.E.3d 254 (Ind. 2014).

CHAPTER EIGHT

Statutes and Regulations

The following federal statutes and regulations address school safety and security issues.

I. SAFE AND DRUG-FREE SCHOOLS AND COMMUNITIES ACT

20 USC § 7101 et seq.

SUBCHAPTER IV - 21ST CENTURY SCHOOLS

PART A - SAFE AND DRUG-FREE SCHOOLS AND COMMUNITIES
7101. Short title.
7102. Purpose.
7103. Authorization of appropriations.

SUBPART 1 - STATE GRANTS
7111. Reservations and allotments.
    (a) Reservations.
    (b) State allotments.
    (c) Limitation.
7112. Reservation of State funds for safe and drug-free schools.
    (a) State reservation for the chief executive officer of a State.
    (b) In State distribution.
    (c) State activities.
7113. State application.
    (a) In general.
    (b) Interim application.
    (c) Approval process.
7114. Local educational agency program.
    (a) In general.
    (b) Eligibility.
    (c) Development.
    (d) Contents of applications.

PART A - SAFE AND DRUG-FREE SCHOOLS AND COMMUNITIES

Sec. 7101. Short title
This part may be cited as the "Safe and Drug-Free Schools and Communities Act."

Sec. 7102. Purpose
The purpose of this part is to support programs that prevent violence in and around schools; that prevent the illegal use of alcohol, tobacco, and drugs; that involve parents and communities; and that are coordinated with related Federal, State, school, and community efforts and resources to foster a safe and drug-free learning environment that supports student academic achievement, through the provision of Federal assistance to -

(1) States for grants to local educational agencies and consortia of such agencies to establish, operate, and improve local programs of school drug

and violence prevention and early intervention;

(2) States for grants to, and contracts with, community-based organizations and public and private entities for programs of drug and violence prevention and early intervention, including community-wide drug and violence prevention planning and organizing activities;

(3) States for development, training, technical assistance, and coordination activities; and

(4) public and private entities to provide technical assistance; conduct training, demonstrations, and evaluation; and to provide supplementary services and community-wide drug and violence prevention planning and organizing activities for the prevention of drug use and violence among students and youth.

Sec. 7103. Authorization of appropriations

There are authorized to be appropriated -

(1) $650,000,000 for fiscal year 2002, and such sums as may be necessary for each of the 5 succeeding fiscal years, for State grants under subpart 1 of this part; and

(2) such sums for fiscal year 2002, and for each of the 5 succeeding fiscal years, for national programs under subpart 2 of this part.

SUBPART 1 - STATE GRANTS

Sec. 7111. Reservations and allotments

(a) Reservations

(1) In general

From the amount made available under section 7103(1) of this title to carry out this subpart for each fiscal year, the Secretary -

(A) shall reserve 1 percent or $4,750,000 (whichever is greater) of such amount for grants to Guam, American Samoa, the United States Virgin Islands, and the Commonwealth of the Northern Mariana Islands, to be allotted in accordance with the Secretary's determination of their respective needs and to carry out programs described in this subpart;

(B) shall reserve 1 percent or $4,750,000 (whichever is greater) of such amount for the Secretary of the Interior to carry out programs described in this subpart for Indian youth; and

(C) shall reserve 0.2 percent of such amount for Native Hawaiians to be used under section 7117 of this title to carry out programs described in this subpart.

(2) Other reservations

From the amount made available under section 7103(2) of this title to carry out subpart 2 of this part for each fiscal year, the Secretary -

(A) may reserve not more than $2,000,000 for the national impact evaluation required by section 7132(a) of this title;

(B) notwithstanding section 3 of the No Child Left Behind Act of 2001, shall reserve an amount necessary to make continuation grants to grantees under the Safe Schools/Healthy Students initiative (under the same terms and conditions as provided for in the grants involved).

(b) State allotments

(1) In general

Except as provided in paragraph (2), the Secretary shall, for each fiscal year, allot among the States -

(A) one-half of the remainder not reserved under subsection (a) of this section according to the ratio between the school-aged population of each State and the school-aged population of all the States; and

(B) one-half of such remainder according to the ratio between the amount each State received under section 6334 of this title for the preceding year and the sum of such amounts received by all the States.

(2) Minimum

For any fiscal year, no State shall be allotted under this subsection an amount that is less than the greater of -

(A) one-half of 1 percent of the total amount allotted to all the States under this subsection; or

(B) the amount such State received for fiscal year 2001 under section 4111 as such section was in effect the day preceding January 8, 2002.

(3) Reallotment

(A) Reallotment for failure to apply

If any State does not apply for an allotment under this subpart for a fiscal year, the Secretary shall reallot the amount of the State's allotment to the remaining States in accordance with this section.

(B) Reallotment of unused funds

The Secretary may reallot any amount of any allotment to a State if the Secretary determines that the State will be unable to use such amount within 2 years of such allotment. Such reallotments shall be made on the same basis as allotments are made under paragraph (1).

(4) Definition

In this section the term "State" means each of the 50 States, the District of Columbia, and the Commonwealth of Puerto Rico.

(c) Limitation

Amounts appropriated under section 7103(2) of this title for a fiscal year may not be increased above the amounts appropriated under such section for the previous fiscal year unless the amount appropriated under section 7103(1) of this title for the fiscal year involved are at least 10 percent greater that (!2) the amounts appropriated under such section 7103(1) of this title for the previous fiscal year.

Sec. 7112. Reservation of State funds for safe and drug-free schools

(a) State reservation for the chief executive officer of a State

(1) In general

The chief executive officer of a State may reserve not more than 20 percent of the total amount allocated to a State under section 7111(b) of this title for each fiscal year to award competitive grants and contracts to local educational agencies, community-based organizations (including community anti-drug coalitions) other public entities and private organizations, and consortia thereof. Such grants and contracts shall be used to carry out the comprehensive State plan described in section 7113(a) of this title through programs or activities that complement and support activities of local educational agencies described in section 7115(b) of this title. Such officer shall award grants based on -

(A) the quality of the program or activity proposed; and

(B) how the program or activity meets the principles of effectiveness described in section 7115(a) of this title.

(2) Priority

In making such grants and contracts under this section, a chief executive officer shall give priority to programs and activities that prevent illegal drug use and violence for -

(A) children and youth who are not normally served by State educational agencies or local educational agencies; or

(B) populations that need special services or additional resources (such as youth in juvenile detention facilities, runaway or homeless children and youth, pregnant and parenting teenagers, and school dropouts).

(3) Special consideration

In awarding funds under paragraph (1), a chief executive officer shall give special consideration to grantees that pursue a comprehensive approach to drug and violence prevention that includes providing and incorporating mental health services related to drug and violence prevention in their program.

(4) Peer review

Grants or contracts awarded under this section shall be subject to a peer review process.

(5) Use of funds

Grants and contracts under this section shall be used to implement drug and violence prevention activities, including -

(A) activities that complement and support local educational agency activities under section 7115 of this title, including developing and implementing activities to prevent and reduce violence associated with prejudice and intolerance;

(B) dissemination of information about drug and violence prevention; and

(C) development and implementation of community-wide drug and violence prevention planning and organizing.

(6) Administrative costs

The chief executive officer of a State may use not more than 3 percent of the amount described in paragraph (1) for the administrative costs incurred in carrying out the duties of such officer under this section.

(b) In State distribution

(1) In general

A State educational agency shall distribute not less than 93 percent of the amount made available to the State under section 7111(b) of this title, less the amount reserved under subsection (a) of this section, to its local educational agencies.

(2) State administration costs

(A) In general

A State educational agency may use not more than 3 percent of the amount made available to the State under section 7111(b) of this title for each fiscal year less the amount reserved under subsection (a) of this section, for State educational agency administrative costs, including the implementation of the uniform management information and reporting system as provided for under subsection (c)(3) of this section.

(B) Additional amounts for the uniform management information system

In the case of fiscal year 2002, a State educational agency may, in addition to amounts provided for in subparagraph (A), use 1 percent of the amount made available to the State educational agency under section 7111(b) of this title for each fiscal year less the amount reserved under subsection (a) of this section, for implementation of the uniform management information and reporting system as provided for under subsection (c)(3) of this section.

(c) State activities

(1) In general

A State educational agency may use not more than 5 percent of the amount made available to the State under section 7111(b) of this title for each fiscal year less the amount reserved under subsection (a) of this section, for activities described in this subsection.

(2) Activities

A State educational agency shall use the amounts described in paragraph (1), either directly, or through grants and contracts, to plan, develop, and implement capacity building, technical assistance and training, evaluation, program improvement services, and coordination activities for local educational agencies, community-based organizations, and other public and private entities. Such uses -

(A) shall meet the principles of effectiveness described in section 7115(a) of this title;

(B) shall complement and support local uses of funds under section 7115(b) of this title;

(C) shall be in accordance with the purposes of this part; and

(D) may include, among others activities -

(i) identification, development, evaluation, and dissemination of drug and violence prevention strategies, programs, activities, and other information;

(ii) training, technical assistance, and demonstration projects to address violence that is associated with prejudice and intolerance; and

(iii) financial assistance to enhance drug and violence

prevention resources available in areas that serve large numbers of low-income children, are sparsely populated, or have other special needs.

(3) Uniform management information and reporting system

(A) Information and statistics

A State shall establish a uniform management information and reporting system.

(B) Uses of funds

A State may use funds described in subparagraphs (A) and (B) of subsection (b)(2) of this section, either directly or through grants and contracts, to implement the uniform management information and reporting system described in subparagraph (A), for the collection of information on -

(i) truancy rates;

(ii) the frequency, seriousness, and incidence of violence and drug-related offenses resulting in suspensions and expulsions in elementary schools and secondary schools in the State;

(iii) the types of curricula, programs, and services provided by the chief executive officer, the State educational agency, local educational agencies, and other recipients of funds under this subpart; and

(iv) the incidence and prevalence, age of onset, perception of health risk, and perception of social disapproval of drug use and violence by youth in schools and communities.

(C) Compilation of statistics

In compiling the statistics required for the uniform management information and reporting system, the offenses described in subparagraph (B)(ii) shall be defined pursuant to the State's criminal code, but shall not identify victims of crimes or persons accused of crimes. The collected data shall include incident reports by school officials, anonymous student surveys, and anonymous teacher surveys.

(D) Reporting

The information described under subparagraph (B) shall be reported to the public and the data referenced in clauses (i) and (ii) of such subparagraph shall be reported to the State on a school-by-school basis.

(E) Limitation

Nothing in this subsection shall be construed to authorize the Secretary to require particular policies, procedures, or practices with respect to crimes committed on school property or school security.

Sec. 7113. State application

(a) In general

In order to receive an allotment under section 7111(b) of this title for any fiscal year, a State shall submit to the Secretary, at such time as the Secretary may require, an application that -

(1) contains a comprehensive plan for the use of funds by the State educational agency and the chief executive officer of the State to provide safe, orderly, and drug-free schools and communities through programs and

activities that complement and support activities of local educational agencies under section 7115(b) of this title, that comply with the principles of effectiveness under section 7115(a) of this title, and that otherwise are in accordance with the purpose of this part;

(2) describes how activities funded under this subpart will foster a safe and drug-free learning environment that supports academic achievement;

(3) provides an assurance that the application was developed in consultation and coordination with appropriate State officials and others, including the chief executive officer, the chief State school officer, the head of the State alcohol and drug abuse agency, the heads of the State health and mental health agencies, the head of the State criminal justice planning agency, the head of the State child welfare agency, the head of the State board of education, or their designees, and representatives of parents, students, and community-based organizations;

(4) describes how the State educational agency will coordinate such agency's activities under this subpart with the chief executive officer's drug and violence prevention programs under this subpart and with the prevention efforts of other State agencies and other programs, as appropriate, in accordance with (5) provides an assurance that funds reserved under section 7112(a) of this title will not duplicate the efforts of the State educational agency and local educational agencies with regard to the provision of school-based drug and violence prevention activities and that those funds will be used to serve populations not normally served by the State educational agencies and local educational agencies and populations that need special services, such as school dropouts, suspended and expelled students, youth in detention centers, runaway or homeless children and youth, and pregnant and parenting youth;

(6) provides an assurance that the State will cooperate with, and assist, the Secretary in conducting data collection as required by section 7132 of this title;

(7) provides an assurance that the local educational agencies in the State will comply with the provisions of section 7881 of this title pertaining to the participation of private school children and teachers in the programs and activities under this subpart;

(8) provides an assurance that funds under this subpart will be used to increase the level of State, local, and other non-Federal funds that would, in the absence of funds under this subpart, be made available for programs and activities authorized under this subpart, and in no case supplant such State, local, and other non-Federal funds;

(9) contains the results of a needs assessment conducted by the State for drug and violence prevention programs, which shall be based on ongoing State evaluation activities, including data on -

(A) the incidence and prevalence of illegal drug use and violence among youth in schools and communities, including the age of onset, the perception of health risks, and the perception of social disapproval among such youth;

(B) the prevalence of risk factors, including high or increasing rates of reported cases of child abuse or domestic violence;

(C) the prevalence of protective factors, buffers, or assets; and

(D) other variables in the school and community identified through scientifically based research;

(10) provides a statement of the State's performance measures for drug and violence prevention programs and activities to be funded under this subpart that will be focused on student behavior and attitudes, derived from the needs assessment described in paragraph (9), and be developed in consultation between the State and local officials, and that consist of -

(A) performance indicators for drug and violence prevention programs and activities; and

(B) levels of performance for each performance indicator;

(11) describes the procedures the State will use for assessing and publicly reporting progress toward meeting the performance measures described in paragraph (10);

(12) provides an assurance that the State application will be available for public review after submission of the application;

(13) describes the special outreach activities that will be carried out by the State educational agency and the chief executive officer of the State to maximize the participation of community-based organizations of demonstrated effectiveness that provide services such as mentoring programs in low-income communities;

(14) describes how funds will be used by the State educational agency and the chief executive officer of the State to support, develop, and implement community-wide comprehensive drug and violence prevention planning and organizing activities;

(15) describes how input from parents will be sought regarding the use of funds by the State educational agency and the chief executive officer of the State;

(16) describes how the State educational agency will review applications from local educational agencies, including how the agency will receive input from parents in such review;

(17) describes how the State educational agency will monitor the implementation of activities under this subpart, and provide technical assistance for local educational agencies, community-based organizations, other public entities, and private organizations;

(18) describes how the chief executive officer of the State will award funds under section 7112(a) of this title and implement a plan for monitoring the performance of, and providing technical assistance to, recipients of such funds; and

(19) includes any other information the Secretary may require.

(b) Interim application

(1) Authority

Notwithstanding any other provision of this section, a State may submit for fiscal year 2002 a 1-year interim application and plan for the use of funds under this subpart that is consistent with the requirements of this section and contains such information as the Secretary may specify in regulations.

(2) Purpose

The purpose of such interim application and plan shall be to afford the State the opportunity to fully develop and review such State's application and comprehensive plan otherwise required by this section.

(3) Exception

A State may not receive a grant under this subpart for a fiscal year after fiscal year 2002 unless the Secretary has approved such State's application and comprehensive plan as described in subsection (a) of this section.

(c) Approval process

(1) Deemed approval

An application submitted by a State pursuant to this section shall undergo peer review by the Secretary and shall be deemed to be approved by the Secretary unless the Secretary makes a written determination, prior to the expiration of the 120-day period beginning on the date on which the Secretary received the application, that the application is not in compliance with this subpart.

(2) Disapproval

The Secretary shall not finally disapprove the application, except after giving the State educational agency and the chief executive officer of the State notice and an opportunity for a hearing.

(3) Notification

If the Secretary finds that the application is not in compliance, in whole or in part, with this subpart, the Secretary shall -

(A) give the State educational agency and the chief executive officer of the State notice and an opportunity for a hearing; and

(B) notify the State educational agency and the chief executive officer of the State of the finding of noncompliance, and in such notification, shall -

(i) cite the specific provisions in the application that are not in compliance; and

(ii) request additional information, only as to the noncompliant provisions, needed to make the application compliant.

(4) Response

If the State educational agency and the chief executive officer of the State respond to the Secretary's notification described in paragraph (3)(B) during the 45-day period beginning on the date on which the agency received the notification, and resubmit the application with the requested information described in paragraph (3)(B)(ii), the Secretary shall approve or disapprove such application prior to the later of -

(A) the expiration of the 45-day period beginning on the date on which the application is resubmitted; or

(B) the expiration of the 120-day period described in paragraph (1).

(5) Failure to respond

If the State educational agency and the chief executive officer of the State do not respond to the Secretary's notification described in paragraph (3)(B) during the 45-day period beginning on the date on which the agency received the notification, such application shall be deemed to be disapproved.

Sec. 7114. Local educational agency program

(a) In general

(1) Funds to local educational agencies

A State shall provide the amount made available to the State under this subpart, less the amounts reserved under section 7112 of this title to local educational agencies for drug and violence prevention and education programs and activities as follows:

(A) 60 percent of such amount based on the relative amount such agencies received under part A of subchapter I of this chapter for the preceding fiscal year.

(B) 40 percent of such amount based on the relative enrollments in public and private nonprofit elementary schools and secondary schools within the boundaries of such agencies.

(2) Administrative costs

Of the amount received under paragraph (1), a local educational agency may use not more than 2 percent for the administrative costs of carrying out its responsibilities under this subpart.

(3) Return of funds to State; reallocation

(A) Return

Except as provided in subparagraph (B), upon the expiration of the 1-year period beginning on the date on which a local educational agency receives its allocation under this subpart -

(i) such agency shall return to the State educational agency any funds from such allocation that remain unobligated; and

(ii) the State educational agency shall reallocate any such amount to local educational agencies that have submitted plans for using such amount for programs or activities on a timely basis.

(B) Carryover

In any fiscal year, a local educational agency, may retain for obligation in the succeeding fiscal year -

(i) an amount equal to not more than 25 percent of the allocation it received under this subpart for such fiscal year; or

(ii) upon a demonstration of good cause by such agency and approval by the State educational agency, an amount that exceeds 25 percent of such allocation.

(C) Reallocation

If a local educational agency chooses not to apply to receive the amount allocated to such agency under this subsection, or if such agency's application under subsection (d) of this section is disapproved by the State educational agency, the State educational agency shall reallocate such amount to one or more of its other local educational agencies.

(b) Eligibility

To be eligible to receive a subgrant under this subpart, a local educational agency desiring a subgrant shall submit an application to the State educational agency in accordance with subsection (d) of this section. Such an application shall be amended, as necessary, to reflect changes in the activities and programs of the local educational agency.

(c) Development

(1) Consultation

(A) In general

A local educational agency shall develop its application through timely and meaningful consultation with State and local government representatives, representatives of schools to be served (including private schools), teachers and other staff, parents, students, community-based organizations, and others with relevant and demonstrated expertise in drug and violence prevention activities (such as medical, mental health, and law enforcement professionals).

(B) Continued consultation

On an ongoing basis, the local educational agency shall consult with such representatives and organizations in order to seek advice regarding how best to coordinate such agency's activities under this subpart with other related strategies, programs, and activities being conducted in the community.

(2) Design and development

To ensure timely and meaningful consultation under paragraph (1), a local educational agency at the initial stages of design and development of a program or activity shall consult, in accordance with this subsection, with appropriate entities and persons on issues regarding the design and development of the program or activity, including efforts to meet the principles of effectiveness described in section 7115(a) of this title.

(d) Contents of applications

An application submitted by a local educational agency under this section shall contain -

(1) an assurance that the activities or programs to be funded comply with the principles of effectiveness described in section 7115(a) of this title and foster a safe and drug-free learning environment that supports academic achievement;

(2) a detailed explanation of the local educational agency's comprehensive plan for drug and violence prevention, including a description of -

(A) how the plan will be coordinated with programs under this chapter, and other Federal, State, and local programs for drug and violence prevention, in accordance with section 7846 of this title;

(B) the local educational agency's performance measures for drug and violence prevention programs and activities, that shall consist of -

(i) performance indicators for drug and violence prevention

programs and activities; including -

        (I) specific reductions in the prevalence of identified risk factors; and

        (II) specific increases in the prevalence of protective factors, buffers, or assets if any have been identified; and

      (ii) levels of performance for each performance indicator;

    (C) how such agency will assess and publicly report progress toward attaining its performance measures;

    (D) the drug and violence prevention activity or program to be funded, including how the activity or program will meet the principles of effectiveness described in section 7115(a) of this title, and the means of evaluating such activity or program; and

    (E) how the services will be targeted to schools and students with the greatest need;

    (3) a description for how the results of the evaluations of the effectiveness of the program will be used to refine, improve, and strengthen the program;

    (4) an assurance that funds under this subpart will be used to increase the level of State, local, and other non-Federal funds that would, in the absence of funds under this subpart, be made available for programs and activities authorized under this subpart, and in no case supplant such State, local, and other non-Federal funds;

    (5) a description of the mechanisms used to provide effective notice to the community of an intention to submit an application under this subpart;

    (6) an assurance that drug and violence prevention programs supported under this subpart convey a clear and consistent message that acts of violence and the illegal use of drugs are wrong and harmful;

    (7) an assurance that the applicant has, or the schools to be served have, a plan for keeping schools safe and drug-free that includes -

    (A) appropriate and effective school discipline policies that prohibit disorderly conduct, the illegal possession of weapons, and the illegal use, possession, distribution, and sale of tobacco, alcohol, and other drugs by students;

    (B) security procedures at school and while students are on the way to and from school;

    (C) prevention activities that are designed to create and maintain safe, disciplined, and drug-free environments;

    (D) a crisis management plan for responding to violent or traumatic incidents on school grounds; and

    (E) a code of conduct policy for all students that clearly states the responsibilities of students, teachers, and administrators in maintaining a classroom environment that -

      (i) allows a teacher to communicate effectively with all students in the class;

      (ii) allows all students in the class to learn;

      (iii) has consequences that are fair, and developmentally

appropriate;

      (iv) considers the student and the circumstances of the situation; and

      (v) is enforced accordingly;

(8) an assurance that the application and any waiver request under section 7115(a)(3) of this title will be available for public review after submission of the application; and

(9) such other assurances, goals, and objectives identified through scientifically based research that the State may reasonably require in accordance with the purpose of this part.

(e) Review of application

(1) In general

In reviewing local applications under this section, a State educational agency shall use a peer review process or other methods of assuring the quality of such applications.

(2) Considerations

In determining whether to approve the application of a local educational agency under this section, a State educational agency shall consider the quality of application and the extent to which the application meets the principles of effectiveness described in section 7115(a) of this title.

(f) Approval process

(1) Deemed approval

An application submitted by a local educational agency pursuant to this section shall be deemed to be approved by the State educational agency unless the State educational agency makes a written determination, prior to the expiration of the 120-day period beginning on the date on which the State educational agency received the application, that the application is not in compliance with this subpart.

(2) Disapproval

The State educational agency shall not finally disapprove the application, except after giving the local educational agency notice and opportunity for a hearing.

(3) Notification

If the State educational agency finds that the application is not in compliance, in whole or in part, with this subpart, the State educational agency shall -

      (A) give the local educational agency notice and an opportunity for a hearing; and

      (B) notify the local educational agency of the finding of noncompliance, and in such notification, shall -

            (i) cite the specific provisions in the application that are not in compliance; and

            (ii) request additional information, only as to the noncompliant provisions, needed to make the application compliant.

(4) Response

If the local educational agency responds to the State educational agency's notification described in paragraph (3)(B) during the 45-day period beginning on the date on which the agency received the notification, and resubmits the application with the requested information described in paragraph (3)(B)(ii), the State educational agency shall approve or disapprove such application prior to the later of -

(A) the expiration of the 45-day period beginning on the date on which the application is resubmitted; or

(B) the expiration of the 120-day period described in paragraph (1).

(5) Failure to respond

If the local educational agency does not respond to the State educational agency's notification described in paragraph (3)(B) during the 45-day period beginning on the date on which the agency received the notification, such application shall be deemed to be disapproved.

Sec. 7115. Authorized activities

(a) Principles of effectiveness

(1) In general

For a program or activity developed pursuant to this subpart to meet the principles of effectiveness, such program or activity shall -

(A) be based on an assessment of objective data regarding the incidence of violence and illegal drug use in the elementary schools and secondary schools and communities to be served, including an objective analysis of the current conditions and consequences regarding violence and illegal drug use, including delinquency and serious discipline problems, among students who attend such schools (including private school students who participate in the drug and violence prevention program) that is based on ongoing local assessment or evaluation activities;

(B) be based on an established set of performance measures aimed at ensuring that the elementary schools and secondary schools and communities to be served by the program have a safe, orderly, and drug-free learning environment;

(C) be based on scientifically based research that provides evidence that the program to be used will reduce violence and illegal drug use;

(D) be based on an analysis of the data reasonably available at the time, of the prevalence of risk factors, including high or increasing rates of reported cases of child abuse and domestic violence; protective factors, buffers, assets; or other variables in schools and communities in the State identified through scientifically based research; and

(E) include meaningful and ongoing consultation with and input from parents in the development of the application and administration of the program or activity.

(2) Periodic evaluation

(A) Requirement

The program or activity shall undergo a periodic evaluation to assess its progress toward reducing violence and illegal drug use in schools to be served based on performance measures described in section

7114(d)(2)(B) of this title.

(B) Use of results

The results shall be used to refine, improve, and strengthen the program, and to refine the performance measures, and shall also be made available to the public upon request, with public notice of such availability provided.

(3) Waiver

A local educational agency may apply to the State for a waiver of the requirement of subsection (a)(1)(C) of this section to allow innovative activities or programs that demonstrate substantial likelihood of success.

(b) Local educational agency activities

(1) Program requirements

A local educational agency shall use funds made available under section 7114 of this title to develop, implement, and evaluate comprehensive programs and activities, which are coordinated with other school and community-based services and programs, that shall -

(A) foster a safe and drug-free learning environment that supports academic achievement;

(B) be consistent with the principles of effectiveness described in subsection (a)(1) of this section;

(C) be designed to -

(i) prevent or reduce violence; the use, possession and distribution of illegal drugs; and delinquency; and

(ii) create a well-disciplined environment conducive to learning, which includes consultation between teachers, principals, and other school personnel to identify early warning signs of drug use and violence and to provide behavioral interventions as part of classroom management efforts; and

(D) include activities to -

(i) promote the involvement of parents in the activity or program;

(ii) promote coordination with community groups and coalitions, and government agencies; and

(iii) distribute information about the local educational agency's needs, goals, and programs under this subpart.

(2) Authorized activities

Each local educational agency, or consortium of such agencies, that receives a subgrant under this subpart may use such funds to carry out activities that comply with the principles of effectiveness described in subsection (a) of this section, such as the following:

(A) Age appropriate and developmentally based activities that -

(i) address the consequences of violence and the illegal use of drugs, as appropriate;

(ii) promote a sense of individual responsibility;

(iii) teach students that most people do not illegally use drugs;

(iv) teach students to recognize social and peer pressure to use drugs illegally and the skills for resisting illegal drug use;

(v) teach students about the dangers of emerging drugs;

(vi) engage students in the learning process; and

(vii) incorporate activities in secondary schools that reinforce prevention activities implemented in elementary schools.

(B) Activities that involve families, community sectors (which may include appropriately trained seniors), and a variety of drug and violence prevention providers in setting clear expectations against violence and illegal use of drugs and appropriate consequences for violence and illegal use of drugs.

(C) Dissemination of drug and violence prevention information to schools and the community.

(D) Professional development and training for, and involvement of, school personnel, pupil services personnel, parents, and interested community members in prevention, education, early identification and intervention, mentoring, or rehabilitation referral, as related to drug and violence prevention.

(E) Drug and violence prevention activities that may include the following:

(i) Community-wide planning and organizing activities to reduce violence and illegal drug use, which may include gang activity prevention.

(ii) Acquiring and installing metal detectors, electronic locks, surveillance cameras, or other related equipment and technologies.

(iii) Reporting criminal offenses committed on school property.

(iv) Developing and implementing comprehensive school security plans or obtaining technical assistance concerning such plans, which may include obtaining a security assessment or assistance from the School Security and Technology Resource Center at the Sandia National Laboratory located in Albuquerque, New Mexico.

(v) Supporting safe zones of passage activities that ensure that students travel safely to and from school, which may include bicycle and pedestrian safety programs.

(vi) The hiring and mandatory training, based on scientific research, of school security personnel (including school resource officers) who interact with students in support of youth drug and violence prevention activities under this part that are implemented in the school.

(vii) Expanded and improved school-based mental health services related to illegal drug use and violence, including early identification of violence and illegal drug use, assessment, and direct or group counseling services provided to students, parents, families, and school personnel by qualified school-based mental health service providers.

(viii) Conflict resolution programs, including peer mediation programs that educate and train peer mediators and a designated faculty supervisor, and youth anti-crime and anti-drug councils and activities.

(ix) Alternative education programs or services for violent or drug abusing students that reduce the need for suspension or expulsion or that serve students who have been suspended or expelled from the regular educational settings, including programs or services to assist students to make continued progress toward meeting the State academic achievement standards and to reenter the regular education setting.

(x) Counseling, mentoring, referral services, and other student assistance practices and programs, including assistance provided by qualified school-based mental health services providers and the training of teachers by school-based mental health services providers in appropriate identification and intervention techniques for students at risk of violent behavior and illegal use of drugs.

(xi) Programs that encourage students to seek advice from, and to confide in, a trusted adult regarding concerns about violence and illegal drug use.

(xii) Drug and violence prevention activities designed to reduce truancy.

(xiii) Age-appropriate, developmentally-based violence prevention and education programs that address victimization associated with prejudice and intolerance, and that include activities designed to help students develop a sense of individual responsibility and respect for the rights of others, and to resolve conflicts without violence.

(xiv) Consistent with the fourth amendment to the Constitution of the United States, the testing of a student for illegal drug use or the inspecting of a student's locker for weapons or illegal drugs or drug paraphernalia, including at the request of or with the consent of a parent or legal guardian of the student, if the local educational agency elects to so test or inspect.

(xv) Emergency intervention services following traumatic crisis events, such as a shooting, major accident, or a drug-related incident that have disrupted the learning environment.

(xvi) Establishing or implementing a system for transferring suspension and expulsion records, consistent with section 1232g of this title, by a local educational agency to any public or private elementary school or secondary school.

(xvii) Developing and implementing character education programs, as a component of drug and violence prevention programs, that take into account the views of parents of the students for whom the program is intended and such students, such as a program described in subpart 3 of part D of subchapter V of this chapter.

(xviii) Establishing and maintaining a school safety hotline.

(xix) Community service, including community service performed by expelled students, and service-learning projects.

(xx) Conducting a nationwide background check of each local educational agency employee, regardless of when hired, and prospective employees for the purpose of determining whether the employee or prospective employee has been convicted of a crime that bears upon the employee's fitness -

(I) to be responsible for the safety or well-being of children;

(II) to serve in the particular capacity in which the employee or prospective employee is or will be employed; or

(III) to otherwise be employed by the local educational agency.

(xxi) Programs to train school personnel to identify warning signs of youth suicide and to create an action plan to help youth at risk of suicide.

(xxii) Programs that respond to the needs of students who are faced with domestic violence or child abuse.

(F) The evaluation of any of the activities authorized under this subsection and the collection of objective data used to assess program needs, program implementation, or program success in achieving program goals and objectives.

(c) Limitation

(1) In general

Except as provided in paragraph (2), not more than 40 percent of the funds available to a local educational agency under this subpart may be used to carry out the activities described in clauses (ii) through (vi) of subsection (b)(2)(E) of this section, of which not more than 50 percent of such amount may be used to carry out the activities described in clauses (ii) through (v) of such subsection.

(2) Exception

A local educational agency may use funds under this subpart for activities described in clauses (ii) through (v) of subsection (b)(2)(E) of this section only if funding for these activities is not received from other Federal agencies.

(d) Rule of construction

Nothing in this section shall be construed to prohibit the use of funds under this subpart by any local educational agency or school for the establishment or implementation of a school uniform policy if such policy is part of the overall comprehensive drug and violence prevention plan of the State involved and is supported by the State's needs assessment and other scientifically based research information.

Sec. 7116. Reporting

(a) State report

(1) In general

By December 1, 2003, and every 2 years thereafter, the chief executive officer of the State, in cooperation with the State educational agency, shall submit to the Secretary a report -

(A) on the implementation and outcomes of State programs under section 7112(a)(1) of this title and section 7112(c) of this title and local educational agency programs under section 7115(b) of this title, as well as an assessment of their effectiveness;

(B) on the State's progress toward attaining its performance measures for drug and violence prevention under section 7113(a)(10) of this title; and

(C) on the State's efforts to inform parents of, and include parents in, violence and drug prevention efforts.

(2) Special rule

The report required by this subsection shall be -

(A) in the form specified by the Secretary;

(B) based on the State's ongoing evaluation activities, and shall include data on the incidence and prevalence, age of onset, perception of health risk, and perception of social disapproval of drug use and violence by youth in schools and communities; and

(C) made readily available to the public.

(b) Local educational agency report

(1) In general

Each local educational agency receiving funds under this subpart shall submit to the State educational agency such information that the State requires to complete the State report required by subsection (a) of this section, including a description of how parents were informed of, and participated in, violence and drug prevention efforts.

(2) Availability

Information under paragraph (1) shall be made readily available to the public.

(3) Provision of documentation

Not later than January 1 of each year that a State is required to report under subsection (a) of this section, the Secretary shall provide to the State educational agency all of the necessary documentation required for compliance with this section.

Sec. 7117. Programs for Native Hawaiians

(a) General authority

From the funds made available pursuant to section 7111(a)(1)(C) of this title to carry out this section, the Secretary shall make grants to or enter into cooperative agreements or contracts with organizations primarily serving and representing Native Hawaiians for the benefit of Native Hawaiians to plan, conduct, and administer programs, or portions thereof, that are authorized by and consistent with the provisions of this subpart.

(b) Definition of Native Hawaiian

For the purposes of this section, the term "Native Hawaiian" means any individual any of whose ancestors were natives, prior to 1778, of the area which now comprises the State of Hawaii.

SUBPART 2 - NATIONAL PROGRAMS

Sec. 7131. Federal activities

(a) Program authorized

From funds made available to carry out this subpart under section

7103(2) of this title, the Secretary, in consultation with the Secretary of Health and Human Services, the Director of the Office of National Drug Control Policy, and the Attorney General, shall carry out programs to prevent the illegal use of drugs and violence among, and promote safety and discipline for, students. The Secretary shall carry out such programs directly, or through grants, contracts, or cooperative agreements with public and private entities and individuals, or through agreements with other Federal agencies, and shall coordinate such programs with other appropriate Federal activities. Such programs may include -

(1) the development and demonstration of innovative strategies for the training of school personnel, parents, and members of the community for drug and violence prevention activities based on State and local needs;

(2) the development, demonstration, scientifically based evaluation, and dissemination of innovative and high quality drug and violence prevention programs and activities, based on State and local needs, which may include -

(A) alternative education models, either established within a school or separate and apart from an existing school, that are designed to promote drug and violence prevention, reduce disruptive behavior, reduce the need for repeat suspensions and expulsions, enable students to meet challenging State academic standards, and enable students to return to the regular classroom as soon as possible;

(B) community service and service-learning projects, designed to rebuild safe and healthy neighborhoods and increase students' sense of individual responsibility;

(C) video-based projects developed by noncommercial telecommunications entities that provide young people with models for conflict resolution and responsible decisionmaking; and

(D) child abuse education and prevention programs for elementary and secondary students;

(3) the provision of information on drug abuse education and prevention to the Secretary of Health and Human Services for dissemination;

(4) the provision of information on violence prevention and education and school safety to the Department of Justice for dissemination;

(5) technical assistance to chief executive officers, State agencies, local educational agencies, and other recipients of funding under this part to build capacity to develop and implement high-quality, effective drug and violence prevention programs consistent with the principles of effectiveness in section 7115(a) of this title;

(6) assistance to school systems that have particularly severe drug and violence problems, including hiring drug prevention and school safety coordinators, or assistance to support appropriate response efforts to crisis situations;

(7) the development of education and training programs, curricula, instructional materials, and professional training and development for preventing and reducing the incidence of crimes and conflicts motivated by hate in localities most directly affected by hate crimes;

(8) activities in communities designated as empowerment zones or enterprise communities that will connect schools to community-wide efforts to reduce drug and violence problems; and

(9) other activities in accordance with the purpose of this part, based on State and local needs.

(b) Peer review

The Secretary shall use a peer review process in reviewing applications for funds under this section.

Sec. 7132. Impact evaluation

(a) Biennial evaluation

The Secretary, in consultation with the Safe and Drug-Free Schools and Communities Advisory Committee described in section 7134 of this title, shall conduct an independent biennial evaluation of the impact of programs assisted under this subpart and of other recent and new initiatives to combat violence and illegal drug use in schools. The evaluation shall report on whether community and local educational agency programs funded under this subpart -

(1) comply with the principles of effectiveness described in section 7115(a) of this title;

(2) have appreciably reduced the level of illegal drug, alcohol, and tobacco use, and school violence and the illegal presence of weapons at schools; and

(3) have conducted effective parent involvement and training programs.

(b) Data collection

The National Center for Education Statistics shall collect data, that is subject to independent review, to determine the incidence and prevalence of illegal drug use and violence in elementary schools and secondary schools in the States. The collected data shall include incident reports by schools officials, anonymous student surveys, and anonymous teacher surveys.

(c) Biennial report

Not later than January 1, 2003, and every 2 years thereafter, the Secretary shall submit to the President and Congress a report on the findings of the evaluation conducted under subsection (a) of this section together with the data collected under subsection (b) of this section and data available from other sources on the incidence and prevalence, age of onset, perception of health risk, and perception of social disapproval of drug use and violence in elementary schools and secondary schools in the States. The Secretary shall include data submitted by the States pursuant to subsection 7116(a) of this title.

Sec. 7133. Hate crime prevention

(a) Grant authorization

From funds made available to carry out this subpart under section 7103(2) of this title the Secretary may make grants to local educational agencies and community-based organizations for the purpose of providing assistance to localities most directly affected by hate crimes.

(b) Use of funds

(1) Program development

Grants under this section may be used to improve elementary and secondary educational efforts, including -

(A) development of education and training programs designed to prevent and to reduce the incidence of crimes and conflicts motivated by hate;

(B) development of curricula for the purpose of improving conflict or dispute resolution skills of students, teachers, and administrators;

(C) development and acquisition of equipment and instructional materials to meet the needs of, or otherwise be part of, hate crime or conflict programs; and

(D) professional training and development for teachers and administrators on the causes, effects, and resolutions of hate crimes or hate-based conflicts.

(2) Application

In order to be eligible to receive a grant under this section for any fiscal year, a local educational agency, or a local educational agency in conjunction with a community-based organization, shall submit an application to the Secretary in such form and containing such information as the Secretary may reasonably require.

(3) Requirements

Each application under paragraph (2) shall include -

(A) a request for funds for the purpose described in this section;

(B) a description of the schools and communities to be served by the grants; and

(C) assurances that Federal funds received under this section shall be used to supplement, and not supplant, non-Federal funds.

(4) Comprehensive plan

Each application shall include a comprehensive plan that contains -

(A) a description of the hate crime or conflict problems within the schools or the community targeted for assistance;

(B) a description of the program to be developed or augmented by such Federal and matching funds;

(C) assurances that such program or activity shall be administered by or under the supervision of the applicant;

(D) procedures for the proper and efficient administration of such program; and

(E) fiscal control and fund accounting procedures as may be necessary to ensure prudent use, proper disbursement, and accurate accounting of funds received under this section.

(c) Award of grants

(1) Selection of recipients

The Secretary shall consider the incidence of crimes and conflicts motivated by bias in the targeted schools and communities in awarding grants under this section.

(2) Geographic distribution

The Secretary shall attempt, to the extent practicable, to achieve an equitable geographic distribution of grant awards.

(3) Dissemination of information

The Secretary shall attempt, to the extent practicable, to make available information regarding successful hate crime prevention programs, including programs established or expanded with grants under this section.

(d) Reports

The Secretary shall submit to Congress a report every 2 years that shall contain a detailed statement regarding grants and awards, activities of grant recipients, and an evaluation of programs established under this section.

Sec. 7134. Safe and Drug-Free Schools and Communities Advisory Committee

(a) Establishment

(1) In general

There is hereby established an advisory committee to be known as the "Safe and Drug Free Schools and Communities Advisory Committee" (referred to in this section as the "Advisory Committee") to -

(A) consult with the Secretary under subsection (b) of this section;

(B) coordinate Federal school- and community-based substance abuse and violence prevention programs and reduce duplicative research or services;

(C) develop core data sets and evaluation protocols for safe and drug-free school- and community-based programs;

(D) provide technical assistance and training for safe and drug-free school- and community-based programs;

(E) provide for the diffusion of scientifically based research to safe and drug-free school- and community-based programs; and

(F) review other regulations and standards developed under this subchapter.

(2) Composition

The Advisory Committee shall be composed of representatives from -

(A) the Department of Education;

(B) the Centers for Disease Control and Prevention;

(C) the National Institute on Drug Abuse;

(D) the National Institute on Alcoholism and Alcohol Abuse;

(E) the Center for Substance Abuse Prevention;

(F) the Center for Mental Health Services;

(G) the Office of Juvenile Justice and Delinquency Prevention;

(H) the Office of National Drug Control Policy;

(I) State and local governments, including education agencies; and

(J) researchers and expert practitioners.

(3) Consultation

In carrying out its duties under this section, the Advisory Committee shall annually consult with interested State and local coordinators of school-

and community-based substance abuse and violence prevention programs and other interested groups.

(b) Programs

(1) In general

From amounts made available under section 7103(2) of this title to carry out this subpart, the Secretary, in consultation with the Advisory Committee, shall carry out scientifically based research programs to strengthen the accountability and effectiveness of the State, chief executive officer's, and national programs under this part.

(2) Grants, contracts or cooperative agreements

The Secretary shall carry out paragraph (1) directly or through grants, contracts, or cooperative agreements with public and private entities and individuals or through agreements with other Federal agencies.

(3) Coordination

The Secretary shall coordinate programs under this section with other appropriate Federal activities.

(4) Activities

Activities that may be carried out under programs funded under this section may include -

(A) the provision of technical assistance and training, in collaboration with other Federal agencies utilizing their expertise and national and regional training systems, for Governors, State educational agencies and local educational agencies to support high quality, effective programs that -

(i) provide a thorough assessment of the substance abuse and violence problem;

(ii) utilize objective data and the knowledge of a wide range of community members;

(iii) develop measurable goals and objectives; and

(iv) implement scientifically based research activities that have been shown to be effective and that meet identified needs;

(B) the provision of technical assistance and training to foster program accountability;

(C) the diffusion and dissemination of best practices and programs;

(D) the development of core data sets and evaluation tools;

(E) program evaluations;

(F) the provision of information on drug abuse education and prevention to the Secretary of Health and Human Services for dissemination by the clearinghouse for alcohol and drug abuse information established under section 290aa(d)(16) of title 42; and

(G) other activities that meet unmet needs related to the purpose of this part and that are undertaken in consultation with the Advisory Committee.

Sec. 7135. National Coordinator Program

(a) In general

From funds made available to carry out this subpart under section 7103(2) of this title, the Secretary may provide for the establishment of a National Coordinator Program under which the Secretary shall award grants to local educational agencies for the hiring of drug prevention and school safety program coordinators.

(b) Use of funds

Amounts received under a grant under subsection (a) of this section shall be used by local educational agencies to recruit, hire, and train individuals to serve as drug prevention and school safety program coordinators in schools with significant drug and school safety problems. Such coordinators shall be responsible for developing, conducting, and analyzing assessments of drug and crime problems at their schools, and administering the safe and drug-free grant program at such schools.

Sec. 7136. Community service grant program

(a) In general

From funds made available to carry out this subpart under section 7103(2) of this title, the Secretary may make grants to States to carry out programs under which students expelled or suspended from school are required to perform community service.

(b) Allocation

From the amount described in subsection (a) of this section, the Secretary shall allocate among the States -

(1) one-half according to the ratio between the school-aged population of each State and the school-aged population of all the States; and

(2) one-half according to the ratio between the amount each State received under section 6334 of this title for the preceding year and the sum of such amounts received by all the States.

(c) Minimum

For any fiscal year, no State shall be allotted under this section an amount that is less than one-half of 1 percent of the total amount allotted to all the States under this section.

(d) Reallotment

The Secretary may reallot any amount of any allotment to a State if the Secretary determines that the State will be unable to use such amount within 2 years of such allotment. Such reallotments shall be made on the same basis as allotments are made under subsection (b) of this section.

(e) Definition

In this section, the term "State" means each of the 50 States, the District of Columbia, and the Commonwealth of Puerto Rico.

Sec. 7137. School Security Technology and Resource Center

(a) Center

From funds made available to carry out this subpart under section 7103(2) of this title, the Secretary, the Attorney General, and the Secretary of Energy may enter into an agreement for the establishment at the Sandia

National Laboratories, in partnership with the National Law Enforcement and Corrections Technology Center - Southeast and the National Center for Rural Law Enforcement in Little Rock, Arkansas, of a center to be known as the "School Security Technology and Resource Center" (hereafter in this section "the Center").

(b) Administration

The Center established under subsection (a) of this section shall be administered by the Attorney General.

(c) Functions

The center established under subsection (a) of this section shall be a resource to local educational agencies for school security assessments, security technology development, evaluation and implementation, and technical assistance relating to improving school security. The Center will also conduct and publish school violence research, coalesce data from victim communities, and monitor and report on schools that implement school security strategies.

Sec. 7138. National Center for School and Youth Safety

(a) Establishment

From funds made available to carry out this subpart under section 7103(2) of this title, the Secretary of Education and the Attorney General may jointly establish a National Center for School and Youth Safety (in this section referred to as the "Center"). The Secretary of Education and the Attorney General may establish the Center at an existing facility, if the facility has a history of performing two or more of the duties described in subsection (b) of this section. The Secretary of Education and the Attorney General shall jointly appoint a Director of the Center to oversee the operation of the Center.

(b) Duties

The Center shall carry out emergency response, anonymous student hotline, consultation, and information and outreach activities with respect to elementary and secondary school safety, including the following:

(1) Emergency response

The staff of the Center, and such temporary contract employees as the Director of the Center shall determine necessary, shall offer emergency assistance to local communities to respond to school safety crises. Such assistance shall include counseling for victims and the community, assistance to law enforcement to address short-term security concerns, and advice on how to enhance school safety, prevent future incidents, and respond to future incidents.

(2) Anonymous student hotline

The Center shall establish a toll-free telephone number for students to report criminal activity, threats of criminal activity, and other high-risk behaviors such as substance abuse, gang or cult affiliation, depression, or other warning signs of potentially violent behavior. The Center shall relay the reports, without attribution, to local law enforcement or appropriate school hotlines. The Director of the Center shall work with the Attorney General to establish guidelines for Center staff to work with law enforcement around the Nation to relay information reported through the hotline.

(3) Consultation

The Center shall establish a toll-free number for the public to contact staff of the Center for consultation regarding school safety. The Director of the Center shall hire administrative staff and individuals with expertise in enhancing school safety, including individuals with backgrounds in counseling and psychology, education, law enforcement and criminal justice, and community development to assist in the consultation.

(4) Information and outreach

The Center shall compile information about the best practices in school violence prevention, intervention, and crisis management, and shall serve as a clearinghouse for model school safety program information. The staff of the Center shall work to ensure local governments, school officials, parents, students, and law enforcement officials and agencies are aware of the resources, grants, and expertise available to enhance school safety and prevent school crime. The staff of the Center shall give special attention to providing outreach to rural and impoverished communities.

Sec. 7139. Grants to reduce alcohol abuse

(a) In general

The Secretary, in consultation with the Administrator of the Substance Abuse and Mental Health Services Administration, may award grants from funds made available to carry out this subpart under section 7103(2) of this title, on a competitive basis, to local educational agencies to enable such agencies to develop and implement innovative and effective programs to reduce alcohol abuse in secondary schools.

(b) Eligibility

To be eligible to receive a grant under subsection (a) of this section, a local educational agency shall prepare and submit to the Secretary an application at such time, in such manner, and containing such information as the Secretary may require, including -

(1) a description of the activities to be carried out under the grant;

(2) an assurance that such activities will include one or more of the proven strategies for reducing underage alcohol abuse as determined by the Substance Abuse and Mental Health Services Administration;

(3) an explanation of how activities to be carried out under the grant that are not described in paragraph (2) will be effective in reducing underage alcohol abuse, including references to the past effectiveness of such activities;

(4) an assurance that the applicant will submit to the Secretary an annual report concerning the effectiveness of the programs and activities funded under the grant; and

(5) such other information as the Secretary determines appropriate.

(c) Streamlining of process for low-income and rural LEAs

The Secretary, in consultation with the Administrator of the Substance Abuse and Mental Health Services Administration, shall develop procedures to make the application process for grants under this section more user-friendly, particularly for low-income and rural local educational agencies.

(d) Reservations

(1) SAMHSA

The Secretary may reserve 20 percent of any amount used to carry out this section to enable the Administrator of the Substance Abuse and Mental Health Services Administration to provide alcohol abuse resources and start-up assistance to local educational agencies receiving grants under this section.

(2) Low-income and rural areas

The Secretary may reserve 25 percent of any amount used to carry out this section to award grants to low-income and rural local educational agencies.

Sec. 7140. Mentoring programs

(a) Purpose; definitions

(1) Purpose

The purpose of this section is to make assistance available to promote mentoring programs for children with greatest need -

(A) to assist such children in receiving support and guidance from a mentor;

(B) to improve the academic achievement of such children;

(C) to improve interpersonal relationships between such children and their peers, teachers, other adults, and family members;

(D) to reduce the dropout rate of such children; and

(E) to reduce juvenile delinquency and involvement in gangs by such children.

(2) Definitions

In this part:

(A) Child with greatest need

The term "child with greatest need" means a child who is at risk of educational failure, dropping out of school, or involvement in criminal or delinquent activities, or who lacks strong positive role models.

(B) Eligible entity

The term "eligible entity" means -

(i) a local educational agency;

(ii) a nonprofit, community-based organization; or

(iii) a partnership between a local educational agency and a nonprofit, community-based organization.

(C) Mentor

The term "mentor" means a responsible adult, a

postsecondary school student, or a secondary school student who works with a child -

        (i) to provide a positive role model for the child;

        (ii) to establish a supportive relationship with the child; and

        (iii) to provide the child with academic assistance and exposure to new experiences and examples of opportunity that enhance the ability of the child to become a responsible adult.

    (D) State

The term "State" means each of the several States, the District of Columbia, the Commonwealth of Puerto Rico, the United States Virgin Islands, Guam, American Samoa, and the Commonwealth of the Northern Mariana Islands.

    (b) Grant program

    (1) In general

The Secretary may award grants from funds made available to carry out this subpart under section 7103(2) of this title to eligible entities to assist such entities in establishing and supporting mentoring programs and activities for children with greatest need that -

    (A) are designed to link such children (particularly children living in rural areas, high-crime areas, or troubled home environments, or children experiencing educational failure) with mentors who -

        (i) have received training and support in mentoring;

        (ii) have been screened using appropriate reference checks, child and domestic abuse record checks, and criminal background checks; and

        (iii) are interested in working with children with greatest need; and

    (B) are intended to achieve one or more of the following goals with respect to children with greatest need:

        (i) Provide general guidance.

        (ii) Promote personal and social responsibility.

        (iii) Increase participation in, and enhance the ability to benefit from, elementary and secondary education.

        (iv) Discourage illegal use of drugs and alcohol, violence, use of dangerous weapons, promiscuous behavior, and other criminal, harmful, or potentially harmful activity.

        (v) Encourage participation in community service and community activities.

        (vi) Encourage setting goals and planning for the future, including encouragement of graduation from secondary school and planning for postsecondary education or training.

        (viii) Discourage involvement in gangs.

    (2) Use of funds

    (A) In general

Each eligible entity awarded a grant under this subsection shall use the grant funds for activities that establish or implement a mentoring program, that may include -

(i) hiring of mentoring coordinators and support staff;

(ii) providing for the professional development of mentoring coordinators and support staff;

(iii) recruitment, screening, and training of mentors;

(iv) reimbursement to schools, if appropriate, for the use of school materials or supplies in carrying out the mentoring program;

(v) dissemination of outreach materials;

(vi) evaluation of the mentoring program using scientifically based methods; and

(vii) such other activities as the Secretary may reasonably prescribe by rule.

(B) Prohibited uses

Notwithstanding subparagraph (A), an eligible entity awarded a grant under this section may not use the grant funds -

(i) to directly compensate mentors;

(ii) to obtain educational or other materials or equipment that would otherwise be used in the ordinary course of the eligible entity's operations;

(iii) to support litigation of any kind; or

(iv) for any other purpose reasonably prohibited by the Secretary by rule.

(3) Availability of funds

Funds made available through a grant under this section shall be available for obligation for a period not to exceed 3 years.

(4) Application

Each eligible entity seeking a grant under this section shall submit to the Secretary an application that includes -

(A) a description of the plan for the mentoring program the eligible entity proposes to carry out with such grant;

(B) information on the children expected to be served by the mentoring program for which such grant is sought;

(C) a description of the mechanism the eligible entity will use to match children with mentors based on the needs of the children;

(D) an assurance that no mentor will be assigned to mentor so many children that the assignment will undermine the mentor's ability to be an effective mentor or the mentor's ability to establish a close relationship (a one-to-one relationship, where practicable) with each mentored child;

(E) an assurance that the mentoring program will provide children with a variety of experiences and support, including -

(i) emotional support;

(ii) academic assistance; and

(iii) exposure to experiences that the children might not otherwise encounter on their own;

(F) an assurance that the mentoring program will be monitored to ensure that each child assigned a mentor benefits from that assignment and that the child will be assigned a new mentor if the relationship between the original mentor and the child is not beneficial to the child;

(G) information regarding how mentors and children will be recruited to the mentoring program;

(H) information regarding how prospective mentors will be screened;

(I) information on the training that will be provided to mentors; and

(J) information on the system that the eligible entity will use to manage and monitor information relating to the mentoring program's -

(i) reference checks;

(ii) child and domestic abuse record checks;

(iii) criminal background checks; and

(iv) procedure for matching children with mentors.

(5) Selection

(A) Competitive basis

In accordance with this subsection, the Secretary shall award grants to eligible entities on a competitive basis.

(B) Priority

In awarding grants under subparagraph (A), the Secretary shall give priority to each eligible entity that -

(i) serves children with greatest need living in rural areas, high-crime areas, or troubled home environments, or who attend schools with violence problems;

(ii) provides high quality background screening of mentors training of mentors, and technical assistance in carrying out mentoring programs; or

(iii) proposes a school-based mentoring program.

(C) Other considerations

In awarding grants under subparagraph (A), the Secretary shall also consider -

(i) the degree to which the location of the mentoring program proposed by each eligible entity contributes to a fair distribution of mentoring programs with respect to urban and rural locations;

(ii) the quality of the mentoring program proposed by each eligible entity, including -

(I) the resources, if any, the eligible entity will dedicate to providing children with opportunities for job training or postsecondary education;

(II) the degree to which parents, teachers, community-based organizations, and the local community have participated, or will participate, in the design and implementation of the proposed mentoring program;

(III) the degree to which the eligible entity can ensure that mentors will develop longstanding relationships with the children they mentor;

(IV) the degree to which the mentoring program will serve

children with greatest need in the 4th through 8th grades; and

(V) the degree to which the mentoring program will continue to serve children from the 9th grade through graduation from secondary school, as needed; and

(iii) the capability of each eligible entity to effectively implement its mentoring program.

(D) Grant to each State

Notwithstanding any other provision of this subsection, in awarding grants under subparagraph (A), the Secretary shall select not less than one grant recipient from each State for which there is an eligible entity that submits an application of sufficient quality pursuant to paragraph (4).

(6) Model screening guidelines

(A) In general

Based on model screening guidelines developed by the Office of Juvenile Programs of the Department of Justice, the Secretary shall develop and distribute to each eligible entity awarded a grant under this section specific model guidelines for the screening of mentors who seek to participate in mentoring programs assisted under this section.

(B) Background checks

The guidelines developed under this subsection shall include, at a minimum, a requirement that potential mentors be subject to reference checks, child and domestic abuse record checks, and criminal background checks.

SUBPART 3 - GUN POSSESSION

Sec. 7151. Gun-free requirements

(a) Short title

This subpart may be cited as the "Gun-Free Schools Act."

(b) Requirements

(1) In general

Each State receiving Federal funds under any subchapter of this chapter shall have in effect a State law requiring local educational agencies to expel from school for a period of not less than 1 year a student who is determined to have brought a firearm to a school, or to have possessed a firearm at a school, under the jurisdiction of local educational agencies in that State, except that such State law shall allow the chief administering officer of a local educational agency to modify such expulsion requirement for a student on a case-by-case basis if such modification is in writing.

(2) Construction

Nothing in this subpart shall be construed to prevent a State from allowing a local educational agency that has expelled a student from such a student's regular school setting from providing educational services to such student in an alternative setting.

(3) Definition

For the purpose of this section, the term "firearm" has the same meaning given such term in section 921(a) of title 18.

(c) Special rule

The provisions of this section shall be construed in a manner consistent with the Individuals with Disabilities Education Act [20 U.S.C. 1400 et seq.].

(d) Report to State

Each local educational agency requesting assistance from the State educational agency that is to be provided from funds made available to the State under any subchapter of this chapter shall provide to the State, in the application requesting such assistance -

(1) an assurance that such local educational agency is in compliance with the State law required by subsection (b) of this section; and

(2) a description of the circumstances surrounding any expulsions imposed under the State law required by subsection (b) of this section, including -

(A) the name of the school concerned;

(B) the number of students expelled from such school; and

(C) the type of firearms concerned.

(e) Reporting

Each State shall report the information described in subsection (d) of this section to the Secretary on an annual basis.

(f) Definition

For the purpose of subsection (d) of this section, the term "school" means any setting that is under the control and supervision of the local educational agency for the purpose of student activities approved and authorized by the local educational agency.

(g) Exception

Nothing in this section shall apply to a firearm that is lawfully stored inside a locked vehicle on school property, or if it is for activities approved and authorized by the local educational agency and the local educational agency adopts appropriate safeguards to ensure student safety.

(h) Policy regarding criminal justice system referral

(1) In general

No funds shall be made available under any subchapter of this chapter to any local educational agency unless such agency has a policy requiring referral to the criminal justice or juvenile delinquency system of any student who brings a firearm or weapon to a school served by such agency.

(2) Definition

For the purpose of this subsection, the term "school" has the same meaning given to such term by section 921(a) of title 18.

SUBPART 4 - GENERAL PROVISIONS

Sec. 7161. Definitions

In this part:

(1) Controlled substance

The term "controlled substance" means a drug or other substance identified under Schedule I, II, III, IV, or V in section 812(c) of title 21.

(2) Drug

The term "drug" includes controlled substances; the illegal use of alcohol and tobacco; and the harmful, abusive, or addictive use of substances, including inhalants and anabolic steroids.

(3) Drug and violence prevention

The term "drug and violence prevention" means -

(A) with respect to drugs, prevention, early intervention, rehabilitation referral, or education related to the illegal use of drugs;

(B) with respect to violence, the promotion of school safety, such that students and school personnel are free from violent and disruptive acts, including sexual harassment and abuse, and victimization associated with prejudice and intolerance, on school premises, going to and from school, and at school- sponsored activities, through the creation and maintenance of a school environment that is free of weapons and fosters individual responsibility and respect for the rights of others.

(4) Hate crime

The term "hate crime" means a crime as described in section 1(b) of the Hate Crime Statistics Act of 1990.

(5) Nonprofit

The term "nonprofit," as applied to a school, agency, organization, or institution means a school, agency, organization, or institution owned and operated by one or more nonprofit corporations or associations, no part of the net earnings of which inures, or may lawfully inure, to the benefit of any private shareholder or individual.

(6) Protective factor, buffer, or asset

The terms "protective factor," "buffer," and "asset" mean any one of a number of the community, school, family, or peer individual domains that are known, through prospective, longitudinal research efforts, or which are grounded in a well- established theoretical model of prevention, and have been shown to prevent alcohol, tobacco, or illegal drug use, as well as violent behavior, by youth in the community, and which promote positive youth development.

(7) Risk factor

The term "risk factor" means any one of a number of characteristics of the community, school, family, or peer- individual domains that are known, through prospective, longitudinal research efforts, to be predictive of alcohol, tobacco, and illegal drug use, as well as violent behavior, by youth in the school and community.

(8) School-aged population

The term "school-aged population" means the population aged five through 17, as determined by the Secretary on the basis of the most recent satisfactory data available from the Department of Commerce.

(9) School based mental health services provider

The term "school based mental health services provider" includes a State-licensed or State-certified school counselor, school psychologist, school social worker, or other State-licensed or -certified mental health professional qualified under State law to provide such services to children and adolescents.

(10) School personnel

The term "school personnel" includes teachers, principals, administrators, counselors, social workers, psychologists, nurses, librarians, and other support staff who are employed by a school or who perform services for the school on a contractual basis.

(11) School resource officer

The term "school resource officer" means a career law enforcement officer, with sworn authority, deployed in community oriented policing, and assigned by the employing police department to a local educational agency to work in collaboration with schools and community based organizations to -

(A) educate students in crime and illegal drug use prevention and safety;

(B) develop or expand community justice initiatives for students; and

(C) train students in conflict resolution, restorative justice, and crime and illegal drug use awareness.

Sec. 7162. Message and materials

(a) "Wrong and harmful" message

Drug and violence prevention programs supported under this part shall convey a clear and consistent message that the illegal use of drugs and acts of violence are wrong and harmful.

(b) Curriculum

The Secretary shall not prescribe the use of specific curricula for programs supported under this part.

Sec. 7163. Parental consent

Upon receipt of written notification from the parents or legal guardians of a student, the local educational agency shall withdraw such student from any program or activity funded under this part. The local educational agency shall make reasonable efforts to inform parents or legal guardians of the content of such programs or activities funded under this part, other than classroom instruction.

Sec. 7164. Prohibited uses of funds

No funds under this part may be used for -

(1) construction (except for minor remodeling needed to accomplish the purposes of this part); or

(2) medical services, drug treatment or rehabilitation, except for pupil services or referral to treatment for students who are victims of, or

witnesses to, crime or who illegally use drugs.

Sec. 7165. Transfer of school disciplinary records

(a) Nonapplication of provisions

This section shall not apply to any disciplinary records with respect to a suspension or expulsion that are transferred from a private, parochial or other nonpublic school, person, institution, or other entity, that provides education below the college level.

(b) Disciplinary records

In accordance with the Family Educational Rights and Privacy Act of 1974 (20 U.S.C. 1232g), not later than 2 years after January 8 2002, each State receiving Federal funds under this chapter shall provide an assurance to the Secretary that the State has a procedure in place to facilitate the transfer of disciplinary records, with respect to a suspension or expulsion, by local educational agencies to any private or public elementary school or secondary school for any student who is enrolled or seeks, intends, or is instructed to enroll, on a full- or part-time basis, in the school.

II. GUN-FREE SCHOOL ZONES ACT

18 U.S.C. § 922(q)

(q)(1) The Congress finds and declares that –

(A) crime, particularly crime involving drugs and guns, is a pervasive, nationwide problem;

(B) crime at the local level is exacerbated by the interstate movement of drugs, guns, and criminal gangs;

(C) firearms and ammunition move easily in interstate commerce and have been found in increasing numbers in and around schools, as documented in numerous hearings in both the Committee on the Judiciary of the House of Representatives and the Committee on the Judiciary of the Senate;

(D) in fact, even before the sale of a firearm, the gun, its component parts, ammunition, and the raw materials from which they are made have considerably moved in interstate commerce;

(E) while criminals freely move from State to State, ordinary citizens and foreign visitors may fear to travel to or through certain parts of the country due to concern about violent crime and gun violence, and parents may decline to send their children to school for the same reason;

(F) the occurrence of violent crime in school zones has resulted in a decline in the quality of education in our country;

(G) this decline in the quality of education has an adverse impact on interstate commerce and the foreign commerce of the United States;

(H) States, localities, and school systems find it almost impossible to handle gun-related crime by themselves – even States, localities, and school systems that have made strong efforts to prevent, detect, and punish gun-related crime find their efforts unavailing due in part to the failure or inability of other States or localities to take strong measures; and

(I) the Congress has the power, under the interstate commerce clause and other provisions of the Constitution, to enact measures to ensure the integrity and safety of the Nation's schools by enactment of this subsection.

(2)(A) It shall be unlawful for any individual knowingly to possess a firearm that has moved in or that otherwise affects interstate or foreign commerce at a place that the individual knows, or has reasonable cause to believe, is a school zone.

(B) Subparagraph (A) does not apply to the possession of a firearm –

(i) on private property not part of school grounds;

(ii) if the individual possessing the firearm is licensed to do so by the State in which the school zone is located or a political subdivision of the State, and the law of the State or political subdivision requires that, before an individual obtains such a license, the law enforcement authorities of the State or political subdivision verify that the individual is qualified under law to receive the license;

(iii) that is –

(I) not loaded; and

(II) in a locked container, or a locked firearms rack that is on a motor vehicle;

(iv) by an individual for use in a program approved by a school in the school zone;

(v) by an individual in accordance with a contract entered into between a school in the school zone and the individual or an employer of the individual;

(vi) by a law enforcement officer acting in his or her official capacity; or

(vii) that is unloaded and is possessed by an individual while traversing school premises for the purpose of gaining access to public or private lands open to hunting, if the entry on school premises is authorized by school authorities.

(3)(A) Except as provided in subparagraph (B), it shall be unlawful for any person, knowingly or with reckless disregard for the safety of another, to discharge or attempt to discharge a firearm that has moved in or that otherwise affects interstate or foreign commerce at a place that the person knows is a school zone.

(B) Subparagraph (A) does not apply to the discharge of a firearm –

(i) on private property not part of school grounds;

(ii) as part of a program approved by a school in the school zone, by an individual who is participating in the program;

(iii) by an individual in accordance with a contract entered into between a school in a school zone and the individual or an employer of the individual; or

(iv) by a law enforcement officer acting in his or her official capacity.

(4) Nothing in this subsection shall be construed as preempting or preventing a State or local government from enacting a statute establishing gun free school zones as provided in this subsection.

CHAPTER NINE

Forms

Page

Form I-1: Staff Skills Inventory

(To be conducted annually)

Name: _____   Room #: _____

Please check any of the following areas in which you have expertise or training:

Emergency Response:

__ First Aid   __ Search and Rescue   __ Emergency Management

__ CPR   __ Law Enforcement   __ CISD (Critical Incident
                                                       Stress Debriefing)

__ EMT   __ CB Radio   __ Other (Specify)

__ Firefighting   __ Ham Radio
                                                   _____

Mobile/cellular phone to be used in emergency:

_____

____ I speak the following foreign languages:

_____

_____

_____

_____

Source: Virginia Department of Education

Form I-2: Crisis Team Member List

Position/Name	Work Phone	Cell Phone
Principal _____	_____	_____
Ass't Principal _____	_____	_____
Guidance Director _____	_____	_____
School Nurse _____	_____	_____
Resource Officer _____	_____	_____
School Psychologist _____	_____	_____
Social Worker _____	_____	_____
Secretary _____	_____	_____
Teacher _____	_____	_____
Administrator _____	_____	_____
Counselor _____	_____	_____
Custodian _____	_____	_____

Source: Virginia Department of Education

Form I-3: Authorization to Release Children in Emergency

Dear Parents/Guardians:

Our school has developed an emergency business plan for use in the event of a disaster. The emergency plan is devoted to the welfare and safety of your child during school hours. It is available for inspection in the school office.

We are requesting your assistance at this time:
Should there be an emergency, such as a major fire, tornado or explosion, your child may be required to remain in the care of the school until it is deemed safe by an Emergency Services authority that the child can be released. At that point, children may be released only to properly authorized parents/guardians and/or designees. Therefore, please list as many names (with local telephone numbers and addresses) as possible, of those persons to whom you would allow your child's release in the event of an emergency. Be sure to notify those persons listed that you have authorized their supervision in case of an emergency.

If you are unable to come to school, it is essential that others be designated to care for your child. No child will be released to the care of unauthorized persons.

We appreciate your cooperation in this important matter.

CHILD: _____ **TEACHER:** _____ **GRADE:_____**

You may release my child to any of the persons listed below:

Name   *Phone*   *Address*   *Relationship*

_____ _____ _____ _____

_____ _____ _____ _____

_____ _____ _____ _____

_____ _____ _____ _____

_____ _____ _____ _____

Parent/Guardian: _____ Date:_____
                        Signature

Home Phone: _____ Cell/Work Phone: _____

Source: Virginia Department of Education

Form I-4: Situation Involving Weapon

These are steps for key personnel to take in situations involving a weapon at school.

Staff:
1. Notify principal or other designated individual.

2. Remain calm.

3. Avoid heroics.

4. Don't threaten.

5. Keep a safe, non-intimidating distance.

6. Avoid abrupt, sporadic movements.

7. Look to see whether there is a place you can dive or jump to.

8. Negotiate minimally until the principal, a designee or law enforcement personnel arrive.

Administrator or Designee:

1. Assess the situation and decide whether to call a lockdown or to handle the situation on a need-to-know basis.

2. Call 911.

3. Contact the superintendent at telephone number _____.

4. Inform another administrator or designee of the threat, ensuring classes do not change until an "all clear" has been issued.

5. Provide as much information as possible.

   • Be prepared to act as a resource and liaison between school and police.

   • Have a map of the school and grounds available for police.

6. Gather as much detailed information as possible and try to determine:

   • Location, identity and detailed description of individual.

Situation Involving Weapon *(continued)*

•   Location and description of weapon.

•   Any pertinent background information regarding the individual, including possible reason for carrying a weapon.

7. Isolate the individual. If the location of the weapon is known, prevent access to it.

8. Remain calm. Try not to raise your voice. If raising your voice becomes necessary, speak decisively and with clarity. Your tone and demeanor will strongly influence the outcome of the crisis.

9. Avoid heroics. Look for a place where you can dive or jump to, and keep a safe, non-intimidating distance.

10. Do not use force or touch the person or weapon. Avoid sudden moves or gestures.

11. Negotiate minimally until law enforcement arrives.

12. Meet with police when they arrive and follow their instructions.

Source: University of Arkansas System, Criminal Justice Institute, School Violence Resource Center

Form I-5: Violent Situations

These are general guidelines to follow when dealing with a violent or potentially violent individual at school.

Staff:
1. Notify principal or other designated individual.

2. Follow the following guidelines:

- Be empathetic. Try not to be judgmental regarding the person's feelings. They are real and must be attended, even if they are not based on reality.

- Clarify messages. Listen to what is really being said. Ask reflective questions. Use both silence and restatements.

- Respect personal space. Stand at least 1.5 to 3 feet away from the person who is acting out. Encroaching on personal space tends to escalate the situation.

- Be aware of your body position. Standing eye to eye and toe to toe sends a message of challenge. Standing one-leg length away and at an angle off to the side makes it less likely that the situation will escalate.

- Permit verbal venting if possible. Allow the individual to release as much energy as possible by venting verbally. If this cannot be allowed, state directives and reasonable limits during lulls in the venting process.

- Set and enforce reasonable limits. If the individual becomes belligerent, defensive or disruptive, state limits and directives clearly and concisely.

- Remain calm, rational and professional. How you respond will directly affect the individual's conduct.

- Use physical techniques only as a last resort. Use the least restrictive effective method. Using physical techniques on someone who is only acting out verbally can escalate the situation.

- Ignore challenge questions, as answering them can fuel a power struggle. When the individual challenges your

Violent Situations *(continued)*

position, training, etc., redirect the individual's attention to the issue at hand.

- Keep your nonverbal cues non-threatening. Be aware of your body language, movement and tone of voice. The more an individual loses control, the less he listens to your actual words. More attention is paid to nonverbal cues.

-From the National Crisis Prevention Institute

Administrator or Designee:

1. Follow the same above guidelines.

Source: University of Arkansas System, Criminal Justice Institute, School Violence Resource Center

Form I-6: Parent Letter Regarding Weapon at School

Dear Parent,

During third period today a student reported that another student had a hand gun in his backpack. The backpack was secured by administration, and the local police department was immediately notified. The police quickly responded, and the student and backpack were detained by police. The administration is working with the police department in an ongoing investigation.

I want to assure you that the safety of our students and staff is our top priority. The confiscation of the backpack and the detention of the student is due to the efforts of our staff and the local police department. Our administration and the local police department will continue to work together to make sure that all parties involved are held accountable.

Our school's staff and your school district are committed to keeping our campus safe. There are no additional safety issues related to this incident. We will continue to be diligent in the enforcement of our rules and will work in conjunction with law enforcement to keep our campus a safe place to learn.

Respectfully,

Principal

Source: John Speer, Principal, Millenium High School, Goodyear, AZ

Form I-7: Checklist of Characteristics of Youth Who Have Caused School-Associated Violent Deaths

While there is no foolproof system for identifying potentially dangerous students who may harm themselves and/or others, this checklist provides a starting point. These characteristics should serve to alert school administrators, teachers and support staff to address needs of troubled students through meetings with parents, provision of school counseling, guidance and mentoring services, as well as referrals to appropriate community health/social services and law enforcement personnel. Further, such behavior should also provide an early warning signal that safe school plans and crisis prevention/ intervention procedures must be in place to protect the health and safety of all school students and staff members so schools remain safe havens for learning.

- Has a history of tantrums and uncontrollable angry outbursts

- Characteristically resorts to name calling, cursing or abusive language

- Habitually makes violent threats when angry

- Has previously brought a weapon to school

- Has a background of serious disciplinary problems at school and in the community

- Is on the fringe of his/her peer group with few or no close friends

- Is preoccupied with weapons, explosives or other incendiary devices

- Has previously been truant, suspended or expelled from school

- Displays cruelty to animals

- Has little or no supervision and support from parents or a caring adult

- Has witnessed or been a victim of abuse or neglect in the home

**Checklist of Characteristics of Youth Who Have Caused
School-Associated Violent Deaths** *(continued)*

- Had been bullied and/or bullies or intimidates peers or younger children

- Tends to blame others for difficulties s/he causes her/himself

- Consistently prefers TV shows, movies or music expressing violent themes and acts

- Prefers reading materials dealing with violent themes, rituals and abuse

- Reflects anger, frustration and the dark side of life in school essays or writing projects

- Is involved with a gang or antisocial group on the fringe of peer acceptance

- Is often depressed and/or has significant mood swings

- Has threatened or attempted suicide.

Source: National School Safety Center

Form I-8: Model Policy for Body Cams

Be it enacted by the *[NAME]*:

SECTION 1.

a.   Only law enforcement officers with the authority to conduct searches and make arrests shall be permitted to wear a body camera. Such body cameras shall be worn in a location and manner that maximizes the camera's ability to capture video footage of the officer's activities.

b.   Both the video and audio recording functions of the body camera shall be activated whenever a law enforcement officer is responding to a call for service or at the initiation of any other law enforcement or investigative encounter between a law enforcement officer and a member of the public, except that when an immediate threat to the officer's life or safety makes activating the camera impossible or dangerous, the officer shall activate the camera at the first reasonable opportunity to do so. The body camera shall not be deactivated until the encounter has fully concluded and the law enforcement officer leaves the scene.

c.   A law enforcement officer who is wearing a body camera shall notify the subject(s) of the recording that they are being recorded by a body camera as close to the inception of the encounter as is reasonably possible.

d.   Notwithstanding the requirements of subsection (b):

  1.   Prior to entering a private residence without a warrant or in non-exigent circumstances, a law enforcement officer shall ask the occupant if the occupant wants the officer to discontinue use of the officer's body camera. If the occupant responds affirmatively, the law enforcement officer shall immediately discontinue use of the body camera;

  2.   When interacting with an apparent crime victim, a law enforcement officer shall, as soon as practicable, ask the apparent crime victim, if the apparent crime victim wants the officer to discontinue use of the officer's body camera. If the apparent crime victim responds affirmatively, the law enforcement officer shall immediately discontinue use of the body camera; and

Model Policy for Body Cams *(continued)*

3. When interacting with a person seeking to anonymously report a crime or assist in an ongoing law enforcement investigation, a law enforcement officer shall, as soon as practicable, ask the person seeking to remain anonymous, if the person seeking to remain anonymous wants the officer to discontinue use of the officer's body camera. If the person seeking to remain anonymous responds affirmatively, the law enforcement officer shall immediately discontinue use of the body camera.

e. All law enforcement offers to discontinue the use of a body camera made pursuant to subsection (d), and the responses thereto, shall be recorded by the body camera prior to discontinuing use of the body camera.

f. Body cameras shall not be used surreptitiously.

g. Body cameras shall not be used to gather intelligence information based on First Amendment protected speech, associations, or religion, or to record activity that is unrelated to a response to a call for service or a law enforcement or investigative encounter between a law enforcement officer and a member of the public.

h. Law enforcement officers shall not activate a body camera while on the grounds of any public, private or parochial elementary or secondary school, except when responding to an imminent threat to life or health.

i. Body camera video footage shall be retained by the law enforcement agency that employs the officer whose camera captured the footage, or an authorized agent thereof, for six (6) months from the date it was recorded, after which time such footage shall be permanently deleted.

j. Notwithstanding the retention and deletion requirements in subsection (i):

1. Video footage shall be automatically retained for no less than three (3) years if the video footage captures images involving:

A. Any use of force;

B. Events leading up to and including an arrest for a

Model Policy for Body Cams *(continued)*

felony-level offense, or events that constitute
a felony-level offense; or

C.   An encounter about which a complaint has been
registered by a subject of the video footage.

2.   Body camera video footage shall also be retained for
no less than three (3) years if a longer retention period
is voluntarily requested by:

A.   The law enforcement officer whose body camera
recorded the video footage, if that officer
reasonably asserts the video footage has
evidentiary or exculpatory value;

B.   Any law enforcement officer who is a subject of
the video footage, if that officer reasonably
asserts the video footage has evidentiary or
exculpatory value;

C.   Any superior officer of a law enforcement officer
whose body camera recorded the video footage
or who is a subject of the video footage, if that
superior officer reasonably asserts the video
footage has evidentiary or exculpatory value;

D.   Any law enforcement officer, if the video footage
is being retained solely and exclusively for police
training purposes;

E.   Any member of the public who is a subject of
the video footage;

F.   Any parent or legal guardian of a minor who is a
subject of the video footage; or

G.   A deceased subject's next of kin or legally
authorized designee.

k.   To effectuate subsections (j)(2)(E), (j)(2)(F) and (j)(2)(G),
any member of the public who is a subject of video footage,
the parent or legal guardian of a minor who is a subject of
the video footage, or a deceased subject's next of kin or
legally authorized designee, shall be permitted to review that
specific video footage in order to make a determination as to
whether they will voluntarily request it be subject to a three

Model Policy for Body Cams *(continued)*

(3) year retention period.

l.   The following video footage shall be exempt from the public inspection requirements of the *[NAME OF STATE OPEN RECORDS ACT/FOIA LAW]*:

    1.   Video footage not subject to a minimum three (3) year retention period pursuant to subsection (j);

    2.   Video footage that is subject to a minimum three (3) year retention period solely and exclusively pursuant to subsection (j)(1)(C), where the subject of the video footage making the complaint requests the video footage not be made available to the public;

    3.   Video footage that is subject to a minimum three (3) year retention period solely and exclusively pursuant to subsection (j)(2)(A), (j)(2)(B), (j)(2)(C) or (j)(2)(D); and

    4.   Video footage that is subject to a minimum three (3) year retention period solely and exclusively pursuant to subsection (j)(2)(E), (j)(2)(F), or (j)(2)(G), where the person making the voluntary request requests the video footage not be made available to the public.

m.   Any video footage retained beyond six (6) months solely and exclusively pursuant to subsection (j)(2)(D) shall not be admissible as evidence in any criminal or civil legal or administrative proceeding.

n.   No law enforcement officer shall review or receive an accounting of any body camera video footage that is subject to a minimum three (3) year retention period pursuant to subsection (j)(1) prior to completing any required initial reports, statements and interviews regarding the recorded event.

o.   Video footage not subject to a minimum three (3) year retention period shall not be viewed by any superior officer of a law enforcement officer whose body camera recorded the footage absent a specific allegation of misconduct, nor shall it be subject to automated analysis or analytics of any kind.

p.   Video footage shall not be divulged or used by any law

Model Policy for Body Cams *(continued)*

enforcement agency for any commercial or other non-law enforcement purpose.

q.   Where a law enforcement agency authorizes a third party to act as its agent in maintaining body camera footage, the agent shall not be permitted to independently access, view or alter any video footage, except to delete videos as required by law or agency retention policies.

r.   Should any law enforcement officer, employee or agent fail to adhere to the recording or retention requirements contained in this chapter, or intentionally interfere with a body camera's ability to accurately capture video footage:

1.   Appropriate disciplinary action shall be taken against the individual officer, employee or agent;

2.   A rebuttable evidentiary presumption shall be adopted in favor of criminal defendants who reasonably assert that exculpatory evidence was destroyed or not captured; and

3.   A rebuttable evidentiary presumption shall be adopted on behalf of civil plaintiffs suing the government, a law enforcement agency and/or law enforcement officers for damages based on police misconduct who reasonably assert that evidence supporting their claim was destroyed or not captured.

s.   The disciplinary action requirement and rebuttable presumptions in subsection (r) may be overcome by contrary evidence or proof of exigent circumstances that made compliance impossible.

t.   Any body camera video footage recorded in contravention of this or any other applicable law shall be immediately destroyed and shall not be admissible as evidence in any criminal or civil legal or administrative proceeding.

u.   Nothing in this chapter shall be read to contravene any laws governing the maintenance and destruction of evidence in criminal investigations and prosecutions.

v.   As used in this section, "law enforcement officer" means any person authorized by law to conduct searches and

Model Policy for Body Cams *(continued)*

effectuate arrests and who is employed by the state, or a county, municipality, or metropolitan form of government.

w.   As used in this section, "subject of the video footage" means any law enforcement officer or any suspect, victim, detainee, conversant, injured party or other similarly situated person who appears on the body camera recording, and shall not include people who only incidentally appear on the recording.

SECTION 2. This act shall take effect *[DATE]*.

Source: American Civil Liberties Union, May 2015.

Form I-9: Threat Assessment Checklist:
Student Information

When conducting an assessment to determine whether a student is a risk, school or police officials should gather three types of general information on that student:

1. Identifying information

2. Background information

3. Current life information

Identifying information includes the student's:

- Name

- Physical description

- Date of birth, and

- Identifying numbers, such as SSN, student ID, etc.

Background information includes the student's:

- Residences

- Family/home situation

- Academic performance

- Social networks

- History of relationships and conflicts

- History of harassing others or being harassed by others

- History of violence toward self and others

- History of being a victim of violence or bullying

- Known attitude toward violence

- Criminal behavior

- Mental health/substance abuse history

Threat Assessment Checklist:
Student Information *(continued)*

- Access to and use of weapons, and

- History of grievances and grudges.

Current life information includes the student's:

- Present stability of living and home situation

- Nature and quality of current relationships and personal support

- Recent losses or losses of status (shame, humiliation, recent breakup or loss of significant relationship)

- Current grievances or grudges

- Perceptions of being treated unfairly

- Known difficulty coping with a stressful event

- Any "downward" progression in social, academic, behavioral or psychological functioning

- Recent hopelessness, desperation and/or despair, including suicidal thoughts, gestures, actions, or attempts, and

- Pending crises or change in circumstances.

Source: The U.S. Secret Service,
   http://www.secretservice.gov/ntac/ssi_guide.pdf

Form II-1: Situation Involving Severe Weather

These are steps for key personnel to take in situations involving severe weather.

Tornadoes, Hurricanes and Thunderstorms

If a tornado watch or severe thunderstorm warning is received during school hours:

1. The principal or a designee should notify all school staff.

2. Teachers continue regular classroom activities.

3. School will dismiss at the normal hour in the regular manner. Drivers will follow regular routes using extra caution.

4. Review school procedures for establishing safe areas.

If there has been a tornado warning stating that a tornado has actually been sighted:

1. The principal or designee will receive the warning by way of radio tuned to a weather channel, a call from the superintendent or a designated representative, or the civil defense office.

2. The principal will inform the staff.

3. Staff and students will immediately proceed to an area predetermined by the school and assume a position protecting the face and head.

4. Teacher will take attendance and notify the principal or a designated representative if anyone is missing.

5. The school secretary or other designated individual will close all vaults and secure important records.

6. All qualified personnel will render first aid if necessary.

7. Staff and students will not return to their classrooms until the principal or a designated representative declares an "all clear."

If no warning has been issued, but a tornado has been sighted and is approaching the school, the principal or a designated representative will direct all individuals to proceed as follows:

Situation Involving Severe Weather *(continued)*

Plan 1 - If time permits, take classes to designated areas.

Plan 2 - If time does not permit removal to designated areas:

- Go to the nearest enclosed hallway, not to open corridors.

- Avoid open spaces and outside hallways.

- Avoid areas with large roof expanse such as the gymnasium, cafeteria or auditorium.

Take Cover Procedures

For the protection of all building occupants, it is important that everyone is informed and understands what to do in the event of severe weather that makes it necessary for the school population to take cover. The following take-cover procedures should be taught in each class:

1. Discuss the take-cover warning.

2. Practice the take-cover position.

3. Encourage students to remain calm and not to panic in the event of a crisis situation.

4. Discuss the "all clear" code.

Staff:

1. Take students to a hallway or other approved location. Seat them on the floor in the hall with their backs against the lockers/walls. If necessary, double up against the lockers/walls. If there is no time to move the students, have them get on the floor away from glass.

2. Instruct students to put their heads down against their knees, cover their necks with their hands and their faces with their arms.

TORNADO WATCH OR SEVERE THUNDERSTORMS

Administrators or designee:

1. The superintendent or a designee will decide whether to close the schools based on current weather information.

Situation Involving Severe Weather *(continued)*

2. If the schools close early, all procedures for the emergency closing of schools will be in effect.

If the weather becomes severe enough during the night or on the weekends to close the schools, all procedures for the emergency closing of schools will be put into effect.

*Source: University of Arkansas System, Criminal Justice Institute,
    School Violence Resource Center*

Form II-2: Sample Notice to Parents
Regarding Lockdown Drill

Date

Dear Parents/Guardians:

In keeping with our ongoing efforts to maintain a safe school, we will be conducting a lockdown drill on _____ (DATE) at _____ (TIME). Your child's teacher will prepare each class for this drill by discussing its specifics with the class ahead of time.

Please talk to your child about this drill.

- Calmly explain that a lockdown is something that the school does to keep students safe when a danger is present, such as when someone gains unauthorized access into the building.

- Assure your child that we hope a lockdown is never needed but that practicing the drill will help keep him or her safe.

- Compare the drill to a school drill they already are familiar with, such as a fire drill or a weather emergency drill.

- Remind your child that by practicing the drill we are better prepared to stay safe.

Form II-3: Gas Leak Response

Gas leaks are often identified by an odor similar to the odor of rotten eggs. If a gas leak is suspected, key personnel should take these steps:

Staff:
1. Notify principal or other designated individual.

2. If you are instructed to evacuate:

- Leave lights on.

- Do not lock doors.

- Instruct students to take with them any items that are easily accessible.

Administrator or Designee:
1. Determine whether you need to evacuate or shelter in place.

2. If evacuation is required:

- Assign staff members to check halls, restrooms, locker rooms and other areas for students.

- If inside, allow fresh air ventilation, if possible.

- If outside, move upwind from any odor.

3. Contact appropriate administrator at telephone number _____.

4. Contact insurance representative at telephone number _____.

5. Determine whether first aid is needed.

6. Establish safe places for classes to reconvene.

Source: University of Arkansas System, Criminal Justice Institute, School Violence Resource Center

Form II-4: Hazardous Spill Response

In the event of a hazardous spill, key personnel should take these steps.

Staff:
1. Notify principal or other designated individual.
2. Avoid direct or indirect contact with material spill.
3. Remove any contaminated clothing.
4. If you are instructed to evacuate:

- Leave lights on.

- Do not lock doors.

- Instruct students to take with them any items that are easily accessible.

Administrator or Designee:
1. Determine whether you need to evacuate or shelter in place.
2. Evacuate the area:

- If spill is outside, move students inside.

- If spill is inside, move students to location with different ventilation system.

- Assign staff members to check halls, restrooms, locker rooms and other areas for students.

- Avoid direct or indirect contact with material spill.

- Remove contaminated clothing.

3. Contact appropriate administrator at telephone number _____.
4. Contact insurance representative at telephone number _____.
5. Determine whether first aid is needed.
6. Establish safe places for classes to reconvene.

Source: University of Arkansas System, Criminal Justice Institute, School Violence Resource Center

Form II-5: Crisis Kit Checklist

Use this checklist to help make sure you have the materials you need to respond to a crisis. Gather and store crisis kit items at strategic locations inside and outside the school. Store the items in a large bag, plastic garbage bag or barrel. Possible storage areas include principals' offices, local fire and police departments, police car trunks, and designated school locations. Update the information in the kits as needed, and make sure you have enough supplies based on your school's size.

- Emergency response telephone numbers

- Placards with directional words like PARENTS, COUNSELORS, MEDIA, CLERGY, VOLUNTEERS and KEEP OUT

- Color-coded name tags and sign-in sheets for service personnel

- Blank white poster board for signs and duct tape to attach signs to tables

- Notebooks, pens and markers

- Preprinted referral pads to be given to counselors and clergy indicating name of counselor/clergy, name of person to be referred for follow-up, concerns and date

- Walkie-talkies to communicate with members of the crisis response team and other emergency personnel. Include extra batteries

- Ankle bands or wrist bands to identify victims

- First aid supplies

- Blankets

- School site layout, floor plans and aerial maps

- Current roster of student and staff with pictures, addresses, phone numbers, emergency contacts and medical information

- Attendance rosters

- Brief summary of school history, number of teachers and staff, and name of principal

Crisis Kit Checklist *(continued)*

- District fact sheet with enrollment, number of schools, etc.

- County map with school district bus routes marked

- Bus rosters and routes

- Resources list of support personnel, such as a contact person for the local phone company

- Caution tape

- Telephone directory for school system

Source: U.S. Department of Education

Form II-6: Emergency Telephone Numbers

Call 911 in any situation that presents an immediate danger to life and property. In addition, the following is a list of other important numbers.

	PHONE	FAX
Poison Control Center	_____	_____
Police	_____	_____
Sheriff's Office	_____	_____
Superintendent	_____	_____
Assistant Superintendent	_____	_____
Director of Transportation	_____	_____
Bus Transportation	_____	_____
Insurance	_____	_____

Source: University of Arkansas System, Criminal Justice Institute, School Violence Resource Center

Form II-7: Sample Letter Home Following Crisis Event

Date

Dear Parents/Guardians,

We regret to inform you about an unfortunate event affecting our school. Yesterday [provide a brief factual statement regarding the event]. An investigation is under way. Until it is complete, we will not have all the details about this tragedy.

The school's crisis team has begun meeting with students and staff. We anticipate that some may need continuing support for awhile to help them deal with the emotional upset that such an event produces. Enclosed are some materials that you may find helpful in talking about the matter at home.

If you have any questions or concerns that you think we can help address, please feel free to call the school at [phone number] and ask for any of the following staff members: [identify staff members].

The following community agencies are ready to help anyone who is feeling overwhelmed by their emotions:

- [Provide name and number of community health center].

- [Provide name and number of other available services provider].

We know events such as this are stressful. We are taking every step we can to be responsive to the needs of our students and their families.

Sincerely,

Principal

Source: U.S. Department of Education

Form II-8: Initial Announcement of Crisis Event

TO:
FROM:

We have just been advised of a tragedy involving a member of our school. I am sad to announce that _____
has died/has been in a serious accident. As soon as we have more information, we will pass it on to you. People will be available in the building to help those of you who need extra support in dealing with this situation. Your teachers will advise you of the location and times available for this support.

As soon as we know the family's/families' wishes regarding _____ we will share that information with you. We ask that all students remain in their classrooms and adhere to their regular schedules.

Source: Virginia Department of Education

Form II-9: Parent Information Sheet - Post-Disaster

Helping Your Child After a Disaster

Children may be especially upset and express feelings about the disaster. These reactions are normal and usually will not last long. Listed below are some problems you may see in your child:

- Excessive fear of darkness, separation, or being alone

- Clinging to parents, fear of strangers

- Worry

- Increase in immature behaviors

- Not wanting to go to school

- Changes in eating/sleeping behaviors

- Increase in either aggressive behavior or shyness

- Bed-wetting or thumb-sucking

- Persistent nightmares; and/or

- Headaches or other physical complaints.

The following will help your child:

- Talk with your child about his/her feelings about the disaster. Share your feelings, too.

- Talk about what happened. Give your child information he/she can understand.

- Reassure your child that you are safe and together. You may need to repeat this reassurance often.

- Hold and touch your child often.

- Spend extra time with your child at bedtime.

- Allow your child to mourn or grieve over a lost toy, a lost blanket, a lost home.

Parent Information Sheet - Post-Disaster *(continued)*

- If you feel your child is having problems at school, talk to his/her teacher so you can work together to help your child.

Please reread this sheet from time to time in the coming months. Usually a child's emotional response to a disaster will not last long, but some problems may be present or recur for many months afterward.

Your community mental health center is staffed by professionals skilled in talking with people experiencing disaster-related problems.

Source: Virginia Department of Education

Form II-10: Thank You Letter - Faculty/Staff

SCHOOL LETTERHEAD

Dear Faculty and Staff Members:

We would like to thank you for your support during the recent crisis at our school. Your professionalism and dedication were evident as we all worked to quiet and soothe scared students and allay their fears while still tending to instructional responsibilities.

We know that this has been an extremely difficult time for you as well as the students. Without your courage and concern, our school could not possibly have come through this crisis as well as we did.

Thank you once again. Your expertise and commitment have enabled all of us to work together as a team and overcome this tragic situation.

Sincerely,

Principal

Guidance Chair

Source: Virginia Department of Education

Form II-11: Bomb Threat Report Form

Make numerous copies and keep them at the main telephone or switchboard for immediate use.

Questions to Ask

1. When is bomb going to explode?
2. Where is it right now?
3. What does it look like?
4. What kind of bomb is it?
5. What will cause it to explode?
6. Did you place the bomb?
7. Why?
8. What is your address?
9. What is your name?

Caller's Voice

____ Calm	____ Nasal
____ Angry	____ Stutter
____ Excited	____ Lisp
____ Slow	____ Raspy
____ Rapid	____ Deep
____ Soft	____ Ragged
____ Loud	____ Clearing Throat
____ Laughter	____ Deep Breathing
____ Crying	____ Cracking Voice
____ Normal	____ Disguised
____ Distinct	____ Accent
____ Slurred	____ Familiar
____ Whispered	

Exact Wording of Threat

_____

_____

_____

Time:_____ Date: _____
Sex of caller: ____ Culture: ____
Age: _____ Length of call: ____

Number at which call was received:

_____

If voice was familiar, who did it sound like? _____

Background Sounds

____ Street	____ Animal Noises
____ PA System	____ Static
____ Voices	____ Music
____ Motor	____ House Noises
____ Local	____ Office Machines
____ Booth	____ Long Distance

Remarks:

_____

_____

_____

Threat Language

____ Well-spoken
____ Foul language
____ Taped
____ Incoherent
____ Message read

Source: Virginia Department of Education

Form II-12: Intruder Response

In the event that an intruder gains unauthorized access to school premises, key personnel should take these steps.

Staff:
1. Notify principal or other designated individual.

2. Take attendance and remain with students.

3. Wait for instructions.

Administrator or Designee:
1. Assess situation and determine threat level.

2. Call 911 if danger is indicated.

3. Contact appropriate administrator at telephone number _____.

4. If lockdown is needed, notify teachers.

5. Keep telephone lines open for emergency use.

6. Provide police with maps of building and grounds.

Source: University of Arkansas System, Criminal Justice Institute, School Violence Resource Center

Form II-13: Students/Staff Needing Special Assistance for Evacuation

Name	Grade/Homeroom	Assistance Needed/Assister

Main Building

_____   _____   _____

_____   _____   _____

_____   _____   _____

_____   _____   _____

_____   _____   _____

_____   _____   _____

_____   _____   _____

_____   _____   _____

Annex A

_____   _____   _____

_____   _____   _____

_____   _____   _____

_____   _____   _____

_____   _____   _____

_____   _____   _____

Source: Virginia Department of Education

Form II-14: 911 Script and Phone List – Cheerleader Injury

(Post by phones)

In case of emergency, call: _____

When the call is answered, talk slowly and clearly and say:

"We are located at (school or name of location). Our address is (street address, city, state and zip code). Our phone number is (a number that can be called back). One of our cheerleaders has injured her (describe nature of injury) and needs an ambulance. Please come to (provide the specific location at the site, such as "Main Gym" or "Tyler Field") located at (provide specifics of the location, such as "on the corner of Main Street and Tiger Drive"). We will have someone there to direct you."

Stay on the line until the dispatcher says you can hang up!

Additional Numbers:

Training Room Number: (_____) _____ - _____

Campus Security Number: (_____) _____ - _____

Other Numbers: (Principal, etc.)

_____   (_____) _____ - _____

_____   (_____) _____ - _____

_____   (_____) _____ - _____

Source: American Association of Cheerleading Coaches and Administrators

Form II-15: Parental Consent Form for Mercury Testing

Parents,

Please fill out the information below for your child (one for each student) and sign.

Student's name _____

SSN _____

Address _____

Sex (Circle one):   M   F

Date of birth _____

Phone number _____

Race (Circle one):
American Indian	Alaska Native	Asian
Black/African American	Native Hawaiian	
Other Pacific Islander	Underreported/Refuse to report	

Ethnicity (Circle one):
 | Hispanic/Latino | Non-Hispanic/Latino |
 | Underreported/Refuse to report | |

I give CONSENT to the LOCAL health department and its staff for my child named at the top of this form to have mercury levels checked with a urine test. (If this consent form is not signed and dated, then your child will not be tested.)

Signature of parent/legal guardian _____

Date (mm/dd/yy) _____

Source: Birmingham City Schools

Form II-16: Crisis Procedure Checklist

A crisis plan must address many complex contingencies. There should be a step-by-step procedure to use when a crisis occurs. For example:

_____Assess life/safety issues immediately.

_____Provide immediate emergency medical care.

_____Call 911 and notify police/rescue first. Call the superintendent second.

_____Convene the crisis team to assess the situation and implement the crisis response procedures.

_____Evaluate available and needed resources.

_____Alert school staff to the situation.

_____Secure all areas.

_____Implement evacuation and other procedures to protect students and staff from harm. Avoid dismissing students to unknown care.

_____Adjust the bell schedule to ensure safety during the crisis.

_____Alert person in charge of various information systems to prevent confusion and misinformation. Notify parents.

_____Contact appropriate community agencies and the school district's public information office, if appropriate.

_____Implement post-crisis procedures.

Source: U.S. Department of Education

Form II-17: What Are "Education Records"?

When you can – and can't – release information can be tricky business, thanks to the Family Educational Rights and Privacy Act (FERPA). As a general rule, FERPA requires schools to protect students' privacy. However, exceptions to FERPA confidentiality requirements apply in emergency situations.

Led by the Federal Bureau of Investigation and the Federal Emergency Management System, several government agencies – the Departments of Education, Homeland Security, Justice, Health and Human Services – completed the "Guide for Developing High-Quality School Emergency Operations Plans."

This guide provides examples of emergency-related exceptions to FERPA confidentiality rules.

Before we discuss the exceptions, we need to know what an "education record" is.

These types of records generally are considered to be education records, meaning they are protected under FERPA:

1. Transcripts

2. Disciplinary records

3. Standardized test results

4. Health (including mental health) and family history records

5. Records on services provided to students under the IDEA

6. Records on services and accommodations provided to students under Section 504 and Title II of the ADA

These types of records generally are not considered to be education records, meaning they are not protected by FERPA:

1. Records that are kept in the sole possession of the maker and used only as personal memory aids

---

What Are "Education Records"? *(continued)*

2. Law enforcement unit records

3. Grades on peer-graded papers before they are collected and recorded by a teacher

4. Records created or received by a school after an individual is no longer in attendance and that are not directly related to the individual's attendance at the school

5. Employee records that relate exclusively to an individual in that individual's capacity as an employee

6. Information obtained through a school official's personal knowledge or observation rather than from the student's education records

Source: Guide for Developing High-Quality School Emergency Operations Plans, http://rems.ed.gov/docs/REMS_K-12_Guide_508.pdf

---

Form II-18: Threat and Hazard Types and Examples

Planning teams must consider the probability, magnitude, warning time and duration of each possible threat or hazard. Some threat and hazard examples to consider include:

Natural Hazards

• Earthquakes

• Tornadoes

• Lightning

• Severe wind

• Hurricanes

• Floods

• Wildfires

• Extreme temperatures

• Landslides or mudslides

• Tsunamis

• Volcanic eruptions

• Winter precipitation

Technological Hazards

• Explosions or accidental release of toxins from industrial plants

• Accidental release of hazardous materials from within the school, such as gas leaks or laboratory spills

• Hazardous material releases from major highways or railroads

• Radiological releases from nuclear power stations

• Dam failure

Threat and Hazard Types and Examples *(continued)*

- Power failure

- Water failure

Biological Hazards

- Infectious diseases, such as pandemic influenza, extensively drug-resistant tuberculosis, *Staphylococcus aureus* and meningitis

- Contaminated food outbreaks, including Salmonella, botulism and *E.coli*

- Toxic materials present in school laboratories

Adversarial, Incidental and Human-caused Threats

- Fire

- Active shooters

- Criminal threats or actions

- Gang violence

- Bomb threats

- Domestic violence and abuse

- Cyber attacks

- Suicide

(Source: Guide for Developing High-Quality School Emergency Plans, www.dhs.gov/sites/default/files/publications/REMS%20K-12%20Guide%20508_0.pdf)

Form II-19: FEMA's Earthquake Preparedness Checklist

To keep students and staff safe in an earthquake, prepare them by conducting safety drills.

If students are <u>inside the school</u>, they should:

- Drop to the ground, take cover under a sturdy table or desk and hold on until the shaking stops.

- Cover their faces and heads in their arms and crouch in a corner if sturdy desks or tables aren't available for shelter.

- Stay away from glass, windows or anything that might fall, such as light fixtures.

- Stay inside until the shaking stops.

- Avoid the elevators.

If students are <u>outside</u>, they should:

- Stay outside.

- Get away from utility wires, buildings, streetlights and other structures. (Most earthquake-related deaths occur from flying debris, collapsing buildings and falling objects.)

If students are on the school bus, drivers should be trained to:

- Stop as quickly as safety permits.

- Avoid stopping near or under buildings, trees, overpasses, underpasses or utility wires.

- Keep students on the bus.

- Proceed with caution after the quake has stopped.

- Avoid roads, bridges or ramps that may have been structurally damaged.

- Contact the school if possible.

Source: http://www.ready.gov/earthquakes

Form II-20: Checklist: Reunification After a Crisis

When the feds updated their guidance to help school officials align their emergency planning practices with new national safety and security standards, they included plans to reunite families after a crisis.

As part of the "Family Reunification Annex," the emergency planning team must contemplate the best ways for school officials to:

- Protect parents' and students' privacy

- Verify that an adult has the authority to take custody of a student

- Facilitate communication between the parent check-in area and the student assembly area

- Ensure students do not leave on their own

- Address language barriers that may exist, and

- Keep families updated.

Source: Guide For Developing High-Quality School
Emergency Operations Plans

Form II-21: Bomb Threat Procedures

Most bomb threats are received by phone. Bomb threats are serious until proven otherwise. Act quickly, but remain calm and obtain information with the checklist below.

If a bomb threat is received by phone:

- Remain calm. Keep the caller on the line as long as possible. DO NOT HANG UP, even if the caller does.

- Listen carefully. Be polite and show interest.

- Try to keep the caller talking to learn more information.

- If possible, write a note to a colleague to call the authorities, or as soon as the caller hangs up, immediately notify them yourself.

- If your phone has a display, copy the number and/or letters on the window display.

- Complete the Bomb Threat Checklist immediately. Write down as much detail as you can remember. Try to get exact words.

- Immediately upon termination of the call, DO NOT HANG UP, but from a different phone, contact authorities immediately with information and await instruction.

If a bomb threat is received by a handwritten note:

Call: _____

If a bomb threat is received via email:

Do NOT delete the message. Call:_____

Signs of a suspicious package:

- No return address

- Excessive postage

- Stains

Bomb Threat Procedures *(continued)*

- Strange odor

- Strange sounds

- Unexpected delivery

- Poor handwriting

- Misspelled words

- Incorrect titles

- Foreign postage

- Restrictive notes

Refer to your local bomb threat emergency response plan or evacuation criteria. Do NOT:

- Use two-way radios or cellular phones. Radio signals have the potential to detonate a bomb.

- Touch or move a suspicious package.

Source: U.S. Department of Homeland Security

Form II-22: Sample Statement to the Media: School Violence

Date

From the office of [school and principal]

Re: Incident involving [school] students

An incident involving two [school] students in the [grade] occurred yesterday at about [time]. The incident occurred [location].

The incident resulted in the non-fatal shooting of one of the students. The injured student was taken to [hospital] and is expected to make a full recovery. The second student was taken into police custody.

An ongoing investigation is being conducted, but no more is known at this time.

The school's Emergency Management Response Team has taken the following actions in response to this incident:

- The Emergency Management Response Team met last night and planned a staff meeting before the school day.

- We notified staff of the meeting using our automated phone system. The team provided information to staff at the meeting and answered questions on what is known about the incident and steps to be taken in response.

- Crisis counseling for students is being provided by personnel from [community partners and resources].

- A review of the [school's] weapons policy is under way and school security is on alert for potential related violence.

Source: The Department of Homeland Security and The Federal Emergency Management Agency

---

Form II-23: Sample Parent Letter: Pre-Incident

Date

Dear Parents/Guardians:

Should an emergency or disaster situation ever arise in our area while school is in session, we want you to be aware that the schools have made preparations to respond effectively to such situations. In fact, schools in [STATE] are built to meet stringent construction standards and they may be safer than your own home in the event of a disaster.

Should we have a major incident during school hours, your student(s) will be cared for at this school. Our School District has a detailed emergency operations plan that has been formulated to respond to major incidents.

Your cooperation is necessary in any incident.

1. Do not telephone the school. Telephone lines may be needed for emergency communication.

2. In the event of a serious emergency, students will be kept at their school until they are picked up by an identified, responsible adult who has been identified as such on a School District green emergency card that is required to be filled out by parents at the beginning of every school year. Please be sure you consider the following criteria when you authorize another person to pick up your child at school:

   a. He/she is 18 or older.

   b. He/she is usually at home during the day.

   c. He/she could walk to the school, if necessary.

   d. He/she is known to your child.

   e. He/she is both aware of and able to assume this responsibility.

3. Turn your radio to [radio stations] for emergency announcements. If students are to be kept at school, radio stations will be notified. If electrical service is not affected, information will be relayed via the School District to cable

Sample Parent Letter: Pre-Incident *(continued)*

on Channel _____. In addition, information regarding day-to-day school operations will be made available by calling the District Office.

4. Impress upon your children the need for them to follow directions of any school personnel in times of an emergency.

STUDENTS WILL BE RELEASED ONLY TO PARENTS AND PERSONS IDENTIFIED ON THE SCHOOL DISTRICT EMERGENCY CARD. DURING AN EXTREME EMERGENCY, STUDENTS WILL BE RELEASED AT DESIGNATED REUNION GATES LOCATED ON SCHOOL CAMPUSES. PARENTS SHOULD BECOME FAMILIAR WITH THE SCHOOL EMERGENCY OPERATIONS PLAN AND BE PATIENT AND UNDERSTANDING WITH THE PARENT-STUDENT REUNIFICATION PROCESS. PLEASE INSTRUCT YOUR STUDENT TO REMAIN AT THE SCHOOL UNTIL YOU OR A DESIGNEE ARRIVES. BECAUSE LOCAL TELEPHONE SERVICE MAY BE DISRUPTED, ALSO LIST AN OUT-OF-STATE CONTACT ON THE EMERGENCY CARD, AS CALLS MAY STILL BE MADE OUT OF THE AREA WHILE INCOMING CALLS ARE AFFECTED.

The decision to keep students at school will be based on whether streets in the area are open. If this occurs, radio stations will be notified. In the event that a natural disaster takes place during the time that students are being transported, students will be kept on the bus and the driver will ask for assistance through radio contact with the school and district personnel. Any child who is home waiting for the bus will not be picked up (if roads are impassable) and remains the responsibility of the parent or guardian. In the event that a natural disaster occurs in the afternoon, the driver will make every attempt to continue delivering students to their homes. Should road conditions prevent the driver from delivering students to home or to school, the students will be delivered to the nearest school site and that school will communicate with the home school to inform them of the students' whereabouts.

In case of a hazardous release event (chemical spill) near the school, Shelter-in-Place procedures will be implemented to provide in-place protection. All students and staff will clear the fields, report to their rooms, and all efforts will be made to prevent outside air from entering classrooms during the emergency. "Shelter-in-Place" signs will be placed in classroom windows or hung outside classroom doors during a drill or an emergency. Students arriving at school during a Shelter-in-

Sample Parent Letter: Pre-Incident *(continued)*

Place drill or event should report to the school office or to a previously designated area at the school because classrooms will be inaccessible. When the danger incident has subsided, an all-clear will be given. Please discuss these matters with your immediate family.

Planning ahead will help alleviate concerns during an emergency.

Sincerely,

[Principal]

[School]

Source: The Department of Homeland Security and The Federal Emergency Management Agency

Form II-24: Involving Students in Prevention Checklist

Directions: Use the following checklist to assess the school's current level of safety related to opportunities for student involvement. If an element is in place, write "Yes." If changes need to be made, write "Improve." If an element is not in place, write "No." If your school plans to add this missing element, write "Implement." If it's not applicable, write "NA."

- Students are represented on the school planning or exercise team. _____

- The school provides opportunities for student leadership related to prevention and safety issues. _____

- The school provides adequate recognition opportunities for all students. _____

- Students are provided encouragement and support in establishing clubs and programs focused on safety. _____

- Students are adequately instructed in their responsibility to avoid becoming victims of violence (i.e., by avoiding high-risk situations and seeking help from adults). _____

- Students have the opportunity to participate in a conflict resolution program. _____

- Students have the opportunity to learn about bullying prevention, as well as conflict resolution, the prevention of sexual harassment and prevention of suicide. _____

- The school provides some form of an anonymous hotline whereby students may report incidents or suspicious activity. _____

Source: The Department of Homeland Security and The Federal Emergency Management Agency

Form II-25: Vulnerability/Hazard Assessment Checklist: Emergency Operations Plan

Directions: Please assess the following areas and answer with Yes, No, N/A (Not applicable), or N/AS (Not assessed).

The Emergency Operations Plan:

- Is all-hazard in nature addressing four phases of emergency management. _____

- Is reviewed and updated on an annual basis. _____

- Is developed by a school safety planning team, representative of essential stakeholders, including local law enforcement, emergency medical services and fire department personnel. _____

- Contains an updated map of the school's floor plan and site plan with room numbers, evacuation routes, utility shut offs, locations of first aid kits and other detailed information. _____

- Contains an established chain of command to respond to an emergency following Incident Command System (ICS) structure. _____

- Contains designated primary and alternate incident command posts. _____

The Emergency Operations Plan contains emergency procedures for:

- a bomb threat. _____

- a hostage taking. _____

- an intrusion. _____

- a kidnapping._____

- acts of violence, such as a school shooting, etc. _____

- a hazardous materials incident._____

- transportation accidents, including train derailments. _____

Vulnerability/Hazard Assessment Checklist:
Emergency Operations Plan *(continued)*

- natural disasters. _____

- persons with limited mobility. _____

- persons with special health needs. _____

- alternative evacuation sites. _____

- a plan for sustaining school occupants for 72 hours. _____

- a component for post-crisis response, such as the availability of mental health services for students and staff. _____

The following emergency drills are conducted and documented regularly:

- Lockdown. _____

- Evacuation of the building – per fire marshal code. _____

- Reverse evacuation. _____

- Bus evacuation._____

- Shelter-in-place. _____

- Severe weather._____

- After Action Reviews are conducted after drills, exercises and actual emergencies. _____

Reunification procedures include:

- Two confidential reunification sites _____

- Traffic control plan. _____

- Holding area for students is out of sight from parents. ____

- Requiring parents/guardians to provide photo identification prior to release of students. _____

Source: Readiness and Emergency Management for Schools, REMS.ed.gov

Form II-26: Vulnerability/Hazard Assessment Checklist: Instructional Facility

Directions: Please assess the following areas and answer with Yes, No, N/A (Not applicable), or N/AS (Not assessed).

- The facility has an electronic security system._____

- All buildings are equipped with closed-circuit digital video system. _____

- Video security system housings are designed to protect against tampering, vandalism and exposure to extreme temperature or moisture. _____

- Video security systems have an uninterruptible power supply and are connected to the building's emergency power supply. _____

- The video security system is protected with adequate firewalls so it cannot be broken into. _____

- Security camera recordings are retained for 30 days. _____

- The electronic security alarm system (including fire alarm system) is connected to local law enforcement or central reporting where appropriate agencies will be contacted.____

- The alarm system is in compliance with the Americans with Disabilities Act (ADA) requirements including provisions for hearing and/or visual impairments._____

- Staff members monitor hallways during school hours. ____

- Staff members monitor stairwells during school hours. ____

- Staff members monitor restrooms during school hours. ____

- Students are not allowed in the school building without direct staff supervision._____

- If the building is used after school or on weekends, staff/security is present. _____

Vulnerability/Hazard Assessment Checklist:
Instructional Facility *(continued)*

- The school requires background checks and fingerprinting of all school staff. _____

- Filters or other mechanisms are in place to monitor suspicious Internet activity on school computers. _____

- There is a written process for pre-employment, recruitment and training for personnel and/or monitors. _____

- Magnetometers (metal detectors) and x-ray equipment are installed and work effectively to deter student misbehavior. _____

- School-based law enforcement officers are located on-site. _____

- School-based law enforcement is dedicated to a single school. _____

- School-based law enforcement provides a visible and regular presence on campus during school hours. _____

- School-based law enforcement officers have an office with a view of the building entrance or main hallways. _____

- School-based law enforcement officers have written position descriptions and they are shared with school administration. _____

- School-based law enforcement officers conduct daily visual inspections of the school for suspicious packages and other items._____

- Local law enforcement/security personnel provide after-hours patrol of the school site. _____

- Background checks required for security personnel. _____

After the school day, staff members are assigned to check:

- All classrooms are locked. _____

- All bathrooms are unoccupied and/or locked. _____

Vulnerability/Hazard Assessment Checklist:
Instructional Facility *(continued)*

- All exterior doors are locked. _____

- All security lights are set. _____

- Security alarms are set. _____

Source: Readiness and Emergency Management for Schools, REMS.ed.gov

Form III-1: Bus Transportation Accident Response

Steps for key personnel to take in the event of a bus transportation accident:

Bus Driver:
1. Notify dispatch using proper procedures.
2. Secure the bus, making sure no passengers leave and no one boards the bus.
3. Set out warning devices such as triangle or cones.
4. Determine whether anyone has been injured.
5. Move the bus to a safer location on the side of the road, if possible.
6. Passenger safety is the most important thing to keep in mind. If the bus is not badly damaged and is not in danger of being struck, keep the passengers on the bus until help arrives.
7. Refer media to administration.

Dispatch:
1. Take control. Remain calm and help the driver make proper decisions.
2. Call designated management staff.
3. Call appropriate law enforcement agency or 911.

Transportation Personnel:
1. Upon arrival, assess for immediate safety concerns.
2. Complete accident reports and take pictures.
3. Refer media to administration.

Schools:
1. Contact parents and relay necessary information.
2. Conduct follow-up on any student who received medical treatment within three days of accident.

Source: University of Arkansas System, Criminal Justice Institute, School Violence Resource Center

Form III-2: Parent Letter - Notice of Bus Accident

Dear Parents,

This morning, prior to school, there was an accident involving a school bus and an automobile. There were known injuries to the passengers of the car. The children on Bus # _____ witnessed the aftermath of the accident but were not involved in it.

The children from the bus involved in the accident were taken to the library by the guidance counselors and administration. The children were asked if they were injured in any way and their parents were then contacted. Because your child was on Bus # ____ he or she may show delayed reaction to the accident. Please be alert over the next several days to symptoms of delayed reaction, including:

- a desire to be alone, unusually quiet

- loss of appetite

- problems with sleeping, nightmares

- difficulty with concentration

- crying

- angry outburst, short temper

- headaches, upset stomach

- depressed, sad

Your child may also exhibit some physical complaints. Please contact (principal's name) to fill out an accident report. The school will be offered support services for students needing help dealing with the accident. We will also provide counseling services to parents in helping their children to cope. Please don't hesitate to call if you have any questions or concerns.

Sincerely,

Principal of School

Source: Virginia Department of Education

Form III-3: Policy Regarding Social Networking Websites

All employees, faculty and staff of the _____ school district who participate in social networking websites (such as MySpace or Facebook) shall not post any data, documents, photographs or inappropriate information on any website that might result in a disruption of classroom activity. This determination will be made by the Superintendent. Employees, faculty and staff should not give social networking website passwords to students. Fraternization via the Internet between employees, faculty or staff and students is prohibited, and violation of any of these policies may result in disciplinary action, up to and including termination. Nothing in this policy prohibits employees, faculty, staff or students from using educational websites such as _____, since these sites are used solely for educational purposes. Access of social networking websites for individual use during school hours is prohibited.

Source: Lamar County (Mississippi) School District

Form III-4: Letter to Parents Regarding Sexting

Dear Parents and Guardians,

Today, our staff spoke with students in their first-period classes about some troubling behavior in which teens are engaging and which has occurred at the national, state and local levels. The behavior is commonly referred to as "sexting" (the act of sending sexually explicit material via cell phone). This week, we learned that this behavior is occurring at our school and at other schools in our district.

In an effort to better educate our students about this topic, teachers at our school were directed to read the following to students at the conclusion of morning announcements:

Some students at our school and other schools in our district have been sending and receiving inappropriate pictures on their cell phones. The pictures have been sexually explicit in nature. This practice is commonly referred to as "sexting." This is a particularly dangerous behavior for middle school students to engage in because they are minors.

If you or anyone you know has engaged in this activity, you must remove those pictures from your phone or any other place they may be (computer, etc.) and not engage in this behavior in the future. It is important for you to know that engaging in this behavior is a serious offense.

Our intent is to educate you about this matter and to help protect you from the serious social and criminal consequences that can occur if you engage in this behavior. Our overall goal is to keep you safe and to provide a safe and supportive learning environment here at our school.

Teachers were also instructed to remind students that electronic communications can spread rapidly anywhere in the world and can be tracked.

We care deeply about the students and the community we serve, and we appreciate your support as we educate our students about this issue. Please use this as an opportunity to talk to your child about proper cell phone use and the potential consequences of misuse. If you have any questions on the matter, please contact me at [PHONE].

Sincerely,

Principal

Source: Kristen Rae, Principal, Chinook Middle School, Lacey, WA

Form III-5: Harassment/Bullying Incident Report Form

Date: _____   Time: _____   Room/Location: _____

□ Staff   □ Student(s) Accused of Bullying/Harassment:

_____   Grade: ____   Class: _____

_____   Grade: ____   Class: _____

□ Staff   □ Student(s) Affected:

_____   Grade: ____   Class: _____

_____   Grade: ____   Class: _____

Inappropriate behaviors observed by adult(s) (check all that apply):

□	Name calling	□	Spitting
□	Stalking	□	Demeaning Comments
□	Inappropriate Gesturing	□	Stealing
□	Staring/Leering	□	Damaging Property
□	Writing/Graffiti	□	Shoving/Pushing
□	Threatening	□	Hitting/Kicking
□	Taunting/Ridiculing	□	Flashing a Weapon
□	Inappropriate Touching	□	Intimidation/Extortion
□	Cyberbullying	□	Other _____

Harassment/Bullying Incident Report Form *(continued)*

Describe the incident:

_____

_____

Did the injury involve physical injury?

☐   Yes   ☐   No

Names of witnesses:

_____

_____

_____

Physical Evidence:

☐ Graffiti   ☐ Notes   ☐ E-Mail   ☐ Websites _____

☐ Videotape ☐ Audiotape ☐ Other _____

Staff signature: _____ Title: _____

Parent(s) contacted: Date: _____   Time: _____

                   Date: _____   Time: _____

Administrative action taken:

_____

_____

Source: Oklahoma State Department of Education

Form III-6: Student Pledge for iPad Use

1. I will take good care of my iPad.

2. I will never leave the iPad unattended. Unattended iPads will be taken to the office.

3. I will never loan out my iPad to other individuals.

4. I will know where my iPad is at all times.

5. I will charge my iPad completely before the beginning of the school day.

6. I will keep food and beverages away from my iPad since they may damage the device.

7. I will not disassemble any part of my iPad or attempt any repairs or jailbreak my iPad.

8. I will protect my iPad by keeping it in the school-provided protective case.

9. I will use my iPad in ways that are appropriate, meet district expectations and are educational in nature.

10. I will not deface or place decorations (stickers or markers, etc.) on the iPad. I will not deface the serial number.

11. I understand that my iPad is subject to inspection at any time without notice and remains property of the school district. I will not put a security code on my iPad.

12. I will follow the policies outlined in the district's iPad Handbook at all times.

13. I will file a police report in case of theft, vandalism and other acts covered by insurance.

14. I will be responsible for all damage or loss caused by neglect or abuse.

Student Pledge for iPad Use *(continued)*

15. I agree to return the district iPad and power cords in good
    working condition.

16. I will not utilize unauthorized photos, videos and/or audio recordings
    of myself or any other person in an inappropriate manner.

I agree to the stipulations set forth in the Student Pledge for iPad Use.

Student's name (Please Print): _____

Grade: _____

Student signature: _____

Date: _____

Parent/guardian name (Please print): _____

Parent/guardian signature: _____

School iPads and accessories must be returned to _____
at the end of each school year. Students who graduate early, withdraw, are
suspended or expelled, or terminate enrollment at _____ for
any other reason must return their iPad on the date of termination.

Source: Oakley High School, Oakley, Kansas

Form III-7: Confidential
Gender Support Plan

School/District _____ Date _____

Student Information

Student's preferred name _____

Student's legal name _____

Student's gender _____ Assigned sex at birth _____

Grade level _____ Date of birth _____

Siblings/Grades _____

Parents/Guardians/Caregivers and relation to student _____
_____

Participants in meeting _____
_____

Parent/Guardian Involvement

Are guardians of this student aware of and supportive of their child's gender transition?   Yes   No

If not, what considerations must be accounted for in implementing this plan?_____
_____

Confidentiality, Privacy and Disclosure

How public or private will information about this student's gender be?

- Will district staff be aware? If so, specify the adult staff members: _____
  _____

- Will site level leadership/administration know? If so, specify

Confidential Gender Support Plan *(continued)*

the adult staff members: _____
_____

- Will teachers and other staff members know? If so, specify the adult staff members: _____
_____

- Is the student sharing the information with a limited number of classmates or friends? If so, specify the students: _____
_____

- Is the student openly "out" with adults and peers?   Yes   No

- Other issues not listed: _____
_____

If the student has asserted a degree of privacy, what are the expectations of the institution if that privacy is compromised? How will a teacher/staff member respond to questions about the student's gender from:

- Other students? _____
_____

- Staff members? _____
_____

- Parents/community members? _____
_____

Student Safety

Who will be the student's "go-to adult" on campus?   _____

If this person is not available, what should the student do? _____
_____

What, if any, will be the process for periodically checking in with the student and/or family?   _____
What are the expectations in the event the student is feeling unsafe and how will the student signal for help:

- During class: _____

Confidential Gender Support Plan *(continued)*

- Outside:_____

- In the halls: _____

- Other safety concerns or questions (specify): _____
  _____

Names, Pronouns and Student Records

Name/gender marker entered into the Student Information System:
_____

Name to be used when referring to the student? _____

Pronouns to be used when referring to the student? _____

Can the student's preferred name and gender marker be reflected in
the SIS? If so, how? _____
_____

If not, what adjustments can be made to protect the student's
privacy?
_____
_____

Who will be the point person for ensuring these adjustments are
made and communicated as needed?_____

How will instances be handled when the incorrect name/pronoun is
used? _____
_____

How will the student's privacy be accounted for and maintained in
the following situations or contexts:

- During registration: _____

- Completing enrollment: _____

- With substitute teachers: _____

- Standardized tests: _____

Confidential Gender Support Plan *(continued)*

- School photos: _____

- IEPs/Other services: _____
  _____

- After-school programs: _____

- Lunch lines: _____

- Taking attendance: _____

- Teacher grade books: _____

- Official school-home communication: _____
  _____

- Unofficial school-home communication (PTA/other): _____
  _____

- Summons to office: _____

- Yearbook: _____

- Student ID/Library cards: _____

- Posted lists: _____

- Distribution of texts/other school supplies: _____
  _____

- Assignment of IT accounts: _____
  _____

- PA announcements: _____

If student's guardians are not aware and supportive of the student's gender status, how will school-home communications be handled?
_____

What are some other ways the school needs to anticipate information about the student's preferred name and gender marker potentially being compromised? How will these be handled?_____
_____

Confidential Gender Support Plan *(continued)*

Use of Facilities

The student may use the following restrooms on campus: _____
_____

The student may change clothes in the following places: _____
_____

If the student has questions/concerns about the facilities, who will be the contact person?_____

What are the expectations regarding the use of facilities during class trips? _____
_____

What are the expectations regarding rooming for overnight trips?
_____

Are there any questions or concerns about the student's access to facilities?_____
_____

Extracurricular Activities

Does the student participate in an after-school program? _____

What steps will be necessary for supporting the student there? _____
_____

In what extracurricular programs or activities will the student be participating? (sports, theater, clubs, etc.) _____
_____

What steps will be necessary for supporting the student there? _____
_____

Other Considerations

Are there any specific social dynamics with other students, families or staff members that need to be discussed or accounted for? _____
_____

Confidential Gender Support Plan *(continued)*

Does the student have a sibling at school? If so, are there factors to consider regarding the sibling's needs? _____

_____

Does the school have a dress code? How will it be handled? _____

_____
_____

Are there lessons, units, content or other activities coming up this year to consider? (growth and development, social justice units, name projects, dance instruction, Pride events, school dances, etc.)__

_____
_____

What training(s) will the school engage in to build capacity for working with gender-expansive students? _____

_____
_____

Support Plan Review and Revision

How will this plan be monitored over time? _____

_____
_____

What will be the process should the student, family or school wish to revisit any aspect of the plan or seek additions to the plan? _____

_____
_____

What are the follow-ups or action items and who is responsible for them? _____

_____

Date and time of next meeting _____

Source: Schools in Transition: A Guide for Supporting Transgender Students in K-12 Schools, from the Human Rights Campaign Foundation

Form III-8: Confidential
Gender Transition Plan

School/District _____ Date _____

Student Information

Student's preferred name _____

Student's legal name _____

Student's gender _____ Assigned sex at birth _____

Grade level _____ Date of birth _____

Siblings/Grades _____

Parents/Guardians/Caregivers and relation to student _____
_____
_____

Participants in meeting _____
_____
_____

Parent/Guardian Involvement

Are guardians of this student aware of and supportive of their child's gender transition?   Yes   No

If not, what considerations must be accounted for in implementing this plan?_____
_____
_____

Initial Plan Meeting

When will the initial plan meeting take place? _____

Where will it occur? _____

Confidential Gender Transition Plan *(continued)*

Who will be the members of the team supporting the student's transition? _____

Student Transition Details

What is the specific information that will be conveyed to other students (be specific)? _____
_____

What requests will be made? _____

With whom and when will this information be shared?

- Peers in transitioning student's class only? Date: _____

- Peers in student's grade level? Date: _____

- With some/all students at school? Date: _____

- Other (specify)? Date: _____

Who will lead the lessons/activities framing the student's announcement? _____

What will the lessons/activities be? _____
_____

Will the student be present for the lesson/sharing of info about the transition? If yes, what, if any, role does the student want to play in the process? _____

Once the information is shared, what parameters/expectations will be set regarding approaching the student? _____

Key Decisions Prior to Student's Transition

<u>Communicating with Other Families</u>

Will any sort of information be shared with other families about the student's transition? _____

Confidential Gender Transition Plan *(continued)*

With whom? _____

How will it be distributed?_____

What specific info will be shared?_____

Questions/Notes:_____
_____

Training for School Staff

Will there be specific training about this student's transition with
school staff? If so, when_____

Will there be continued training? If so, what will be the context of
the training? _____
_____

Questions/Notes:_____
_____

Parent Information Night About Gender Diversity

Will there be specific training for school community members? If so,
when and who will conduct it? _____
_____

What will be the context of the training? _____
_____

Questions/Notes:_____
_____

Identifying and Enlisting Adult Allies

Are there any parents/adults in the community that will be enlisted to
support the child's transition? If so, who?_____
_____

When will you meet with the person and what will you request?____
_____

Identifying and Enlisting Peer Allies

Confidential Gender Transition Plan *(continued)*

Are there any students that will be enlisted to support the child's
transition? If so, who? _____

_____

When will you meet with them and what will you request? _____

_____

<u>Siblings</u>

Does the student have any siblings at the school? If so, what needs to
be considered for them? _____

_____

Training in the classroom? _____Emotional support? _____

Timeline

Which of the following will take place in relation to the student's
gender transition, when will it occur and who will be made
responsible for making it happen?

Activity	Date	Lead
Initial Planning Meeting		
Lessons/activities with other students		
Communications with other families		
Training for school staff		
Identifying and enlisting parent allies		
Identifying and enlisting parent allies		
Other:		

*Source: Schools in Transition: A Guide for Supporting Transgender
Students in K-12 Schools, from the Human Rights Campaign Foundation*

Form III-9: School Violence Prevention and Intervention Checklist

Directions: Use the following checklist to assess the school's current level of safety related to prevention and intervention efforts. If an element is in place, write YES. If changes need to be made, write IMPROVE. If an element is not in place, write NO.

- Students have access to conflict resolution programs. _____

- Students are assisted in developing anger management skills. _____

- Prevention of harassment is emphasized school wide._____

- Bilingual and multicultural resources are available to students and staff members. _____

- Programs are available for students who are academically at-risk. _____

- Students may ask for help without the loss of confidentiality. _____

- Students and parents are aware of community resources. __

- A bully prevention program is in place. _____

- The school has a well-developed network of service providers to which students can be referred._____

- Crisis prevention is an integral part of the school's safety plan; that is, practice of emergency drills and evacuation, a partnership with law enforcement officials, metal detection capability and adequate adult monitoring at all times._____

- Adequate suicide prevention support systems are in place for students. _____

- The school has implemented a character education program in accordance with state codes. _____

Sources: The Department of Homeland Security and The Federal Emergency Management Agency

Form III-10: Sample Statement to the Media:
School Bus Accident

Date

From the office of [school and principal]

Re: School Bus Accident

Students from [school and grade] and [teacher's name] were
returning from a field trip when their school bus was involved
in an accident on [road, highway, interstate]. The accident occurred
at approximately [time].

Emergency medical teams have arrived and are transporting
students to [nearby hospital]. [School administrator] is at the
accident scene. [District administrator] is on the way to the
hospital to assess the situation.

We are notifying parents and guardians of students involved in the
accident. In addition, parents and others may call our hotline at
[phone number] for more information.

Our Emergency Response Team is implementing our emergency
protocol for bus accidents.

[School] will keep parents, guardians, students and the community
informed of any developments in this situation.

*Sources: The Department of Homeland Security and The Federal
Emergency Management Agency*

Form IV-1: Sample Parent Letter Following Weapons Incident

Dear Parents and Guardians,

I am writing as a follow-up to my previous phone message regarding the student who carried disassembled pieces of a gun onto a (school name) bus today, and the subsequent steps taken to ensure student safety.

As explained in my message, the disassembled parts could not be discharged. Still, the pieces were quickly confiscated thanks to the responsible actions of another student who promptly reported their presence. This eliminated any possible danger to students and staff. We then contacted police, who are investigating the incident.

Please tell your children that the very presence of any weapon, even in pieces, poses serious potential threat. That is why the weapons are strictly prohibited in school and there are serious consequences for violators.

In today's situation, students were never in immediate danger. Continued safety was assured because a student did the right thing by reporting the matter to an adult.

Please discuss what happened with students who are old enough to understand. Reassure them that they are safe at school, but let them know they play an important role in maintaining that safety.

I will continue to keep you informed of all situations that affect our commitment to student safety. Working together, we can all keep (school name) a safe place to learn and grow.

Thank you for your understanding and support.

Sincerely,

Source: Ellis Elementary School,
Prince William County Schools, Virginia

Form IV-2: Student Knife Contract

We can work together to keep knives out of school. At [*school name*], every student has the right to feel safe and be safe at school.

- There is no reason for a student to have a knife at school

- No knives are allowed to be taken to school by students

- It is against the law for a student to have a knife at school

- A student who has a knife at school may receive serious consequences

What kinds of knives are banned?

You are not allowed to have any type of knife at school, including:

- Flick knives, ballistic knives, sheath knives, push daggers, trench knives, butterfly knives, star knives, butter knives, fruit knives or craft knives

- Any item that can be used as a weapon, for example, a chisel

What will happen if I bring a knife to school?

If you have a knife at school:

- The principal may call the police

- Police may search you and your property

- You may be disciplined, such as [include specific examples according to school policy]

- You may face criminal charges

How can I help to keep [school name] safe?

- Make sure you know the laws and rules about knives

- Ask your parents not to put knives or knife tools in your lunch box, pencil case or craft kit

Student Knife Contract *(continued)*

- Contact your teacher immediately if you are being bullied or threatened at school

- Immediately tell your teacher or another adult if you think someone had a knife at school, or if someone mentioned bringing a knife to school

- Immediately tell a teacher if a student is threatening anyone with an object that could cause injuries.

Source: Adapted from Queensland Government, Australia

Form VI-1: Questionnaire for Chaperones

Thank you for volunteering to serve as a chaperone for the following field trip: [INSERT TRIP DESCRIPTION AND DATE OF TRIP]. We value your willingness to help our school and our students.

Please complete, sign and date this form and return it to _____ no later than _____. Once we review the completed form, we will notify you whether you have been selected to serve as a chaperone on this trip. If the answer to any question below is "Yes," please explain in the space provided.

1. ___ Yes ___ No   Have you ever been disciplined for any type of misconduct in connection with your employment?

2. ___ Yes ___ No   Have you ever been convicted of a criminal offense?

3. ___ Yes ___ No   Are you on probation in any state?

4. ___ Yes ___ No   Have you ever been acquitted or found not guilty of any criminal offense for reasons related to insanity or diminished mental capacity?

5. ___ Yes ___ No   Are any criminal charges currently pending against you?

I certify that I am at least 21 years of age and have completed this form truthfully and to the best of my knowledge.

PRINT NAME: _____   SIGNATURE: _____

DATE: _____

ADDRESS: _____

PHONE: _____

Form VI-2: Guidelines for Chaperones

Thank you for agreeing to serve as a chaperone for the following field trip:
[INSERT TRIP DESCRIPTION AND DATE OF TRIP].

As a chaperone, you serve as a role model and help students learn. The
following guidelines for chaperones apply to this trip. Please review them
carefully. Please sign and date this form and return it to _____
no later than _____. Once again, thank you for your assistance.

1. Chaperones are required to remain with their assigned group at all times,
   until chaperoning duties are finished.

2. Chaperones agree to continuously monitor their group's activities.

3. Chaperones will not use any alcohol or tobacco products during the trip
   at any time.

4. Chaperones will refrain from using profane or inappropriate language
   at any time during the trip.

5. Chaperones are NEVER to touch a child unless the child is presenting
   an immediate threat to the health or safety of himself or others.

6. Chaperones are not to administer medications to students.

7. Chaperones may not bring along non-student siblings or other children
   on the trip.

8. Chaperones will report any safety or health concerns to a teacher
   immediately.

I have read the above guidelines and agree to abide by them.

NAME: _____

SIGNATURE: _____

DATE: _____

Form VI-3: Field Trip Permission Slip

On _____, your child's class will be taking a field trip to _____.
We will be leaving the school at _____
and returning at _____. The cost of this trip is _____.

If cost is a concern, please contact the school principal.

Please complete and return the bottom portion of this form no later than
_____. Your child will not be permitted to attend if this slip is not
completed and returned.

I give permission for my child, _____, of room _____,
to attend the field trip to _____ on _____.
I am enclosing a check or money order in the amount of _____
made payable to _____, to cover the cost of this trip.

I hereby grant permission for school personnel to arrange for the provision
of medical treatment to _____ in the event of a medical
emergency. If such an emergency occurs, please contact
_____ at phone number _____ or
_____ at phone number _____

If your child is allergic to any medications, please list them here (if none,
write "none"): _____.

NAME: _____

SIGNATURE _____

PHONE: _____

RELATIONSHIP TO STUDENT_____

Form VI-4: Mentor Contract

Name: _____   Date: _____

By choosing to participate in this mentoring program, I agree to:
- Follow all rules and guidelines as outlined by the program coordinator, mentor training, program policies, and this contract
- Provide the support and advice to help my mentee succeed
- Make a one-year commitment to being matched with my mentee
- Meet at least eight hours per month with my mentee
- Make at least weekly contact with my mentee
- Obtain parent/guardian permission for all meeting times at least three days in advance, if possible
- Be on time for scheduled meetings or call my mentee at least 24 hours beforehand if I am unable to make a meeting
- Submit monthly meeting times and activities to the program coordinator, and regularly and openly communicate with the program coordinator as requested
- Inform the program coordinator of any difficulties or areas of concern that may arise in the relationship
- Keep any information that my mentee tells me confidential except as may cause him or others harm
- Always obey traffic laws when in the presence of my mentee and keep a copy of his/her health insurance coverage in the automobile at all times when traveling together
- Never be in the presence of my mentee when I have or am consuming alcohol, tobacco, or controlled substances
- Participate in a closure process when that time comes
- Notify the program coordinator if I have any changes in address, phone number, or employment status
- Attend in-service mentor training sessions twice per year

_____ (please initial) I understand that upon match closure, future contact with my mentee is beyond the scope of this program and may happen only by the mutual consensus of the mentor, the mentee, and parent/guardian.

I agree to follow all the above stipulations of this program as well as any other conditions as instructed by the program coordinator.

_____   _____
(Signature)   (Date)

Source: U.S. Department of Education

Form VI-5: Mentor Acceptance Letter

Date

Mr. John Doe
123 Main Street
Anytown, USA

Dear Mr. Doe,

Congratulations!

On behalf of our mentoring program, we are happy to inform you of
your acceptance as a mentor. Without the enthusiasm of volunteers like
you, we would not be able to accomplish our mission.

We thank you for taking the time and effort to join our program and
look forward to continuing to support you and assist you as a mentor.
At this time, we are working in finding you a suitable match and will
contact you when we have found you a mentee.

Sincerely,

Principal/Program Coordinator

Source: U.S. Department of Education

Form VI-6: Mentor Rejection Letter

Date

Mr. John Doe
123 Main Street
Anytown, USA

Dear Mr. Doe,

On behalf of our mentoring program, I wanted to express my sincere thanks for your interest in our program. I understand that you have given a considerable amount of time to this process and we greatly appreciate your effort. Unfortunately, we are unable to accept your application to be a mentor for our program.

Thank you again for your time and interest in our program.

Sincerely,

Principal/Program Coordinator

Source: U.S. Department of Education

Form VI-7: Parent/Guardian Mentoring Contract

Name: _____   Date: _____

   By allowing my son/daughter to participate in the mentoring program, I agree to:
- Allow my child to participate in the program and to be matched with a mentor
- Follow and encourage my child to follow all rules and guidelines as outlined by the program coordinator, mentee training, program policies, and this contract
- Support my child in this match by allowing him to meet with his mentor at least eight hours per month and have weekly contact with him/her for a year
- Support my child being on time for scheduled meetings or have him/her call the mentor at least 24 hours beforehand if unable to make a meeting
- Regularly and openly communicate with the program coordinator as requested
- Inform the program coordinator if I observe any difficulties or have areas of concern that may arise in the match relationship
- Participate in a closure process when that time comes
- Notify the program coordinator if I have any changes in address or phone number
- Provide the program coordinator and the mentor with any updated health insurance information for my child

   _____ (please initial) I understand that upon match closure, future contact between my child and his/her mentor is beyond the scope of this mentoring program, and can happen only by the mutual consensus of the mentor, the mentee, and their parent/guardian.

   I agree to follow all the above stipulations of this program as well as any other conditions as instructed by the program coordinator.

_____   _____
(Signature)   (Date)

Source: U.S. Department of Education

Form VI-8: Mentor Contact and Information Release Form

Youth's Name: _____ Date: _____

School: _____

I hereby grant permission for the mentoring program to make contact with my child and conduct a personal interview for the purpose of applying to be a mentee. The program may also make contact with my child on school premises for the purpose of screening and interviewing as well as ongoing support of his/her participation in the mentoring program.

I authorize the program to obtain any needed information regarding my child from his/her school's staff, including academic and behavioral records and conversations with teachers, counselors, and other administrative staff.

Further, I understand that basic information about my child will be anonymously (without names) shared with a prospective mentor(s) to aid in determining a suitable match. Once a mentor/mentee match is determined, my child's identity and other relevant information will be shared with the mentor to the extent it aids in facilitating a successful match.

_____ _____
Parent/Guardian Signature   Date

Parent/Guardian Name: _____

Street Address: _____

City: _____ State: _____ Zip: _____

Source: U.S. Department of Education

Form VI-9: Playground Safety Checklist

Use this checklist to make sure your playground area is a safe place to play.

1. Make sure the surfaces surrounding playground equipment either have at least 12 inches of wood chips, mulch, sand, or pea gravel, or are mats made of safety-tested rubber or rubber-like materials.

2. Check that protective surfacing extends at least six feet in all directions from play equipment. For swings, be sure surfacing extends, in front and back, twice the height of the suspending bar.

3. Make sure play structures more than 30 inches high are spaced at least nine feet apart.

4. Check for dangerous hardware, such as open "S" hooks or protruding bolt ends.

5. Make sure spaces that could trap children, such as openings in guardrails or between ladder rungs, measure less than 3.5 inches or more than nine inches.

6. Check for sharp points or edges in equipment.

7. Make sure there are no tripping hazards, such as exposed concrete footings, tree stumps and rocks.

8. Make sure elevated surfaces such as platforms and ramps have guardrails to prevent falls.

9. Regularly check to ensure that equipment and surfacing are in good condition.

10. Carefully supervise children at all times.

Source: U.S. Consumer Product Safety Commission

Form VI-10: Concussion Quiz for Coaches, Athletes and Parents

Mark each of the following statements as True (T) or False (F).

1. A concussion is a brain injury.

2. Concussions can occur in any organized or unorganized recreational sport or activity.

3. You can't see a concussion and some athletes may not experience and/or report symptoms until hours or days after the injury.

4. Following a coach's rules for safety and the rules of the sport, practicing good sportsmanship at all times, and using the proper sports equipment are all ways that athletes can prevent a concussion.

5. Concussions can be caused by a fall or by a bump or blow to the head or body.

6. Concussions can happen even if the athlete hasn't been knocked out or lost consciousness.

7. Nausea, headaches, sensitivity to light or noise, and difficulty concentrating are some of the symptoms of concussion.

8. Athletes who have a concussion should not return to play until they are symptom-free and have received approval from a doctor or health care professional.

9. A repeat concussion that occurs before the brain recovers from the first can slow recovery or increase the likelihood of having long-term problems.

ANSWER KEY: 1. True. 2. True. 3. True. 4. True. 5. True. 6. True. 7. True. 8. True. 9. True.

Source: Centers for Disease Control and Prevention

Form VI-11: Behavior Contract/Prom Permission Slip

Student's Name _____
Guest's Name _____

Student Release Information

I have read the rules on this form, the Behavior Contract/Prom
Permission Slip, and agree to abide by them. I understand the
consequences for any inappropriate behavior. I understand the dance is
a school event, and like all school events, is TOBACCO, DRUG AND
ALCOHOL FREE. **MY DATE AND I AGREE TO REMAIN DRUG
AND ALCOHOL FREE FOR THIS EVENT!**

Student signature _____
Printed name _____Date _____
I understand that I may be called if my child has a problem at
this event. The phone numbers where I may be reached are
(home) _____ and (cell) _____
Parent/Guardian signature _____
Relationship to student _____Date _____

Guest Release Information

I have read the rules on this form, the Behavior Contract/Prom
Permission Slip, and agree to abide by them. I understand the
consequences for any inappropriate behavior. I understand the dance is
a school event, and like all school events, is TOBACCO, DRUG AND
ALCOHOL FREE. MY DATE AND I AGREE TO REMAIN DRUG
AND ALCOHOL FREE FOR THIS EVENT!

Guest signature _____
Printed name _____Date _____
Grade ____Age ____ School attending _____
I understand that I may be called if my child has a problem at
this event. The phone numbers where I may be reached are
(home) _____ and (cell) _____
Parent/Guardian signature _____
Relationship to student _____Date _____

Please have an administrator from the guest's school sign below and
include the administrator's business card. **NOTE: Please do not sign if
guest has been suspended or expelled.**

Administrator's signature_____
Administrator's printed name _____
Phone number _____

Behavior Contract/Prom Permission Slip *(continued)*

The prom will be held on _____, beginning at ___ and ending at ___ at _____ _____. Students who purchase tickets are required to inform their guests of all contract rules. Students and guests are required to abide by all school rules and terms of this contract. Any student or guest exhibiting disruptive behavior will be removed from the dance, and the student/guest will be released to a chaperone or police if parents cannot be reached. Students will be held accountable for the behavior of their guest. No reimbursement or refund will be given if students and guests are asked to leave for not following this agreement.

Tickets
Tickets will be on sale beginning _____. They will be available at _____.
Ticket prices are $_____. Accepted forms of payment include ____ _____.

Refunds will be considered up until 48 hours before the dance. **Absolutely no refunds after that point.** Students who are removed or denied entry will not receive refunds.

Students must bring a clear copy of their student ID. Guests must bring a clear photocopy of a current high school photo ID card or a government-issued photo ID that shows date of birth. Copies must be legible to be accepted.
We do not make copies – bring your own.

Admittance
Admittance is subject to administrator's approval. **Admittance is a privilege, not a right**, which may be revoked for a lack of responsibility at the school, including but not limited to: unpaid fines, unfulfilled detentions, serious (suspensions or expulsions) or chronic discipline issues, unsatisfactory attendance or failing grades.

All attendees must present valid picture identification at the registration table at the dance to be admitted.
NO VALID ID, NO ENTRANCE!

All attendees must be willing to submit to alcohol/drug testing. All students and their guests may be searched for weapons and illegal substances prior to entry of the dance.

No one will be admitted after _____ without prior written consent from _____. Attendees are required to stay until _____ before they are released from the dance. Students and guests who leave the prom will not be readmitted.

Behavior Contract/Prom Permission Slip *(continued)*

All students and guests must be picked up by _____.

Rules

All school rules and regulations are enforced at any school event.
Any student or guest suspected of using alcohol or any controlled or
illegal substance will be removed from the dance. Parents will be called
to escort the student home. Smoking tobacco at school events is
prohibited. Any student who is under the influence of any substance
is subject to suspension.

Students who purchase tickets are required to inform their guests about
the contract rules. Guests are required to abide by the rules and the
terms of this contract. Any student or guest exhibiting disruptive
behavior will be removed from the dance, and the student/guest will
be released to a chaperone or police if parents cannot be reached.
Students will be held accountable for the behavior of their guest. No
reimbursement or refund will be given if students and guests are asked
to leave for not following this agreement.

Students who violate any school rule or the terms of this contract will
face disciplinary action.

Conduct

No dancing such as freaking, moshing or slamming will be permitted.
No back-to-front dancing, bending over, no leg or hip riding, both feet
must be on the floor and any other dancing deemed inappropriate by
administration. **NOTE: Violation of the dancing policy will consist
of removal from the dance floor and forfeit attendance at the next
school sponsored formal dance.** No reimbursement will be given to
attendees who are asked to leave for violating the dance policy.

Dress Code

Formal attire is required for prom. The following dress code restrictions
will be in effect. Violations may result in non-admittance. If dress code
violations occur after admittance, students and/or guests may be
removed from the dance. If anyone has specific questions regarding
the appropriateness of their dress, please consult with
_____ or _____
prior to the event.

Females: Dresses that expose skin in the midriff area are not
           acceptable, including revealing sides and low-cut backs.

           Bandeau/tube/scarf tops and excessively low cut or plunging
           necklines are prohibited.

Behavior Contract/Prom Permission Slip *(continued)*

Dresses must be an appropriate length, which is _____.

Any other clothing deemed inappropriate by the school dress code is prohibited.

Males: Collared shirts, slacks, ties required.

No jeans or shorts are permitted.

Undershirts may not be worn in place of collared shirt.

Bare chest may not be exposed.

Any other clothing deemed inappropriate by the school dress code is prohibited.

Checklist to include with completed form:

_____ Photocopies of all attendees' IDs (attach to form).

_____ Payment for tickets.

_____ Permission slip signed by all parties and filled out completely.

_____ Administrator's signature for guest admittance.

Source: Mission Viejo High School

Form VI-12: Playground Safety Checklist for Kids

Directions: Circle the answer to each question.

Supervision

Are adults at the playground?   Yes   No

Can adults see children in crawl spaces?   Yes   No
(Hint: Crawl spaces are areas where kids can hide.)

Are the rules posted?   Yes   No

Age Appropriate

Are the play areas separated   Yes   No
for younger and older kids?

Is the equipment at the correct height?   Yes   No
(Hint: Equipment should be below 8 feet
for kids between the ages of 5 and 12.)

Are signs about rules and safety posted?   Yes   No

Fall Surfacing

Does the surface have appropriate materials?   Yes   No
(Hint: Appropriate materials are sand, pea gravel,
wood products, shredded rubber or rubber mats.)

Are the materials 12 inches deep?   Yes   No

Is the playground clean?   Yes   No

Equipment Maintenance

Are the spaces in the equipment less   Yes   No
than 3½ inches or greater than 9 inches?
(Hint: Spaces that are between 3½
and 9 inches can cause strangulation.)

Is the equipment in good condition?   Yes   No

Is the equipment surface smooth?   Yes   No

**If you circled "No," then that's a problem area and you should
tell someone, such as a teacher, parent or principal.**

Playground Safety Checklist for Kids *(continued)*

What you can do to help make your playground safe:

- Check your playground for safe conditions.

- Pick up the trash.

- Help make adults aware of things that need to be fixed.

- Play on the playground only when it's safe.

- Teach other kids about the importance of playground safety.

Source: National Program for Playground Safety

Form VI-13: Youth Pledge: Responsible Walking and Bicycling

You know how to walk and bike, but take a second to review what it means to be a responsible pedestrian and bike "Roll Model" to others.

Remember, younger kids look up to you and follow your lead and some older adults learned differently or don't remember. You can be an example to others.

By signing this pledge, I agree to be a responsible "Roll Model" by promising to ...

- Walk on the sidewalk if there is one. If not, I'll walk on the side of the road facing traffic.

- Cross streets safely. I will:

  — Cross in crosswalks or at intersections.

  — Stop at the edge of the street and look left, right, and left again, crossing only when it's clear. As I'm crossing, I'll continue to look for traffic in all directions.

  — Stop at the outside edge of parked cars and look left, right and left again, crossing only when it's clear. I'll keep scanning (looking) for traffic as I cross.

- Stay alert, scanning and listening for traffic. I will:

  — Stop using personal electronic equipment, such as my phone or mp3 player when walking and biking around traffic.

  — Watch out for my own safety by adjusting my position, so I can see and get out of the way of traffic (cars, buses, trucks, pedestrians and bicyclists) and avoid obstacles (overgrown bushes, potholes, parked cars, etc.).

- Wear my bike helmet correctly (level on my head, covering my forehead and buckled) every time I ride, and I will encourage my friends and family to do the same.

Youth Pledge: Responsible Walking
and Bicycling *(continued)*

- Always bike in the same direction as traffic, whether riding on the sidewalk or road.

- Wear bright or fluorescent colors when I walk or bike during the day, to be seen.

- When I walk or bike at dusk/dawn, in fog or rain, and at night, I will:

  — Wear reflective gear (vest, dots, strips, laces, etc.) on my clothes, shoes, backpack, helmet and bike.

  — Use front white lights and red rear lights/reflectors on my bike as required by law.

  — Use a flashlight or wear lights when walking.

- Stay 10 feet (five big steps) away from the street when waiting for buses.

- Stop, look and listen for approaching trains before I cross railroad tracks.

- Walk/bike with my friends or in a group whenever possible.

Youth signature:_____

Date: _____

Peer witness: _____

Date: _____

Source: National Highway Traffic Safety Administration, www.nhtsa.gov

Form VI-14: Quiz: 10 Playground Safety Questions

- **Is the playground surface safe?**

  Unsafe surfaces such as concrete – and sometimes even grass – have the risk of severely injuring or killing. Falling is the No. 1 cause of injuries on the playground, and therefore it is important to restrict children from playing on equipment placed on hard surfaces like asphalt, concrete and packed earth or grass. Acceptable playground surfacing should be certified wood fiber, shredded rubber or poured-in-place surfacing.

- **Is there enough room underneath and around playground equipment?**

  The general rule is to allow a minimum use zone of six feet around playground equipment. Refer to the ASTM f1487 Standard or the Consumer Product Safety Commission guidelines for specific zone use requirements.

- **Is there enough space between the playground equipment?**

  The general rule is to allow a minimum use zone of six feet around playground equipment. Refer to the ASTM f1487 Standard or the Consumer Product Safety Commission guidelines for specific zone use requirements.

- **Is the playground appropriate for children?**

  Each playground should be designed appropriately to meet the needs of children that vary in age and ability.

- **Does the equipment put children at risk from protruding objects?**

  Jutting pieces of hardware should not be on the equipment. Protruding objects could severely cut or injure children.

- **Does the playground equipment present a strangulation risk?**

  Look for anything that has the potential to snag on clothing, jewelry or strings.

Quiz: 10 Playground Safety Questions *(continued)*

- **Are there any moving parts that could pinch children?**

  There should be no access points where kids could possibly be pinched.

- **Is there anything that might cause children to trip? Surfaces should be smooth and free of tripping hazards.**

  Ensure the ground is level by checking for tree stumps, roots or rocks.

- **Is the playground well maintained?**

  Playground equipment and hardware should be well kept. Rust and other deterioration are signs to reevaluate maintenance procedures. Regular inspection is important to keep the playground in good condition.

- **Has the playground been renovated since 1993?**

  Out-of-date equipment can be extremely dangerous. Throughout the 60s, 70s and 80s, playgrounds were commonly equipped with heavy metal swings, which can potentially injure children who walk in front of them. Frequent renovation is essential in order to secure playground safety.

Sources: The Voice of Play – an initiative of the nonprofit International Play Equipment Manufacturers Association voiceofplay.org

Form VII-1: Parent Letter Regarding Child with Allergy

Dear Parents,

This letter is to inform you that a student in your child's classroom has a severe peanut/nut allergy. Strict avoidance of peanut/nut products is the only way to prevent a life-threatening allergic reaction. We are asking your assistance in providing the student with a safe learning environment.

If exposed to peanuts/nuts the student may develop a life-threatening allergic reaction that requires emergency medical treatment. The greatest potential for exposure at school is to peanut products and nut products. To reduce the risk of exposure, the classroom will be peanut/nut free. Please do not send any peanut- or nut-containing products for your child to eat during snack-time in the classroom. Any exposure to peanuts or nuts through contact or ingestion can cause a severe reaction. If your child has eaten peanuts or nuts prior to coming to school, please be sure your child's hands have been thoroughly washed prior to entering the school.

Since lunch is eaten in the cafeteria, your child may bring peanut butter, peanut or nut products for lunch. In the cafeteria there will be a designated peanut-free table where any classmate without peanut or nut products can sit. If your child sits at this table with a peanut or nut product, s/he will be asked to move to another table. This plan will help to maintain safety in the classroom while allowing non-allergic classmates to enjoy peanut/nut products in a controlled environment. Following lunch, the children will wash their hands prior to going to recess or returning to the class. The tables will be cleaned with soap, water and paper towels after each lunch.

We appreciate your support of these procedures. Please complete and return this form so that we are certain that every family has received this information. If you have any questions, please contact me.

x _____
Signature of Principal/Teacher/Nurse

I have read and understand the peanut/nut-free classroom procedures. I agree to do my part in keeping the classroom peanut and nut free.

Child's name:_____

Parent's signature: _____

Date: _____

Source: Massachusetts Department of Education

Form VII-2: Substitute Teacher Letter
Regarding Child with Allergy

Dear Substitute Teacher,

The students listed below in this class have life-threatening food allergies.

Please maintain the food allergy avoidance strategies that we have developed to protect these students.

Should a student ingest, touch or inhale the substance to which they are allergic (the allergen), a severe reaction (anaphylaxis) may follow requiring the administration of epinephrine (Epi-pen®).

The Allergy Action Plan, which states who has been trained to administer epinephrine, is located _____.
Epinephrine is a life-preserving medication and should be given in the first minutes of a reaction.

Student   Allergies

_____

_____

_____

_____

_____

Please treat this information confidentially to protect the privacy of the students. Your cooperation is essential to ensure their safety. Should you have any questions please contact the school nurse _____ or the principal _____.

_____
Classroom teacher

Source: Massachusetts Department of Education

Form VII-3: Sample Diabetes Management Plan

Effective Dates: _____

This plan should be completed by the student's personal health care team and parents/guardian. It should be reviewed with relevant school staff and copies should be kept in a place that is easily accessed by the school nurse, trained diabetes personnel, and other authorized personnel.

Student's Name: _____

Date of Birth: _____ Date of Diagnosis: _____

Grade: _____ Homeroom Teacher: _____

Physical Condition: _____ Type 1 Diabetes _____ Type 2 Diabetes _____

Contact Information

Mother/Guardian: _____

Address: _____

Telephone: Home: _____ Work: _____Cell:_____

Father/Guardian: _____

Address: _____

Telephone: Home: _____ Work: _____ Cell: _____

Other Emergency Contacts:

Name: _____

Relationship: _____

Telephone: Home: _____ Work: _____ Cell: _____

Notify parents/guardian or emergency contact in the following situations:

_____

_____

Sample Diabetes Management Plan *(continued)*

Blood Glucose Monitoring

Target range for blood glucose: _____ 70-150 _____ 70-180 _____ Other: _____

Usual times to check blood glucose:_____

Times to do extra blood glucose checks (*check all that apply*):

_____ before exercise

_____ after exercise

_____ when student shows signs of hyperglycemia

_____ when student shows signs of hypoglycemia

_____ other (explain): _____

Can student perform own blood glucose checks? _____ Yes _____ No

Type of blood glucose meter student uses: _____

Insulin

Usual Lunchtime Dose

Base dose of Humalog/Novolog/Regular insulin at lunch (circle type of rapid-/short-acting insulin used) is _____ units or does flexible dosing using _____ units/_____ grams carbohydrate. Use of other insulin at lunch: (circle type of insulin used): intermediate/NPH/lente _____ units or basal/Lantus/Ultralente _____ units.

Insulin Correction Doses

Parental authorization should be obtained before administering a correction dose for high blood glucose levels. _____ Yes _____ No

_____ units if blood pressure is _____ to _____ mg/dl

_____ units if blood pressure is _____ to _____ mg/dl

_____ units if blood pressure is _____ to _____ mg/dl

_____ units if blood pressure is _____ to _____ mg/dl

_____ units if blood pressure is _____ to _____ mg/dl

Can student give own injections? _____ Yes _____ No

Can student determine correct amount of insulin? _____ Yes _____ No

Can student draw correct dose of insulin? _____ Yes _____ No

_____ Parents are authorized to adjust the insulin dosage under the following circumstances: _____

Sample Diabetes Management Plan *(continued)*

For Students with Insulin Pumps

Type of pump: _____ Basal rates: _____ 12 am to _____

_____ _____ to _____

_____ _____ to _____

Type of insulin in pump: _____

Type of infusion set: _____

Insulin/carbohydrate ratio: _____ Correction factor: _____

Student Pump Abilities/Skills	*Needs Assistance*
Count carbohydrates	_____ Yes _____ No
Bolus correct amount for carbohydrates consumed	_____ Yes _____ No
Calculate and administer corrective bolus	_____ Yes _____ No
Calculate and set basal profiles	_____ Yes _____ No
Calculate and set temporary basal rate	_____ Yes _____ No
Disconnect pump	_____ Yes _____ No
Reconnect pump at infusion set	_____ Yes _____ No
Prepare reservoir and tubing	_____ Yes _____ No
Insert infusion set	_____ Yes _____ No
Troubleshoot alarms and malfunctions	_____ Yes _____ No

For Students Taking Oral Diabetes Medications

Type of medication: _____ Timing: _____

Other medications: _____ Timing: _____

Meals and Snacks Eaten at School

Is student independent in carbohydrate calculations and management? ___ Yes ___ No

Meal/Snack	*Time*	*Food content/amount*
Breakfast	_____	_____
Mid-morning snack	_____	_____
Lunch	_____	_____
Mid-afternoon snack	_____	_____
Dinner	_____	_____

Sample Diabetes Management Plan *(continued)*

Snack before exercise? ____ Yes ____ No

Snack after exercise? ____ Yes ____ No

Other times to give snacks and correct amount: _____

Preferred food snacks: _____

Foods to avoid, if any: _____

Instructions for when food is provided to the class (e.g., as part of a class party or food sampling event):

_____

_____

Exercise and Sports

A fast-acting carbohydrate such as _____ should be available at the site of exercise or sports.

Restrictions on activity, if any: _____

Student should not exercise if blood-glucose level is below _____ mg/dl or above _____ mg/dl or if moderate to large urine ketones are present.

Hypoglycemia (Low Blood Sugar)

Usual symptoms of hypoglycemia: _____

_____

Treatment of hypoglycemia: _____

_____

Urine should be checked for ketones when blood-glucose levels are above ____ mg/dl.

Treatment for ketones: _____

Supplies to Be Kept at School

____ Blood-glucose meter, test strips, batteries   ____ Insulin pump and supplies

____ Lancet device, lancets, gloves, etc.   ____ Insulin pen, needles cartridges

____ Urine ketone strips   ____ Carbohydrate containing snack

____ Insulin vials and syringes   ____ Glucagon emergency kit

Sample Diabetes Management Plan *(continued)*

Signatures

This Diabetes Medical Management Plan has been approved by:

_____   _____
Student's Physician/Health Care Provider   Date

I give permission to the school nurse, trained diabetes personnel, and other designated staff members of _____ school to perform and carry out the diabetes care tasks as outlined by _____'s Diabetes Medical Management Plan. I also consent to the release of the information contained in this Diabetes Medical Management Plan to all staff members and other adults who have custodial care of my child and who may need to know this information to maintain my child's health and safety.

Acknowledged and received by:

_____   _____
Student's Parent/Guardian   Date

_____   _____
Student's Parent/Guardian   Date

Source: U.S. Department of Health and Human Services

Form VII-4: Parent Letter Regarding MRSA

Dear Parents,

This letter is being sent to provide information regarding Methicillin-Resistant Staphylococcus Aureus (MRSA) infections in schools.

MRSA infection is a type of staph infection that is resistant to some antibiotics. It has existed for decades but has just recently begun to become more prevalent in non-health care settings, including schools. Although MRSA infection is a cause for some concern, it is completely preventable and completely curable.

Our school district has posted information about MRSA infection and precautions that your child can take on our Web site at _____. Further information is available from the Centers for Disease Control and Prevention at www.cdc.gov. We are providing additional information in this letter to tell you what we are doing at our schools to guard against an outbreak. We are also offering suggestions you can follow at home.

Steps Being Taken at Our Schools:

School restrooms, locker rooms and team rooms are being disinfected on a daily basis, and the artificial turf on our athletic playing field is being disinfected once per week. We have placed spray bottles with disinfectant and gel disinfectant dispensers in all weight rooms. Supervisory personnel are instructing all students who use the weight room to disinfect weight room equipment before and after use. These students are also being instructed to use the gel disinfectant on their hands when they leave the weight room.

Steps to Take at Home:

The best way to prevent MRSA infection is to practice good hygiene habits. Keeping hands clean with soap and water or an alcohol-based hand soap is very important. Students should take a shower after engaging in sports activity. Cuts and scrapes must be kept clean and completely covered until they are completely healed. Contact with other people's wounds and bandages is to be avoided, as is the sharing of personal items, such as towels, toothbrushes and razors.

Thank you for your assistance.

Sincerely,

Superintendent

Form VII-5: Model Notification of FERPA Rights

The Family Educational Rights and Privacy Act (FERPA) affords parents and students over 18 years of age ("eligible students") certain rights with respect to the student's education records. These rights are:

1. The right to inspect and review the student's education records within 45 days of the day the School receives a request for access. Parents or eligible students should submit to the School principal [or appropriate school official] a written request that identifies the record(s) they wish to inspect. The School official will make arrangements for access and notify the parent or eligible student of the time and place where the records may be inspected.

2. The right to request the amendment of the student's education records that the parent or eligible student believes are inaccurate or misleading. Parents or eligible students may ask the School to amend a record that they believe is inaccurate or misleading. They should write the School principal [or appropriate official], clearly identify the part of the record they want changed, and specify why it is inaccurate or misleading. If the School decides not to amend the record as requested by the parent or eligible student, the School will notify the parent or eligible student of the decision and advise them of their right to a hearing regarding the request for amendment. Additional information regarding the hearing procedures will be provided to the parent or eligible student when notified of the right to a hearing.

3. The right to consent to disclosures of personally identifiable information contained in the student's education records, except to the extent that FERPA authorizes disclosure without consent. One exception, which permits disclosure without consent, is disclosure to school officials with legitimate educational interests. A school official is a person employed by the School as an administrator, supervisor, instructor, or support staff member (including health or medical staff and law enforcement unit personnel); a person serving on the School Board; a person or company with whom the School has contracted to perform a special task (such as an attorney, auditor, medical consultant, or therapist); or a parent or student serving on an official committee, such as a disciplinary or grievance committee, or assisting another school official in performing his or her tasks. A school official has a legitimate educational interest if the official needs to review an education record in order to fulfill his or her professional responsibility.

[Optional] Upon request, the School discloses education records without consent to officials of another school district in which a student seeks or intends to enroll.

Model Notification of FERPA Rights *(continued)*

[NOTE: FERPA requires a school district to make a reasonable attempt to notify the parent or eligible student of the records request unless it states in its annual notification that it intends to forward records on request.]

4. The right to file a complaint with the U.S. Department of Education concerning alleged failures by the School to comply with the requirements of FERPA. The name and address of the Office that administers FERPA are:

Family Policy Compliance Office

U.S. Department of Education

400 Maryland Avenue, SW

Washington, DC 20202-5901

[NOTE: In addition, an institution may want to include its directory information public notice, as required by Section 99.37 of the regulations, with its annual notification of rights under FERPA.]

Source: U.S. Department of Education

Form VII-6: Dealing with Suicidal Students

These are steps for key personnel to take when it appears that a student is at risk for committing suicide.

Staff:
1. Notify principal or other designated individual.

2. Respond by listening empathetically and gathering information.

3. Refer the student to a guidance counselor.

Guidance:
1. Gather information and check for lethality indicators.

2. Contact the student's parents or guardians.

3. If your assessment indicates the student is currently a suicidal risk, keep the student with you until a parent/guardian arrives for pickup.

4. Contact the school resource officer.

5. Provide the parents/guardians with a list of agencies for referral.

6. If the parents/guardians refuse to accept/seek help, contact the appropriate children and families services agency at phone _____.

7. Document all actions taken by school personnel.

8. Complete these follow-up steps:

   • Try to have the student commit to contact you or another adult if suicidal feelings return.

   • Make guidance appointments for the student on a continuing basis and monitor how the student is coping.

   • Contact parents/guardians to check on progress with referral agencies and to make them aware of student's behavior at school.

   • Keep the principal, other administrators and the student's teachers apprised of the student's situation.

Dealing with Suicidal Students *(continued)*

Social Worker:
1. May assist by contacting parents/guardians who cannot be reached by school personnel.

Administrator or Designee:

1. If suicide is attempted at school, contact superintendent or designee at telephone number _____.

2. If suicide is attempted at school, contact insurance representative at telephone number _____.

3. Provide support as needed.

4. Follow up with guidance department.

Source: University of Arkansas System, Criminal Justice Institute, School Violence Resource Center

Form VII-7: Announcement of Student Suicide

(To be read to students by the classroom teacher.)

TO: School Faculty
FROM: Principal
SUBJECT: (Crisis)
DATE:

John Doe committed suicide early Saturday morning. As a faculty, we extend our sympathy to John's family and friends.

We encourage all students to consider the tragic nature of this death and to realize that death is final. John's death is a reminder to us all that the act of taking one's own life is not an appropriate solution to any of life's problems nor is it an act of courage. Please let your teachers know if you would like to talk to a counselor or other staff member.

Funeral services for John will be held in _____
and there will not be a memorial service in this area. Expressions of sympathy may be sent to _____.

Source: Virginia Department of Education

Form VII-8: Announcement - Student Death
From Accident or Illness

As many of you are aware, we were sorry to hear that _____,
a student in the _____ grade of our school, died on _____ from
injuries in a car crash. As soon as we learn the funeral plans, we will
announce them. Those of you who want to discuss your feelings about
_____'s death should obtain a hall pass from your teacher to
go to the library. This help will be available throughout the school day.
Let us have a moment of silence. Thank you for your cooperation today.

Source: Virginia Department of Education

Form VII-9: Parent Letter: Unexpected Student Death

Dear Parents,

Yesterday, we learned that one of our first graders, _____, died while in the hospital. _____ had his tonsils removed over the past weekend. Complications set in after his parents took him home where he died yesterday afternoon.

Today, at school, each teacher read a short message about _____ to his/her class. We discussed what happened and how _____ died. We also stressed that many people have their tonsils out every day and have no problems with it. Our guidance counselor and our school psychologist were available throughout the day to talk with any student that may have had a particularly difficult time dealing with the news.

Any death is difficult for children to understand. _____'s death is particularly difficult due to his young age and its unexpectedness. The fact that _____ died while at the hospital and the fact that it was related to having his tonsils out may also be frightening for children, especially those who may need to have their own tonsils out in the future.

We recommend that you take some time to discuss death with your child. We suggest allowing your child to talk about how he/she feels and any fears or concerns he/she may have as a result of hearing this news. We are enclosing a list of suggestions to help you talk with your child about _____'s death and/or the death of any loved one.

If you feel that your child would benefit from talking with our guidance counselor or our school psychologist, please call us at the school and share your concerns.

The faculty, staff and students extend our heartfelt sympathies to the family and to all their friends. We, at the school, will miss _____ very much. He was our friend and we loved him.

Sincerely,

School Principal

Source: Virginia Department of Education

Form VII-10: Student/Parent Letter - Sudden Student Death

SCHOOL LETTERHEAD

Date

Dear Students and Parents:

On Friday, John Doe, a fifth-grade student at [School] was in a terrible accident. Apparently, John was hit by a car that was speeding and had crossed over the median strip to the wrong side of the road. John died instantly.

John's death is a tragic, emotional loss for the entire [School] family. I am sure all of us will make every effort to comfort and support John's family as they attempt to deal with this traumatic loss. There are no adequate words to express our sense of grief and sympathy for the family.

Because John's death is felt so deeply by so many, on Monday and thereafter as needed, we will bring in our crisis team to discuss this accident and loss with students and faculty.

We encourage each of you to discuss this loss with your child. In order to help you do so we are holding a parent meeting on [date], and [time], in the cafeteria of [School]. The topic will be ways to help children cope with loss and will be presented by
_____ , a local mental health professional.

John's family, friends, and the school are suffering deeply. Please join us in supporting John's family.

Sincerely,

Principal

(School)

Source: Virginia Department of Education

Form VII-11: Parent Letter Regarding Nutrition Habits

Dear Parent:

Children who learn to live healthy, live longer. By establishing healthy habits early in life, children can dramatically reduce their health risks and increase their chances for longer, more productive lives. We all want the best for our children. Here's how you can help.

The Brentwood Middle School Health Council encourages you to support our efforts to create a healthy school nutrition environment. We are promoting healthy food choices throughout our school – in the school meal programs, in vending machines, and at school-sponsored events. We are also supporting nutrition education and physical activity. You can help your children lead the healthiest lives possible by supporting our efforts to create a healthy school nutrition environment, and by reinforcing healthy habits at home.

Please join us and other parents on Tuesday, October 17 at 7:00 p.m. in the school auditorium for a meeting to learn more about the healthy school nutrition environment project and how you can get involved. Our keynote speaker, Dr. Roger Peterson, a national expert on education, will talk about the importance of nutrition to good health and academic performance.

Please call me at (827) 339-2525 if you have questions. Hope to see you on October 17.

Sincerely,

David Dewhurst, PhD

Principal

Source: United States Department of Agriculture

Form VII-12: Parent Letter Regarding Asthma

Dear Parent:

The school team at _____ school is looking forward to an excellent year for your child, _____.

Our School Asthma Management Program will provide the following health services:

- Access to the school nurse

- Help for students with asthma in following their asthma action plans

- Asthma education for all students in grade(s) _____

- Asthma in-service training for all school staff

- Indoor Air Quality (IAQ) Tools for Schools to promote a healthy environment

In order to provide the best possible school asthma management for your child, we request your assistance with the following:

Please

- Obtain an asthma action plan (a statement of your child's treatment goals, medication and peak flow plan, and environmental risk reduction measures) from your physician. Please be sure guidelines are included for managing symptoms during special school or off-site events (recess, gym, outdoor play, field trips, parties, art class, etc.). You may use the attached form.

- Meet with the school nurse – before school entry and as needed – to explain your child's condition, medication, devices, and environmental triggers.

- Submit a Medication Administration form for any medication that is administered in school. Please provide pharmacy-labeled medications, personally bring them to school, and keep them refilled as needed.

Parent Letter Regarding Asthma *(continued)*

- Meet with teachers to setup expectations for maintaining communication and continuity during absences.

- Prepare your child. Discuss and rehearse the medication plan; discuss how to handle symptoms, triggers, food restrictions, and school policies.

- Keep the school staff up to date on any changes in your child's asthma action plan.

- Keep your physician up to date on school services and supports for helping your child manage his or her asthma.

Thank you for working with us to assist your child.

Sincerely,

Principal (signature)

School Nurse (signature)

Source: U.S. Department of Education, U.S. Department of Health and Human Services

Form VII-13: Physician Letter Regarding Asthma

Dear _____:

The school team at _____ school is looking forward to an excellent year for your patient, _____.

Our School Asthma Management Program will provide the following health services:

- Access to the school nurse

- Help for students with asthma in following their asthma action plans

- Asthma education for all students in grade(s) _____

- Asthma in-service training for all school staff

- Indoor Air Quality (IAQ) Tools for Schools to promote a healthy environment

In order to provide the best possible school asthma management for your patient, we request your assistance with the following:

- Complete an asthma action plan or provide comparable information on another form and return to us at school.

- Complete a medication administration form for any medications that may need to be administered in school and return it to us at school. (Students may self-carry and administer their quick relief medications if you and the parents or guardians indicate approval on the form.)

- Inform us of additional patient needs.

- Assist us in supporting family priorities. Connect parents or guardians with each other, support groups, and resources such as the Allergy and Asthma Network/Mothers of Asthmatics (AAN/MA), the American Lung Association (ALA), and the Asthma and Allergy Foundation of America (AAFA).

Physician Letter Regarding Asthma *(continued)*

Let us know if you need information on educational rights and responsibilities (Individuals with Disabilities Education Act [IDEA] and Section 504 of the Rehabilitation Act of 1973) for your patients.

We look forward to working with you. Thank you for your help.

Sincerely,

Principal (signature)

School Nurse (signature)

Source: U.S. Department of Education, U.S. Department of Health and Human Services

Form VII-14: Parent Letter Regarding Flu

Dear Parent,

As you may know, flu can be easily spread from person to person. Therefore, we are taking steps to reduce the spread of flu in [School name]. We want to keep the school open to students and functioning in a normal manner during this flu season. **But, we need your help to do this.**

We are working closely with the [county/state education agency] and the [county/state] health department to monitor flu conditions and make decisions about the best steps to take concerning schools. We will keep you updated with new information as it becomes available.

If the flu becomes more severe, we may take additional steps to prevent the spread such as:

- conducting active fever and flu symptom screening of students and staff as they arrive at school

- making changes to increase the space between people such as moving desks farther apart and postponing class trips, and

- dismissing students from school for at least 7 days if they become sick.

For now we are doing everything we can to keep our school functioning as usual. Here are a few things you can do to help.

- **Teach your children to wash their hands** often with soap and water or an alcohol-based hand rub. You can set a good example by doing this yourself.

- **Teach your children not to share personal items** like drinks, food or unwashed utensils, and to cover their coughs and sneezes with tissues. Covering up their coughs or sneezes using the elbow, arm or sleeve instead of the hand when a tissue is unavailable.

- **Know the signs and symptoms of the flu.** Symptoms of the flu include fever (100 degrees Fahrenheit, 37.8 degrees Celsius or greater), cough, sore throat, a runny or stuffy

Parent Letter Regarding Flu *(continued)*

nose, body aches, headache, and feeling very tired. Some people may also vomit or have diarrhea.

- **Keep sick children at home** for at least 24 hours after they no longer have fever or do not have signs of fever, without using fever-reducing drugs. Keeping children with a fever at home will reduce the number of people who may get infected.

- **Do not send children to school if they are sick.** Any children who are determined to be sick while at school will be sent home.

For more information, [see the attached flyer/additional information and] and visit www.flu.gov, or call 1-800-CDC-INFO for the most current information about the flu. For more information about flu in our community and what our school is doing, visit [school/health department Web site] or call [appropriate phone number]. We will notify you of any additional changes to our school's strategy to prevent the spread of flu.

Sincerely,

[School administrator's name and signature]

Source: Centers for Disease Control

Form VII-15: Parent Letter Regarding Severe Flu

Dear Parent,

As you may know flu is spreading easily from person to person and school-age children are among the groups most affected. We are taking steps to prevent the spread of flu in [School name]. Currently, flu conditions in [name of county or area or in the United States] have become more severe. We want to keep the school open and functioning as normal for as long as possible. **We need your help to do this.**

We are working closely with the [county/state education agency] and the [county/state] health department to monitor flu conditions and make decisions about the best steps to take. Since flu conditions have become more severe, we are now implementing the following steps to prevent the spread of flu within our school.

- **Extending the time sick students or staff stay home** for at least 7 days, even if they feel better sooner. People who are still sick after 7 days should continue to stay home until at least 24 hours after their symptoms have gone away.

- **Allowing high risk students and staff to stay home.** Certain groups are at higher risk of developing serious complications from flu. These groups include children under the age of 5 years, pregnant women, people of any age who have chronic medical conditions (such as asthma, diabetes, or heart disease), and people age 65 years and older. These students and staff should consult their doctor to make the decision to stay home.

- **Conducting active fever and symptom screening** of students and staff upon arrival at school. School staff will ask students about symptoms suggestive of a respiratory infection such as fever, cough, sore throat, runny or stuffy nose, body aches and fatigue. Any student who has at least 2 of these symptoms will be separated from others, offered a surgical mask, and sent home as soon as possible.

- **Increasing social distances** (the space between people) at school. We will be rotating teachers between classrooms while keeping the same group of students in one classroom, canceling classes that bring students together from multiple

Parent Letter Regarding Severe Flu *(continued)*

classrooms, holding classes outdoors when possible, moving desks farther apart, dividing classes into smaller groups, discouraging use of school buses and public transit, moving classes to larger spaces to allow more space between students, and postponing class trips.

- **Dismissing students.** We will keep students home for [5-7] days and then reassess with the [county/state education agency] and the [county/state] health department. We will keep you informed of when students may return to school. During dismissal we will continue school work from home through [homework packets, web-based lessons, phone calls, etc.]. Staff will remain at school to develop and deliver lessons and materials and continue to provide [important services, school lunches, etc.]. We will also be [canceling, postponing] all school-related mass gatherings. This includes [sporting events, school dances, performances, rallies, commencement ceremonies, etc.].

Here are a few things you can do to help since flu conditions are now more severe.

- **Teach your children to wash their hands** often with soap and water. You can set a good example by doing this yourself.

- **Teach your children not to share personal items** like drinks, food or unwashed utensils, and to cover their coughs and sneezes with tissues. If they don't have a tissue, they should cough or sneeze into their upper sleeve, not their hands.

- **Know the signs and symptoms of the flu.** Symptoms of the flu include fever (100 degrees Fahrenheit, 37.8 degrees Celsius or greater), cough, sore throat, a runny or stuffy nose, body aches, headache, and feeling very tired. Some people may also vomit or have diarrhea.

- **Extend the time sick children stay home** for at least 7 days, even if they feel better sooner. People who are still sick after 7 days should continue to stay home until at least 24 hours after symptoms have gone away.

- **If a household member is sick, keep any school-age brothers or sisters home for 5 days** from the time the

Parent Letter Regarding Severe Flu *(continued)*

household member became sick. Parents should monitor
their health and the health of other school-age children for
fever and other symptoms of the flu.

*   **Don't send children to school if they are sick.** Any
    children who are sick at school will be sent home. Staying
    home when sick will allow your children to rest and allows
    you to monitor their health closely. Keeping your sick child
    home is the responsible thing to do. It protects fellow
    students and school staff, especially those who are at higher
    risk of severe illness from the flu.

For more information, [see the attached flyer/additional information
and] visit www.flu.gov, or call 1-800-CDC-INFO for the most current
information about the flu. For more information about flu in our
community and what our school is doing, visit [school/health
department Web site] or call [appropriate phone number]. We will
notify you of any additional changes to our school's strategy to prevent
the spread of flu.

Sincerely,

[School administrator's name and signature]

Source: Centers for Disease Control

Form VII-16: Eating and Feeding Evaluation
Children with Special Needs

PART A		
Student's Name		Age
Name of school	Grade Level	Classroom
Does the child have a disability? If Yes, describe the major life activities affected.	Yes	No
Does the child have special nutritional feeding needs? If yes, complete Part B of this form and have it signed by a licensed physician.	Yes	No
If the child is not disabled, does the child have special nutritional or feeding needs? If Yes, complete Part B and have it signed by a recognized medical authority.	Yes	No
If the child does not require special meals, the parent can sign at the bottom and return the form to the school food service.		

PART B
List any dietary restrictions or special diet.
List any allergies or food intolerances to avoid.
List foods to be substituted.
List foods that need the following change in texture. If all foods need to be prepared in this manner, indicate "All."   Cut up or chopped into bite-size pieces: Finely ground: Pureed:
List any special equipment or utensils that are needed.
Indicate any other comments about the child's eating or feeding patterns.

Parent's Signature	Date:
Physician or Medical Authority's Signature	Date:

Source: U.S. Department of Agriculture

Form VII-17: Information Card Regarding Students with Special Dietary Needs (For Food Service Staff)

Source: U.S. Department of Agriculture

Student's Name	Teacher's Name
Special Diet or Dietary Restrictions	
Food Allergies or Intolerances	
Food Substitutions	

Foods Requiring Texture Modifications:
Chopped:
Finely Ground:
Pureed or Blended:

Other Diet Modifications:
Feeding Techniques
Supplemental Feedings

Physician or Medical Authority:
Name: Telephone: Fax:

Additional Contact: Name: Telephone: Fax:	Additional Contact: Name: Telephone: Fax:

School Food Service Representative/Person Completing Form: Title: Signature:

Form VII-18: Food Allergy Action Plan

Name: _____

DOB: _____ Weight: _____

Allergy: _____

Asthma: Yes _____ (if yes, higher risk for a severe reaction) No _____

Place student's photo here

Extremely reactive to the following foods: _____

Therefore:

_____If checked, give epinephrine immediately for ANY symptoms if allergen was *likely* eaten.

_____If checked, give epinephrine immediately if allergen was *definitely* eaten, even if no symptoms are noted.

Any **SEVERE SYMPTOMS** after suspected or known ingestion:

One or more of the following:

LUNG:	Short of breath, wheeze, repetitive cough
HEART:	Pale, blue, faint, weak pulse, dizzy, confused
THROAT:	Tight, hoarse, trouble breathing/swallowing
MOUTH:	Obstructive swelling (tongue and/or lips)
SKIN:	Many hives over body

Or **combination** of symptoms from different body areas:

SKIN:	Hives, itchy rashes, swelling (e.g., eyes, lips)
GUT:	Vomiting, diarrhea, crampy pain

➡

1. **INJECT EPINEPHRINE IMMEDIATELY**
2. Call 911
3. Begin monitoring (see box below)
4. Give additional medications*
   a. Antihistamine
   b. Inhaler (bronchodilator) if asthma

*Antihistamines & inhalers/bronchodilators are not to be depended upon to treat a severe reaction (anaphylaxis). USE EPINEPHRINE.

MILD SYMPTOMS ONLY:

MOUTH:	Itchy mouth
SKIN:	A few hives around mouth/face, mild itch
GUT:	Mild nausea/discomfort

➡

1. **GIVE ANTIHISTAMINE**
2. Stay with student; alert healthcare professionals and parents
3. If symptoms progress (see above), USE EPINEPHRINE
4. Begin monitoring (see box below)

Medication/Doses

Epinephrine (brand and dose): _____

Antihistamine (brand and dose): _____

Other (e.g., inhaler-bronchodilator if asthmatic): _____

Food Allergy Action Plan *(continued)*

Monitoring
Stay with student; alert healthcare professionals and parents. Tell rescue squad
epinephrine was given; request an ambulance with epinephrine. Note time when
epinephrine was administered. A second dose of epinephrine can be given 5 minutes or
more after the first if symptoms persist or recur. For a severe reaction, consider keeping
student lying on back with legs raised. Treat student even if parents cannot be reached.

_____ _____   _____ _____
Parent/Guardian signature   Date   Physician/Healthcare Provider signature   Date

Source: Centers for Disease Control

Form VII-19: Suicide Notification Statement for Students

It is with great sadness that I have to tell you that one of our students, _____, has taken [his, her] own life. All of us want you to know that we are here to help you in any way we can.

A suicide death presents us with many questions that we may not be able to answer right away. Rumors may begin to circulate, and we ask that you not spread rumors you may hear. We'll do our best to give you accurate information as it becomes known to us.

Suicide is a complicated act. It is usually caused by a mental disorder such as depression, which prevents a person from thinking clearly about his or her problems and how to solve them. Sometimes these disorders are not identified or noticed; in other cases, a person with a disorder will show obvious symptoms or signs. One thing is certain: There are treatments that can help. Suicide should never, ever be an option.

Each of us will react to _____'s death in our own way, and we need to be respectful of each other. Feeling sad is a normal response to any loss. Some of you may not have known _____ very well and may not be as affected, while others may experience a great deal of sadness. Some of you may find you're having difficulty concentrating on your schoolwork, and others may find that diving into your work is a good distraction.

We have counselors available to help our school community deal with this sad loss and to enable us to understand more about suicide.

If you'd like to talk to a counselor, just let your teachers know.

Please remember that we are here to help you.

Respectfully,

Principal

Source: American Foundation for Suicide Prevention and Suicide Prevention Resource Center. 2011. After a suicide: A Toolkit for Schools. Newton, MA: Education Development Center, Inc.

Form VII-20: Emergency Information for Individuals with Autism

Legal Name _____ Nickname _____

Parent/Guardian _____

Siblings _____

Signature consent (to release form to emergency responders)

_____

Address _____

City_____ State _____ Zip _____

Home phone _____ Cell phone _____

Work phone _____

Date of Birth _____ Age _____ Gender _____ Height _____ Weight _____

Eye color _____ Hair color _____

Scars (other identifying marks) _____

Medical Diagnosis _____

Special Diet or Diet Restrictions _____

_____

_____

_____

Medications (List name, dose and time to be taken) _____

_____

_____

_____

_____

Medication allergies _____

Other allergies _____

Health Insurance _____ Plan _____

Policy _____

Pharmacy _____ Phone number _____

Primary Care Physician _____ Phone number _____

Specialist _____ Phone number _____

Emergency Information for Individuals with Autism *(continued)*

Emergency Contacts

Name _____

Address _____

City_____ State _____ Zip _____

Home phone _____ Cell phone _____

Work phone _____

Name _____

Address _____

City_____ State _____ Zip _____

Home phone _____ Cell phone _____

Work phone _____

Name _____

Address _____

City_____ State _____ Zip _____

Home phone _____ Cell phone _____

Work phone _____

Common problems for the individual _____

_____

_____

Things to avoid _____

_____

Favorite places _____

_____

Source: Autism Safety Project, www.autismsafetyproject.org

Form VII-21: Food Allergy Policy Checklist

A comprehensive policy for the management of life-threatening food allergies in school and school-associated settings should be developed by school boards in partnership with school personnel (school administrators, 504 coordinators, licensed healthcare providers [e.g., registered nurse, physician], school health advisory council members, teachers, school nutrition staff, bus companies/drivers, after-school program personnel, etc.), students, families, and others particularly affected by, or involved in, the implementation of the policy.

A comprehensive policy addresses all of the following essential components:

1. Identification of students with food allergies and provision of school health services

2. Individual written management plans

3. Medication protocols: storage, access and administration

4. Healthy school environment: comprehensive and coordinated approach

5. Communication and confidentiality

6. Emergency response

7. Professional development and training for school personnel

8. Awareness education for students

9. Awareness education and resources for parents/guardians

10. Monitoring and evaluation

Source: The National School Boards Association, www.nsba.org/Board-Leadership/SchoolHealth/SelectedNSBAPublications/Food-Allergy/Safe-at-School-and-Ready-to-Learn.pdf

Form VII-22: Sample Response to Anaphylactic Shock

The purpose of this posting is to make all parents, staff and students aware of a medical issue involving a (school name) student having an extreme allergy to Axe Body Spray.

This allergy is potentially life-threatening for this student.

Most recently this student has been transported to the hospital by ambulance for emergency medical treatment due to this student being exposed to Axe Body Spray while attending school.

My request to all (school name) members is that we take into consideration this student's allergy to Axe Body Spray and refrain from using it as your cologne or fragrance of choice while attending (school name).

On behalf of this student's family and myself, thank you for your consideration.

Source: Freedom High School, Bethlehem, Pennsylvania, posted on the school's website

Form VII-23: Checklist: Steps to Take Within 24 Hours of a Nonfatal Food Allergy Reaction

- Call parent or guardian to follow up on student's condition

- Review anaphylactic or allergic episode with parent or guardian and student:

  — identify allergen and route of exposure

  — discuss signs and symptoms with parent or guardian

  — review action steps taken

  — discuss positive and negative outcomes

  — discuss any needed revision to care plan based on the experience or outcome

- Discuss family's role with parent or guardian to improve outcomes

- Discuss school and home concerns to improve prevention, response and student outcomes

- Ask parent or guardian to replace epinephrine dose that was administered, if necessary

- Ask parent or guardian to follow up with health care provider

Source: Centers for Disease Control

Form VII-24: Sample Letter to Parents About Student Vaccinations

We all need shots (also called vaccinations or immunizations) to help protect us from serious diseases.

To help keep our community safe, [*your school name*] is proudly participating in National Immunization Awareness Month.

Shots can prevent serious diseases like the flu, measles and tuberculosis (TB). It's important to know which shots you need and when to get them.

- **[Add details about your local activities.]**

- **[Include quote from your organization.]**

Everyone age 6 months and older needs to get a flu shot every year. Other shots work best when they are given at certain ages.

Talk to your doctor or nurse to make sure that everyone in your family gets the shots they need.

Also, talk to school officials about required vaccinations – or required waivers – for student enrollment.

For more information, contact [*insert your school's point of contact.*].

Source: U.S. Department of Health and Human Services, www.healthfinder.gov

Form VII-25: Parent Letter Regarding Flu Prevention

Dear students, faculty, staff and parents,

As you may know, flu can be spread easily from person to person. Therefore, we are taking steps to prevent the spread of flu at [*name of institution*] for as long as possible, **but we need your help to accomplish this**.

We are working closely with the [*County/State*] health department to monitor flu conditions and make decisions about the best steps to take concerning our institution. We will keep you updated with new information as it becomes available to us.

For now, we are doing everything we can to keep our institution operating as usual. Here are a few things you can do to help:

- **Practice good hand hygiene** by washing your hands with soap and water, especially after coughing or sneezing. Alcohol-based hand cleaners also are effective.

- **Practice respiratory etiquette** by covering your mouth and nose with a tissue when you cough or sneeze. If you don't have a tissue, cough or sneeze into your elbow or shoulder, not into your hands. Avoid touching your eyes, nose, or mouth; germs are spread this way.

- **Know the signs and symptoms of the flu.** A fever is a temperature taken with a thermometer that is equal to or greater than 100 degrees Fahrenheit or 38 degrees Celsius. Look for possible signs of fever: if the person feels very warm, has a flushed appearance, or is sweating or shivering.

- **Stay home if you have flu or flu-like illness for at least 24 hours after you no longer have a fever** (100 degrees Fahrenheit or 38 degrees Celsius) or signs of a fever (have chills, feel very warm, have a flushed appearance, or are sweating). This should be determined without the use of fever-reducing medications (any medicine that contains ibuprofen or acetaminophen). Don't go to class or work.

- **Talk with your health care providers about whether you should be vaccinated for seasonal flu.** Also if you are at higher risk for flu complications from 2009 H1N1 flu, you should consider getting the H1N1 vaccine when it becomes available. People at higher risk for 2009 H1N1 flu complications include pregnant women and people with

Parent Letter Regarding Flu Prevention *(continued)*

chronic medical conditions (such as asthma, heart disease, or diabetes). For more information about priority groups for vaccination, visit *www.cdc.gov/h1n1flu/vaccination/acip.htm*.

If this year's flu season becomes more severe, we may take the following additional steps to prevent the spread of the virus:

- **Allow students, faculty, and staff at higher risk for complications to stay home.** These students, faculty, and staff should make this decision in consultation with their health care provider.

- **Find ways to increase social distances** (the space between people) in classrooms such as moving desks farther apart, leaving empty seats between students, holding outdoor classes and using distance learning methods.

- **Extend the time sick students, faculty, or staff stay home or in their residence.** During severe flu conditions sick people should stay home for at least 7 days, even if they feel better sooner. Those who are still sick after 7 days should continue to stay home until at least 24 hours after symptoms have gone away. Symptoms of flu include fever or chills *and* cough or sore throat. In addition, symptoms can include runny nose, body aches, headache, tiredness, diarrhea or vomiting.

- **Suspend classes.** This decision will be made together with local and state public health officials. The length of time classes should be suspended will depend on the goal of suspending classes as well as the severity and extent of illness.

For more information about flu in our community and what our institution is doing, visit [*institution's website*] or call [*appropriate phone number*].

For the most up-to-date information on flu, visit *www.flu.gov*, or call 1-800-CDC-INFO (232-4636). We will notify you by [*e-mail, institution's website, text message, Facebook, Twitter, etc.*] of any additional changes to our school's strategy to prevent the spread of flu on our campus.

Sincerely,

[*Institution administrator's name and signature*]

Source: www.flu.gov

Form VII-26: Restraint and Seclusion Checklist: 15 Principles

The ED, in collaboration with SAMHSA, has identified 15 principles that should be considered when developing and implementing policies and procedures to ensure that any use of restraint or seclusion in school does not occur, except when there is a threat of imminent danger of serious physical harm to the student or others, and occurs in a manner that protects the safety of all children and adults at the school.

1. Every effort should be made to prevent the need for the use of restraint and for the use of seclusion.

2. Schools should never use mechanical restraints to restrict a child's freedom of movement, and schools should never use a drug or medication to control behavior or restrict freedom of movement (except as authorized by a licensed physician or other qualified health professional).

3. Physical restraint or seclusion should not be used except in situations where the child's behavior poses imminent danger of serious physical harm to self or others and other interventions are ineffective and should be discontinued as soon as imminent danger of serious physical harm to self or others has dissipated.

4. Policies restricting the use of restraint and seclusion should apply to all children, not just children with disabilities.

5. Any behavioral intervention must be consistent with the child's rights to be treated with dignity and to be free from abuse.

6. Restraint or seclusion should never be used as punishment or discipline (e.g., placing in seclusion for out-of-seat behavior), as a means of coercion or retaliation, or as a convenience.

7. Restraint or seclusion should never be used in a manner that restricts a child's breathing or harms the child.

8. The use of restraint or seclusion, particularly when there is repeated use for an individual child, multiple uses within the same classroom, or multiple uses by the same individual, should trigger a review. And, if appropriate, revision of strategies currently in place to address dangerous behavior,

Restraint and Seclusion Checklist: 15 Principles *(continued)*

if positive behavioral strategies are not in place, staff should consider developing them.

9. Behavioral strategies to address dangerous behavior that results in the use of restraint or seclusion should address the underlying cause or purpose of the dangerous behavior.

10. Teachers and other personnel should be trained regularly on the appropriate use of effective alternatives to physical restraint and seclusion, such as positive behavioral interventions and supports, and only for cases involving imminent danger of serious physical harm, on the safe use of physical restraint and seclusion.

11. Every instance in which restraint or seclusion is used should be carefully and continuously and visually monitored to ensure the appropriateness of its use and safety of the child, other children, teachers and other personnel.

12. Parents should be informed of the policies on restraint and seclusion at their child's school or other educational setting, as well as applicable Federal, State or local laws.

13. Parents should be notified as soon as possible following each instance in which restraint or seclusion is used with their child.

14. Policies regarding the use of restraint and seclusion should be reviewed regularly and updated as appropriate.

15. Policies regarding the use of restraint and seclusion should provide that each incident involving the use of restraint or seclusion should be documented in writing and provide for the collection of specific data that would enable teachers, staff and other personnel to understand and implement the preceding principles.

Source: The U.S. Department of Education

Form VII-27: Seclusion/Restraint Documentation

Student's name: _____

School: _____

DOB: _____ Grade: _____

Student ID: _____

Person completing form: _____

Date of incident: _____ Time of incident: _____

Circle those that apply

- IEP

- Behavior Intervention Plan (BIP)

- 504 plan

Description of the incident leading up to seclusion, isolation and/or physical restraint: _____

_____

_____

_____

_____

Please indicate and describe any of the following interventions that were used

Seclusion: confinement of a student alone in an enclosed space from which the student is physically prevented from leaving by locking hardware. Seclusion is allowed in emergency situations while awaiting the arrival of law enforcement personnel.

Description and duration: _____

_____

_____

_____

_____

Seclusion/Restraint Documentation *(continued)*

<u>Seclusion</u>: confinement of a student alone in an enclosed space from which the student is physically prevented from leaving by locking hardware. Seclusion is allowed in emergency situations while awaiting the arrival of law enforcement personnel.

Description and duration: _____

_____

_____

_____

_____

_____

<u>Isolation</u>: the confinement of a student alone in an enclosed space without locking hardware. Isolation is allowed after de-escalating procedures have failed, student's behavior poses a serious, probable threat of imminent physical harm to self or others, with parental approval as specified in the student's IEP, 504 plan or BIP.

Description and duration: _____

_____

_____

_____

_____

_____

<u>Physical restraint</u>: the use of person-to-person physical contact to restrict the free movement of all or a portion of a student's body. It includes briefly holding a student without undue force for instruction or other purposes, briefly holding a student to calm them, taking a student's hand to transport them for safety purposes, physical escort or intervening in a fight. Physical restraint is allowed when less restrictive measures have not effectively de-escalated the situation, or with parental approval as specified in a student's IEP, 504 plan or BIP.

Description and duration: _____

_____

_____

_____

_____

_____

Seclusion/Restraint Documentation *(continued)*

<u>Mechanical restraint</u>: Only as specified in the student's IEP, 504 plan or BIP with two exceptions: a. vehicle safety restraints shall be used according to state and federal regulations and b. mechanical restraints employed by law enforcement officers in school settings should be used in accordance with their policies and appropriate professional standards.

Description and duration: _____

_____

_____

_____

_____

Staff involved in the incident

Name and title _____

Name and title _____

Name and title _____

Name and title _____

Name and title _____

Was the student injured?   Yes   No

Description of injury, if applicable: _____

_____

_____

_____

Was any staff injured?   Yes   No

Description of injury, if applicable: _____

_____

_____

_____

Nurse Observation

Date: _____ Time: _____

Observations: _____

_____

_____

_____

Seclusion/Restraint Documentation *(continued)*

Parent/Guardian notification

Name and title: _____

Date: _____ Time: _____

Email or phone number: _____

_____

A student's parent or guardian shall be notified through verbal or electronic means of the emergency situation involving the use of seclusion, isolation or restraint as soon as possible, but no later than the end of the day of the incident. A student's parent or guardian shall also receive a written report of the emergency situation within 5 school days of the incident. The report shall include all of the following:

- Date, time of day, location, duration and description of the incident and interventions

- Events that led up to the incident

- Nature and extent of any injury to the student

- Name of district employee the parent or guardian can contact regarding the incident

- Plan to prevent the need for future use of seclusion, isolation or restraint

- Documentation that a nurse observed the student following the restraint

Description of consequences or discipline (if any) as a result of the incident: _____

_____

_____

_____

Signature of person completing this form _____

Source: Rockwood School District, Missouri

Form VII-28: How Asthma-Friendly is Your School?

Students who have asthma need proper support at school to keep their asthma under control and be fully active. Use this checklist to find out how well your school serves students who have asthma:

- Are the school buildings and grounds free of tobacco smoke at all times?

- Are all school buses, vans and trucks free of tobacco smoke?

- Are all school events, like field trips and athletic events (both at "home" and "away") free from tobacco smoke?

- Does your school have a policy or rule that allows students to carry and use their own asthma medicines?

- If some of your students do not carry their asthma medicines, do they have quick and easy access to their medicines?

- Does your school have a written emergency plan for teachers and other staff to follow to take care of a student who has an asthma attack?

- In an emergency, such as a fire, weather event or lockdown, or if a student forgets his or her medicine, does your school have a standing orders and quick-relief medicines for students to use?

- Do all students who have asthma have updated asthma action plans on file at the school?

- Is there a school nurse or other school health staff in your school building during the school day?

- Does a school nurse or other school health staff identify, assess and monitor students who have asthma at your school?

- Does a school nurse or other school health staff help students with their medicines and help them to participate fully in exercise and other physical activity, including PE, sports, recess and field trips?

- If a school nurse or other school health staff is not full-time in your school, is a nurse readily and routinely available to write and review plans and

How Asthma-Friendly is Your School? *(continued)*

give the school guidance?

- Does an asthma education expert teach all school staff about asthma, asthma action plans and asthma medicines?

- Is asthma information incorporated into health, science, first aid and other classes as appropriate?

- Can students who have asthma participate fully and safely in a range of exercise and other physical activity, including PE, sports, recess and field trips?

- Are students' quick-relief medicines nearby before, during and after exercise and other physical activity?

- Can students who have asthma choose a physical activity that is different from others in class when it is medically necessary?

- Can students who have asthma choose another activity without fear of being ridiculed or receiving reduced grades?

- Does the school help to reduce or prevent students' contact with allergens or irritants – indoors and outdoors – that can make their asthma worse?

- Does your school have a no-idling policy for vehicles on school grounds, such as buses or carpools?

- Does your school monitor daily local Air Quality Index (AQI) information to help reduce students' exposure to unhealthy air quality?

- Does your school partner with parents and health care providers to address students' asthma needs?

- Does your school work with an asthma specialist in the community?

- Are any of the following present?

    — Cockroach droppings

    — Excessive dust and/or carpets, pillows, cloth-covered or upholstered furniture, or stuffed toys that harbor dust mites

How Asthma-Friendly is Your School? *(continued)*

— Mold or persistent moisture

— Pets with fur or hair

— Strong odors or sprays, such as paint, perfume, bug spray or cleaning products

Uncontrolled asthma can hinder a student's attendance, participation, performance and progress in school.

School staff, health care providers and families should work together to make schools more asthma-friendly to promote student health and education.

Source: National Heart, Lung and Blood Institute, www.nhlbi.nih.gov

Form VII-29: Sample Suicide Notification Letter: When Family Requests That the Cause of Death Remain Undisclosed

I am writing with great sadness to inform you that one of our students, _____, has died. Our thoughts and sympathies are with [his/her] family and friends.

All of the students were given the news of the death by their teacher in [advisory/homeroom] this morning. I have included a copy of the announcement that was read to them.

The family has requested that information about the cause of death not be shared at this time. We are aware that there have been rumors that this was a suicide death. Since the subject has been raised, we want to take this opportunity to remind our community that suicide, when it does occur, is a very complicated act. It is usually caused by a mental disorder such as depression, which can prevent a person from thinking clearly about the problems in his or her life and how to solve them. Sometimes these disorders are not identified or noticed; other times, a person with a disorder will show obvious symptoms or signs.

Members of our Crisis Response Team are available to meet with students individually and in groups today as well as over the coming days and weeks. Please contact the school office if you feel your child is in need of additional assistance; we have a list of additional school and community mental health resources.

Information about the funeral will be made available as soon as we have it. If your child wishes to attend, we strongly encourage you to accompany him or her to the service. If the funeral is scheduled during school hours, students who wish to attend will need parental permission to be released from school.

Please do not hesitate to contact me or the school counselors with any questions or concerns.

Sincerely,

[Principal]

Source: American Foundation for Suicide Prevention and Suicide Prevention Resource Center. 2011. After a Suicide: A Toolkit for Schools. Newton, MA: Education Development Center, Inc.

Form VII-30: After a Student Suicide:
Crisis Response Team Leader's Checklist

Once a suicide death has been confirmed, the school should immediately implement a coordinated crisis response in order to effectively manage the situation, provide opportunities for grief support, maintain an environment focused on normal educational activities, help students cope with their feelings and minimize the risk of suicide contagion.

- Inform the school superintendent of the death.

- Contact the deceased's family to offer condolences, inquire what the school can do to assist, discuss what students should be told and inquire about funeral arrangements.

- Call an immediate meeting of the Crisis Response Team to assign responsibilities.

- Establish a plan to immediately notify faculty and staff of the death via the school's crisis alert system (usually phone or email).

- Schedule an initial all-staff meeting as soon as possible (ideally before school starts in the morning).

- Arrange for students to be notified of the death in small groups such as homerooms or advisories (not by overhead announcement or in a large assembly) and disseminate a death notification statement for students to homeroom teachers, advisors, or others leading those groups.

- Draft and disseminate a death notification letter for parents.

- Disseminate handouts on facts about suicides, mental disorders and talking about suicide to faculty.

- Speak with the superintendent and Crisis Response Team throughout the day.

- Determine whether additional grief counselors, crisis responders, or other resources may be needed from outside the school.

Source: American Foundation for Suicide Prevention and Suicide Prevention Resource Center. 2011. After a Suicide: A Toolkit for Schools. Newton, MA: Education Development Center, Inc.

Form VII-31: Mental Health Help:
When Students Face Death

Have you ever watched a movie or read a book where a character dies? Did it make you sad? Was it scary? All living things, from plants to pets to people, die. It's a hard part of life and sometimes hard to understand why. Even though it can be a sad and scary time, it is important you talk to your friends and family when someone you know dies.

What is grieving?

Grieving and coping are ways people adjust with a difficult change in their lives. There is no right or wrong way to grieve. You might cry or feel angry and that's OK. It's hard when someone you love dies.

Remembering people or pets who have died is one way to keep them a part of us. You can:

- Look at pictures

- Visit the grave or a special place

- Think about how much the person meant to you

- Draw a picture, and

- Write a story or poem.

Who can I talk to?

Are you wondering if other people in your life will die soon?

It's important to talk about any fears or questions you may have instead of hiding them or pretending you aren't scared. Talk to a parent or another grown-up you trust. That person will answer your questions the best that they can.

At first it can be hard to talk about missing someone, but talking may be the best way to help you start to feel better.

The best thing we can do is accept death as a part of life. It happens and sometimes it's not fair, but we can't do anything to change that. You may always miss the person, but one day you will be able to think about them and smile at the good times you had together. The more time passes, the less sad you will feel. Remembering the person and the good memories will help you feel better.

Source: kids.usa.gov

THE JUDICIAL SYSTEM

To allow you to determine the relative importance of a judicial decision, the cases included in *Keeping Your School Safe & Secure: A Practical Guide* identify the particular court from which a decision has been issued. For example, a case decided by a state's highest court generally will be of greater significance than a state intermediate court case. Hence a basic knowledge of the structure of our judicial system is important to an understanding of school law.

Almost all the reports in this volume are taken from appellate court decisions. Although most education law decisions occur at trial court and administrative levels, appellate court decisions have the effect of binding lower courts and administrators so that appellate court decisions have the effect of law within their court systems.

State and federal court systems generally function independently of each other. Each court system applies its own law according to statutes and the determinations of its highest court. However, judges at all levels often consider opinions from other court systems to settle issues which are new or arise under unique fact situations. Similarly, lawyers look at the opinions of many courts to locate authority which supports their clients' cases.

Once a lawsuit is filed in a particular court system, that system generally retains the matter until its conclusion. Unsuccessful parties at the administrative or trial court level generally have the right to appeal unfavorable determinations of law to appellate courts within the system. When federal law issues or constitutional grounds are present, lawsuits may be appropriately filed in the federal court system. In those cases, the lawsuit is filed initially in the federal district court for that area.

On rare occasions, the U.S. Supreme Court considers appeals from the highest courts of the states if a distinct federal question exists and at least four justices agree on the question's importance. The federal courts occasionally send cases to state courts for application of state law. These situations are infrequent and, in general, the state and federal court systems should be considered separate from each other.

The most common system, used by nearly all states and also the federal judiciary, is as follows: a legal action is commenced in district court (sometimes called trial court, county court, common pleas court or superior court) where a decision is initially reached. The case may then be appealed to the court of appeals (or appellate court), and, in turn, this decision may be appealed to the supreme court.

Several states, however, do not have a court of appeals; lower court decisions are appealed directly to the state's supreme court. Additionally, some states have labeled their courts in a nonstandard fashion.

In Maryland, the highest state court is called the Court of Appeals. In the state of New York, the trial court is called the Supreme Court. Decisions of this court may be appealed to the Supreme Court, Appellate Division. The highest court in New York is the Court of Appeals. Pennsylvania has perhaps the most complex court system. The lowest state court is the Court of Common Pleas. Depending on the circumstances of the case, appeals may be taken to either the Commonwealth Court or the Superior Court. In certain instances the Commonwealth Court functions as a trial court as well as an appellate court. The Superior Court, however, is strictly an intermediate appellate court. The highest court in Pennsylvania is the Supreme Court.

While supreme court decisions are generally regarded as the last word in legal matters, it is important to remember that trial and appeals court decisions also create important legal precedents. For the hierarchy of typical state and federal court systems, please see the diagram below.

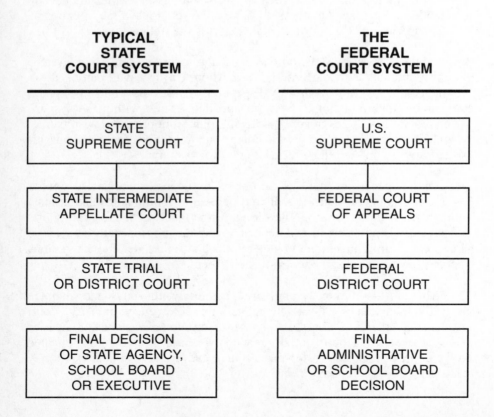

Federal courts of appeals hear appeals from the district courts which are located in their circuits. Below is a list of states matched to the federal circuits in which they are located.

First Circuit	— Maine, Massachusetts, New Hampshire, Puerto Rico, Rhode Island
Second Circuit	— Connecticut, New York, Vermont
Third Circuit	— Delaware, New Jersey, Pennsylvania, Virgin Islands
Fourth Circuit	— Maryland, North Carolina, South Carolina, Virginia, West Virginia
Fifth Circuit	— Louisiana, Mississippi, Texas
Sixth Circuit	— Ohio, Kentucky, Michigan, Tennessee
Seventh Circuit	— Illinois, Indiana, Wisconsin
Eighth Circuit	— Arkansas, Iowa, Minnesota, Missouri, Nebraska, North Dakota, South Dakota
Ninth Circuit	— Alaska, Arizona, California, Guam, Hawaii, Idaho, Montana, Nevada, Northern Mariana Islands, Oregon, Washington
Tenth Circuit	— Colorado, Kansas, Oklahoma, New Mexico, Utah, Wyoming
Eleventh Circuit	— Alabama, Florida, Georgia
District of Columbia Circuit	— Hears cases from the U.S. District Court for the District of Columbia
Federal Circuit Appeals	— Sitting in Washington, D.C., the U.S. Court of Federal Circuit, hears patent and trade appeals and certain appeals on claims brought against the federal government and its agencies.

HOW TO READ A CASE CITATION

Generally, court decisions can be located in case reporters at law school or governmental law libraries. Some cases can also be located on the Internet through legal websites or official court websites.

Each case summary contains the citation, or legal reference, to the full text of the case. The diagram below illustrates how to read a case citation.

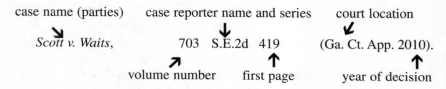

Some cases may have two or three reporter names such as U.S. Supreme Court cases and cases reported in regional case reporters as well as state case reporters. For example, a U.S. Supreme Court case usually contains three case reporter citations.

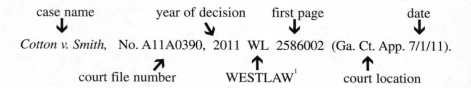

The citations are still read in the same manner as if only one citation has been listed.

Occasionally, a case may contain a citation which does not reference a case reporter. For example, a citation may contain a reference such as:

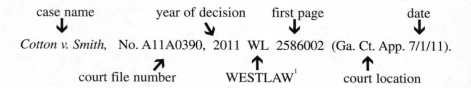

The court file number indicates the specific number assigned to a case by the particular court system deciding the case. In our example, the Georgia Court of Appeals has assigned the case of *Cotton v. Smith* the case number of "No.

[1]WESTLAW® is a computerized database of court cases available for a fee.

A11A0390" which will serve as the reference number for the case and any matter relating to the case. Locating a case on the Internet generally requires either the case name and date of the decision, and/or the court file number.

Below, we have listed the full names of the regional reporters. As mentioned previously, many states have individual state reporters. The names of those reporters may be obtained from a reference law librarian.

P.	**Pacific Reporter**	
	Alaska, Arizona, California, Colorado, Hawaii, Idaho, Kansas, Montana, Nevada, New Mexico, Oklahoma, Oregon, Utah, Washington, Wyoming	
A.	**Atlantic Reporter**	
	Connecticut, Delaware, District of Columbia, Maine, Maryland, New Hampshire, New Jersey, Pennsylvania, Rhode Island, Vermont	
N.E.	**Northeastern Reporter**	
	Illinois, Indiana, Massachusetts, New York, Ohio	
N.W.	**Northwestern Reporter**	
	Iowa, Michigan, Minnesota, Nebraska, North Dakota, South Dakota, Wisconsin	
So.	**Southern Reporter**	
	Alabama, Florida, Louisiana, Mississippi	
S.E.	**Southeastern Reporter**	
	Georgia, North Carolina, South Carolina, Virginia, West Virginia	
S.W.	**Southwestern Reporter**	
	Arkansas, Kentucky, Missouri, Tennessee, Texas	

F.   **Federal Reporter**
              Decisions from the thirteen federal courts of appeals.

F.Supp.   **Federal Supplement**
              Decisions from federal district courts within the thirteen federal judicial circuits. *See The Judicial System, p. 575* for specific circuits.

Fed.Appx.   **Federal Appendix**
              Contains unpublished decisions of the U.S. Circuit Courts of Appeal.

U.S.   **United States Reports**
S.Ct.   **Supreme Court Reporter** ⟩ U.S. Supreme Court Decisions
L.Ed.   **Lawyers' Edition**

GLOSSARY

Americans with Disabilities Act (ADA) - The ADA is a federal law that bars discrimination on the basis of disability in several contexts, including employment, access to programs and services provided by public entities, and access to places of public accommodation.

Assumption of Risk - A defense to a claim of negligence, in which the defendant asserts that the injured plaintiff is barred from recovery because he knowingly and voluntarily exposed himself to the hazard that caused his injury.

Biometrics - Methods and techniques used to identify individuals on the basis of a behavioral or physical characteristic or trait.

Class Action Suit - Federal Rule of Civil Procedure 23 allows members of a class to sue as representatives on behalf of the whole class provided that the class is so large that joinder of all parties is impractical, there are questions of law or fact common to the class, the claims or defenses of the representatives are typical of the claims or defenses of the class, and the representative parties will adequately protect the interests of the class. In addition, there must be some danger of inconsistent verdicts or adjudications if the class action were prosecuted as separate actions. Most states also allow class actions under the same or similar circumstances.

Clery Act - see Jeanne Clery Disclosure of Campus Security Policy and Campus Crime Statistics Act.

Crime Prevention Through Environmental Design (CPTED) - An approach to increasing safety in a variety of contexts, including the school context, that recognizes the important role that the design of the built environment can play in reducing the risk of criminal activity.

Cyberbullying - Student bullying that is perpetrated via the Internet, mobile phone or other electronic technology.

Due Process Clause - The clauses of the Fifth and Fourteenth Amendments to the Constitution which guarantee the citizens of the United States "due process of law" (see below). The Fifth Amendment's Due Process Clause applies to the federal government, and the Fourteenth Amendment's Due Process Clause applies to the states.

Due Process of Law - The idea of "fair play" in the government's application of law to its citizens, guaranteed by the Fifth and Fourteenth Amendments. Substantive due process is just plain *fairness*, and procedural due process is accorded when the government utilizes adequate procedural safeguards for the protection of an individual's liberty or property interests.

Enjoin - see Injunction.

Equal Protection Clause - The clause of the Fourteenth Amendment which prohibits a state from denying any person within its jurisdiction equal protection of its laws. Also, the Due Process Clause of the Fifth Amendment which pertains to the federal government. This has been interpreted by the Supreme Court to grant equal protection even though there is no explicit grant in the Constitution.

Establishment Clause - The clause of the First Amendment which prohibits Congress from making "any law respecting an establishment of religion." This clause has been interpreted as creating a "wall of separation" between church and state. The test frequently used to determine whether government action violates the Establishment Clause, referred to as the *Lemon* test, asks whether the action has a secular purpose, whether its primary effect promotes or inhibits religion, and whether it requires excessive entanglement between church and state.

Exclusionary Rule - A rule that allows criminal suspects to have excluded from consideration any evidence that is seized in violation of the Fourth Amendment.

42 U.S.C. §§ 1981, 1983 - Section 1983 of the federal Civil Rights Act prohibits any person acting under color of state law from depriving any other person of rights protected by the Constitution or by federal laws. A vast majority of lawsuits claiming constitutional violations are brought under § 1983. Section 1981 provides that all persons enjoy the same right to make and enforce contracts as "white citizens." Section 1981 applies to employment contracts. Further, unlike § 1983, § 1981 applies even to private actors. It is not limited to those acting under color of state law. These sections do not apply to the federal government, though the government may be sued directly under the Constitution for any violations.

Family Educational Rights and Privacy Act (FERPA) - A federal law that protects the privacy of student education records.

Fourth Amendment - Federal constitutional amendment that protects individuals from unreasonable searches and seizures.

Free Exercise Clause - The clause of the First Amendment which prohibits Congress from interfering with citizens' rights to the free exercise of their religion. Through the Fourteenth Amendment, it has also been made applicable to the states and their sub-entities. The Supreme Court has held that laws of general applicability which have an incidental effect on persons' free exercise rights are not violative of the Free Exercise Clause.

Government Accountability Office (GAO) - A federal agency that acts as the investigative arm of Congress. The GAO examines matters relating to the receipt and payment of public funds.

H1N1 Flu – Also referred to as swine flu based on early indications that it resembled influenza viruses that normally occur in pigs, 2009 H1N1 is an influenza virus that was first detected in humans in the United States in April 2009. In June 2009, the World Health Organization (WHO) declared that a pandemic of this flu had begun. Typically, those who contracted the virus recovered without the need for specialized medical treatment. But certain people, including people age 65 or older, people younger than five, pregnant women, and people with certain preexisting medical conditions, were at high risk of developing severe complications. In August 2010, the WHO announced that the virus had "largely run its course" but also noted the likelihood of continued localized outbreaks.

Incorporation Doctrine - By its own terms, the Bill of Rights applies only to the federal government. The Incorporation Doctrine states that the Fourteenth Amendment makes the Bill of Rights applicable to the states.

Individualized Educational Program (IEP) - The IEP is designed to give children with disabilities a free, appropriate education. It is updated annually, with the participation of the child's parents or guardian.

Individuals with Disabilities Education Act (IDEA) - Also known as the Education of the Handicapped Act (EHA), the Education for All Handicapped Children Act (EAHCA), and the Handicapped Children's Protection Act (HPCA). Originally enacted as the EHA, the IDEA is the federal legislation which provides for the free, appropriate education of all children with disabilities.

Injunction - An equitable remedy (see Remedies) wherein a court orders a party to do or refrain from doing some particular action.

Jeanne Clery Disclosure of Campus Security Policy and Campus Crime Statistics Act - A federal law requiring colleges and universities to disclose information regarding crime on and around campus.

Jurisdiction - The power of a court to determine cases and controversies. The Supreme Court's jurisdiction extends to cases arising under the Constitution and under federal law. Federal courts have the power to hear cases where there is diversity of citizenship or where a federal question is involved.

Miranda **Warning** - Warning that police must provide to an individual in police custody before proceeding with questioning.

MRSA - MRSA, which stands for Methicillin-resistant staphylococcus aureus, is a type of staph bacteria that is resistant to certain antibiotics.

National Incident Management System (NIMS) - a system developed by the Secretary of Homeland Security to provide a national template that helps government, private, and nongovernmental organizations effectively coordinate efforts during crisis events.

Negligence per se - Negligence on its face. Usually, the violation of an ordinance or statute will be treated as negligence per se because no careful person would have been guilty of it.

Overbroad - A government action is overbroad if, in an attempt to alleviate a specific evil, it impermissibly prohibits or chills a protected action. For example, a law attempting to deal with street litter by prohibiting the distribution of leaflets or handbills could be challenged as overbroad.

Rehabilitation Act - Section 504 of the Rehabilitation Act prohibits employers who receive federal financial assistance from discriminating against otherwise qualified individuals solely on the basis of disability.

Remand - The act of an appellate court in returning a case to the court from which it came for further action.

Remedies - There are two general categories of remedies, or relief: legal remedies, which consist of money damages, and equitable remedies, which consist of a court mandate that a specific action be prohibited or required. For example, a claim for compensatory and punitive damages seeks a legal remedy; a claim for an injunction seeks an equitable remedy. Equitable remedies are generally unavailable unless legal remedies are inadequate to address the harm.

Res Judicata - The judicial notion that a claim or action may not be tried twice or re-litigated, or that all causes of action arising out of the same set of operative facts should be tried at one time. Also known as claim preclusion.

Safe and Drug-Free Schools and Communities Act - Federal law supporting programs that prevent violence in and around schools, prevent illegal alcohol, tobacco and drug use, and foster a safe and drug-free school environment.

Section 1981 & Section 1983 - see 42 U.S.C. §§ 1981, 1983.

Sheltering-in-place - A planned response to the danger presented by the possible release of environmental contaminants that calls for students and personnel to take refuge in a safe interior location.

Sovereign Immunity - The idea that the government cannot be sued without its consent. It stems from the English notion that the "King can do no wrong." This immunity from suit has been abrogated in most states and by the federal government through legislative acts known as "tort claims acts."

Special Relationship Doctrine - A legal doctrine by which a state defendant can be held liable for a person's injury if the state defendant took actions that created a legal duty to protect the person from injury.

Standing - The judicial doctrine which states that in order to maintain a lawsuit a party must have some real interest at stake in the outcome of the trial.

State-Created Danger Doctrine - A legal doctrine by which a state defendant can be held liable for a person's injury if the state's actions either created or significantly increased the danger that caused the injury.

Statute of Limitations - A statute of limitation provides the time period in which a specific cause of action may be brought.

Swine Flu - see H1N1 flu.

Summary Judgment - Also referred to as pretrial judgment. Similar to a dismissal. Where there is no genuine issue as to any material fact and all that remains is a question of law, a judge can rule in favor of one party or the other. In general, summary judgment is used to dispose of claims which do not support a legally recognized claim.

Supremacy Clause - Clause in Article VI of the Constitution which states that federal legislation is the supreme law of the land.

Title IX - Federal law barring discrimination on the basis of sex under any educational program or activity that receives federal financial assistance.

Title VI - A part of the Civil Rights Act of 1964 that prohibits discrimination based on race, color or national origin in programs or activities that receive federal financial assistance.

Title VII of the Civil Rights Act of 1964 (Title VII) - Title VII prohibits discrimination in employment based upon race, color, sex, national origin, or religion. It applies to any employer having fifteen or more employees. Under Title VII, where an employer intentionally discriminates, employees may obtain money damages unless the claim is for race discrimination. For those claims, monetary relief is available under 42 U.S.C. § 1981.

Vacate - The act of annulling the judgment of a court either by an appellate court or by the court itself. The Supreme Court will generally vacate a lower court's judgment without deciding the case itself, and remand the case to the lower court for further consideration in light of some recent controlling decision.

Writ of Certiorari - The device used by the Supreme Court to transfer cases from the appellate court's docket to its own. Since the Supreme Court's appellate jurisdiction is largely discretionary, it need only issue such a writ when it desires to rule in the case.

INDEX